1989

Causes, Coping and Consequences of Stress at Work

Causes, Coping and Consequences of Stress at Work

Edited by

Cary L. Cooper
Manchester School of Management,
University of Manchester
Institute of Science and Technology

and

Roy Payne
Manchester Business School,
University of Manchester

JOHN WILEY & SONS
Chichester · New York · Brisbane · Toronto · Singapore

Library of Congress Cataloging-in-Publication Data

Cooper, Cary L.
    Causes, coping, and consequences of stress at work/by Cary L.
Cooper and Roy Payne.
      p. cm.—(Wiley series on studies in occupational stress)
    ISBN 0 471 91879 2
    1. Job stress. I. Payne, Roy. II. Title. III. Series.
HF5548.85.C654 1988
158.7—dc19   87–35399
                                                                                   CIP

British Library Cataloguing in Publication Data

Cooper, Cary L. (Cary Lynn), *1940–*
    Causes, coping and consequences of stress
at work.—(Wiley series on studies in
occupational stress).
    1. Job stress
    I. Title   II. Payne, R. L. (Roy L.)
    158.7   HF5548.85
    ISBN 0 471 91879 2

Printed in Great Britain by St Edmundsbury Press, Bury St Edmunds

List of contributors

JULIAN BARLING — *Department of Psychology, Queens University, Canada*

STEPHEN D. BLUEN — *University of the Witwatersrand, South Africa*

ROB BRINER — *MRC/ESRC Social and Applied Psychology Unit, University of Sheffield, UK*

RONALD J. BURKE — *Faculty of Administrative Studies, York University, Canada*

CARY L. COOPER — *Manchester School of Management, University of Manchester, Institute of Science and Technology, UK*

JEFFREY R. EDWARDS — *The Colgate Darden Graduate School of Business Administration, University of Virginia, USA*

BEN (C) FLETCHER — *Department of Psychology, Hatfield Polytechnic, UK*

MICHAEL FRESE — *Department of Psychology, University of Munich, West Germany*

YITZHAK FRIED — *Department of Management, Wayne State University, USA*

BARBARA A. GUTEK — *Department of Psychology, Claremont Graduate School, USA*

G. ROBERT J. HOCKEY — *MRC/ESRC Social and Applied Psychology Unit, University of Sheffield, UK*

JOHN M. IVANCEVICH — *College of Business Administration, University of Houston, USA*

MARY LEVENS — *Brain–Behaviour Research Institute, La Trobe University, Australia*

MICHAEL T. MATTESON — *College of Business Administration, University of Houston, USA*

LAWRENCE R. MURPHY — *National Institute for Occupational Safety and Health, Centers for Disease Control, USA*

ROY PAYNE — *Manchester Business School, University of Manchester, UK*

RENA L. REPETTI — *University of Pennsylvania, USA*

DEBORAH L. SILVER — *Department of Psychology, Claremont Graduate School, USA*

GEORGE SINGER — *Brain–Behaviour Research Institute and School of Behavioural Sciences, La Trobe University, Australia*

MEREDITH WALLACE — *Brain–Behaviour Research Institute and School of Behavioural Sciences, La Trobe University, Australia*

DIETER ZAPF — *Department of Psychology, University of Munich, West Germany*

Contents

Editorial Foreword to the Series

This book, *Causes, Coping and Consequences of Stress at Work*, is the twelfth* book in the series of *Studies in Occupational Stress*. The main objective of this series of books is to bring together the leading international psychologists and occupational health researchers to report on their work on various aspects of occupational stress and health. The series will include a number of books on original research and theory in each of the areas described in the initial volume, such as Blue Collar Stressors, The Interface Between the Work Environment and the Family, Individual Differences in Stress Reactions, The Person–Environment Fit Model, Behavioural Modification and Stress Relation, Stress and the Socio-technical Environment, The Stressful Effects of Retirement and Unemployment and many other topics of interest in understanding stress in the workplace.

We hope these books will appeal to a broad spectrum of readers—to academic researchers and postgraduate students in applied and occupational psychology and sociology, occupational medicine, management, personnel etc.—and to practitioners working in industry, the occupational medical field, mental health specialists, social workers, personnel officers, and others interested in the health of the individual worker.

CARY L. COOPER.
*University of Manchester Institute of
Science and Technology*
STANISLAV V. KASL,
Yale University

* Two earlier titles are now out of print.

Introduction

In 1978, we edited one of the first volumes dedicated to research carried out in occupational stress. The book was entitled *Stress at Work* and is still one of the most frequently quoted volumes in the field. Our publishers, John Wiley & Sons, came to us nearly a decade later to ask us to undertake the same task, of up-dating research in this growing area, by bringing together some of the leading international researchers to focus on the central topics of contemporary concern.

This current volume is divided into five sections. Part I deals with Stress at Work in Perspective, featuring a chapter on the Epidemiology of Occupational Stress, which indicates how close the medical and psychological traditions are growing; a development which was absent in our 1978 endeavour. Part II explores the Factors in the Person's Environment. The chapters in this section examine the stress of repetitive manual work, managerial and professional stress in large organizations, new technology and operator stress, the nonwork factors and stress at work, and the psychological stressors associated with industrial relations. Although *Stress at Work* explored blue collar and managerial/white collar stress, the 1980s and 1990s are forcing us to examine in greater detail stress in the office, the impact of new technology, the pressures of industrial relations difficulties and the continuing problems of repetitive manual work, many research issues which were not prevalent in the 1960s and 1970s.

Part III explores the Factors in the Person. The chapters in this part of the volume focus on individual differences and coping strategies. Whereas in the 1970s the research was centred almost entirely on Type A behaviour, today's and tomorrow's literature highlights, and will continue to highlight, personality as both a precursor and moderator of stress. Type A behaviour is only one aspect of stress, with more focus on hardiness, locus of control, trait anxiety and a range of personality characteristics. In addition, the significance of coping, both as a determinant and consequence of stress, is central to this discussion of contemporary stress research.

Part IV looks at The Person in the Work Environment. This is composed of chapters which examine health promotion in the workplace, as well as management interventions for stress reduction and prevention. These topics were unheard of in the 1970s, when all we focused on was how the *individual* could cope, with a 'passing nod' to the socio-technical apprroach to job redesign as a possible approach to stress reduction. Times have changed; we now have numerous organizational approaches to stress-prevention and stress-management interventions and training. These chapters highlight the increasingly numerous approaches and research evaluation in this area.

Part V examines the Issues in Research on Stress at Work. This looks primarily at methodological issues and the future of physiological assessments in work situations. With the ever-spiralling research in occupational stress, the methodological concerns are multiplying on issues of self-report measures, longitudinal designs and validity of questionnaires and other instruments. In addition, more researchers are wanting to employ physiological measures in field situations, such as monitoring equipment and biochemical analysis kits. These were problems only touched on in *Stress at Work*, issues which are now actual rather than potential challenges, and ones demanding more academic attention.

Twenty years ago, Kornhauser in his classic book on the *Mental Health of the Industrial Worker* reflected on what individuals at work needed, not only to survive the '9 to 5' but to positively enjoy it:

> Mental health is not so much a freedom from specific frustrations as it is an overall balanced relationship to the world, which permits a person to maintain a realistic, positive belief in himself and his purposeful activities. Insofar as his entire job and life situation facilitate and support such feelings of adequacy, inner security, and meaningfulness of his existence, it can be presumed that his mental health will tend to be good. What is important in a negative way is not any single characteristic of his situation but everything that deprives the person of purpose and zest, that leaves him with negative feelings about himself, with anxieties, tensions, a sense of lostness, emptiness and futility.

Let's hope that research into stress in the workplace will provide some of the vehicles for the management and elimination of the more noxious aspects of work environments.

Cary L. Cooper
Roy Payne

PART I

Stress at Work in Perspective

Causes, Coping and Consequences of Stress at Work
Edited by C. L. Cooper and R. Payne
© 1988 John Wiley & Sons Ltd

Chapter 1

The Epidemiology of Occupational Stress

Ben (C) Fletcher

This chapter outlines the extent of the occupational stress problem, attempts to identify which sectors of the workforce suffer most, and considers some of the occupational factors which may have injurious effects on physical health, well-being and life expectancy. It provides a review and analysis of epidemiological and other evidence which may imply a central role for occupational *psychological stressors* as causal precursors of *strain*. Strain refers to the state of being stressed as evidenced by physiological, psychological or medical indices (see Fletcher and Payne, 1980b). The chapter is primarily concerned with disease states and their associated biochemical and psychological risk factors.

There are a number of ways in which the relationship between work stressors and health can be established. Epidemiological methods provide one tool. It is necessary in any research initiative, however, to utilize the results obtained by other methodologies to inform the nature and content of the work. This is especially true when considering the contribution of occupational stressors in disease, since there has been no large-scale systematic attempt to assess their possible influence in epidemiological studies in the same way that the role of (say) blood pressure or dietary fat has been examined in coronary heart disease (CHD). Epidemiological studies have been done which assess the role of specific work factors (e.g. work overload and underload, Jenkins, 1982; occupational mobility and work changes, Syme, Hyman and Enterline, 1964; Syme, Borhani and Buechley, 1965; Haynes, Feinleib and Kannel, 1980; occupational responsibility or level, Hinkle *et al.* 1968; Rosenman *et al.*, 1964, 1970; blue vs white collar work, Haynes and Feinleib, 1982; support from boss, Haynes *et al.* 1978; occupational type, Rosenman *et al.*, 1964, 1970; etc.) However, no study has examined more than just a few crude work related variables. There may be sensible reasons for this. It may be considered unlikely, for example, to find that 'poor fringe benefits' is independently related to disease likelihood, despite the fact that 30% of the workforce feels it affects them either 'often' or 'all the time' (Fletcher, Glendon and Stone, 1987). The work environment includes a constellation of psychological factors which are likely to interact in different ways in different jobs for different people. Epidemiological methods

3

cannot reveal such interactions: that is a limitation of the discipline, not of the methodologies. It is necessary, therefore, to take account of different types of evidence if we are to make progress in occupational stress. We are probably now at a stage when such cross-fertilization is possible and worthwhile.

THE CASE FOR CONSIDERING PSYCHOLOGICAL STRESS IN DISEASE

The title, 'the epidemiology of occupational stress', would not traditionally imply a major role for psychological variables in the causal chain because this steps outside the realm of the 'casually documented' or 'theoretically neutral' sets of variables usually considered. Behavioural epidemiology usually considers such behavioural factors as eating excessive saturated fats, smoking, inadequate exercise, inadequate dietary fibre, excessive dietary sodium, alcohol, calorie intake, non-use of seat belts and sexual habits (Sexton, 1979). It is becoming increasingly necessary, however, for analytic epidemiological methods to take a wider account of the possible role of psychological causes (which may, for the most part, not be conscious or affective) if its methods are to provide useful insights about the aetiology of disease. There is, for example, a considerable corpus of documented evidence in the occupational stress and health literature to make such exercises worthwhile. Kasl (1978) in his well received and thoughtful review of epidemiological contributions to the study of work stress, saw the necessity to trawl the literature with a wider net than provided for by traditional epidemiological tools.

There are a number of reasons for suggesting that greater emphasis should be placed on psychological factors in epidemiological investigations. First, since the time of Kasl's review there has been an increasing number of studies of occupational stress which have utilized epidemiological methods (comparative observation, case-controlled or experimental epidemiology, prospective studies, etc.).

Second, more recent models of occupational stress take it as axiomatic that strain must be predicted by taking account of the individual's perceptions of work stressors. Failure to do so will result in little of the predictable variance being accounted for, and the subsequent failure of important psychological factors in strain being revealed. The Person–Environment Fit models (e.g. Cox, 1978; French, Caplan and Van Harrison, 1982; Van Harrison, 1978; 1988—chapter 8, this volume), for example, require the measurement of a person's perception of their own abilities to meet the perceived environmental job demands. Measurement of environmental factors alone is insufficient, especially since under-demand or underutilization of ability is one of the better predictors of work strain (Margolis, Kroes and

Quinn, 1974). The Demands, Supports and Constraints model (Payne, 1979; Payne and Fletcher, 1983) also proposes that a reasonable understanding of work stress can best be achieved by measuring the balance of these three variables for each individual, or at least for a group of individuals who do very similar work.

Third, establishing differences in the patterns of morbidity and mortality by occupational classifications or work title, and then searching for possible work-based explanations, is unlikely to be very helpful in determining aetiology. Kasl (1978) suggests a number of difficulties which would scupper such attempts including (a) self-selection, (b) company selection, (c) health reasons, (d) determining exposure, (e) inadequate documentation or record, (f) bias in follow-up, (g) other confounding variables such as smoking, diet and exercise, (h) small case numbers. As Kasl notes, such an epidemiological paradigm 'is probably too simple to be a methodological guide to the study of work stress' (p. 11). More important, perhaps, is the need to realise that 'occupation' may be too crude a variable to provide causally useful data. French *et al.* (1982), for example, in their stress and health study of 2010 people from 23 occupations, perceived that the term 'occupation' 'is really a surrogate for a variety of charateristics of the job and of the person' (p. 88). It is more important to determine what job factors or job characteristics produce strain than to consider the pattern of strain across occupations. They give two overriding reasons for favouring this approach: (a) symptoms do not reveal causes—knowing that some occupations have high strain levels does not provide information about the stressors, (b) occupations reflect a whole constellation of factors, only some of which affect strain. Traditional epidemiology leaves us the problems of isolating those work factors that are stressful, as well as being generally unhelpful about the role played by nonwork stressors both on the effects of work, and directly on strain itself (Fletcher and Payne, 1980a). French *et al.* (1982) report that occupational psychological factors predicted between 14 and 45% of the variance in strain measures, compared with only 2–6% of the variance when occupation title was used as the predictor. Shifting the emphasis away from 'occupations' to 'occupational factors' does not, of course, remove the burden of proof. Such factors may only be considered relevant if they have been determined by scientific techniques.

Fourth, if psychological factors are important causal agents in the ontogenesis of disease, ignoring them may well lead to models with poor predictive power, fruitless searches for other causal factors, and incomplete understanding of the disease process. There is, however, considerable controversy in the biomedical field about the potential role psychological factors may play in disease. Perhaps those sceptical about the possible contribution of psychological factors would do well to apply the same rigours of proof in all fields. It should be borne in mind that psychology may not be predictive at the level of the individual, although it is at the group level (a point well made for the occupational stress area by Payne, Jick and Burke, 1982). It is sometimes forgotten that, in general, psychology shares with medicine a probabalistic framework for diagnosis and empirical research which sits uncomfortably with deterministic or mechanistic models (Fletcher, 1980). Although considerable research is required to determine exactly what role psychological factors play in the onset of diseases it seems certain that they play some role (Fletcher, 1989). There are, for example, fundamental links between the central nervous system and the hormonal and immune systems (e.g. Ader and Cohen, 1985), the human immune systems delayed hypersensitivity reaction can be markedly affected by expectancy effects (e.g. Smith and McDaniels, 1983), there is evidence from human studies of a biochemical substrate for psychosomatic immune-related effects (Ruff *et al.* 1985), and considerable evidence that the cardiovascular system (Engel, 1986) and the immune systems (Ader and Cohen, 1985) are conditionable and, therefore, integral *behavioural* systems. There is also an increasing amount of evidence linking psychological causes with all manner of infectious diseases (e.g. Jemmott and Locke, 1984; Solomon, 1981), cancer (e.g. Cooper, 1984; Cox and Mackay, 1982; Fox, 1982), coronary heart disease (e.g. Krantz, Baum and Singer, 1983; Ostfeld and Eaker, 1985) and other variables hypothesized to influence health (e.g. Henry and Stephens, 1977; Holmes and David, 1984; Matthews *et al.* 1986). Whilst the research is not without its controversies and inconsistencies it should be remembered that such work is attempting to link a complex constellation of poorly understood variables with crude measuring tools to determine influences that are dynamic and generally chronic in effect, may have been triggered way back in the past, with less-than-optimal research designs, using all kinds of people, only a small number of whom will exhibit the outcome under consideration, and then perhaps will do so primarily as a consequence of other influences.

THE SIZE OF THE WORK STRESS PROBLEM

Methodological Considerations

It is difficult to estimate the size of any problem when the outcome variables have multifactorial 'causes' and one is particularly interested in one aspect of aetiology (i.e. work stress). This is not an issue peculiar to the psychological investigation of disease. It should be borne in mind that the standard physiological and medical risk factors for coronary heart disease (CHD) or lung cancer are not good predictors of the degree or incidence of the clinical manifestation of the diseases. For example, Eysenck (1984) has pointed out that only 10% of smokers die of lung cancer and 10% of people who die of lung cancer are non-smokers. In addition, the 10-year incidence of CHD will be made up of 40% who have no evidence of significant risk factors, and only 10% of those with such risks will have developed CHD (Inter-Society Commission for Heart Disease Resources, 1972).

It is even more difficult to estimate the size of the problem when there is little consensus about the measurement of the relevant variables. This is often the case with psychological variables as is evident in, for example the assessment of psychological factors in epidemiological studies of cardio-vascular disease (e.g. Ostfeld and Eaker, 1985). Occupational strain is no exception in this respect, although it does present the additional difficulty related to the often mentioned 'lack of definition of stress'. The World Health Organisation, for example, mirrors a common view that this definitional difficulty provides a cloak of misconception for the magician psychologist. In its Expert Committee report on the prevention of coronary heart disease (WHO, 1982) they advised:

> With respect to 'stress' or 'response to stress', the lack of definition and quantitative measurement is severely limiting. . . . The Expert Committee noted the danger that public and professional misconceptions about 'stress', whereby it is assigned a primary role in the genesis of CHD, may divert attention from demonstrated needs in prevention (p. 32).

The definitional difficulty is compounded by the potentially multifaceted manifestations of stress. Cox (1978), for example, lists multiple examples of six categories of work strains: cognitive, physiological, health, organizational, behavioural, and subjective. Each strain (blood pressure, work absence, smoking behaviour, heart disease, etc.) has numerous contributing causes which makes it difficult to apportion the contribution, if any, of work stressors. Little is gained by an examination of those epidemiological studies which attempt to estimate the contribution work stressors make to any strain [as, for example, in the excellent prospective Framingham Heart Study (Haynes *et al.* 1978; Haynes, Feinleib and Kannel, 1980; Haynes and Feinleib, 1982)]. Multiple regression and other multiple logistic risk assessment techniques are not utilized as often as they might be, perhaps partly because large numbers are required for the subpopulations under examination, and because the contribution of psychological work factors is itself difficult and, to some extent, dependent upon a conceptual clarity which is not present in the discipline.

There is a sense in which the very nature of epidemiological research excludes adequate measurement of psychological factors in the workplace. Unless studies tap a large proportion of the universe of potentially contributing occupational factors, it would be surprising if the few factors measured (or implied) did account for much of the observed variance in the outcome measures. A critical reading of the epidemiological literature would soon convince the reader that traditional risk factors in disease (e.g. smoking behaviour, blood pressure, obesity, cholesterol levels, etc. in coronary heart disease) themselves account for only a small proportion of the predictable variance, that relative and attributable risks from combined risk variables often show synergistic relationships exist (making the measurement of their combinations necessary), that single risk factors do not predict disease outcomes with unequivocal consistency, and that it is the weight of evidence, not absolute proof, that needs consideration. Remember that Keys *et al.* (1972) suggested that all the traditional risk factors together explain less than 50% of the variance in CHD. In a prospective study by Lehr, Messinger and Rosenman (1973), which sampled 12 biochemical/biological risk factors and 12 simple 'social' factors, the former did not account for much of the variance in the CHD discriminant analysis, and factors such as 'parental religious difference', 'father's occupation' and 'behaviour pattern' (which can hardly be said to explore the rich tapestry of psychological factors!) were more discriminating than two thirds of the biological risks.

It has been fashionable to question the contribution psychology may make in epistemological investigations of disease by referring to the small correlations often reported. For example, in occupational stress the stressor–strain relationships are commonly around 0.2. Some commentators (e.g. Fletcher and Payne, 1980a; Kasl, 1978) have suggested this indicates the relative non-importance of the stressor in strain aetiology. A correlation of this size accounts for only 4% of the predictable variance, and should be considered small. It will, however, be reliably detected in large sample studies. Small correlations may also mask results of considerable clinical importance. In a study of work stress by Frese (1985) workers in the highest stress group had up to nine times the excess risk of being psychosomatically impaired compared to low stress groups even though stressor–strain relationships were around 0.2. Methodological reasons may also mitigate against obtaining high correlations [poor measuring tools which increase the error variance, the use of homogeneous samples (e.g. from similar occupations) which restrict the variance, etc.].

What is required are studies that truly attempt to examine causal models of work stressor–strain against alternatives. Such studies are rare, but do support the contention that occupational factors are true causes of strain. The study by Frese (1985), for example, examined a series of four hypotheses commonly offered as alternatives to the causal view that work stressors produce strain. His study of blue-collar workers took account of subjective self-report stressor assessment by including stressor assessment by colleagues and independent observers, it involved a longitudinal component to investigate whether being under strain was the cause of the stressors, it assessed whether the work stressor–strain relationship was only present for a subsample of the population by considering the difference for 'overestimaters' and 'underestimaters', and it enabled the partialling out of some factors which are often considered to intervene between the stressor–strain relationship such as job insecurity, age, socio-economic status (SES), the financial situation and political factors. The resulting analyses supported the contention that stressors in the workplace were independent causal contributors to strain (psychosomatic complaints).

Parkes (1982) reports the results of a longitudinal natural experiment on 164 student nurses. During a three-month period each nurse did both surgical and medical ward duties which allowed counterbalancing of important factors. In addition, it allowed an evaluation of the impact of stressors on affective strain, sickness and work performance in terms of changes within individuals. She found that medical wards were associated with higher levels of affective disorders, which could be primarily attributed to lower levels of job discretion and higher levels of social support, not differences in job demands. Keenan and Newton (1987) report a 4-year longitudinal study of engineers in which four areas of occupational stressors were identified by factor analysis. In general only one of these areas ('people difficulties') was related to the measures of psychological strain used.

Such studies also demonstrate the need to account for a multitude of factors in order to provide a realistically convincing argument that work stressors have important medical consequences. Unfortunately, similar studies utilizing disease-based measures of strain, rather than psychometrically assessed strain, are methodologically and pragmatically unfeasible.

A third reason why observed work stressor–strain relationships are small is that work is only one of many contributing factors to strain. The interface between the domestic and occupational environments, as well the interaction of both with personality or individual perceptions, requires careful investigation. It has been pointed out (Fletcher and Payne, 1980a) that when studies have taken some account of both work and nonwork factors, nonwork factors appear, on the face of it, to be more important contributors to mental and physical ill-health. This is too simplistic a view. We need to consider the wider effects of work without assuming the independence of work and domestic life. Recent research, for example, suggests that occupational factors may be related to the extent of activity in leisure and political participation (Karasek, 1978), and that occupational stress may be transmitted to spouses and affect their health (e.g. Fletcher, Gowler and Payne, 1980; Sloan and Cooper, 1986).

The Costs of Stress

The multifaceted effects of stress, and the problems inherent in this field of research makes the estimation of the costs of occupational stress virtually impossible. Nonetheless, attempts have been made. Kearns (1986) suggests that 60% of absence from work is caused by stress-related disorders and that in the UK alone 100 million working days are lost each year because people cannot face going to work. Cooper (1986) presents financial statistics indicating that £1.3 billion per annum is lost as a result of alcoholism in industry, and that American employers spend some $700 million per annum replacing men below retiring age due to CHD incapacity. It is, of course, difficult to know what savings would be made (and at what cost) if work could be made physically and psychologically healthy. Certainly some practitioners believe that instituting better work practices, essentially better management, would probably reduce the problem (Stone, 1985), as would trends to redesign jobs to increase either group or individual autonomy, feedback, task identity, variety and significance (e.g. Wall, 1980; Hogan and Martell, 1987). The fact that many large companies are investing money to help reduce the stress problems for their employees (e.g. Cooper, 1986; Fletcher and Hall, 1984) is probably a significant indicator that they believe it is more than mental health that is improved by such exercises. It should be borne in mind, however, that age-standardized mortality rates for one major group of diseases (cardiovascular diseases—ICD No. 390–458) are showing considerable decreases in the 10-year period to 1982 (28.4% for men and 30.4% for women, USA; 16.7% for men and 19.6% for women, England and Wales) (Uemura and Pisa, 1985). It would not be generally agreed that psychological occupational stressors have been reduced during the same period.

Just as pathogens do not necessarily result in clinical manifestations of disease, stressors do not invariably produce strain. Occupational stressors are factors in the work environment which increase the probability of strain reactions. In the same way mediators (such as individual differences) are factors which increase the likelihood that a change in the normal stressor–strain relationship will occur (the X-Y-Z sequence bio-behavioural model in Elliot and Eisendorfer, 1982, provides a similar formal attempt to unite the stimulus-based models of the biological sciences and the response-based models of the social scientists). The development of such hedged statements from data is how empirical sciences advance, even if this is done in the context of mechanistic or deterministic models. The degree of strain which is actually exhibited, therefore, provides only the tip of the underlying problem. This is one reason it makes no sense to concentrate investigations of the cause of stress by close examination of those individuals with strain (whatever the strain). The answers derived from such investigations will be contaminated by what Fletcher and Payne (1980b) have called 'secondary stressors'. These are factors which are only associated with the strain measures because the organism is under strain as a result of 'primary stressors' which result in a lowered tolerance threshold to stressors. Only primary stressors are true causes of strain.

The reliance on exhibited strain is an inbuilt limitation to epidemiological studies. Indeed, epidemiological research expends considerable resources on attempting to limit the possible contaminations due to such factors. It is a commonly held view, for example, that prospective designs are superior for determining cause–effect relationships (e.g. Fox, 1978; Kasl, 1983) because they are necessary to show that observed case-control differences are not a consequence of the illness itself. 'Cause' is not, however, a solely time-based concept and, as I have argued elsewhere, can, depending on the context, be better revealed by cross-sectional designs which provide a richer examination of psychosocial issues with a larger useable sample pool (Fletcher, 1989). Traditional epidemiological studies are largely hamstrung by this fundamental limitation. What is needed is an understanding of how much of a limitation it is.

Stressors in the Workplace

Figure 1 presents a simple stressor–strain model of the role of occupational factors in psychological and physical disease, based on numerous similar conceptualizations (e.g. Cooper and Marshall, 1976; Cooper, 1986; French

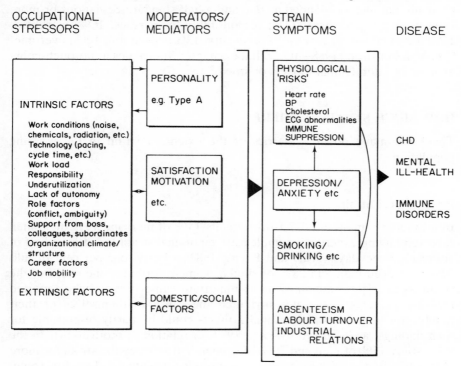

Figure 1   A stressor–strain model of occupational stress

et al., 1982, Kagan and Levi, 1974; Schuler, 1982). Such models make no real attempt to predict the levels of strain, or the subtle interactions between their many variables, or to facilitate in the conceptual understanding of what occupational stress is. They are useful, however, as thumbnail sketches to envelope and list the critical factors which any predictive model should deal with, and to provide a chart of the current state of knowledge (and belief). Epidemiological models of chronic disease (e.g. Medalie, 1985) take account of a considerably greater number of factors (e.g. social networks, family system, age, sex, geographical, cultural and political factors).

Other psychologists who have measured a large number of work stressors [e.g. French *et al.* (1982) measured some 22 subjective work factors and 26 person–environment variables, Fletcher *et al.* (1987) measured 129 work stressors] have concluded that a more theoretically positive stance is justified (see Van Harrison, 1978, 1988—this volume, chapter 8). French *et al.* (1982), for example, view stressors as those factors which produce a misfit between a person's perception of their work environment and their perception of their own abilities and motives. Viewed in this way, a considerable minority of their working male sample ($N=300$) showed a large degree of misfit on some occupational factors (defined as one-and-a-half standard deviations or more from perfect fit): income, 33%; responsibility for persons, 16%; workload, 14%; role ambiguity, 14%; job complexity, 13%; education, 10%; overtime, 9%. Van Harrison (1988—this volume, chapter 8) includes a thorough-going analysis of interactional models of stress.

HOW MUCH STRAIN IS THERE?

There are many possible metrics of the extent of strain in the working population.

Psychological Strain

In a random sample of 3077 British adults 14% of men and 19% of women reported having experienced unpleasant emotional strain for at least half of yesterday (weekday) (Warr and Payne, 1982a). Forty-four per cent of full-time employed men and 28% of similar women attributed the cause of the strain to their job—the single most important cause. People who reported pleasure yesterday generally attributed the cause to themselves or their family, not their job (attributional artifacts could be partly responsible for such findings, as discussed by Farr, 1977, in relation to motivation). In the same study 15% of men and 20% of women had suffered the strain for more than one month. Whilst work may produce negative affect for some, however, it may contribute positively to health too. Warr and Payne (1983), for example, found that over 15%, of employed men and women derived pleasure from their jobs for at least half of yesterday.

In a longitudinal study of coping behaviour in young engineers Newton and Keenan (1985) observed that 33% had suffered a stress incident at work within the last 14 days. Whilst most individuals attempted to cope in positive way (e.g. 30% talk to others, 18% took direct action for resolution, 11% took preparatory action) a significant proportion (30%) either expressed helplessness, resentment or withdrawal behaviour.

In the Framingham Heart Study of 1822 men and women over 45 years old over 48% of the sample described themselves as being 'often troubled by feelings of tenseness, tightness, restlessness, or inability to relax', and 37% as being 'usually pressed for time' (Haynes *et al.*, 1978). High stress jobs have also been associated with higher rates of nervousness. For example, in a comparison of high risk jobs with controls Johansson, Aronson and Lindstrom (1978) observed that 'slight nervous disturbance' was reported by 36% more of the individuals in the former than the latter group.

In an examination of a sample of 1% of physically healthy community residents aged 15–69 in a large city Finlay-Jones and Burvill (1977) report some 13.6% of men and 18.9% of women have General Health Questionnaire (GHQ) scores indicating a growing need for medical and psychiatric treatment. Fletcher *et al.*'s (1987) randomized survey revealed that 14% had case levels of anxiety and 12% case levels of depression. Dohrenwend *et al.* (1980), from an analysis of epidemiological studies done in North America and Europe since 1945, have estimated that the prevalance (for a few months to a year) of functional mental disorders is between 16 and 25%. In addition, another 13% would have severe psychological/somatic illness not accompanied by recognizable mental disorder.

Examinations of particular occupational groups have also revealed levels of minor psychiatric morbidity levels which should give some cause for concern. Pratt (1978) reports that 21% of his teacher sample had elevated GHQ scores. Over 21% of student nurses scored at case levels on the Crown–Crisp Experiential Index (CCEI) in Parkes' (1982) study. Fletcher and Payne (1982), using the CCEI, found 19% of teachers to be depressed beyond the level of psychiatric outpatients. In addition, 22% had felt as if they were going to have a nervous breakdown, of which 53% attributed the cause primarily to their job. Fletcher and Morris (1987), in an examination of stress in licensed London taxi drivers, found 16% with clinical scores for free-floating anxiety, 13% with depression, 34% with phobic anxiety, 26% with obsessional neurosis, 15% with somatic anxiety and 43% with hysterical personalities (using the CCEI). In a prospective National Survey of Health and Development of 1415 26-year-old men, Cherry (1978) reports that 38% of the sample said they were under some or severe nervous strain at work whereas only 8% were under some or severe strain at home or in their personal lives. Almost 50% of those under severe strain also reported physical health symptoms. Of the 13 work causes considered, 36% reported 'pressure of work' as the cause of the strain, 24% 'responsibility' and 12% 'contact with people'. In a follow-up 6 years later Cherry (1984) questions whether the strain symptoms related to pre-existing indicators of susceptibility rather than to the apparently stressful nature of their jobs. MacIver (1969) suggests that it has not been difficult for industrial psychiatrists to accept that 25% of the industrial population have significant emotional problems. He suggests that these problems will be exhibited in the form of neuroses (including depression) in about 5%, personality disorders in 5%, alcoholism in 3% and psychophysiologic disorders in around 10%. Even this estimate, however, seems to underestimate the size of the problem. As long ago as 1947, for example, Fraser's excellent work for the Industrial Health Research Board of the Medical Research Council revealed that some 9% of men and 13% of women in light and medium engineering factories had exhibited definite and disabling neurosis (anxiety, depression, obsessionality, hysteria, psychosis, etc.) in the six months of the study. A further 19% of men and 23% of women had suffered from minor neuroses (which included psychosomatic illness). Each neurosis was responsible for up to one third of all absences from work, causing a loss, for the workforce as a whole, of 1.1% (men) and 2.4% (women) of possible working days. For example, women exhibiting definite neuroses (without physical illness) were absent on 13% of possible working days as a result of the neuroses. A number of work factors were found to be associated with more than the usual incidence of neuroses including working in excess of 75 hours per week, work found boring or disliked, light or sedentary work, work requiring skill inappropriate to the worker's intelligence, work requiring constant attention, especially allied with constrained scope or responsibility and work offering little variety. Fraser's (1947) work can be seen to have predated much of the modern impetus in stress research (including the 'Life Events' work of Holmes, Rahe and others, the emphasis on low demand and lack of autonomy, and the Person–Environment Fit model).

A number of studies have examined the prevalence rates of stress reactions in large work organizations. For example, Zaleznik et al. (1977) report the results of an analysis of 2131 employees in the middle and high occupational brackets of a large company. Since they estimated that 15% of the employees did not complete the questionnaires due to illness or schedule conflicts the prevalence rates they report are likely to underestimate the degree of strain. Nonetheless, 24% reported suffering insomnia, 21% restlessness and agitation, 19% fatigue, 16% felt their work adversely affected their health, 13% felt the need to withdraw and 11% were worried about having a nervous breakdown. Ferguson (1973 a, b), in a study of 516 telegraphists, reports that 33% had or have had disabling neurosis as determined by medical interview/examination (neurosis was defined as anxiety state, neurasthenia, nervous exhaustion or debility, or nervous dyspepsia).

Such estimates of emotional distress may have important implications for absence behaviour, labour turnover and efficiency at work, as well as indicating that a significant proportion of the workforce is unhappy. Perhaps more important for epidemiology, however, is that such mental ill-health predisposes employees to physical manifestations of ill-health too. In Russek's well known early research of 100 CHD patients (89 infarction and 11 angina-on-effort) with case-controls, for example, he says that: 'prolonged emotional strain associated with job responsibility . . . preceded the attack in 91% of the patients as compared with an occurrence of similar strain in only 20% of normal control subjects' (Russek, 1965, p. 189; see also Russek and Zohman, 1958). In a more recent study Maschewsky (1982) compared 313 infarction survivors with 220 controls. All subjects were employed and aged between 30 and 64. Of 48 psychologically relevant dimensions only having 'nervous strain in the last 10 years' discriminated between the groups at better than the 5% level. Such effects are, of course, centrally implied by models of stress like those depicted in Figure 1, and are supported by the weight of empirical evidence, even if many of the individual studies do not allow strong causal conclusions or reveal inconsistences (Fletcher, 1989).

Physiological Risk Factors and Physical Illness

Fraser's (1947) early work with 3500 factory workers showed that 14% of men and 18% of women had suffered a definite disabling physical illness causing 7 days or more absence in the preceding 6 months. A further 24% of men and 22% of women had suffered more minor physical illness necessitating absence of less than 7 days. Clearly, many types of physical illness would contribute to the absence behaviour and the prevalence and incidence of some these will be considered.

In the International Cooperative Study of some 8841 Dutch male workers over 39 years old Reeder, Schrama and Dirken (1973) found that 14.3% of the workforce showed abnormal electrocardiograms and 23.7% had serum cholesterol levels in excess of 279 mg%. Other studies of specific occupational groups have also been made. Cooper, Mallinger and Kahn (1978) report that 16.7% of their dentist sample showed ECG abnormalities. Marmot *et al.* (1978) report that 12.6% of administrative grade civil servants had elevated plasma cholesterol levels. Zaleznik *et al.* (1977), in their study of managers, found that 8.4% of them reported having had more than 10 days or more off recently due to cardiovascular problems. In addition, 8% reported presently having rapid heart beats and 7% having suffered them previously. In the Swiss part of the International Collaborative Study the male population over

30 years of age of a Zurich factory were examined ($N=885$) (Schar, Reeder and Dirken, 1973). Ninety-four per cent of the sample were blue-collar workers. Because of the type of work required the workforce was quite selected and showed a low prevalence of elevated cholesterol, glucosurea, proteinurea and cardiovascular pathology. Nonetheless their health history revealed that 36.6% had a severe illness or accident, 6.9% some cardiovascular–renal disease and 6.4% a cerebrovascular stroke, infarction or pathological hypertension.

The prevalence rates of ischaemic heart disease derived from major recent studies reveal that a sizeable minority of the working population suffer from significant coronary conditions. For example, the French–Belgian Collaborative Group (1982) examined men aged 40–60. They showed that factory workers in Brussels–Ghent had prevalence rates between 16 and 24% depending upon the age group, and civil servants in Marseilles 7–22% (diagnostic criteria used the Rose questionnaire and Minnesota Codes for the ECGs). In the Framingham Heart Study the prevalance of total CHD (myocardial infarction and anginal) was some 9% (Haynes *et al.*, 1978). That CHD prevalence varies with the stressfulness of work was suggested in an early study by Russek (1962). The stressfulness of particular professions was assessed independently of the case sample by qualified specialists. In the three professional groups considered (medicine, dentistry and law) the high stress occupations within each profession were associated with considerably higher prevalence rates of CHD. For example, GPs and anaesthesiologists (high stress) showed an age-adjusted rate of 12% which was 2.7 times that of pathologists and dermatologists (low stress). Of course, in addition to occupational differences there are large international differences. In a comparison of the CHD mortality rates of 27 industrialized countries, for example, the highest rates were 2.7 (men)/3.8 (women) times those of the lowest rate (Uemura and Pisa, 1985). These international league tables place both France and Belgium in the lowest quartile, the United States of America in the middle of the table, and the United Kingdom nearer the top.

Incidence rates are derived from prospective studies of populations initially free of manifest CHD. The prospective phase of the British Regional Heart Study (Shaper *et al.*, 1985) examined a random sample of 7735 men aged 40–59. The average annual incidence rate of major ischaemic heart disease was 6.2/1000 (ICD No. 410–414). In a 5-year prospective study of Israeli civil servants and municipal workers an annual incidence rate of 5.2/1000 was observed for clinical myocardial infarction (Goldbourt, Medalie and Neufeld, 1975) and 5.7/1000 for angina pectoris without infarction (Medalie and Goldbourt, 1976). Since it has been estimated that more than $700 million/annum is spent by American companies alone to replace premature CHD employees (Cooper, 1986), such incidence rates in the working population can be very costly.

Some estimates of the prevalence of hypertension suggest that as many as 18% of population have blood pressures exceeding 160/95 mmHg (Health and Nutrition Examination Survey, 1977). Both systolic and diastolic pressures have been shown to predict CHD mortality (e.g. Lichtenstein, Shipley and Rose, 1985) even though recent evidence confirms that diastolic pressure may be more important (Tverdal, 1987). Studies of working populations indicate prevalence rates rather lower than this. Charlesworth, Williams and Baer (1984), for example, found that 10% of a corporation's workforce had blood pressures over 140/90 mmHg, or were under treatment for essential hypertension. Fletcher and Heath (in preparation) in a blood pressure screening study (N=3095) report that 14% of working men and 21% of employed women had high blood pressure (in excess of 140/90 up to 45 years old, or 150/90 for older people). In a study of 17,530 male civil servants 12.8% had systolic pressures in excess of 159 mmHg (Marmot et al., 1978). Clearly, since high blood pressure is largely asymptomatic and poorly monitored by health services, self-report studies suggest even lower rates. In such a study of a managerial workforce, for example, Zaleznik et al. (1977) found that only 6.2% reported currently having high blood pressure. Males are more likely to have high blood pressure, particularly when they are younger. Wadsworth et al. (1985) in a birth cohort study of 36-year-olds reports 17.3% of men and 9.5% of women had diastolic pressures above 90 mmHg, and 12.3% of men and 6.2% of women had systolic pressures above 140 mmHg.

The extent of pill consumption has been linked with job stressors such as job demands and lack of job discretion (Karasek, 1979). Pill consumption is common. In an examination of a sub-sample from the Caerphilly Heart Study, Elliott et al. (1987) report that over 8% of the men were on antihypertensive drugs (with a further 31% with blood pressure above 159/94 mmHg). In the Zaleznik et al. (1977) study over 21% took vitamin pills, 3% took sleeping pills, and 10% took other types of pill. Ferguson (1973 a, b) reported that 12% of his telegraphist sample took some form of sedative and 13% analgesics. Although alcohol consumption shows occupationally-linked patterns (e.g. Plant, 1977) the rates appear to be related more to access, armed forces and old social traditions than occupational stressors. It has been shown, however, that 9% of employed men and 7% of employed women cope with the unpleasant emotional strain they felt yesterday by drinking more alcohol than usual (Warr and Payne, 1982b). Six per cent of employed men cope by taking medicine or tablets, 15% smoke more and 6% eat more than usual (the comparable figures for employed women were 15%, 9% and 17%).

Headaches have also been associated with occupational stress. For example, Johansson et al. (1978) found that individuals in high-stress-risk jobs in a saw mill had prevalence rates 36% higher than the control groups. Turner and Stone (1979) in a random sample survey found that 88% of people report having headaches of whom 23% suffer between 1 and 3 per week. Green (1977), in a sample of 14,893 people, report 19% of men and 26% of women suffered from migraine which necessitated an average of four days absence from work per year. Waters (1970), on the basis of a postal survey, reports that as many as 28% of men and 41% of women will have had a unilateral headache in the preceding year, although proper clinical diagnoses reduce these prevalence estimates somewhat (Waters and O'Conner, 1971).

Work and Positive Stress Effects

Occupational factors are clearly not entirely responsible for the above patterns of morbidity and mortality. Work may, for example, have positive health benefits as well as negative ones. Unemployment and retirement from work are associated with excess risk of psychological dysfunction (Cobb and Kasl, 1977; Jackson and Warr, 1984; Kasl, 1980; Warr, 1982, 1983) although the evidence that loss of a job leads to increased risk of cardiovascular disease is, at best, equivocal (Kasl and Cobb, 1980).

   Specific occupational factors may be beneficial to health. Energy expenditure at work is one such protective factor. In a 22-year follow-up of 3686 longshoremen from a birth-cohort study, Paffenbarger *et al.* (1977) classified jobs into those requiring high energy output (an average of 1876 kcal over basal output per 8-hour working day), intermediate (1473 kcal) and light (865 kcal). The age adjusted rates of fatal heart attacks for each cohort showed that high energy expenditure at work was associated with the lowest incidence rates although obesity, abnormal glucose metabolism and high serum cholesterol did not add to the risk. For example, the adjusted rates per 1000 were 4.3 for high and 7.7 for intermediate energy expenditure. Sudden death within one hour of an infarction was also less likely amongst the high energy output group. More recent epidemiological work by Paffenbarger *et al.* (1984) has confirmed that habitual leisure-time exercise among those who are likely to do more sedentary work (a study of 16,936 Harvard alumni) is associated with improved lifestyle, cardiovascular health and longevity. An important point to remember is that energy expenditure is likely to have important psychological benefits that may be at least partly responsible for the protective benefits. For example, Schar *et al.* (1973) found that higher energy expenditure was correlated with higher work satisfaction and lower social stress, neuroticism and subjective work strain.

Prevalence of 'Risky' Personalities at Work

It has been thought for many years that some individuals have personalities which particularly predispose them to the effects of occupational stressors.

One such individual difference that has been examined in some detail is Type A 'coronary prone behaviour'. Type A behaviour is characterized by sustained drive towards poorly defined goals, preoccupation with deadlines, competitiveness and desire for advancement and achievement, mental and behavioural alertness or aggressiveness, chronic haste and impatience (see Friedman and Rosenman, 1959; Jenkins, Zyzanski and Rosenman, 1971; Price, 1982; Payne, 1988—this volume, chapter 6; Fletcher, 1989). Such behaviours are seen as being promoted by environmental factors (Friedman and Rosenman, 1974) and it is from this perspective that the work environment may be important. Typically more than 50% of a workforce would be classified as Type A's by one of the commonly used validated measures. In a study of managers from 12 different companies Howard, Cunningham and Rechnitzer (1976) report that 61% were Type A's, 44% of whom exhibited the more extreme Type A1 behaviour. High growth companies also tended to have more Type A managers—up to 76% in one company. In this study the A1 types tended to report more emotional distress and cardiovascular strain symptoms, had higher systolic and diastolic blood pressure, serum cholesterol and triglycerides levels, lower maximum oxygen uptake (VO_2 in ml/kg min), and more of them smoked. Type A behaviour is by no means confined to the managerial levels—Hurrell (1985), for example, examined 2803 paced letter sorters and 2715 non-paced postal service workers. Some 54% of the workforce (men and women) were classified as Type A with a disproportionately high representation among paced male workers. Those prospective studies which include sufficient numbers of blue- and white-collar workers to enable sound comparisons do suggest that white-collar workers score more highly on Type A scales (e.g. Haynes and Feinleib, 1982).

Type A behaviour has been shown to be an important risk factor in the development of CHD as shown by prospective studies such as the Western Collaborative Group Study (e.g. Rosenman *et al.* 1966; Rosenman *et al.* 1975) and the Framingham Heart Study (e.g. Haynes and Feinleib, 1982). These studies are particularly valuable because they begin with Type A and B individuals who were initially free of manifest CHD and allowed for the independent assessment of the role behaviour type and the traditional CHD risk factors. In the early 2.5-year follow-up of the Western Group Study (Rosenman *et al.*, 1966) Type A men showed a 3.4 times greater risk of developing CHD than Type B men. Younger Type A men (39–49 years old) showed a 6.5 times excess risk. By the time of the 8.5-year follow up (Rosenman *et al.*, 1975, 1976) Type A excess risk for CHD was 2.2 times and for non-CHD deaths 1.4 times that of Type B. In the earlier report behavioural type was a better predictor of relative CHD risk than other prognostically significant indices such as high/low beta/alpha lipoprotein ratios, serum cholesterol levels, or parental CHD history. In the later report multivariate adjustments for eight traditional CHD risk factors still left a residual Type A risk double that for Type B men. In the Framingham Study, which included both men and women (aged 45–64), the 10-year incidence rates of angina and myocardial infarction complicated by angina showed considerable excess risk from Type A behaviour (1.9 and 2.6 men; 2.6 and 2.1 women). (But see Johnston, Cook and Shaper, 1987; Ragland and Brand, 1988.)

As Kasl (1978) has pointed out, however, it is unclear what this psychosocial risk factor implies about the occupational environment. The majority of the research has been derived from primarily white-collar managerial samples, although there is evidence from blue-collar workers that the Type A/B distinction has a direct influence on some mood states (e.g. tension–anxiety, anger–hostility) (Hurrell, 1985). Such factors may be predictive of diseases like CHD and cancer although the evidence is by no means impressive (Fletcher, 1989). It does appear that Type As are more likely to smoke (e.g. Haynes & Feinleib, 1982; Howard, Cunningham and Rechnitzer, 1986) and less likely to give up smoking than Type Bs (Caplan *et al.* 1975). Smoking behaviour has been associated with work stressors such as objective quantitative work load (e.g. number of office visits, phone calls, meetings per unit time) responsibility for the work of others, equipment and other's futures (French and Caplan, 1970), ambiguity about one's future, role ambiguity (Caplan *et al.*, 1975), job complexity and workload variance (French *et al.*, 1982). It is likely, therefore, that work factors may promote injurious behaviours, particularly for Type A individuals.

The work environment will, of course, affect different individuals in different ways and if Type A behaviour were shown to moderate the effects of work stressors, this would have important implications for work and health. Some researchers have proposed that the behavioural distinction does indeed moderate the work stressor–strain relationship and present models to this effect (e.g. Davidson and Cooper, 1980), although some empirical work would not support this view (e.g. Hurrell, 1985). Certainly, however, Type A people exhibit a number of effects which are of relevance to the work environment. Howard *et al.* (1986), for example, report a 2-year prospective study of 278 managerial staff, who were classified as Type A or Type B individuals. They were particularly interested in how changes in the work stressor role ambiguity (Kahn *et al.*, 1964; Van Sell, Brief and Schuler, 1981) were affected by behaviour type and job satisfaction, and the relationship of these variables to coronary risk factors. For Type A managers the multiple regressions showed that changes in ambiguity were significantly related to systolic blood pressure, diastolic blood pressure and triglyceride levels. These effects were also moderated by intrinsic satisfaction such that larger changes were present for those with initially higher or lower levels of satisfaction. Other analyses also showed cholesterol level changes were related to changes in role ambiguity. A totally different picture was obtained for Type B managers. The regression indicated that only systolic blood pressure was related to ambiguity changes, and that the effect was in the opposite direction: increases in ambiguity were associated with decreases in blood pressure. Other research has shown that Type As respond to stressors at work in a different way to Type Bs. Newton and Keenan (1985), for example, demonstrate that Type As are less likely to use potentially helpful coping strategies in response to a work stress incident: instead they tend to show greater helplessness and resentment.

Laboratory studies also demonstrate Type A/B differences in response to stressors which are of relevance to the work environment. For example, on a treadmill task Type As will do more work than Type Bs, although they will not admit to being as fatigued (Carver, Coleman and Glass, 1976). They also appear to deny distress more often than Type Bs under conditions of physiological arousal which led Pittner and Houston (1980) to conclude that they are more likely to consciously try to cope with a difficult situation. Type As are also more physiologically reactive and labile than Type Bs (e.g. Houston, 1983; Krantz and Manuck, 1984, 1985). Reactivity may itself be a risk factor for the later development of chronic disease. When faced with a stressor Type As show larger cardiovascular and endocrinal responsivity. Their reactivity is also affected by such factors as competitive conditions in the presence of a harassing opponent (Glass *et al.*, 1980) and whether or not they can exert control over the situation (Glass, 1977; 1983; Matthews and Glass, 1984). Recent research, however, suggests that whatever role behavioural type plays in work stress it is unlikely to be a consciously mediated one. Kahn *et al.* (1980) and Krantz *et al.* (1982) have reported that Type As undergoing surgery requiring general anaesthetic show greater preoperative–introoperative physiological changes than Type Bs. Thus, the sympathetic nervous system responsivity is not a result of the behavioural type, but the cause of it (Krantz and Durel, 1983).

OCCUPATION, MORBIDITY AND MORTALITY

This section presents, in broad terms, some data on which sectors of a workforce suffer most from strain. It may have been noted from the above discussion of the French–Belgian-Collaborative Group study (1982) that the prevalence and incidence rates of heart disease of the factory workers were larger than those of the civil servants. This was true for both hard (infarction) events and angina pectoris and for each of the four age bands considered. For the 40–44-year-olds, for example, the incidence rate of hard coronary events and angina was 4.4 times higher for the factory workers.

The relationship between broad occupationally derived social variables and mortality and morbidity rates is the subject of considerable debate. The relevance of such a debate to occupational stress is that it has become increasingly clear that purely physical environmental agents/facilities cannot adequately account for the disease patterns. Syme and Berkman (1976) in their review of social class, susceptibility and sickness, for example, state that poor housing, crowding, racial factors, low income, poor education, unemployment, poor nutrition, poor use and availability of medical services, strenuous employment, non-hygenic settings and increased exposure to toxic agents are all inadequate to explain the associations which have been observed between a large number of diseases and social class. Improvements in such factors, for example, does not appear to affect the social class gradient markedly. It is suggested that at least some of the relationship between occupational and social categories and disease is due to psychological factors which compromise the disease defences and affect general susceptibility.

In the past there has been considerable controversy over the relationship between illness/mortality rates and occupational category, particularly when the latter forms the basis of socioeconomic classifications (e.g. Biorck, Blomqvist and Sievers, 1958; Stamler *et al.*, 1960; Lee and Schneider, 1958; Pell and D'Alonzo, 1963). Antonovsky (1968), in his well-known review of social class and the major cardiovascular diseases, concluded that for cardiovascular diseases, circulatory diseases, hypertensive heart disease, diseases of the heart, arteriosclerotic and degenerative heart disease, or coronary heart disease, 'no fewer studies report inverse class gradients than direct gradients, and both are outnumbered by the number of studies showing no clear gradient' (p. 102). Cerebral haemorrhage (ICD 330–334) and 'other myocardial degeneration' (422) did show consistent inverse class gradients. There is some evidence that the relationships have probably changed over time (e.g. Jenkins, 1982; Morgenstern, 1985), which suggests that more attention should be paid to more recent studies.

One reason for many of these early inconsistencies may have been that many different ways of measuring socioeconomic variables were employed (Kessler, 1982; Lehman, 1967; Morgenstern, 1985) and some of the confusion is probably due to failures to compare like with like. When epidemiological studies have adopted two different classificatory procedures the results have not always been consistent (e.g. Finlay-Jones and Burvill, 1977).

The difficulty of assessing the true role of occupational factors in mortality and morbidity as revealed by social class gradients is greatly confounded by the degree to which the occupation determines the classification. The Edward's Scale (1934), commonly used in the USA, is weighted by average income and educational level to produce six categories: professional and technical, managers, administrators and proprietors, sales and clerical, skilled craftsmen and foremen, semi-skilled operatives, and unskilled labourers. The Duncan Index and its derivatives (Duncan, 1961; Blau and Duncan, 1967; Stevens and Featherman, 1981) includes account of prestige ratings, whilst the Warner Index (Warner, Meeker and Eells, 1949) includes reference to other social aspects besides occupational status such as source of income and quality of domicile. Hollingshead and Redlich's (1958) index did include reference to educational level and quality of neighbourhood as well as occupational status, although the neighbourhood dimension does not add much predictability to the scale (Hollingshead, 1971).

The British Registrar General's Social Class Scale divides occupations into six different categories: professional and similar (A or I), intermediate (B or II), non-manual skilled (C1 or IIIN), manual skilled (C2 or IIIM), partly skilled (D or IV) and unskilled occupations (E or V). The basis of this scale is the level of work skill required by the job:

> The occupation groups included in each of these categories have been selected in such a way as to bring together, so far as is possible, people with similar levels of occupational skill . . . and no account is taken of differences between individuals in the same occupation group e.g. differences of education or level of remuneration' (OPCS Classification of Occupations, 1980, p. xi)

Other scales (e.g. Wright and Perrone's Class Typology, Robinson and Kelly's Class Typology) are concerned more with the degree of authority and control in the workplace. Whilst each of these scales categorizes workers according to different criteria (the value of which may change with time) such broad groupings do have some value in assessing the impact of broad spectrum stressors on health. All schemes which attempt to categorize a group of occupational descriptions or labels under common characteristics are bound to have limitations, especially when the descriptions are themselves dubious catchers of reality (e.g. the description 'company director'). The use of 'social class' descriptors can also be particularly problematic when using standardized statistics of morbidity and mortality, such as the Standardized Mortality Ratio (SMR), because of numerator/denominator bias, as revealed by longitudinal study (OPCS *Decennial Supplement*, 1986a) although such bias is particularly problematic only for the unskilled category. Such problems with statistics like the SMR are considerably outweighed by their advantages.

In addition, it has been suggested that some of the discrepancies in the literature may be a result of previous failures to take account of such factors as 'social mobility' and 'status discordance' (see Jenkins, 1971; Kasl, 1978). More recent reviews, however, provide a more sceptical view (Berkman, 1980; Jenkins, 1976), and it has been suggested that if there are health effects of such factors they are probably dependent on individual and situational factors (Morgenstern, 1985). Kessler (1982), for example, shows that the relative importance of social status as a predictor of strain levels varies with the sex and labour force status of those under consideration.

Socioeconomic variables do represent one of the most commonly measured psychosocial factors in epidemiology and it is necessary to attempt to dissect what contribution occupational psychological factors may play in these observed patterns of disease. This can be difficult because the different scales weight occupational factors to different degrees. It has been suggested, for example, that when occupational rank is related to (e.g.) risk of coronary heart disease within an organizational context, the relationship is likely to be an inverse one. Using broader community and regional settings, however, changes the nature of the relationship (Lehman, 1967). A consideration of recent evidence strongly supports the contention that, for almost any significant measure of strain, the higher a worker is up the occupational ladder, the less likely they are to suffer significant illness (Fletcher and Payne, 1980a; Fletcher, Gowler and Payne, 1979; Fletcher, 1979). Some of this evidence will be considered below, taking account of a range of strains from biomedical risks, through morbidity rates, to life expectancy. Whilst there are exceptions to the inverse gradient between occupational level and strain, and each occupational classification and strain measure has its own associated limitations, the weight of evidence is relatively consistent. As to what the pattern means, that is another question.

Psychological Strain

Kornhauser's (1965) famous work with Detroit car workers showed clearly that 'The higher the occupation the better the mental health on the average' (p. 56). He found that when the workers were classified into job levels by reference to work skill, variety, responsibility and pay, mental health scores (which were relatively assessed) showed a consistent correlation with the occupational gradient. For example, considering just middle-aged blue-collar workers, the proportions in each occupational group with high mental health were: skilled workers 56%, high semi-skilled 41%, ordinary semi-skilled 38%, repetitive semi-skilled 26%, repetitive machine-paced 26%. These occupational differences were present when a number of other factors were partialled out including age, education level, job satisfaction, perceived utilization of ability and opportunity for advancement, income level in boyhood, and a range of other childhood variables including deprivation, anxiety, happiness and aspirations. Kornhauser thus concluded that 'they still show group differences in mental health corresponding to their occupational level—differences roughly comparable in size to those for the total occupational group' (p. 73). This supported the view that the job was a major contributing cause to the level of mental health of the workers.

Warr and Payne's (1982a) survey of experiences of strain and pleasure among adults also revealed significant relationships with socioeconomic status. Men (19%) and women (23%) from socioeconomic groups DE were more likely to have experienced emotional strain for at least half of yesterday than those of C2 status (13% men, 19% women) or ABC1 (11% men, 11% women). In addition, they were considerably more likely to have experienced the strain for at least one month. The DE women were also more likely to react to the strain by smoking more, compared with the C2 and ABC1 women (20%, 15%, 10% respectively) (Warr and Payne, 1982b).

When considering validated indices of mental health a similar pattern is revealed. Crown and Crisp (1979), in their normative data for the CCEI, demonstrate that those in social classes A and B have lower scores than those from C and D for the scales of free-floating anxiety, phobic anxiety, obsessionality (women), depression (men) and somatic anxiety (men and women). Finlay-Jones and Burvill (1977), in their 1% 'healthy' community showed that the lowest two occupational groupings had a greater prevalence of minor psychiatric cases than the top four (18.5% vs 11.2%). It should be re-emphasized, however, that different measures of socioeconomic status have been shown to produce inconsistent patterns (e.g. Finlay-Jones and Burvill, 1977; Goldberg, 1972). Some studies also show a J-shaped relationship between socioeconomic status and mental health, such that the highest levels show an increase, not a decrease, in ill-health (e.g. Goldberg, 1972, Appendix 7; Hepworth, 1980). Hepworth (1980), for example, reports GHQ scores of unemployed men, categorized by the Registrar General's classification of their former occupations. The GHQ scores obtained (and percentage of samples above the cut-off point indicating at least minor moribidity) were: managerial, 3.2 (46%); skilled non-manual, 2.8 (25%); skilled manual, 4.0 (61%); partly skilled, 6.2 (80%); unskilled 6.5 (70%) (but see Payne, Warr and Hartley, 1984). Using an earlier version of the same socioeconomic scale, Finlay–Jones and Burvill (1977) also observed an increased case prevalence in the 'professional and similar' workers (15.6%), compared with the 'intermediate' (primarily managerial) group (11.5%). A similar effect has been observed for the prevalence of arteriosclerotic diseases amongst white collar males in a large organization (Lee and Schneider, 1958), with 5-year rates of 11.8% for 'top executives', 7.7% for 'executives', 6.6% for 'minor executives' and 15.3% for non-executives (see also Holme *et al.*, 1982).

The broadly negative relationship between occupational or social position and psychological distress which has been consistently documented in epidemiological surveys may not be simply due to the lower strata being exposed to a greater level of stressors. Kessler and Cleary (1980), for example, suggest that statistical adjustment for differential exposure to stressors does not account for much of the variance. Instead one needs to consider that a significant aspect of the relationship is due to differences in responsiveness to stressors. According to this view those in the lower occupational levels are more likely to develop symptoms when exposed to a stressor: their general psychological defences (and biological defences) are weaker than those higher up the ladder. Such possibilities imply that minor differences in stressor levels (which may be difficult to detect reliably) would be amplified in strain manifestations.

Whatever the reason for these patterns of psychiatric morbidity, there is some evidence that the higher the status of the workers the more likely they are to admit or believe they have stress problems. Cherry (1978) reports that 54% of professional workers admitted suffering from nervous strain, compared with only 10% of unskilled manual workers: the myth of executive stress in action. Perhaps this is why the majority of stress courses are for managerial employees! In view of this it is not too surprising to find examples of studies which show that those higher up the occupational ladder are more likely to use professional help for personal problems. Kulka, Veroff and Douvan (1979), for example, report the results of two national surveys of the American adult population done in 1957 and 1976. They found that the higher the income or educational level the more likely a person was to show 'readiness for self-referral'. They also report that help-seeking behaviour was largely independent of psychological symptom levels.

Disease Risk Factors

Some biochemical risk factors have been shown to be positively related to occupational level. One such factor is purine uric acid. High levels of uric acid may lead to crystallization in the joints or the urinary tract, causing gout or kidney stones. Evidence suggests that uric acid levels rise with occupational status and social class. Dunn *et al.*, (1963), for example, found that 43% of executives had a serum urate level of greater than 6 mg%, compared with 12% of craftsmen. The uric acid levels also showed a monotonic increase with number of years of schooling. Other factors (e.g. diet, aspirin consumption, obesity) could not account for the observed relationship. These early findings have been replicated and extended. There is also other evidence that levels are related to achievement and achievement-oriented behaviour and are affected by work stress and losing one's job (see a review by Mueller *et al.*, 1970).

Other biochemical indices have also been shown to be lower among low level jobs. Caplan *et al.* (1975), for example, showed marked occupational differences in serum cortisol levels, a stress hormone of the adrenal-cortical axis. Low levels were observed in machine assemblers, with significantly elevated levels in scientists and administrators. Payne *et al.*, (1985) have also reported that members of a cardiac surgery firm showed cortisol levels above the normal range of 72% of measurements, with mean levels higher the more senior the doctor, but this relationship was not replicated (Payne and Rick, 1986).

Some studies have also observed plasma cholesterol levels to be higher in those higher up the occupational ladder. Marmot *et al.* (1978) reported that the higher the civil service grade, the more likely a person was to have cholesterol levels above 260 mg% (12.6% of the highest grade, and 7.8% of the lowest), and the higher the mean level (201 vs 192 mg%). The authors attributed this to the richer fat diet of the higher administrative grades. Other studies, however, have not found a direct relationship between occupational level and cholesterol levels. The Oslo Study, in which 14,677 men aged between 40 and 49 were screened for coronary risk factors, observed an inverse gradient between levels and socioeconomic class (Holme *et al.*, 1976). This discrepancy is not simply a function of the crudeness of the social class scale in the latter study since the same data broken down into specific occupational groups shows that, for symptom-free men, lower status occupations such as tram drivers, metal foundry workers, construction machinery operators and taxi drivers are associated with the highest plasma cholesterol levels (Holme *et al.*, 1976). Nor should it be thought that the discrepancy is necessarily a function of specific occupational stressors being appropriate to white-collar jobs, and not blue-collar jobs (although the reverse may be true). Low level jobs (defined by the Duncan scale or by specific job title) are characterized by underutilization of abilities, low participation, flexibility and autonomy, but occupational level is also inversely correlated with 'executive stressors' such as role conflict, role ambiguity and ambiguity over one's future (Caplan *et al.*, 1975). The existing data are, however, inadequate to make anything but the broadest of generalizations.

When other coronary risk factors are considered the literature would support the contention that, on the whole, there is an inverse gradient between occupational level and coronary risk. Obviously, the more marked the differences between occupational level the clearer the picture is.

In their study of employment grade and CHD in British civil servants, Marmot *et al.* (1978) show that a man's grade was a strong predictor of the presence of the major coronary risk factors in their 7½-year longitudinal study. Four grades were considered: messengers/unskilled personnel, clericals, professionals/executives, and administrators (in order of grade). For the risk factors of systolic blood pressure, smoking behaviour, obesity and physical inactivity the higher the grade the higher the age-adjusted means and the higher the percentage of cases showing 'elevated' values. For example, the mean systolic pressure of administrators was 134 mmHg, with 11% showing elevated values (above 159 mmHg). The figures obtained for messengers were 138 mmHg and 17%. The differences were present for those in the under-40-year-old and 40–49-year-old age bands (Marmot & Khaw, 1982). In addition, 61% of messenger grade men smoked and only 15% had never smoked, compared with 29% and 33% for the administrators. Fifty-six per cent of the messenger grades were physically inactive compared with only 26% of the administrators (Marmot *et al.*, 1978). Similar patterns have been demonstrated in other studies of coronary risk. In the Oslo Study, for example, data for 43 occupational groups is presented (Holme *et al.* 1977). In general, those in the blue-collar occupations exhibited considerably higher multiplicative coronary risk scores (based on factors such as blood pressure, serum cholesterol, triglycerides and smoking behaviour) than those in white-collar jobs. Those in pedagogical work (e.g. university lecturers and professors) showed the lowest risk. Executives and managers had relatively low risk, clerical and sales personnel medium risk, higher risks for transport workers (e.g. bus and taxi drivers), and considerably raised risks for metal foundry workers and machinery operators. For example, the levels of risk factors for 'leading administrators and executive officials' were: 29% smoked, triglycerides 2.0 mmol/1, blood pressure 131/83 mmHg, cholesterol 272 mg/dl. For 'administrative, executive and managerial workers' the relative figures were: 37%, 2.12 mmol/1, 134/86 mmHg, 266 mg/dl; and for metal foundry workers: 58%, 2.5 mmol/1, 141/89 mmHg, 280 mg/dl.

Disease and Life Expectancy

In their massive study of 270,000 employees of Bell Telephone Company, Hinkle *et al.* (1968) report the results of a 3-year study in which 6347 events of disability or death were due to coronary heart disease. The age-standardized incidence rates of first events of disabling coronary heart disease were inversely related to occupational level. The rates/1000 were 1.85 for executives, 2.85 for general area managers, 3.91 for local area managers and supervisors, 4.52 for foremen and 4.33 for skilled manual workers. Although educational level at the time of hiring was shown to have a marked effect on these rates, those at the lowest level (workers) were still about twice as likely to suffer a coronary event, compared with executives, whether one considers only the population with college education (4.15/1000 vs 1.65/1000), or only those without college education (4.46/1000 vs 2.46/1000).

The study by Hinkle *et al.* (1968) clearly demonstrated the importance of educational factors in affecting the likelihood of a person suffering a coronary event which 'has been approximately 30 per cent lower among college men than among no-college men under all circumstances. . . . Up to now we have not encountered any exception to this rule' (p. 243), which suggests that factors outside the workplace play a major role in determining coronary risk (Hinkle *et al.* even proposed that the workforce could be divided into two populations with notably different biological features). One should not, however, ignore the interaction between the work environment and the pre-existing personal characteristics. The Framingham Study, for example, has shown that Type A coronary risk is not reflected in a greater incidence of CHD for blue-collar workers, although among white-collar workers the excess risk for Type As is over 2.4 that of Type Bs (Haynes and Feinleib, 1982). It should also be borne in mind that the occupational/social status gradient generally observed for CHD is not explicable solely in terms of differences in the risk factor gradients discussed in the previous section. A number of studies have shown that even when traditional risk factors are controlled for the gradient does not change appreciably (Holme *et al.*, 1982; Marmot *et al.*, 1978; Rose and Marmot, 1981). In the Marmot *et al.* (1978) longitudinal study of civil servants, for example, the messengers in the lowest grades had 3.6 times the CHD mortality of those in the highest administrative grades. Although men in the lower grades tended to show higher risks in terms of most of the traditional risk factors (see above) the excess risk accounted for by such factors was minimal, leaving a large part of the intergrade differences in CHD mortality rates unexplained. The authors suggested that 'psychosocial differences between the grades' (p. 249) may have been the major discriminating risk factor.

What occupational psychosocial factors may be responsible for the pattern of CHD observed is a contentious issue. Figure 1 contains a list of possible contributing work stressors. The stressors associated with increased risk include work overload (e.g. Jenkins, 1982; Russek, 1965; Theorell and Floderus-Myrhed, 1977), although it is also clear that the low level jobs are associated with strain indicators because of factors related to work underload. In a study by Margolis *et al.* (1974) underutilization of abilities correlated with overall strain more strongly than did most other stressors. Kritsikis, Heinemann and Eitner (1968) observed that workers on conveyor line systems had a particularly high prevalence of angina pectoris. The job redesign literature emphasizes, at a theoretical and pragmatic level, that changes in the work environment which increase worker autonomy, task identity, significance, variety and feedback all serve to increase mental health (Broadbent, 1985) even if these changes are made only at the level of the work group, leaving the basic work processes of the individual largely undisturbed (Wall, 1980; Wall and Clegg, 1981). It seems likely that the occupational factors relating to overload and underload, although both affecting the endocrinal systems in similar ways, may have their influence through separate psychological mechanisms. If one considers overload and underload as being separate unipolar dimensions (each being stressors) rather than a single bipolar dimension, a good degree of sense can be made of the literature.

One conceptualization of occupational stress which simultaneously accommodates both types of stressor is the Demands–Supports–Constraints model (Payne, 1979; Payne and Fletcher, 1983). Essentially the model proposes that orthogonal factors, job demand and job support-constraint, determine the risk of strain. The higher the job demand, the lower the support and the higher the constraint, the greater the risk. Thus the model accounts for the apparent paradox that underload is associated with strain by proposing that such jobs are usually accompanied by low levels of support or high levels of

Table 1 Deaths in Great Britain from major causes 1979–1980 and 1982–83 for occupied men aged 20–64, married women (classified by husband's occupation) and single women aged 20–59

Cause of death (ICD No. 9th revision)	Deaths occupied men (%)	Deaths married women (%)	Deaths single women (%)	SMRs for men						SMRs for married women						SMRs for single women					
				I	II	IIIN	IIIM	IV	V	I	II	IIIN	IIIM	IV	V	I	II	IIIN	IIIM	IV	V
Diseases of circulatory system (390–459)	48	27	22	69	80	102	108	113	151	54	68	84	119	140	191	60	57	81	128	123	128
Ischaemic Heart Disease (410–414)	37	14	10	70	82	104	109	112	144	46	63	80	122	144	194	51	57	82	153	127	142
Acute myocardial Infarction (410)	28	10	7	71	83	105	109	111	143	43	62	83	122	145	192	64	56	88	157	121	140
Neoplasms (140–239)	29	49	41	69	77	89	113	117	154	89	95	101	110	117	132	96	94		133	117	112
Trachea, bronchus, lung (162)	11	7	4	43	63	80	120	126	178	50	73	81	122	138	170	85	72		168	157	158
Digestive organs and peritoneum (150–159)	8	9	7	80	83	92	110	115	141	91	93	101	110	120	130	75	75		130	136	132
Stomach (151)	2	2	1	50	67	83	119	127	158	77	79	86	118	128	161	82	78		154	135	181
Colon (153)	2	3	2	114	99	105	103	101	116	107	104	116	108	105	98	94	79		141	146	90
Lymphatic and haematopoietic tissue (200–208)	2	3	3	107	97	98	105	104	121	95	104	98	106	115	119	104	96		151	114	113
Female Breast (174)		5	13	—	—	—	—	—	—	109	105	114	104	107	104		99		126	101	100
External causes of injury and poisoning (E800–E999)	9	7	16	67	70	78	93	121	226	75	81	91	79	105	150		81		79	103	154
Motor vehicle accidents (E810–E825)	3	2	5	65	79	81	106	118	181	89	85	96	75	103	123		99		105	106	159
Suicide and self inflicted injury (E950–E959)	3	3	5	89	80	95	86	114	198	91	91	111	77	94	123		85		65	109	111
Diseases of respiratory system (460–519)	7	6	7	36	50	83	102	129	210	47	64	76	118	143	220		54		83	93	97
Diseases of Digestive System (520–579)	3	3	3	67	79	91	92	112	204	70	85	76	112	116	196		72		97	89	126
Stomach and duodenum ulcer (531–533)	0.6	0.5	0.6	39	55	80	94	124	261	54	58	79	114	136	280		82		87	86	135
Diseases of nervous system and sense organs (320–389)	1	2	3	69	61	100	80	109	185	98	85	92	110	128	132		61		95	66	88

Table 1 (continued)

Cause of death (ICD No. 9th revision)	Deaths occupied men (%)	Deaths married women (%)	Deaths single women (%)	SMRs for men						SMRs for married women						SMRs for single women					
				I	II	IIIN	IIIM	IV	V	I	II	IIIN	IIIM	IV	V	I	II	IIIN	IIIM	IV	V
Endocrinal, nutritional and metabolic diseases, and immunity disorders (240–279)	1	1	2	72	76	110	99	118	156	49	60	88	114	145	242	88	43	79	141	84	96
Diabetes mellitus (250)	0.7	0.8	1	67	76	113	100	123	155	47	59	92	114	147	247	94	51	75	130	86	113
Diseases of genitourinary system (580–629)	0.6	1	1	43	69	106	94	116	185	45	63	105	113	134	241	24	50	56	98	93	139
Infectious and parasitic diseases (001–139)	0.5	0.7	0.9	65	62	93	89	117	215	68	86	73	112	128	187	76	61	89	94	64	85
Mental disorders (290–319)	0.4	0.4	0.7	35	48	55	84	97	342	63	66	83	95	116	227	67	44	76	41	65	61
All causes (001–999)	N= 326573	N= 90713	N= 10209	66	76	94	106	116	165	75	83	93	111	125	160	75	68	80	111	107	117

Reproduced from Fletcher 1989.

constraint. It is this configuration which elevates the coronary risk [Karasek's (1979) Demand-Discretion model, although somewhat simpler in conceptualization, makes similar predictions]. Jobs which are high in demand may also carry excess risk, but not if they are 'active' jobs which are also characterized by high levels of job discretion or decision latitude. Executive and managerial roles may be very demanding (even overloading) but they are also associated with high levels of control or support which effectively nullifies the demandingness and reduces coronary risk. Jobs which are high on demand and low in discretion (some machine-paced work?) will lead to high levels of strain, because the lack of decision latitude acts as a severe constraint to prevent optimal coping. Effectively the demandingness of the job is not held in check by the positive benefits of personal freedom and supportive environment in which they carry out their jobs. Unskilled operatives may not be placed under high levels of demand, but such jobs are very low in support and decision latitude which itself carries excess coronary risk independently of the level of demand.

The Demands-Discretion model has been successfully applied to the prediction of a range of strains including felt exhaustion, pill consumption, absence, satisfaction (Karasek, 1979) endocrine and metabolic processes (Karasek, Russell and Theorell, 1982) and coronary heart disease (Alfredsson, Karasek and Theorell, 1982; Karasek *et al.*, 1982). In the Alfredsson *et al.* (1982) study, for example, psychosocially relevant aspects of 118 different occupations were identified by conducting a nationwide interview survey of 3876 working men. These results were then used to attempt to discriminate 334 myocardial infarct cases from double case-control men matched for age, sex and area of residence. A number of 'occupational' psychosocial characteristics were significant discriminators, including shiftwork, monotony, low autonomy over work tempo, not learning new things, and heavy lifting. The *combination* of high demand and low discretion has also provided more accurate predictions of CHD than either dimension separately (Karasek *et al.*, 1982).

Karasek's model may not particularly be relevant to *occupational* stress. Its predictiveness has been confined to large socially and occupationally heterogeneous samples in which a package of nonwork variables is probably the major discriminator. When applied to occupationally homogeneous groups the predicted interactions are very small or nonexistent (Payne and Fletcher, 1983). This supports the view that a much richer tapestry of occupational psychological factors needs to be sampled in stress studies sampling specific or socially homogeneous occupational groups (e.g. Fletcher and Payne, 1982). The Demands–Supports–Constraints framework may prove rather more useful in such contexts.

The relationship obtained between occupational status and disease discussed above is present for a whole array of diseases. Table 1 presents the latest mortality statistics (Fletcher, 1989) for all the major causes of death of working age people for occupied men aged 20–64 years, and single women aged 20–59 classified according to their own occupation (based on the OPCS *Classification of Occupations*, 1980). The figures relate to deaths in the years 1979–80 and 1982–3 and have been abstracted from the OPCS *Occupational Mortality Decennial Supplement* microfiche tables (OPCS, 1986b). Perusal of Table 1 shows that for almost every major cause of death the higher the occupational class the lower the SMRs. The relationship is not confined to infectious diseases and those (such as respiratory diseases) for which relatively clear physical environmental agents may be responsible. Nor should it be suggested that such factors as diet and smoking behaviour are the major discriminating variables. Not only do these factors fail to explain the pattern shown here, but such explanations naively ignore the role psychological work stressors play in determining the presence of such risk factors themselves. The pattern is also unlikely to be due to psychosomatic differences in social class. For example, patients in lower socioeconomic categories do not have a higher perception of pain or neuroticism about illness than those in higher classes (Larson and Marcer, 1984).

There are, of course, many factors involved in good health and life expectancy and it would not be sensible to assert that all (or even many) of these factors are occupationally and psychologically determined. There is a direct gradient, for example, between occupational status, or number of years of formal education completed, and the number of common surgical operations a person is likely to have undergone (Coulter and McPherson, 1985). Such findings are independent of known morbidity rates by socioeconomic status, and clearly imply that broader factors are responsible for surgical contact rates. What is needed, however, is a sympathetic consideration of the possible role of psychological (and particularly occupational) factors in disease and death. The final section of this paper raises one such issue in greater depth.

OCCUPATIONAL MORTALITY AND THE TRANSMISSION OF OCCUPATIONAL RISKS

A consideration of occupational mortality statistics implicates a major role being played by occupational psychological stressors on job encumbents and their spouses (Fletcher, Gowler and Payne, 1980; Fletcher, 1982, 1983, 1985, 1988). Put another way, work stressors affect the life expectancy of men and their wives in quite subtle but powerful ways. Fletcher (1983), for example, analysed the mortality statistics of 1,088,995 people aged 15–64 years who died in the 8-year period 1959–1963, 1970–1972. Occupational mortality statistics for over 200 different jobs were considered. There were marked differences in mortality rates for different occupations which were independent of social class. In addition, however, correlations of around 0.9 were reported

Table 2 SMRs for selected occupations 1970–1972, for men and married women (classified by husband's occupation) aged 15–64, for different causes of death
(From Fletcher, 1985)

Occupation unit (and OPCS number)	All causes		Malignant neoplasms		Circulatory diseases		Respiratory diseases		Accidents etc.	
	Men	Women	Men	Women	Men	Women	Men	Women	Men	Women
Gardeners and groundsmen (5)	92	108	101	104	83	105	89	88	104	105
Coalminers — underground (7)	141	161	119	138	132	198	252	208	156	115
— surface (8)	160	136	127	114	168	161	226	183	83	57
Ceramic formers (13)	131	125	144	110	113	124	268	202	65	72
Fettlers, metal drawers (23)	110	112	113	112	99	99	155	121	101	127
Electricians (27)	95	97	103	99	103	96	80	95	85	85
Electrical engineers (30) (so described)	317	295	323	330	342	285	211	210	301	263
Foremen (engineering) (31)	47	61	52	67	51	62	34	54	17	17
Sheet and metal workers (33)	110	111	129	120	112	111	112	118	76	88
Machine tool setters (38)	86	94	101	91	86	103	91	104	46	56
Machine tool operators (39)	156	197	163	192	148	198	137	192	211	258
Tool makers, tool room fitters (40)	105	106	118	113	111	111	81	84	83	71
Motor mechanics (41)	107	112	117	121	113	109	90	86	102	101
Plumbers (45)	101	112	117	115	99	119	91	97	89	79
Inspectors (metal and electrical) (53)	91	88	89	86	100	93	92	87	50	46
Fibre repairers (64)	130	153	127	112	133	193	152	217	108	84
Makers of paper and paperboard (83)	93	116	106	107	97	138	115	133	38	48
Paper product makers (84)	50	55	65	51	54	73	44	31	3	12
Plasterers etc. (95)	112	124	124	123	103	128	137	171	93	39
Bricklayers, labourers (97)	273	241	225	186	239	250	419	419	403	173
Textile labourers (110)	109	105	86	71	114	132	139	138	93	78
Coke, ovens and gas workers (112)	131	111	122	94	113	115	240	180	108	92
Other labourers (114)	201	198	182	164	164	212	271	256	377	246

Table 2 (continued)

Occupation unit (and OPCS number)	All causes		Malignant neoplasms		Circulatory diseases		Respiratory diseases		Accidents etc.	
	Men	Women	Men	Women	Men	Women	Men	Women	Men	Women
Deck and engineroom ratings etc. (116)	233	186	221	167	180	197	250	221	488	206
Telephone operators (127)	129	120	116	116	133	134	118	81	124	117
Bus conductors (131)	118	128	118	118	112	120	165	181	83	78
Civil service executives (142)	78	78	83	87	93	76	45	68	24	26
Policemen (152)	109	109	115	115	131	124	76	67	80	107
Caretakers (165)	106	109	114	110	106	107	99	97	84	79
Managers in engineering (175)	65	66	71	82	76	55	31	37	40	58
Managers in building (176)	54	55	62	60	60	52	25	51	32	38
Medical practitioners (181)	81	92	61	98	85	66	34	25	180	322
Nurses (183)	112	114	94	130	122	110	76	118	147	134
University teachers (192)	49	67	49	86	47	41	17	41	63	78
Primary and secondary school teachers (193)	66	80	57	97	81	66	38	50	54	100
Accountants (209)	88	89	93	112	97	63	47	66	66	84
Armed forces (UK) (221)	147	150	166	177	145	120	129	116	149	158

Figures abstracted from OPCS *Occupational Mortality 1970–72* Microfiche tables (OPCS, 1978).

between the occupationally derived SMRs of men and those of married women *classified by their husband's occupation, not their own*. It was suggested therefore, that the life expectancy of a married woman may be significantly affected by the occupation her husband is engaged in. An alternative interpretation of such similarities between male and married female SMRs suggests that neither is affected by occupational factors because the life expectancy of both is largely determined by the 'way of life' they lead (e.g. OPCS, 1978a, 1986a,; Fox and Adelstein, 1978). Such an explanation, however, ignores the occupational specificity present in the mortality data and the large literature on the health consequences of psychological aspects of work, and requires the rather unlikely assumption that work has little impact on the job encumbent.

There is evidence from other studies showing that the life expectancy of marital partners is affected by spouse characteristics. For example, in the Framingham Heart Study a prospective analysis of 269 spouse pairs over a 10-year period showed that men married to women with 13 or more years of education were 2.6 times more likely to develop CHD than those whose wives had a grammar school education. In addition, men married to wives in white-collar jobs were up to 5.4 times more likely to develop CHD than if their wives were blue-collar workers (Haynes, Eaker and Feinleib, 1983, see also Kessler, 1982, p. 759). A differential rate of CHD in Type A and Type B men has also only been shown to be present for men whose wives' characteristics might be deemed stressful (Eaker, Haynes and Feinleib, 1983). Several studies have also shown that work factors may have a spillover onto other family members. Male police officers under work stress, for example, show more anger, less involvement in family affairs and are more likely to have unsatisfactory marriages (Jackson and Maslach, 1982). Other work factors such as working hours (Mott *et al.* 1965; Winnett and Neale, 1981), job mobility (Cooper, 1979) and job related travel (Culbert and Renshaw, 1972) have also been shown to have stress effects on marital partners. The interaction between work and family roles does appear to result in stress effects when considered together (Bhagat *et al.*, 1985; Cooke and Rousseau, 1984), especially when job-involvement is high (Frone and Rice, 1987). It has also been shown that work stressors can result in prolonged physiological after-effects. For example, Rissler (1977) studied the after-effects of overtime on worktime and evening urinary levels of adrenaline in a 2-month longitudinal study. During the 4-week block of overtime evenings adrenaline levels were elevated by more than 200% over pre-overtime levels, suggesting that unwinding after overtime may be a slow process with significant spillover into the home.

I have argued elsewhere (Fletcher, 1983) that several commonsense explanations of the link between the occupationally derived SMRs (e.g. common social class, transfer of physical risks, bereavement effects) are inadequate, and that any explanation needs to centre on the occupational stress risks present in the male's work environment. For example, the effects of suffering a bereavement on the surviving spouse produce only a short-term elevation in death rate for widowers (Parkes, Benjamin and Fitzgerald, 1969) with little indication that widows are similarly affected (Bowling, 1987). Beral (1974) has also reported marked occupational differences for cervical cancer mortality of married women (classified by their husband's occupation) which were independent of the observed social class gradient. An alternative explanation I have offered (e.g. Fletcher, 1983, 1987, 1989) suggests that the job a person does moulds their cognitive structure. This in turn affects the domestic environment in which both partners live and, therefore, the psychological stressors they are both exposed to. This would imply that psychological factors do have a pervasive role in morbidity and eventual death.

If occupational psychological stressors are partly responsible for the life expectancy of both partners, then one might expect that occupations would carry specific disease and cause-of-death risks. If this were so the psychological transmission hypothesis would imply that marital partners should show related causes of death. That is, there should be a significant likelihood of marital partners dying from the same cause. There is some support for this assertion. Parkes *et al.* (1969) in a study of 4486 widowers showed an elevation in their death rates of some 40% for the 6 months after bereavement. Of the 213 who died, 48 died from a cause concordant with their spouses which showed a slight excess over expected rates in five of the six disease groups considered (arteriosclerotic and degenerative heart disease; other heart and circulatory disorders; pneumonia, influenza and bronchitis; cancer; and all other causes). Whilst not all studies confirm these findings (Helsing and Szklo, 1981; Helsing, Comstock and Szklo, 1982) other studies have shown similar concordances for tuberculosis, influenza and pneumonia, cancer and CHD (Ciocco, 1940), lung cancer in the non-smoking wives of smoking husbands (Hirayama, 1981) and chronic bronchitis possibly related to the dusty male working environments (McLaughlin, 1966).

It is difficult to demonstrate that occupational stressors are responsible for the concordance in the causes of death of married people across the whole spectrum of occupations. A first step is to consider the correlations between SMRs of men and married women when both are classified according to the occupation of the husband (Fletcher, 1983, 1987, 1988). For different year categories (1959–1963, 1970–1972, 1979–1980 and 1982–1983), taking into consideration the deaths of nearly 1.5 million deaths from nearly 500 occupational classifications, these correlations are very large for specific major causes of death as well as for 'all causes' of death. They are also present when each social class is considered separately (Fletcher, 1987, 1988). The correlations are present for organic disease clusters (e.g. cancer, CHD) and 'non-organic' causes (e.g. suicide, accidents, poisonings and violence). In addition partialling out SMRs of all causes of death for men and married women for each specific cause also leaves marked residual partial correlations as does excluding statistical outliers. Table 2 presents the SMRs of men and married women for different causes of death for some of the well known occupational categories for one of the year groupings. One can see that coalminers (and women married to coalminers), for example, have a high mortality risk for respiratory diseases but a considerably lower risk of dying from a malignant neoplasm. Machine tool setters (and women married to them) have low accident mortality risk but normal respiratory diseases mortality. Machine tool operators, on the other hand, have high accident SMRs. Medical practitioners (and women married to them) have very low SMRs for respiratory diseases but a higher SMR for accidents etc. than coalminers. Policemen and their wives have low SMRs for respiratory diseases but elevated SMRs for circulatory diseases. The number of such comparisons which can be made is strikingly large and is present in each of the year groupings considered.

Whilst such evidence can never 'prove' that psychological occupational factors play a major role in the disease risks of men and their wives they should not be dismissed lightly. The findings are from a very large sample of deaths, include an analysis for the major causes of death, and are based on the entire range of occupations, not a selected subset. The evidence also adds weight to the small-scale studies which suggest that work and domestic roles have an interactive effect on health, and the increasing body of research showing that very subtle psychological factors may mediate the onset of all kinds of physical diseases, psychologically related causes of death, and of injurious behaviours (e.g. smoking, diet) linked to disease. That the psychological impact of work is not confined to the workplace is, of course, no surprise. That its effects may be so far reaching gives a wry twist to the phrase 'work as a way of life'.

CONCLUSIONS

This chapter has attempted to highlight a number of important points for stress research. It has suggested that greater emphasis should be placed on psychological factors in epidemiological investigations of objective strain indicators, that occupational psychological aspects are probably an important category of stressors, that a significant proportion of the workforce will be exhibiting significant strain at any one point in time, that the major sectors of the workforce under strain are those in low level jobs with little support and discretion (although a few biochemical risk factors show a positive relationship with occupational grade), that work stress probably has a major impact on the life expectancy of the job encumbant, as well as considerable spill-over on those outside the work environment.

The occupational stress literature has considerably greater clarity that it did 10 years ago. It is time, however, for a more subtle appraisal of occupational psychological factors in disease. This will require greater consideration of the rich tapestry of psychological factors that define as individual's job and an emphasis away from crude epidemiological variables (e.g. job title) which only serve to confound rather than clarify the role of work on health. The time is ripe for such research: individuals, organizations and economies are all likely to benefit from the endeavour.

REFERENCES

Ader, R. and Cohen, N. (1985). CNS-immune system interactions: conditioning phenomena, *The Behavioural and Brain Sciences*, **8**, 379–94.

Alfredsson, L., Karasek, R. A. and Theorell, T. (1982). Myocardial infarction risk and psychosocial environment—an analysis of the male Swedish Working Force, *Social Science and Medicine*, **16**, 463–467.

Antonovsky, A. (1968). Social class and the major cardiovascular diseases, *Journal of Chronic Diseases*, **21**, 65–106.

Beral, V. (1974). Cancer of the cervix: a sexually transmitted infection? *The Lancet*, **i**, 1037–40.

Berkman, L. F. (1980). Physical health and the social environment: a social epidemiological perspective. In L. Eisenberg and A. Kleinman (eds) *The Relevance of Social Science for Medicine*, pp. 51–75, Reidel, New York.

Bhagat, R. S., McQuaid, S. J., Lindholm, H. and Segovis, J. (1985). Total life stress: a multimethod validation of the construct and its effects on organisationally valued outcomes and withdrawal behaviours, *Journal of Applied Psychology*, **70**, 202–14.

Biorck, G., Blomqvist, M. K. and Sievers, J. (1958). Studies on myocardial infarction in Malmo 1935–1954—II. Infarction rate by occupational group, *Acta Medica Scandinavia*, **161(1)**, 21–32.

Blau, P. and Duncan, O. D. (1967). *The American Occupational Structure*, John Wiley and Sons, New York.

Bowling, A. (1987). Mortality after bereavement: a review of the literature on survival periods and factors affecting survival, *Social Science and Medicine*, **24**, 117–24.

Broadbent, D. E. (1985). The clinical impact of job design, *British Journal of Clinical Psychology*, **24**, 33–44.

Caplan, R. D., Cobb, S., French, J. R. P., Van Harrison, R. and Pinneau, S. R. (1975). *Job Demands and Worker Health*, DHEW Publication No. (NIOSH) 75–160, US Government Printing Office.

Carver, C. S., Coleman, A. E. and Glass, D. C. (1976). The coronary-prone behaviour pattern and suppression of fatigue on a treadmill test, *Journal of Personality and Social Psychology*, **33**, 460–6.

Charlesworth, E. A., Williams, B. J. and Baer, P. E. (1984). Stress management at the worksite for hypertension: compliance, cost–benefit, health care and hypertension-related variables, *Psychosomatic Medicine*, **46(5)**, 387–97.

Cherry, N. (1978). Stress, anxiety and work: A longitudinal study, *Journal of Occupational Psychology*, **51**, 259–70.

Cherry, N. (1984). Nervous strain, anxiety and symptoms amongst 32-year-old men at work in Britain, *Journal of Occupational Psychology*, **57**, 95–105.

Ciocco, A. (1940). On the interdependence of the length of life of husband and wife, *Human Biology*, **13**, 505–25.

Cobb, S. and Kasl, S. V. (1977). *Termination: the Consequences of Job Loss*, US Department of Health, Education and Welfare, Cincinatti.

Cooke, R. A. and Rousseau, D. M. (1984). Stress and strain from family roles and work-role expectations, *Journal of Applied Psychology*, **69**, 252–60.

Cooper, C. L. (1979) *The Executive Gypsy: The Quality of Managerial Life*, Macmillan Press, London.

Cooper, C. L. (ed.) (1984), *Psychosocial Stress and Cancer*, John Wiley and Sons, Chichester.

Cooper, C. L. (1986). Job distress: recent research and the emerging role of the clinical occupational psychologist, *Bulletin of the British Psychological Society*, **39**, 325–31.

Cooper, C. L. and Marshall, J. (1976). Occupational sources of stress: a review of the literature relating to coronary heart disease and mental ill-health, *Journal of Occupational Psychology*, **49**, 11–28.

Cooper, C. L., Mallinger, M. and Kahn, R. (1978). Identifying sources of occupational stress among dentists, *Journal of Occupational Psychology*, **51**, 227–34.

Coulter, A. and McPherson, K. (1985). Socioeconomic variations in the use of common surgical operations, *British Medical Journal*, **291**, 183–7.

Cox, T. (1978). *Stress*, University Park Press, Baltimore.

Cox, T. and Mackay, C. (1982). Psychosocial factors and psychophysiological mechanisms in the aetiology and development of cancers, *Social Science and Medicine*, **16**, 381–96.

Crown, S. and Crisp, A. H. (1979). *Manual of the Crown–Crisp Experiential Index*, Hodder and Stoughton, London.

Culbert, S. A. and Renshaw, J. R. (1972). Coping with the stresses of travel as an opportunity for improving the quality of work and family life, *Family Process*, **11**, 321–7.

Davidson, M. J. and Cooper, C. L. (1980). Type A coronary-prone behaviour in the work environment, *Journal of Occupational Medicine*, **22**(6), 375–83.

Dohrenwend, B. P., Dohrenwend, B. S., Gould, M. S., Link, B., Neugebauer, R. and Wunsch-Hitzig, R. (1980). *Mental Illness in the United States: Epidemiological estimates*, Praeger, New York.

Duncan, O. D. (1961). A socioeconomic index for all occupations. In A. J. Reiss (ed.) *Occupation and Social Status*, pp. 109–38, Free Press, New York.

Dunn, J. P., Brooks, G. W., Mausner, J., Rodnan, G. P. and Cobb, S. (1963). Social class gradient of serum uric acid levels in males, *Journal of the American Medical Association*, **185**, 431–6.

Eaker, E. D., Haynes, S. G. and Feinleib, M. (1983). Spouse behaviour and coronary heart disease in men: prospective results from the Framingham Heart Study—II. Modification of risk in Type A husbands according to the social and psychological status of their wives, *American Journal of Epidemiology*, **118**, 23–41.

Edwards, A. M. (1934). *Comparative occupation statistics for the United States*, pp. 164–9, US Government Printing Office, Washington, DC.

Elliot, G. R. and Eisdorfer, C. (eds) (1982). *Stress and Human Health: Analysis and Implications of Research*, Springer, New York.

Elliott, P. Fehily, A. M. Sweetnam, P. M. and Yarnell, J. W. G. (1987). Diet, alcohol, body mass, and social factors in relation to blood pressure: the Caerphilly Heart Study, *Journal of Epidemiology and Community Health*, **41**, 37–43.

Engel, B. T. (1986). An essay on circulation as behaviour, *The Behavioural and Brain Sciences*, **9**, 285–318.

Eysenck, H. J. (1984). Personality, stress and lung cancer. In S. Rachman (ed.) *Contributions to Medical Psychology*, Vol. 3, Pergamon Press, Oxford.

Farr, R. M. (1977). On the nature of attributional artifacts in qualitative research: Herzberg's two factor theory of work motivation, *Journal of Occupational Psychology*, **50**, 3–14.

Ferguson, D. (1973a). A study of neurosis and occupation, *British Journal of Industrial Medicine*, **30**, 187–98.

Ferguson, D. (1973b). A study of occupational stress and health, *Ergonomics*, **16**(5), 649–63.

Finlay-Jones, R. A. and Burvill, P. W. (1977). The prevalence of minor psychiatric morbidity in the community, *Psychological Medicine*, **7**, 474–89.

Fletcher, B. (C) (1979). Stress, illness and social class, *Occupational Health*, **31**(9), 405–11.

Fletcher, B. (C) (1980). Discussion contributions. In A. J. Chapman and D. M. Jones (eds) *Models of Man*, British Psychological Society.

Fletcher, B. (C) (1982). Work stress and its effect on wives, *Occupational Health*, **34**(9), 421–6.

Fletcher, B. (C) (1983). Marital relationships as a cause of death: an analysis of occupational mortality and the hidden consequences of marriage—some U.K. data,. *Human Relations*, **36**(2), 123–34.

Fletcher, B. (C) (1985). Marriages of death: males' occupation as a predictor of married women's cause of death, *Bulletin of the British Psychological Society*, **38** A35 (Abstract).

Fletcher, B. (C) (1987). Work stress, marriage and disease-concordance. Presented to the *British Psychological Society*, London Conference, December.

Fletcher, B. (C) (1988). Occupation, marriage, and disease-specific mortality concordance, *Social Science and Medicine*, in press.

Fletcher, B. (C) (1989). *Occupational Stress, Disease and Life Expectancy*, Chichester, John Wiley and Sons.

Fletcher, B. (C) and Hall, J. (1984). Coping with personal problems at work, *Personnel Management*, February 1984, 30–3.

Fletcher, B. (C) and Heath, S. (1989). The occupational psychological correlates of casual blood pressure: the role of job demands and job discretion in blue and white-collar workers, in preparation.

Fletcher, B. (C) and Morris, D. (1987). The health of London licensed taxi drivers: evidence obtained using the Crown–Crisp Experiential Index, the Job Diagnostic Survey, and the Demands, Supports and Constraints Questionnaire. Presented to the *British Psychological Society*, London Conference, December.

Fletcher, B. (C) and Payne, R. L. (1980a). Stress at work: a review and theoretical framework, Part I, *Personnel Review*, **9**(1), 19–29.

Fletcher, B. (C) and Payne, R. L. (1980b). Stress at work: a review and theoretical framework, Part II, *Personnel Review*, **9**(2), 4–8.

Fletcher, B. (C) and Payne, R. L. (1982). Levels of reported stressors and strains amongst schoolteachers: some U.K. data, *Educational Review*, **34**, 267–78.

Fletcher, B. (C), Glendon, I. and Stone, F. (1987). The epidemiology of 129 occupational stressors, depression and free floating anxiety: a national random sample survey, unpublished manuscript.

Fletcher, B. (C)., Gowler, D. and Payne, R. L. (1979). Exploding the myth of executive stress, *Personnel Management*, **11**(5), 30–5.

Fletcher, B. (C)., Gowler, D. and Payne, R. L. (1980). Transmitting occupational risks, *The Lancet*, **ii**, 1193.

Fox, A. J. and Adelstein, A. M. (1978). Occupational mortality: work or a way of life? *Journal of Epidemiology and Community Health*, **32**, 73–8.

Fox, B. H. (1978). Premorbid psychological factors as related to cancer incidence, *Journal of Behavioural Medicine*, **1**(1), 45–133.

Fox, B. H. (1982). A psychological measure as a predictor of cancer. In J. Cohen, J. W. Cullen and L. R. Martin (eds) *Psychosocial aspects of cancer*, Raven Press, New York.

Fraser, R. (1947). The incidence of neurosis among factory workers, *Medical Research Council Industrial Health Research Board Report No. 90*, HMSO, London.

French–Belgian Collaborative Group (1982). Ischemic heart disease and psychological patterns: prevalence and incidence studies in Belgium and France, *Advanced Cardiology*, **29**, 25–31.

French, J. R. P. and Caplan, R. D. (1970). Psychosocial factors in coronary heart disease, *Industrial Medicine*, **39**(9), 383–97.

French, J. R. P., Caplan, R. D. and Van Harrison, R. (1982). *The Mechanisms of Job stress and Strain*, John Wiley and Sons, Chichester.

Frese, M. (1985). Stress of work and psychosomatic complaints: a causal interpretation, *Journal of Applied Psychology*, **70**, 314–28.

Friedman, M. and Rosenman, R. H. (1959). Association of specific overt behaviour pattern with blood and cardiovascular findings: blood cholesterol level, bloodclotting time, incidence of arcus senilis, and clinical coronary artery disease, *Journal of the American Medical Association*, **169**, 1986.

Friedman, M. and Rosenman, R. H. (1974). *Type A Behaviour and your Heart*, Alfred A. Knopf, New York.

Frone, M. R. and Rice, R. W. (1987). Work–family conflict: the effect of job and family involvement, *Journal of Occupational Behaviour*, **8**, 45–53.

Glass, D. C. (1977). *Behaviour patterns, stress and coronary disease*, Lawrence Erlbaum, Hillsdale, NJ.

Glass, D. C. (1983). Psychosocial influence and the pathogenesis of arteriosclerosis. In J. A. Herd and S. M. Weiss *Behaviour and Arteriosclerosis*, Plenum Press, New York.

Glass, D. C., Krakoff, L. R., Contrada, R., Hilton, W., Kehoe, K., Mannucci, E. G., Collins, C., Snow, B. and Elting, E. (1980). Effect of harassment and competition upon cardiovascular and plasma catecholamine responses in Type A and Type B individuals, *Psychophysiology*, **17**, 453–63.

Goldberg, A. (1972). *The detection of psychiatric illness by questionnaire*, Maudsley Monograph No. 21, Oxford University Press, Oxford.

Goldbourt, U., Medalie, J. H. and Neufeld, H. N. (1975). Clinical myocardial infarction over a five year period—III. A multivariate analysis of incidence, the Israel ischemic heart disease study, *Journal of Chronic Diseases*, **28**, 217–37.

Green, J. E. (1977) Migraine abroad: a survey of migraine in England. 1975–1976, *Headache*, **17**, 67–8.

Haynes, S. G. and Feinleib, M. (1982). Type A behaviour and the incidence of coronary heart disease in the Framingham Heart Study, *Advanced Cardiology*, **29**, 85–95.

Haynes, S. G., Eaker, E. D. and Feinleib, M. (1983). Spouse behaviour and coronary heart disease in men: prospective results from the Framingham Heart Study, *American Journal of Epidemiology*, **118**, 1–41.

Haynes, S. G., Feinleib, M. and Kannel, W. B. (1980). The relationship of psychosocial factors to coronary heart disease in the Framingham Study—III. Eight-year incidence of coronary heart disease, *American Journal of Epidemiology*, **111**, 37–58.

Haynes, S. G., Feinleib, M., Levine S., Scotch, N. and Kannel, W. B. (1978). The relationship of psychosocial factors to coronary heart disease in the Framingham Study—II. Prevalence of coronary heart disease, *American Journal of Epidemiology*, **107**(5), 384–402.

Health and Nutrition Examination Survey (1977). *Public Health Reports*, **92**(1), 91.

Helsing, K. J. and Szklo, M. (1981). Mortality after bereavement, *American Journal of Epidemiology*, **114**, 41–52.

Helsing, K. J., Comstock, G. W. and Szklo, M. (1982). Causes of death in a widowed population, *American Journal of Epidemiology*, **116**, 524–32.

Hendrix, W. H., Ovalle, N. K. and Troxler, R. G. (1985). Behavioural and physiological consequences of stress and its antecedent factors, *Journal of Applied Psychology*, **70**(1), 188–201.

Henry, J. P. and Stephens, P. M. (1977). *Stress, Health, and the Social Environment: A Sociobiologic Approach to Medicine*, Springer, New York.

Hepworth, S. (1980). Moderating factors of the psychological impact of unemployment, *Journal of Occupational Psychology*, **53**, 139–45.

Hinkle, L. E. (1974). The effect of exposure to culture change, social change, and changes in interpersonal relationships on health. In B. S. Dohrenwend and B. P. Dohrenwend (eds) *Stressful Life Events: Their Nature and Effect*, pp. 9–44, John Wiley and Sons, New York.

Hinkle, L. E. Jr, Whitney, L. H., Lehman, E. W., Dunn, J., Benjamin, B., King, R., Plakun, A. and Fehinger, B. (1968). Occupation, education and coronary heart disease, *Science*, **161**, 238–46.

Hirayama, T. (1981). Non-smoking wives of heavy smokers have a higher risk of lung-cancer: a study from Japan, *British Medical Journal*, 183–5.

Hogan, E. A. and Martell, D. A. (1987). A confirmatory structural equations analysis of the Job Characteristics Model. *Organisational Behaviour and Human Decision Processes*, **39**, 242–263.

Hollingshead, A. B. (1971). Comment on 'the indiscriminate state of social class measurement, *Social Forces*, **49**, 563–7.

Hollingshead, A. and Redich, R. (1958). *Social Class and Mental Illness: A Community Study*, John Wiley and Sons, New York.

Holme, I., Helgeland, A., Hjermann, I., Leren, P. and Lund-Larsen, P. G. (1976). Coronary risk factors and socioeconomic status. The Oslo Study, *The Lancet*, **ii**, 1936.

Holme, I., Helgeland, A., Hjerman, I., Leren, P. and Lund-Larsen, P. G. (1977). Coronary risk factors in various occupational groups: the Oslo Study, *British Journal of Preventative and Social Medicine*, **31**, 96–100.

Holme, I., Helgeland, A., Hjermann, I., Leren, P. and Lund-Larsen, P. G. (1982). Socioeconomic status as a coronary risk factor: the Oslo Study, *Acta Medica Scandinavia*, **660** (Supplement), 147–151.

Holmes, T. H. and David, E. M. (1984). *Life change events research 1966–1978*, Praeger, New York.

Houston, B. K. (1983). Psychophysiological responsibility and the Type A behaviour pattern, *Journal of Research in Personality*, **17**, 22–39.

Howard, J. H., Cunningham, D. A. and Rechnitzer, P. A. (1976). Health patterns associated with Type A behaviour: a managerial population, *Journal of Human Stress*, **2**, 24–31.

Howard, J. H., Cunningham, D. A. and Rechnitzer, P. A. (1986). Role ambiguity,

Type A behaviour, and job satisfaction: moderating effects on cardiovascular and biochemical responses associated with coronary risk, *Journal of Applied Psychology*, **71**, 95–101.

Hurrell, J. J. (1985). Machine-paced work and the Type A behaviour pattern, *Journal of Occupational Behaviour*, **58**, 15–25.

Inter-Society Commission for Heart Disease Resources (1972). Primary Prevention of the artriosclerotic diseases. *Circulation*, **42**, 1–44.

Jackson, P. R. and Warr, P. B. (1984). Unemployment and psychological ill-health: the moderating role of duration and age, *Psychological Medicine*, **14**, 605–614.

Jackson, S. E. and Maslach, C. (1982). After-effects of job-related stress: families as victims, *Journal of Occupation Behaviour*, **3**, 63–77.

Jemmott, J. B. and Locke, S. E. (1984). Psychosocial factors, immunologic meditation, and human susceptibility to infectious diseases: how much do we know? *Psychological Bulletin*, **95**(1), 78–108.

Jenkins, C. D. (1971). Psychologic and social precursors of coronary disease, *New England Journal of Medicine*, **284**, 244–55, 307–17.

Jenkins, C. D. (1976). Recent evidence supporting psychologic and social precursors of coronary disease, *New England Journal of Medicine*, **294**, 987–94.

Jenkins, C. D. (1982). Psychosocial risk factors for coronary heart disease, *Acta Medica Scandanavia*, **660** (Supplement), 123–36.

Jenkins, C. D., Zyzanski, S. J. and Rosenman, R. H. (1971). Progress toward validation of a computer-scored test for Type A Coronary-Prone Behaviour Pattern, *Psychosomatic Medicine*, **33**, 193–202.

Johansson, G., Aronson, G. and Lindstrom, B. O. (1978). Social, psychological and neuroendocrine stress reactions in highly mechanised work, *Ergonomics*, **21**, 583–99.

Johnston, D. W., Cook, D. G. and Shaper, A. G. (1987). Type A behaviour and ischaemic heart disease in middle aged British men, *British Medical Journal*, **295**, 86–89.

Kagan, A. R. and Levi, L. (1974). Health and environment–psychosocial stimuli: a review, *Social Science and Medicine*, **8**, 225–41.

Kahn, J. P., Kornfield, D. S., Frank, K. A., Heller, S. S. and Hoar, P. F. (1980). Type A behaviour and blood pressure during coronary artery bypass surgery, *Psychosomatic Medicine*, **42**, 407–14.

Kahn, R. L., Wolfe, D. M., Quinn, R. P., Snoek, J. D. and Rosenthal, R. A. (1964). *Organisational Stress: Studies in Role Conflict and Ambiguity*, John Wiley and Sons, New York.

Karasek, R. A. (1978). Job socialisation, a longitudinal study of work, political and leisure activity in Sweden. *IX World Congress of Sociology* (RC30), 15 August, 1978, Swedish Institute for Social Research, Stockholm University.

Karasek, R. A. (1979). Job demands, job decision latitude and mental strain: implications for job design, *Administrative Science Quarterly*, **24**, 285–308.

Karasek, R. A., Russell, R. S. and Theovell, T. (1982). Physiology of stress and regeneration in job related cardiovascular illness, *Journal of Human Stress*, **8**(1), 29–42.

Karasek, R. A., Theorell, T. G. T., Schwartz, J., Pieper, C. and Alfredsson, L. (1982). Job, psychological factors and coronary heart disease, *Advanced Cardiology*, **29**, 62–7.

Kasl, S. V. (1978). Epidemiological contributions to the study of work stress. In C. L. Cooper and R. L. Payne (eds) *Stress at Work*, John Wiley and Sons, New York.

Kasl, S. V. (1980). The impact of retirement. In C. L. Cooper and R. L. Payne (eds) *Current Concerns in Occupational Stress*, pp. 137–86, John Wiley and Sons, Chichester.

Kasl, S. V. (1983). Pursuing the link between stressful life experiences and disease: A time for reappraisal. In C. L. Cooper (ed.) *Stress Research: Issues for the Eighties*, John Wiley and Sons, Chichester.

Kasl, S. V. and Cobb, S. (1980). The experience of losing a job: Some effects on cardiovascular functioning, *Psychotherapy and Psychosomatics*, **34**, 88–109.

Kearns, J. (1986). Stress at work: the challenge of change, *BUPA Series The Management of Health: 1 Stress and the City*, BUPA.

Keenan, A. and Newton, T. J. (1987). Work difficulties and stress in young professional engineers, *Journal of Occupational Psychology*, **60**, 133–45.

Kessler, R. C. (1982). A disaggregation of the relationship between socioeconomic status and psychological distress, *American Sociological Review*, **47**, 752–764.

Kessler, R. C. and Cleary, P. D. (1980). Social class and psychological distress, *American Sociological Review*, **45**, 463–78.

Keys, A., Aravanis, C., Blackburn, H., Van Buchem, F. S. P., Buzina, R., Djordjevic, B. S., Fidanza, F., Karvonen, M. J., Menotti, A., Puddu, V. and Taylor, H. L. (1972). Probability of middle-aged men developing coronary heart disease in 5 years, *Circulation*, **45**, 815–28.

Kornhauser, A. (1965). *Mental Health of the Industrial Worker: A Detroit Study*, John Wiley and Sons, New York.

Krantz, D. S. and Durel, L. A. (1983). Psychobiological substrates of the type A behaviour pattern, *Health Psychology*, **2**, 393–411.

Krantz, D. S. and Manuck, S. B. (1984). Acute psychophysiologic reactivity and risk of cardiovascular disease: a review and methodological critique, *Psychological Bulletin*, **96**(3), 435–64.

Krantz, D. S. and Manuck, S. B. (1985). Measures of acute physiologic reactivity to behavioural stimuli: assessment and critique. In A. M. Ostfeld and E. D. Eaker (eds) *Measuring Psychosocial Variables in Epidemiologic Studies of Cardiovascular Disease*, US Department of Health and Human Services, NIH Publication No. 85–2270.

Krantz, D. S., Baum, A. and Singer, J. (eds) (1983). *Handbook of Psychology and Health. Vol. III. Cardiovascular Disorders and Behaviour*, Lawrence Erlbaum Associates, Hillsdale, NJ.

Krantz, D. S., Arabian, J. M., Davia, J. E. and Parker, J. S. (1982). Type A behaviour and coronary artery bypass surgery: intraoperative blood pressure and perioperative complications, *Psychosomatic Medicine*, **44**, 273–84.

Kritsikis, S. P., Heinemann, A. L. and Eitner, S. (1968). Die Angina Pectoris in Aspekt ihrer Korrelation mit biologischer Disposition, psychologischen und soziologischen Emmussfaktoren, *Deutsch. Gesundheit*, **23**, 1878–85.

Kulka, R. A., Veroff, J. and Douvan, E. (1979). Social class and use of professional help for personal problems: 1957 and 1976, *Journal of Health and Social Behaviour*, **20**, 2–17.

Larson, A. G. and Marcer, D. (1984). The who and why of pain: analysis by social class, *British Medical Journal*, **288**, 883–6.

Lee, R. E. and Schneider, R. F. (1958). Hypertension and arteriosclerosis in executive and nonexecutive personnel, *Journal of the American Medical Association*, **167**, 1447–50.

Lehman, E. W. (1967). Social class and coronary heart disease: a sociological assessment of the medical literature, *Journal of Chronic Diseases*, **20**, 381–91.

Lehr, I., Messinger, H. B. and Rosenman, R. H. (1973). A socibiological approach to the study of coronary heart disease, *Journal of Chronic Diseases*, **26**, 13–30.

Lichtenstein, M. J., Shipley, M. J. and Rose, G. (1985). Systolic and diastolic blood pressure as predictors of coronary heart disease mortality in the Whitehall study, *British Medical Journal*, **291**, 243–5.

MacIver, J. (1969). The epidemiology mental illness in industry, *Journal of International Psychiatric Clinicians*, **6**, 271–6.

McLaughlin, A. I. G. (1966). Chronic bronchitis and occupation, *British Medical Journal*, 101–102.

Margolis, B. L., Kroes, W. H. and Quinn, R. P. (1974). Job stress: an unlisted occupational hazard, *Journal of Occupational Medicine*, **16**, 659–61.

Marmot, M. G. and Khaw, K. T. (1982). Implications for population studies of the age trend in blood pressure, *Contributions to Nephrology*, **30**, 101–7.

Marmot, M. G., Rose, G., Shipley, M. and Hamilton, P. J. S. (1978). Employment grade and coronary heart disease in British civil servants, *Journal of Epidemiology and Community Health*, **32**, 244–9.

Maschewsky, W. (1982). The relation between stress and myocardial infarction: a general analysis, *Social Science and Medicine*, **16**, 455–62.

Matthews, K. A. and Glass, D. C. (1984). Type A behaviour, stressful life events, and coronary heart disease. In B. S. Dohrenwend and B. P. Dohrenwend (eds) *Stressful life events and their contexts*, Rutgers University Press, edition.

Matthews, K. A., Weiss, S. A., Detre, T., Dembroski, T. M., Falkner, B. & Williams, R. B. (1986). *Handbook of Stress, Reactivity and Cardiovascular Disease*, John Wiley and Sons, Chichester.

Medalie, J. H (1985). Personality characteristics: content discussion. In A. M. Ostfeld and E. D. Eaker (eds) *Measuring Psychosocial Variables in Epidemiologic Studies of Cardiovascular Disease*, NIH Publication No. 85–2270, US Department of Health and Human Services.

Medalie, J. H. and Goldbourt, U, (1976). Angina pectoris among 10,000 men—II. Psychosocial and other risk factors as evidenced by a multivariate analysis of a five-year incidence study, *American Journal of Medicine*, **60**, 910–20.

Morgenstern, H. (1985). Socioeconomic factors: concepts measurement, and health effects. In A. M. Ostfeld and E. D. Eaker (eds) *Measuring Psychosocial Variables in Epidemiologic Studies of Cardiovascular Disease*, NIH Publication No. 85–2270, US Department of Health and Human Services.

Mott, P. E., Mann, F. C., McLoghlin, Q. and Warwick, D. P. (1965). *Shift Work: The Social Psychological, and Physical Consequences*, University of Michigan Press, Ann Arbor.

Mueller, E. F., Kasl, S. V., Brooks, G. W. and Cobb, S. (1970). Psychosocial correlates of serum urate levels, *Psychological Bulletin*, **73(4)**, 238–57.

Newton, T. J. and Keenan, A. (1985). Coping with work-related stress, *Human Relations*, **38**(2), 107–26.

OPCS (1978). *Registrar General's Decennial Supplement, England and Wales, 1970–72, Occupational Mortality* Series DS No. 1, HMSO, London.

OPCS (1978b). *Registrar General's Decennial Supplement, England and Wales, 1970–72, Occupational Mortality*, Microfiche Tables 1–6, HMSO, London.

OPCS (1980). *Classification of Occupations and Coding Index*, HMSO, London.

OPCS (1986a). *Occupational Mortality 1979–80, 1982–3, Decennial Supplement*, Part I, Commentary, Series DS No. 6, HMSO, London.

OPCS (1986b). *Occupational Mortality 1979–80, 1982–3, Decennial Supplement*, Part II, Microfiche Tables, Series DS No. 6, HMSO, London.

Ostfeld, A. M. and Eaker, E. D. (eds) (1985). *Measuring Psychosocial Variables in Epidemiologic Studies of Cardiovascular Disease*, NIH Publication No. 85–2270, US Department of Health and Human Services.

Paffenbarger, R. S., Hale, W. E., Brand, R. J. and Hyde, R. T. (1977). Work-energy level, personal characteristics, and fatal heart attack: a birth cohort effect, *American Journal of Epidemiology*, **105**(3), 200–13.

Paffenbarger, R. S., Hyde, R. T., Wing, A. L. and Steinmetz, C. H. (1984). A natural history of athleticism and cardiovascular health, *Journal of the American Medical Association*, **252**, 491–5.

Parkes, C. M., Benjamin, B. and Fitzgerald, R. G. (1969). Broken heart: a statistical study of increased mortality among widowers, *British Medical Journal*, **1**, 740–3.

Parkes, K. R. (1982). Occupational stress among student nurses: a natural experiment, *Journal of Applied Psychology*, **67**(6), 784–96.

Payne, R. L. (1979). Demands, supports, constraints and psychological health. In C. J. Mackay and T. Cox (eds) *Responses to Stress: Occupational Aspects*, International Publishing Corporation, London.

Payne, R. L. (1988). Individual differences and occupational stress. This volume, Chapter 6.

Payne, R. L. and Fletcher, B. (C) (1983). Job demands, supports, and constraints as predictors of psychological strain among school teachers, *Journal of Vocational Behaviour*, **22**, 136–47.

Payne, R. L. and Rick, J. T. (1986). Psychobiological markers of stress in surgeons and anaesthetists. In T. H. Schmidt, T. M. Dembroski and G. Blumchen (eds) *Biological and Psychological factors in Cardiovascular Disease*, Springer, Berlin.

Payne, R. L., Jick, T. D. and Burke, R. J. (1982). Whither stress research? An agenda for the 1980s, *Journal of Occupational Behaviour*, **3**, 131–45.

Payne, R. L., Warr, P. and Hartley, J. (1984). Social class and psychological ill-health during unemployment, *Sociology of Health and Illness*, **6**(2), 152–174.

Payne, R. L., Rick, J. T. Smith, G. H. and Cooper, R. (1985). Multiple indicators of stress in a group of cardiothoracic surgeons, MRC/ESRC Memo 612.

Pell, S. and D'Alonzo, C. A. (1963). Acute myocardial infarction in a large industrial population, *Journal of the American Medical Association*, **185**, 831–8.

Pittner, M. S. and Houston, B. K. (1980). Response to stress, cognitive coping strategies, and the Type A behaviour pattern, *Journal of Personality and Social Psychology*, **39**, 147–157.

Plant, M. A. (1977). Alcoholism and occupation: a review, *British Journal of Addiction*, **72**, 309–16.

Pratt, J. (1978). Perceived stress among teachers: the effects of age and background of children taught, *Educational Review*, **30**, 3–14.

Price, V. A. (1982). What is Type A? A cognitive social learning model, *Journal of Occupational Behaviour*, **3**, 109–129.

Ragland, D. R. and Brand, R. J. (1988). Type A behaviour and mortality from coronary heart disease, *New England Journal of Medicine*, **318**, 66–69.

Reeder, L. G., Schrama, P. G. M. and Dirken, J. M. (1973). Stress and cardiovascular health: an international cooperative study—I. *Social Science and Medicine*, **7**, 573–84.

Rissler, A. (1977). Stress reactions at work and after work during a period of quantitative overload, *Ergonomics*, **20**, 13–16.

Robinson, R. V. and Kelly, J. (1979). Class as conceived by Marx and Darendorf: effects on income in equality and politics in the United States and Great Britain, *American Sociological Review*, **44**, 38–58.

Rose, G. and Marmot, M. G. (1981). Social class and coronary heart disease, *British Heart Journal*, **45**, 13–19.

Rosenman, R. H., Brand, R. J., Sholtz, R. I. and Friedman, M. (1976). Multivariate prediction of coronary heart disease during 8.5 year follow-up in the Western Collaborative Group Study, *American Journal of Cardiology*, **37**, 903–10.

Rosenman, R. H., Brand, R. J., Jenkins, C. D., Friedman, M., Straus, R. and Wurm, M. (1975). Coronary heart disease in the Western Collaboration Group Study: final follow-up experience of 8.5 years, *Journal of the American Medical Association*, **233**, 872–7.

Rosenman, R. H., Friedman, M., Straus, R., Jenkins, C. D., Zyzanski, S. J. and Wurm, M. (1970). Coronary heart disease in the Western Collaborative Group Study: a follow-up experience of 4.5 years, *Journal of Chronic Diseases*, **23**, 173–90.

Rosenman, R. H., Friedman, M., Wurm M., Jenkins, C. D. and Messinger, H. B. Strauss, R. (1966). Coronary heart disease in the Western Collaborative Group Study, *Journal of the American Medical Association*, **195**, 86–92.

Rosenman, R. H., Friedman, M., Straus, R., Wurm, M., Kositchek, R., Hahn, W. and Werthessen, N. T. (1964). A predictive study of coronary heart disease: the Western Collaborative Group Study, *Journal of the American Medical Association*, **189**, 15–22.

Ruff, M. R., Pert, C. B., Weber, R. J., Wahl, L. M., Wahl, S. M. and Paul, S. M. (1985). Benzodiazepine receptor-mediated chemotaxis of human monocytes, *Science*, **229**, 1281–3.

Russek, H. I. (1962). Emotional stress and coronary heart disease in American physicians, dentists and lawyers, *American Journal of Medical Science*, **243**, 716–25.

Russek, H. I. (1965). Stress, tobacco and coronary disease in North American professional groups, *Journal of the American Medical Association*, **192**, 189–94.

Russek, H. I. and Zohman, B. L. (1958). Relative significance of heredity, diet and occupational stress in coronary heart disease of young adults, *Americal Journal of Medical Science*, **235**, 266–75.

Schar, M., Reeder, L. G. and Dirken, J. M. (1973). Stress and cardiovascular health: an international cooperative study—II. The male population of a factory in Zurich, *Social Science and Medicine*, **7**, 585–603.

Schuler, R. S. (1982). An integrative transactional process model of stress in organisations, *Journal of Occupational Behaviour*, **3**, 5–19.

Sexton, M. M. (1979). Behavioural epidemiology. In O. V. Pomerlean and J. P. Brady (eds), *Behavioural Medicine: Theory and Practice*, Baltimore, Williams and Wilkins.

Shaper, A. G., Pocock, S. J., Walker, M., Phillips, A. N., Whitehead, T. P. and MacFarlane, P. W. (1985). Risk factors for ischaemic heart disease: the prospective phase of the British Regional Heart Study, *Journal of Epidemiology and Community Health*, **39**, 197–209.

Sloan, S. J. and Cooper, C. L. (1986). *Pilots under Stress*, Routledge and Kegan Paul, London.

Smith, G. R. and McDaniels, S. M. (1983). Psychologically mediated effect on the delayed hypersensitivity reaction to tuberculin in humans, *Psychosomatic Medicine*, **45**, 65–70.

Solomon, G. F. (1981). Emotional and personality factors in the onset and course of autoimmune disease, particularly rheumatoid arthritis. In R. Ader (ed), *Psychoneuroimmunology*, New York, Academic Press.

Stamler, J., Lindberg, H. A., Berkson, D. M., Shaffer, A., Miller, W. and Poindexter, A. (1960). Prevalence and incidence of coronary heart disease in a strata of the labor force of a Chicago industrial corporation, *Journal of Chronic Diseases*, **11**, 405–20.

Stevens, G. and Featherman, D. L. (1981). A revised socioeconomic index of occupational status, *Social Science Research*, **10**, 364–95.

Stone, F. (1985). Measures to reduce stress at work, unpublished PhD thesis, University of Aston.

Syme, S. L. and Berkman, L. F. (1976). Social class, susceptibility and sickness, *American Journal of Epidemiology*, **104**(1), 1–8.

Syme, S. L., Borhani, N. O. and Buechley, R. W. (1965). Cultural mobility and coronary heart disease in an urban area, *American Journal of Epidemiology*, **82**, 334–46.

Syme, S. L., Hyman, M. M. and Enterline, P. E. (1964). Some social and cultural factors associated with the occurrence of coronary heart disease, *Journal of Chronic Diseases*, **17**, 277–89.

Theorell, T. and Floderus-Myrhed, B. (1977). Work load and myocardial infarction—a prospective psychological analysis, *International Journal of Epidemiology*, **6**(1), 17–21.

Turner, D. B. and Stone, A. J. (1979). Headache and its treatment: A random sample survey, *Headache*, **19**(2), 74–7.

Tverdal, A. (1987). Systolic and diastolic blood pressure as predictors of coronary heart disease in middle aged Norwegian men, *British Medical Journal*, **294**, 671–3.

Uemura, K. and Pisa, Z. (1985). Recent trends in cardiovascular disease mortality in 27 industrialised countries, *World Health Statistics Quarterly*, **38**, 142–62.

Van Harrison, R. (1978). Person–environment fit and job stress. In C. L. Cooper and R. L. Payne (eds) *Stress at Work*, pp. 175–205, John Wiley and Sons, New York.

Van Harrison, R. Interaction of models in stress research. This volume, chapter 8.

Van Sell, M., Brief, A. P. and Schuler, R. S. (1981). Role conflict and role ambiguity: Integration of the literature and directions for future research, *Human Relations*, **34**, 43–71.

Wadsworth, M. E. J., Cripps, H. A., Midwinter, R. E. and Colley, J. R. T. (1985). Blood pressure in a national birth cohort at the age of 36 related to social and familial factors, smoking and body mass, *British Medical Journal*, **291**, 1534–8.

Wall, T. (1980). Group work redesign in context: a two phrase model. In K. D. Duncan, M. M. Gruneberg and D. Wallis (eds) *Changes in Working Life*, John Wiley and Sons, Chichester.

Wall, T. D. and Clegg, C. W. (1981). A longitudinal study of group work redesign, *Journal of Occupational Behaviour*, **2**, 31–49.

Warner, W. L., Meeker, M. and Eells, K. (1949). *Social Class in America*, Social Science Research Associates, Chicago.

Warr, P. B. (1982). Psychological aspects of employment and unemployment, *Psychological Medicine*, **12**, 7–11.

Warr, P. B. (1983). Work, Jobs and unemployment, *Bulletin of the British Psychological Society*, **36**, 305–11.

Warr, P. B. and Payne, R. L. (1982a). Experiences of strain and pleasure among British adults. *Social Science and Medicine*, **16**, 1691–7.

Warr, P. B. and Payne, R. L. (1982b). Unpleasant emotional strain and feelings of pleasure: point prevalence, attributions of cause and coping responses, MRC/ESRC SAPU, Memo No. 497.

Warr, P. B. and Payne, R. L. (1983). Affective outcomes of paid employment in a random sample of British workers, *Journal of Occupational Behaviour*, **4**, 91–104.

Waters, W. E. (1970). Community studies of the prevalence of headache, *Headache*, **9**, 178–86.
Waters, W. E. and O'Connor, P. J. (1971). Epidemiology of headache and migraine in women, *Journal of Neurology, Neurosurgery and Psychiatry*, **34**, 148–53.
Winnett, R. A. and Neale, M. S. (1981). Flexible work schedules and family time allocation: assessment of a system change on individual behaviour using self-report logs, *Journal of Applied Behaviour Analysis*, **14**, 39–46.
Wright, E. O. and Perrone, L. (1977). Marxist class categories and income inequality, *American Sociological Review*, **42**, 32–55.
World Health Organisation (1982). *Prevention of Coronary Heart Disease: Report of a WHO Expert Committee*, WHO Technical Report Series 678, Geneva.
Zaleznik, A., Kets de Vries, M. F. R. and Howard, J. (1977). Stress reactions in organisations: syndromes, causes and consequences, *Behavioural Science*, **22**, 151–62.

PART II

Factors in the Person's Environment

Causes, Coping and Consequences of Stress at Work
Edited by C. L. Cooper and R. Payne
© 1988 John Wiley & Sons Ltd

Chapter 2

Blue Collar Stress

Meredith Wallace, Mary Levens, and George Singer

The distinction between blue and white çollar workers traditionally corresponded to the distinction between those on an hourly vs those on a weekly
contract of pay. With changes in awards this distinction has now lost its
meaning. Other bases for distinctions have been unskilled vs skilled work;
manual vs non-manual; bureau of census occupational groupings; educational
level; hourly vs weekly termination of employment and so on. With new
awards, new technology and social equity philosophy many of the implications of the distinction are lost.

Studies of blue collar workers based on one or more of these divisions
have shown contradictory evidence of greater stress in blue collar workers.
In these and other studies attempts have been made to identify mediating
variables for increased stress and stress related health effects. These include
lack of control, understimulation, uncertainty, deskilling, alienation and
home stress. Unequivocal evidence for the effects of these mediating variables and their greater incidence in blue collar workers is lacking.

In this chapter we will examine existing data on stress and stress related
illnesses and behaviours. Comparison will be made using equivalents to the
classical divisions of blue collar or white collar workers, and also using
classifications based on the meditating variables discussed earlier. The independent variables which are included in the analysis are: migrant status,
education, wages/staff employment and level of earning. Work related variables include autonomy, control, support, degree of security, skill level,
physical work, physical environment, and the level of stimulation provided
by the job. Home stress and personal relationships are also examined. The
level of stress, stress related illness and stress associated behaviours are
assessed from self report scales.

INTRODUCTION

In this chapter the validity of the traditional division of the work force into
blue and white collar workers is debated. Since changes in technology may
lead to the redistribution of occupations within work force divisions and

since these changes may influence health and social variables, the alternative divisions of the work force based on sex, education and income are examined.

The chapter starts with a review of the definitions of blue collar work and its health and social consequences, then selected data from our own research are reported. Finally, the justification for retaining the classification of the work force into blue and white collar workers is discussed.

DEFINITION OF BLUE COLLAR WORKERS

'Blue collar' is a term used to denote a section of the working population. It implies unskilled, manual work in its narrowest usage but may be broadened to cover 'service workers' including porters, janitors, waiters, cooks, barbers and watchmen. That is, blue collar are those whose jobs involve rote manual labour (Shostak, 1980).

The distinction between blue and white collar workers traditionally corresponded to that between those on an hourly and those on a weekly contract of pay. For example, Lupton (1976) refers to 'a class of persons in industrial societies who are variously denoted "industrial operatives", "payroll", "hourly paid" or simply, "manual workers" ' (p. 171). They are distinct from 'manager' and 'white collar' workers. Other bases for distinctions are unskilled vs skilled work; manual vs non-manual; workers vs clerical and managerial; hourly vs weekly termination of employment.

Fisher (1985) defines blue collar workers as 'the skilled and unskilled groups in service or production industries, who carry out the essential manual and monitoring operations required by the production process' (p. 20). Shostak (1980) uses blue collar to refer to manual workers, but also in referring to the 'working class'.

More formal groupings of occupations have been made by government offices such as the UK Office of Population Census and Surveys who use six divisions: professional, employers and managers, intermediate and junior non-manual, skilled manual and own account non-professional, semi-skilled manual and personal service, and unskilled manual. 'Blue collar' has been used to refer to the last three divisions, the last two or merely the last group.

The broad categories of occupations used in the Tecumseh Community Health Study (House *et al.*, 1986) were derived from the US Bureau of Census occupational groupings. The men in this study were divided into three status groups: high (all white collar); medium (foremen and craftsmen) and low (operatives, labourers and service workers). Women were divided into high status (professional and managerial) medium status (clerical and sales) and low status (all blue collar).

Attempts to distinguish between blue and white collar give rise to two problems. First, the definition of blue collar has never been clear—the examples above indicate consistency only in that the least skilled groups are included in all uses of the term. Where the upper limit of the blue collar domain falls varies from one occasion, and one country, to the next. A simple dichotomy between blue and white collar implies the inclusion of a large number of occupations in the 'blue' category. Even in more detailed schemes it can be difficult to place people working in service organizations such as the police, ambulance, fire brigades and nurses.

The second problem is the intention of the distinction. If the blue collar label is meant to imply certain job characteristics such as heavy physical effort, manual labour and harsh physical work environments, then even a restriction of the term to 'unskilled work' does not guarantee that these conditions will always apply. Although there are still many occupations such as mining, fishing, farming, timber felling and working in an abattoir where these characteristics obtain, they are not necessarily 'unskilled'. On the other hand, totally unskilled work in a modern factory may involve little physical effort and minimum manual labour in clean and pleasant surroundings.

Dissatisfaction with occupational classifications has been expressed by researchers working in the areas of social epidemiology and medical sociology. In a review of associations between health and occupational class, gender, and other personal characteristics, Macintyre (1986) comments that:

> The ubiquity and persistence of the RG (Registrar General's) classification in government and health statistics has tended to lead to the reification of occupational class; that is, it is sometimes treated as though it were a fixed and material attribute of individuals that somehow 'causes' certain outcomes, rather than as a convenient system of social classification imposed on a complex social reality by investigators with certain research purposes . . . (p. 400)

> None of [these social positions] is likely directly to cause health outcomes; rather they are markers for the complex set of social conditions and processes which may be causally implicated. (p. 401)

and Schneider (1986), in a critique of the Hollingshead scale points out that:

> As the US shifts from an industrial to a service economy, semiskilled, so called 'blue collar' jobs are replaced by low level clerical and service jobs such as keypunch, computer operator, or sales clerk. While classified as 'white collar' these jobs are roughly equivalent to the factory work of earlier decades and often provide less in monetary return. (p. 211)

A specific example of the effects of modern technology comes from Edgren (1981):

> In such highly technical production systems as modern pulp manufacturing the boundary between the factory (blue collar) and office (white collar) disappears. There is a participation in both the practical and production process and in the administrative decision making process by most employees. (p. 70)

In fact there are a number of disappearing boundaries. Blue collar incomes are boosted by overtime and awards compensating for physical working conditions. Physical effort has been removed from many blue collar jobs by new technology and by legislative control of work practices. Blue collar workers may have to acquire skills to use new technology while white collar workers may suffer deskilling. These days, white collar workers also face redundancy and early retirement more often than in the past.

An analysis of the work force in terms of a division into blue and white collar groupings is no longer a meaningful exercise. With this blurring of the distinction are there implications for jobs that were once physically heavy, but are now button pushing jobs? Is there a new type of stress associated with deskilling? Further, are there any *a priori* meaningful distinctions in the workforce? And if so, are there differences in the stressors and strains which are related to these distinctions? Are there increased health risks associated with being a member of some subgroup in the workforce?

Distinctions which might replace the occupational class division include education and pay levels, while personal characteristics such as sex, physical handicap and ethnic origin might delineate subgroups who are more or less vulnerable to occupational stressors.

MODELS OF 'STRESS AT WORK'

Various models of stress have driven research in the occupation area and have determined the selection of both independent and dependent variables. These models will be very briefly outlined before some of the sources of stress in the workplace are discussed.

A review of epidemiological studies of work stress in *Stress at Work* led Kasl (1978) to conclude that 'stress at work' had not achieved any kind of closure as a concept, but he identified two major 'versions' of stress at work: the first was concerned with an excess of environmental demands over the capability to meet them, and the second, broader version was that of an inadequate person-environment fit, which includes the relation of needs in the person to sources of satisfaction in the work environment to meet such needs.

A model of occupational stress which allows prediction of specific outcomes is the two dimensional model of Karasek (1979). This model has less emphasis on cognitive appraisal, and adds the independent dimension of control (job decision latitude) to the dimension of job demands.

Karasek incorporates the idea of job control (job decision latitude) and work load factors in a causal chain between job and worker distress. Essentially his model indicates that psychological strain results from the 'joint effects of the demands of a work situation and the range of decision-making discretion available to the worker facing those demands' (Karasek, 1979,

p. 298). Ideally, job demands and job decision latitude should be highly correlated, but in fact, Karasek reports there is considerable empirical evidence from both US and Sweden that the correlation is quite low (Karasek, 1981).

According to Karasek, individuals who work in high demand/low control jobs are likely to report the highest frequency of stress symptoms and have the highest levels of stress-related illnesses (including cardiovascular disease). Low demand/low control jobs can lead to passivity and boredom. Low demand/high control jobs produce the lowest levels of stress symptoms but with insufficient stimulation people can lose interest in work activities. High demand/high control jobs produce reasonably high stress levels and high levels of social activity.

Nonwork outcomes are specifically addressed by Karasek who considers that the job functions as a place for the social learning of attitudes which the individual transfers to his or her free time. That is, 'active' work (high demand/high control) leads to more varied leisure activities with more involvement in community activities, while 'passive' work leads to passive leisure (less variety in leisure activities).

In general the Karasek two-dimensional view of job stress provides a basis for understanding some of the major differences between blue and white collar occupations. Blue collar disadvantages are seen to comprise a greater range of industrial hazards and uncomfortable physical working conditions and, by virtue of status, a reduced possibility of control at work and in the matter of leaving work (Fisher, 1985). In fact the disadvantages may no longer be exclusively related to blue collar work: while some physical hazards may be much reduced, others may be much more widely spread throughout the workforce.

In the next section some of the aspects of occupations which feature in these theories as sources of stress will be discussed.

SOURCES OF STRESS IN BLUE COLLAR WORK

A large number of factors have now been suggested as sources of occupational stress. Those which might be particularly associated with blue collar work fall into three groups: (1) heavy work and other physical conditions such as heat, noise, dust, presence of toxic substances; (2) paced, and/or repetitive work, demand for speed; work which is monotonous, requires no skill or over which there is no control; (3) tasks characterized primarily by various types of information processing activities and decisional complexity, often performed under time constraints.

Ergonomic factors such as static muscular workload, high sensory demands and machine-paced muscular workload were found to be major contributors to occupational discomfort in surveys of Swedish industrial workers in 1970 and 1980 (Ostberg and Nilsson, 1985). These factors have also been of major importance in occupational health in Australia in the 1980s (Wallace and Buckle, 1987). They are typically associated with short cycle, monotonous machine paced tasks and also characterize work with visual display terminals.

Additive and synergistic effects have been reported from combinations of physical and environmental stressors (Poulton, 1978) which may also interact with work characteristics such as: kind of work, duration of work, familiarity with the work and with the stressor, the level of incentive and the presence of other stressors in the working situation (Sharit and Salvendy, 1982).

A list of stressors claimed to be specifically relevant to blue collar workers identifies four objective factors: 'a man's pay, a man's safety at work, the quality of his work setting and the stability of his job' (Shostak, 1980, p. 11), and four subjective factors: status, supervision, sociability (work group affiliations) and satisfaction (Shostak, 1980).

Stressors which are not so specifically characterized as blue collar but which are associated with work include role ambiguity (Caplan *et al.*, 1980) which is a measure of the workers's perceptions of the clarity of the work situation and role conflict, a measure of the conflicting demands that a worker sees as present in the job.

Sharit and Salvendy (1982) conclude a review of occupational stressors with the observation that 'the number of factors qualifying as potential sources of occupational stress is seemingly limitless. However, if any one variable were to be singled out as the predominant underlying source of occupational stress, it would be uncertainty' (p. 150). They predict that with current rapid technological changes in work processes, uncertainty will probably become a more prevalent source of occupational stress since increasingly, operators are working on systems about which they understand very little.

Cooper and Marshall (1978) identified 40 interacting factors which they grouped into seven major categories of occupational (managerial) stressors: (1) factors intrinsic to the job including working conditions such as pacing, demand for physical effort, repetitive tasks and both quantitative and qualitative work overload; (2) role in the organization, conceptualized as role ambiguity, role conflict, responsibility for people and other role stressors such as having too little responsibility, lack of managerial support, little participation in decision making and keeping up with rapid technological change; (3) relationships at work; (4) career development (presumed to be especially relevant for managers); (5) organizational structure and climate; (6) extra-organizational sources of stress including family problems, life crises, financial difficulties and conflict of company with family demands; (7) characteristics of the individual, focused mainly on personality differences between high and low stressed individuals, and in particular, the relationship between Type A behaviour patterns and the incidence of coronary heart disease.

Although these are designated as managerial stressors, many are relevant to all workers. While the items listed as factors intrinsic to the job are often included in blue collar studies, considerations of extra-organizational sources of stress tend to be restricted to studies of white collar managers.

OUTCOME VARIABLES: THE INDICATORS OF STRAIN

The study of stress reactions includes physiological variables such as heart rate, cardiovascular disease, blood pressure, ulcers; risk behaviours such as smoking and escapist drinking; indicators of mental ill health, including depressed mood and lowered self esteem, self reports of job satisfaction or behaviours such as absenteeism which reflect job dissatisfaction (Cooper and Marshall, 1978; Kasl, 1978).

A number of intervening and buffering variables have been included in the stress process model. This is because it is argued that differences in the personal and social resources that people have available to them lead to different vulnerabilities for mental and physical illness in the face of environmental strain. These variables, such as individual coping ability and social support, may also be assessed.

SURVEYS OF HEALTH BY OCCUPATION

Conclusions about the health of blue collar and white collar workers have been based on information drawn from large cross-sectional surveys. The data usually show that blue collar workers are at a disadvantage on the health variables which are surveyed and that the disadvantage extends to illnesses which are not necessarily work related or stress related. When data on illnesses such as cardiovascular disease are examined conclusions about occupational links are not always supported.

The usual problems about 'exposure' are encountered in drawing inferences from these data. One difficulty is to tease out the relative importance of direct occupational risks as compared with general living conditions. Social epidemiologists are becoming interested in the contribution of gender, marital status, ethnicity and other social variables but there is little information available at this time.

Demographic Studies and Cross-sectional Surveys

On the basis of the Black Report (Townsend and Davidson, 1982) and other surveys, there is considerable evidence to support the claim that 'blue collar workers are "at risk" ' in terms of health (Cooper and Smith, 1985, p. 1). Mortality and morbidity statistics from a number of countries indicate that there are more deaths and more illness in the working population among blue collar and unskilled workers than among white collar and professional groups [for example, UK Population census, 1970–1972 and UK General Household Survey, 1974 and 1975, and the Black Report (Townsend and Davidson, 1982)]. Similar data on mortality and morbidity comes from America (reports from the NIH, US Department of Health and Human Service), Sweden (Lundberg, 1986), Australia (McMichael and Hartshorne, 1980) and other countries.

As an example, the following differences have been found in chronic and acute illnesses between occupational classes in the UK. Between 1971 and 1976 the rate of limiting long-standing illness per 1000 population, self reported to the General Household Survey, was three times greater among unskilled manual workers than among professional workers (Macintyre, 1986). For men, the rate of acute illness was 130% higher among unskilled workers than among professionals (Townsend and Davidson, 1982). In 1982 men in semi-skilled and unskilled manual jobs were over twice as likely as men in professional jobs to have been absent from work in the 4 weeks prior to interview because of their own illness or injury (Macintyre, 1986).

Health information is usually presented as mortality data or morbidity data based either on self report or medical report. It has been argued that morbidity rates are to be preferred when studying occupational groupings because not all illnesses are fatal: there may be differences between groups in non-fatal illnesses, but not in fatal ones. Also, morbidity rates give some idea of pain and suffering (Lundberg, 1986). Self report illness data can be defended on the grounds that some individuals who are ill will not have visited a doctor or been absent from work (this can be affected by the level of sickness benefits available, for instance) and that self reported symptoms in fact form the basis of a physician's diagnosis (Lundberg, 1986).

Other health variables which are associated with occupational-social class differences in the UK are reviewed by Macintyre (1986) and include mental health (based on screening instruments such as the General Health Questionnaire) and self perceived health (as distinct from self reported illness). Energy, pain, sleep and physical mobility were rated worse by lower occupational groups.

A problem with basing conclusions about blue collar health or, even more difficult, blue collar stress on these studies is that the general findings about illness and occupations do not always hold up when specific illnesses or occupations are studied.

Coronary heart disease (CHD) is often regarded as an index of work stress. The relationship is far from clearcut since there are a number of factors involved in the aetiology of CHD. In the next section epidemiological data are presented on the relationship between the occurrence of CHD and job classification. It must be remembered that these are correlational data and should not be regarded as demonstrating causal relationships.

Surveys of Coronary Heart Disease (CHD)

While there is a consensus that health inequalities exist in many countries, the pattern for specific diseases is not so clear. A comparison of class differences (based on occupations) in health between Britain and Sweden confirmed a pattern of inequality in long-standing illness, with the semi-skilled and unskilled classes having the highest risks (Lundberg, 1986). An index of 'circulatory problems' (based on questions about aches, pain in the chest, weak heart, high blood pressure and breathlessness) was also found to increase with age and lower social group (Lundberg, 1986). However, studies in the US have reported no consistent linear gradient in CHD mortality and morbidity due to socio-economic status for white males (Kasl, 1978).

The Framingham Heart Study (Haynes and Feinleib, 1980) found that among the males in the sample, clerical and sales workers had the lowest incidence, professional and managers the highest, with blue collar workers showing a coronary heart disease incidence intermediate between the two. The Tecumseh study (House *et al.*, 1986) reported no occupational differences in health (including CHD) for men, but found female clerical and sales workers (medium status occupations) had twice the prevalence of CHD that other women had.

The relationship between CHD and specific aspects of jobs which might be particularly associated with blue collar occupations has yielded some positive findings. There is reasonably good supporting evidence that working excessive hours or having more than one job may be associated with CHD (Kasl, 1978). When a random sample from the Swedish male work force was studied it was found that jobs with low decision latitude provided an independent risk factor in coronary disease (Karasek *et al.*, 1981). On the other hand, analysis of data collected for the Minnesota Heart Survey (Sorensen *et al.*, 1985) revealed few effects of job experiences such as work hours, deadlines and occupational mobility on risk factors (physical exercise, smoking, total serum cholesterol and blood pressure) for coronary heart disease.

OCCUPATION, SOCIAL CLASS AND LIFESTYLE: THE PROBLEM OF 'EXPOSURE'

Occupation and social class are closely related. Occupation is frequently the basis for determining social class (Schneider, 1986) and may define an entire set of social conditions and experiences such as housing, leisure activities and diet which will closely affect lifestyle (Sorensen *et al.*, 1985).

The interplay of occupational and non-occupational factors such as lifestyle in disease aetiology has been emphasized by McMichael (1981) who points out that distinctive and relevant 'exposures' occur both on and off the job and often both influence the same disease processes. Data from some recent studies suggest that there are non-occupational aspects of social class which have a substantial influence (Macintyre, 1986; Marmot, Shipley and Rose, 1984; McMichael 1981, 1985). Some behaviours such as smoking, drinking and eating, while not job related, seem to be more prevalent among blue collar workers and unskilled workers than among professional and managerial workers (Badura, 1984; McMichael and Hartshorne, 1980; Townsend and Davidson, 1982). These behaviours make it difficult to interpret health data in terms of occupation groupings.

INTERPRETATION OF THE HEALTH INEQUALITIES DATA

The causes of death and the nature of the illnesses which are more prevalent in blue collar workers are not restricted to those which might be 'stress-related'.

Is it correct to claim that 'blue collar workers . . . seem to be a vulnerable group to occupational stressors and their manifestations'? (Cooper and Smith, 1985, p. 1). This is difficult to support since (a) the illnesses on which the occupations (classes) differ are not restricted to those which could be argued to be stress related, (b) it is difficult to distinguish between the effects of work environment and lifestyle, and (c) while it is acknowledged that the experience of stress seems to increase susceptibility to other disease agents and hence increases the overall likelihood of becoming ill, the link between health and stress is not firmly established.

Kasl (1978) warns that 'facile *a posteriori* judgments of stressfulness should not be routinely invoked to "explain" morbidity or mortality differences by occupation' (p. 10).

In the next section research into stress and occupational status will be discussed.

STUDIES OF OCCUPATION GROUPINGS AND STRESS

A major study of the relationship between stress and 23 blue and white collar occupations was reported by Caplan *et al.* (1980) and French *et al.* (1982). Occupations which were classed as unskilled blue collar (assembly line workers, forklift drivers) were highest on job dissatisfaction, boredom, depression and somatic complaints. Skilled blue collar employees (tool-makers and diemakers) and white collar nonprofessionals (such as police, foremen, train dispatchers) did not differ from professional white collar groups. Role conflict, role ambiguity and quantitative workload show a 'surprising lack of association with the blue collar versus white collar distinction, except that those low on workload are mostly blue collar jobs' (Kasl, 1978, p. 32). Imprecise operationalization of variables such as role ambiguity and role conflict makes interpretation of the evidence from the study difficult (Kasl, 1978).

French *et al.* (1982) analysed some of the data from this study to test the P–E fit model. Correlations between strains (defined as any deviations from the normal state or responses of the person), and income and education showed that (a) too little income was associated with increased strain and (b) strains (job dissatisfaction, boredom and somatic complaints) increased primarily when the person had more education than was typically required to perform the job.

A more recent report of the relationship between occupational characteristics and stresses found only slight evidence of associations between job characteristics or stresses and health behaviour and morbidity (House *et al.*, 1986). Measures collected between 1967 and 1969 in the Tecumseh Community Health Study on 1215 employed men, 763 employed women and 555 housewives were related to biomedical and questionnaire assessments taken at the same time, and to mortality over the succeeding 9–12 year period. Occupations were grouped into high, medium and low status.

This study extended the usual set of health behaviour and morbidity measures to include effects on the family which were assessed with the question: 'How often is feeling your job tends to interfere with your family life a source of pressure?' The question forms part of the Job Pressure Index which the researchers regard as one of the determinants of health behaviours, which in turn affect various forms of morbidity. The few positive associations found were strongest between job pressures or demands and health behaviour and morbidity. In contrast, job rewards and satisfactions and occupation–education discrepancies showed little consistent relation to health measures (House *et al.*, 1986).

A direct investigation of the effects of some of the factors postulated to be stressors in blue collar work was carried out on postal sorters where two forms of the job (manual and mechanized) could be compared (Chamberlain and Jones, 1987). The jobs differed in skills and knowledge required, and in the work organization and environment. The manual job was self paced and allowed a greater element of discretion, more physical movement and social interaction while the mechanized job was low on variety, autonomy, social interaction and high on pacing.

Stress was assessed with an anxiety–stress questionnaire designed to measure tensions and pressures. Higher levels of stress were found in mail sorters than in other jobs in the same workplace (such as supervision) but there were no differences between the groups of sorters in mean levels of stress. However, stress was closely related to dissatisfaction in the mechanized but not the manual group and it was manifested differently. In manual sorters and supervisors, stress appeared as fatigue, but in the mechanized group it took the form of anxiety. It was concluded that there was no 'dose-relationship' between the mechanized work and stress. There was evidence of a strong association between dissatisfaction and anxiety which might have been determined by the organizational factors connected with a particular kind of work.

This is somewhat in contrast to the findings reviewed by Kasl (1978). He concluded that studies conducted in the 1970s had, in general, failed to support the prediction that those who performed routine, machine paced work would have significantly lower levels of job satisfaction. Blue collar workers were found to be 'not appreciably different' from the remainder of the US employed population on variables such as health, depression, self esteem and life satisfaction (Quinn *et al.*, 1971, Quinn and Shepard, 1974; both cited in Kasl, 1978).

Broad, generalized claims about the relationship between job characteristics, job satisfaction and mental health may need careful scrutiny. For instance, assembly line work is frequently cited as one of the worst occupations. It is described as producing the greatest levels of boredom and job dissatisfaction and the highest levels of anxiety, depression, irritation and psychosomatic disorders (Shostak, 1980). However, a study of repetition and pacing in the UK car industry (Broadbent, 1981) found that repetition was associated with dislike of the job, but had no strong effect on anxiety. Paced work, while not necessarily disliked, was associated with anxiety, and the effect was worse for meticulous workers. The same association between anxiety and pacing was reported in a study of laundry workers (Broadbent, 1981).

RESEARCH INTO SOCIAL FACTORS WHICH MAY INTERACT WITH OCCUPATIONAL STRESS

Biographical variables such as gender, age, marital status, educational level and ethnic background have often been omitted in occupational stress research although social epidemiologists are now recognizing their importance in determining health (Badura, 1984).

In general, women score significantly worse than men on health variables across all occupational levels (Lundberg, 1986). Most data relate to CHD and blood pressure, but findings differ. A significant interaction between high blood pressure and occupational status was found in a study of over 1169 employed women (Zimmerman and Hartley, 1982) but it did not vary by employment or occupational status in the Framingham data (Haynes and

Feinleib, 1980). The Tecumseh study found no significant differences among the three occupational levels of employed women for any morbidity variables, although the middle status clerical and sales women had a significantly higher incidence of CHD than other employed women and housewives (House *et al.*, 1086). In the Minnesota Heart Survey, women reported more stress symptoms than men but they had significantly lower mean levels of serum cholesterol and systolic blood pressure (Sorensen *et al.*, 1985).

The question of whether there is an interaction between education and occupation in predicting health has been answered in the negative by several studies (e.g. House *et al.*, 1986; Karasek, 1981; McKenna and Scholl, 1985). However there does appear to be a relationship between education and health related behaviours (Badura, 1984).

Education also has an effect on job satisfaction and self report of physical health where there is a discrepancy between the worker's level of education and the education required for the job.

The possible interaction between social factors and health raises the question of whether the disadvantages previously thought to attach to being a blue collar worker actually relate to other factors such as being female, being poor or less well educated?

To answer these questions, we present in detail an analysis of data collected from a number of occupations. The analysis is intended to explore the relationships between biographical variables (sex, education and migrant status), occupational distinctions (blue/white collar, earnings, job characteristics) and perceptions of health, occupational stress and social and family functioning.

THE RESEARCH DATA BANK

The analyses and findings reported here are based on a data bank established by the Brain–Behaviour Research Institute at La Trobe University (Melbourne, Australia). The data bank contains information collected by questionnaire from Australian workers in various occupational groups.

The questionnaire has a modular structure which provides for the investigation of different aspects of work and lifestyle of diverse occupational groups, and also for cross-sample comparisons. The basic modules include biographical, health, sleep, social and family details, attitudes to the job and workplace description. Optional modules provide for sections concerning shiftwork, chemical use and business management. Apart from demographic information the sections concerning health, sleep, social and family details, and job details which are not occupation specific provide the information for cross-sample comparisons. The basic format and content of all questionnaires is similar but each survey instrument is modified for different occupational groups.

Versions of this instrument have been used to survey police and prison officers, social workers, dairy farmers, electricity and chemical workers. The instrument gives results that distinguish between shiftworkers and dayworkers, both within and between occupational groups such as police and prison officers, two police groups, police and electricity workers (Ong *et al.*, 1985; Levens and Singer, 1987a, b). Males and females were also found to differ within and between two police forces (Singer, 1986; Levens and Singer, 1987a).

Each occupational group was surveyed separately between 1984 and 1987. Questionnaires were mailed to random samples of the target group together with a postage paid return envelope and a covering letter from the sponsoring organization. The sample structure and valid return rates varied between surveys as did the sample size. Stratified sampling of the police forces by rank, and of the social workers by agency was employed. Sample sizes ranged from 426 to 889 except for the group of chemical workers where the sample size of 22 represented the total factory work force. Valid return rates were between 70 and 100% with the exception of the dairy industry group for whom the valid return rate was 33.4%.

A representative sample of approximately 919 subjects was drawn randomly from the data base. The sample was stratified by sex. The number of subjects from each survey and sex group are shown in Table 1. Mean age and length of employment are also shown.

Table 1 Sample size, mean age, years of employment and sex for each survey group

Survey	Sex		Sample size	Mean age	Mean years of employment
	Male	Female			
Electricity workers	195	0	195	38.69	14.55
Police officers (1)	131	73	164	32.44	12.99
Chemical workers	5	0	5	46.60	7.60
Social workers	19	75	93	35.38	3.17
Police officers (2)	150	65	215	35.48	14.27
Prison officers	152	10	162	41.44	8.45
Dairy farmers	38	2	90	43.23	22.09
Dairy apprentices	4	1	5	18.20	2.20
Whole subsample	743	186	919	37.35	12.73

All surveys included items allowing common bivariate classification of subjects by country of birth, rank in the industry or organizational hierarchy, income and level of education. The distinction between groups for these variables was made as follows. Subjects were classed as Australian born or not. Subjects reporting earning $A 500 or more per week including overtime payment were classed as high income while those earning below $A 500 per week were classed as low income.

Level of education refers to the highest level of education reached. The higher educated group had completed at least one post-secondary qualification. The lower educated group included those who had completed apprenticeship or certificate qualifications, as well as all subjects reporting schooling up to, but not further than, completion of secondary school (12 years).

The distinction between rank in the industry or organizational hierarchy varied for different occupational groups. The 327 white collar workers included commissioned and non-commissioned police officers, prison officers with the rank of chief and above, chemical laboratory technicians, resident managers of dairy farms, electricity workers on staff and all social workers. The blue collar group of 593 included shift foremen and process workers, non-officer ranks in the police groups, ranks below chief for prison officers, electricity workers on wages and, from the farming group, sole owners, business partners, share farmers, farm labourers and apprentices.

Table 2 The distribution of cases over each independent variable for white and blue collar workers

Group	Sex		Australian		Earnings		Education	
	Male	Female	born	Migrant	High	Low	High	Low
White collar	242	85	264	63	222	104	91	223
Blue collar	493	100	433	157	152	417	35	492

The dependent variables were mean scale scores computed for selected sets of items representing dimensions of health, social and family life, job characteristics and attitudes. Each item required respondents to indicate frequency of occurrence or degree of agreement with a statement on a five point rating scale. The ratings for individual items were recorded where appropriate to ensure uniform direction of meaning before computing mean scale scores. Twenty-one scales were derived from 141 items. There were nine scales describing dimensions of health, eight job scales, five scales covering family and social issues and one scale concerning sleep.

Statistical Analyses

A univariate two-way analysis of variance for completely randomized design followed by analysis for simple main effects was conducted separately on each dependent variable (scale scores) for every unique pair of independent variables (bivariate classifications). A type 1 error rate of 0.01 was adopted for both *a priori* and *post hoc* tests.

The total subsample was included in all analyses of health and social and family scales. The dairy farmers and apprentices were excluded from the analyses for job scales since the items used to assess their job and workplace characteristics differed too greatly from those used in other surveys. The reason for this was that the farming group worked in relatively isolated operations unlike the other survey samples which represent employee groups.

Results

Health

Very few differences were found between groups on the health variables. The health scales which distinguished between groups concerned respiratory system complaints, gastrointestinal system complaints, symptoms of fatigue, symptoms which could possibly be associated with cardiac problems and allergy symptoms. The following differences were found:

Greater fatigue and more allergies were reported by blue collar males than blue collar females.

Both male blue collar workers and female white collar workers reported more frequent gastrointestinal problems than did male white collar workers.

Australian born (all groups) suffer fewer allergies than migrants.

Symptoms which might be related to cardiac problems were reported to be more frequent in white collar Australian born workers than in blue collar Australian born workers. No differences were found between blue and white collar migrant workers on this scale.

White collar workers in the lower education group showed more gastrointestinal problems than blue collar workers with a lower educational level and more than white collar workers with a higher level of education.

White collar workers in the high earner group suffered more frequent gastrointestinal problems than did white collar low earners.

No differences between any groups were found for the three scales related to mood (symptoms of depressed mood, symptoms of manic mood and indicators of mood balance) nor on the musculoskeletal symptom scale.

A separate scale denoting quality and quantity of sleep differentiated only between white collar males and white collar females. White collar females reported getting better sleep than did white collar males.

Job Characteristics

The eight job scales covered autonomy in one's own job role, physical and mental workload, demand for skills, job related support at work, personal relationships in the workplace, control or participation in decision making, the physical work environment and quality of facilities.

Table 3 presents a summary of the variables which differentiated between the blue and white collar workers in terms of their job characteristics for both levels of the four subgroupings.

Table 3 Summary of variables differentiating between blue and white collar workers in terms of job characteristics

| Blue collar | Blue collar vs white collar | | | |
	Sex	Migrant	Education	Earnings
Less autonomy	*	*	*	*
Lighter physical and mental workload	*	*	*	*

Gender differences

No significant differences were found for the job scales describing job control and the physical environment.

Six of the eight job scales showed 12 differences between blue and white collar and male and female groups. Only two of these differentiated between blue and white collar workers regardless of sex. Blue collar workers reported having less autonomy and lighter mental and physical workload than did white collar workers.

None of the scales differentiated between males and females for both blue and white collar workers. Sex differences were found within groups on some scales. Blue collar females had heavier physical and mental workloads than blue collar males.

When blue collar and white collar workers were examined separately, males in both groups felt they had more autonomy at work than females.

White collar males reported greater job support as well as more autonomy, better relationships with colleagues at work but their facilities such as canteen, first-aid, resting and social amenities were poorer than for white collar women.

Blue collar females had better relationships with colleagues at work than white collar females, but the latter had a greater demand for their job skills and better facilities in the workplace. The only differences between blue collar and white collar males was in terms of job support: blue collar males reported less support and feedback from the boss and from workmates.

Differences by country of birth

The job scales describing support and relationships in the work place and the physical work conditions did not differentiate between any groups.

Seven differences on five of the eight job scales were found between blue and white collar migrant and Australian born workers. Again, only the autonomy and workload scales showed differences between blue and white collar workers regardless of country of origin. Blue collar workers reported less autonomy and lighter physical and mental workloads than did white collar workers.

Australian born workers reported more control in the job than migrant workers. Blue collar Australian born workers perceived their facilities at work to be worse than did migrant blue collar workers. The white collar Australian born workers, when compared with white collar migrant workers, felt they had less autonomy in their job and carried a greater physical and mental workload.

Among Australian born workers, those with blue collar status complained there was less demand for their job skills. There were no differences between blue and white collar migrant born workers.

Education differences

The eight job scales differentiated between groups of blue and white collar workers and higher or lower education. Of the 12 differences found, blue collar workers again reported having less autonomy and lighter mental and physical workloads than did white collar workers.

None of the scales distinguished between the lower and higher education groups overall but some differences were found within the blue or white collar classification.

Generally, a higher level of education was associated with reports of greater physical and mental workloads, less support on the job and poor work relationships. When blue collar workers are considered, those educated to a higher level reported less autonomy and greater physical and mental workload. White collar workers with a higher level of education also claimed to have less autonomy and reported less social support at work and worse relationships with colleagues. They did, however, have better facilities than lower educated white collar workers.

When workers with a higher level of education were examined in terms of their work status, the blue collar workers reported less demand for their skills, less control and worse facilities at work. Workers with a lower level of education differed only in terms of physical working conditions, with blue collar workers being worse off than white collar.

Differences in terms of income

The scales describing support in the work place and participation in work place decision-making did not differentiate between any of the groups.

Autonomy and workload were reported to be less by blue collar workers than by white collar workers. There were three other job scales which showed differences between groups. However, there were no other overall differences between blue and white collar or between higher and lower earners.

Differences in income are associated with only a few differences in reports of job characteristics. White collar higher income earners assessed their autonomy as higher than those with lower incomes, but rated their facilities at work as worse. Blue collar high earners reported worse physical work conditions than white collar higher earners and blue collar low earners found less demand for their skills than white collar low earners.

Summary

It will be seen from the data presented in this section that there are differences between blue collar and white collar jobs, particularly in terms of autonomy, physical and mental workload and demand for work skills. A comparison of blue and white collar workers by sex reveals many more differences between males and females than are found when comparisons are made by place of birth. This suggests that being born in Australia or elsewhere does not have a wide ranging effect on the way blue or white collar workers experience their jobs.

The level of education makes a considerable difference to the way a job affects a blue or white collar worker. Differences were found for all eight job characteristics scales (there were 12 significant differences on these scales). This contrasts with the comparison between high and low earners, where only four differences were found when blue and white collar workers were compared on these characteristics.

Social and Family Interactions

The five scales concerning social and family issues described the quality of relationships within the family, the difficulty of engaging in activities requiring regular commitments of time, difficulty in doing occasional chores, the perceived quality of performance of one's own parenting role and the degree to which the job interferes with leisure time. Table 4 presents a summary of the variables which differentiated between blue and white collar workers in terms of their social and family problems for both levels of each of the subgroupings.

Gender differences

Only one of the five family scales differentiated between blue and white collar workers regardless of sex. Blue collar workers had fewer opportunities for occasional activities than white collar workers. Other differences between blue collar and white collar groups were found only for females. Women

Table 4 Summary of the variables which differentiate between blue and white collar workers in terms of social and family problems

| Blue collar | Blue collar vs white collar | | | |
	Sex	Migrant	Education	Earnings
Fewer difficulties with occasional chores	*			
Fewer parenting problems			*	
Fewer difficulties with family closeness			*	

who were blue collar workers found fewer problems in their role as parents, fewer difficulties with the sort of activities that make for good family relationships, such as having enough time for children and family outings and thought of themselves as good providers and protectors of their family, but they reported it was more difficult to undertake regular social and sporting activities.

On the other hand, some overall differences were found between males and females on four scales, regardless of their place in the workforce. Males reported more difficulties with family closeness and with regular activities than females and they felt they did less well in their role as parent and partner. They complained more than females did that the job interfered with the time available to spend with friends and spouse, to meet new people or to carry out their own plans.

There were no sex differences within either blue or white collar groups. Nor were there any differences between blue and white collar males.

Differences by country of birth

No significant differences were found between groups on the scales describing difficulty with necessary activities or interference of the job with spare time activities.

The same three scales which differentiate generally between blue and white collar workers (family closeness, parenting and time available for occasional activities such as appointments and shopping) showed differences within groups.

The blue and white collar distinction made no difference to migrant workers, but it did affect Australian born workers. The Australian blue collar worker had more difficulty with family closeness but fewer parenting problems and found it easier to carry out occasional chores.

There were no differences between Australian born and migrant workers when considered without reference to their work status. Blue collar migrant workers reported more difficulties in activities relating to family closeness and more parenting problems that Australian blue collar workers. White collar Australian workers had more difficulty than white collar migrant workers with occasional chores.

Education differences

In total, 10 significant differences were found on the five social and family scales.

When the sample was subdivided into work status groups, blue collar workers with a higher level of education reported more difficulties with occasional chores than blue collar workers with lower level education. Their white collar counterparts reported fewer difficulties with family closeness than the white collar lower level education group.

A division of the sample in terms of level of education produced significant differences on four scales. Those with some educational qualifications above secondary level appear to be better off in terms of their family and the social aspects of their life than the group with lower educational levels. The higher educated group reported fewer problems with parenting, less job interference with social and family activities and fewer difficulties with their regular social and sporting activities. The lower educated white collar workers reported greater difficulty with family closeness than their higher educated colleagues.

Despite the general finding that a higher level of education was associated with better social and family life, the blue collar workers with a higher level of education reported more difficulties with social and sporting activities than white collar workers in the same educational category, although they managed to carry out occasional chores with less problems. Conversely, blue collar workers in the lower education group were better off than equivalent white collar workers in terms of their regular social and sporting activities.

Differences in terms of income

Seven significant differences were found on the five social and family scales.

Level of income was associated with differences on two scales. Higher earners had more difficulty with family closeness and more problems as parents than lower earners. When blue collar workers were considered it was found that a higher income was associated with more job interference in family activities (possibly because they were working overtime to obtain the higher level of income.)

Among white collar workers, high earners had more difficulty with sporting and social activities than low earners. There were no differences between blue and white collar workers in the higher income group. In the lower income group, blue collar workers were in a better position than white collar workers: they had less difficulty with family closeness, fewer parenting problems and were more able to carry out occasional chores.

Discussion

The data bank has been used to compare shiftworkers with dayworkers. In all of these comparisons a range of significant differences were found with regard to a few health variables as well as with regard to some social and family aspects and job characteristics. These differences between shift and day workers were invariant for different industries, sex differences and place of birth. Most of the biological differences could be predicted from data and theories of circadian rhythms or as a result of social displacements caused by shiftwork.

In the present comparison between blue and white collar workers there is no firm basis for predictions nor are there clear cut demarcation lines between blue collar and white collar. The latter may be the result of changes due to new technologies which narrow the gap between skilled and unskilled work and also a narrowing of the gap with regard to income and educational differences.

The fact that there are few differences in health variables between blue collar and white collar workers when the demarcation between them is made according to traditional criteria may be unexpected but is convincing when it is compared with differences found for shiftworkers. Even when interactions between the blue collar and white collar classification, sex, place of birth, education and income are examined there is no general picture of better or worse health for any of the subgroups.

With regard to job characteristics, there are two significant differences: one for the degree of autonomy and the other for perceived workload. These differences are qualified by some of the interactions. For instance, males whether blue or white collar workers felt they had more autonomy and blue collar females reported more heavier physical and mental workloads. Australian born workers report more job control than migrants.

There are further qualifying interactions when level of education and income are considered. The patterns which emerge here come closer to the traditional concepts of the blue collar workers. On social and family interactions, blue collar workers report fewer difficulties with occasional chores, fewer parenting problems and fewer difficulties with family closeness. These are unexpected and therefore surprising.

In summary, there are strong grounds for dissatisfaction with the traditional classification of the workforce into blue and white collar workers. This situation holds no matter which of the traditional divisions are used to operationalize the concept. This may account for the conflicting and ambiguous results of research. Our attempts to use alternative grouping variables, on the premise that disadvantages thought to attach to blue collar workers relate to other social factors such as gender, poverty or education, were unsuccessful. It is possible that our surveys have missed out on large pockets of 'typical' blue collar workers, but it is more likely that new technologies and increased social services have eliminated the meaningfulness of the blue vs white collar distinction. Other aspects of work arrangement, such as a shift work vs day work dichotomy, may provide an appropriate basis for classifying the work force. Differences in quality of life may also be found in regard to employment status and the poverty line.

REFERENCES

Badura, B. (1984). Life-style and health: some remarks on different viewpoints, *Social Science and Medicine*, **19**, 341–7.
Broadbent, D. E. (1981). Chronic effects from the physical nature of work. In G. Gardell and G. Johansson, (eds) *Working Life*, John Wiley and Sons, Chichester.
Chamberlain, A. G. and Jones, D. M. (1987). Satisfactions and stresses in the sorting of mail, *Work and Stress*, **1**, 25–34.
Caplan, R. D., Cobb, S., French, J. R. P., Harrison, R. V. and Pinneau, S. R. (1980). *Job Demands and Worker Health: Main Effects and Occupational Differences*, Institute for Social Research, Ann Arbor.
Cooper, C. L. and Marshall, J. (1978). Sources of managerial and white collar stress. In C. L. Cooper and R. Payne (eds) *Stress at Work*, John Wiley and Sons, Chichester.
Cooper, C. L. and Smith, M. J., (1985). Introduction: Blue collar workers are 'at risk'. In C. L. Cooper and A. J. Smith (eds) *Job Stress and Blue Collar Work*, John Wiley and Sons, Chichester.
Edgren, J. (1981). Discussant's comments. In G. Gardell and G. Johansson (eds) *Working Life*, John Wiley and Sons, Chichester.
Fisher, S. (1985). Control and blue collar work. In C. L. Cooper and M. J. Smith (eds). *Job Stress and Blue Collar Work*, John Wiley and Sons, Chichester.
French, J. R. P., Caplan, R. D. and Harrison, R. V. (1982). *The Mechanisms of Job Stress and Strain*, John Wiley and Sons, Chichester.
Haynes, S. G. and Feinleib, M. (1980). Women, work and coronary heart disease: prospective findings from the Framingham Heart Study, *American Journal of Public Health*, **70**, 133–41.
House, J. S., Strecher, V., Metzner, H. L. and Robbins, C. A. (1986). Occupational stress and health among men and women in the Tecumseh Community Health Study, *Journal of Health and Social Behavior*, **27**, 62–77.
Karasek, R. A., (1979). Job demands, job decision latitude and mental strain: implications for job redesign, *Administrative Science Quarterly*, **24**, 285–308.
Karasek, R. A. (1981). Job socialisation and job strain: the implications of two related psychosocial mechanisms for job design. In G. Gardell and G. Johansson (eds) *Working Life*, John Wiley and Sons, Chichester.
Karasek, R., Baker, D., Marxer, F., Ahlbom, A. and Theorell, T. (1981). Job decision latitude, job demands and cardiovascular disease: a prospective study of Swedish men, *American Journal of Public Health*, **71**, 694–705.
Kasl, S. V. (1978). Epidemiological contributions to the study of work stress. In C. L. Cooper and R. Payne (eds) *Stress at Work*, John Wiley and Sons, Chichester.
Levens, M. and Singer, G. (1987a). A comparison of the quality of life of Victorian and South Australian police officers; parts 2 and 3, Brain–Behaviour Research Institute, La Trobe University, Melbourne.
Levens, M. and Singer, G. (1987b). Quality of life: comparison of West Australian

prison officers and Victorian police officers; parts 2 and 3, Brain–Behaviour Research Institute, La Trobe University, Melbourne.

Lundberg, O. (1986). 'Class and health: comparing Britain and Sweden, *Social Science and Medicine*, **23**, 511–7.

Lupton, T. (1976). Shop floor behavior. In R. Dubin (ed.) *Handbook of Work, Organisation and Society*, Rand McNally, Chicago.

Macintyre, S. (1986). The patterning of health by social position in contemporary Britain: directions for sociological Research, *Social Science and Medicine*, **4**, 393–415.

McKenna, J. F. and Scholl, R. W. (1985). The interactive patterns of occupations and workers in predicting excessive occupational stress, *Stress Medicine*, **1**, 93–100, (see p. 94).

McMichael, A. J. (1981). 'Occupational disease': disentangling the effects of work environment and lifestyle, *Community Health Studies*, **5**, 71–8.

McMichael, A. J. (1985). Social class (as estimated by occupational prestige) and mortality in Australian males in the 1970s, *Community Health Studies*, **9**, 220–30.

McMichael, A. J. and Hartshorne, J. M. (1980). Cardiovascular disease and cancer mortality in Australia, by occupation, in relation to drinking, smoking and eating, *Community Health Studies*, **4**, 76–80.

Marmot, M. G., Shipley, M. J., Rose, G. (1984). Inequalities in death—specific explanations of a general pattern? *Lancet*, **i**, 1003–6.

Ong, B., Levens, M., Wallace, M. and Singer G. (1985). Police Association of South Australia: quality of life survey 1984–5; parts 1, 2 and 3', Brain–Behaviour Research Institute, La Trobe University, Melbourne.

Ostberg, O. and Nilsson, C. (1985). Emerging technology and stress. In Cooper, C. L. and Smith, M. J. (eds) *Job Stress and Blue Collar Work*, John Wiley and Sons, Chichester.

Poulton, E. C. (1978). Blue collar stressors. In Cooper and R. Payne (eds) *Stress at Work*, John Wiley and Sons, Chichester.

Schneider, J. A. (1986). Rewriting the SES: demographic patterns and divorcing families, *Social Science and Medicine*, **23**, 211–22.

Sharit, J. and Salvendy, G. (1982). Occupational stress: review and reappraisal, *Human Factors*, **24**, 129–62.

Shostak, A. B. (1980). *Blue-collar Stress* Addison–Wesley, Reading, MA.

Singer, G., (1986). Discussion paper for the Conference on Legislative and Award Restrictions to Women's Employment, Office of the Prime Minister and Cabinet, Canberra.

Sorensen, G., Pirie, P., Folsom, A., Luepker, R., Jacobs, D. and Gillum, R. (1985). Sex differences in the relationship between work and health: the Minnesota Heart Survey, *Journal of Health and Social Behavior*, **26**, 379–94.

Townsend, P. and Davidson, N. (1982). *Inequalities in Health: The Black Report*, Penguin, Harmondsworth.

Wallace, M. and Buckle, P. (1987). Ergonomic aspects of neck and upper limb disorders. In, D. J. Oborne (ed.) *International Reviews of Ergonomics*, Vol. 1, 173–200.

Zimmerman, M. K. and Hartley, W. S. (1982). 'High blood pressure among employed women: A multi-factor discriminant analysis, *Journal of Health and Social Behavior*, **23**, 205–20.

Causes, Coping and Consequences of Stress at Work
Edited by C. L. Cooper and R. Payne
© 1988 John Wiley & Sons Ltd

Chapter 3

Sources of Managerial and Professional Stress in Large Organizations*

Ronald J. Burke

This chapter will examine sources of managerial and professional stress in large organizations. An increased understanding of sources of managerial and professional stress provides major benefits to both research and intervention. This material will provide scholars with a summary of what has been found and highlight future research directions (Burke, 1987). This material should also enlighten practice. In order to do something positive about managerial and professional work stressors, it is important to identify them. The success of any intervention effort to reduce work stressors and heighten individual satisfaction and well-being will depend on accurate diagnosis since different work stressors require different actions.

The chapter begins with a review of categories of work stressors present in models of occupational stress. It then provides a limited summary of recent findings for six categories of stressors: physical environment, role stressors, organizational structure and job characteristics, relationships with others, career development and work–family conflict. Some attention is then given to research examining the effects of managerial and professional sources of stress on nonwork experiences of job incumbents, and experiences of their spouses. Considerable attention is then devoted to increasingly important contemporary sources of managerial and professional stress: mergers and acquisitions, organizational retrenchment and decline, job future ambiguity and insecurity, and occupational locking-in.

The chapter will discuss advances in work stressor research during the past decade: the use of more comprehensive models and more sophisticated analysis approaches, the use of meta-analyses, attempts to develop innovative measures of work stressors, increased use of longitudinal designs in field studies, laboratory simulations and natural experiments, increasing efforts to measure both objective and subjective work stressors, and investigations of

* Preparation of this chapter was supported in part by Imperial Oil Ltd and the Social Sciences and Humanities Research Council of Canada. I would like to thank Esther Greenglass and Gene Deszca for their helpful comments, Greg McGuire and Victoria Greco for their assistance in identifying material for the chapter and Maria Simone for preparing the manuscript.

acute work stressors. The chapter concludes with an examination of organizational interventions specifically designed to reduce occupational sources of
stress: goal setting, participative decision making, job redesign to improve
person–environment fit, orientation program, and programs to manage staff
reductions.

FRAMEWORKS FOR UNDERSTANDING MANAGERIAL AND PROFESSIONAL STRESS

Several writers have developed frameworks to aid our understanding of work
stress (Quick and Quick, 1984; Cherniss, 1980; Ivancevich and Matteson,
1980; Cooper and Marshall, 1976, 1978a, b; Beehr and Newman, 1978).
These frameworks are consistent with person–environment fit approaches.
That is, each includes a panel of variables encompassing sources of occupational stressors in the work environment and a panel of variables dealing
with individual differences.

Various authors provide different categories of work stressors. Thus
Cooper and Marshall (1976, 1978a) offer five clusters of work stressors: those
intrinsic to the job, and those resulting from one's role in the organization,
career development, relationships with others, and organizational structure
and climate. Quick and Quick (1984) propose four categories of stressors:
task demands, role demands, physical demands (elements in one's physical
setting or environment) and interpersonal demands. Ivancevich and Matteson
(1980) also divide stressors into four categories: physical environment, individual level (a mixture of role and career development variables) group level
(primarily relationship-based) and organizational level (a mixture of climate,
structure, job design and task characteristics). Schuler (1982) identifies seven
categories of work stressors in organizations: job qualities, relationships,
organizational structure, physical qualities, career development, change and
role in the organization. Some authors also include extra-organizational stressors (e.g. family) as well (Cooper and Marshall, 1976, 1978a; Ivancevich and
Matteson, 1980).

There is considerable overlap among these frameworks, both in terms of
the categories themselves, as well as stressors included within each category.
We will use six categories of sources of managerial and professional work
stressors to organize our review: the physical environment and those resulting
from one's role in the organization, organizational structure and job characteristics, relationships with others, career development and work–family
conflict.

PHYSICAL ENVIRONMENT

The importance of physical characteristics of the environment as stressors at
the management level has been largely overlooked in stress research. This

inattentiveness to the importance of environmental factors is a reflection of the nature of the typical manager's job within the organization. Management and executive level organizational operations are largely conducted in an office environment which is not subjected to the same types of hazardous and noxious agents which often put lower-level employees at risk. In addition, management level employees are assumed to have a great deal of personal control over their physical environment, thereby possessing the ability to significantly reduce or remove immediate environmental stressors.

The most frequently mentioned environmental stressors include density and crowding as an example of overload (Suedfeld, 1979; Rule and Nesdale, 1976; Keating, 1979) and/or lack of privacy (Cohen, 1980b); high noise levels (Rule and Nesdale, 1976) and vibrations and/or soundwaves (Quick and Quick, 1984); temperature extremes (Cohen, 1980a); air movement and background colour (Jokl, 1984) and illumination. Behavioural toxicology would also highlight the importance of environmental contamination, including air, water and noise pollution (Gochman, 1979; Russell, 1978). Finally, the increased employment of computer video terminals has recently drawn attention as an environmental stressor (Chadrow, 1984).

Sutton and Rafaeli (1987) conducted a field study of 109 clerical workers which explored work station characteristics as potential occupational stressors. They studied two categories of physical stressors: intrusions from atmospheric conditions (hotness, coldness, poor quality lighting) and intrusions from other employees (noise and distractions, lack of control over privacy, high population density). Two categories of employee reactions were examined: satisfaction with the work station itself and general reactions to work, which included traditional affective, behavioural and physiological variables examined in work stress research. Finally, role overload was envisioned as a moderator variable, and was used to test two hypotheses—detachment and aggravation—of the effects of physical stressors.

The detachment hypothesis suggested that overloaded employees would concentrate harder on doing their jobs and thus be less bothered by intrusions from the physical environment. The aggravation hypothesis suggested that intrusions would be particularly upsetting to overloaded employees. The data indicated that, when moderating effects of role overload were present, they supported the detachment hypothesis rather than the aggravation hypothesis. The results also indicated that, for the clerical employees in the sample, characteristics of work stations were not occupational stressors.

There has been some research conducted on traditional vs open offices in which stress-related variables were examined (Zalesny and Farace, 1987; Oldham and Brass, 1979; Oldham and Rotchford, 1983; Davis, 1984). Managers and professionals, for example, reported lower perceived privacy following a change from a traditional to an open office design (Zalesny and

Farace, 1987). These individuals perceived the loss of their private offices, traditional symbols of organizational status and prestige, as a loss of status.

Szilagyi and Holland (1980) examined the effects of change in social density (amount of space and numbers of people within that space) resulting from physical movement to a new building on role stress variables. Data were collected from 96 professional employees in a petroleum-related organization using questionnaires administered at two points in time, 4 months before and 4 months after the move. The results showed significantly *less* role conflict and role ambiguity among those individuals with increased social density following the move. The authors attribute this finding to the nature of professional work. That is, the highly skilled professionals in this sample require a high degree of interaction and information to do their work. Thus a physical environment that help in the performance of these jobs is likely to reduce role stressors.

ROLE IN THE ORGANIZATION

Role conflict and ambiguity are the most widely examined source variables in managerial stress research (Beehr, 1985). The original study of role conflict conducted by Kahn *et al.* (1964), and subsequent research efforts, have identified five types of role conflict in organizations: intersender conflict, intrasender conflict, interrole conflict, person–role conflict and role overload (Beehr, 1985; Van Sell, Brief and Schuler, 1981). Research on role conflict and ambiguity is extremely homogenous, as anywhere from 50% (Van Sell *et al.*, 1981) and 85% (Jackson and Schuler, 1985) of this literature employs scales developed by House and Rizzo (1972a, b).

Summarizing across the role conflict and role ambiguity literature, the following variables are often found to be positively correlated with role conflict and ambiguity: tension and fatigue (Singh, Agarwala and Malhan, 1981; Schuler, Aldag and Brief, 1977); absenteeism (Breaugh, 1980), leaving the job, and anxiety, (Hamner and Tosi, 1974), and both psychological and physical general strain (Orpen, 1982). Jackson and Schuler (1985) also found the following variables to be positively correlated with role conflict: task/skill variety, locus of control, education and propensity to leave the organization.

Variables found to be consistently negatively correlated with role conflict and ambiguity include job satisfaction (Singh *et al.* 1981; Breaugh, 1980), physical withdrawal, supervisory satisfaction, performance, job involvement (Schuler *et al.*, 1977), decision making, job involvement, organizational commitment, (Fisher and Gitelson, 1983), tolerance for conflict and group cohesion (Randolph and Posner, 1981) and reported influence (Hamner and Tosi, 1974). Submitting the literature to meta-analysis techniques, Jackson and Schuler (1985) found significant negative correlations between role conflict and/or ambiguity and the following variables: participation, task identity, feedback, job satisfaction across several sublevels, and commitment and involvement. It has been also clearly demonstrated that role conflict and role ambiguity are consistently correlated with each other (Jackson and Schuler, 1985; Van Sell *et al.*, 1981).

Popovich and Licota (1987) propose that sexual harassment in work settings may be explained using a role model approach building on the existing literature on role conflict and role ambiguity. Sexual harassment becomes a role problem when an individual's sex role or gender role interferes with their functions as an employee. A recent study of over 250 victims of sexual harassment (Crull, 1982) reported that almost all of the women experienced debilitating stress reactions as a result. These reactions included psychological and physical symptoms as well as difficulties with job performances.

Antecedents of Role Stressors

Early stress research (Miles and Perreault, 1976; Kahn *et al.* 1964) showed that boundary roles expose job incumbents to role conflict and role ambiguity. More recent research (Miles, 1980; Pearce, 1981) has increased our understanding of antecedents of role stressors.

Parkington and Schneider (1979) proposed that service employees would experience role stress when they perceived management emphasizing system requirements at odds with client needs; that is, the greater the discrepancy between perceptions of management and customer demands, the greater the experienced role ambiguity and role conflict. These role stressors would in turn, be related to dissatisfaction with the organization, feelings of frustration, perceived poor customer service and increased propensity to leave. Data were collected from a sample of bank branch employees (*N*-263) from 23 branches of a large commercial bank. The following findings were noted: service orientation discrepancy had an indirect effect on employee outcomes through role ambiguity and role conflict, and role conflict and role ambiguity were both significantly correlated with the employee outcomes. Thus, role ambiguity and role conflict served as the psychological mechanisms through which discrepancies in perceived service orientation resulted in negative employee outcomes.

Miles and Perreault (1976) examined antecedents and consequences of role conflict among 195 professional level employees. Antecedents of role conflict lay in the objective role requirements of the job incumbent. They identified four role conflict types: person–role, intersender, intrasender, and overload. Potential antecedents of role conflict included: the importance of selected role activities or role requirements (e.g. integration and boundary spanning activities, personnel supervision and scientific research), and characteristics of the focal person's role set (e.g. average organizational distance of important role senders, degree of formal authority role senders as a group have relative to the focal person). Objective conditions which were high on conflict potential (i.e. heavy role requirements emphasizing supervisory activities, integration and boundary-spanning activities and scientific research activities, and/or role sets characterized by high distance or superior-authority role senders) would be related to different and greater role conflicts.

Data were collected from professional-level personnel from nine governmental research and development organizations. Objective conditions were measured in the following ways. Each focal person indicated how many distinct intra- and interorganizational boundaries separated him/her from each of his/her role senders. The role-set average on this measure served as a measure of the organizational distance of role senders. Focal persons also reported how much formal authority role senders had relative to their own. In addition, responsibility for performing various role requirements (personnel supervision, integration and boundary spanning, scientific research). The following findings emerged: four of the five objective conditions were significantly associated with level of role conflict. There were: scientific research, distance of role senders, integration and boundary spanning activities and personnel supervision activities. Role set authority was not related to level of experienced role conflict.

There is also a body of research and theory which links dyadic goal setting within organizations to role stress variables (Quick, 1979a). That is, goal setting processes serve a role making function through defining, clarifying and enacting organizational roles. In addition, dyadic goal setting increases role congruence, the degree of agreement between the job incumbents actual role behaviors and the behaviors expected by various role senders. Quick (1979b) developed a research framework for examining the dyadic goal setting process in organizations. This framework introduced the concept of manager–subordinate consensus which results from the goal setting process and serves to reduce the negative effects of role stressors.

Ivancevich (1979) conducted an analysis of participation in decision making among project engineers and role stressors (role conflict and role ambiguity) and individual outcomes related to role stressors (fatigue, physical symptoms, tensions). He hypothesized that project engineers having lower PDM than they would like would report greater job-related stress. Data were collected from 154 project engineers employed by a large engineering and development and construction firm. All had managerial responsibilities. Decision deprived project engineers reported greater physical symptoms and job tension but no differences on measures of role conflict, role ambiguity and fatigue. Further analyses focusing on degree of decisional deprivation showed that project engineers reporting higher levels of decisional deprivation reported greater role conflict and role ambiguity, greater physical symptoms and more job tension.

Schuler (1980b) proposed a role and expectancy perception model of participation in decision making. He found that participation in decision making was associated with employee satisfaction when participation reduced role conflict and role ambiguity and clarified performance—reward expectancies. Lee and Schuler (1982) replicated and extended these findings in a study of employees in a medium-sized service organization.

Morris, Steers and Koch (1979) studied the influence of organization structure and role conflict and ambiguity for three occupational groupings. Six structural variables were examined: work-group size, span of subordination, supervisory space, functional dependence, formalization and participation in decision making. Data were collected from 252 nonacademic employees of a major university using questionnaires. These individuals represented three occupational groupings: professional, secretarial clerical and blue-collar. The average intercorrelation among the six structural variables was 0.08, ranging from 0.00 to 0.24. Multiple regression analyses yielded four significant and independent correlates of role conflict (participation in decision making, supervisory span, span of subordination, formalization) and three significant and independent correlates of role ambiguity (participation in decision making, span of subordination, formalization). Morris *et al.* (1979) also found that occupational grouping increased the amount of explained variance in both role conflict and role ambiguity. This was attributed to higher levels of role conflict and role ambiguity among professionals.

Finally, Chonko (1982) examined the relationship of span of control to sales representatives' experienced role conflict and role ambiguity. He hypothesized that role conflict would decrease and role ambiguity would increase as span of control widens. One hundred and twenty-two sales representatives provided data using questionnaires. The data indicated that *both* role ambiguity and role conflict increased as the span of control of one's supervision increased.

ORGANIZATIONAL STRUCTURE AND JOB CHARACTERISTICS

Ivancevich, Matteson and Preston (1982) examined the prevalence of five work stressors among three managerial levels (lower, middle, upper). The work stressors were: quantitative work overload, qualitative work overload, lack of career progression, supervisor relations and role conflict. Significant, group differences were present on four of the five work stressors (not on qualitative work overload). It was found that middle level managers reported significantly more stress than did lower or upper level managers.

In the same article, Ivancevich *et al.* (1982) compared the prevalence of six work stressors among 29 operating room nurses and 27 medical–surgical nurses. The six work stressors included: quantitative work overload, qualitative work overload, time pressures, role conflict, supervisor relations and physician relations. The medical–surgical nurses reported higher levels of quantitative work overload and time pressures stress.

Parasuraman and Aluto (1981) carried out an investigation of antecedents of work stressors. They divide antecedents into three categories: contextual variables (subsystem, shift), role variables (job level) and task variables (autonomy, complexity, interdependence, routinization and closeness of supervision). They considered seven work stressors in their study, but few of these have been examined by others. These included: inter-unit conflict, technical problems, efficiency problems, role frustration, staff shortages, short lead times and too many meetings.

The data were obtained from organizational records and questionnaires completed by 217 employees of a medium-sized food processing firm. The results indicated that both job level (low, medium, high) and subsystem (administration, prediction-limited variety, prediction-wide variety, technical support and boundary) were significantly related to levels of work stressors. Work shift had an effect that approached statistical significance. There were significant main effects of job level and subsystem on five of the seven stressors (technical problems, efficiency problems, role frustration, short lead times and too many meetings).

These findings show that both horizontal and vertical differentiation have important relationships to levels of experienced work stressors. The administrative subsystem exhibited fewer technical and efficiency problems, short lead times and role frustrations. The higher job autonomy and lower routinization and closeness of supervision may also have helped its members cope better with various stressors. Technical problems were more common in the two production subsystems. The data also revealed systematic differences in the pattern of work stressors across organizational levels. For managers and supervisors, the highest level group, the main stressors were those of quantitative overload and time constraints (efficiency problems, short lead times, too many meetings). Individuals in middle or lower levels reported role frustrations and technical problems.

Walsh, Taber and Beehr (1980) tested an integrative model of perceived job characteristics and found that role clarity functioned, along with challenge, as an intervening variable between the job characteristics and job satisfaction. Role clarity also appeared to be a necessary precondition for perceived challenge. Finally, role clarity was influenced by the feedback from supervisor and feedback from task variables.

RELATIONSHIPS WITH OTHERS

Most frameworks include relationships with others in one's organization as a source of occupational stress (Schuler, 1982). Leiter and Meechan (1986) examined social interactions and burnout (emotional exhaustion, depersonalization, lack of personal accomplishment) as measured by the Maslach Burnout Inventory (Maslach and Jackson, 1981). Social interactions among 35 staff of a residential rehabilitation and mental health center were organized into three separate sociograms (client-oriented contacts, program-oriented contacts, informal social contacts). Three measures were derived from those sociograms: mutual references, accuracy and concentration. The following findings were observed. First, the more a participant's social contacts were concentrated within a formally defined work area, the higher the emotional exhaustion, particularly for informal contacts. Second, the greater the ambiguity (i.e. the lower the accuracy score) with respect to social interactions with clients, the greater the personal accomplishment. Third, professionals who were ambiguous about their social interaction with other staff members (low accuracy) and concentrated their social interactions with workers of their own formal subgroup scored higher on depersonalization. The second finding was contrary to expectations and suggested an artifact of the specific measures used, or a positive quality of ambiguity.

Leiter (1987) examined the effects of social involvement with co-workers (work-related and social communication) and psychological burnout among human service workers. The results indicated that psychological burnout (as measured by the MBI) was higher for workers who communicated extensively with co-workers regarding work but having relatively few informal supportive communications with co-workers. Theory and research focusing on psychological burnout contends that social interactions are the critical stressors (Leiter and Maslach, 1987; Maslach and Jackson, 1984). Leiter and Maslach (1987) found that nurses, when asked to identify sources of stress in their jobs, cited interactions with co-workers ten times more often than interactions with patients.

Leiter (1987) makes a useful distinction between aspects of communication (relationships) which are work-oriented (supervision, consultation, administration) and informal and socially supportive (friendships, nonwork related interactions). Leiter proposes and finds support for differentiated patterns of the two kinds of social interactions and the three components of psychological burnout assessed by the MBI.

Beehr (1981) hypothesized that sources of work stress come from one's co-workers (i.e. the social system). Thus individuals in stressful jobs would be more dissatisfied with their co-workers since these individuals were senders of role expectations. He obtained data from a diverse sample of 651 job incumbents employed in five mid-western US organizations using a structured interview. Three role stressors (role ambiguity, role overload, underutilization of skills) were included along with five aspects of role strain. In addition, several facets of job dissatisfaction (e.g. co-workers, non-social aspects of the job, workload, role clarity) were assessed. The data indicated that the three role stressors were significantly correlated with measures of strain; each role stressor was most strongly correlated with dissatisfaction with the stress itself, second most strongly correlated with dissatisfaction with co-workers and least strongly correlated with dissatisfaction with the non-social aspects of the work role. Beehr concludes that job incumbents who experience job stress blame the social system resulting in dissatisfaction with co-workers who embody the social system.

CAREER DEVELOPMENT

Although taxonomies of work stressors usually include a Career Development cluster (Cooper and Marshall, 1978a; Schuler, 1982) and there is a large body of career research (Hall, 1986), work stress researchers have not paid much attention to career development factors (Glowinkowski and Cooper, 1985). We have organized the writing in this area in terms of career stage beginning with work stressors associated with starting a managerial or professional career and concluding with an examination of work stressors at the conclusion of a career.

Starting a Career

Katz (1985) reviewed material dealing with organizational stress and early socialization experiences. The first year is for many a very frustrating period full of stress, anxiety and disillusionment. Potential sources of early career stress include: reality shock from the clash of naive or incorrect expectations with reality; inadequate socialization experiences, particularly of a sink or swim nature; ambiguity and uncertainty, concern about establishing one's organizational role identity; learning to deal with one's manager and co-workers; understanding the reward system and situational norms.

Cherniss (1980) developed a model to account for work experiences of human service professionals in early career which resulted over time in negative personal change (psychological burnout). The model proposes that particular work setting characteristics (e.g. workload, scope of client contacts) interact with individuals characteristics (e.g. career orientations, extra-work demands and supports). These factors, in concert, result in particular sources of stress being experienced to varying degrees by human service professionals. Cherniss identified five sources of experienced stress by professionals in human services: doubts about competence referred to concerns that the professional was falling short; problems with clients referred to difficult and ungrateful recipients of assistance; bureaucratic interference referred to rules, policies and procedures which interfere with getting the job done; lack of stimulation and fulfillment referred to feelings of routine, boredom and monotony; lack of collegiality referred to little social support from work colleagues. These work stressors, in turn, were predicted to lead to psychological burnout. Empirical support has been provided for this model (Burke, Shearer and Deszca, 1984; Burke, 1987).

In one of the few investigations of early career stressors, Fisher (1985) examined the role played by social support on the job from co-workers and supervisors in helping newcomers deal with unmet-expectations stress. A longitudinal design employing three waves of data collection was used. Nurses were surveyed at the end of their professional training, just prior to beginning work on their first job, after three months on the job and again after six months. Unmet expectations was measured by the differences between expectations prior to employment and conditions experienced on the job. Six work outcomes were considered: job satisfaction, organizational commitment, intention to leave the organization, self-rated performance, professional commitment and intention to leave the profession. Social support from supervisors and co-workers were also included. Unmet expectation stress and outcomes were significantly related at both three and six months. Social support was found to be negatively and significantly correlated with unmet-expectation stress, and to adjustment outcomes as predicted.

Developing a Career

Bartolome and Evans have written extensively on the tensions and ambiguity 'successful' middle managers report in their attempts to balance commitments to professional versus private lives (Bartolome and Evans, 1979, 1980; Evans and Bartolome, 1980a, 1980b, 1986). Eighty percent of the 532 male middle managers in their sample attached a high value to *both* work–career and family–leisure. Yet they spent 62% of their time and 71% of their energy on their professional lives. In addition, the boundary between professional and personal lives allowed movement in only one direction—job concerns pervade family and leisure lives. Bartolome and Evans (1979) found only half of their managers to be satisfied with the way they were distributing time and energy between professional and private life.

They propose the life stage of the manager as the most important single factor in determining how managers experience their lifestyles. Thus, managers cope with the tensions and ambiguities inherent in their lifestyles by limiting the focus of their attention and concerns to one or a few aspects of their lives at any one stage. The career is central while the family is secondary in the early stage. At a later stage, the family is central while the career is secondary. Bartolome and Evans define life stages by the different central preoccupations. They identified three stages: the first stage from the mid-20s to the mid-30s is a time of overriding investment to work and career; the second stage, from the mid-30s to the early 40s is marked by investment in private life; the third stage, from the early 40s to the 50s is characterized by either an integration of professional and private life or the maintenance of a fragmentation of the two.

Maintaining a Career

Korman and his colleagues (Korman and Korman, 1980; Lang, 1985; Korman, Wittig–Berman and Lang, 1981) conducted a series of studies of alienation among successful careerists. They used the phrase *career success and personal failure* to illustrate the paradoxical juxtaposition of career success and personal and social alienation. They developed and tested a research framework suggesting the experience of certain features of organizational and family life, and realities of the aging process (mid-life), were antecedents of personal and social alienation among managers and professionals.

Four organizational and life experience factors were proposed: (1) disconfirmed expectancies, realization that things one had expected to happen have not happened; (2) contradictory life demands, a realization that life (and work) is full of contradictions and trade-offs and one cannot have it all, though believing one was promised it all, (3) sense of external control, a realization that one has not determined the course of one's life but instead has been doing things to please others; (4) loss of affiliative satisfactions, a realization that one has few meaningful interpersonal relations. In addition, Korman and Korman (1980) identify the male mid-life stage as a key influence on personal and social alienation. This career and life stage is characterized by an awareness of one's advancing age and mortality, goals one may never attain, decreased job mobility and changes in one's family patterns.

Three research studies (Korman *et al.*, 1981; Lang, 1985, Burke and Deszca, 1982) have used this career success and personal failure framework. None of them, however, examined the specific effects of the mid-life stage. These studies, using questionnaires, provide support for the proposed framework. Korman *et al.*, (1981) collected data from 90 alumni of a large US school of business and 67 MBA students. Correlations between the four life experience factors and various personal and social alienation scales were as predicted. Burke and Deszca (1982), using identical measures, collected data from managers and professionals in a wide range of jobs and functions. They also found significant relationships between the four work and life experience factors and personal and social alienation. Finally, Lang (1985) examined the role of factors such as family and college background, expectations at college graduation for positive outcomes in personal, interpersonal and work areas and current fulfillment in each of these areas. Results showed that young managers and professionals whose backgrounds included high socio-economic status and graduation from elite colleges were more likely to report alienation when fulfillment was lacking. Thus the role of unrealistic early expectations emerges as a major cause of lack of fulfillment and alienation.

Ending a Career

McGoldrick and Cooper (1985) list potential sources of stress individuals face in the final stage of their working career. These include: (1) the aging process itself, resulting in psychological changes in later years; (2) changes in work abilities, both mental and physical; (3) the individual's perceptions of work and retirement; (4) the work environment and the individual's job; (5) the individual's nonwork circumstances. More specifically, individuals must deal with their changing psychological, physiological and social circumstances. The approach of retirement itself may be a threat which signifies old age, uselessness and dependence.

Major work stressors for older managers and professionals would include dealing with new technology, lack of promotion possibilities, dealing with potential skill obsolescence, retraining, discrimination, concerns about meeting performance expectations, sources of stress in the nonwork sphere include one's marital relationship, home circumstances, own health and health of spouse, financial security dependents and family.

Both Kasl (1980) and McGoldrick and Cooper (1985) review research on the effects of retirement on the physical and emotional health of individuals. The data is clear in showing retirement to *not* have a negative effect on the physical and mental health of retirees. Research does indicate, however, that poor health and inadequate finances were the two major sources of stress during retirement.

Career Transitions

The concept of transition has received increasing attention in career research in recent years (Louis, 1980; Nicholson, 1984). A career transition may result in a change of job or profession, or a change in one's orientation to work in the same job. Career transitions impose costs to individuals undergoing the transition, their families and their organizations (Brett, 1980). Louis (1980) provides a useful typology of career transitions and a series of propositions for understanding them.

Latack (1984) undertook an empirical study of career transitions viewing transitions as stress-coping processes influenced by both work and nonwork factors. Her model hypothesized that the process through which a career transition creates stress depends on the magnitude of the career transition. Thus, the greater the magnitude of career transition, the greater the role ambiguity and role overload.

Data were collected from 109 managers and professionals in a manufacturing firm and an osteopathic hospital using questionnaires, organizational records and performance ratings of supervisors. Two measures of career transition magnitude, objective and subjective, were used. The objective measure of career transition magnitude correlated with job-related stress (anxiety). And both measures of magnitude of career transition correlated with a measure of personal life transition. But magnitude of career transition was uncorrelated with role ambiguity, and correlated *opposite* to predictions with role overload. When path analysis was used to examine the model, little support was found for the assumption that transitions lead to stress, at least for managers and professionals in advanced career stages. This conclusion must be conditioned by the fact that all career transitions in this study were positive (promotions) and may have produced little pressure for adaptation.

WORK–FAMILY CONFLICT

Kopelman, Greenhaus and Connolly (1983) provide a theoretical model for describing the relationship between role conflict at work, in the family and between the two, as well as satisfiaction at home, at work and with life in general. They define *work conflict* as the extent to which an individual experiences incompatible role pressures within the work domain, and *family conflict* as the extent to which incompatible role pressures are experienced within the family. For both types of conflict, the model postulates that incompatibility may arise from multiple role senders, one role sender, or a lack of fit between the focal person and role requirements. The model also includes *interrole conflict* which is described as the extent to which a person experiences pressures within one role that are incompatible with pressures from another role. In two studies which tested the theoretical model, Kopelman *et al.* (1983) report strong links between domain conflict and domain satisfaction, i.e. work conflict and job satisfaction, and between domain satisfaction and life satisfaction. The investigators, however, failed to find a significant relationship between interrole conflict and domain satisfaction. This may be due to the operation of unmeasured, mediating variables, namely coping strategies, given that previous research has found a significant relationship between effective coping with interrole conflict, and role and life satisfaction.

Another theoretical model of role conflict (Greenhaus and Beutell, 1985) suggests that pressures from work or family can heighten conflict between work and family roles. Greenhaus and Beutell (1985) identified three ways that role pressures can be incompatible: (1) time spent in one role may leave little time to devote to other roles; (2) strain within one role domain may 'spillover' into another one; (3) behavior appropriate to one role domain may be dysfunctional in another, i.e. shifting gears from work to family. Thus, variables that have an impact on time, strain or behavior, can heighten work–family conflict. The model proposes that any role characteristics that affects a persons' time involvement, strain or behavior within a role can produce conflict between that role and another role.

Empirical studies using the model are being conducted (Burke and Greenglass, 1987). For example, Beutell (1986), in a sample of 115 married couples with children, reported that the best predictor of conflict involving the work role was the wife's employment status, with women highly involved in their employment experiencing more conflict with home maintenance and parental roles. These findings are consistent with the notion that time-based conflict is the most prevalent type of work–family conflict.

Antecedents of Work–family Conflict

Holahan and Gilbert (1979) investigated sex differences in specific pairs of work and family roles and their relationship to attitudinal, self-concept and satisfaction variables. Focusing directly on life roles (Professional, Spouse, Parent and Self as Self-Actualized Person), rather than on time demands, Holahan and Gilbert constructed scales to measure potential role conflict in specific pairs of roles (e.g. Professional vs Parent). Holahan and Gilbert found that Professional vs Self roles were associated with the highest conflict for both non-parent and parent groups alike. The addition of the parent role provided additional conflict with each of the roles in the area of most conflict, namely Professional vs Self.

Pleck, Staines and Lang (1980), in an analysis of the 1977 Quality of Employment Survey data, reported that 34% of men believed that their job and family lives interfered with each other. Greenhaus and Kopelman (1981) studied 229 male alumni of an eastern US technical college. Subjects were employed in technical, administrative and marketing positions as well as being self-employed. Using responses to open-ended items, Greenhaus and Kopelman report that approximately half the sample experienced interrole conflict. They found that conflict between work and family was positively related to work-role salience. While wives' employment status had no effect on conflict, men whose wives were employed in managerial/professional positions experienced significantly more intense work–family conflict than men whose wives were employed in non-managerial/non-professional positions. Further results indicated that incidence of work–family conflict was higher when children were pre-schoolers rather than when children were older. As expected, men who placed greater importance on work and men whose children were young and living at home were the most likely to experience work–family conflict.

Another factor related significantly to work–family conflict is that of career commitment. Individuals who place high priority on their careers invest more time and energy in their work role, expect more of themselves and undertake more challenging assignments than those who are less career-committed. Holahan and Gilbert (1979) demonstrated that career aspirations were positively correlated with role conflict for females in dual career couples but negatively correlated with role conflict in males. They found that when husband's career salience was high, and there were children present in the home, working women experienced greater role conflict than when their husband's career salience was low. They also report than when the work role was of equally high importance to both husband and wife, role conflict was low relative to those couples with disparate work salience. They suggest that highly career-committed couples may have worked out a system of mutual understanding and accommodation (see Gupta and Jenkins, 1985).

WORK STRESSORS AND NONWORK EXPERIENCES

Burke and Weir (1981) and Burke (1982a) investigated the effects of work stressors of job incumbents on several areas of nonwork experience and satisfaction. The general hypothesis underlying the research was that greater work stressors would have an adverse effect on nonwork experiences of the job incumbents. In addition, adverse effects would be more pronounced on areas closest to the work–family interface (marital satisfaction or home and family functioning) and less pronounced on areas extending over other roles (life satisfaction, emotional and physical well-being).

Burke and Weir (1981) collected data from 127 senior administrators in correctional institutions. Eighteen occupational demands and a variety of outcome measures were considered. The overall pattern of findings indicated that the occupational demands for administrators had negative impacts on nonwork experiences. The negative impact was more pronounced in some nonwork areas (life worries, marital and life satisfactions, personal, home and family life, number of concrete stressful events outside work) than in others (social participation, supportive social relationships, objectively examined physical health). Particular work stressors had consistently negative effects (e.g. role ambiguity, role conflict, pace of change) whereas others had mixed effects (e.g. concentration, lack of influence, underutilization of skills).

WORK STRESSORS OF JOB INCUMBENTS AND SPOUSE WELL-BEING

Very little research attention has been given to the ways in which work stressors experienced by the job incumbent affect others in his or her home situation. Burke and Weir (1980) and Burke (1982b) investigated the relationship of 18 work stressors experienced by 85 male senior administrators of correctional institutions, and 41 senior administrators of probation/parole/

aftercare services, and the well-being of their spouses. Data were collected by means of questionnaires completed independently by the husbands and their wives. The results indicated that wives whose husbands reported greater work stressors reported less marital and life satisfaction, decreased social participation and increased psychosomatic symptoms and negative feeling states. In no case was wives' well-being enhanced as a function of increased work stressors on husbands. As might be expected, those areas most negatively influenced by husbands' occupational demands were those closest to the husband–wife relationship. Areas of satisfaction and well-being that were likely to be influenced by several sources of experience, were least likely to be influenced by husbands' work stressors.

Particular occupational demands were consistently related to greater levels of dissatisfaction or distress in spouses. It was not possible however to attribute this effect to greater absolute levels of these demands being experienced. These occupational demands included: quality pressures, stress from the rate or pace of change and stress in communicating to others at work. Another cluster of occupational demands was less detrimental effect on the various areas of wife satisfaction and well-being. These included: stressors unique to the correctional milieu, the number of hours worked per week, job complexity, role ambiguity, quantitative overload, inequity in pay, boundary-spanning activities and responsibility for things. Finally, there were some occupational demands encountered by the administrators which had little or no affect on any area of wives' satisfaction and well-being. These included: concentration, responsibility for people, underutilization of skills, lack of influence, job future ambiguity, role conflict and feeling locked-in.

CONTEMPORARY SOURCES OF MANAGERIAL AND PROFESSIONAL STRESS

Work stressors of potential interest to both researchers and job incumbents vary with changing circumstances over time. Four sources of work stressors have begun to receive increased research attention during the past few years: mergers and acquisitions, retrenchment and budget cutbacks, job future ambiguity and insecurity, and occupational locking-in. These four newly emerging sources of work stressors share some common features. First, they may be interrelated since all represent the effects of the economic recession and attempts by organizations to survive and to increase productivity. Second, being relatively recent areas of research, relatively little empirical work has been completed. Third, these areas have vast implications for both practice and intervention at both individual and organizational levels.

Mergers and Acquisitions

Marks and Mirvis (1986) indicate that 3284 US. companies were acquired by other companies in 1985, with the dollar value of these acquisitions estimated at $150 billion. They also indicate statistics showing that between 50 and 80% of all mergers are financial disappointments.

Mirvis (1985) illustrates some of the heightened work stressors in a case study of negotiations over the combination of a small manufacturing firm into a multi-billion dollar conglomerate following its acquisition. Strategic and tactical conflicts surfaced between the two firms during the first year of negotiations following the sale which Mirvis traced to the parties' emotional reactions to the combination. Work stressors that were heightened during this period (and preceding the sale) were: each party's sense of uncertainty and threat (Gill and Foulder, 1978), loss of personal and organizational identities, feeling of conflict associated with the ambivalence of loss versus gain, feeling of conflict associated with dependence and counter-dependence—proactive vs reactive control, feelings of conflict because of incompatibilities in company managements, business systems, organizational cultures and goals for the combination itself (Sales and Mirvis, 1984; Sinetar, 1981).

Marks and Mirvis (1985a) found the 'merger syndrome'—a defensive, fear the worst response—a common response to the uncertainty and stress of a merger. The top of the acquired organization reports disbelief, uncertainty, fear and stress. Lower levels in the organization circulate rumours of mass layoffs and forced relocations, pay freezes and the loss of benefits, and plant closings. And these concerns are not limited to hostile takeovers. Crisis management is the order the day (Marks and Mirvis, 1985b). Senior management seal themselves off, becoming less accessible, limiting their lines of communication and leaving their staff uniformed about what is going on.

Merger syndrome is manifested by increased centralization and decreased communication that leaves employees in the dark about what is happening in the merger. Rumours are fueled and run rampant through grapevine and rumour mill. In addition, 'worst case' scenarios are developed and employees become preoccupied with the merger. The result is that employees are distracted, productivity decreases and key people leave the company. Marks and Mirvis cite a *Wall Street Journal* survey which found that nearly 50% of executives in acquired firms seek other jobs within one year and another 25% planned to leave within three years.

Organization Retrenchment and Decline

The late 1970s and early 1980s have been characterized by economic slowdown, plant closings and layoffs, and budget cutbacks. This mood of austerity has affected private and public sector organizations alike, and is continuing through the 1980s. More organizations are working towards balanced budgets and fiscal responsibility—becoming 'leaner and meaner' (Levine, 1980; Hirschhorn, 1983).

These initiatives, however, have been found to increase work stressors of job incumbents (Jick, 1985). Let us consider some dimensions of objective sources of budget cut stress (Murray and Jick, 1985; Jick and Murray, 1982). Jick and Murray (1982) identify two dimensions: severity (size of cuts, impact on goals, programs or survival prospects, frequency of cuts, organization slack, availability of alternate funds) and time pressure (amount of fore-warning, response time, duration of cuts, information clarity). It was hypo-thesized that the greater the severity and time pressure associated with budget cuts, the greater the likelihood of experienced stress in an organization.

Jick (1983), summarizing research fundings, writes that in cases of threat-ened or actual cuts:

* The greater the size of the budget cuts, the higher the likelihood of experienced stress/uncertainty.
* The greater the extent to which the cuts affect changes in goals, programs or organizational survival, the higher the likelihood of experienced stress/ uncertainty.
* The higher the frequency of cuts, the higher the likelihood of experienced stress/uncertainty.
* The less organizational slack and the fewer the opportunities for alternate funding, the higher the likelihood of experienced stress/uncertainty.
* The fewer the management assurances regarding job security or departmental survival, the higher the likelihood of experienced stress/uncertainty.
* The more the cuts are selective rather than uniform, the higher the likelihood of experienced stress/uncertainty (due to more opportunity for inequity).
* The less forewarning information of impending budget cuts, the higher the likelihood of experienced stress/uncertainty when the cuts finally occur.
* The lower the information clarity regarding impending budget cuts, the higher the likelihood of experienced stress/uncertainty.
* The lower the response time available between the mandate to cut and the actual cuts, the higher the likelihood of experienced stress/ uncertainty.
* The longer the mandated duration of the budget cuts, the higher the likelihood of experienced stress/uncertainty.

(Jick, 1983, pp. 270–1)

Jick (1983, p. 272) has proposed that individuals in organizations undergoing cutbacks will be subject to various sources of stress. These include: role confusion, job insecurity, work overload, career plateauing, poor incentives, office politics and conflict, lack of participation in decision-making, tense organizational climate, ideological disagreement, and job and personal life conflicts. Cameron, Whetten and Kim (1987) identified twelve dysfunctional *organizational* consequences of any organization decline. These include: centralization, the absence of long-range planning, the curtailment of innovation, scapegoating, resistance to change, turnover, decreased morale, loss of slack, the emergence of special interest groups (politics), loss of credibility of top management, conflict and in-fighting, and across-the-board rather than prioritized cuts.

Rosselini (1981) observed that federal budget cuts had a significant role in a recent increase in federal employees usage of health services. In light of anticipated staff reductions, almost triple the number of federal employees were treated at the Department of Health and Human Services for stress-related symptoms such as dizziness, stomach upset and high blood pressure. Blundell (1978) reported that government employees in Denver whose staff had been reduced and reorganized were found to be so fearful and concerned about their future that productivity suffered.

Schlenker and Gutek (1987) examined the effects on professionals in a large social service agency of being reassigned to non-professional jobs. It was possible to study the effects of work role loss separate from the loss of one's employment and salary. In the administration of staffing cuts, one group of social workers were abruptly reassigned to non-professional jobs while keeping the same salary and benefits. Data were collected about 9 months following the reassignments, sufficient time for workers to adjust to their demotions as much as they were likely to. The sample of 132 included six reassigned workers and 66 non-reassigned workers. Individuals who were reassigned (demoted) reported significantly less self-esteem, significantly less job and life satisfaction and significantly greater intention to turnover. No differences were found on measures of professional role involvement, professional role identification (commitment to social work) and work-related depression.

Job Future Ambiguity and Insecurity

One of the most dramatic changes in organizations during the past few years has been the change of traditionally secure managerial and professional jobs into insecure ones (Hunt, 1986). Several factors have come together to produce this phenomenon. These include: an increase in acquisitions and mergers, retrenchment and decline due to increasing competitive pressures, a loss of managerial and professional jobs in the manufacturing sectors as jobs move to third world countries and the service and information sectors, increasing competition for managerial and professional jobs by younger, better educated men and women, and the introduction of new technology which makes old skills, knowledge and attitudes absolute (Handy, 1984; Meagre, 1986; Gill, 1985; Levine, 1980).

Research has indicated that this dramatic change in expectations of previously guaranteed employment has had a marked psychological impact on those affected. These effects can be seen in managers and professionals who have lost their jobs, and managers and professionals who are insecure about their jobs. Managers and professionals who lose their jobs indicate increases in depression, anxiety, and poorer emotional health and social functioning (Kaufman, 1982; Leana and Ivancevich, 1987; Fineman, 1983; Latack and Dozier, 1986; Fryer and Payne, 1986). The consistently negative effects of unemployment are attributed to loss of psychological and economic benefits inherent in managerial and professional jobs.

Although the number of managers and professionals who have actually lost jobs may be relatively small, some writers (Greenhalgh and Rosenblatt, 1984) postulate a 'ripple effect'. That is, managers and professionals who are currently employed but see that it is increasingly harder to get and hold managerial and professional jobs will become increasingly insecure about their own jobs. They should become increasingly concerned about maintaining their own jobs, decreased promotional and career development opportunities within their organization and the prospects of finding another job similar to the one they now have should they lose it.

Research on the stressful effects of job insecurity is just beginning to emerge (Brockner, 1987; Greenhalgh, 1983a, b; Jick, 1985; Hartley and Klandermans, 1987). The small amount of data that exists indicates that the effects of job insecurity appear to be similar to job loss itself. Depolo and Sarchieli (1987) compared the emotional well-being of individuals who had lost their jobs with 'survivors' in the same organization. They found no difference between the two groups. Interestingly, the level of emotional well-being was extremely low in both groups. Cobb and Kasl (1977) conducted a longitudinal study of job loss and reported that workers anticipating job loss were in greater distress than when they actually lost their jobs.

Several studies have examined the effects of insecurity on work commitment and job behavior. These studies (Greenhalgh, 1982; Jick, 1985) show that survivors exhibit levels of reduced work commitment and effort. In addition, other research findings show increased resistance to change among survivors (Fox and Staw, 1979; Greenhalgh, 1982). Thus job insecurity becomes a critical factor in accelerating organizational decline.

Occupational Locking-in

Kay (1975) identified several factors associated with increasing discontent in middle management ranks. One of these was a boxed-in feeling when individuals had almost no opportunity to move from their present jobs or when the only position for which they were qualified was the one they currently held. Quinn (1975) used the term locking-in to refer to the same phenomenon. Quinn distinguished three components of locking-in: (a) low probability of securing another job as good as or better than the present one; (b) little opportunity to modify a presently disliked employment situation by securing a change in job assignments; (c) low likelihood that a worker who was dissatisfied with his job could take psychological refuge in the performance of other roles not linked to his job. Thurley and Word-Penney (1986) suggest this phenomenon will be present through the 1980s and beyond.

Burke (1982) conducted a study in which self-reported locking-in of 127 administrators was related to personal and situational demographic character- istics and personality variables, occupational and life demands and satisfac- tions, and life style and emotional and physical well-being measures. Individ- uals reporting greater locking-in were older, less educated, had more chil- dren, longer organizational tenure, made fewer previous geographic moves and were less interested in further promotion. Locking-in was also associated with interpersonal passivity, emotional instability, an external locus of control and reduced Type A propensities. Work experiences and satisfactions were generally unrelated to degree of locking-in although administrators more locked-in reported greater underutilization at work and greater life dissatis- faction. Locking-in, however, was not associated with negative emotional and physical health consequences.

Wolpin and Burke (1986) replicated this study with 72 senior administrators of probation, parole, and aftercare services from a single government depart- ment. Locking-in was found to be related to both personality and social competence variables in that managers reporting greater locking-in were more passive and had lower levels of initiative and drive. In addition, more locked-in managers appeared to lack interpersonal skills and sensitivities. More locked-in managers in this sample reported less marital satisfaction, greater negative feeling states (depression and worthlessness) and less life satisfaction. Finally, more locked-in administrators exhibited poor self- reported physical health.

Martin and Schermerhorn (1983) developed a research model to examine the impact of work and nonwork influences on health in which 'inability to leave' functioned as a critical variable. The ability to leave was viewed as one means that managers and professionals might use to cope with stress experienced from aspects of both their work and nonwork domains.

ADVANCES IN WORK STRESSOR RESEARCH

There have been several significant developments in research on sources of managerial and professional stress in the 10 years since the first edition of *Stress at Work* appeared. These include advances in the comprehensiveness of research frameworks, more complex analysis strategies (e.g. path analysis), the use of meta-analysis, innovative measures of sources of managerial and professional stress, increasing use of longitudinal field studies, laboratory simulations and natural experiments, as well as advances in particular content areas such as the examination of objective and subjective stressors, and acute vs chronic stressors.

More Complex Models and Analysis Strategies

Recent work stress research has shown an increasing tendency toward more sophisticated and complex research designs and analysis strategies. Two of the most noteworthy are the increasing use of path analytic approaches to evaluate complex research frameworks and longitudinal research designs.

Hendrix, Ovalle and Troxler (1985) noted the need for work stress researchers to employ a multidisciplinary approach which simultaneously examines psychological (behavioral) and physiological (medical) consequences. They attempted to develop, through exploratory path analysis, a preliminary structural model of stress within a framework combining both behavioral and medical disciplines. Job and life stress were hypothesized to result from intraorganizational, extraorganizational and individual factors. In turn, job stress was hypothesized to directly affect job satisfaction and indirectly affect intention to quit through job satisfaction. Cholesterol ratio was hypothesized to be affected by stress and individual difference characteristics.

They collected data from 370 employees working for the US Department of Defense and a private sector organization, and in a wide variety of jobs. All variables, with the exception of the cholesterol ratio, were obtained from questionnaires. Ten work stressors were considered. Overall job stress reflected the extent that individuals felt their jobs overall to be stressful and the degree their jobs produced stress by thwarting personal growth. Each of the 10 work stressors were significantly related to overall job stress, job satisfaction and intention to quit. None, however, were related to the cholesterol ratio. Path analysis was then used to elimate variables not having statistically significant path coefficients. The revised model indicated that many of the relationships in the hypothesized model were not supported. Some of the work stressors directly affected job satisfaction and others directly affected job stress. Job stress had only an indirect effect on intention to quit through job satisfaction. Work stressors had no effect on the cholesterol ratio. The latter was primarily affected by individual difference characteristics.

Meta-Analysis

A significant body of empirical findings have accumulated during the past 20 years in the occupational stress field. Most of this work has examined role stressors but several other sources of managerial and professional stress have received attention. The accumulation of this work makes it possible to to determine the state of knowledge about particular work stressors, the degree of agreement within this literature and conclusions that seem warranted. Two types of literature reviews, content and empirical, have been undertaken. Most have been content-oriented (Cooper and Marshall, 1980; Cooper and Payne, 1978, 1980; Quick and Quick, 1984; Ivancevich and Matteson, 1980). In addition, specific content reviews have been carried out on role stressors (Van Sell *et al.* 1981; Schuler *et al.*, 1977).

Hunter, Schmidt and Jackson (1982) refined a methodology, meta-analysis, which provides a technique for combining empirical findings across studies. Fisher and Gitelson (1983) and Jackson and Schuler (1985) conducted meta-analyses of the role conflict and role ambiguity literature. Fisher and Gitelson considered 43 studies; Jackson and Schuler examined 96 studies, which included most of those in the Fisher and Gitelson review.

Jackson and Schuler (1985) analyzed 29 correlates of role conflict and role ambiguity. These included 10 organizational context variables, five individual characteristics, 10 affective reactions and four behavioral reactions. Meta-analysis provides an estimate of the true strength of relationship between each role stressor and other correlates as well as whether the strength of this relationship varied as a function of a third variable or moderator. Meta-analysis appears to be a promising analysis tool in the occupational stress field. Researchers would be encouraged to apply the technique to other occupational stressors as empirical findings continue to accumulate.

Innovative Measures of Work Stressors

Objective measures

Shaw and Riskind (1983) assessed job stress potential by relating objective job characteristics to a variety of work stressors. Data on job characteristics were obtained from the Position Analysis Questionnaire (PAQ) data bank, and job stress data were taken from three previously published sources. The PAQ is a job analysis inventory of 194 different job elements used to derive scores on 32 divisional job dimensions. The concept of job stress potential suggests that job characteristics can be identified that relate to how incumbents, as a group, experience stress on a job. The three published studies included data on occupational stressors (e.g. job complexity, role conflict, role ambiguity, job responsibility, skill utilization) as well as a variety of psychological (e.g. anxiety and depression, job satisfaction), physiological (cardiovascular and respiratory disease, incidence of mortality) and behavioral strains (e.g. dispensary visits). Divisional job dimension scores (PAQ) for each of the jobs represented in the three separate samples were then used to predict work stressors and strains reported in those jobs. The findings showed fairly strong relationships of the divisional dimensions and the stressor and strain variables. About one quarter of the correlations between the 32 job dimensions and 18 measures of work stressors and strain reached statistical significance.

Measures based on job products

Dougherty and Pritchard (1985) developed new measures of role ambiguity, conflict and overload based on specific job products produced by a group of attorneys working in the headquarters of a large energy company, (e.g. making presentation to product groups, producing written advice for clients).

The role variables were measured in the following ways.

Role overload. Attorneys recorded, for each product, the number of hours per week required to adequately produce that product. The total number of hours summed over all products was one measure of overload. A second measure asked attorneys to indicate, for each product, how frequently they did *not* have time to adequately perform that duty.

Role ambiguity. Two types of ambiguity—task and performance evaluation—were measured. For performance evaluation ambiguity, each attorney indicated for each product, the lowest and the highest rating which their supervisor might give concerning the importance of the product for one's overall performance evaluation. A large discrepancy would indicate more ambiguity. For task ambiguity each attorney rated, for each product, how frequently they had problems knowing how to proceed in performing the work.

Role conflict. This measure was based on attorneys' perceived agreement with their supervisor on the importance of job products. Each attorney indicated the importance of each product in their own evaluation of performance, and also rated the importance of the product in their supervisor's evaluation of their performance. The larger the discrepancy, the greater the role conflict.

The 40 attorneys also completed widely used measures of role conflict ambiguity and overload, and provided data on a number of outcome measures (job satisfaction, propensity to resign, tension-anxiety), job involvement, intrinsic motivation, organizational commitment, objective absence frequency obtained from company records, and both self and company ratings of job performance.

The product-based measures of role ambiguity, conflict and overload had high internal consistency reliabilities, high concurrent validity indicated by high correlations with traditional measures of these three role stressors, and reasonable discriminant validity. The product-based measures yielded relationships to outcome variables which were similar to traditional measures. There was some evidence of superiority for the new product-based measures over the traditional global measures in problems of method variance. This approach to the measurement of role stressors looks promising for further research.

Repertory grid methodology

Crump, Cooper and Maxwell (1981) undertook an examination of work stressors among air traffic controllers and coronary heart disease risk factors using repertory grid methodology. The sample consisted of 67 licensed controllers at a large UK airport. Repertory grid methodology obtains, from individuals, their own interpretation of work events. These interpretations consist of *elements* (e.g. work overload) and *constructs* which the individuals used to discriminate between elements (e.g. controllable vs uncontrollable).

The research involved five stages. In the first stage, the elicitation of work stressors, 27 controllers responded to a three question, open-ended questionnaire in which task, job and home stressors were listed. In the second stage, the identification of dimensions used by controllers to distinguish similarities and differences between work stressors, interviews were held with each of the 27 controllers. The work stressors identified in the first stage were presented in triads and controllers were asked to indicate which two were similar to each other and different from the third, and why. The third stage involved a content analysis of the material generated in the first two stages into a manageable number of elements and constructs. This involved combining similar elements, and constructs, in a single category. The fourth stage, yielded a consensus list of 15 work stressors and 10 dimensions. The work stressors included: high workload, equipment failure, shiftwork problems and the work environment (noise, light, temperature, work space). The dimensions included: short term vs long term, able to avoid vs unable to avoid, and controllable vs uncontrollable. The fifth stage included administering the repertory grid to the total sample of controllers. The controllers indicated the extent to which each dimension applied to each work stressor on a seven point Likert scale.

Most of the variation in grid ratings was accounted for by stress and time, control, ability to resolve and personal impact. The most stressful situations involved being overloaded, equipment failure and poor controllers' ability, all of which were defined as being uncontrollable and representing inadequate coping. The non-stressful work demands included shift work, variable workload and the work environment, which were defined as long term, frequent and unproblematic, routine features of the job. The use of the repertory grid approach provides useful qualitative, information about sources of occupational stress and also opens up the possibility of quantitative analyses as well.

Longitudinal Research Designs

There has been an increase in the use of longitudinal research designs to understand work stressors and individual and organizational outcomes. A study by Jackson, Schwab and Schuler (1986) is illustrative of this trend. They were interested in examining potential antecedents and consequences of psychological burnout operationalized by the Maslach Burnout Inventory (Maslach and Jackson, 1981). They hypothesized that both unmet expectation in general and specific aspects of employees' job experiences (size of caseload, role conflict, lack of participation in decision making, lack of performance contingent rewards, lack of support from colleagues and supervisors, lack of autonomy concerning how to do one's job, non-contingent punishment) would be related to one or more of the components of burnout.

Data were collected from 277 teachers at two point in time separated by one year. Questionnaire survey at Time 1, asked about current job conditions, the fit between job and expectations and psychological burnout. Questionnaire survey at Time 2 measured turnover intentions and psychological burnout. The analysis using regression techniques used Time 1 descriptors of hypothesized job conditions to predict Time 2 burnout scores. The major findings were: unmet expectations about the job were not not associated with psychological burnout. Emotional exhaustion was most strongly associated with role conflict. Lack of personal accomplishment was associated with lack of support, particularly from one's principal. Depersonalization was also associated with lack of support from one's principal.

A laboratory study of occupational stressors

Manning, Ismail and Sherwood (1981) employed a simulation methodology to assess the cause and effect relationship between role conflict on physiological variables (three cardiovascular variables and four biochemical variables), affective responses (satisfaction and feeling states) and an objective and a subjective measure of job performance. The subjects were 50 female nurses enrolled in a university degree program. Twenty-five were randomly accepted to both a treatment and a control condition. All had previous hospital work experience.

All subjects participated in a simulated hospital experience that required them to perform tasks similar to those performed in an actual hospital. The simulation was conducted in a room equipped as a clinic. Five tasks were performed: monitor a cardiac patient, alphabetize computer billing forms for patients, take the pulse rate and temperature of a patient, administer an intravenous to a patient, aid a patient who had fallen out of bed. Role conflict was manipulated by conflict or overlap in the timing of requests for subjects to perform the simulated tasks. In the role conflict condition, subjects were given new tasks before they had a chance to complete the previous task (simultaneous demands). In the non-role conflict situation, subjects were able to complete a particular task before being requested to do another task. Nurses experiencing role conflict during the 40 minute simulation were significantly different from nurses in the control condition on eight outcome variables: higher pulse rate, lower systolic blood pressure, lower uric acid, less satisfaction, less positive and more negative affect, and lower job performance on both objective and self-report measures. This experiment demonstrated that simulations which employ rigorous control of variables in a realistic situation can be a useful methodology for researchers of managerial and professional stress.

A natural field experiment

Parkes (1982) conducted a natural experiment in a hospital setting in which female student nurses were randomly assigned, following 8 weeks of classroom instruction, to clinical experience in both medical and surgical wards working with both male and female patients. That is, four groups were involved. Participants provided data at five points in time: the week prior to their first work assignment, and at the middle and end of each of the 13 week work allocations. Both subjective (job demand, job discretion, social support) and objective (type of work, number of beds, number of admissions and deaths for each ward over each allocation period) assessments of the work environment were obtained. In addition, measures of affective states (symptom level, work satisfaction) and behavior (total number of days of short-term noncertificated sickness and absence, supervisors ratings of work performance) were included.

The following findings were noted. First, each of the measures of perceived work environment showed significant main effects associated with type of nursing (medical/surgical) and sex of patients, except that job demand did not differ significantly between medical and surgical wards. Second, measures of the perceived work environment contributed to observed differences in affective distress between medical and surgical wards, while reducing differences between male and female wards. The design made it possible to definitely conclude that the different work settings gave rise to the effects on mental health.

Objective vs subjective work stressors

Wells (1982) investigated the association between objective job conditions and perceptions of occupational stressors in a study of social support. Although his research was carried out on a large sample of blue collar workers, it serves as an illustration of this type of research. Data were collected from 1809 blue collar employees from a large manufacturing firm using questionnaires. In addition, information on job conditions was obtained from company records and job descriptions, and for those dimensions not rated by the company, ratings were obtained from company, union and members of the research staff familiar with the plant.

Five perceived occupational stressors were examined: responsibility, quality concerns, role conflict, job vs non-job conflict and workload. Five objective job demands, particularly relevant to the five perceived work stressors were also assessed. These were: interpersonal demands, quantitative workload, qualitative workload, whether the employee was paid a piecework wage or an hourly wage and type of shift work.

The following pattern of findings were observed. Interpersonal demands were significantly associated with role conflict. Interpersonal demands and qualitative workload were significantly associated with quality concerns. Qualitative workload and type of shift was significantly associated with job non-job conflict. Interpersonal demands, quantitative workload and piecework were significantly associated with workload. Finally, interpersonal demands, qualitative workload, piecework and quantitative workload (negatively) were significantly associated with responsibility. Although these relationships were generally modest in size. There was reasonable support for the association of objective job conditions and perceived work stressors.

Acute vs chronic work stressors

Eden (1982) reports the results of a study that was longitudinal and examined the effects of acute work stressors. The study also considered both objective and subjective work stressors. Most models of occupational stress, and the studies growing out of these models, have emphasized chronic stressors. Eden, on the other hand, studied what he termed *critical job events*, defined as a time-bounded peak of performance demand made on the incumbent as part of his job. The quasi-experimental design that was used was an interrupted time series with multiple replications. Data were obtained from 39 female first-year students in a hospital-affiliated school of nursing. Objective stress was operationalized by two CJEs, independent of students' perceptions, sandwiched by three, low objective stress time periods. The two CJEs selected were the first comprehensive patient care, which occurred after 4 months of intensive classroom instruction, and the final exam, which took place 4½ months following the first comprehensive patient care. Subjective work stress and psychological strain were measured by questionnaire. Items were focused on the present (i.e. today) to make them relevant measures of acute stress. These stress measures included: quantitative overload, qualitative overload and role ambiguity. The strain measures included: anxiety, depression, psychosomatic complaints and self-esteem. Physiological measures of pulse rate, diastolic blood pressure, cholesterol and serum uric acid were also taken.

The study design encompassed five stages. In stage 1, baseline measures (questionnaires, blood pressure, pulse rate) were taken in the fourth month. In stage 2, weeks later, data were collected just prior to delivering their first comprehensive patient care (first CJE). In stage 3, about 2 months later, data were collected during a routine week. In stage 4, about 2 1/2 months later, data were collected on the morning of the final exam (the second CJE). In stage 5, the final measures were taken about one month following the final exam.

The effects of the CJEs were determined by analyzing change in the mean levels of the dependent variables from stage to stage. The data showed a consistent confirmatory pattern of significantly rising and falling strain for anxiety, systolic blood pressure and pulse rate. Qualitative overload and serum uric acid changed as predicted four times out of five. The remaining variables, with exception of cholesterol, showed only partial support for the hypothesis. The longitudinal design employed and the largely confirmatory pattern of rising and falling levels of subjective work stressors and strain demonstrate the hypothesized *causal* effects of acute objective stress on strain.

CONCLUSIONS

The volume of stress research continues to grow. Newman and Beehr (1979) noted that occupational stress first appeared as a key word in *Psychological Abstracts* in 1973, indicating that there was not enough published material prior to this time to warrant this heading. Pioneering work stress researchers such as a Jack French and his colleagues (French, Kahn and Mann, 1962; French and Caplan, 1972) and Alan McLean (1966) began their research programs 25 years ago. But it is only within the last 10 years that a broad interest in occupational stress by academics has emerged (Beehr and Bhagat, 1985; Cooper, 1983, Cooper and Payne, 1978, 1980; Ivancevich and Matteson, 1980; Quick and Quick, 1984; *Addison-Wesley Series*, 1979; *Journal of Organizational Behavior Management*, 1987). And research in occupational stress is currently being undertaken in various countries around the world as seen in the table of contents of the *Journal of Human Stress, The Journal of Occupational Behavior* and *Work and Stress*. It is not an exaggeration to conclude that occupational stress has become a central topic in the field of organizational behavior (Staw, 1984).

REFERENCES

Addison Wesley Series on Occupational Stress (1979). Addison-Wesley, Reading, MA.

Bartolome, F. and Evans, P. (1979). Professional lives versus private lives—shifting patterns of managerial commitment, *Organizational Dynamics* **8**, 3–29.

Bartolome, F. and Evans, P. (1980). Must success cost so much? *Harvard Business Review*, **80**, 137–68.

Beehr, T. A. (1981). Work-role stress and attitudes towards coworkers, *Group and Organizational Studies*, **6**, 201–10.

Beehr, R. A. (1985). Organizational stress and employee effectiveness: a job characteristics approach. In T. A. Beehr and R. S. Bhagat (eds) *Human stress and Cognition in Organizations*, pp. 57–82, John Wiley and Sons, New York.

Beehr, T. A. and Bhagat, R. S. (1985). *Stress and cognition in organizations: An Integrated Perspective*, John Wiley and Sons, New York.

Beehr, T. A. and Newman, J. E. (1978). Job stress, employee health, and organizational effectiveness: a facet analysis, model, and literature review, *Personnel Psychology*, **31**, 665–99.

Beutell, N. J. (1986). Conflict between work-family and student-family roles: some sources and consequences, Working paper, Division of Research, W. Paul Stillman School of Business, Seton Hall University.

Blundell, W. E. (1978). As the axe falls so does productivity of grim U.S. workers. *Wall Street Journal*, 17 August.

Breaugh, J. A. (1980). A comparative investigation of three measures of role ambiguity, *Journal of Applied Psychology*, **65**, 584–9.

Brett, J. M. (1980). The effect of job transfer on employees and their families. In C. L. Cooper and R. Payne (eds.) *Current Concerns in Occupational Stress*, pp. 99–136, John Wiley and Sons, New York.

Brockner, J. (1987). The effects of work layoffs on survivors: a psychological analysis. In R. P. McGlynn (ed.) *Interfaces in Psychology*, Vol. 5, Texas Tech Press, Lubbock, TX.

Burke, R. J. (1982a). Impact of occupational demands on nonwork experiences of senior administrators, *Psychological Reports*, **112**, 195–211.

Burke, R. J. (1982b). Occupational demands on administrators and spouses' satisfaction and well-being, *Psychological Reports*, **51**, 823–36.

Burke, R. J. (1982). Occupational locking-in: some empirical findings, *Journal of Social Psychology*, **118**, 177–85.

Burke, R. J. (1987). Burnout in police work: an examination of the Cherniss model, *Group and Organization Studies*, **12**, 174–188.

Burke, R. J. (1987). The present and future status of stress research, *Journal of Organizational Behavior Management*, **8**, 249–267.

Burke, R. J. and Deszca, E. (1982). Type A behavior and career success and personal failure, *Journal of Occupational Behavior*, (1984). **5**, 161–70.

Burke, R. J. and Greenglass, E. R. (1987). Work and family. In C. L. Cooper and I. T. Robertson (eds) *International Review of Industrial and Organizational Psychology*, pp. 273–320, John Wiley and Sons, New York.

Burke, R. J. and Weir, T. (1980). Work demands on administrators and spouse well-being, *Human Relations*, **33**, 253–78.

Burke, R. J. and Weir, T. (1981). Impact of occupational demands on non-work experiences, *Group and Organization Studies*, **6**, 472–85.

Burke, R. J., Shearer, J. and Deszca, G. (1984). Burnout among men and women in police work: an examination of the Cherniss model, *Journal of Health and Human Resources Administration*, **7**, 162–88.

Cameron, K. S., Whetten, D. A. and Kim, M. U. (1987). Organizational dysfunctions of decline, *Academy of Management Journal*, **30**, 126–37.

Chadrow, M. E. (1984). Job satisfaction, occupational stress and video-display-terminal work: an interactional model of person–environment fit. *Dissertation Abstracts International*, **44**(8–b), 2548.

Cherniss, C. (1980). *Professional Burnout in Human Service Organizations*, Praeger, New York.

Chonko, L. B. (1982). The relationship of span of control to sales representatives' experienced role conflict and role ambiguity, *Academy of Management Journal*, **25**, 452–6.

Cobb, S. and Kasl, S. V. (1977). *Termination: The Consequences of Job Loss*, NIOSH Research Report, Cincinatti.

Cohen, S. (1980a). Afteraffects of stress on human performance and social behavior: a review of research and theory. *Psychological Bulletin*, **88**, 82–108.

Cohen, S. (1980b). Cognitive processes as determinants of environmental stress. In I. G. Sarason and C. D. Spielberger (eds) *Stress and anxiety. Vol. 7. The Series in Clinical and Community Psychology*, pp. 171–83, Hemisphere, Washington, DC.

Cooper, C. L. (1983). *Stress Research: Issues for the Eighties*, John Wiley and Sons, New York.

Cooper, C. L. and Marshall, J. (1976). Occupational sources of stress: a review of the literature relating coronary heart disease and mental ill health, *Journal of Occupational Psychology*, **49**, 11–28.

Cooper, C. L. and Marshall, J. (1978a). Sources of managerial and white collar stress. In C. L. Cooper and R. Payne (eds) *Stress at Work*, pp. 81–105, John Wiley and Sons, New York.

Cooper, C. L. and Marshall, J. (1978b). *Understanding Executive Stress*, Macmillan, London.

Cooper, C. L. and Marshall, J. (1980). *White Collar and Professional Stress*, John Wiley and Sons, New York.

Cooper, C. L. and Payne, R. (1978). *Stress at Work*, John Wiley and Sons, New York.

Cooper, C. L. and Payne, R. (1980). *Current Concerns in Occupational Stress*, John Wiley and Sons, New York.

Crull, P. (1982). Stress effects of social harassment on the job: implications for counselling, *American Journal of Orthopsychiatry*, **52**, 539–43.

Crump, J. H., Cooper, C. L. and Maxwell, U. B. (1981). Stress among air traffic controllers: occupational sources of coronary heart disease risk, *Journal of Occupational Behavior*, **2**, 293–303.

Davis, T. R. V. (1984). The influence of the physical environment in offices, *Academy of Management Review*, **9**, 271–83.

Depolo, M. and Sarchielli, G. (1987). Job insecurity, psychological well-being and social representation: a case of cost sharing. In H. W. Scroiff and G. Debus (eds) *Proceedings of the West European Conference on the Psychology of Work and Organization*, Elsevier, Amsterdam.

Dougherty, T. W. and Pritchard, R. D. (1985). The measurement of role variables: exploratory examination of a new approach, *Organizational Behavior and Human Decision Processes*, **35**, 141–55.

Eden, D. (1982) Critical job events, acute stress, and strain: a multiple interpreted time series, *Organizational Behavior and Human Performance*, **30**, 312–29.

Evans, P. and Bartolome, F. (1980a). The relationship between professional and private life. In C. B. Derr (ed.) *Work, Family and Career*, Praeger, New York.

Evans, P. and Bartolome, F. (1980b). *Must Success Cost so Much?* Grant McIntyre, London.

Evans, P. and Bartolome, F. (1986). The dynamics of work–family relationships in managerial lives, *International Review of Applied Psychology*, **35**, 371–95.

Fineman, S. (1983). *White Collar Unemployment: Impact and Stress*, John Wiley and Sons, Chichester.

Fisher, C. D. (1985). Social support and adjustment to work: a longitudinal study, *Journal of Management*, **11**, 39–53.

Fisher, C. D. and Gitelson, R. (1983). A meta-analysis of the correlates of role conflict and ambiguity, *Journal of Applied Psychology*, **68**, 320–33.

Fox, F. V. and Staw, B. M. (1979). The trapped administrator: effects of job insecurity and policy resistance upon commitment to a course of action, *Administrative Science Quarterly*, **24**, 449–71.

French, J. R. P., Jr and Caplan, R. D. (1972). Occupational stress and individual strain. In A. J. Marrow, (ed.) *The Failiure of Sucess*, AMACOM, New York.

French, J. R. P., Jr, Kahn, R. L. and Mann, F. C. (1962). Work, health and satisfaction, *Journal of Social Issues*, **18**, 1–129.

Fryer, D. and Payne, R. (1986). Being unemployed: a review of the literature on the psychological experience of unemployment. In C. L. Cooper and I. Robertson (eds) *International Review of Industrial and Organizational Psychology*, John Wiley and Sons, New York.

Gill, C. (1985). *Work, Unemployment and the New Technology*, Policy Press, Cambridge.

Gill, J. and Foulder, I. (1978). Managing a merger: the acquisition and its aftermath, *Personnel Management*, **10**, 14–17.

Glowinkowski, S. P. and Cooper, C. L. Current issues in organizational stress research, *Bulletin of the British Psychological Society*, **38**, 212–16.

Gochman, I. R. (1979). Arousal, attribution, and environmental stress. In I. G. Sarason and C. D. Spielberger (eds) *Stress and Anxiety*, Vol. 7. *The Series in Clinical and Community Psychology* pp. 67–92, Hemisphere, Washington, DC.

Greenhalgh, L. (1982). Maintaining organizational effectiveness during organizational retrenchment, *Journal of Applied Behavioral Science*, **18**, 155–70.

Greenhalgh, L. (1983a). Organizational decline, *Research in the Sociology of Organizations*, **2**, 231–76.

Greenhalgh, L. (1983b). Managing the job insecurity crisis, *Human Resources Management*, **4**, 431–44.

Greenhalgh, L. and Rosenblatt, Z. (1984). Job insecurity: toward conceptual clarity, *Academy of Management Review*, **9**, 438–48.

Greenhaus, J. H. and Beutell, N. J. (1985). Sources of conflict between work and family roles, *Academy of Management Review*, **10**, 76–88.

Greenhaus, J. H. and Kopelman, R. C. (1981). Conflict between work and nonwork roles: implications for the career planning process; *Human Resources Planning*, **4**, 1–10.

Gupta, N. and Jenkins, G. D. (1985). Dual career couples: stress, stressors, strains and strategies. In T. A. Beehr and R. S. Bhagat (eds) *Human Stress and Cognition in Organizations*, pp. 141–175, John Wiley and Sons, New York.

Hall, D. T. (ed) (1986). *Career Development in Organizations*, Jossey-Bass, San Francisco.

Hamner, W. C. and Tosi, H. L. (1974). Relationship of role conflict and role ambiguity to job involvement measures, *Journal of Applied Psychology*, **59**, 497–9.

Handy, C. (1984). *The Future of Work*, Blackwell, Oxford.

Hartley, J. and Klandermans, P. G. (1987). Individual and collective responses to job insecurity. In H. W. Scroiff and G. Debus (eds) *Proceedings of the West*

European Conference on the Psychology of Work and Organization, Elsevier, Amsterdam.

Hendrix, W. H., Ovalle, N. K. and Troxler, R. G. (1985). Behavioral and physiological consequences of stress and its antecedent factors, *Journal of Applied Psychology*, **70**, 188–201.

Hirschhorn, L. (1983). *Cutting Back*, Jossey-Bass, San Francisco.

Holahan, C. K. and Gilbert, L. A. (1979). Conflict between major life roles: women and men in dual career couples, *Human Relations*, **32**, 451–67.

House, R. J. and Rizzo, J. R. (1972a). Toward the measurement of organizational practices: scale development and validation, *Journal of Applied Psychology*, **56**, 388–96.

House, R. J. and Rizzo, J. R. (1972b). Role conflict and ambiguity as critical variables in a model of organizational behavior, *Organizational Behavior and Human Performance*, **7**, 467–505.

Hunt, J. W. (1986). Alienation among managers—the new epidemic or the social scientists' invention? *Personnel Review*, **15**, 21–6.

Hunter, J. E., Schmidt, F. L. and Jackson, G. B. (1982). *Meta-analysis: cumulating Research Findings Across Studies*, CA, Sage, Beverly Hills.

Ivancevich, J. M. (1979). An analysis of participation in decision making among project engineers, *Academy of Management Journal*, **22**, 253–69.

Ivancevich, J. M. and Matteson, M. T. (1980). *Stress and Work: A Managerial Perspective*, Scott, Foresman and Co. Glenview, II.

Ivancevich, J. M. Matteson, M. T. and Preston, C. (1982). Occupational stress, Type A behavior, and physical well-being, *Academy of Management Journal*; **25**, 373–91.

Jackson, S. E. and Schuler, R. S. (1985). A meta-analysis and conceptual critique of research on role ambiguity and role conflict in work settings, *Organizational Behavior and Human Decision Processes*, **36**, 16–78.

Jackson, S. E., Schwab, R. L. and Schuler, R. S. (1986). Toward on understanding of the burnout phenomenon. *Journal of Applied Psychology*, **71**, 630–40.

Jick, T. D. (1983). The stressful effects of budget cuts in organizations. In L. A. Rosen (ed.) *Topics in Managerial Accounting*, pp. 267–80, McGraw-Hill, New York.

Jick, T. D. (1985). As the axe falls: budget cuts and the experience of stress in organizations. In T. A. Beehr and R. S. Bhagat (eds). *Human Stress and Cognition in Organizations: an integrated perspective*, pp. 83–114, John Wiley and Sons, New York.

Jick, T. D. and Murray, V. V. (1982). The management of hard times: budget cutbacks in public sector organizations, *Organization Studies*, **3**, 141–70.

Jokl, M. W. (1984). The psychological effects on man of air movement and the colour of his surroundings, *Applied Ergonomics*, **15**, 119–126.

Journal of Organizational Behavior Management (1987). Special Issue—Stress: Theory, Research and Suggestions, **8**, 1–267.

Kahn, R. L., Wolfe, D. M., Quinn, R. P., Snoek, J. D. and Rosenthal, R. (1964). *Organizational Stress: Studies in Role Conflict and Ambiguity*, John Wiley and Sons, New York.

Kasl, S. V. (1980). The impact of retirement. In C. L. Cooper and R. Payne (eds) *Current Concerns in Occupational Stress*, pp. 137–86. John Wiley and Sons, New York.

Katz, R. (1985). Organizational stress and early socialization experiences. In T. A. Beehr and R. S. Bhagat (eds) *Human Stress and Cognition in Organizations*, pp. 117–40, John Wiley and Sons, New York.

Kaufman, H. G. (1982). *Professionals in Search of Work: Coping with the Stress of Job Loss and Underemployment*, John Wiley and Sons, New York.

Kay, E. (1975). Middle management. In J. O'Toole (ed.) *Work and the Quality of Life*, MIT Press, Cambridge, MA.

Keating, J. P. (1979). Environmental stressors: misplaced emphasis. In I. G. Sarason & C. D. Speilberger (eds). *Stress and Anxiety*, Vol. 6. *The Series in Clinical and Community Psychology*, pp. 55–66, Hemisphere, Washington, DC.

Kopelman, R. E., Greenhaus, J. H. and Connelly, T. F. (1983). A model of work, family, and interrole conflict: a construct validation study, *Organizational Behavior and Human Performance*, **32**, 198–215.

Korman, A. K. and Korman, R. W. (1980). *Career Success/Personal Failure*, Prentice-Hall, Englewood Cliffs, NJ.

Korman, A. K., Wittig-Berman, U. and Lang, D. (1981). Career success and personal failure: alienation in professionals and managers, *Academy of Management Journal*, **14**, 342–60.

Lang, D. (1985). Preconditions of three types of alienation in young managers and professionals, *Journal of Occupational Behavior*, **6**, 171–82.

Latack, J. C. (1984). Career transitions within organizations: an exploratory study of work, nonwork, and coping strategies, *Organizational Behavior and Human Performance*, **34**, 296–322.

Latack, J. C. and Dozier, J. B. (1986). After the axe falls: job loss on a career transition, *Academy of Management Review*, **11**, 375–92.

Lenna, C. R. and Ivancevich, J. M. (1987). Involuntary job loss: institutional interventions and a research agenda, *Academy of Management Review*, **12**, 301–12.

Lee, C. and Schuler, R. S. (1982). A constructive replication and extension of a role and expectancy perception model of participation in decision making, *Journal of Occupational Psychology*, **55**, 109–18.

Leiter, M. P. (1988). Burnout as a function of communication patterns in a multidisciplinary mental health team, In *Group and Organization Studies*, in press.

Leiter, M. P. and Maslach, C. (1988). The impact of interpersonal environment on burnout and organizational commitment, *Journal of Occupational Psychology*, in press.

Leiter, M. P. and Meechan, K. A. (1986). Role structure and burnout in the field of human services, *Journal of Applied Behavioral Sciences*, **22**, 47–52.

Levine, C. H. (ed.) (1980). *Managing Fiscal Stress*. Chatham House, Chatham, NJ.

Louis, M. R. (1980). Career transitions: varieties and commonalities, *Academy of Management Review*, **5**, 329–40.

Manning, M. R., Ismael, A. H. and Sherwood, J. J. (1981). Effects of role conflict on selected physiological, effective, and performance variables, *Multivariate Behavioral Research*, **16**, 125–41.

Marks, M. L. and Mirvis, P. H. (1985a). Merger syndrome: stress and uncertainty, *Mergers & Acquisitions*, **20**, 50–5.

Marks, M. L. and Mirvis, P. H. (1985b). Merger syndrome: management by crisis, *Mergers & Acquisitions*, **20**, 70–6.

Marks, M. L. and Mirvis, P. H. (1986). The merger syndrome, *Psychology Today*, **20**, 36–42.

Martin, T. N. and Schermerhorn, J. R. (1983). Work and non-work influences on health: a research agenda using inability to leave as a critical variable, *Academy of Management Review*, **8**, 650–9.

Maslach, C. and Jackson, S. W. (1981). Measurement of experienced burnout, *Journal of Occupational Behavior*, **2**, 99–113.

Maslach, C. and Jackson, S. E. (1984). Burnout in organizational settings, *Applied Social Psychology Annual*, **5**, 133–53.

McGoldrick, A. F. and Cooper, C. L. (1985). Stress at the decline of one's career: the act of retirement. In T. A. Beehr and R. S. Bhagat (eds) *Human Stress and Cognition in Organization*, pp. 177–201, John Wiley and Sons, New York.

McLean, A. (1966). Occupational mental health: review of an emerging art, *The American Journal of Psychiatry*, **61**, 961–76.

Meagre, N. (1986). Temporary work in Britain, *Employment Gazette*, **94**, 7–14.

Miles, R. H. (1980). Boundary roles. In C. L. Cooper and R. Payne (eds). *Current Concerns in Occupational Stress*, pp. 61–96, John Wiley and Sons, New York.

Miles, R. H. and Perreault, W. D. (1976). Organizational role conflict: its antecedents and consequences, *Organizational Behavior and Human Performance*, **17**, 19–44.

Mirvis, P. H. (1985). Negotiations after the sale: the roots and ramifications of conflict in an acquisition, *Journal of Occupational Behavior*, **6**, 65–84.

Morris, J. H., Stters, R. M. and Koch, J. L. (1979). Influence of organizational structure on role conflict and ambiguity for the three occupational groupings, *Academy of Management Journal*, **22**, 58–71.

Murray, V. V. and Jick, T. D. (1985). Taking stock of organizational decline management: some issues and illustrations from an empirical study, *Journal of Management*, **11**, 111–23.

Newman, J. E. and Beehr, T. A. (1979). Personal and organizational strategies for handling job stress: a review of research and opinion, *Personnel Psychology*, **32**, 1–44.

Nicholson, N. (1984). A theory of work role transitions, *Administrative Science Quarterly*, **29**, 172–91.

Oldham, G. R. and Brass, D. J. (1979). Employee reactions to an open-plan office: a naturally occurring quasi-experiment, *Administrative Science Quarterly*, **24**, 267–84.

Oldham, G. R. and Rotchford, N. L. (1983). Relationships between office characteristics and employee reactions: a study of the physical environment. *Administrative Science Quarterly*, **28**, 542–56.

Orpen, C. (1982). Type A personality as a moderator for the effects of role conflict, role ambiguity and role overload on individual strain, *Journal of Human Stress*, **8**, 8–14.

Parasuraman, S. and Alutto, I. A. (1981). An examination of the organizational antecedents of stressors at work, *Academy of Management Journal*, **24**, 48–67.

Parkes, K. R. Occupational stress among student nurses: a natural experiment, *Journal of Applied Psychology*, **67**, 784–96.

Parkington, J. J. and Schneider, B. Some correlates of experienced job stress: a boundary role study. *Academy of Management Journal*, **22**, 270–81.

Pearce, J. L. (1981). Bringing some clarity to role ambiguity research, *Academy of Management Review*, **6**, 665–74.

Pleck, J. H., Staines, G. L. and Lang, L. (1980). Conflicts between work and family life, *Monthly Labor Review*, 29–32.

Popovich, P. M. and Licota, B. J. (1989). A role model approach to sexual harassment, *Journal of Management*, **13**, 149–62.

Quick, J. C. (1979a). Dyadic goal setting with organizations: role making and motivational considerations. *Academy of Management Review*, **4**, 369–80.

Quick, J. C. (1979b). Dyadic goal setting and role stress: a field study, *Academy of Management Journal*, **22**, 241–52.

Quick, J. C. and Quick, J. D. (1984). *Organizational Stress and Preventive Management*, McGraw-Hill, New York.

Quinn, R. P. (1975). Locking-in as a moderator of the relationship between job satisfaction and mental health, unpublished manuscript, Survey Research Center, University of Michigan, Ann Arbor, Michigan.

Randolph, W. A. and Posner, B. Z. (1981). Explaining role conflict and role ambiguity via individual and interpersonal variables in different job categories, *Personnel Psychology*, **34**, 89–102.

Rossellini, L. (1981). Federal cuts increasing workers' stress levels, *New York Times*, 16 December.

Rule, B. G. and Nesdale, A. R. (1976). Environmental stressors, emotional arousal, and aggression. In C. D. Spielberger and I. G. Sarason (eds) *Stress and Anxiety*. Vol. 3. *The Series in Clinical and Community Psychology*, pp. 87–103, Hemisphere, Washington, DC.

Russell, R. W. (1978). Environmental stresses and the quality of life, *Australian Psychologist*, **13**, 143–59.

Sales, A. L. and Mirvis, P. H. (1984). Acquisition and collision of cultures. In R. Quinn and J. Kimberly (eds) *Managing Organizational Transitions*, Dow Jones, New York.

Schlenker, J. A. and Gutek, B. A. (1987). Effects of role loss on work-related attitudes, *Journal of Applied Psychology*, **72**, 286–93.

Schuler, R. S. (1980). A role of expectancy perception model of participation in decision making, *Academy of Management Journal*, **23**, 331–40.

Schuler, R. S. (1982). An integrative transactional process model of stress in organizations, *Journal of Occupational Behavior*, **3**, 5–20.

Schuler, R. S., Aldag, R. J. and Brief, A. P. (1977). Role conflict and ambiguity: a scale analysis, *Organization Behavior and Human Performance*, **20**, 111–28.

Shaw, J. B. and Riskind, J. H. (1983). Predicting job stress using data from the Position Analysis Questionnaire, *Journal of Applied Psychology*, **68**, 253–61.

Sinetar, M. (1981). Mergers, morale, and productivity, *Personnel Journal*, **60**, 863–7.

Singh, B., Agarawala, U. N. and Malhan, N. K. (1981). The nature of managerial role conflict, *Indian Journal of Industrial Relations*, **17**, 1–26.

Staw, B. M. (1984). Organizational behavior: a review and reformulation of the fields outcome variables. In M. R. Rosenzweig and L. W. Porter (eds) *Annual Review of Psychology*, Vol. 35, pp. 627–66, Annual Reviews, Palo Alto, CA.

Suedfeld, P. (1979). Stressful levels of environmental stimulation. In I. G. Sarason and C. D. Spielberger (eds) *Stress and Anxiety*. Vol. 6. *The Series in Clinical and Community Psychology*, pp. 109–27, Hemisphere, Washington, DC.

Sutton, R. I. and Rafaeli, A. (1987). Characteristics of work stations as potential occupational stressors, *Academy of Management Journal*, **30**, 260–76.

Szilagyi, A. D. and Holland, W. E. (1980). Changes in social density: relationships with functional interaction and perceptions of job characteristics, role stress, and work satisfaction, *Journal of Applied Psychology*, **65**, 28–33.

Thurley, K. and Ward-Penny, C. (1986). Changes in the roles and functions of middle management: a literature survey of English language publications. In *Report to the European Foundation for the Improvement of Living and Working Conditions*. London, London School of Economics.

Van Sell, M., Brief, A. P. and Schuler, R. S. (1981). Role conflict and ambiguity: integration of the literature and directions for future research, *Human Relations*, **34**, 43–71.

Walsh, J. T., Taber, T. D. and Beehr, T. A. (1980). An integrated model of perceived job characteristics, *Organization Behavior and Human Performance*, **25**, 252–267.

Wells, J. A. (1982). Objective job conditions, social support and perceived stress among blue-collar workers, *Journal of Occupational Behavior*, **3**, 79–94.

Wolpin, J. and Burke, R. J. (1986). Occupational looking-in: some correlates and consequences, *International Review of Applied Psychology*, **35**, 327–45.

Zalesny, M. D. and Farace, R. V. (1987). Traditional versus open offices: a comparison of sociotechnical social relations, and symbolic meaning perspectives, *Academy of Management Journal*, **30**, 240–59.

Causes, Coping and Consequences of Stress at Work
Edited by C. L. Cooper and R. Payne
© 1988 John Wiley & Sons Ltd

Chapter 4

Operator Stress and Computer-based Work

Rob Briner and G. Robert J. Hockey

INTRODUCTION

The introduction of computers into the workplace is frequently cited as a major source of increased occupational stress. This chapter examines the evidence for this assertion, though there has been a surprising dearth of systematic studies on which to draw. It would be surprising, of course, if the stress associated with adaptation to new technology were fundamentally different from that associated with other kinds of modern work environments. On the other hand it is likely that the major shifts in work practice which these changes have produced have given rise to problems and situations at work which are of a different order from those we have been used to (for example, the massive emphasis on cognitive work, and the possibility of remote access to information). In practice, we have related our findings, where possible, to the general conclusions of the occupational stress literature, in order to achieve a more broadly-based set of conclusions. In order to do justice to the complexity of the issues, however, we have been obliged to focus on one particular branch of computer work, that concerned with developments in office technology. Other areas of work in which new technology has made a major impact, such as manufacturing and process control, are referred to where it has seemed helpful to do so.

How can we recognize stress? Stress is defined here in terms of a mismatch or unresolved tension between an existing state and a target state (Hockey, 1984). The consequences of such a state may be observed in various outcome variables: subjective discomfort or unhappiness, difficulties in job performance, or in biochemical and physiological indicators of health. The problem of interpretation of these outcome variables is that the adaptive processes involved in environmental regulation appear to operate through the use of compensatory control processes. This means that a mismatch in one subsystem (say, performance) may be reduced effectively, though only at the expense of costs in some other sub-system (subjective strain, or hormonal activity). In order to infer stress in a situation it is thus necessary to identify

115

trade-offs between different components of the adaptive process. While there is evidence of this kind in the experimental stress literature (Lundberg and Frankenhaeuser, 1978) few of the studies we have found on computer-based stress provide any such data.

What are the potential sources of stress in computer operators? Table 1 summarizes the major problems, on which we have concentrated in our review. Many of these are, of course, those we are used to considering in other areas of occupational stress, though they are associated with unexpected complications when applied here. Others, notably those arising from changes in job demands, appear to have some features which are unique to the new technology arena.

Table 1 Principal sources of stress in computer-based work

Human factors constraints	Work demands
Workstation layout	Changes in work pattern
VDU and keyboard design	Increased cognitive load
Hardware characteristics	Temporal and structural changes
Interface design	Constraints on planning and work strategies
	Opportunities for control and discretion
Organizational decisions	
Introduction strategies	
Implementation and job impact	**Personal characteristics**
Training and user support	Stress tolerance
Long-term strategies	Cognitive skills
Constraints on communication and social interaction	

In the next three sections we consider human factors, organizational and work demands issues in turn. The available empirical evidence is scanty and rather indirect, and our interpretation necessarily tentative, though some broad conclusions and a number of research needs may be confidently spelled out. Finally, we examine the moderating influence of individual differences. Many of the ambiguities of the literature (not only in the new technology field, but in occupational stress in general) may be considered to arise from a failure to recognize the central role of abilities, expectations and strategies in the patterning of interactions with the environment. We highlight areas in which such sources of inter-individual variability may be particularly important, and suggest some further directions for research.

HUMAN FACTORS SOURCES OF STRESS

Human factors (or ergonomics) research has tended to concentrate on hardware properties of computing environments, such as the design of workstations, keyboards and visual display units (VDUs). In recent years, however, there has been a rapid growth in the literature on interface and software problems. The reasons for this are twofold. First, the increasing power of computers has given designers the opportunity to plan and choose the way in which users communicate with the system. Second, human factors research has itself moved away from looking at the purely physical properties of work environments towards the psychological dimensions of human–machine interaction.

Hardware and software design have important implications for the frustration and stress experienced by users, though the large diversity of computing environments and of end users mean that that the effects of design on stress are by no means consistent. For example, as Armbruster (1983) points out, in some university and software development environments human factors considerations have almost been ignored with no apparent ill effects in terms of work satisfaction or frustration. These users are highly motivated to work with computers, and to use them within a broad and stimulating work context. Contrast such groups with data entry employees who can spend as long as 75% of their working day looking at a VDU (Dainoff, Happ and Crane 1981) and report high levels of work load and fatigue (Binaschi *et al.*, 1983). For this latter group, the design of workstations, VDUs, and software may be more critical.

Hardware Considerations

Workstation design

There is a large research literature on human factors in VDU workstation design (Grandjean, 1987) and input devices (Greenstein and Arnaut, 1987), widely regarded in popular accounts as being implicated in health of operators. There are reports that VDU operators suffer from a wide range of health complaints, from muscular aches and visual discomfort to emotional distress (Dainoff, 1982; Smith, 1984). This evidence is somewhat ambiguous, though it has been a contributory factor in the development of recommendations for workstation layout, lighting levels and work scheduling (Health and Safety Executive, 1983; Mackay, 1980). Discomfort is often related not to design itself, but to the requirement to maintain a particular posture during prolonged work (Mackay, 1980). Other well-documented workstation principles refer to glare reduction, and the heat and noise sometimes associated with computer terminals, VDUs and printers. These are unlikely to contribute significantly to stress in such workplaces, though they may be a source of irritation.

Keyboard design is now well developed (Greenstein and Arnaut, 1987) and most systems relatively easy to use. Specific layout problems with keyboards can lead to frustration for users however. For example, placing the 'break' key next to the 'return' key will mean that the user may press 'break' by mistake, and so lose or disrupt work. Other input devices and cursor control devices such as the 'mouse' (hand operated) and 'mole' (foot operated) can have advantages for some users in some tasks (Card, English and Burr, 1978; Karat, McDonald and Anderson, 1986); however, for a skilled typist, using a mouse may simply be an annoying distraction.

Evidence for effects on health

The VDU itself has attracted more attention than any other hardware item, both from human factors researchers and trade unions. Some health problems have been associated with radiation levels of VDU screens (Grandjean, 1987). However, measurements of the radiation levels emitted from VDUs have not exceeded international safety guidelines (Mackay, 1980) and in some cases have been found to be no greater than background levels (Cakir, Hart and Stewart, 1980). Many studies have found higher levels of reported visual fatigue and eye strain in VDU users, but there is no evidence that these symptoms are a direct consequence of the physical properties of VDUs (Dainoff, 1982; Oborne, 1985).

Most of the evidence on the health effects of VDUs comes from verbal reports of VDU operators. The reasons why people report symptoms are very complicated and have been the subject of considerable debate in the stress and illness area for a number of years. Very few studies have attempted to validate these subjective reports, by relating them to performance or bodily indicators of stress. Dainoff *et al.* (1981) found that VDU work had no effect on measures of visual function, even though users reported subjective symptoms of eye strain. Symptom reports are not necessarily a direct measure of underlying bodily states or cognitive function (Nisbitt and Wilson, 1982), though they may be indicative of compensatory processes at work. Such data can only be evaluated satisfactorily if measurements are taken across a range of stress indicators (Hockey, 1986a).

Another problem with studies of symptom reporting concerns the use of appropriate control groups. Several studies report that the discomfort in VDU operators is of the same magnitude as that found in other office groups, such as full-time copy-typists, manual telephone directory operators, or hard-copy proof-readers. Laubli and Grandjean (1984) point out, however, that a quite different picture emerges when the comparable control groups are drawn from less strenuous traditional office jobs. In such studies the incidence of reported visual and musculoskeletal discomfort is higher amongst VDU operators. The selection of control groups, in this as in other areas of occupational psychology, remains a major methodological difficulty for field studies.

In general, although the ergonomic design of workstations, keyboards and

VDUs plays a role in the distress experienced by users, the evidence suggests that the type of work carried out at VDUs is the main cause of health complaints (Elias, Tisserand and Christmann, 1983; Howarth and Istance, 1985; Sauter *et al.*, 1981; Smith *et al.*, 1983). The type of work performed by users will be determined by the task demands, work load and organizational structure, which will be discussed in later sections. In addition, however, the operating characteristics of the computer system will affect the way an operator uses the system. This is discussed in the next section.

Software and System Considerations

Compared with hardware ergonomics, very little is known about the effects of system/software design on user satisfaction and well-being. Turner and Karasek (1984) suggest a number of reasons for this. First, the cognitive processes involved are not as well understood as the physiological limitations of humans. Second, the characteristics of the interface are much harder to measure than the physical characteristics of hardware. Because of the lack of theory and empirical evidence in this area, the general issues of how software may affect user well-being will be addressed in terms of dialogue structure and more general features of computer systems.

Dialogue structure

The way in which the user communicates with, and receives information from the system will influence the user's feelings of comfort, control and confidence during interactions. Shneiderman (1987) makes a distinction between three types of dialogue structure or interaction style: menu selection; command languages; direct manipulation. In menu selection the user is presented with a list of commands at each function level from which they choose an item. There are obvious short-term advantages for the novice user. However, more experienced users may find menus a hinderance. Although tasks and decision making are clearly structured for the user, after experience with the system the user may want to break out of this rigid way of interaction. The same problems apply to 'idiot-proof' and 'user-friendly' systems. If there is little flexibility in these dialogue structures the user will find the experience of interaction unstimulating, constraining and frustrating. In using a command language, the user has to recall and issue appropriate commands. This type of dialogue can give the user a greater feeling of control. Instead of simply recognizing and selecting the desired command as in menu systems, he or she can initiate and determine the course of interaction.

There are some problems for the user in command language dialogues, such as the increased memory load, particularly if the command language is not structured in a meaningful way, or command abbreviations are not related to the full command name. The large number of commands often available can mean that users only use the commands they can remember, or feel comfortable with. In this situation, the user is certainly not getting the most out of the system and may experience frustration in trying to complete tasks using only the small number of commands they can remember. The novice user may be overwhelmed by command languages and find it difficult to progress quickly. Shneiderman (1987) gives the example of driving a car as a direct manipulation interface. There is a very close relationship between the actions of the driver, the change in position and speed of the car, and the feedback the driver receives about the position and speed of the car through the windscreen. In menu selection and command language dialogues, such a task might mean issuing commands such as 'brake gently' or 'turn right 15 degrees' and then waiting for feedback from the system to see the effects. Direct manipulation interfaces attempt to reduce the information processing distance between what the user wants to do and the functions of the machine, and the feedback given to the user from the system quickly and clearly tells the user the state of the system. In such interfaces the user has a feeling of direct engagement with the system (Hutchins, Hollan and Norman, 1985). For this reason direct manipulation often makes use of objects and icons which the user can manipulate in the same way as objects in the real world. Laurel (1986) describes these feelings of directness as 'first-personness'. Most interfaces have second-person characteristics in that the interface forms an intermediary between the user and the system. Hutchins *et al.* (1985) suggest that direct manipulation interfaces reduce the effort required to accomplish goals. In this way, such interfaces could reduce the kinds of stresses and frustrations associated with menu selection and command dialogues.

System characteristics

Slow response times in computer systems have been found to reduce job satisfaction (Barber and Lucas, 1983) and increase stress and mental strain (Johansson and Aronsson, 1984). On the other hand, very fast response times may increase the pace of the interaction to an uncomfortable level where users feel they must always respond to the system promptly (Shneiderman, 1980). The optimum response time will depend on the task. Variability in system response time and system crashes may also cause stress in users. Johansson and Aronsson (1984) reported that workers in an insurance company worked very quickly in the morning to try and complete as much work as possible, in case the system failed in the afternoon. In addition, when response times were unusually long, workers experienced anxiety and uncertainty as they could not be sure if the long response times were due to high load on the system, or whether the system had failed. Another general feature of computer systems is that they should provide information to the user about the state of the system. For example, by providing an indication of how long response time is going to be and by issuing clear and helpful error messages. If computer systems do not allow for error recovery, users may feel anxious at crucial stages of tasks where they know that a mistake could be expensive in terms of losing hours of work, or causing the machine to fail.

Summary

The experience of working with a computer will be greatly influenced by the human factors dimensions of hardware and software. Although task demands will probably play a more important role in determining the extent to which this experience is stressful, putting more effort into design may help to alleviate such problems. The demands of work, although partly defined by characteristics of the technology, depend also on the way in which work is organized around such technology. We now examine these issues.

ORGANIZATIONAL SOURCES OF STRESS

The common use of the word 'impact' when discussing the effects of computer systems on organizations and work environments (e.g. DeVaris, 1981; Blackler and Brown, 1985) suggests that when computer systems and organizations are brought together the result is a collision which sends shock waves through the organization. The effects of computer systems on organizations are indeed complex and wide ranging (see Kling and Scacchi, 1982). We can consider the implications of system design for the people who use and work with the system as similar to the implications of urban planning for people in the community (Kling, 1983). For the user, or potential user, two general periods of stress can be identified. The first occurs during the introduction of the system; the second is associated with long-term adaptation to new working patterns.

The Introduction of Computer Systems

Any change may result in stress. The change to new technology may be particularly stressful since it is new and completely unknown to many potential users. Moreover, Norman (1984) suggests that there is a mystique surrounding computers which creates a large knowledge gap between those who know something about computers and those who know little or nothing. The attitudes towards computers of inexperienced users are generally more negative than those of experienced users (Arndt, Clevenger and Meiskey, 1985; Zoltan, 1981) which suggests that potential users' initial expectations of working with computers will change as they find out more about them. The lack of knowledge among potential users about what computers can and cannot do, and what it is like to work with one is likely to be a source of stress during the initial period of adaptation.

In addition, long term fears about changes in work practices and work conditions will contribute to the response to computer systems: the loss of old skills and the demands of learning new ones; possible redundancy; lowering of status; greater supervision. The concern of workers over the effects of VDUs (and more generally of working with computers) is reflected in the initiative taken by many trade unions in publishing relevant health and safety reports and recommendations (Pearce, 1984). More recently trade unions have placed more emphasis on software and job stress (Pearce, 1984), and on the effects of computers on social contacts and power relations at work (Nygaard, 1980) rather than concentrating exclusively on ergonomic characteristics of VDUs. There is little empirical evidence on the attitudes and stressful experiences of users during the period of adaptation to computer systems. However, such effects may be understood by discussing the method of system implementation intended to minimize or reduce such effects, namely, user participation.

User participation

The design of computer systems and their implementation may be considered to be part of the same process, since the former has a marked influence on the latter (Mumford, 1979). User participation in system design is intended to improve the design and implementation of systems which in turn may lead to increased user acceptance (Helmreich, 1985), satisfaction with the system, greater efficiency and a stress-free transition from the old to the new (Mumford, 1983). While many different strategies of participation are possible, this process can work for a number of reasons. First, participation in itself will give users feelings of control and involvement, and so have a beneficial effect irrespective of the contributions made by them to the final design. Second, if users are able to tell designers exactly what their job currently involves, the implemented system should be better suited to their job requirements. Third, participation will also inform users about the new system and so act as a form of training.

Although user participation in system design thus appears to be an ideal solution to the problems of stress during the introduction of a computer system, a number of problems do exist. For example, employees may not be interested in participating, and perceive participation as some kind of management trick (Bjorn–Andersen, 1984): participation is seen to be encouraged only as a means of smoothing the implementation process and not because of any genuine interest on the part of management in involving users in the design (Eason, 1982). This problem is, of course, common to participative design in all work situations, though there may be features of computer technology and office environments which make user participation particularly problematic. The first difficulty is connected with the level of existing knowledge workers have about computer technology. It is difficult to participate in the design of technology without having at least some technical knowledge. For example, an experienced typist would know something about building a better typewriter, but how could they suggest design features of a word-processor program, without considerable knowledge of existing word-processors, or evaluate suggested interface options? In the case of computer technology, which can often be very different from older technologies, user participation in design and implementation can only be achieved by first educating potential users about computers. Second, the use of prototypes for users to test during the design of software is often restricted by time and costs. Third, in order to participate, users must be able to articulate the content and functions of their job. In the case of office procedures this may be difficult. Sheil (1983), during interviews with office workers, found that the information processing and administrative procedures were not clearly defined. What happened in practice was different from the formal descriptions given by the workers.

Ultimately, of course, the problems experienced by computer operators faced with new systems may be solved by adapting either the system or the user. The first solution requires a degree of participation and involvement in the design of software. The second involves training and continued user support. Although the initial period of adaptation to computer systems may be stressful, and genuine user participation in design may ease the transition, the long-term effects on the work environment and work problems are likely to be a greater source of stress. The need for involvement, participation and support will not disappear with initial adaptation to the implemented system, as new problems and difficulties will become apparent.

Long-term Effects of Computerised Work

The effects on organizations of changing to computer-based working are ambiguous, with findings of both deskilling and of upgrading and enrichment of jobs (Attewell and Rule, 1984). These diverse findings are partly due to the broad range of computer applications included in these studies. To say that someone works with a computer tells us almost nothing about the content or nature of that job. But even when the application is the same (for example, word-processing), the views expressed about the effects of such an application range from what Rowe (1986) describes as those of 'optimists' such as Giuliano (1985), to 'pessimists' such as Downing (1980).

Optimists see the possibilities of improved and enriched work, while the

pessimists view the effects of word-processing and office automation as negative, leading to increased control and degrading of jobs. Another perspective
views the effects of new technology in a less deterministic way, seeing such
effects as a consequence of management choices about how to implement
and organize work around the technology, rather than as a consequence of
the technology itself (e.g. Buchanan and Boddy, 1982).

Computer monitoring of work performance

The advent of computer working has enabled the close monitoring of worker
performance. For each worker many aspects of their work performance and
productivity such as keystroke, error and task completion rates can be
recorded and used by supervisors and management. In addition some
computer work such as data entry is paid on a keystroke/hour basis. Higher
levels of stress, lower levels of satisfaction and a deterioration in relations
with peers, supervisors and senior management have been reported by
clerical workers using computers with performance monitoring systems
(Irving, Higgins and Safayeni *et al*, 1986). Such close monitoring can cause
workers to feel constrained and under considerable pressure, particularly
when many aspects of their work performance, such as the quality of work
produced, are not reflected in such quantitative measures. It appears that
workers may not be opposed to computer performance monitoring in principle (Irving *et al.*, 1986). As long as performance levels are set in a participative and flexible way (Long, 1984) and other performance measures that
take into account the quality of work are used, many stressful aspects of
these systems may be removed.

Communication and social interaction

It is ironic that although computers are used in communications, enabling
large amounts of information to be transferred from one location to another,
the effect of computer systems in the workplace is often to decrease direct
communication between workers and cause social isolation. Many writers
have commented that the introduction of computer working can reduce social
contact between workers (e.g. Bjorn-Andersen, 1983; Cohen, 1984; Gregory
and Nussbaum, 1982), but little systematic research has been directed towards
this issue. However, it is clear that people expect more from their job than
income: social interaction and social support are important aspects of the
work environment. The most basic reason why working with computers can
result in social isolation is that more time is spent interacting with the
computer than with many of the machines, such as typewriters, that
computers have replaced. In an office, for example, where files are stored
on computer and electronic mail is used, many of the activities which require

movement and social interaction have been replaced by the computer system. Secretaries no longer need to move around the office to collect papers from filing cabinets or to take information to other workers. Indeed one of the aims of workstation design is to enable the user to work without having to leave their desk. In some circumstances this could be useful, and actually reduce the stress and frustration sometimes associated with interruption of cognitive activities (for example, failing to locate information in an office filing system). But the complete removal of the need to interact with co-workers in accomplishing tasks, coupled with computer performance monitoring means that some computer workers have to remain almost constantly at their terminals, with minimal interaction with others. Cohen (1984) suggests that the promotion of social support at work should be encouraged to overcome some of the problems of social isolation, for example by providing places for lunch breaks and allowing operators to take breaks together. In addition, the layout of desks and other furniture may maximise whatever social interaction is possible.

Learning and user support

Provision of a thorough formal initial training is an important part of implementation. Apart from the confidence and knowledge it gives to users, it also indicates the positive attitude and commitment of management to investing in their employees. Such training is costly, however, and is often omitted in favour of the more usual practice of giving the employee a computer with a (sometimes badly written) manual and telling them to 'get on with it'. Such practice can only serve to maximise the fears and anxieties of the employee, both about the task itself and his or her long-term prospects in the organization. Although formal training will ensure that employees can get started with the new system, transferring these skills to the job will present new problems not covered in the training course, requiring further directed learning. Extended formal training of this kind is rarely provided, so that operators have to learn from each other.

The provision of a social support network within the social and work environment can facilitate learning beyond the initial period of formal training (where any is given). Remembering command names, long sequences of commands, or trying to learn the more complicated functions of an application program are frustrating aspects of computer working which may continue for months or even years after the introduction of a system. If the social resources for helping workers with such problems are not available, or not easily accessed, then such problems, though perhaps small in themselves, may result in unhappiness and anxiety. In general, computer users often prefer informal sources of help (Alty and Coombs, 1980; Lang, Ault and Lang, 1982), while manuals and other documentation may not always be relevant or useful (Carroll, 1984, 1985). What can be done on an organizational level to encourage the use of informal sources of training? Local experts and the development of a sense of community are important ways to encourage operators to help each other (Bannon, 1986). If workers can turn to an 'expert' colleague for help then not only may their problem be solved more quickly, but the knowledge in itself that someone is readily available to help may increase their confidence to try to solve the problem by themselves. Such an expert could also be accessed by a telephone or electronic mail 'hotline'. A sense of community can ensure that information is freely exchanged; operators share and resolve the difficulties they may be having with the system, and do not feel embarrassed about asking for help. These aspects of the social environment are particularly important in computer working, as the system may be continually changing and evolving as new versions of software packages appear and new hardware becomes available. By making sure that the social resources can meet the learning needs of the workers many of the irritations and problems caused when users cannot use the system can be overcome.

Role change

If computers are introduced into already existing jobs then it is likely that old and well defined roles between co-workers and between workers and management will change as the job itself is likely to change. In the case of word-processing environments, Bjorn-Andersen (1983) indicates that secretaries will spend less time on typing and move into the roles of private secretaries, personal assistants or even co-workers, taking on some of the tasks previously done by management. In practice, however, word-processing may not reduce the time spent typing since, for example, authors and initiators of documents often demand more drafts and more changes to documents when word-processors are used; the costs of modification are so greatly reduced. Another role change which may occur as a consequence of the change from conventional typing to word-processing is that typists may lose contact with the authors and be unable to complete a whole job for someone they will interact with. This change may come about because of the technological and economic advantages of pooling word-processing resources (Boddy and Buchanan, 1981; Buchanan and Boddy, 1982).

  If technology changes the nature of work, then the relationships between people at work will change in subtle, but important ways. Such changes can be stressful. In a comparative study by Cooper and Cox (1985), word-processing operators reported more stress and more job dissatisfaction than copy-typists. The single category of work stressor which predicted most of the mental ill-health and job dissatisfaction was lack of role clarity. This includes having little power in the office, no existing pay grades, no identifiable career structure and unclear job expectations. Contradicting these findings, some research has reported an increase in job satisfaction after the introduction of word-processors (e.g. Bird, 1980). This example of word-processing shows that computers can both improve jobs and make them less satisfying and more stressful. Although such changes may be subtle and difficult to predict they may have a major influence on the well-being of operators. An awareness of the potential impact of such changes may help to reduce the negative effects of working with computers when strategic management choices are made about the implementation and organization of work around computer systems.

Summary

The increasing use of computers at work means that a great many jobs are changing. Such changes are likely to be stressful in themselves, but even after the initial period of adaptation to the system the social and organizational restructuring brought about by the use of the system will have significant implications for the well-being of those who work with it. A review by Kahn and Cooper (1986) comments that a remarkable number of factors have been put forward to explain the causes of stress in computer working. This is not so remarkable when we consider the complexity of the relationship between work and stress, and the perhaps unique ability of computer systems to change the way in which organizations function. To attempt to understand these effects in terms of individual cognitive adjustment it is necessary to consider how computers affect the ability of operators to meet the specific demands of their jobs.

JOB AND TASK DEMANDS

It is often assumed that the job and task demands associated with computer working are likely to result in stress, either because these demands are too high (information overload) or too low (underload or boredom). However, the relationship between environmental demands and stress is complex. Although the pattern of demands in computer working are different from those in other types of work, they are not necessarily more stressful. In some cases, the use of computers can actually reduce job stress (Kalimo and Leppanen, 1985). Where computer working is stressful, job design is often the main cause (Eason, 1984), particularly when the job involves all-day computer working (e.g. Grandjean, 1987; Stellman *et al.*, 1987). A full discussion of the relationship between job design, job demands and stress is beyond the scope of this chapter. However, some general points can be made.

The Nature of Demands

Broadly speaking, job demands can be thought of as involving intrinsic task requirements, the level of uncertainty, time pressure, and the rate, amount and difficulty of work (e.g. Karasek, 1979; Turner, 1984). Resources available to meet such demands include skills, coping and appraisal, social support and tools. The ability to use these resources will be affected by the amount of discretion (job decision latitude) available, which in turn will be determined by job design and characteristics of the technology. While job design should aim to do more than prevent stress [e.g. promote well-being and job satisfaction, and meet needs for personal growth (Hackman and Oldham, 1975)] in this chapter we will mainly concentrate on the stressful components of job design.

There are many ways of classifying tasks and demands (Companion and Corso, 1982; Fleishman and Quaintance, 1984). This can be done, for example, in terms of the abilities required to perform the task, the description of task behaviours, and the objective and intrinsic characteristics of the task. Most of these classification systems are too detailed to be useful for the description of the wide and varied jobs involved in computer working. In addition, the new task demands associated with computer working may not fit easily within these classification systems. Rather than take any one of these approaches, the focus will be on the demands of computer working that are known to be, or thought to be stressful from a cognitive ergonomics point of view (e.g. Cakir, 1986). In this way, some of the more computer-specific job and task demands can be identified.

Adaptation to Computer Working

Occupational stress may be said to occur when people fail to adapt to changes that occur in their working lives. Adaptation to the introduction of computers into the workplace involves learning to meet the new demands of the job in a way that does not involve excessive personal or physiological adjustment.

Costs of adaptation

The effort required to meet particular demands (and therefore the costs of coping) will vary, depending on the resources available and the discretion to deploy resources strategically. Karasek (1979, 1982), who refers to discretion as 'job decision latitude', found that the highest levels of mental strain and coronary heart disease occur in those groups of workers who experience high job demands and low job decision latitude. Uncontrollable and unpredictable demands also have the effect of removing active control over resources deployment. Uncontrollable demands, such as those in machine-paced work, have been found to be more stressful than those in self-paced work (Johansson, Aronsson and Lindstrom *et al.*, 1978). Unpredictable demands and interruptions to workflow, such as system breakdowns, may also be difficult to cope with because of a disruption of cognitive control processes (Johansson and Aronsson, 1984).

Because of the wide range of computer applications and the lack of relevant research, the specific job and task demands of computer working are difficult to agree upon. However, we can perhaps identify the ways in which computer working may impose new kinds of job demands, change the resources available to meet those demands and affect the operator's active control over such resources.

Short-term and long-term adaptation to computer work

As we have argued elsewhere in this chapter it is probably important to distinguish between the stress involved in short-term adjustment to the presence of a new computer system, and the long-term adaptation to the chronic demands of computer working. Even where the use of computers eventually reduces levels of chronic job stress, the transition period may be stressful (Huuhtanen, 1984).

As computer technology is introduced, the pattern of job demands imposed on operators is likely to change quite significantly. As noted above, any change in demands will require adaptive effort to cope with the change. Once new patterns have been fully established, such demands may or may not be more stressful than previous demands. However, in the short term, the extent of the differences between old and new demands are likely to be the main source of stress, as is evident in the literature on task performance in stressful environments (Hockey, 1984).

What changes in job demands and job content can be expected when operators switch from more traditional technologies to computer-based working? Unfortunately, there is little published research on this topic. There are some case studies of organizational and social changes following the introduction of computers into manufacturing environments (Butera and Thurman, 1984), though these do not attempt to look at changes in job characteristics and demands in any systematic way. This state of affairs is characteristic of research in the new technology field in general (Wall *et al.*, 1987). Such weak empirical evidence makes it particularly difficult to assess the level of adjustment required during the change to working with the new technology. While the level of adjustment required will depend on many variables (e.g. training, differences between the old and new job, and method of implementation), there may be some particular task related sources of stress which can be identified during the transition.

Demands of Computer Work

While there is a tendency to view the changes in job and task demands following the introduction of a computer system simply in terms of deskilling or upgrading (Attwell and Rule, 1984), in practice, such changes are likely to be quite diverse. This is not surprising when we consider the wide range of jobs and tasks that can be accomplished by using computers, and the many ways in which computers themselves can be used within the same jobs and tasks depending on the hardware and software of the system. We now consider those demands which are particularly associated with using computers to complete tasks, in contrast to more traditional methods. Such changes in demands will of course vary, depending on how job functions are allocated between the user and the computer system (Hacker and Schonfelder, 1986) and the level of previous demands.

Cognitive demands

Although it is self-evident that computer working will make greater demands on cognitive resources than more traditional methods, what particular changes in demands can we expect? There are clear implications for the involvement of cognitive processes such as memory, attention and decision-making.

The most obvious is a greater involvement of working memory, particularly in interactive computer working. Because of the complex mental model the user must develop of the system (Norman, 1986), greater demands will be placed on working memory (for example, as the user retrieves parts of the model in order to use the system). In many forms of interactive computer working, the user must be able to remember long sequences of commands in order to complete tasks. This puts extra demands on working memory, particularly if the current state of the system is not well specified.

The requirement to use a computer is likely to make considerable demands on attention processes. In order to issue appropriate commands, the user must be aware of the current state of the system, and maintain a suitable balance of cognitive resources to complete the task. This requires close monitoring and concentration. In addition, certain characteristics of computer systems may impose an uncomfortable attentional requirement. The user may feel 'coupled' or 'yoked' (Sauter *et al.*, 1981) to the computer, particularly as computer response times, in contrast to human response times, are much faster (Johansson and Aronsson, 1984). A flashing cursor or prompt constantly reminds the user that the system is ready for more input, so increasing the pace and rhythm of work. Attentional resources are also stretched by the need in some tasks to carry out several activities at the same time (Salvendy, 1982); for example new developments in user interfaces requiring the management of several windows on the screen.

A third area of involvement of cognitive resources is that of decision-making and planning. Computer working can create higher or lower levels of control and discretion, depending on job design and job tasks. Low levels of decision-making and planning are most apparent when the user is engaged in repetitive work (such as data entry) for most or all of the working day. Rigid dialogue structures, where the user cannot choose their own job strategies can also reduce discretion and control. Conversely, computer working can increase levels of decision-making and planning by giving the user more job-related information and communication facilities. The use of computer-based decision aids in jobs such as process control and intensive care monitoring enables operators to optimize their use of diagnostic and planning decision processes which may otherwise be overwhelmed by the complexity of the situation (e.g. Hollnagel, Mancini and Woods, 1986). In cases such as these the computer is clearly seen to be a tool which can help the operator to perform his or her job. On the other hand, in jobs, with little opportunity for decision-making or planning, the computer is not a tool; it is the whole job.

Other work demands

In addition to the load placed on cognitive resources, the use of computers in work also requires adjustment to a range of other task factors; in particular, changes in variety, pacing and task structure.

The variety of tasks can be greatly reduced after the introduction of computer systems. In the case of the change from copy-typing to word-processing for example (Buchanan and Boddy, 1982), work can simply become the input of text. While copy-typing includes many other tasks, such as putting paper in the typewriter, moving around the office to fetch files, word-processing can result in long periods of typing without any change in activity. However, if computers are used to remove some of the repetitive elements of jobs, then significant role changes can occur allowing greater work variety (Bjorn-Andersen, 1983; Wainwright and Francis, 1984).

We have already pointed out that the fast response times of computers may lead to a continuous and rapid pace of work. On the other hand, slow response times and system breakdowns can be stressful (Johansson and Aronsson, 1984). Pacing in computer working thus may become more externalized; the operator feels 'pulled along' at the pace of the display. Task structure may also become externally controlled. While task and job goals are fairly fixed, the structure of those tasks, or how the user decides to meet these goals may be quite flexible. In the computer environment this structure may similarly become fixed and rigid: it is constrained by the design of the user–system dialogue structure. For example, in an electronic filing system a database may have to be searched according to a fixed sequence of option choices, whereas operators would normally have preferred individual strategies for retrieving information. Such external control will be exacerbated by computer performance monitoring, when both the rate of work and any deviations from a fixed task structure can be recorded.

Special demands in computer working

Although we cannot be sure that there are unique demands in computer working, certain aspects of computer systems and jobs may interact to produce demands which are novel, particularly in work environments such as offices. In those jobs which are highly computer-dependent, the most significant and perhaps unique demands are connected with the level of coupling involved. When all or many of the operator's job functions are performed using the computer, and the dialogue structure is rigid, the level of discretion and control will be greatly reduced. While in other forms of working, discretion and control may also be reduced, a computer has the potential to control almost all aspects of work demands, including rate of work, task structure and workload.

Wisner (1981) has suggested that computer technology may create jobs that are almost purely cognitive, and Sheil (1983) argues that information technology in the office separates information processing from the social processes that formerly embodied such functions. This implies that computer systems present the operator with a unique pattern of demands, one requiring only cognitive or information processing skills. Previously the job functions were performed by using both cognitive and social skills. However, computer systems can facilitate and formalize information processing in such a way as to reduce the requirement for social contact and group working.

Summary

The job and tasks demands involved in computer working are difficult to specify, particularly where computer systems are used more as tools, perhaps for only part of the working day. For those jobs which involve intensive computer working however, it is apparent that the software of the system can determine to a great extent the specific job and task demands. While some of these demands may be unique to computer working, many of them are unique to office environments. There is a clear need for research to assess the job and task demands of computer working. In particular, what effects such demands can have on well-being, and the determinants of such demands (e.g. software, job design). This empirical approach to the assessment of job and task demands has only recently been developed in some areas of information technology, such as advanced manufacturing technology

(Wall *et al.*, 1987). It is now perhaps appropriate, with the increasing spread of information technology in offices, to use such an approach in these working environments.

INDIVIDUAL DIFFERENCES IN COMPUTER STRESS

As in other areas of occupational stress, remarkably little attention has been paid to a consideration of the role of individual differences in determining the nature and extent of stress in computer operators. Apart from desirable interface design goals of including provision for individualization of 'user models' in the software of a system (e.g. Rich, 1983), such information has more fundamental implications for training and stress management. In the space available to us here we are able only to comment on two broad approaches to the problem: variability in personality factors and variability in cognitive behaviour.

Variability in Personality

Differences in personality can be expected to contribute broadly to patterns of stress and coping, for example, the 'stress-prone' type of individual. In fact, predictions based on personality assessment have generally been rather disappointing, and this has been true also of computing stress. Such general approaches may also be misleading: a particular example will illustrate the problem.

A focal issue in computer stress has been 'computer anxiety' or 'computer-phobia'. It is commonly believed that some individuals are particularly prone to anxiety when faced with computer-based tasks, particularly when meeting them for the first time, and that this is a major source of stress. While there have been few direct studies of this phenomenon, the available evidence suggests in fact that computer anxiety is not part of a general personality trait. Howard and Smith (1986) found the strongest predictor of computer anxiety to be specific mathematical anxiety, while correlations with general 'stress tolerance' measures such as trait anxiety and locus of control were not significant. General personality indices of stress tolerance need to be developed, of course, though they may be less clearly related to obvious characteristics such as trait anxiety and temperament. In any case, they may not be applicable to situations where clearly defined problems provide a more specific focus for adaptive behaviour. A cognitive approach may be better equipped to deal with these.

What seems particularly important in the search for a measure of stress tolerance is to be specific about the nature of stress. In successfully nego-tiating the transition from a traditional to a computerized office, say, the individual faces at least three forms of stressful experience: the anticipation of the change, the period of implementation and the long-term adaptation to new working conditions. While specific fears, attitudes and factors such as confidence in one's own ability may be good predictors of the earlier phases of coping with these changes, long-term coping may be more clearly associated with factors such as adaptability and tolerance of environmental change, and the availability of strategies capable of maintaining a suitable level and pattern of coping activity. As far as we are aware there is no relevant research on these issues.

Cognitive Variability

Cognitive differences between individuals are likely to play a major part in determining the level and manner of their interaction with computer systems. Although cognitive style has been implicated in this transaction (van de Veer *et al.*, 1985; Robertson, 1985), such an approach may be fundamentally flawed, since it fails on grounds of both validity and reliability (Hockey, in press). In short, cognitive style dimensions such as field dependence are highly correlated with specific abilities, such as perceptual integration (Widiger, Knudson and Rorer, 1980), and are highly situation specific. More promising are approaches based on ability. Although traditional measures of general intelligence do not offer possibilities for differentiating between different patterns of human–computer interaction, they are a good predictor of general adaptive ability (Sternberg, 1986). Perhaps more useful, where different task environments are concerned, are measures of specific abilities. Spatial ability in particular has been shown to exert an appreciable influence on both learning and using word-processing systems (Sebrechts *et al.*, 1984; Gomez, Egan and Bowers, 1986).

Hockey (in press) has argued that cognitive variability may arise from two sources: cognitive competence (patterns of information processing skills) and executive or control skill. Differences in the patterning of basic skills (e.g. in using memory or dividing attention between activities) will result in different profiles of cognitive-based performance. These differences may, however, be greatly minimized for individuals with a high level of executive skill, since they are better able to maintain relatively uncomfortable patterns of cognitive activity, particularly over long periods. The use of such active control in problem solving is, however, effortful and attracts physiological costs, such as increased catecholamine excretion (Lundberg and Frankenhaeuser, 1978) and reduced vagal control of blood pressure (Mulder and Mulder, 1981).

In terms of the present chapter, two implications of this distinction may be mentioned. First, differences in competence are likely to be reflected in differential experiences of difficulty for operators engaged in a range of computer tasks. To be specific, differences in difficulty have to do with the match between task demands and cognitive competence, rather than with general ability or broad differences between tasks. If the introduction of computer working changes the operator's task in such a way that the mismatch is increased we would expect him or her to experience at least a transient state of stress. Second, in order to predict whether such a stress state is likely to persist or be resolved (or, perhaps more fundamentally, what form the adaptive process will take), we should have some knowledge about the individual's executive skill. A high capacity for control allows task goals to be attained with minimal disturbance. This will normally reduce stress by removing the primary source of cognitive discomfort (the perception of failure to attain goals), though the outcome will depend also on the costs of control. Hockey (1986b) has described several alternative control strategies which are associated with different patterns of performance, subjective state and physiological costs. When tasks are too difficult to manage without excessive effort, individuals may protect either performance levels or their physiological state, but not both. The dynamics of such strategy decisions need to be explored systematically if we are to understand the contribution of cognitive variability to coping with computer stress.

CONCLUSIONS

The impact of computing systems on working life is associated with changes not only in the details of jobs, but in the way in which work is organized and integrated within the social structure of the organization. While stress is a natural consequence of any work, we have argued in this chapter that the change to working in a computer environment may present more difficulties of coping and adaptation than many work situations. Although there is little systematic evidence that currently allows us to define this area of research clearly, the parallels with other aspects of occupational stress have allowed us to attempt a preliminary integration of this scattered literature. Problems associated with hardware seem unlikely to play a significant role in future developments, except where the technology allows the introduction of systems which are too complex for comfortable working. Software developments are also reducing the major sources of stress associated with earlier human–computer dialogue designs. Major practical problems remain to be solved concerning the ways in which computer working is introduced and integrated into organizational practice, though the broad principles appropriate for minimizing operator stress are quite well established. The most promising areas for further research appear to be those of work demands and individual differences. Only when the nature of the work is known can the impact of technological changes be clearly assessed. The extent to which such changes will actually result in stress for an operator is likely to be most strongly determined by general cognitive and temperamental predispositions and skills.

REFERENCES

Alty, J. L. and Coombs, M. J. (1980). Face-to-face guidance of university computer users—I. A study of advisory services, *International Journal of Man–Machine Studies*, **12**, 389–405.

Arndt, S., Clevenger, J. and Meiskey, L. (1985). Students' attitudes toward computers, *Computers and the Social Sciences*, **1**, 181–90.

Armbruster, A. (1983). Ergonomic requirements. In H. J. Otway and M. Peltu (eds) *New Office Technology: Human and Organizational Aspects*, Frances Pinter, London.

Attewell, P. and Rule, J. (1984). Computing and organizations: what we know and what we don't know, *Communications of the ACM*, **27**, 1184–92.

Bannon, L. J. (1986). Helping users help each other. In D. A. Norman and S. W. Draper (eds) *User Centered System Design: New Perspectives on Human–Computer Interaction*, Lawrence Erlbaum, Hillsdale, NJ.

Barber, R. E. and Lucas, H. C. (1983). System response time, operator productivity, and job satisfaction, *Communications of the ACM*, **26**, 972–86.

Binaschi, G., Albonico, G., Gelli, E. and di Popolo, M. R. M. (1983). Study on subjective symptomatology of fatigue in VDU operators. In E. Grandjean and E. Vigliani (eds) *Ergonomic Aspects of Visual Display Terminals*, Taylor and Francis, London.

Bird, E. (1980). *Information Technology in the Office: The Impact on Women's Jobs*, Equal Opportunities Commission, Manchester.

Bjorn-Andersen, N. (1983). The changing roles of secretaries and clerks. In H. J. Otway and M. Peltu (eds) *New Office Technology: Human and Organizational Aspects*, Frances Pinter, London.

Bjorn-Andersen, N. (1984). User-driven system design, *Work and People*, **10**, 17–23.

Blackler, F. and Brown, C. (1985). Evaluation and the impact of information technologies on people in organizations, *Human Relations*, **38**, 213–31.

Boddy, D. and Buchanan, D. A. (1981). Word processing in a marine engineering consultancy: Y-ARD, *Effective Computer Applications*, **1**, 36–59.

Buchanan, D. A. and Boddy, D. (1982). Advanced technology and the quality of working life: the effects of word processing on video typists, *Journal of Occupational Psychology*, **55**, 1–11.

Butera, F. and Thurman, J. E. (eds) (1984). *Automation and Work Design*, North-Holland, Amsterdam.

Cakir, A. (1986). Short paper: Towards an ergonomic design of software, *Behaviour and Information Technology*, **5** (1), 63–70.

Cakir, A., Hart, D. J. and Stewart, T. F. M. (1980). *Visual Display Terminals: A Manual Covering Ergonomics, Workplace Design, Health and Safety, Task Organization*, John Wiley and Sons, New York.

Card, S. K., English, W. K. and Burr, B. J. (1978). Evaluation of mouse, rate-controlled isometric joystick, step keys, and text keys for text selection on a CRT, *Ergonomics*, **21**, 601–13.

Carroll, J. M. (1984). Minimalist training, *Datamation*, 1 November, 125–36.

Carroll, J. M. (1985). Minimalist design for active users. In B. Shackel (ed.) *Human–Computer Interaction—INTERACT '84*, North-Holland, Amsterdam.

Cohen, B. G. F. (1984). Organizational factors affecting stress in the clerical worker. In B. G. F. Cohen (ed.) *Human Aspects in Office Automation*, Elsevier, Amsterdam.

Companion, M. A. and Corso, G. M. (1982). Task taxonomies: a general review and evaluation, *International Journal of Man–Machine Studies*, **17**, 459–72.

Cooper, C. L. and Cox, A. (1985). Occupational stress among word processor operators, *Stress Medicine*, **1**, 87–92.

Dainoff, M. J. (1982). Occupational stress factors in visual display terminal (VDT) operation: a review of empirical research. *Behaviour and Information Technology*, **1**, 141–76.

Dainoff, M. J., Happ, A. and Crane, P. (1981). Visual fatigue and occupational stress in VDT operators, *Human Factors*, **23**, 421–38.

DeVaris, P. E. (1981). The impact of electronics on humans and their work environments. In *Proceedings of the Conference on Human Factors in Computer Systems*, Gaithersburg, Maryland, March 1982. Association for Computing Machinery, New York.

Downing, H. (1980). Word processors and the oppression of women. In T. Forester (ed.) *The Microelectonics Revolution*, Basil Blackwell, Oxford.

Eason, K. D. (1982). The process of introducing information technology, *Behaviour and Information Technology*, **1**, 197–213.

Eason, K. D. (1984). Job design and VDU operation. In B. G. Pearce (ed.) *Health hazards of VDTs?* John Wiley and Sons, Chichester.

Elias, R., Tisserand, C. M. and Christmann, H. (1983). Investigations in operations working with CRT display terminals: relationships between task content and psychophysiological alterations. In E. Grandjean and E. Vigliani (eds) *Ergonomic Aspects of Visual Display Terminals*, Taylor and Francis, London.

Fleishman, E. A. and Quaintance, M. K. (1984). *Taxonomies of Human Performance: The Description of Human Tasks*, Academic Press, Orlando, FL.

Giuliano, V. E. (1985). The mechanization of office work. In T. Forester (ed.) *The Information Technology Revolution*, Basil Blackwell, Oxford.

Gomez, L. M., Egan, D. E. and Bowers, C. (1986). Learning to use a text editor: some learner characteristics that predict success. *Human–Computer Interaction*, **2**, 1–23.

Grandjean, E. (1987). *Ergonomics in computerized offices*, Taylor and Francis, London.

Greenstein, J. S. and Arnaut, L. Y. (1987). Human factors aspects of manual computer input devices. In G. Salvendy (ed.) *Handbook of Human Factors*, John Wiley and Sons, New York.

Gregory, J. and Nussbaum, K. (1982). Race against time: automation in the office. An analysis of the trends in office automation and the impact on the office workforce. *Office: Technology and People*, **1**, 197–236.

Hacker, W. and Schonfelder, E. (1986). Job organisation and allocation of functions between man and computer—I. Analysis and assessment. In F. Klix and H. Wandke (eds) *Man-Computer Interaction Research: MACINTER—I*, Elsevier, Amsterdam.

Hackman, J. R. and Oldham, G. R. (1975). Development of the Job Diagnostic Survey, *Journal of Applied Psychology*, **60**, 159–70.

Health and Safety Executive (1983). *Visual Display Units*, HMSO, London.

Helmreich, R. (1985). Human aspects of office systems—user acceptance research results. In B. Shackel (ed.) *Human–Computer Interaction—INTERACT '84*, North–Holland, Amsterdam.

Hockey, G. R. J. (1984). Varieties of attentional state: the effects of environment. In R. Parasuraman and D. R. Davies (eds) *Varieties of Attention*, Academic Press, New York.

Hockey, G. R. J. (1986a). Changes in operator efficiency as a function of environmental stress, fatigue, and circadian rhythms. In K. R. Boff, L. Kaufman and J. P. Thomas (eds) *Handbook of Perception and Human Performance*. Vol. 2. *Cognitive Processes and Performance*, John Wiley and Sons, New York.

Hockey, G. R. J. (1986b). A state control theory of adaptation and individual differences in stress management. In G. R. J. Hockey, A. W. K. Gaillard and M. G. H. Coles (eds) *Energetics and Human Information Processing*, Martinus Nijhoff, Dordrecht.

Hockey, G. R. J. (in press). Styles, skills and states: Implications of cognitive variability for the role of mental models in HCI. In D. Ackerman and M. J. Tauber (eds) *Mental Models and Human–Computer Interaction*.

Hollnagel, E., Mancini, G. and Woods, D. D. (1986). *Intelligent Decision Support in Process Environments*. Springer, Berlin.

Howard, G. S. and Smith, R. D. (1986). Computer anxiety in management: myth or reality? *Communications of the ACM*, **7**, 611–15.

Howarth, P. A. and Istance, H. O. (1985). The association between visual discomfort and the use of visual display units. *Behaviour and Information Technology*, **4**, 131–49.

Hutchins, E. L., Hollan, J. D. and Norman, D. A. (1985). Direct manipulation interfaces, *Human–Computer Interaction*, **1**, 331–8.

Huutanen, P. (1984). Implementation of an ADP-system to calculate salaries: evaluation of the implementation process and changes in job content and work load. In E. Grandjean (ed.) *Ergonomics and Health in Modern Offices*, Taylor and Francis, London.

Iriving, R. H., Higgins, C. A. and Safayeni, F. R. (1986). Computerized performance monitoring systems: use and abuse, *Communications of the ACM*, **29**, 794–801.

Johansson, G. and Aronsson, G. (1984). Stress reactions in computerized administrative work, *Journal of Occupational Behaviour*, **5**, 159–81.

Johansson, G., Aronsson, G. and Lindstrom, B. O. (1978). Social psychological and neuroendocrine reactions in highly mechanised work, *Ergonomics*, **21**, 583–99.

Kahn, H. and Cooper, C. L. (1986). Computing stress. *Current Psychological Research & Reviews*, Summer, 148–62.

Kalimo, R. and Leppanen, A. (1985). Feedback from video display terminals, performance control and stress in text preparation in the printing industry, *Journal of Occupational Psychology*, **58**, 27–38.

Karasek, R. A. (1979). Job demands, job decision latitude, and mental strain: implications for job redesign. *Administrative Science Quarterly*, **24**, 285–308.

Karasek, R. A. (1982). Job decision latitude, job design, and coronary heart disease. In G. Salvendy and M. J. Smith (eds) Machine pacing and occupational stress, Taylor and Francis, London.

Karat, J., McDonald, J. E. and Anderson, M. (1986). A comparison of menu selection techniques: touch panel, mouse and keyboard, *International Journal of Man–Machine Studies*, **25**, 73–88.

Kling, R. (1983). Social goals in systems planning and development. In H. J. Otway and M. Peltu (eds) *New Office Technology: Human and Organizational Aspects*, Frances Pinter, London.

Kling, R. and Scacchi, W. (1982). The web of computing: computer technology as social organization. In *Advances in Computers*, Vol. 21, Academic Press, New York.

Lang, K, Auld, R. and Lang, T. (1982). The goals and methods of computer users, *International Journal of Man–Machine Studies*, **17**, 375–99.

Laubli, T. and Grandjean, E. (1984). The magic of control groups. In E. Grandjean (ed.) *Ergonomics and Health in Modern Offices*, Taylor and Francis, London.

Laurel, B. K. (1986). Interface as mimesis. In D. A. Norman and S. W. Draper (eds) *User Centered System Design: New Perspectives on Human–Computer Interaction*, Lawrence Erlbaum, Hillsdale, NJ.

Long, R. J. (1984). The application of microelectronics to the office: organisational and human implications. In N. Piercy (ed.) *The Management Implications of New Information Technology*, Croom Helm, London.

Lundberg, U. and Frankenhaueser, M. (1978). Psychophysiological reactions to noise as modified by personal control over noise intensity, *Biological Psychology*, **6**, 55–59.

Mackay, C. (1980). *Human Factors Aspects of Visual Display Unit Operation*, Health and Safety Executive Research Paper 10, HMSO, London.

Mulder, G. and Mulder, L. J. M. (1981). Task-related cardiovascular stress. In J. Long and A. D. Baddeley (eds) *Attention and Performance*, Vol. 9, Lawrence Erlbaum, Hillsdale, NJ.

Mumford, E. (1979). Conclusions. In N. Bjorn–Andersen, B. Hedberg, D. Mercer, E. Mumford and A. Sole (eds) *The impact of systems change in organisations*, Sijthoff and Noordhoff, Alphen aan den Rijn, The Netherlands.

Mumford, E. (1983). Successful systems design. In H. J. Otway and M. Peltu (eds) *New Office Technology: Human and Organizational Aspects*, Frances Pinter, London.

Nisbitt, R. E. and Wilson, T. D. (1977). Telling more than we can know: verbal reports on mental processes, *Psychological Review*, **8**, 231–59.

Norman, D. A. (1984). Worsening the knowledge gap: the mystique of computation builds unnecessary barriers. In H. R. Pagels (ed.) *Computer Culture: The Scientific, Intellectual, and Social Impact of the Computer. Annals of the New York Academy of Sciences*, Vol. 426, The New York Academy of Sciences, New York.

Norman, D. A. (1986). Cognitive engineering. In D. A. Norman and S. W. Draper (eds) *User Centered System Design: New Perspectives on Human–Computer Interaction*, Lawrence Erlbaum, Hillsdale, NJ.

Nygaard, K. (1980). Workers' participation in system development. In A. Mowshowitz (ed.) *Human Choice and Computers*, Vol. 2, North–Holland, Amsterdam.

Oborne, D. J. (1985). *Computers at Work: A Behavioural Approach*, John Wiley and Sons, Chichester.

Pearce, B. G. (1984). Trades unions and ergonomic problems. In B. G. Pearce (ed.) *Health Hazards of VDTs?* John Wiley and Sons, Chichester.

Rich, E. (1983). Users are individuals: individualizing user models, *International Journal of Man-Machine Studies*, **18**, 199–214.

Robertson, I. T. (1985). Human information-processing strategies and style, *Behaviour and Information Technology*, **4**, 19–29.

Rowe, C. (1986). *People and Chips: The Human Implications of Information Technology*, Paradigm Publishing, London.

Salvendy, G. (1982). Human–computer communication with special reference to technological developments, occupational stress, and educational needs, *Ergonomics*, **25**, 435–47.

Sauter, S. L., Harding, G. E., Gottlieb, M. S. and Quackenboss, J. J. (1981). VDT-computer automation of work practices as a stressor in information-processing jobs: some methodological considerations. In G. Salvendy and M. J. Smith (eds) *Machine pacing and occupational stress*, Taylor and Francis, London.

Sebrechts, M. M., Deck, J. G., Wagner, R. K. and Black, J. B. (1984). How human abilities affect component skills in word processing, *Behaviour Research Methods, Instruments, and Computers*, **16**, 234–7.

Sheil, B. A. (1983). Coping with complexity, *Office: Technology and People*, **1**, 295–320.

Shneiderman, B. (1980). *Software Psychology*, Winthrop, Cambridge, MA.

Shneiderman, B. (1987). *Designing the User Interface: Strategies for Effective Human--computer Interaction*, Addison–Wesley, Reading, MA.

Smith, M. J. (1984). Health issues in VDT work. In J. Bennett, D. Case, J. Sandelin and M. J. Smith (eds) *Visual Display Terminals: Usability Issues and Health Concerns*, Prentice–Hall, Englewood Cliffs, NJ.

Smith, M. J., Stammerjohn, L. W., Cohen, B. F. and Lalich, N. R. (1983). Job stress in video display operations. In E. Grandjean and E. Vigliani (eds) *Ergonomic Aspects of Visual Display Terminals*, Taylor and Francis, London.

Stellman, J. M., Klitzman, S., Gordon, G. C. and Snow, B. R. (1987). Work environment and the well-being of clerical VDT workers, *Journal of Occupational Behaviour*, **8**, 95–114.

Sternberg, R. J. (1986). Intelligence is mental self-government. In R. J. Sternberg and D. K. Detterman (eds), *What is Intelligence?* Ablex, Norwood, NJ.

Turner, J. A. (1984). Computer mediated work: the interplay between technology and structured jobs, *Communications of the ACM*, **27**, 1210–17.

Turner, J. A. and Karasek, R. A. (1984). Software ergonomics: effects of computer application design parameters on operator task performance and health, *Ergonomics*, **27**, 663–90.

Veer, G. C. van der, Tauber, M. J., Waren, Y. and Muylwijk, B. van. (1985). On the interaction between system and user characteristics, *Behaviour and Information Technology*, **4**, 289–308.

Wainwright, J. and Francis, A. (1984). *Office Automation, Organisation and the Nature of Work*, Gower, Aldershot.

Wall, T. D., Clegg, C. W., Davies, R. T., Kemp, N. J. and Mueller, W. S. (1987). Advanced manufacturing technology and work simplification: an empirical study, *Journal of Occupational Behaviour*, **8**, 233–50.

Widiger, T. A., Knudson, R. M. and Rorer, L. G. (1980). Convergent and discriminant validity of measures of cognitive style and abilities, *Journal of Personality and Social Psychology* **39**, 116–29.

Wisner, A. (1981). Organizational stress, cognitive load and mental suffering. In G. Salvendy and M. J. Smith (eds), *Machine Pacing and Occupational Stress*, Taylor and Francis, London.

Zoltan, E. (1981). How acceptable are computers to professional persons? In *Proceedings of the Conference on Human Factors in Computer Systems*, Gaithersburg, Maryland, March 1982, Association for Computing Machinery, New York.

Chapter 5

Nonwork Roles and Stress at Work

Barbara A. Gutek, Rena L. Repetti, and Deborah L. Silver

In recent years, researchers have begun to realize that people do not work in a vacuum; behavior on the job is often influenced by experiences in other role arenas. This chapter reviews research on the effects of outside influences on job stress. Several caveats are in order before we begin. First, influences outside of the workplace, sometimes referred to as 'nonwork' in the organizational literature (Kabanoff, 1980; Near, Rice and Hunt, 1980), are reduced for the most part to family variables. The emphasis is justified in that family life is generally the most important aspect of a person's life (Andrews and Withey, 1976; Etzion, 1984; Pleck and Lang, 1978) and contributes heavily, along with job satisfaction, to general life satisfaction (Campbell, Converse and Rodgers, 1976; Kabanoff, 1980; Near *et al.*, 1984; Rice, 1984). Other nonwork factors such as health or leisure are much less frequently studied as factors affecting job stress.

Second, because the literature on nonwork roles lacks specificity in defining job stress and other job-relevant variables (Gutek, Nakamura and Nieva, 1981), we use the term job stress loosely, more loosely than most of the other chapters in this volume. We include research examining the effects of nonwork roles on job satisfaction, job commitment and perceived productivity, as well as studies that focus on psychological strain, an expected outcome of job stress (Bhagat *et al.*, 1985; Repetti, 1987a; see Kahn *et al.*, 1964, for a frequently used model of job stress and psychological strain). Of the studies that do measure job stress, most eschew complex or multiple measures of job stress in favor of one or a few items in a self-report inventory. In addition, as a result of selection of subjects or sampling procedure, samples are frequently restricted to one occupational group or one organization.

Third, unlike most of the literature on work, women rather than men tend to be the subjects. The development of interest in nonwork factors that affect work coincided with an increase in women's employment and research on working women (Gutek, Larwood and Stromberg, 1986). Social scientists have reasoned that because women traditionally have primary responsibility for family and household affairs, family matters should be especially likely to affect their work performance and experience of stress at work (cf. Kanter, 1977a; Pleck, 1977). Related to this point is the fourth caveat—research investigating work–nonwork relationships must be viewed within a rapidly changing context. Because of the importance of social and historical factors, findings from older research pieces may not be replicated in the present. Therefore, our review emphasizes recent findings.

LINKING PROCESSES

Our discussion of the ways in which circumstances outside work may affect job stress will center on three types of connections between an employed person's life at work and life outside work. First, we address the number and compatibility of demands and benefits associated with family and paid work domains, role processes. Second, the employed person's emotional state or psychological well-being is viewed as a medium through which outside conditions can influence and change experiences at work, a spillover process. Finally, we consider how values, skills and attitudes may be transmitted from one domain to the other, a socialization process. The three connecting processes, which may function independently or simultaneously, help to organize our discussion of the empirical research literature with the ultimate goal of explaining *how* a day, or a year, at work may be colored both by specific family events or by more stable home characteristics.

Role processes analyze the distribution of an individual's time, energy and opportunities between social roles, for example, paid worker and parent. Three approaches, each with different sets of assumptions and predictions, can be identified in the literature. The *interrole conflict* approach accounts for situations in which the behaviors required to enact occupational and family roles are incompatible. Survey respondents typically identify interrole scheduling conflicts as one of the most significant problems they face (Fournier and Engelbrecht, 1982; Pleck and Staines, 1982; Pleck, Staines and Lang, 1980). A *role overload* position assumes that the two role arenas compete for personal resources and predicts that an individual can easily become overburdened by the combination of demands. Problems with time and scheduling in work and family roles are usually viewed as examples of interrole conflict, whereas a limited amount of personal energy to meet multiple demands and resulting fatigue are viewed as examples of role overload. Both role processes are usually associated with the individual's subjective experience of role strain or job dissatisfaction (Cooke and Rousseau, 1984; Parasuraman and Cleek, 1984). In contrast, a *role accumulation* perspective suggests that the benefits of multiple roles sum, so that opportunities for social interaction, personal development and self esteem increase by combining roles (Sieber, 1974). Each approach describes a different mechanism through which family structure and roles are linked to occupational role enactment.

Consider a week-long visit from relatives. The effect that this family event might have on one's occupational role can be analyzed from each of the three role perspectives. Strain may increase because a planned family outing on the weekend conflicts with a need for extra work at the office. From a role overload perspective, an evening of family celebration might leave the employee fatigued at work the next day. According to the role accumulation theory, however, the mere presence of additional family members may have a positive impact on the employee. Role theorists have suggested that because of a supportive atmosphere, family activities may actually create energy that can be used in other role arenas (Marks, 1977).

Spillover processes describe the effects that family events can have on job adjustment due to a change in the employed person's emotional well-being. Although the term spillover has been used in a number of different ways by authors in this area (see e.g. Nieva and Gutek, 1981; Gutek, 1985; Crouter, 1984), the term is most often used in a general way to characterize a relationship between work and nonwork that results in similar experiences and reactions in the two domains (Near *et al.*, 1984; Rousseau, 1978). As such, spillover is usually contrasted with compensation, a process in which an individual seeks opposite experiences and satisfactions at work and at home in order to make up for deficiencies in one of the settings (Champoux, 1978; Evans and Bartolome, 1984; Kabanoff, 1980; Kornhauser, 1965; Rousseau, 1978). In this chapter, the term spillover is used in a more specific manner, referring to a short-term process through which an affective state generated in one setting spills over into the other setting (Piotrkowski, 1979; Repetti, 1987b).

When feelings engendered at home are later expressed at work, the effects may be observed in an employee's motivation and job performance as well as in the interpersonal realm. For example, the joy associated with a child's first steps may permeate work–family boundaries and be noticed by co-workers. Of course, dysphoric mood states are also transferred to the workplace. Consider an employee whose unsatisfying marriage constrains her personal relations at work because she is preoccupied with marital worries and is reluctant to burden co-workers with her problems.

Investigators studying spillover processes have been concerned with the way that experiences from work are conveyed in the family as well as the way experiences in the family are expressed at work (Valdez and Gutek, 1987). In fact, most research has focused on the injection of job stress into the home (Kanter, 1977a; Piotrkowski, Rapoport and Rapoport, 1987). For example, in a study involving bank tellers, Repetti (1987b) interviewed one woman who claimed, 'When I've had a bad day, the first people that hit me are the people at home, so I take it out on them I guess' (p. 117).

Socialization processes suggest that values, skills and attitudes learned at home influence an employed person's behavior within the job setting. Learning may occur some time in the past, for example vocational socialization acquired from parents during childhood (Mortimer, 1976), or it may take place in the present, such as a supervisor's ability to be supportive because being a parent calls for patience and understanding on a daily basis. In both cases it is assumed that important behavioral and attitudinal styles shaped over time in the family have long-term consequences for work adjustment.

Not all behavioral styles that are functional at home will be adaptive at work. For example, family systems theory suggests that a high level of cohesion, or emotional bonding among family members, is an effective response to stress (Olson, 1986). Yet disengagement, quite the opposite of cohesion, has been found in at least one study to be the most efficacious coping mechanism in the workplace (Pearlin and Schooler, 1978). Sex differences in family training may be particularly dysfunctional for employed women. Hoffman (1972) has argued that daughters often are not encouraged in their early independence strivings and, as a result, become less oriented toward achievement. Dexter (1985) has taken the position that the early family experiences of daughters do not prepare them to exercise power, a critical skill in management.

Before reviewing substantive research findings in more detail, it is important to highlight a few points about linkages between family and occupational variables.

Circularity

The relation between family system variables and job stress is reciprocal. Although this chapter emphasizes the effects that family circumstances can have on an employed member's job stress, a substantially larger body of research addresses the opposite question: how do occupational experiences affect the family? A growing literature in the social sciences, often labeled 'work–family research' is primarily devoted to studying the carry-over of job experiences into the family (e.g. Repetti, 1987b; Piotrkowski *et al.*, 1987). Kanter (1977a) contended that the effects of work on family are studied more than the effects of family on work because of 'a comfortable economic determinism—the centrality of work in setting the conditions for family life' (p. 53). She noted that although it is commonly assumed families must adjust to conditions of work, conditions of work could adjust to family circumstances.

While many of the ideas and empirical findings discussed in the chapter originated in research on the effects that jobs have on families, correlational designs render the perspective from which the investigation is conducted a moot point. For example, a statistically significant correlation between marital satisfaction and job satisfaction may be interpreted as support for opposite causal propositions — one asserting that a high level of job satisfaction leads to greater satisfaction with one's marriage and the other asserting that marital happiness leads to increased satisfaction at work. For this reason, experimental and quasi-experimental research designs are needed in order to advance the field beyond simple conclusions that work and family variables are related to one another. Orpen (1978), for example, examined cross-lagged correlations between measures of work and nonwork satisfaction taken one year apart and found evidence that job satisfaction has a stronger effect on nonwork satisfaction than vice-versa.

Neutrality

The three connecting mechanisms—role processes, spillover, and socialization—are neutral with regard to valence; each can result in either a positive or a negative outcome. Similarly, the net effect of nonwork roles on job outcomes does not have a predetermined valence. It is the nature of experiences at home as well as job characteristics that determine whether the carry-over process results in an increase or decrease in strain. To cite a common example, a person socialized in team sports has an advantage in jobs that emphasize collaboration or team participation (cf. Harragan, 1977). On the other hand, a person socialized to be nurturant may be less stressed than others in jobs requiring interpersonal skills like empathy and the provision of emotional support. When considered out of context, it is often impossible to specify how a particular family event will affect an individual's job adjustment. The context to be considered should include individual, family and occupational characteristics.

Group asymmetries

Certain group differences seem to play an important role in determining the degree and manner in which a particular family circumstance influences occupational life. Sex is probably the single most important individual characteristic to consider. Gender asymmetries (Crosby, 1987) exist for two reasons—men and women tend to hold different types of jobs and they usually play very different roles in the family. For example, a child's illness may be more likely to affect women at work because mothers typically carry a disproportionate share of the responsibility for child care. Socioeconomic status, which is associated with a number of occupational and family characteristics, acts as another important group moderator variable. High prestige jobs may entail greater time commitments and job involvement but also offer greater security and more scheduling flexibility (Nieva and Gutek, 1981). The latter two job characteristics, job security and flexible schedules, are critical coping resources during family crises. A family's developmental stage may be the source of another group asymmetry. Based on their interviews with managers, Evans and Bartolome (1984) have suggested that different linking processes become more salient at different points in the family's life cycle.

PLAN OF THE CHAPTER

In this chapter, we review the research on outside influences on job stress and related job outcomes, using the linking processes and issues described above to organize our discussion. Most of the literature focuses on family variables and this review is no exception. First, we examine the roles of spouse and parent as these affect job stress and satisfaction. In doing so, we review characteristics of other family members—husband or wife and children—that influence stress at work. We then examine two particular aspects of family life that might affect levels of job stress, social support provided by family members and the division of labor in the family. After examining influences of specific roles, we review a related body of work on the effects of the number and stability of social roles on job stress. Whether a person has two major roles (e.g. worker and spouse) or three (e.g. worker, spouse, parent) may be important, independent of the characteristics of any single role. In the final section, we evaluate the overall effects of nonwork roles on stress at work and discuss characteristics of research in this area, as well as areas that sorely require additional attention.

REVIEW OF THE LITERATURE ON NONWORK ROLES

Marriage and Divorce

Marriage

When the job attitudes of married and single people are compared, there is a consistent finding—the married portion of the sample reports higher levels of job satisfaction (Bersoff and Crosby, 1984; Crosby, 1984; Valdez and Gutek, 1987). Spillover processes may account best for the more positive work experiences reported by married employees (Crosby, 1982). Moderate positive correlations have been reported between positive moods at home and on the job (Piotrkowski and Katz, 1983). Others have found greater marital satisfaction and adjustment associated with increased job satisfaction (Bailyn, 1970; Barling and Rosenbaum, 1986; Kemper and Reichler, 1976), more positive job mood (Piotrkowski and Crits–Christoph, 1981), lower levels of job tension and stress (Barling and Rosenbaum, 1986; Houston and Kelly, 1985) and, among dual-earner couples, greater approval of the paid employment role for women (Repetti, 1987b).

It seems paradoxical that, despite the apparent greater contentment of married employees, marriage often appears to limit occupational achievement, particularly for women. Based on her analysis of the literature, Laws (1979) concluded that for women, marriage and children had a much greater negative impact on employment than employment had on marriage and children. Studies of successful professionals frequently show that high achieving men are married whereas high achieving women tend to be unmarried (e.g. Herman and Gyllstrom, 1977; Houseknecht, Vaughan and Stratham, 1987), suggesting that occupational attainment may be more difficult for a woman if she is married than if she is unmarried. In a retrospective study, Stewart (1980) found that those women who married and those who had children were less persistent in their career pursuits. There is also evidence that a wife's postmarital educational gains show little relation to subsequent occupational attainment (Sharda and Nangle, 1982). In another study, Houseknecht *et al.* (1987) found that women who remained single in graduate school achieved greater occupational attainment than those women who married while still students. Furthermore, Houseknecht *et al.* (1987) found that women who married after completion of graduate school achieved less occupationally than women who remained unmarried. In short, women appear to sacrifice potential career attainment when they marry.

Role processes seem to offer the best explanation for the negative effects that marriage can have on women's occupational attainment. Mortimer, Hall and Hill (1978) have described how certain attributes of a husband's job may constrain both his time and motivation to contribute to family-role activities which, in turn, reduces career opportunities for wives. Presumably single women, with fewer family responsibilities, do not face the same blocks to career success. Compared with singles, married women do report more role conflict in areas such as time and household management (Nevill and Damico, 1975). It is employed women in low quality marriages who appear to suffer most from interrole conflict, interrole overload and home management stress (Repetti, in press; Thomas, Albrecht and White, 1982). Interrole conflict probably also helps to explain why a substantial minority of employed married women work part-time (Johnson, 1979).

Men's experiences serve as a sharp contrast to women's. While women appear to have lower career attainment when they marry, men seem to do better. Talbert and Bose (1977) found that compared with singles, married male clerks received an average annual pay *differential* of $650, regardless of their location in the retail stores which were studied. Similarly, in an analysis of national longitudinal data, Pfeffer and Ross (1982) found that married men earned an average of $2000–$3801 more than unmarried men. Being married was also predictive of men's occupational prestige, but only for managers, not professional or blue collar men.

Pfeffer and Ross (1982) interpreted their findings as supportive of two hypotheses: wife as a career resource and conformance to social expectations.

The notion of wife as a valuable career resource comes from Kanter (1977b) who identified four contributions of a wife's work to her husband's career: direct substitution for the work of a paid employee, indirect support including entertaining, consultation and advice giving, and emotional support which keeps the husband motivated and interested in his work. Kanter (1977b) found evidence of all four types of contributions in her study of wives of corporate managers. In a recent study, Roby and Uttal (1988) found that some male married union stewards report that their wives helped to write their speeches, handled their correspondence, and the like, whereas none of the female married union stewards reported that their husbands performed such tasks for them. Fowlkes (1980) has similarly shown how wives often contribute both directly and indirectly to the successful careers of male professors and physicians. She found, for example, that these women some-times served such functions as 'girl Friday' and junior colleague. Earlier, Papanek (1973) had described the two-person single career, which was defined by the formal and informal demands placed on *both* members of a couple by an institution employing only the husband. Indeed, in 1971 a popular business magazine advised executives to have their wives act as 'traveling secretaries' when accompanying their husbands on business trips (*Dun's Review*, 1971).

Pfeffer and Ross (1982) also interpreted their findings as supportive of conformance to social expectations. They argued that within our society, men are supposed to support a wife and are rewarded for doing so. For men, marriage represents an opportunity to take on 'the good provider role' (Bernard, 1981) whereas for women marriage can represent a source of conflict with her employment.

Studies investigating the effects of marriage on job satisfaction (favorable) and career attainment and income (favorable for men; perhaps negative for women) usually treat the relationships as causal, but most are cross-sectional. Given the associations, it is equally plausible to suggest that occupational experiences affect marriages as to suggest the reverse. Indeed, a growing literature examines the effects of a wife's employment status and both spouses' job conditions on marriages (e.g. Gove and Peterson, 1980; Piotrkowski *et al.*, 1987; Repetti, 1987b).

Experimental and quasi-experimental research designs are promising, but infrequently used for investigating linkages between work and family systems. For example, in a recent time-sample study involving air traffic controllers, Repetti (1987c) collected measures of perceived job stress and marital inter-action on three consecutive days and found evidence of reciprocal relations between the two sets of variables. Controllers' ratings of a fast pace and increased air traffic volume at work were associated with social withdrawal during interactions with their spouses on subsequent days. At the same time, angry and tense marital interactions on previous days were followed by perceptions of increased taskload at work. The findings support the proposition that conditions at work influence marital behavior and that experiences at home affect perceptions of stress levels at work.

Divorce

Just as a marital relationship can have a significant impact on one's work life, so too can the termination of a marriage through divorce. Crosby (1985) conducted in-depth interviews with recently divorced managers and found that the large majority described at least a few months of impaired job functioning following the divorce. Poor concentration was the single greatest problem both prior to the divorce and after; motivational deficits and absence from work were also mentioned. Another manifestation of work disturbance, shortened tempers, was identified by Crosby as 'deflected anger' because it appeared to represent a spillover of feelings from the divorce to the job setting. According to managers, the spillover of anger sometimes interfered with good decision-making at work.

Crosby (1985) also uncovered positive outcomes of divorce. The separation and divorce process seemed to arouse or energize some managers, leading to increased productivity at work. Another benefit was learning what occurred as a result of the traumatic experience—many managers reported that they became more sensitive and tolerant of co-workers and subordinates.

Divorce appears to have different effects on men and women's job commitments. Economists have suggested that the rise in frequency of divorce may account for one-third of the unexplained increase in women's postwar labor-force participation (Johnson and Skinner, 1986). Other studies indicate that currently divorced and separated mothers are more likely to be employed and to seek employment compared with remarried mothers (Beller and Graham, 1985). Although separation and divorce appear to increase the average number of hours a woman spends in paid employment, the dissolution of a marriage seems to marginally reduce the work effort of men (Crosby, 1985; Johnson and Skinner, 1986). This gender asymmetry may be due to the different accommodations that are made in men's and women's family roles following a divorce. Husbands' withdrawal from their jobs may be associated with the loss of their wives' home labor. Women may increase their hours in the labor-force to compensate for the loss of their husband's income.

Is there evidence that occupational experiences influence the divorce process? Women's labor-force participation does not appear to directly affect divorce probabilities (Johnson and Skinner, 1986). However, an interesting finding from Crosby's (1985) study was the extent to which work helped participants recover from the divorce. In their occupational roles, the managers claimed they found friends, an opportunity to rebuild self-esteem, a separate identity, absorbing activities, and some structure and purpose to their day. Most of the participants clearly believed that their jobs helped them adjust to the divorce.

Spouse's Characteristics

Characteristics of one's spouse also affect job-related stress. Two characteristics of the spouse, occupation and attitudes, have been the subject of substantial research.

Spouse's occupation

Before reviewing this literature, it is important to note some prominent gender asymmetries. Research on men is concerned simply with their wives' employment status, i.e. whether they are housewives vs employed in any job, whereas research on women is concerned with specific characteristics of husbands' occupations. It is taken for granted, perhaps erroneously, that husbands are employed. For a woman, the characteristics of her husband's job, such as the demands on his time and the expectation that his wife will act as an organizational member (e.g. corporate wife, faculty wife) are viewed as a contributors to her job stress.

Several studies have indicated that wives' employment is associated with negative job outcomes. Pfeffer and Ross (1982) reported that men whose wives are not employed earn more than men with employed wives. A wife's employment in a high-status job early in marriage may be somewhat detrimental to her husband's chances for future occupational mobility (Sharda and Nangle, 1982). Osherman and Dill (1983) found that having a wife with a career was negatively related to a husband's feeling successful at work, but not related to his feeling 'actualized' at work. In the Staines, Pottick and Fudge (1986) study, wives' employment had a small but statistically significant negative effect on husbands' job satisfaction ($r = -0.164$).

Various explanations for the link between wife's employment and husband's deleterious job outcomes have been advanced. Some men may have been socialized to expect that their participation in the workplace will serve as a means for participation in the family (Aldous, 1969) and as a means for gaining psychological satisfaction as the family provider (Bernard, 1981; Yankelovich, 1974). When their wives are employed, these men may feel that their identity as the good provider is threatened (Aldous, 1969; Yankelovich, 1974) and that they are losing family power (Ross, Mirowsky and Huber, 1983).

Others have argued that husbands may experience role overload and conflict when their wives are employed, especially if in demanding occupations (Lewis and Cooper, 1988; Ross *et al.*, 1983; Sekaran, 1986). The pressure wives may exert on husbands to attend to family matters (Sekaran, 1986) and increase participation in domestic activities (Young and Willmott, 1973) has been thought to create psychological strain for men (Sekaran, 1986). If husbands reallocate time and energy from work to family roles, their career development may suffer (Sekaran, 1986) as they may be penalized in the competition for job advancement (Pfeffer and Ross, 1982). However, as discussed below, recent evidence indicates that men with employed wives actually contribute very little extra household labor, relative to men whose wives are not employed.

Using the 1977 Quality of Employment data, Staines *et al.* (1986) explored four hypotheses regarding a possible negative effect of women's employment on husbands' job satisfaction. They were unable to find support for three of the four hypotheses: (1) potential added domestic burdens of having an employed wife, (2) possible constraints on mobility, (3) husband's disapproval of wife's employment status. They did find some support for their fourth hypothesis, that the wife's employment is taken as an indication that the husband is inadequate as a breadwinner. More specifically, when husbands' self-reports of inadequancy as a breadwinner were included in a multiple regression equation, the relation between their wives' employment status and their level of job satisfaction became nonsignificant. The findings of Staines *et al.* (1986) support Bernard's (1981) analysis of the good provider role. Bernard (1981) argued that a good provider not only provides money to pay for the family's goods and services, but provides in sufficient abundance that the other family members do not have to supply any money, and, in fact, can donate a considerable amount of time to spending the money brought home by the good provider. [Galbraith (1973) argued that in the 20th century, women have been assigned the role of consumer, which complements the male provider role.] Thus, socialization processes may explain the negative effects that a wife's employment sometimes seems to have on a husband's job satisfaction and job stress.

The issue of circularity deserves mention in this context. While researchers have been intrigued with the issue of negative impact of wives' jobs on men's job satisfaction and mental health, it should be noted that most studies employ cross-sectional data. Thus, the negative relationship could be interpreted in the other direction, i.e. a husband's dissatisfaction with his job and with his adequacy as a breadwinner might facilitate his wife's entry into the labor force.

There is little research on the impact of a man's occupation on his wife's job stress and satisfaction. Pleck (1977) argued that men are expected to allow work to interfere with their family lives whereas women are expected to allow family matters to interfere with their work lives. To the extent to which these expectations hold, a woman might be expected to experience job stress associated with constraints placed on her by her husband's job, e.g. limited ability to relocate for her own career, increased risk of inter-rupting her own career to relocate for her husband's career, reduction in her own career aspirations to accommodate her husband's career ambitions, or selection of part-time rather than full-time employment to accommodate her husband's career ambitions (see Nieva and Gutek, 1981, chapter. 3). In a comprehensive review of research on relocation and occupational advance-ment, Markham (1987) concluded that people who voluntarily relocate for their own career advancement gain an advantage over those who remain behind and that, compared with men, women move to advance their careers less often and are less willing to move.

Other research has shown that in dual-career couples, the couple more often moves to support the husband's career advancement than the wife's (e.g. Bryson *et al.*, 1976). In a series of studies, Wallston and her colleagues (Berger, Foster and Wallston, 1978; Foster, Wallston and Berger, 1980; Wallston, Foster and Berger, 1978) found that even when a young couple has an egalitarian strategy for selecting jobs (e.g. 'We will take the best job offer between us and the other partner will find a job in that location'), husbands get better offers and wives tend to make accommodations in their careers.

Certain attributes of her husband's occupation may also be related to a woman's career involvement. Winter, Stewart and McClelland (1977) found that wives of business executives were less likely than wives of other college graduates to be involved in a demanding career. A variety of studies of business executives show that they tend to be married to non-employed spouses (reviewed in Pfeffer and Ross, 1982; see also Kanter, 1977b).

These studies, like the studies of men's spouses, seem best explained by socialization processes. And like the studies of men's spouses, circularity is an issue in the study of employed women. We can infer that women's job possibilities are constrained by their husbands' occupational characteristics and that this creates job stress for them. On the other hand, women who are less interested in demanding, full-time careers may be more likely to select husbands who are executives or whose jobs demand frequent relo-cation. They may prefer to be part of a two-person career (Papanek, 1973) rather than to have their own career.

Spouses' attitudes

Spouses' attitudes, like their occupations, can have an effect on levels of job stress. Gender role attitudes held by the spouses of employed men and women may affect their adjustment to the demands of work and family roles. Research in this area is dominated by studies of husbands' reactions to their wives' career involvement. There is relatively little examination of wives' reactions to their husbands careers.

Women may be at risk when their occupational prestige or income equals or exceeds that of their spouses'. Tension between spouses in this situation can result in marital dissolution or downward occupational movement for women (see Hiller and Philliber, 1982). Sekaran (1986) discussed the compromises that successful women often make in order to avoid discomfort at home:

> The most common mechanism that wives have adopted to cope with competitive feelings in their husbands are to reject promotions, to try not to be too successful, and to keep a careful watch on how far they can outstrip their husbands without arousing strong competitive feelings. (p. 33)

The conclusion can easily be drawn that a reduction in work commitment, which wives of men with traditional sex-role attitudes may assume, creates tension for women on and off the job (Lewis and Cooper, 1988).

Not all of the evidence, however, suggests that women whose occupational status is superior to their husbands' experience strain and reduce their work commitment. Richardson (1979) found no association between wives' occupational prestige levels and marital happiness in a re-analysis of national sample data, and argued that this belief is a myth which is maintained because it is consistent with conventional sex-role attitudes. Sekaran (1986) claimed that women who achieve greater occupational status than their husbands are more able to establish egalitarian values in the family. Hiller and Philliber (1982) have argued that when spouses have traditional sex-role expectations and identities there is pressure on the wife not to exceed her husband's occupational achievements, but that androgynous couples are comfortable with either spouse having superior occupational attainments.

In the case of dual-earner couples, the very fact that both husband and wife are employed is a challenge to the prescribed norms under which each partner was socialized. A key factor in successful arrangements within dual-earner couples seems to be an appropriate match between husbands' and wives' expectations and attitudes (Bailyn, 1970; Sekaran, 1986). Beutell and Greenhaus (1982) found that similarity in career salience, irrespective of whether it is high or low, is associated with low work–family conflict. Similarly, the impact of a wife's employment on her own and her husband's depression depends on whether her employment is consistent with the preferences of both partners (Ross *et al.*, 1983). In contrast, dissimilarity between husbands' and wives' attitudes about family roles and wives' employment can cause tension which weakens mutual support systems and produces stress (Eiswirth–Neems and Handal, 1978).

Children and Childcare

Children, like spouses, appear to be a mixed blessing for employed people. Since the number and timing of children can be controlled to some extent today, men and women are able to consider the potential impacts of children on their work and adjust either accordingly. Today both sexes, but especially women, take their jobs into account when they consider having children. According to the US Department of Labor (1980), over one quarter of the women between ages 18 and 34 in 1979 reported that they do not expect to have children. This choice may reflect the belief that children will inhibit their career progress by creating role conflict and strain for them. In a study of factors influencing the timing of parenthood, Gormly, Gormly and Weiss (1987) found that 30% of college women but only 5% of college men indicated that they prefer to have children *after* they establish a career or achieve career goals.

In another study, Bronstein *et al.* (1987) found that women applicants for a position of assistant professor did not volunteer any information about their family status in their applications, whereas male applicants were much more open about their family status. In letters of recommendation, women's families were presented as obstacles, e.g. 'Despite the fact that Mary has a husband in law school and two preschool children, she performed brilliantly in our program.' In contrast, the men's families, especially their wives, were often presented as assets by the recommenders. The research by Bronstein *et al.* (1987) suggests that whether or not husbands and children actually are a source of interrole conflict for women, they are perceived to be so by others. In fact, employed mothers do complain more about a shortage of time than do fathers (Voydanoff and Kelly, 1984).

Gwartney–Gibbs (1988) has shown that the mere presence of children is an impediment to women's career advancement and Olson and Frieze (1987) showed that for women MBAs, the mere presence of children exerts a negative influence on salary. Pregnancy and the birth of a child also often lead to women's career changes (Thomas *et al.*, 1982) and temporary departures from the labor-force (Ewer, Crimmins and Oliver, 1979). Evidence suggests, however, that a self-selection process results in more career-oriented employees among those mothers who opt to return to work after the birth of an infant (Hock, Christman and Hock, 1980). Despite this, new mothers frequently discover that their job responsibilities have been reduced due to supervisorial expectations that they will not exhibit a high level of job involvement (Lewis, 1986, cited in Lewis and Cooper, 1988). Perhaps to compensate for the temporary loss of income from their wives, fathers of young children are likely to work longer hours than at later points in the family's life cycle (Moen and Moorehouse, 1983).

It is not only the presence, number and ages of children that affect parents' work lives. Research with employed women and their children suggests that better mother–child relations are associated with such desirable occupational outcomes as increased job satisfaction and positive job mood (Harrell and Ridley, 1975; Piotrkowski and Katz, 1983). Despite parental misgivings about combining children and a career, children, like spouses, appear to have a positive effect on parents' job satisfaction (Bersoff and Crosby, 1984; Crosby, 1984). Other researchers have found that mothers of children with few behavior problems report greater job satisfaction and less work–family role conflict (Barling and Van Bart, 1984). Investigators are not yet able to distinguish the effect that children have on parents' job experiences from the effect that parental enjoyment of work has on children. At the moment it seems plausable to assume that a spillover from family to work can only be beneficial when parents have good relations with their children.

Mothers' employment experiences cannot be understood without considering childcare arrangements. Indeed, a substantial proportion of employed female respondents to national surveys cite the unavailability of satisfactory childcare as a major problem they face and a constraint on the number of hours they work (National Commission on Working Women, 1979; Presser, 1986). Angrist, Lave and Mickelson (1977) studied samples of professional/managerial and clerical/technical women and found that one-third of the women reported that they take time off from work to care for a sick child. Salkevar (1981) also found that the number of hours a mother devotes to paid employment depends on the health of her children. A study of Canadians (Northcott, 1983) showed that employed mothers stay at home with sick children much more frequently than employed fathers do.

As McCartney and Phillips (in press) point out, historically there has been an uneasy relation between motherhood and childcare in the United States. They assert that 'the ideal of the stay-at-home mother continues to provide the norm against which personal decisions are judged', resulting in today's many 'conflicted' employed mothers. Hock (1985) has identified and measured maternal separation anxiety, a distressing emotional state that occurs when a parent is apprehensive about transfering the care of her infant to a caregiver. Gnezda and Hock (1983) found that women who displayed low maternal separation anxiety scored high on a measure of career investment. In another study, satisfaction with substitute childcare predicted mothers' greater job satisfaction (Harrell and Ridley, 1975). Mothers apparently find their jobs more pleasurable and involving when they are comfortable with the care their children receive while they are at work.

Social scientists have only begun to address the question of how fathers' occupational adjustment might be affected by relations with their offspring and by caregiver arrangements. The limited research that is available indicates that fathers are not as concerned nor as involved as employed mothers are with planning for childcare. Mothers express a stronger desire for work-setting facilities and policies, such as on-site daycare and family emergency days off (Sekaran, 1983), and assume greater responsibility for the planning and management of substitute care (Anderson and Leslie, 1987).

Social policy experts agree that there is a childcare problem in the United States and have called for organizational and government programs to address the needs of dual-earner families, including initiatives to facilitate greater father involvement in parenting (Kammerman, Kahn and Kingston, 1983; Pleck, 1986; Zigler and Gordon, 1982). The failure of government and organizations to acknowledge the needs of employed parents is at least partly influenced by the traditional assumption that men support children and nonemployed women raise them. However, there is evidence of change on the horizon.

How have some organizations responded to the childcare needs of their employees? In a thorough review of family-responsive corporate policies, Galinsky (1986) cited examples of practices related to work hours and location, such as flexitime, flexiplace, compressed work weeks, part-time work, job sharing and personal days off. Each of these are designed to provide employed parents with as much flexibility and freedom of choice as possible in meeting their multiple occupational and family responsibilities. Direct forms of support for childcare being adopted by some companies include resource and referral services for employees, reimbursement for the employee's childcare costs and the provision of sick childcare. Although actual on-site corporate childcare centers are rare, there are examples of alternative organizational initiatives like company support for existing local centers and the provision of start-up costs to employees to develop their own program (Galinsky, 1986).

Spouse and Family Support

Social support has been identified as a resource that helps individuals cope with job stress through supportive relationships with others (House 1981). Spouse and family support are often included in studies that investigate both work and nonwork sources of social support (Beehr, 1976; Ganster, Fusilier and Mayes, 1986). Family cohesion, or the emotional bonding among family members, is sometimes used as an indicator of family support. Families in general, and spouses in particular, serve as significant sources of social support for coping with both minor daily hassles and major stressful life events (Barbarin, Hughs and Chesler, 1985; Caplan, 1976; Cohen and Wills, 1985; McCubbin *et al.*, 1980). It is therefore not surprising that family support often plays an important role in an employed person's occupational life. In open-ended interviews and questionnaires, employed people often cite their families as one of their most important emotional resources for coping with job stress. In Crouter's (1984) interviews with employees of a large manufacturing plant, examples of positive spillover from home to job often focused on the supportive nature of family relationships.

An interesting consistency emerges when married people are asked to describe the kinds of work-related support that spouses provide; listening and offering advice about how to handle a problematic situation is the type of assistance that most often comes to mind. Repetti (1987b) learned from interviews with female clerical workers that an understanding and supportive husband can go a long way toward mitigating the immediate results of a stressful day at work. For example, one bank worker said: 'It's nice that my husband is always home to lend an ear . . . I get a lot of support and good advice from him' (p. 118). Weiss' (1985) intensive interviews with male professionals revealed that wives sometimes served as 'human relations consultants' by discussing problems that their husbands were having at work with peers, bosses or subordinates (see also Kanter, 1977b). When over 900 women were asked how they helped their spouses in job-related work, they most often described listening and acting as a sounding board as the support they provided, as well as the most frequent form of support they received from their husbands (Lopata, Barnewolt and Norr, 1980).

By what mechanism might support from family members reduce job stress? Indirect or buffering effects have been identified in the general literature on social support (Cohen and Wills, 1985). A buffering effect would suggest that family support reduces the relation between stressful experiences at work and the employed person's adjustment, such that under conditions of high family support job problems have less of an effect on the individual. According to the research cited above, employed men and women do perceive a mitigating function of family support.

Results from two studies, both based on quantitative analyses of self-report data, also suggest that spouse support can limit the deleterious effects of job-related stress. In one study, farm women's perceptions of spousal support (measured by their satisfaction with husbands' assistance in the household and with farm duties) were found to reduce the effect that the experience of role overload had on the women's level of distress. The more support a wife received from her husband, the weaker was the relation between her distress level and feelings of being overloaded with conflicting job- and family-role demands (Berkowitz and Perkins, 1984). Vanfossen (1981) similarly found that instrumental support from husbands reduced the impact that role overload had on depression, in a sample of employed women. Women who felt that they had more to do than they could handle suffered less if they also believed that they could rely on their husbands for help with family problems. Overloaded women who were not as sure of their husbands' support had higher rates of depression. For the husbands in Vanfossen's study, expressive support derived from a close and intimate marital relationship reduced the impact that a poor social climate at work had on depression.

In addition to buffering the effects of difficult conditions at work, support from a spouse and other family members may act directly on an employed individual's occupational life. In one study (Burke and Weir, 1977), after controlling for current job and life stressors, satisfaction with help from one's spouse in coping with tensions was a significant predictor of men's and women's job satisfaction. Repetti (1987b) reported that female bank workers' ratings of strong family cohesion, an indicator of support, were associated with perceptions of a more positive social climate at work.

Evidence suggests that wives are better providers of both instrumental and emotional support than are husbands. Employed women appear to facilitate their husbands' job performance more than their husbands help them (Gutek and Stevens, 1979; Lopata *et al.*, 1980), often by providing direct assistance (Fowlkes, 1980; Kanter, 1977b). Wong (1986) found the same gender asymmetry when she examined husbands' and wives' reports of spouse support with regard to interrole conflict and role overload associated with combining a job and parenting. The sex difference cannot be explained by an overall response bias because the wives in Wong's study reported more co-worker support than did the husbands. Using multiple indicators of emotional support from a spouse, Vanfossen (1981) found that men reported more support from wives than women reported receiving from husbands.

Interestingly, it appears that the group receiving the least amount of support may need it most. As noted above, women usually face greater role conflict and role strain than men do when employment and family roles are combined. In Wong's (1986) study, women reported less satisfaction than did men with the way they were combining work and parenting. Yet, women also received lower levels of spouse support in this domain. Other research indicates that the quality of family relations, including family cohesion, plays a more important role in stress resistance for women than for men (Holahan and Moos, 1985).

So far our discussion has focused on the beneficial effects that supportive family members have on occupational adjustments. However, there may be a reciprocal link between job conditions and spouse and family support. Evidence for a spillover effect from job to family comes from a study of unemployed men in which unemployment was followed by a decrease in levels of spouse support and family cohesion. The spillover appeared to be mediated, at least in part, by the effect of unemployment on the husband's psychological well-being (Atkinson, Liem and Liem, 1986). It is also important to consider whether the effects of family support are really universally beneficial (see Ganster *et al.*, 1986). Social support researchers have pointed out that even the well-intended may inadvertently reinforce sick role behavior, dependence and feelings of shame or guilt (Rook, 1985). In addition, ineptly provided support may exacerbate rather than alleviate the recipient's feelings of distress (Wortman and Lehman, 1985). Some investigators have suggested that support from family members might encourage ineffective strategies for coping with problems at work, thereby increasing the negative effects of job stress (Bartone, 1987; Kobasa and Puccetti, 1983).

Division of Labor in the Family

'Family labor' as defined here includes tasks required to maintain a household and childcare responsibilities. The division of family labor between husbands and wives is typically the result of social expectations which foster allocation along traditional sex-role lines. Despite the increase in women's labor-force participation, there has been little, if any, concurrent change in the division of family labor (Angrist, Lave and Mickelson, 1977; Ross *et al.*, 1983); women still perform the vast majority of housework and childcare tasks (Berk and Berk, 1979; Piotrkowski and Repetti, 1984; Pleck, 1985). In a review of the literature on husbands' family-role involvement, Nieva and Gutek (1981, chapter 4) concluded that husbands do not necessarily increase their participation in housework and childcare as wives increase their labor force participation. The men who increase their participation in family labor are those who have employment histories similar to their wives (Weingarten, 1978) or have egalitarian sex role ideologies (Perucci, Potter and Rhoads, 1978).

In a recent review and reanalysis of two national sample data sets, Pleck (1985) concluded that husbands of employed wives 'do not increase their family work in the narrow sense, but do show an increase in the broader forms of family participation' (pp. 148–149), notably in 'total child contact'. Pleck's (1985) review of fathers' participation in family labor clarified some of the contradictory findings in the area by showing that husbands of employed wives engage in a larger proportion of total family labor than husbands' of nonemployed wives; however, this increase is due not to husbands' greater time commitments, but to employed wives' decreased participation in family labor. Bernardo, Shehan and Leslie (1987) came to the same conclusion; that is, as employed wives reduce their own participation in housework, husbands of employed wives increase their housework time in relative terms, but not in absolute terms.

Because women typically maintain major responsibility for the home and the family, it has been argued that they are likely to experience interrole conflict and overload as they attempt to juggle the demands of work and family domains (see, e.g. Jick and Mitz, 1985; Lewis and Cooper, 1983, 1988; Pleck, 1977; Szinovacz, 1977). The psychological strain which results from interrole conflict and role overload may reduce the time, effort and attention that mothers can devote to their jobs (Sekaran, 1986). Crouter

(1984) summarized the manner by which family roles interact with and affect the work situation:

> As long as society sees childcare and household work as primarily mothers' responsibilities, many mothers are likely to experience spillover from family to work in the form of absenteeism, tardiness, energy deficit, pre-occupation with family related matters, and reluctance to accept work-related responsibilities that conflict with family time and activities. (p. 437)

Lewis and Cooper (1988) have argued that couples tend to cope with overload along traditional lines; i.e. women reduce paid workload and increase domestic involvement. These authors contend that this 'solution' inherently produces an additional stressor as women find themselves facing skill under-utilization in low-level jobs or part-time work (see also Berger *et al.*, 1978).

In addition to the role strain experienced by employed women as the result of managing work and family demands, an unequal division of family labor produces psychological difficulties that may spillover into the work domain and influence effective work functioning. An inequitable division of family labor has been linked to depression (Schafer and Keith, 1980), job dissatisfaction (Lewis, 1986, cited in Lewis and Cooper, 1988), and marital dissatisfaction (Yogev and Brett, 1985). Repetti (1987d, in press) found that three work-role characteristics, work social climate, supervisory support and job satisfaction, interacted with perceived inequity in the division of family labor to produce depression among women. She concluded that, 'women who believe they are over-burdened by an unfair share of labor at home may be more vulnerable to stressful conditions at work' (p. 20).

Number and Stability of Roles

The concept of role and its relatives such as role conflict, role overload and role strain appear prominently in the literature on work–nonwork linkages. While most of the research focuses on specific roles such as worker, spouse or parent, there is also a growing literature on number of roles or multiple roles. This research tends to equate roles and focuses on the sheer number of different role assignments instead of the characteristics of each role which might lead to job stress. Multiple roles can be viewed as sources of stress, sources of satisfaction, or both (Herman and Gyllstrom, 1977; Repetti, 1987d in press; Valdez and Gutek, 1987). Although the research on multiple roles is still in its infancy, it tends to focus on possible negative effects, especially for women, under the assumptions that people have limited energy and resources and may become overburdened by too many roles (Pietromonaco, Manis and Frohardt–Lane, 1986).

What little research there is suggests that multiple roles are more often associated with positive rather than negative effects (Repetti and Crosby,

1984), although few studies specifically examine job stress as an outcome variable (see Russell, Altmeier and Van Velzen, 1987, for an exception). In fact, there is empirical evidence that the benefits of multiple roles can be observed not only in improved mental health (Repetti and Crosby, 1984), but also in occupational life. Crosby (1982), for example, found that women who occupied the roles of employee, spouse, and parent were more satisfied with their jobs than women who were only employees and spouses. Russell *et al.* (1987) found that teachers who were married reported less burnout than teachers who did not have a spouse role. Compared with married teachers, the unmarried teachers reported less personal accomplishment in their jobs (one component of burnout). In a representative survey of workers in Los Angeles County, Valdez and Gutek (1987) found similar results: with age of subjects controlled, the lowest levels of job satisfaction were found among women who had not been married. Pietromonaco *et al.* (1986) found that women with three, four or five roles had higher self-esteem and were more satisfied with their jobs that women with one or two roles. Interestingly, when asked to discuss the major source of stress, women with families typically mentioned problems associated with family members while women without partners or children typically mentioned the absence of partners or children as the chief source of stress.

Studies on multiple roles are generally consistent with Sieber's (1974) early discussion of role accumulation. Sieber discussed four possible positive consequences of multiple roles, using professional men in most of his examples. The four types of rewards identified by Sieber are: role privileges, status security, resources and personality enrichment. Multiple roles can provide multiple sources of expertise and competence that sometimes complement each other, adding to one's prestige and competence in any one area. Performing several roles may increase one's privileges, resources and contacts, and increase one's social standing. Performing well in multiple roles can increase one's self-esteem and sense of competence. In addition to the four possible positive consequences identified by Sieber (1974), multiple roles can provide buffers against failure or frustration in any given role (Crosby, 1982; Pietromonaco *et al.*, 1986). As Crosby (1982) stated

> For married workers and especially for parents, the joys of home may wash away the concerns and smooth away the disgruntlements of the office, the factory, or the shop. Perhaps, too, some of the woes of parenthood . . . may put difficulties at work in a new, rather soft light. (p. 74)

The research showing that multiple roles are associated with increased job satisfaction and self-esteem may come as a surprise and seem inconsistent with findings that support interrole conflict predictions. For example, as noted above several studies have shown that employed women are less likely than employed men to have a spouse and/or children, which has been interpreted to mean that women avoid accumulating roles in order to avoid the resulting role stress (cf. Herman and Gyllstrom, 1977). Similarly research showing that both marriage and children reduce the probability of employment among women (cf. Erickson and Klein, 1981) can be interpreted as supporting an interrole conflict hypothesis. Valdez and Gutek (1987) hypothesized that women in especially demanding jobs would have fewer roles than women who work in less demanding jobs. They found that, other factors held constant, women managers were more likely than other women workers to be divorced and both professional and managerial women had fewer children than other employed women. They interpreted their findings as supportive of a role conflict hypothesis.

Gender asymmetries appear to be operative in researchers' attempts to understand the relation between number of roles and job stress. It is probably no coincidence that Sieber's (1974) discussion of positive aspects of role accumulation used the experiences of professional men as examples whereas most of the discussion on possible negative effects of multiple roles uses working women as examples.

An interesting line of inquiry would be the circumstances under which multiple roles lead to positive vs negative consequences. Several researchers (Herman and Gyllstrom, 1977; Gutek *et al*, 1986) suggested that the amount of effort required for each role may be more important than the number of roles, and might possibly explain gender asymmetries. Four nonoverlapping, time-consuming roles may be more stressful than four complementary roles that require relatively little expenditure of energy and time. Given women's greater expenditure of time in parental and possibly spousal roles (Berk and Berk, 1979; Pleck, 1985), men's combined work and family roles may require less time and energy than women's combined work and family roles.

While research on multiple roles grows, there is very little research on stability of roles. The stability of roles, however, may be important because several measures of stress (Dohrenwend *et al*., 1978; Holmes and Rahe, 1967; Russell *et al*., 1987) are based on number of stressful events. Work- and family-related events make up a large portion of both the Social Readjustment Rating Scale (SRRS) (Holmes and Rahe, 1967) and Psychiatric Epidemiology Research Interview (PERI) (Dohrenwend *et al*., 1978), two commonly used indicators of life stress. Family-related events such as getting married, divorced or pregnant are viewed as stressful. Thus, the stability of nonwork roles, might provide additional useful information in explaining stress at work. Vicino and Bass (1978) found that higher life stability (as indicated by few stressful life events) was associated with managerial success. Sarason and Johnson (1979) found that negative personal life changes were significantly related to lower levels of satisfaction with various aspects of one's job; such as supervision, pay and the work itself. Positive life changes, on the other hand, were significantly related to satisfaction with promotional opportunities. Studies of multiple roles and stability of roles or life events suggest that they are potentially fruitful areas for studying nonwork influences on stress at work and should complement the information we already have gained pertaining to the impacts of specific roles on job stress.

CONCLUSIONS AND RECOMMENDATIONS

To conclude the chapter, we return to the three issues discussed at the beginning: circularity, group asymmetries and neutrality. We then make some recommendations about what organizations can do to reduce the level of job stress attributable to nonwork roles and offer some suggestions for future research.

As noted at the beginning of the chapter, relations between work and family are circular or reciprocal; in fact, there seems to be some consensus that work probably impacts family more than family does work (cf. Crouter, 1984; Kanter, 1977a; Piotrkowski *et al.* and 1987). In our review of the literature, the reciprocal causality between the work and family domains was quite apparent. We have also noted numerous group asymmetries, especially gender asymmetries, both in choice of research topics and in research findings. For example, husbands' attitudes towards wives' employment has been studied extensively, but wives' attitudes towards husbands' employment or occupation has not been studied. Research on impacts of children on job stress, on the other hand, has focused more on women than men. While mothers my feel stress because of role overload (Pleck, 1985), fathers might experience some job stress as they attempt to fulfill the role of the good provider (Bernard, 1981; Staines *et al.*, 1986).

Net Effect of Nonwork Roles

The issue of neutrality assumes that nonwork roles can have both positive and negative effects on stress at work. Indeed, the research reviewed here exhibits this fact. The issue that does not come through clearly in our review is the net effect of family influences. Overall, do marriage and children increase or decrease one's job stress? The answer: it depends. Much of the literature focuses on potential negative effects of marriage and children on women's job experiences. Ample evidence exists to support the contention that husbands and children are sources of stress for employed women. The mere facts that employed women are less likely to be married than employed men and that they tend to have fewer children supports the notion that it is difficult for women to combine work and a family. In addition, evidence that husbands of employed wives spend relatively little time doing housework and that mothers are more responsible than fathers for childcare also supports the notion that family roles can create job stress for women.

On the other hand, a small but growing body of research suggests that women who are married, or married with children, are more satisfied with their jobs than are other women. This research suggests that family roles can lower job stress in women. Many women also cite family members as sources of support and women without husbands or children define their absence as a source of stress for them!

By examining the situation for men, researchers might better understand the effects of family roles on women workers' job stress. For men, the net effect of family on job stress is more straightforward. Marriage seems to be uniformly positive for men. Having an employed wife may be slightly less positive than having a wife who is not employed, as an employed wife may slightly reduce his job satisfaction if he feels that her employment indicates that he is inadequate as a provider for the family. The net effect, however, is clearly positive for the average man. Children also appear to have a neutral or positive effect on men's job satisfaction. Children do not appear to create work–family interrole conflict for their fathers in the same way they do for their mothers. This may be due to the fact that children interfere less with father's work than with mothers' work, even though men with employed wives may have more contact with their children than men whose wives are not employed.

Research on multiple roles and role stability further suggests that multiple roles and stable roles are positively related to job satisfaction. This is especially true if one has a good relationship with one's children and spouse, and if the spouse performs an equitable share of household chores and provides social support.

We conclude that it is not the fact of the roles that creates job stress for women, but the way their roles are currently defined. As long as the mother and wife roles require substantially more work than the husband and father roles, women may experience interrole conflict, even if these roles do meet other needs and provide social support.

Recommendations

How might women's roles be changed so that the net effect of family roles can be as positive for women as for men? At least two different strategies could be pursued. One strategy has been implemented in the Soviet Union over the last half century. In the Soviet Union, women are acknowledged to have as much right to employment as men, but they are also given full responsibility for the family domain (Lapidus, 1988). In order to give women opportunity in the labor-force, the State provides support for women in the form of childcare. There is a reciprocal agreement between a woman and the State: she contributes in the form of paid labor and the State in turn provides childcare for her children. (The State, however, does not provide assistance with housework or shopping, which takes a substantial amount of Soviet women's time.)

Although the United States does not have a government policy about work or family, and most Western European countries do not have a policy as explicit as the Soviet Union's, the developing trend in Western countries has been to encourage men to share in family responsibilities as women participate more in the labor-force. The research suggests a slight reduction in gender asymmetry in social roles as both sexes increasingly become responsible for both work and family domains. Whether this trend will continue remains to be seen.

If men do participate more in family responsibilities, they may begin to experience interrole conflict like their wives. In this case, work–family conflict will not be a problem unique to women and employing organizations may come under increasing pressure to make some accommodations to nonwork roles. More flexibility is needed from employers in two areas. First is increased flexibility in time and place of work (Nieva, 1985, pp. 177–8; Galinsky, 1986; Pleck, 1986). Flexitime represents a small step in this direction, but employers could go much further. For example, employees might be given the option of working at home a certain number of days a year in order to accommodate sick children, visits by repair persons, and the like. Second, we recommend increased flexibility in benefit packages. Few flexible benefit packages currently contain childcare options, although there is good reason to believe that childcare would be a highly desirable benefit for many workers (National Commission on Working Women, 1979; Presser, 1986). If working men and women are interested in sharing in both domains, these benefits need to be available to men as well as women.

Research Agenda

Several reviews of the work–family literature already provide suggestions for future research (Bronfenbrenner and Crouter, 1982; Gutek *et al.*, 1981; Nieva, 1985; Piotrkowski *et al.*, 1987; Repetti, 1987b). Rather than repeat those recommendations here, we highlight directions for research that follow directly from the three issues discussed throughout this review: circularity, group asymmetries and neutrality. By pointing out the circular or reciprocal relationships between work–nonwork or work–family domains, we call attention to the need for more longitudinal and experimental research addressing work–nonwork linkages. Without longitudinal data we are unable to determine the extent to which each domain affects the other. We would also like to see more research focusing directly on job stress as an outcome variable. In this review, we have had to include studies with outcomes such as job satisfaction because there is a dearth of studies specifically investigating nonwork influences on job stress or strain.

By treating nonwork influences on job stress as potentially neutral, we can more clearly see both positive and negative effects. Too much research in the past has actively sought to find negative effects, especially of women's employment on children and marriage, and to a lesser extent, negative effects of family on women's jobs. In the past, nonwork influences were considered irrelevant to men's job stress, an assumption that does not seem warranted.

Finally, our focus on gender asymmetries calls attention to the assumptions and values that often guide research on work–family linkages. Researchers, like others, tend to view some questions as more important for women and other questions as more important for men. In some cases, these assumptions may be correct, but in other cases they have contributed to neglect of potentially important topics and reflect our socialized biases. For example, should we not look at the effects of wives' attitudes on husbands' job stress and satisfaction as well as effects of husbands' attitudes on wives' job stress and satisfaction?

We hope that this review will stimulate additional research in the areas that we have outlined. In addition to the great potential for contributions to theory-building, the outcomes of such research can ultimately influence the quality of day-to-day life in both the family and work domains.

REFERENCES

Aldous, J. (1969). Occupational characteristics of males' role performance in the family, *Journal of Marriage and the Family*, **31**, 707–12.

Anderson, E. A., and Leslie, L. A. (1987). The relationship between stress and decision making in working families, unpublished manuscript, University of Maryland.

Andrews, F. M. and Withey, S. B. (1976). *Social Indicators of Well-being*, Plenum Press, New York.

Angrist, S. A., Lave, J. R. and Mickelson, R. (1977). How working mothers manage: socioeconomic differences in work, child care, and household tasks, *Social Science Quarterly*, **56**, 631–7.

Atkinson, T., Liem, R. and Liem, J. H. (1986). The social costs of unemployment: implications for social support, *Journal of Health and Social Behavior*, **27**, 317–31.

Bailyn, L. (1970). Career and family orientations of husbands and wives in relation to marital happiness, *Human Relations*, **23**(2), 97–113.

Barbarin, O. A., Hughes, D. and Chesler, M. A. (1985). Stress, coping and marital functioning among parents of children with cancer, *Journal of Marriage and Family*, **47**, 473–80.

Barling, J. and Rosenbaum, A. (1986). Work stressors and wife abuse, *Journal of Applied Psychology*, **71**, 346–8.

Barling, J. and Van Bart, D (1984). Mothers' subjective employment experiences and the behavior of their nursery school children, *Journal of Occupational Psychology*, **57**, 49–56.

Bartone, P. T. (1987). Moderators of stress in Chicago city bus drivers, unpublished manuscript.

Beehr, T. A. (1976). Perceived situational moderators of the relationship between subjective role assymetry and role strain, *Journal of Applied Social Psychology*, **61**, 35–40.

Beller, A. H. and Graham, J. W. (1985). Variations in economic well-being of divorced women and their children: the role of child support income. In M. David and T. Sneeding (eds), *Horizontal Equity, Uncertainty, and Economic Well-being*, University of Chicago Press, Chicago.

Berger, M., Foster, M. A. and Wallston, B. S. (1978). In R. Rapoport and R. Rapoport (eds) *Working Couples*, Harper, New York.

Berk, R. and Berk S. F. (1979). *Labor and Leisure at Home*, Sage, Beverly Hills.

Berkowitz, A. D. and Perkins, H. W. (1984). Stress among farm women: work and family as interacting systems, *Journal of Marriage and the Family*, **46**, 161–6.

Bernard, J. (1981). The good-provider role: its rise and fall, *American Psychologist*, **36**, 1–12.

Bernardo, D. H., Shehan, C. L. and Leslie, G. R. (1987). A residue of tradition: jobs, careers, and spouses' time in housework, *Journal of Marriage and the Family*, **49**, 381–90.

Bersoff, D. and Crosby, F. (1984). Job satisfaction and family status, *Personality and Social Psychology Bulletin*, **10**, 79–84.

Beutell, N. J. and Greenhaus, J. H. (1982). Interrole conflict among married women: the influence of husband and wife characteristics on conflict and coping behavior, *Journal of Vocational Behavior*, **21**, 99–110.

Bhagat, R. S., McQuaid, S. J., Lindholm, H. and Segovis, J. (1985). Total life stress: a multimethod validation of the construct and its effects on organizationally valued outcomes and withdrawal behaviors, *Journal of Applied Psychology*, **70**, 202–14.

Bronfenbrenner, U. and Crouter, A. C. (1982). Work and family through time and space. In S. B. Kamerman and C. D. Hayes (eds), *Families that Work: Children in a Changing World*, pp. 39–83.

Bronstein, P., Black, L., Pfenning, J. L. and White, A. (1987). Stepping onto the academic career ladder: how are women doing? In B. A. Gutek and L. Larwood (eds) *Women's Career Development*, Sage, Newbury Park.

Bryson, R. B., Bryson, J. B., Licht, M. and Licht, B. (1976). The professional pair: husband and wife psychologists, *American Psychologist*, **31**, 10–16.

Burke, R. J. and Weir, T. (1977). Marital helping relationships: the moderators between stress and well-being, *Journal of Psychology*, **95**, 121–30.

Campbell, A., Converse, P. E. and Rodgers, W. L. (1976). *The Quality of American Life*, Russell Sage Foundation, New York.

Caplan, G. (1976). The family as a support system. In G. Caplan and M. Killilea (eds), *Support Systems and Mutual Help*, Grune and Stratton, New York.

Champoux, J. E. (1978). Perceptions of work and nonwork, *Sociology of Work and Occupations*, **5**, 402–22.

Cohen, S. and Wills, T. A. (1985). Stress, social support, and the buffering hypothesis. *Psychological Bulletin*, **98**, 310–57.

Cooke, R. A. and Rousseau, D. M. (1984). Stress and strain from family roles and work-role expectations, *Journal of Applied Psychology*, **69**, 252–60.

Crosby, F. (1982). *Relative Deprivation and Working Women*, Oxford University Press, New York.

Crosby, F. (1984). Job satisfaction and domestic life. In M. D. Lee and R. N. Kanurgo (eds) *Management of Work and Personal Life*, Praeger, New York.

Crosby, F. (1985). Divorce in Corporate America, unpublished manuscript, Smith College, Northampton, Massachusetts.

Crosby, F. J. (1987). Preface. In F. J. Crosby (ed.) *Spouse, Parent, Worker: On Gender and Multiple Roles*, Yale University Press, New Haven.

Crouter, A. C. (1984). Spillover from family to work: the neglected side of the work–family interface, *Human Relations*, **37**, 425–42.

Dexter, C. (1985). Women and the exercise of power in organizations: from ascribed to achieved status. In L. Larwood, A. H. Stromberg and B. A. Gutek (eds.) *Women and Work: An Annual Review*, Vol. 1, Sage, Newbury Park.

Dohrenwend, B. S., Krasnoff, L., Askenasy, A. R. and Dohrenwend, B. P. (1978). Exemplification of a method for scaling life events: the PERI Life Events Scale, *Journal of Health and Social Behavior*, **19**, 205–29.

Dun's Review (1971). When is a wife deductible? Vol. 98 (July) p. 63.

Eiswirth-Neems, N. A. and Handal, P. J. (1978). Spouse's attitudes toward material occupational status and effects on family climate, *Journal of Community Psychology*, **6**, 168–72.

Erickson, J. A. and Klein, G. (1981). Women's employment and changes in family structure. *Sociology of Work and Occupations*, **8**, 5–23.

Etzion, P. (1984). Moderating effect of social support on the stress–burnout relationship, *Journal of Applied Psychology*, **69**, 615–22.

Evans, P. and Bartolome, F. (1984). The changing pictures of the relationship between career and family, *Journal of Occupational Behavior*, **5**, 9–21.

Ewer, P. A., Crimmins, E. and Oliver, R. (1979). An analysis of the relationship between husband's income, family size and wife's employment in the early stages of marriage, *Journal of Marriage and the Family*, **41**, 727–38.

Foster, M. A., Wallston, B. S. and Berger, M. (1980). Feminist orientation and job-seeking behavior among dual-career couples, *Sex Roles*, **6**, 59–66.

Fournier, D. G. and Engelbrecht, J. D. (1982). Assessing conflict between family life and employment: conceptual issues in instrument development, unpublished manuscript, Oklahoma State University.

Fowlkes, M. R. (1980). *Behind Every Successful Man: Wives of Medicine and Academe*, Columbia University Press, New York.

Galbraith, J. K. (1973). *Economics and the Public Purpose*, Houghton Mifflin, Boston.

Galinsky, E. (1986). Family iife and corporate policies. In T. B. Brazelton and M. Yogman (eds) *In Support of Families*, Harvard University Press, Boston.

Ganster, D. C., Fusilier, M. R. and Mayes, B. T. (1986). Role of social support in the experience of stress at work. *Journal of Applied Psychology*, **71**, 102–10.

Gnezda, M. T. and Hock, E. (1983). Working mothers of infants: desired work status and anxiety, paper presented at the annual meeting of the American Psychological Association, Los Angeles, California.

Gormly, A. V., Gormly, J. B. and Weiss, H. (1987). Motivations for parenthood among young adult college students, *Sex Roles*, **16**, 31–40.

Gove, W. R. and Peterson, C. (1980). An update of the literature on personal and marital adjustment: the effect of children and the employment of wives, *Marriage and Family Review*, 3(3/4), 63–96.

Gutek, B. A. (1985). *Sex and the Workplace: Impact of Sexual Behavior and Harassment on Women, Men and Organizations*, Jossey-Bass, San Francisco.

Gutek, B. A. and Stevens, D. A. (1979). Effects of sex of subject, sex of stimulus cue and androgyny level on evaluations in work situations which evoke sex role stereotypes, *Journal of Vocational Behavior*, **14**, 23–32.

Gutek, B. A., Larwood, L. and Stromberg, A. H. (1986). Women at work. In C. Cooper and I. Robertson (eds) *Review of Industrial/Organizational Psychology*, pp. 217–34, John Wiley and Sons, Chichester.

Gutek, B. A. Nakamura, C. Y. and Nieva, V. F. (1981). The interdependence of work and family roles. *Journal of Occupational Behavior*, **2**, 1–16.

Gwartney-Gibbs, P. A. (1988). Women's work experience and the rusty skills hypothesis: a reconceptualization and re-evaluation of the evidence. In B. A. Gutek, A. H. Stromberg and L. Larwood (eds), *Women and Work: An Annual Review*, Vol. 3. Sage, Newbury Park.

Harrell, J. E. and Ridley, C. A. (1975). Substitute child care, maternal employment and the quality of mother–child interaction, *Journal of Marriage and the Family*, **37**, 556–64.

Harragan, B. L. (1977). *Games Mother Never Taught You*. Warner Books, New York.

Herman, J. B. and Gyllstrom, K. K. (1977). Working men and women: inter- and intra-role conflict, *Psychology of Women Quarterly*, **1**, 319–33.

Hiller, D. V. and Philliber, W. W. (1982). Predicting marital and career success among dual-worker couples, *Journal of Marriage and the Family*, **44**(1), 53–62.

Hock, E. (1985). The transition to day care: effects of maternal separation anxiety on infant adjustment. In R. C. Ainslie (ed.) *the Child and the Day Care Setting: Qualitative Variations and Development*, Praeger, New York.

Hock, E., Christman, K. and Hock, M. (1980). Factors associated with decisions about return to work in mothers of infants, *Development Psychology*, **16**, 535–6.

Hoffman, L. W. (1972). Early childhood experiences and women's achievement motives. In M. T. S. Mednick, S. S. Tangri and L. W. Hoffman (eds), *Women and Achievement: Social and Motivational Analysis*. John Wiley and Sons, New York.

Holahan, C. J. and Moos, R. H. (1985). Life stress and health: personality, coping, and family support in stress resistance, *Journal of Personality and Social Psychology*, **49**, 739–47,

Holmes, T. H. and Rahe, R. H. (1967) The Social Readjustment Rating Scale, *Journal of Psychosomatic Research*, **11**, 213–18.

House, J. S. (1981). *Work Stress and Social Support*, Addison-Wesley, Reading, MA.

Houseknecht, S. K., Vaughan, S. and Stratham, A. (1987). The impact of singlehood on career patterns of professional women, *Journal of Marriage and the Family*, **49**, 353–66.

Houston, B. K. and Kelly, K. (1985). Product–moment correlation coefficients for relations between work-related variables and measures of quality of marital relationships, unpublished data.

Jick, T. D. and Mitz, L. F. (1985). Sex differences in work stress. *Academy of Management Review*, **10**(3), 408–20.

Johnson, B. L. (1979). Changes in marital and family characteristics of workers, 1970–78, *Monthly Labor Review*, **102**(4), 49–52.

Johnson, W. R. and Skinner, J. (1986). Labor supply and marital separation, *American Economic Review*, **76**, 455–69.

Kabanoff, B. (1980). Work and nonwork: A review of models, methods, and findings, *Psychological Bulletin*, **88**, 60–77.

Kammerman, S. B., Kahn, A. J. and Kingston, P. (1983). *Maternity Policies and Working Women*, Columbia University Press, Irvington, NY.

Kahn, R. C., Wolfe, D. M., Quinn, R. P., Snoek, J. D. and Rosenthal, R. A.

(1964). *Organizational Stress: Studies in Role Conflict and Ambiguity*, John Wiley and Sons, New York.

Kanter, R. M. (1977a). *Work and Family in the United States: A Critical Review and Agenda for Research and Policy*, Sage, New York.

Kanter, R. M. (1977b). *Men and Women of the Corporation*, Basic Books, New York.

Kemper, T. D. and Reichler, M. L. (1976). Work integration, marital satisfaction, and conjugal power, *Human Relations*, **29**, 929–944.

Kobasa, S. C. O. and Puccetti, M. C. (1983). Personality and social resources in stress resistance, *Journal of Personality and Social Psychology*, **45**, 839–50.

Kornhauser, A. (1965). *Mental Health of the Industrial Worker*, John Wiley and Sons, New York.

Lapidus, G. W. 1988. The interaction of women's work and family roles in the U.S.S.R. In B. A. Gutek, L. Larwood and A. Stromberg (eds), *Women and Work: An Annual Review*, Vol. 3, Sage, Newbury Park.

Laws J. L. (1979). *The Second X: Sex Role and Social Role*, Elsevier, New York.

Lewis, S. N. (1986). Occupational stress and two-earner couples: a lifestage approach, unpublished doctoral dissertation, University of Manchester Institute of Science & Technology. Cited in Lewis and Cooper (1988).

Lewis, S. N. and Cooper, C. L. (1983). The stress of combining occupational and parental roles: a review of the literature, *Bulletin of the British Psychological Society*, **36**, 341–5.

Lewis, S. N. and Cooper, C. L. (1988). Stress in dual-earner couples. In B. A. Gutek, A. Stromberg and L. Larwood (eds) *Women and Work: An Annual Review*, Vol. 3, Sage, Newbury Park, in press.

Lopata, H. Z., Barnewolt, D. and Norr, K. (1980). Spouses' contributions to each others' roles. In F. Pepitone-Rockwell (ed.) *Dual-career Couples*, Sage, Beverly Hills.

Markham, W. T. (1987). Sex, relocation, and occupational advancement: the 'real cruncher' for women. In A. H. Stromberg, L. Larwood and B. A. Gutek (eds.), *Women and Work: An Annual Review*, Vol. 2, pp. 207–32, Sage, Newbury Park.

Marks, S. R. (1977). Multiple roles and role strain: some notes on human energy, time and commitment, *American Sociological Review*, **43**, 921–36.

McCartney, K. and Phillips, D. (in press). Motherhood and child care. In B. Birns and D. Hays (eds), *The Different Faces of Motherhood*, Plenum Press, New York.

McCubbin, H. I., Joy, C. B., Cauble, A. E., Comeau, J. K. Patterson, J. M. and Needle, R. H. (1980). Family stress and coping: a decade review, *Journal of Marriage and the Family*, **42**, 855–71.

Moen, P. and Moorehouse, M. (1983). Overtime over the life cycle: a test of the life cycle squeeze hypothesis. In H. Z. Lopata and J. H. Pleck (eds), *Research in the Interweave of Social Roles*, Vol. 3. *Families and Jobs*, JAI Press, Greenwich, CT.

Mortimer, J. T. (1976). Social class, work and family: some implications of the father's occupation for familial relationships and son's career decisions, *Journal of Marriage and the Family*, **38**, 241–56.

Mortimer, J. T. Hall, R. and Hill, R. (1978). Husbands' occupational attributes as constraints on wives' employment, *Sociology of Work and Occupations*, **5**, 285–313.

National Commission on Working Women (1979). *National Survey of Working Women: Perceptions, Problems and Prospects*, Center for Women and Work, National Manpower Institute, Washington, DC.

Near, J. P., Rice, R. W. and Hunt, R. G. (1980). The relationship between work and nonwork domains: a review of empirical research, *Academy of Management Review*, **5**, 415–29.

Near, J. P., Smith, C. A., Rice, R. W. and Hunt, R. G. (1984). A comparison of work and nonwork predictors of life satisfaction, *Academy of Management Journal*, **27**(1), 184–90.

Nevill, D. and Damico, S. (1975). Role conflict in women as a function of marital status, *Human Relations*, **28**, 487–97.

Nieva, V. F. (1985). Work and family linkages. In L. Larwood, A. H. Stromberg and B. A. Gutek (eds), *Women and Work: An Annual Review*, Vol. 1, pp. 162–90, Sage, Beverly Hills.

Nieva, V. G. and Gutek, B. A. (1981). *Women and Work: A Psychological Perspective*, Praeger, New York.

Northcott, H. C. (1983). Who stays home? Working parents and sick children, *International Journal of Women's Studies*, **6**, 387–94.

Olson, D. H. (1986). Circumplex model VII: validation studies and FACE III, *Family Process*, **25**, 337–51.

Olson, J. E. and Frieze, I. H. (1987). Income determinants for women in business. In A. H. Stromberg, L. Larwood and B. A. Gutek (eds) *Women and Work: An Annual Review*, Vol. 2, Sage, Newbury Park.

Orpen, C. (1978). Work and nonwork satisfaction: a causal-correlational analysis, *Journal of Applied Psychology*, **63**, 530–2.

Osherman, S. and Dill, D. (1983). Varying work and family choices: their impact on men's work satisfaction, *Journal of Marriage and the Family*, **45**, 339–46.

Papanek, H. (1973). Men, women, and work: reflections on the two-person career, *American Journal of Sociology*, **78**, 852–72.

Parasuraman, S. and Cleek, M. A. (1984). Coping behaviors and managers affective reactions to role stressors, *Journal of Vocational Behavior*, **24**, 179–93.

Pearlin, L. I. and Schooler, C. (1978). The structure of coping, *Journal of Health and Social Behavior*, **19**, 2–21.

Perucci, C. C., Potter, H. R. and Rhoads, D. L(1978). Determinants of male family-role performance, *Psychology of Women Quarterly*, **3**, 53–66.

Pfeffer, J. and Ross, J. (1982). The effects of marriage and a working wife on occupational and wage attainment. *Administrative Science Quarterly*, **27**, 66–80.

Pietromonaco, P. R., Manis, J. and Frohardt-Lane, K. (1986). Psychological consequences of multiple social roles, *Psychology of Women Quarterly*, **10**, 373–82.

Piotrkowski, C. S. (1979). *Work and the Family System*, The Free Press, New York.

Piotrkowski, C. S. and Crits-Christoph, P. (1981). Women's jobs and family adjustment, *Journal of Family Issues*, **2**, 126–7.

Piotrkowski, C. S. and Katz, M. H. (1983). Work experience and family relations among working-class and lower-middle-class families. In H. Z. Lopata and J. H. Pleck (eds), *Research in the Interweave of Social Roles*, Vol. 3. *Jobs and Families*, pp. 187–200, JAI Press, Greenwich, CT.

Piotrokowski, C. S. and Repetti, R. L. (1984). Dual-earner families, *Marriage and Family Review*, **7**(3/4), 99–124.

Piotrkowski, C. S., Rapoport, R. N. and Rapoport, R. (1987). Families and Work. In M. B. Sussman and S. K. Steinmetz (eds) *Handbook of Marriage and the Family*, Plenum Press, New York.

Pleck, J. H. (1977). Work-family role system, *Social Problems*, **63**, 81–88.

Pleck, J. H. (1985). *Working Wives/Working Husbands*, Sage, Beverly Hills.

172   *Causes, Coping and Consequences of Stress at Work*

Pleck, J. H. (1986). Employment and fatherhood: issues and innovative policies. In M. E. Lamb (ed.) *The Father's Role: Applied Perspectives*, John Wiley and Sons, New York.

Pleck, J. H. and Lang, L. (1978). *Men's family role: its nature and consequences*, Working Paper No. 10, Wellesley College Center for Research on Women, Wellesley, MA.

Pleck, J. H. and Staines, G. L. (1982). Work schedules and work–family conflict in two-earner couples. In J. Aldous (ed.) *Two Paychecks: Life in Dual-earner Families*, Sage, Beverly Hills.

Pleck, J. H., Staines, G. L. and Lang, L. L. (1980). Conflicts between work and family life, *Monthly Labor Review*, **103**, 29–32.

Presser, H. B. (1986). Shift work among American women and child care, *Journal of Marriage and the Family*, **48**, 551–63.

Repetti, R. L. (1987a). Individual and common components of the social environment at work and psychological well-being, *Journal of Personality and Social Psychology*, **52**, 710–20.

Repetti, R. L. (1987b). Linkages between work and family roles. In S. Oskamp (ed.) *Applied Social Psychology Annual*, Vol. 7. *Family Processes and Problems*, pp. 98–127, Sage, Beverly Hills.

Repetti, R. L. (1987c). Product–moment correlation coefficients for relations between daily measures of perceived job stress and marital interaction, unpublished data.

Repetti, R. L. (1987d). Family and occupational roles and women's mental health. In R. M. Schwartz (ed.) *Women at Work—1987*, Los Angeles, Institute of Industrial Relations, UCLA.

Repetti, R. L. and Crosby, F. (1984). Gender and depression: exploring the adult role explanation, *Journal of Social and Clinical Psychology*, **2**, 57–70.

Rice, R. W. (1984). Organizational work and the overall quality of life. In S. Oskamp (ed.) *Applied Social Psychology Annual*, Vol 5. *Applications in Organizational Settings*, pp. 155–78, Sage, Beverly Hills.

Richardson, J. G. (1979). Wife occupational superiority and marital troubles: an examination of the hypothesis, *Journal of Marriage and the Family*, **41**, 63–72.

Roby, P., and Uttal, L. (1988). Trade union stewards: coping with union, work, and family responsibilities. In B. A. Gutek, L. Larwood and A. H. Stromberg (eds.) *Women and Work: An Annual Review*, Vol. 3, Sage, Newbury Park, in press.

Rook, K. S. (1985). The functions of social bonds: perspectives from research on social support, loneliness and social isolation. In I. G. Sarason and B. R. Sarason (eds), *Social Support: Theory, Research and Applications*, Martinus Nijhoff, Boston.

Rousseau, D. M. (1978). Characteristics of departments, positions, and individuals: contexts for attitudes and behavior, *Administrative Science Quarterly*, **23**, 521–40.

Ross, C. E. Mirowsky, J. and Huber, J. (1983). Dividing work, sharing work, and in-between: marriage patterns and depression, *American Sociological Review*, **48**, 809–23.

Russell, D. W., Altmeier, E. and Van Velzen, D. (1987). Job related stress, social support, and burnout among classroom teachers. *Journal of Applied Psychology*, **72**, 269–74.

Salkevar, D. S. (1981). Effects of children's health on maternal hours of work: a preliminary analysis, *Southern Economic Journal*, **47**, 156–66.

Sarason, I. G. and Johnson, J. H. (1979). Life stress, organizatonal stress, and job satisfaction, *Psychological Reports*, **44**, 75–9.

Schafer, R. B. and Keith, P. M. (1980). Equity and depression among married couples, *Social Psychology Quarterly*, **43**, 430–5.

Sekaran, U. (1983). How husbands and wives in dual-career families perceive their family and work worlds, *Journal of Vocational Behavior*, **22**, 288–302.

Sekaran, U. (1986). *Dual-career Families*, Jossey-Bass, San Francisco.

Sharda, B. D., and Nangle, B. E. (1982). Marital effects on occupational attainment. In J. Aldous (ed.) *Two Paychecks: Life in Dual-earner Families*, Sage, Beverly Hills.

Sieber, S. D. (1974). Toward a theory of role accumulation, *American Sociological Review*, **39**, 567–78.

Staines, G. L., Pottick, K. J. and Fudge, D. A. (1986). Wives' employment attitudes and husbands' attitudes towards work and life, *Journal of Applied Psychology*, **71**, 118–28.

Stewart, A. J. (1980). Personality and situation in the prediction of women's life patterns, *Psychology of Women Quarterly*, **5**, 195–206.

Szinovacz, M. E. (1977). Role allocation, family structure and female employment, *Journal of Marriage and the Family*, **39**, 781–91.

Talbert, J. and Bose, C. E. (1977). Wage attainment processes: the retail clerk case, *American Journal of Sociology*, **83**, 403–24.

Thomas, S., Albrecht, K. and White, P. (1982). Determinants of marital quality in dual-career couples, paper presented at the annual meeting of the American Psychological Association, Washington, DC.

US Department of Labor (1980). *Perspectives on Working Women: A Data Book*, Bureau of Labor Statistics, Recruiting Office, Washington, DC.

Valdez, R. L. and Gutek, B. A. (1987). Family roles: a help or a hindrance for working women? In B. A. Gutek and L. Larwood (Eds.) *Women's Career Development*, pp. 157–69, Sage, Beverly Hills.

Vanfossen, B. E. (1981). Sex differences in the mental health effects of spouse support and equity, *Journal of Health and Social Behavior*, **22**, 130–43.

Vicino, F. L. and Bass, B. M. (1978). Lifespace variables and managerial success, *Journal of Applied Psychology*, **63**, 81–8.

Voydanoff, P. and Kelly, R. F. (1984). Determinants of work-related family problems among employed parents, *Journal of Marriage and the Family*, **46**, 881–92.

Wallston, B. S., Foster, M. A. and Berger, M. (1978). I will follow him: myth, reality, or forced choice, *Psychology of Women Quarterly*, **3**, 9–21.

Weingarten, K. (1978). The employment pattern of professional couples and their distribution of involvement in the family, *Psychology of Women Quarterly*, **3**, 43–52.

Weiss, R. S. (1985). Men and the family, *Family Process*, **24**, 49–58.

Winter, D., Stewart, A., and McClelland, D. (1977). Husband's motives and wife's career level, *Journal of Personality and Social Psychology*, **35**, 159–66.

Wong, N. W. (1986). Support-specificity: the effects of individual sources of support on the well-being of employed parents, unpublished manuscript.

Wortman, C. B. and Lehman, D. R. (1985). Reactions to victims of life crises: support attempts that fail. In I. G. Sarason and B. R. Sarason (eds) *Social Support: Theory, Research and Applications*, Martinus Nijhoff, Boston.

Yankelovich, D. (1974). The meaning of work. In J. M. Rosow (ed.) *The Worker and the Job*, pp. 19–48, Prentice Hall, Englewood Cliffs, NJ.

Yogev, S. and Brett, J. (1985). Perceptions of the division of housework and child care and marital satisfaction, *Journal of Marriage and the Family*, **47**, 609–18.

Young, M. and Willmott, P. (1973). *The Symmetrical Family—A Study of Work and Leisure in the London Region*, Routledge and Kegan Paul, Boston.
Zigler, E. F. and Gordon, E. W. (eds) (1982). *Day Care: Scientific and Social Policy Issues*, Auburn, Boston.

Causes, Coping and Consequences of Stress at Work
Edited by C. L. Cooper and R. Payne
© 1988 John Wiley & Sons Ltd

Chapter 6

Psychological Stressors Associated with Industrial Relations*

Stephen D. Bluen and Julian Barling

Diverse aspects of industrial relations (IR) are stressful, but no comprehensive, integrated approach to this issue has been taken. The aim of the present chapter is to demonstrate theoretically and practically the importance of investigating IR as a source of stress. The theoretical link between IR and stress derives from the fact that two central dynamics of IR, conflict and change, are also important sources of stress. Thus, conceptually, the stress potential of people involved in IR is high. Several practical examples of the stress of IR involvement are covered. First, the stress associated with various aspects of the labor–management relationship is discussed. Topics covered include (a) establishing the labor–management relationship (b) joint decision making (c) implementing the agreement, and (d) breakdowns in the relationship. Second, the stress inherent in three labor roles (union leaders, shop stewards and workers) and three management roles (upper level managers, supervisors and IR practitioners) is demonstrated. It is concluded that both from a theoretical and a practical orientation, the practice of IR is stressful. Consequently, there is the need to investigate further the stress associated with IR.

> Bob Greene . . . is a former tire salesman who was laid off six weeks ago. Separated from his wife and making child-support payments, he has been trying to get by on $158 a week in unemployment benefits. After years of donating blood to the Red Cross, he decided to sell it instead and now markets up to two pints a week. Says he: 'you can make about $100 a month, enough for a little better meal or an occasional date'. (Long gray line, 1982, p. 51).

> Says Cerrito (who lost her job after 35 years) 'My job was my whole life. That's all I did. It's unbearable now. Staying home is terrible. I can't go on like this'. (Trippett, 1982, p. 50)

> Douglas Steel, 40, a burly man with a bristly mustache, has defied the [British

* Portions of this research were supported by grants from the Human Sciences Research Council of South Africa and the University of the Witwatersrand Senate Research Committee to the first author and by Grant 410–85–1139 from the Social Sciences and Humanities Research Council of Canada to the second author.

mineworkers] strike since the beginning—and has suffered the consequences. Both he and his son (also a working miner) have been jostled and beaten by gangs of strikers. Last month vandals threw a stone and a bottle of bleach mixed with battery acid through his living-room window. Steel's neighbor, also a worker, recently had the brake cables cut on his car. 'There's no way they can keep me from work now,' Steel, a lifelong resident of Shirebrook, says defiantly, 'They'd have to cripple me first'. (Town divided, 1984, p. 8).

Retrenchments, aggressive bargaining, union busting and strikes are all examples of the diverse stressful activities deeply entrenched in the practice of industrial relations (IR). Yet, despite the personal strain ensuing from involvement in the IR process, no comprehensive, integrated approach to this issue has been undertaken. Even Gordon and Nurick (1981), in mapping out an agenda for the field of psychological approaches to union–management relations, did not consider the potentially stressful role of IR. This represents a serious omission if the deleterious consequences of such stressors for the individual are to be considered. Consequently, this chapter examines the stressors and strains of IR: given the importance of conflict and change as sources of stress (Dohrenwend and Dohrenwend, 1974; Kahn *et al.*, 1964), the central role of both conflict and change in the IR process will be discussed. Thereafter, (a) specific stressors inherent in typical labor–management interactions and (b) the stress associated with key labor and management occupations will be presented.

Physical illnesses have frequently been implicated as consequences of stress and include coronary heart disease, tuberculosis, ulcers, hernia, skin disease, fractures, head, back and stomach aches and even premature death (Holmes and Masuda 1974). The effects of stress are not limited to physical illness alone: psychological (depression, acute paranoia, aggression, boredom, psychosomatic complaints, psychological fatigue, lowered self esteem, suicidal proclivity) and behavioral (abuse of drugs, alcohol, caffeine and nicotine, work and academic performance, absenteeism, turnover and early retirement) consequences of stress are not uncommon (Beehr and Newman, 1978; Vinokur and Selzer, 1975).

It is not only the individual who suffers the consequences of stress. The stressed person's aberrant behavior could affect his/her entire life style, in turn disrupting family life and social relationships (Barling and Rosenbaum, 1986). The deleterious effects of stress also affect the organization and the economy. For example, the estimated cost of stress in terms of lost productivity due to stress-induced ill health to the USA is estimated to be between 6 and 20 billion dollars annually, or between 1 and 3% of the Gross National Product (Marshall and Cooper, 1979).

Because the consequences of stress can be so debilitating, it is important to understand diverse stressors so that preventative measures can be adopted. Although there is no universally accepted definition of stress, there is agreement that stress involves some form of environmental demand requiring personal adjustment (e.g. Dohrenwend and Dohrenwend, 1974). Selye likens stress to 'the disease of adaptation'. In stressful situations people adapt to environmental demands and often perform at an accelerated rate. Where there is no respite, exhaustion leads to negative outcomes such as those already mentioned (Selye, 1982).

Work represents one aspect of life fraught with potential stressors. In the last decade, a plethora of literature has been published outlining a variety of organizational stressors and subsequent strains (e.g. Beehr and Newman, 1978; Marshall and Cooper, 1979). Within the domain of organizational stress, there is a paucity of knowledge specific to the stress associated with the practice of IR. The aim of the present chapter is to redress this by demonstrating from both a theoretical and a practical perspective the importance of investigating this source of stress: as will be shown, various union and management roles are exposed to the stressors associated with involvement in the IR process.

CONFLICT AND CHANGE AS SOURCES OF IR STRESS

The two underlying dynamics of IR, conflict and change, are especially relevant in the present discussion. Conflict is central to the IR process as the labor–management relationship is based on a fundamental conflict of interests (Fox, 1973). Change is also crucial within IR, both regarding the need for the IR system to adjust to environmental developments (Kochan, 1980), and in demands for ideologically-based changes to the IR system (Hyman, 1975). Research results show consistently that both conflict and change are important factors in the generation of stress (Dohrenwend and Dohrenwend, 1974; Kahn *et al.*, 1964).

Conflict in IR

The idea that conflict is central to the study of IR is evident from the work of Fox (1973). Fox identified two frames of reference applicable to IR, the unitary and the pluralist perspectives. An organization adopting the unitary perspective is analogous to a healthy functioning sports team. There is but one source of authority and one focus of loyalty. Management and workers strive jointly to meet company goals which are congruent with personal worker goals. People accept their positions in the organization and do not question the authority of the leaders who are perceived as best qualified to manage the organization effectively. There is no challenge to managerial leadership either from within the organization or from external sources.

In turn, management owe a reciprocal allegiance to the workers within the unitary perspective. They motivate and promote an *esprit de corps* among the workforce (Reddish, 1975). Generally there would be a sense of unity and partnership in a company adhering to the unitary perspective. Because the unitary perspective emphasizes harmony, the validity of conflict in organizations is generally denied. Any conflict that does exist is seen as either being negligible or caused by faulty communications, stupidity or the work of agitators.

The existence of the unitary ideology is contrary to demonstrable facts: trade unions, collective bargaining, strikes and lockouts are integral parts of the IR process. Fox (1973) argues that the unitary ideology is only maintained because it serves the interests of management. By adopting the unitary ideology which promotes harmony and denies the existence of structural conflict, a substantial portion of organizational life associated with the manifestations and resolutions of conflict is ignored. In so doing, a great potential for stress associated with IR is left unconsidered.

The pluralist perspective represents a far more accurate description of organizations (Fox, 1973), accepting the existence of several different interest groups, each with their own leaders, loyalties and objectives in any organization (Schein, 1980). In the IR context, the two major groups are management and workers. Each attempts to have its view accepted in the organization. However, the interests of these groups are fundamentally in conflict: management seeks to maximize profits by raising productivity while holding costs (including labor costs) to a minimum. Workers retain wages and security as their prime interest (Flanders, 1968). Hence within the pluralist perspective conflict is not regarded as abnormal. Rather, it is seen as a natural component of the IR system.

Conflict occurs in either organized or unorganized forms. Unorganized conflict is manifest in individual behavior (e.g. absenteeism, labor turnover and poor work performance). Organized conflict (e.g. strikes, boycotts and pickets) involves group behavior and is far more dramatic and visible than unorganized conflict. Within the pluralist perspective conflict is a natural part of labor–management relations: it is not necessarily a sign of organizational malaise. A certain amount of overt conflict is welcomed as a sign that all aspirations are neither being drowned by hopelessness nor suppressed by power (Fox, 1973).

The pluralist ideology has been criticized by supporters of a 'radical' perspective for not addressing the full extent of conflict in IR (e.g. Fox, 1973; Hyman, 1975). Pluralists are criticized for (a) ignoring the total impact of social power and (b) not exploring the broader functions of trade unions as mechanisms for the redistribution of power and rewards in the society (Winchester, 1983). Thus, whether limiting one's focus to the level of the organization or extending it to encompass the entire society, conflict remains a central component in the study of IR within either the pluralist or radical perspectives.

Considerable research evidence has accumulated over the past two decades suggesting that conflict represents an important source of personal stress (Kahn *et al.*, 1964), in turn, leading to strain and threatening psychological well-being (Pondy, 1967). Conflict has frequently been associated with a variety of forms of emotional turmoil such as anxiety, tension and frustration. From the perspective of the organization, common reactions to conflict such as job turnover (Beehr and Newman, 1978), strikes and/or violence (Pondy, 1967) would be dysfunctional to the organization (Kahn *et al.*, 1964).

Given the centrality of conflict in IR, the potential for stress for individuals involved in IR warrants further investigation. Importantly, there is a reciprocal relationship between conflict and change, the second central psychological concept in the study of IR. Conflict can both be a function of (Ratajczak, 1981) and a cause of (Etzioni-Halevy, 1975) change, which in itself is a further major source of psychological stress (cf. Dohrenwend and Dohrenwend, 1974).

Change in IR

Within a systems framework (Dunlop, 1958), IR represents one subsystem of the wider society. Kochan (1980) states that economic (e.g. inflation and unemployment), political (e.g. government regulations), demographic (e.g. younger, more educated workers wanting greater participation in decision making) and technological (e.g. technological advancement causing changes in relations of production) factors exert direct pressure on the IR system which bring about change. Kochan states: 'Ultimately, not only the level of performance, but, indeed, the survival of collective bargaining as an institution, depends on its ability to adapt to the changing characteristics of its environment' (p. 82). Within the IR system the goals, attitudes, expectations, values, power and behaviors of the actors are continually under pressure to adapt to change (Craig, 1975; Kochan, 1980). New labor contracts, new people occupying positions and establishing ties with a trade union are some of the many forces within the IR system that exert pressure for continuous change (Kochan, 1980). Given that labor relations are determined by the interaction of many subsystems, change in any one subsystem will alter the basic character of the labor–management relationship. Consequently, labor and management continually need to redefine and adjust the terms governing their interaction (Allen and Keaveny, 1983).

Ideologically, within the 'critical perspective' (Shalev, 1980), change is a central assumption of IR theory. Cox (1977) criticizes existing IR theory for not questioning the potential for change in or from labor–management relations. Hyman (1975) sees the intended role of trade unions as vehicles for transforming capitalism into socialism by wresting control of the production processes and determining the framework for the economic policy of the society. Thus due to both environmental and ideological pressures, change is central to the study of IR. Large-scale strikes like the lengthy mineworkers strike in Britain in 1984/5 shows the extent of the personal adjustment required:

> For the miners of Shirebrook, this [British mineworkers strike] has been a very costly fight. The union offers no strike pay, apart from the $4 a day for picket-line duty. Derek Crew, 25, returned his rented television and has sold his electric guitar and amplifier to help feed his wife and two children. The family now stretches the food for one meal into three, and his sons, ages three and six, have had to make do with smaller portions. But Crew's resolve has not wavered: 'We'll keep going until we win, even if we have to eat grass'. (Town divided, 1984, p. 8)

Consequently, involvement in the practice of IR demands continual adjustment and adaptation to change both within and between groups.

Conflict and change are central both to IR theory and to stress theory. Conceptually, therefore, the stress potential of people involved in IR is high. The second part of this chapter details how involvement in IR can be stressful. Certain aspects of the labor–management relationship and the particular stress associated with key IR roles will be examined.

PRACTICAL EXAMPLES OF THE STRESS OF IR INVOLVEMENT

The stress involved in the IR process can best be understood further by examining aspects of labor–management interactions. Thereafter, a variety of stressors associated with the typical day-to-day activities of three labor roles (union leaders, shop stewards and workers) and three management roles (upper management, supervisors and IR managers) will be discussed.

The Stress Associated with the Labor–Management Relationship

The union–management relationship is a complex phenomenon composed of many interrelated facets. In an earlier study, Stagner, Derber and Chalmers (1959) analyzed union–management relations in 41 organizations and identified ten discrete factors of the union–management relationship: management satisfaction, local settlement of disputes, union satisfaction with relations, union achievement, bargaining style, skill of the workforce, union satifaction with achievement, size, legalism and effective grievance handling. In addition, union–management relations are influenced by a wide array of external economic, political, demographic and social factors (Kochan, 1980). Not only is the union–management relationship multi-faceted, it is also complicated by the inherent conflict of interests between the parties (Fox, 1973). Thus from a structural view the labor–management relationship is potentially stressful.

The idiosyncratic nature of the union–management relationship is evident from the results of a study by Driscoll (1981). He found that 69% of his sample consisting of labor and management representatives expressed feelings of role conflict for participating in joint co-operative labor–management problem–solving ventures. Not only is labor–management conflict stressful, but attempts at co-operation are also stressful as they induce role conflict. Four aspects of the labor–management relationship need to be considered: establishing the relationship, labor–management decision making, implementing an agreement and breakdowns in the relationship.

Establishing the relationship

Given the traditionally adversarial nature of the union–management relationship (Berger, Olson and Boudreau 1983), establishing such a relationship is potentially stressful for both labor and management. The delicate task of forming a bond between two hostile groups (labor and management) is aggravated further by the negative stereotypes with which trade unions have become associated. Union leaders are often seen by the public (a) as more interested in their own benefits than in the needs of their members, (b) to have accumulated too much power including having influence in political elections, legislation and government and (c) as having lower esteem than business leaders, government officials, religious leaders and college professors (Kochan, 1979).

Management might experience fear in the situation derived from certain stereotypes concerning unions. Trade unions are seen as militant organizations capable of causing financial, social and personal loss. Unions can also be seen as politicizing agents who use their power to change the social order, or as conscientizing agents who alert workers to the negative aspects of the organization and thereby threaten the general IR climate (Goldberg, 1981). The extent of attitudinal differences that exist between labor and management can be seen from a study by Schwartz, Starke and Shiffman (1970). They compared union and management leaders' judgement of 19 common, emotionally–laden IR words. They found that certain words with clear, conventional meanings (e.g. strike, solidarity, grievance) elicited predictable preferences in the union groups and aversions in the management groups.

Managerial responses to approaches by trade unions are typically based either on resentment or fear of the union (Allen and Keaveny, 1983). Management feel resentful of unions encroaching and limiting their decision-making rights. This anger is particularly prevalent when management accept the unitary ideology and reject alternate sources of power and authority. In general, attitudes are notoriously resistant to change and any attempts to enforce such changes (e.g. by trying to replace a unitary with a pluralist perspective) will be strongly resisted.

Finally, unions and management might fear the unknown about each other. Interviews with union and management representatives reveal that both unions and management found the uncertainty surrounding initial union–management contact to be extremely stressful (Bluen and Barling, 1987). Thus establishing the union–management relationship is fraught with fear, resentment and uncertainty and the potential for hostile actions such as planting spies, using force, intimidation and violence (Allen and Keaveny 1983), all of which can be particularly stressful.

Labor–management decision making

According to Dunlop (1958) and Flanders (1968), rules form the central core of the study of IR. Two types of rules exist: procedural rules, which govern the rule-making process and substantive rules which constitute the content of the agreement and include such items as wage rates and conditions of employment. Procedural rules are particularly relevant to the stress process.

Participation in Decision Making. Participation in decision making is a complex process (see Segovis and Bhagat, 1981). At the center of the IR-related participation problem is the question of who chooses to get involved in any participative project. Within the human relations approach, participative schemes are typically imposed by management. They fit in with existing company policy and authority structures and are seen as attempts to make the status quo more palatable by improving the organizational climate surrounding them. Far from genuine power sharing, such ventures are likely to increase managerial control (Koch and Fox, 1978). 'If participation is forced . . . the attitude of both management and non-management personnel are likely to be more antagonistic than when participation in decision making is increased voluntarily' (Jackson, 1983, p. 17). On the other hand, where unions are operating effectively, participation is not given by management, it is demanded by labor. Once the 'voluntary nature' of imposing participation is removed from management, the process would become stressful.

There are several ways in which worker-oriented participation can be stressful. First, because participative decision making is related to the values of participants (Wood, 1973), manifest conflict could arise in the IR context where the values of labor and management compete (Flanders, 1968). Second, participative management in the IR context can actually threaten rather than enhance managerial control. Strauss (1982) cites examples where worker participation in management threatened supervisory power and altered or even eliminated supervisory jobs altogether. Supervisors' power may be taken from them and handed to workers' committees. Strauss (1982) quotes a British Steel worker-director who said:

Management below board level . . . become unsure of themselves, realizing that now I had access to levels of information they didn't have . . . One day the department manager is my boss . . . The next day I'm off to a board meeting and it's a meeting he'd love to go to.

Strauss (1982) raises a further issue, the problem of confidentiality: because workers involved in the decision making process gain access to confidential information, management communications to worker representatives can be censored in the interests of company security. Indeed, worker participation raises a dilemma of trust: do you disclose information to worker-directors who might later use that information against you in labor–management power relations? Or do you withhold the information and thereby jeopardize the effectiveness of the participative endeavor? However, confidentiality is not a major problem. Worker-directors invariably use discretion in deciding what they pass on and the confidentiality of secrets is usually respected (Strauss 1982).

Further problems emerge. Worker representatives may be seen as a threat to the union, while rivalry concerning who truly represents worker interests (i.e. worker representatives, shop stewards or union officials) may develop (Strauss, 1982). Finally, the credibility of participation schemes would be questioned by unionists who see it as a way of exploiting workers to increase profits (Koch and Fox, 1978).

Collective bargaining. Collective bargaining is the second form of union–management decision making to be discussed. Bargaining is a complex process that attempts to resolve manifestations of the fundamental labor–management conflict of interests. Even where cooperation could be mutually advantageous, shared purposes may not develop and interaction may be regulated antagonistically rather than normatively (Deutsch and Krauss, 1960). Consequently, the stress potential of collective bargaining warrants investigation.

Depending on the issues being negotiated and the prevailing, relationship between the parties, the negotiations can either be distributive or integrative (Walton and McKersie, 1965). Distributive bargaining is used when the parties are pursuing incompatible goals (e.g. wages). Because the parties are negotiating over a fixed amount, a gain by one side represents a loss to the other. Consequently the potential for conflict is great. Conversely, the aim in integrative bargaining is to solve problems in a mutually beneficial manner.

Several tactics are used in distributive bargaining to strengthen one's own position and weaken the opposition's. An obvious outcome of such tactics is the risk of increasing the conflict between labor and management (Allen and Keaveny, 1983). These power tactics are inherently stressful. For example, one tactic would be to withhold or distort information (Driscoll, 1981; Schuler, 1979), which has been found to be stressful (Segovis and Bhagat,

1981). Second, Deutsch and Krauss (1960) found that in the bargaining situation there is a tendency to threaten the other party so that they modify their initial bargaining position. Thus, unions threaten to strike while management threaten to lock-out or even to close a plant. Indeed, the entire power balance in negotiations is based on maximizing the other side's cost of disagreeing (e.g. by threatening a strike) and minimizing their costs of agreeing with your proposals (Allen and Keaveny, 1983). Consequently, there is a great deal of uncertainty in the negotiations: neither party is sure of how far the other side is prepared to go in carrying out its threats.

Another aspect of uncertainty in negotiations concerns the final outcome, which can be particularly stressful for negotiators who are being evaluated on the results they obtain (Segovis and Bhagat, 1981; Stephenson, 1981). Also, negotiators do not act in personal capacities. Instead they have a set of obligations to which they must respond. The stress inherent here is particularly pronounced when negotiators have little latitude in determining their positions yet are held accountable for their performance (Stephenson, 1981).

A further stressor facing negotiators is person–role conflict, where negotiators are forced to pursue issues that conflict with their personal values and beliefs. Batstone, Boraston and Frenkel (1978) quote excerpts from an interview with a manager involved in such negotiations 'I've got to follow the company line, and the same's true of [the steward]. Because of our jobs we could well find ourselves fighting, each against what we thought was right' (p. 175). If negotiators do not adhere to their mandates they could find themselves in the distressing position of the party they represent refusing to accept or ratify the agreement (Stepp, Baker and Barrett, 1982).

There are also problems with integrative bargaining even though it is not inherently conflictive. Allen and Keaveny (1983) discuss two dilemmas confronting negotiators. Besides the problem of disclosure mentioned earlier, there is also the issue of trusting what you are told by the other side: to what extent is it the truth and to what extent is it part of the other party's overall strategy to ensure that you believe what they tell you? Thus even though integrative bargaining focuses on mutually beneficial issues it cannot escape the fundamental conflict of interests of the labor–management relationship.

One example of stress in integrative bargaining is joint union–management involvement in quality of worklife (QWL) projects. Although these programs have had positive effects such as improving worker health while reducing stress levels (Davis and Sullivan, 1980), QWL programs can become a source of stress. Because there is a pervasive tendency for both labor and management to be wary of each other, an adversarial orientation may be maintained even in the context of developing 'cooperative' programs (Greenberg and Glaser, 1981). If labor and management can overcome their mutual distrust, they face a further problem concerning role conflict. The substitution of traditional distributive bargaining tactics with a problem-solving, cooperative approach has been found to leave negotiators facing conflicting expectations from the parties they represent (Driscoll, 1981). Thus collective bargaining, whether in a distributive or an integrative form, is a potentially stressful experience.

Implementing the agreement

Stressful aspects regarding the day-to-day activities of IR in organizations will be considered in some detail when the various labor and management roles are discussed. Therefore, only a few observations will be made here.

Negotiation of a wage agreement usually involves changes in wages and working conditions. These adaptations could be stressful (cf. Dohrenwend and Dohrenwend, 1974), especially if they are not favored by the people involved (Rabkin and Streuning, 1976). For example, not getting an expected increment would increase the worker's stress associated with reorganizing his/her budget, standard of living and family problems. Similarly, having to cut back on departmental spending because of negotiated increases in labor costs can be a source of stress for management.

The handling of disciplinary and grievance procedures can also be stressful, as they are concerned with resolving conflict at its source of origin (Van Coller, 1979). As such they usually involve sensitive issues and emotionally-charged situations (Briggs, 1981).

One item of negotiated agreements that is particularly stressful is the retrenchment procedure. Four stressful phases are associated with retrenchment: the anticipation stage, the unemployment stage, the job seeking stage and the reemployment stage (Kasl and Cobb, 1979).

Breakdowns in the labor–management relationship

Thus far, it has been implied that labor and management are able to resolve their differences. In practice however, this does not always occur. Instead there is often a breakdown in the relationship which leads to a strike or lockout or other disruptive situations (e.g. industrial sabotage, boycotts).

The personal consequences of a strike might be beneficial: one school of thought maintains that strikes ensure the release of emotions necessary for the continuation of the free collective bargaining system (Hameed, 1976). The catharsis experience obtained in the early stages of a strike could mean a saving of many more work-hours lost in subsequent strikes or other forms of conflict. Shirom (1982) suggests that strikes bring about better understanding and communication and improve intergroup relations. Furthermore, Stagner and Eflal (1982) found that union leaders acquire additional prestige and influence over their members during a strike. Members are more willing to cooperate in union activities, and any gains achieved through a strike are more highly valued than comparative gains obtained without a strike. Nevertheless, there are numerous aspects of strikes that exert negative personal consequences.

On the other hand, Milburn, Schuler and Walman (1983) state that organizational crises (such as a strike) cause short- medium- and long-term stress responses. Macbride, Lancee and Freeman (1981) measured the psychological responses of striking Canadian air traffic controllers at three points in time: during the strike, four months later and a further six months thereafter. They found that during the strike the controllers had a dramatically high level of psychological distress (e.g. increased feelings of worthlessness, depression and strain) and a deterioration of perceived general functioning, physical health and psychological well-being compared with their responses during each of the two follow-up periods. Nonetheless, the lack of both a pretest measure and a control group limits the generalization of their findings. In a longitudinal study, Barling and Milligan (1987) showed that IR stressors experienced during and at the end of a strike by community college faculty were negatively associated with psychological well-being six months after the termination of the strike. Barling and Milligan (1987) speculate that the psychological stressors inherent in a strike situation are similar to those experienced in the unemployment process: there would be major financial burdens, the link that employment offers with reality and its provision of a consistent daily time structure would be lost, and the dramatic and sudden role changes required (especially for individuals going out on strike for the first time or professional employees), parallel the experience of unemployment (cf. Jahoda, 1982). In addition, feelings of powerlessness, unpredictability and uncontrollability would be consistent with the uncertainty surrounding the outcome of the strike.

What other factors might contribute to the stress of a strike? There is a paucity of psychological literature addressing this issue since access for psycho-social researchers during a strike is extremely difficult. However, an indication of the stress associated with a strike can be obtained from the few case studies and reports that do exist.

A particularly informative account of the personal experiences of different groups of people involved in a strike at an hotel is given by Wood and Pedler (1978). Initially, the workers were scared. Management felt that the spontaneous, unplanned strike had started because the union could not control its members. The first morning of the strike was chaotic for management who had to maintain clientele services despite the strike. The early weeks of the strike were marred by threats, lies, obscenities and physical violence from pickets whose ranks had been swelled by outsiders.

Before the strike, union officials felt pressured by their members who were becoming frustrated with the lack of progress in the union–management negotiations. The workers rather than the union officials initiated the strike, but once it began the union leaders declared it official. Thus the union leaders felt frustrated: they would have planned the strike differently had they initiated it. Also they did not use the full power of the union to win the strike because of the potential damage to public opinion that such a move might cause. Hence the union officials were limited in their actions both by their members and their perceptions of public opinion.

For the non-striking workers the strike was equally stressful. On the first day, they were unsure of what was happening. They were confronted by hostile pickets as they tried to enter the hotel to seek advice from their supervisors; established colleagues called them scabs. The non-strikers were physically afraid and emotionally upset over such incidents. They also feared that at the end of the strike that many of the unskilled and older strikers would find it difficult to find alternative employment. Wood and Pedler (1978) observed that the various parties saw the strike in completely different perspectives. The misunderstandings, inaccurate information and sheer ignorance of the other party's position that characterized the strike led to polarization and an escalation of conflict.

Other reports also demonstrate the stressful nature of strikes. Thompson and Borglum (1973) report that throughout the course of an eight month strike in a multi-plant meat packaging organization in the USA, there were acts of violence against people and property including gunfire, explosions and sabotage. Lane and Roberts (1971) report on the Pilkington strike where serious divisions *within* the union occurred between the leaders and the rank-and-file members. Similarly, the polarization of management and worker attitudes and behavior intensifies hostility between management and workers (Nicholson and Kelly, 1980). Shirom (1982) refers to the spillover effect where the hostility between labor and management carries over to the post-strike stage and becomes manifest in acts such as reduced productivity and sabotage. Finally, the strike can exert negative consequences in both the community and the family where the strike results in a reduction of family income.

Thus far, attention has been focused on the stress associated with four aspects of union–management interactions (establishing the relationship, labor–management decision making, implementing the agreement and breakdowns in the labor-management relationship). In the next section the stress associated with central labor and management roles will be examined. Although no clear distinctions can be drawn between labor–management interactions and the roles played by various people involved in IR, these two aspects of the stress associated with the practice of IR are presented separately to enhance clarity.

STRESS ASSOCIATED WITH DIFFERENT LABOR ROLES

Involvement in trade unions can be extremely stressful for individuals holding diverse roles. Three particular roles can be identified in this regard—the union leader, the shop steward and the rank-and-file member (see Table 1).

Stressors Encountered by the Union Leader

While a plethora of literature exists detailing managerial stress (e.g. Ivancevich and Matteson, 1980), and to a lesser extent, the stress experienced by blue collar workers in general (e.g. Shostak 1980), there is a paucity of research outlining the stress experienced by union leaders. This is a glaring omission in the literature especially when the multitude of stressors union leaders encounter is considered: as an organization, the union contains several stress-inducing contradictions (e.g. the bureaucracy–democracy dilemma, role ambiguity caused by ambivalent attitudes of members, problems meeting with members causing role conflict and limited financial resources causing role overload) which the union leader cannot avoid.

One conflict faced by union leadership is the bureaucracy–democracy dilemma. The democratic principle and the relevance of union policies to the members' everyday lives are held in high regard (Coleman, 1956). Unions are often borne as an expression of opposition to autocratic practices in management (Coleman, 1956). Traditionally and philosophically, the trade union is a democratic institution which differs from other types of associations (notably business organizations) in the extent to which it emphasizes internal democracy (Stein, 1972). Furthermore, one reason workers join unions is to achieve a greater degree of participation on the job (Kochan, 1979). Participating in decisions that influence their working lives is often crucial for workers (Anderson, 1978).

However, if one accepts the universal applicability of Michels' 'iron law of oligarchy' (Michels, 1959) that all organizations have a tendency to move from democratic to bureaucratic practices in both decision making and decision implementing, trade unions frequently betray their democratic philosophy and ideals (Jackson, 1975). In fact, many authors emphasize the need for unions to rationalize their structure, adopt more planning and control mechanisms and develop natural expertise to be more effective (e.g. Anderson, 1978).

Michels himself stated that bureaucratization was facilitated by the incompetence of the masses. Thus the union leader is faced with the often conflicting objectives of running an organization that can deal effectively with management while simultaneously ensuring that the internal processes of the union remain suitably democratic. Ursell, Nicholson and Blyton (1981) refer to this paradox as the inevitable tensions between the pursuit of intra-

IR role	Stressors				
	Role ambiguity	Role conflict	Role overload	Labour–management hostility	General stressors
Union leaders	Ambivalent authority Ambivalent member attitudes.	Irregular work hours: work and family interrole conflict.	Short-staffed: quantitative overload	Conflicting union–management goals	Bureaucracy–democracy dilemma
Shop stewards	Unclear performance guidelines	Irregular work hours: work and family interrole conflict Responsible to many people: inter-sender conflict. Values/behavior clashes: person-role conflict.	Short-staffed: quantitative overload Insufficient training: qualitative overload	Initiation and handling of conflict	
Workers	Dilemma of whether to join a union	Union vs management demands: inter-sender conflict.		Intimidation to join the union Victimisation by anti-union management	Poor objective and subjective working conditions
Upper management		Diverse responsibilities: inter-sender conflict		Union challenge managerial prerogatives Conflicting labour-management goals	
Supervisors	Limited authority	Face-to-face interactions: inter-sender conflict	Insufficient training: qualitative overload		
IR management	Limited authority Regarded suspiciously by both labor and management. Discrepancies between company policy and practice	Intra-organizational and labour-management interactions: intersender conflict Values/behavior clashes: person-role conflict			Uncontrollable environmental forces interrupting IR systems

organizational democracy and interorganizational power. This dichotomy often causes a related source of stress facing the union leader—leadership challenges from within the union. For example, Kochan (1979) found that union members expected a far higher level of internal administrative competence than typically existent.

Union leaders must also contend with ambivalent attitudes of members toward them. Union leaders are given sufficient status and power to achieve the union's objectives, but at the same time are constantly reminded that they are servants of the workers themselves (Coleman, 1956). This role ambiguity, where people are unsure of their ascribed roles, represents a major source of role stress (Kahn *et al.*, 1964) and has been associated with many forms of psychological strain (Van Sell, Brief and Schuler, 1981).

Another structural component of the union leader's role that is stressful is the difficulty of meeting with members. Mindful of productivity, management are unlikely to allow union leaders to interact freely with their members during working hours. Consequently, union leaders typically must attend to union matters after working hours which encroaches on the time they spend with their families. In an empirical investigation, Gullahorn (1956) found that union officials felt a sense of interrole conflict where work and family demands were competing for their attention. Such interrole conflict, like ambiguity, is a primary source of stress with negative psychological consequences (Barling, 1986; Barling and Van Bart, 1984; Suchet and Barling, 1986).

A further structural feature that pressures the union leader is that unions, at least in the UK, are poorly financed (Warr, 1981). Also, there are only approximately 3000 full-time paid officials in the UK, representing a 1:4000 union official–member ratio (Warr, 1981). There are insufficient trade union leaders to do the required work, increasing the chances of the union leader experiencing role overload, another source of stress which has negative consequences similar to the other forms of role stress (Kahn *et al.*, 1964; Van Sell *et al.*, 1981).

Psychological Stressors Encountered by the Shop Steward

Besides their work roles, shop stewards perform a variety of key IR functions. In one empirical investigation, Poole (1973) asked stewards to define their primary duties. Four classes of responses were given: (a) member representative; (b) union representative; (c) active conciliator, peace maker or dispute solver; (d) active negotiator and protector of members. Carrying out these duties involves many varied and complex tasks such as negotiating with management, representing workers, counselling workers and helping with the formulation of union policy. The performance of these diverse functions cause at least five stressors: (a) quantitative role overload caused by excessive work demands; (b) inadequate training leading to qualitative role overload; (c) role ambiguity; (d) role conflict; (e) the potential for labor-management conflict in the job.

First, the shop steward role is stressful because of the sheer enormity of the task. In a survey of Danish shop stewards, Lund (1963) found the average ratio of union members to shop stewards to be 54:1 (range 11–158). Similarly, Warr (1981) estimates the member–steward ratio for the UK to be approximately 40:1. Looking after the interests of so many people is a daunting task. Nicholson (1976) found that three-quarters of a sample of shop stewards reported moderate to severe feelings of quantitative role overload brought about by the breadth and volume of activities demanded of stewards. Interestingly, feelings of role overload were greatest where there was a favorable IR climate reflecting the strenuousness of the work involved in achieving such a climate.

Warren (1971) states that the amount of work involved in being a shop steward may entail working after hours and on week-ends. This interferes with the steward's role as spouse and/or parent. Nicholson (1976) found that several stewards, especially women, felt competing demands on their time made by home and work commitments. Lund (1963) found that the major force pulling workers away from the shop stewards job was the possibility of interpersonal problems with families, workmates and management.

Stewards also encounter qualitative role stress (Kahn *et al.*, 1964). Although the execution of the steward's job requires sophisticated skills, many receive no relevant training, or their training is pitifully inadequate (Nicholson, 1976). One of the stewards in Nicholson's (1976) study reported:

When I first became a shop steward I didn't know one little thing, I didn't know which way to go about anything, and the first time I went to a meeting I was sick in the stomach because I was frightened of saying the wrong thing. (p. 20)

Given that training correlates with role satisfaction (Nicholson, 1976), the absence of training can lead to psychological strain amongst stewards who remain ill-equipped psychologically to tackle the complex tasks they encounter.

A further source of role stress experienced by stewards is role ambiguity. Many stewards experience difficulty in deciding the right course of action due to lack of appropriate guidelines (Nicholson, 1976). The situation may be exacerbated where management adopt a unitary perspective, and deliberately withhold relevant information from the steward, aggravating their ambiguity (Warren, 1981).

Because stewards are expected to fulfil so many diverse roles, they too may suffer the effects of role conflict. Shop stewards' tasks require them to interact with, and take responsibility for, several people who might have competing interests (i.e. management, supervisors, union members, other shop stewards and union officials. Thus stewards can be subjected to inter-sender conflict—pressures from one role sender that are in conflict with pressures from one or more other senders (Kahn *et al.*, 1964). For example, stewards can be required to deal simultaneously with pressures from workers for increased wages and management demands for maintaining the status quo.

Shop stewards also experience person–role conflict (Kahn *et al.*, 1964). The expectations diverse people hold of stewards frequently conflict with the steward's own values, needs or beliefs. Nicholson (1976) found that a common source of person–role conflict was being forced to call members out on strike for what stewards felt were inappropriate issues. In the Grosvenor Hotel strike, union officials accepted their members' decision to strike even though the officials would have planned the strike differently if they had organized it themselves (Wood and Pedler, 1978).

Finally, the inherent conflict in the steward's role is potentially stressful. Nicholson (1976) states that 'it is a role that appears to be almost inherently stressful, since the initiation and handling of conflict are anticipated aspects of role performance' (p. 16). The amount of hostility that shop stewards are expected to display toward management must be sufficient to maintain worker morale but not so much as to cause unnecessary trouble (Shostak, 1980).

Nicholson (1976) concludes by stating:

the complexity and demand characteristics of the shop steward role render it . . . similar to managerial and executive functions though the provision of resources and supportive mechanism is in no way comparable. (p. 24)

Stress in the Worker Role

Before considering the stress specific to IR that workers encounter, it is necessary to mention briefly the variety of stressors facing workers in their normal working environments. House *et al.* (1979) criticize blue collar stress research for limiting its focus to discussions of physical or chemical hazards such as noise, heat, dust and fumes. Psychosocial job stress appears to impair the health of blue collar workers and is worthy of investigation. In his study of 'blue collar stress', Shostak (1980) identifies four verifiable or objective stressors: compensation; health and safety hazards; unpleasant working conditions; the fear and insecurity of work loss. Shostak (1980) also outlines four subjective stressors: the low status attributed to blue collar workers; problems with supervision; the importance of being part of the peer group; job dissatisfaction (Shostak, 1980).

Such an array of stressful circumstances can motivate the worker to seek changes. One avenue open would be to join a trade union in the hope that the union will be able to reduce these stressors and improve the situation. Kochan (1980) found that the most important reason workers joined unions was because of their negative perceptions of the work environment: job dissatisfaction, poor wages and working conditions and perceptions of inequality were the most prominent issues. Wight-Bakke (1975) states that workers join unions if they believe that such a move reduces their frustration and anxieties, help them realize their opportunities and enhance their standard of living. Indeed, the perceived instrumentality of the union consistently predicts the direction of union voting in certification and decertification elections (Summers, Betton and DeCotiis, 1986).

Yet joining a trade union present workers with a host of stressful issues. The positive aspect of joining a union is that it provides security and protection and a means of realizing worker objectives that might otherwise not be attained. However, by joining the union, workers forfeit some autonomy and individuality: Kochan (1979) found 10% of workers who elected not to join a union did so because they feared a loss of independence. The consequences of electing to join or not to join a union can be particularly stressful. By refusing to join, workers may be intimidated and pressured into reversing their decisions. Shostak (1980) states that in the event of a trade union presence in an organization, non-union employees face three stressful issues. First, organizers may put the workshop situation under close inspection, highlighting local employment drawbacks. Second, unionizing campaigns often polarize the workforce into mutually hostile factions. Third, employer response to unionization campaigns can aggravate workplace tensions and undermine the employer–employee relationship in general.

If workers join the union, they risk being victimized by an anti-union management. Allen and Keaveny (1983) state that management's attitude toward trade unions can range from open hostility at one extreme through controlled hostility, accommodation, cooperation and collusion at the other extreme. Open hostility implies a willingness to use almost any method, legal or otherwise, to get rid of the union. Allen and Keaveny (1983) cite examples such as calling in police or troops to control and limit the effects of strikers; discharging pro-union employees; threatening to close the plant; threatening union sympathizers; denying privileges to union supporters or transferring them to lower paying jobs and employing industrial spies 'planted' amongst workers to keep tabs on union activities and leaders. In South Africa, for example, one security company advertised the services of trained employees who infiltrate the workforce and report the names of union leaders and details of any union activities to management so that management could take 'necessary precautionary measures' (Anstey, 1982). Such anti-union measures are adopted simply because workers exercise their rights of freedom of association. However, Kochan (1979) found that only 1% of workers stated that the prime reason for not joining a union was a fear of employer retaliation or closure of the plant resulting from unionization.

Kochan (1980) speaks of companies avoiding dealings with unions by placing extreme pressure on employees not to join. He cites one case where a computer manufacturing company would not employ job applicants who had certain demographic characteristics associated with the propensity to unionize. In that organization, a newspaper reporter wishing to expose this practice, presented the 'appropriate' anti-union image and was hired. She then began behaving as a union sympathizer and was immediately ostracized by her colleagues who were afraid that talking to her about union matters would jeopardize their positions in the company. The reporter was fired from the computer company after three weeks when her pro-union sentiments became known by management.

Finally, where the relationship between labor and management is adversarial, and especially where a previously peaceful relationship becomes conflictive, workers can experience inter-sender role conflict. Pressures from one party would be in direct conflict with those of the other.

Stress Facing Key Management Roles

Management in union-active organizations are also subjected to a unique set of stressors. Trade union presence inhibits managerial power, prerogative, authority and behavior, and challenges managerial traditions, attitudes and values, all of which can increase the stress management face. The stress inherent in three managerial roles usually associated with IR (upper-level management, supervisors, and IR/human resource managers) is examined here (see Table 1).

Stress in the upper-level management role

In addition to traditional forms of work stress (cf. Ivancevich and Matteson, 1980) upper-level management in union-active organizations are confronted with a host of specific stressors. These are derived from the fact that while in the long-term both union and management might acknowledge their mutual interest in the well-being of the organization (Fox, 1973), in the short-term, union objectives can compete and threaten those of management, thereby increasing their stress levels.

The role of upper management is to make rational decisions so that the organization's resources are used productively (Kochan, 1980). Unions active in the organization threaten managerial objectives in several ways. First, by virtue of the numbers and/or the skills of their members, unions constitute an alternate power source capable of influencing the organizational decision making process (Kochan, 1980). Unions challenge managerial prerogative and attempt to limit managerial control over the workforce. They demand a voice in decisions that directly affect workers (Hyman, 1975). Accordingly, management are forced to relinquish a certain amount of power and control to the unions. Invariably, upper management are unwilling to surrender power and resent being told by others what to do (Bluen, 1986).

Consequently the complexity surrounding decision-making increases for upper-level management. Instead of simply making cost–benefit decisions they must consider the views of, and often negotiate with, an alternate party. Unilateral decision making in accordance with general organizational goals may be replaced by struggles for power and joint decision making with a party whose objectives could be antagonistic.

This leads to a second stressor, viz. competing goals. Management has as one of it's prime objectives productivity and profitability. On the contrary, the union's aim is to maximize wages and enhance working conditions and job security (Flanders, 1968). These goals often conflict, rendering the decision-making process that much more demanding.

If trade union objectives extend beyond the traditional limits of American style 'business unionism' (Jackson, 1975) to include macro socio-political aims (Allen, 1971), additional stressors would be encountered. In South Africa, for example, although blacks do not enjoy the right to vote, they do have the right to join trade unions and participate in the official collective bargaining machinery. Consequently many socio-political issues are raised at company level, forcing (white) management to pressure political leaders to seek change. Even if they were willing, management alone cannot satisfy the political demands of the unions. According to Wiehahn (1982) the primary reason South African management fear labor is that they believe the unions will become politicized and use their power to replace the free enterprise system with a socialist government. Indeed, since 1984, South African unions have become involved in organizing periodic, mass stay-aways from work for political reasons.

Stress in the supervisor role

Just as the shop steward is labor's representative, the supervisor is management's link in dealing with IR issues on the shop floor. As such these two groups encounter similar stressors, namely: (a) role conflict; (b) face-to-face contact with workers; (c) qualitative role overload; (d) limited authority.

First, the supervisor must deal with a diverse set of potentially conflicting role senders, notably the entire spectrum of management on the one hand and stewards, workers and unions on the other (Pedler, 1977). Second, the supervisor's role involves face-to-face contact with the workers. As such, not only are supervisors required to ensure productivity but are also largely accountable for 'healthy' labor–management relations: supervisors are usually responsible for the initial handling of grievances, dismissals and disciplinary procedures in the organization (Sartain and Baker, 1972). Thus, the consequences of their actions can have serious ramifications for the IR climate of an organization, and thereby increase the stress experienced by the supervisor. Indeed, in one study, over half the reported strikes resulted from grievances, dismissals and supervision problems at the supervisory level (Allen, 1982). Such disruptive occurrences are likely to exacerbate the relationship of supervisors with their subordinates thereby increasing the stress they experience at work.

The inherent stress in the supervisory role arises 'out of the relative impossibility of reconciling two rather incompatible ideologies or systems of sentiment' (Miller and Form, 1967, p. 212). Like stewards, supervisors can suffer from qualitative role overload if their training has not included the relevant IR and interpersonal skills input to deal effectively with such a sensitive job.

Fourth, the supervisor's authority is extremely limited. Supervisors are required to perform a wide variety of tasks while management afford them little or no authority to fulfil their responsibilities (Miller and Form, 1967). Also, supervisors are usually not involved in negotiating the union–management contract to which they must adhere (Sartain & Baker, 1972). Having to follow a set of externally determined rules may well be stressful for the supervisor. This is especially the case when any changes to be introduced overwhelm the supervisor. For example, supervisors are bombarded with a stream of unending technological changes, yet they cannot protest because they have neither the authority nor the expertise to do so (Miller and Form, 1967). Also, the nature of change may oppose the supervisor's own values and beliefs. For example, because of international, economic and political pressures, many South African organizations have adopted anti-discriminatory employment practices (Godsell, 1981). However, the removal of apartheid from the shop floor remains in conflict with the principles of many white South African supervisors who are faced with adjustment problems irrespective of their political allegiance.

The presence of a trade union further restricts the supervisor's authority and behaviour toward subordinates. Where a militant trade union is active, supervisors are afraid to exercise any control over the workforce whatsoever: they fear the 'retaliatory' steps the union might take and consequent managerial dissatisfaciton for causing such disruptions (Bluen und Barling, 1987). Thus the supervisor must perform a complex task that involves considerable potential for conflict and negative organizational consequences. At the same time, the supervisor has only limited authority regarding formulating and carrying out workplace regulations.

Stress in the IR Practitioner Role

The role of the IR manager is 'to protect the organizational interests of their firm while acknowledging the legitimacy of unions and collective bargaining' (Kochan, 1980, p. 181). Given the structural conflict of interests between labor and management, the role stress inherent in the IR manager's job is apparent. At least four factors (limited authority, role ambiguity, role conflict and environmental forces) exacerbate the stressful nature of the IR function.

The IR manager's authority is limited as a staff rather than line manager (Allen and Keaveny, 1983). In fact, Purcell (1983) points out that 'we are deluding ourselves if we assume that industrial relations activities either would or should form a major or even moderate part in the determination of corporate strategy' (p. 4). The entire status of the IR function is seen as insignificant unless the organization is threatened by large scale labor unrest (Purcell, 1983).

Similarly, Kochan (1980) found an extremely high degree of centralization of responsibility for IR policy in organizations. Most responsibility was held at corporate level by the chief executive or IR vice president with minimal authority passed down to divisional or plant level. Thus, like both the shop steward and the supervisor, the IR specialist must perform a delicate job with a limited amount of authority. Centralized decision making by key line managers can place additional pressure on the IR function if IR-related decisions are taken purely with the profit motive rather than sound IR practices in mind. The consequence of these IR-related decisions can exert negative effects on the IR climate which further exacerbate the IR practitioner's role.

An example of such limited authority is provided by Kochan (1980), who describes the decision-making practices involved in preparing for collective bargaining with a trade union. After collecting objective data (e.g. labor market conditions, grievance reports) and meeting with supervisors and the plant-level management, IR staff representatives then meet their colleagues from other plants in the company. Meeting are held with divisional IR staff, line management, and the corporate IR director while the corporate labor relations staff prepare the company's economic proposals together with the corporate finance staff. Finally, the proposals are presented to the chief executive for approval. Kochan (1980) observes that such intra-organizational bargaining may often involve conflicts of interest between the various groups of management. The IR staff attempt to guide such proposals through the various stages while trying to accommodate the differing managerial interest groups, ever mindful of the potential acceptability of the proposal to labor in the forthcoming negotiations. Not only do IR practitioners have limited authority, they must also contend with much inter-sender conflict both from within managerial ranks and from labor.

The second stressful feature of the IR practitioners' role is its inherent ambivalence. IR practitioners find themselves caught somewhere between labor and management, maintaining some form of balance between the two. Again, they must contend with competing demands both from within management sub-groups, and between them and labor. Miner (1976) states that IR/personnel managers have often been identified more strongly with workers than with management. Because of the inherent ambivalence in their role, IR managers may be seen as sell-outs by both sides.

An already complex situation is exacerbated when considering that the link between managerial policies and actual practices can be somewhat tenuous. Purcell (1983) provides examples of management endorsing sound IR statements about voluntary trade unionism yet at the same time being actively involved in anti-union ventures. Such ambiguous tactics could be stressful not only for IR practitioners executing company policy, but for everyone else associated with the practice of IR.

Third, IR practitioners may suffer from person–role conflict. There could be a clash between their own values and those of management: they might adhere to a pluralist perspective while line management align themselves with the unitary perspective. These differences may distance them from management. At the same time, to the worker, the IR manager is first and foremost a member of management and therefore part of the 'opposition'. Interviews with IR managers reveal that having their personal values scrutinized was stressful (Bluen and Barling, 1987). Thus the role ambiguity of the IR position might cause incumbents to experience social isolation and a lack of peer group support. Social support is an important factor that usually buffers the stressed person from potentially harmful consequences (Karasek, Triantis and Chaudhry, 1982).

A fourth stressful feature of IR practitioners' jobs concerns their accountability for sound labor–management relations in the organization. However, there is a host of environmental and organizational pressures beyond their control that impinge on the practice of IR. For example, a sympathy strike having nothing to do with the particular company would have negative repercussions on the IR climate and hence increase the pressure on the IR incumbent.

Three labor roles and three managerial roles have been examined within the IR context. All six roles carry a great potential for the experience of personal stress. Role ambiguity and role conflict are particularly prevalent forms of stress experienced by people involved in the practice of IR. This is understandable considering that the inherent conflict of interests between labor and management leads to conflicting demands and ambiguous authority levels and role sender expectations. Financial constraints and insufficient training were also identified as major sources of role overload. Finally, considerable stress is derived from hostility and violence experienced in various aspects of the labor–management relationship.

CONCLUSION

Although it has been argued that involvement in the practice of IR is stressful for labor and management alike, the situation is not inevitably negative. First, according to the General Adaptation Syndrome (GAS) (Selye, 1982), individual responses to stress, resemble an inverted U-shaped curve: after an initial stage of shock where the level of functioning is reduced, the individual enters the second stage, the stage of resistance. During the stage of resistance, performance level is far above normal functioning. The stress experienced during this second stage is called 'eustress', positive stress. Maddi and Kobasa (1984) state that many people in business thrive on stress, operating well under pressure and achieving goals that they would normally find hard to attain. Only when the stressors continue indefinitely and no respite is gained from the stressors is the third stage of the stress cycle, the stage of 'exhaustion' (Selye, 1982) encountered. This final stage results in the person experiencing 'dystress', negative forms of stress, which if left unattended, lead to physical and mental illness and, ultimately, premature death (Selye, 1982).

In the IR context, it is possible that although many people involved in the practice of IR are subjected to a variety of stressors, they may respond by adopting a positive, high level of functioning: they may be experiencing eustress where they, their families and the labor–management relationship derive great benefit from their endeavors. Indeed, interviews with certain labor and management representatives revealed that negotiations, IR confrontations and the uncertainty surrounding the course of the labor–management relationship was perceived positively as a challenge. Also, potential resolution of IR problems was seen to be most gratifying to some individuals (Bluen and Barling, 1987).

Positive responses to stress are related to an intriguing aspect of the stress process, namely: why do similar stressors have different effects on different people? Where some people find a situation to be extremely stressful, others might find it to be a welcome challenge and no negative consequences would ensue. Several factors moderate this process. One variable found to buffer the effect of stress is personality. Maddi and Kobasa (1984) identify three personality traits (a high level of commitment, internal locus of control and a sense of welcoming challenge) that were associated with effective stress handling. Thus the 'hardy' person may well perceive the stressors associated with IR as desirable, rather than as a source of stress to be avoided. Perceived personal mastery in a situation also buffers the negative effects of stress (Hobfall and London, 1986).

Another factor found to buffer the effects of stress is social support: people who can rely on family, friends and/or work colleagues for support when they are experiencing stress usually cope better with the situation than those people who cannot rely on receiving any social support (House, 1981). In IR, trade unions represent a potential source of social support for members (Shostak, 1980). Unions can offer material support to striking on retrenched workers and moral support, legal advice, and expert assistance in securing worker rights and interests (Marsden and Duff, 1975). Family and community groups are also potential sources of support. Haywood and Taylor (1981) report that during the nine-month Inco Metals strike involving nearly 12,000 Canadian steelworkers, community and wife support committees were formed and were responsible for reducing the traumatic and discouraging experience of the strike. Thus, by identifying and incorporating relevant factors that buffer people from the harmful effects of IR stress (e.g. the hardy personality and social support), the deleterious consequences of stress in IR can be minimized. Any research on the stress associated with involvement in the IR process therefore must consider those mediating factors that might reduce subsequent strain.

Interestingly, personality resources and social support may fulfil different buffering functions. During acute stressors such as strikes, personality resources may be more appropriate: because of the stable, dispositional nature, personality resources would be more appropriate in situations with a sudden impact. On the other hand, it takes some time to seek and then receive social support. As a result, social support might be more relevant for buffering chronic stressors.

We have argued both from a theoretical and a practical orientation that involvement in the practice of IR is stressful: the prevalence of the underlying dynamics of conflict and change serve as powerful generators of stress in IR. There is a need to investigate systematically the stress specifically associated with the practice of IR. Furthermore, it is suggested that these investigations are conducted with the view to obtaining an integrated perspective of the diverse sources (e.g. union–management conflict, joining a union), moderators (e.g. personality, social support) and physiological (e.g. back-ache, heart disease), psychological (e.g. depression, anxiety, irritability), behavioral (e.g. increased alcohol or smoking rates) and organizational (e.g. job dissatisfaction, absenteeism, labor turnover rates) consequences of stress associated with the practice of IR (Beehr and Newman, 1978). The criticism that current research is restricted to investigations of isolated manifestations of stressors in IR (e.g. strikes, retrenchments and negotiations) can be overcome by adopting such a strategy. In so doing, a greater understanding of IR stress can be obtained. Knowledge gained in this regard may well lead to healthier participants in the IR process.

Finally, an ideological caveat is in order: despite the potentially stressful nature of the IR process, it is not the role of the organizational psychologist to devise ways of avoiding or destroying the IR process. Rather, organizational psychologists must accept the inevitability, legitimacy and even the positive function of conflict, change and the IR process, even though this might require ideological and attitudinal change for some (Barling and Milligan, 1987).

REFERENCES

Allen, B. J. (1982). Industrial relations training in the service sector, *South African Journal of Labour Relations*, **6**(1), 82–6.

Allen, R. E. and Keaveny, T. (1983). *Contemporary Labor Relations*, Addison–Wesley, Reading, MA.

Allen, V. L. (1971). *The Sociology of Industrial Relations: Studies in Method*, Longman, London.

Anderson, J. N. (1978). A comparative analysis of local union democracy, *Industrial Relations*, **17**, 278–95.

Anstey, M. (1982). Editorial feature: Security in the workplace, *Institute for Industrial Relations Information Sheet*, July, 1–4.

Barling, J. (1986). Interrole conflict and marital functioning amongst employed fathers, *Journal of Occupational Behaviour*, **7**, 1–8.

Barling, J. and Milligan, J. (1987). Some psychological consequences of striking: a six month, longitudinal study, *Journal of Occupational Behaviour*, **8**, 127–138.

Barling, J. and Rosenbaum, A. (1986). Work stressors and spouse abuse, *Journal of Applied Psychology*, **78**, 346–348.

Barling, J. and Van Bart, D. (1984). Mother's subjective work experiences and the behaviour of their nursery school children, *Journal of Occupational Psychology*, **57**, 59–56.

Batstone, E., Boraston, I. and Frenkel, S. (1978). *The Social Organisation of Strikes*, Blackwell, Oxford.

Beehr, T. A. and Newman, J. E. (1978). Job stress, employee health, and organizational effectiveness: a facet analysis, model and literature review, *Personnel Psychology*, **31**, 665–99.

Berger, C. J., Olson, C. A. and Boudreau, J. W. (1983). Effects of unions on job satisfaction: the role of work-related and perceived rewards, *Organizational Behavior and Human Performance*, **32**, 289–324.

Bluen, S. D. (1986). Industrial relations: approaches and ideologies. In J. Barling, C. Fullagar and S. Bluen (eds) *Behaviour in Organizations: South African Perspectives*, 2nd edn. McGraw–Hill, Johannesburg.

Bluen, S. D. and Barling, J. (1987). Stress and the industrial relations process: development of the Industrial Relations Event Scale. *South African Journal of Psychology*, **17**, 150–159.

Briggs, S. (1981). The grievance procedure and organizational health. *Personnel Journal*, June, 471–4.

British Steel Corporation Employee Directors (1977) p. 24.

Coleman, J. S. (1956). The compulsive pressures of democracy in unionism. *American Journal of Sociology*, **62**.

Cox, R. W. (1977). Pour une etude prospective des relations de production. (Reflections towards a prospective study of production relations), *Sociologie du Travail*, **19**, 113–37.

Craig, A. W. J. (1975). A framework for the analysis of industrial relations systems. In B. Barrett, E. Rhodes and J. Beishon (eds) *Industrial Relations and the Wider Society*, Collier Macmillan, London.

Davis, L. E. and Sullivan, C. S. (1980). A labor–management contract and quality of working life, *Journal of Occupational Behavior*, **1**, 29–41.

Deutsch, M. and Krauss, R. (1960). The effects of threat upon interpersonal bargaining, *Journal of Abnormal and Social Psychology*, **61**, 181–9.

Dohrenwend, B. S. and Dohrenwend, B. P. (eds) (1974). *Stressful Life Events*, John Wiley and Sons, New York.

Driscoll, J. W. (1981). Coping with role conflict: an exploratory field study of union–management cooperation, *International Review of Applied Psychology*, **30**(2), 177–98.

Dunlop, J. T. (1958). *Industrial Relations Systems*, Holt, New York.

Etzioni–Halevy, E. (1975). Patterns of conflict generation and conflict "absorption": the cases of Israeli labor and ethnic conflicts, *Journal of Conflict Resolution*, **19**, 286–309.

Flanders, A. (1968). Collective bargaining: a theoretical analysis, *British Journal of Industrial Relations*, **6**, 1–26.

Fox, A. (1973). Industrial relations: a social critique of pluralist ideology. In J. Child (ed.) *Man and Organisation*, Allen and Unwin, London.

Godsell, G. (1981). The impact of industrial relations changes on the personnel function, *Psychologia Africana*, **20**, 21–7.

Goldberg, M. (1981). Formulating worker consciousness, *Social Dynamics*, **7**, 32–41.

Gordon, M. E. and Nurick, A. J. (1981). Psychological approaches to the study of unions and union–management relations, *Psychological Bulletin*, **90**, 293–306.

Greenberg, P. D. and Glaser, E. M. (1981). Viewpoints of labor leaders regarding quality of worklife improvement programs, *International Review of Applied Psychology*, **30**, 157–75.

Gullahorn, J. T. (1956). Measuring role conflict, *American Journal of Sociology*, **61**, 299–303.

Hameed, S. M. A. (1976). Cost benefit analysis of a strike: a tentative framework, *Industrial Relations*, **31**, 145–55.

Haywood, L. and Taylor, E. (1981). Strikes and support systems: what happened at Sudbury, *Canada's Mental Health*, March, 18–33.

Hobfall, S. E. and London, P. (1986). The relationship of self-concept and social support to emotional distress among women during war, *Journal of Social and Clinical Psychology*, **4**, 189–203.

Holmes, T. H. and Masuda, M. (1974). Life change and illness susceptibility. In B. S. Dohrenwend and B. P. Dohrenwend (eds) *Stressful Life Events*, John Wiley and Sons, New York.

House, J. S., Wells, J. A., Landermen, L. R., McMichael, A. J. and Kaplan, B. H. (1979). Occupational stress and health among factory workers. *Journal of Health and Social Behavior*, **20**, 139–60.

House, J. S. (1981). *Social Support and Stress*, Addison–Wesley, Reading, MA.

Hyman, R. (1975). *Industrial Relations: A Marxist Introduction*, Macmillan, London.

Hyman, R. (1984). *Strikes*, 3rd edn, Fontana, London.

Ivancevich, J. M. and Matteson, M. T. (1980). *Stress and Work: A Managerial Perspective*, Scott, Foresman, IL.

Jackson, M. (1975). *Industrial Relations*, Croom Helm, London.

Jackson, S. E. (1983). Participation in decision making as a strategy for reducing job related strain. *Journal of Applied Psychology*, **68**, 3–19.

Jahoda, M. (1982). *Employment and Unemployment: A Social Psychological Analysis*, Cambridge University Press, New York.

Kahn, R. L., Wolfe, D. M., Quinn, R. P., Snoek, J. D. and Rosenthal, R. A. (1964). *Organizational Stress: Studies in Role Conflict and Ambiguity*, John Wiley and Sons, New York.

Karasek, R. A., Triantis, K. P. and Chaudhry, S. S. (1982). Coworker and supervisor support as moderators of associations between task characteristics and mental strain, *Journal of Occupational Behavior*, **3**, 181–200.

Kasl, S. V. and Cobb, S. (1979). Some mental health consequences of plant closing and job loss. In L. Ferman and J. Gordus (eds) *Mental Health and the Economy*, Upjohn Institute, Michigan.

Koch, J. L. and Fox, C. L. (1978). The industrial relations setting, organizational forces, and the form and content of worker participation, *Academy of Management Review*, **3**, 572–83.

Kochan, T. A. (1979). How American workers view labor unions, *Monthly Labor Review*, **102**, 23–31.

Kochan, T. A. (1980). *Collective Bargaining and Industrial Relations*, Irwin, IL.

Lane, T. and Roberts, K. (1971). *Strike at Pilkingtons*, Fontana, London.

Long gray line (1982) *Time*, 17 May, 50–51.

Lund, R. (1963). Some aspects of the Danish shop steward system, *British Journal of Industrial Relations*, **1**, 370–82.

Macbride, A., Lancee, W. and Freeman, S. J. J. (1981). The psychosocial impact of a labour dispute, *Journal of Occupational Psychology*, **54**, 125–33.

Maddi, S. R. and Kobasa, S. C. (1984). *The Hardy Executive: Health under Pressure*, Irwin, IL.

Marsden, D. and Duff, E. (1975). *Workless: Some Unemployed Men and their Families*, Penguin, Harmondsworth.

Marshall, J. and Cooper, C. L. (1979). *Executives under Pressure*, Macmillan, London.

Michels, R. (1959). *Political Parties*, Dover, New York.

Milburn, T. W., Schuler, R. S. and Walman, K. M. (1983). Organizational crisis: two strategies and responses, *Human Relations*, **36**, 1161–79.

Miller, D. C. and Form, W. H. (1967). *Industrial Sociology*, 2nd edn, Harper, New York.

Miner, J. B. (1976). Levels of motivation to manage among personnel and industrial relations managers, *Journal of Applied Psychology*, **61**, 419–27.

Nicholson, N. (1976). The role of the shop steward: an empirical case study, *Industrial Relations Journal*, **7**, 15–26.

Nicholson, N. and Kelly, J. (1980). The psychology of strikes, *Journal of Occupational Behaviour*, **1**, 275–84.

Pedler, M. (1977). Negotiations skills training — Part 2, *Journal of European Industrial Training*, **1**(5), 12–16.

Pondy, L. R. (1967). Organizational conflict: concepts and models, *Administrative Science Quarterly*, **12**, 298–320.

Poole, M. (1973). Towards a sociology of shop stewards, *Sociological Review*, **22**, 57–82.

Purcell, J. (1983). The management of industrial relations in the modern corporation—agenda for research, *British Journal of Industrial Relations*, **21**, 1–16.

Rabkin, J. G. and Streuning, E. L. (1976). Life events, stress, and illness, *Science*, **194**, 1013–20.

Ratajczak, Z. (1981). New roles for industrial psychologists: a view from Poland. *International Review of Applied Psychology*, **30**, 303–10.

Reddish, H. (1975). Written memorandum of evidence to the Royal Commission on Trade Unions and Employers' Associations. In B. Barrett, E. Rhodes and J. Beishon (eds) *Industrial Relations and the Wider Society*, Collier Macmillan, London.

Sartain, A. Q. and Baker, A. W. (1972). *The Supervisor and his Job*, 2nd edn, McGraw–Hill, New York.

Schein, E. H. (1980). *Organizational Psychology*, 3rd edn, Prentice–Hall, Englewood Cliffs, NJ.

Schuler, P. S. (1979). A role perception transactional process model for organizational communication—outcome relationships, *Organizational Behavior and Human Performance*, **23**, 268–91.

Schwartz, M. M., Stark, H. F. and Schiffman, H. R. (1970). Responses of union and management leaders to emotionally-toned industrial relations terms, *Personnel Psychology*, **23**, 361–7.

Segovis, J. C. and Bhagat, S. (1981). Participation revisited—implications for organizational stress and performance, *Small Group Behavior*, **12**, 299–327.

Selye, H. (1982). History and present status of the stress concept. In L. Goldberger and S. Breznitz (eds) *Handbook of Stress: Theoretical and Clinical Aspects*, Free Press, New York.

Shalev, H. (1980). Industrial relations theory and the comparative study of industrial relations and industrial conflict, *British Journal of Industrial Relations*, **18**, 26–43.

Shirom, A. (1982). Strike characteristics as determinants of strike settlements: a chief negotiator's viewpoint. *Journal of Applied Psychology*, **67**, 45–52.

Shostak, A. B. (1980). *Blue Collar Stress*, Addison–Wesley, Reading, MA.

Stagner, R., Derber, M., & Chalmers, W. E. (1959). The dimensionality of union–management relations at local level, *Journal of Applied Psychology*, **43**, 1–7.

Stagner, R. and Eflal, B. (1982). Internal union dyanmics during a strike: a quasi-experimental study, *Journal of Applied Psychology*, **67**, 37–44.

Stein, E. (1972). The dilemma of union democracy. In J. Shepheard (ed.) *Organizational Issues in Industrial Society*, Prentice Hall, Englewood Cliffs, NJ.

Stephenson, G. M. (1981). Intergroup bargaining and negotiation. In J. C. Turner and H. Giles (eds) *Intergroup Behaviour*, Blackwell, Oxford.

Stepp, J. R., Baker, R. P. and Barrett, J. T. (1982). Helping labor and management see and solve problems, *Monthly Labor Review*, **105**, 15–20.

Strauss, G. (1982). Workers participation in management: an international perspective. In B. M. Staw and L. L. Cummings (eds) *Research in Organizational Behavior*, Vol. 4, JAI Press, CT.

Suchet, M. and Barling, J. (1986). Employed mothers: interrole conflict, spouse support and marital functioning, *Journal of Occupational Behaviour*, **7**, 167–78.

Summers, T. P., Betton, J. H. and DeCotiis, T. A. (1986). Voting for and against unions: a decision model, *Academy of Management Journal*, **11**, 643–55.

Thompson, D. E. and Borglum, R. P. (1973). A case study of employee attitudes and labor unrest, *Industrial and Labor Relations Review*, **27**, 74–83.

Town divided (1984) *Newsweek*, 20 August, 8.

Trippett, F. (1982). The anguish of the jobless, *Time*, 18 January, 50.

Ursell, G., Nicholson, N. and Blyton, P. (1981). Process of decision making in a trade union branch, *Organizational Studies*, **2**, 45–72.

Van Coller, S. (1979). A framework for developing a management strategy in industrial relations. In K. Jubber (ed.) *South Africa: Industrial Relations and Industrial Sociology*, Juta, Cape Town.

Van Sell, M., Brief, A. P. and Schuler, R. S. (1981). Role conflict and role ambiguity: integration of the literature and directions for future research, *Human Relations*, **34**, 43–71.

Vinokur, A. and Selzer, M. L. (1975). Desirable versus undesirable life events: their relationship to stress and mental distress, *Journal of Personality and Social Psychology*, **32**, 329–37.

Walton, R. E. and McKersie, R. E. (1965). *A Behavioral Theory of Labor Negotiations*, McGraw–Hill, New York.

Warr, P. (1981). Psychological studies of union management relations in the United Kingdom, *International Review of Applied Psychology*, **30**, 311–20.

Warren, A. (1971). The challenge from below: an analysis of the role of the steward in industrial relations, *Industrial Relations Journal*, **2**, 52–60.

Wiehahn, N. E. (1982). Trade unions and politics in South Africa, *South African Journal of Labour Relations*, **6**(2), 36–40.

Wight-Bakke, E. (1975). To join or not to join. In B. Barrett, E. Rhodes and J. Beishon (eds) *Industrial relations and the Wider Society*, Collier Macmillan, London.

Winchester, D. (1983). Industrial relations research in Great Britain, *British Journal of Industrial Relations*, **21**, 100–14.

Wood, M. T. (1973). Power relations and group decision making in organizations, *Psychological Bulletin*, **79**, 280–93.

Wood, S. and Pedler, M. (1978). On losing their virginity: the story of a strike at the Grosvenor Hotel, Sheffield, *Industrial Relations Journal*, **9**, 15–37.

PART III

Factors in the Person

Causes, Coping and Consequences of Stress at Work
Edited by C. L. Cooper and R. Payne
© 1988 John Wiley & Sons Ltd

Chapter 7

Individual Differences in the Study of Occupational Stress

Roy Payne

Students of occupational stress vary in their reasons for studying it, but whatever their individual motives most researchers would be interested in the scientific problem of understanding human stress; they might have additional interests in reducing the .negative effects of stress on health and well-being, and they might also be interested in improving work performance. If they are concerned with these issues they are inevitably involved in understanding the effects of a *process that takes place over time*: that is in the outcomes of events that spread over months or years, rather than days or even weeks. They are less likely to be interested in the stressful consequences of rare and short-lived stresses of the kind which can occur at work, but are more often studied in the laboratory. This is not to say that the stress of promotion interviews, or the sudden collapse of a computer system or some other emergency are not worthy of study, but that they are less likely to have long-term consequences for health, well-being and performance. It is important to recognize, however, that this chapter is largely concerned with the roles that individual differences play in processes that take place over time, and which are potentially stressful to the employees exposed to them.

The first task is to specify the ways in which individual differences are involved in the stress process, and in empirical studies of it. A large range of variables are potentially relevant. Table 1 classifies some of the more obvious ones.

Table 1 Examples of relevant of individual difference variables

Genetic	Acquired	Dispositional
Physique	Social class	Trait anxiety/neuroticism
Constitution	Education	Type A
Reactivity	Age	Self-image/esteem
Sex		Locus of control
Intelligence		Flexibility
		Coping style
		Extraversion–introversion

The list of the dispositional variables could, of course, be much longer. Several writers on stress have begun to look for syndromes or collections of traits that protect people from stress. Maddi and Kobasa (1984) have published a book about the 'hardy executive'. Hardiness refers to the possession of commitment (vs alienation), control (vs powerlessness) and challenge (vs threat). Antonovsky (1987) refers to the sense of coherence which is composed of a sense that the world is comprehensible, manageable and provides one with a sense of meaningfulness. In his attempt to provide a conceptual structure for understanding well-being Warr (1987) distinguishes between five aspects of mental health which include affective well-being, competence, autonomy, level of aspiration and integrative functioning which refers to the balance between the other four dimensions. Warr also points out that all these dimensions of symptoms/characteristics can vary over time and that they can only be treated as characteristics of a person when they occur frequently and have done so for a long time. Warr refers to this as a person's baseline mental health to make the good point that in studies of stress one is concerned with deviations from that baseline. This alone is a justification for studying individual differences in this field. Whilst acknowledging the importance of these recent writers the following review considers a range of single variables such as neuroticism/stability, internal locus of control vs external, Type A vs Type B, though it is clear from both the concepts and the empirical work that at least the first two of these dimensions are contained within the three broad syndromes described above.

To return to Table 1, there are obviously complex influences amongst the variables in each of the three columns. Physiological reactivity may relate to dispositional anxiety, intelligence may affect coping style, and certainly will affect educational achievement. Ignoring this complexity, however, I will simplify the problem by asking how individual differences might be involved in the stress process. They obviously can be involved at all points in the process, so I shall ask the following questions which focus on the beginning, the middle and the end of the stress process. To be precise, there is only an end if coping is effective and removes the stress. The questions are:

(1) Do individual differences play a role in selecting individuals into jobs which differ in stressfulness?
(2) How do individual differences relate to the development of symptoms of psychological strain?
(3) How do individual differences relate to perceptions of stress in the environment.
(4) Do they act as moderators of the stress–strain relationship?
(5) Do they affect the way people cope with stress?

In principle, these questions could be asked for every individual difference variable separately. Space alone dictates that this chapter will not be comprehensive in this sense, so the evidence put forward on each of these issues needs to be considered as illustrative rather than definitive.

INDIVIDUAL DIFFERENCES AND JOB CHOICE

There is ample evidence that both morbidity and mortality vary by occupation and some of the evidence is reviewed in Fletcher and Payne (1980) and even more thoroughly in the chapter by Fletcher (1988) in this book. There is equally ample evidence that the choices people make about jobs and career are not random. Using a series of regression analyses Bachman (1970) found family socio-economic status influences occupational aspiration more than any other variable. Kohn (1969) shows how social class influences values, self-conception and through these the choices people make about the careers they attempt to pursue. Werts and Watley (1970) compared father's occupation with the probability of children's academic achievements in scientific, artistic, oral, leadership, musical and literary spheres. Children excel at their father's occupational skills. Thus both heredity and environment shape the careers people follow. Since some careers are associated with greater ill-health than others it is certain that environment is affecting health but also possible that individuals select themselves into occupations where they are better able to cope with the intellectual and emotional demands the jobs make on them. People who adapt well to shift-work, for example, may be both psychologically and constitutionally different from those who try it and leave because it begins to damage their health and well-being (Frese and Okonek, 1984). Thus in studies of the people who remain in an occupation self-selection is occurring, for the ones who remain tend to be those who are able to cope at least at an adequate level of functioning. Studies of occupational stress have not really been able to take account of this role of individual difference variables because stress tends to be studied at finite times, or for periods too short to show large-scale changes in health or well-being, but it is worth noting that the patterns of individual differences do vary by occupation (Holland, 1976) and they may indirectly affect the emergence of psychological stress and the means people use to deal with it. The role of chronic factors in stress research is dealt with more fully in the section which deals with the role of individual differences in the development of stress symptoms.

HOW DO INDIVIDUAL DIFFERENCES VARIABLES RELATE TO THE DEVELOPMENT OF SYMPTOMS?

The most comprehensive answer to this question can be found in Depue and Monroe (1986). They are concerned with the fact that studies of large numbers of people more or less randomly selected from the general population will inevitably include people who have chronic conditions, and these chronic conditions will lead to these people reporting high levels of negative psychological symptoms. One implication of this is that such a data set will not reflect at all accurately the level of symptoms which are due to recent changes in environmental stressors: i.e. illness is being studied rather than stress. Depue and Monroe suggest four types of chronic disorders. They are: personality traits, psychopathological disorders, which may have genetic and or environmental origins; secondary chronic dysphoria, resulting from a primary, persistent, life threatening or life-altering medical disorder leading to persistent distress; and prolonged life difficulties, such as those arising from long-term unemployment, marital discord or living in dangerous neighbourhoods such as those produced by poverty or urban warfare.

Following Watson and Clark (1984) they argue for the existence of a personality disposition which is well established in a variety of personality studies and which has been shown to be stable over long periods of time. Watson and Clark dubbed this negative affectivity (NA), but more traditionally it might be called trait anxiety. Conley (1985) reports recent studies showing the trait is not only stable over time, but also across situations. Depue and Monroe quote from Hinkle's work (1974) which showed that:

> In contrast to the 25% of subjects who had few episodes of disorder, the 25% experiencing chronic-intermittent patterns of disorder perceived their lives and occupations as difficult and unsatisfactory, reacted sharply to events, were aware of emotional difficulties and marginal social adjustment, tended to be anxious, introverted, and unduly sensitive, and sought much support and encouragement.

That is they were high on NA and that NA has at least a partial overlap with high symptom levels. Payne (1987) found a correlation of 0.63 between the Eysenck's measure of trait neuroticism (Eysenck and Eysenck, 1964) and a measure of recent symptomology (Goldberg's General Health Questionnaire, 1972). This study involved 75 men who had been unemployed for between 2 and 3 years, but the result was replicated on a sample of 381 employed male and female psychiatric nurses (Janman *et al.*, 1988), though the correlation was somewhat smaller, being 0.57. One of the first studies to report this high level of correlation between neuroticism and GHQ was by Henderson, Byrne and Duncan-Jones (1981) who found that neuroticism accounted for 69% of the variance in a combined measure of mental health. Cherry (1978) also notes from a longitudinal study that those who scored high on symptoms at age 32 had also scored high on neuroticism at age 16 years. There is good evidence then that in unselected populations many of the people indicating signs of stress symptoms are doing so, not because they are suffering increases in their stress levels, but because of the disposition to experience the world as a threatening place.

Variations in symptom reporting also occur with other individual difference variables. They vary by social class (Finley-Jones and Burville, 1977; Kessler and Cleary, 1980) with the lower social classes having much higher rates of psychological distress than those of skilled and professional classes. Females also have higher admission rates to mental hospitals than males, and have higher rates of symptom reporting (Sorensen *et al.*, 1985), though the rates may not differ dramatically by sex if the role circumstances of the men and women are similar (Warr and Payne, 1982). Employed single persons are an example of such a group. Rates of symptomatology also vary by age with young and old men having higher scores on GHQ-30 (Health Promotion Research Trust, 1987). This pattern does not hold for women where age and symptom expression do not seem to vary systematically. Amongst the unemployed the middle-aged tend to have poorer mental health than either the young or old, though the main effect of unemployment is to raise the rates of symptoms for most people (Warr and Jackson, 1985). These differences by sex and age are, of course, associated with changes in status and circumstances so age and sex may not be direct causes of the changes in symptom rates themselves.

There is a widespread belief in the stress literature that Type A behaviour is related to Coronary Heart Disease (CHD) and that stress is a contributor to CHD. Recent extensive reviews of Type A (Mathews and Haynes, 1986: Schmidt, Dembroski and Blümchen, 1986; Powell, 1987) show its relationship to CHD are not as clear-cut as is generally supposed. Only just over half the studies predicting a hard criterion of CHD such as death, or myocardial infarction (MI) actually find a significant relationship, and many of these are large, prospective studies which are a more powerful test of the hypothesis. Powell (1987) particularly focuses on methodological issues in this area and valid measurement of the construct is clearly one reason why results are variable.

These difficulties of developing good measures of Type A may partly account for the fact that the relationship between Type A and reports of psychological strain also vary. Keenen and McBain (1979) found no relationship between Type A and self-reported job tension. Burke (1984) similarly found no relationship between Type A and a range of affective measures nor with his measures of psychosomatic symptomatology. Matteson, Ivancevich and Smith (1984) found a moderate sized positive relationship between Type A and a measure of 28 Health Complaints in a study of 355 insurance salesmen, and Kelly and Houston (1985) found quite a strong relationship ($r = 0.41$) between Type A and a measure of job tension in a study of 92 middle-class women living in Kansas.

Costa and McCrae (1985) have recently produced some intriguing results, however, using neuroticism as a predictor of CHD. Results show that neuroticism is a very strong predictor of complaints about chest pains (i.e. angina pectoris). Neuroticism, however, does not predict death from CHD, or MI which obviously involves actual damage to the heart. It seems, however, that Type A behaviour relates quite strongly to self-reports of variables which directly or indirectly measure trait neuroticism. Indeed, Costa and McCrae quote several studies showing that Type A relates to measures of neuroticism-anxiety and conclude, 'Further evidence that the Framingham Type A Scale (FTAS) is more a measure of neuroticism than coronary prone behaviour is given by Smith's findings that FTAS scores correlated 0.50 and 0.41 with STAS and EPI-N scores respectively' (p. 92). (STAS and EPI–N are measures of trait anxiety and neuroticism respectively.) Any predictions that Type A does relate to poorer mental health then does need to discount the effects of trait neuroticism, which appears to have a common relationship with Type A and negative psychological symptoms.

Understanding the influence of Type A on strain is further complicated by the role of other individual difference variables which relate both to Type A and to symptom levels. Waldron *et al.* (1977) have shown that those with higher educational qualifications score higher on measures of Type A, but educational status is negatively correlated with symptoms of psychological ill-health (Fletcher and Payne, 1980). The influence of one individual difference variable might, therefore, counteract the effect of the other.

The confounding role of trait neuroticism appears again in attempts to relate locus of control to symptoms of psychological strain. Spector (1982) reviews studies using locus of control as a variable in organizational settings. In discussing the validity of the construct Spector notes that locus of control is negatively related to trait anxiety (Joe, 1971; Archer 1979), i.e. that externals are more anxious. Gemmill and Heisler (1972) reported a correlation of 0.31 between locus of control and a measure of job tension.

These studies have ignored two criticisms of the general literature on locus of control. One is that it is multi-dimensional (Phares, 1976) and the other that people's beliefs about their ability to control things is more situation or topic specific: thus scales have been developed to assess specific topics such as health (Lau, 1982). The Health Locus of Control Scale also turns out to be multidimensional having four sub-scales: self-control, provider control, chance and general health threat. These were used by Furnham (1983) in a study of 196 people, the sample being heterogeneous in terms of age, sex and employment status. Furnham found correlations of between 0.2 and 0.36 between the four sub-scales and a measure of psychiatric symptomatology developed by Langner (1962).

More recently Hoehn-Saric and McLeod (1985) showed that even within a sample of 112 adults diagnosed as having chronic anxiety disorders those higher on externality scored higher on neuroticism (EPI) and trait anxiety (STAI] and lower on social adjustment. The fact that locus of control and anxiety correlate within such a homogenous population is impressive evidence or the overlap between operational measures of the two constructs. However, the inevitable exceptions that prove the case, but raise doubts rather than disproof, must also be noted. Ray and Katahn (1968), for example, did not find a relationship between these two variables, and Keenan and McBain (1979) found no relationship between locus of control and job tension.

It is perhaps better established that externals tend to report higher levels of depression, and since anxiety correlates strongly with depression there is almost certainly some overlap between measures of affect and locus of control. Spector (1982) expresses the problem in relation to the effect of locus of control on learning or task performance: 'It may well be that anxiety rather than locus of control explains why internals seem to learn better than externals. Obviously, additional research is needed to ascertain the joint role of anxiety and locus of control in task performance' (p. 484). Payne (1988) used hierarchical regression to predict symptoms of anxiety and depression (Goldberg's GHQ measures) amongst unemployed men. The model assumed that environmental difficulties would predict level of symptoms over and above the effect of background variables such as social class, and personal attributes such as locus of control and coping styles. Both locus of control and the environmental difficulties measures did indeed predict symptoms, but if trait neuroticism is entered as the first variable then the effects of any other variables are removed. Any influence of the perceived environment or locus of control is cloaked by the strong influence of neuroticism on perceptions, on locus of control and on levels of anxiety symptoms and depressive symptoms.

Research has recently begun to develop on a construct which has some broad similarity to locus of control, namely optimism–pessimism (Scheier, Weintraub and Carver, 1986) though the detailed theory which underpins it makes some specific predictions which differ from those associated with locus of control *per se* (Scheier and Carver, 1987). For present purposes, however, it is worth noting that optimists have been shown to report fewer physical symptoms two years after their optimism was measured (Reker and Wong, 1983). A similar finding is reported by Scheier and Carver (1985) who also show that optimism is stable over a four-week time period and that it correlates between −0.21 and −0.31 with reports of the presence of up to 39 physical symptoms (dizziness, coughs, soreness, etc.). How optimism–pessimism will relate to trait anxiety/neuroticism is not known.

This brief review of the relationships between individual differences and strain has revealed the usual complexity of findings in the stress literature. It seems reasonable to conclude, however, that several variables have moderate to strong correlations with measures of psychological symptomatology. Not surprisingly, trait neuroticism/anxiety has the strongest relationship: many of the items in the scales which measure them are, of course, the same. It should not be forgotten, however, that the stability of the trait measures over time is considerably greater than that of the symptom measures. Payne (1988) reports a two-year longitudinal study of unemployed men. Test–retest correlations for the symptom measures of anxiety and depression were about 0.60. For those men who became re-employed during this period the test–retest correlations were only about 0.38. Test–retest correlations for trait measures over similar periods of time are much more like 0.85 (Conley, 1985).

What is somewhat more worrying of this literature is that neuroticism appears to have modest correlations with the other individual difference variables which have been studied such as Type A and locus of control. It is difficult to know from most of these studies if the relationships found are due to Type A, locus of control or to neuroticism.

It is an interesting point for the sociology of knowledge that trait anxiety/ neuroticism has been largely ignored in 25 years of stress research. Apart from its use by Kahn *et al.* (1964) in 'Organizational stress' it has rarely been measured in studies of stress, occupational stress in particular. Yet the 'man in the street' would surely suggest that the disposition to be anxious would be an important factor to take into account in studying stress. One does have to wonder just how reliable studies are if they have relied largely on self-report methods and have ignored trait anxiety/neuroticism, for not only may the trait affect the reporting of symptoms, it may also affect perceptions of the stressfulness of the environment. This is the next issue to be examined.

INDIVIDUAL DIFFERENCES AND PERCEPTIONS OF THE STRESSFULNESS OF THE ENVIRONMENT

Much of the literature in stress research is based on empirical studies which rely on subjects to report their perceptions of how stressful they perceive their environment to be. It is well known that even people in the same jobs, working in the same physical environment do not see their environment as having the same level of stress. This is not just a problem for stress research, however, for it also applies to perceptions of organizational or team climate (Glick 1985) and to perceptions of job characteristics such as measured by the Job Description Inventory (Hackman and Oldham, 1975). A considerable amount of this disagreement can be attributed to measurement error, some to real differences in the micro environment as, for example, when a supervisor treats two workers very differently, but some is very likely to arise from individual differences which affect the person's interpretation or appraisal of the threats and/or opportunities which are present in their work situation. This topic then has a substantive interest of its own, but it is particularly important to understand such influences when studies set out to test the proposition that environmental stress leads to psychological strain, and test it by relying on perceptions of environmental stressfulness and self-reports of symptoms. Clearly, any correlation between these two variables could be due to one causing the other, but it could also be due to a third variable, such as an individual difference variable. Kasl (1978) has been particularly concerned about this issue in occupational stress research describing it as 'the triviality trap'.

Trait anxiety/neuroticism is the most obvious variable which might influence perceptions of stressfulness since it defines the person as being in a state of unease about the uncertainty of events. As already indicated, not many studies have included measures of trait anxiety. Kahn (1974) found a modest relationship between an objective measure of role conflict (the sum of pressures to change behaviour as reported by the role senders who had formal influence on the person in the focal role) and perceived role conflict. Further analysis showed, however, that this relationship largely resulted from those in the sample who were high on anxiety proneness. Buck (1972) used perceptual measures of stressors, self-report personality measures (including anxiety) and self reports of felt job pressure. These variables correlated very highly so that over 80% of the variance in job pressure was accounted for by the other variables. However, perceived stressors correlated so highly with the personality variables that adding the stressor variables only accounted for a little more of the variance (9% for managers and 17% for manual workers).

Payne (1988) attempted to predict mental health (GHQ) amongst the unemployed from a model of environmental stress where the level of overall stress was determined by the balance of problems, opportunities and supports in the environment of the unemployed. All measures were self-report but the study was longitudinal the measures being collected on three occasions over a two-year period. At the third phase only trait neuroticism was measured using the Eysenck Personality Inventory (Eysenck and Eysenck, 1964). Trait neuroticism was strongly correlated with perceptions of problems including perceptions of financial problems. It was not correlated with perceptions of support, and opportunities was not measured during the third wave of data collection. Janman *et al.* (1988) also used the demands, supports–constraints framework proposed by Payne (1979) to study mental health (GHQ) in a study of 381 psychiatric nurses. Three independent dimensions of job demands were derived from a principal components analysis of 30 items, and four dimensions of job supports from 37 items. Neuroticism was found to correlate with some of the job demands scales but not others, e.g. 0.26 with aversive demands, but 0.02 with administrative demands. Those higher on neuroticism tended to see the communications as less supportive (-0.19), the administration as less supportive (-0.19) and the union as less supportive (-0.14). Negative affectivity then appears to affect the perceptions of a range of environmental variables, though the size of the effect is much smaller than that with reports of psychological symptoms.

Another individual difference variable which might affect perceptions of the environment is locus of control. In summarizing the characteristics of individuals high on internal locus of control Phares (1976) said this: 'in contrast to externals, internals exert greater effort to control their environment, exhibit better learning, seek new information more actively when that information has personal relevance, use information better, and seem more concerned with information rather than with social demands of situations'. Given these attributes of internals it is not surprising that they are inclined to see less stress in their environment than externals. Payne and Hartley (1987) found a correlation of 0.34 between perceptions of the severity of problems facing 399 unemployed men and an abbreviated measure of Rotter's locus of control scale. Keenan and McBain (1979) found locus of control to correlate −0.18 with role overload, but found no significant relationship with role ambiguity or role conflict.

Organ and Greene (1974) and Batlis (1980) reported correlations between locus of control and role ambiguity, the correlation being 0.42 for a sample of senior scientists and engineers, and 0.21 for supermarket managers. Batlis also reported a correlation of 0.19 with role conflict, but none with role overload.

Summarizing a wider review of the effect of locus of control on perceptions of job characteristics, including some of the studies identified above, Spector (1982) came to the following conclusion: 'The studies included here that reported a relation between I–E and job characteristics were consistent in showing that there may be differences in perceptions, but they were inconsistent in demonstrating a direction of relation'. The few reported here which have been published since 1982 confirm this view since they again show that I–E relates to perceptions of some dimensions of work, but not others. Once again, these relationships may largely be determined by the neuroticism component of locus of control, but Payne's study (1988) is the only one to have measured both variables and perceptions of environmental stressfulness. It does not seem too risky to conclude, however, that locus of control may influence perceptions of the environment just as much as it might influence the reporting of psychological symptoms, and that it is a variable worthy of investigation. Taking its multidimensionality into account, and developing more specific content measures such as an organizational locus of control measure, might throw more light on the role of these sorts of beliefs.

Few studies have looked at the relationship between Type A and locus of control, though Keenen and McBain (1979) used both measures (correlation = 0.10), but Type A has been used in a number of occupational stress studies, usually being conceived as a moderator between stress and strain (e.g. Van Dijkhuizen and Reiche, 1980). The last study concerned 574 employees from six different levels, but like several other studies divided the sample up according to their scores on the Type A–B continuum. In this particular case they only compared the extreme As and Bs, just less than 50 of each. They were able to show that the Type As reported higher levels of quantitative workload, more psychic complaints, higher diastolic blood pressure, more responsibility for people, but higher self-esteem and more use of their abilities. They attribute these differences to the fact that Type A managers seek out situations which demand more from them. It is also well established in the literature that Type A is higher amongst those of higher socio-economic status and education (Health Promotion Research Trust, 1987). These people also tend to occupy more demanding jobs at least as far as the jobs involve more responsibility, greater supervisory load, higher workload and involve more difficult tasks (Dearborn and Hastings, 1987). Keenan and McBain, however, found Type A to relate to work overload ($r = 0.28$) but not to role conflict or ambiguity.

Reporting on the results of the Minnesota Heart Survey, Sorensen *et al.* (1985) found two of the sub-scales of the Jenkins Activity Survey (a questionnaire measure of Type A behaviour) to relate to several aspects of the job situation which are less subjective than the role and job demand measures:

	Work hours	Deadlines	Occupational mobility
Hard driving	0.22*	0.20*	0.21*
Speed	0.16*	0.21*	0.13*

$N=2177$; * $p<0.05$.

These relationships may occur because the Type As self-select into such jobs, or being Types As (and therefore partly neurotic) they may over-report the nature of their job conditions, though in this particular study that seems much less likely.

It cannot, however, be totally discounted. Dearborn and Hastings (1987) studied Type A as a mediator of stress and strain in a sample of 136 employed women. As part of the study the researchers themselves rated the stressfulness of the jobs held by these women, and described this rating as an objective measure of job stress. They also asked the subjects to rate the stressfulness of their jobs. Ratings amongst different raters for the 'objective' measure were in good agreement, and there was a correlation of 0.33 between the objective ratings and the stressfulness as perceived by the job occupants themselves. Type A scores were correlated with both ratings and the first order partial correlation coefficient was calculated between Type A and subjective perceptions of job stress partialling out for objective stress. The partial coefficient was 0.25 indicating that those who are higher on Type A report their jobs as more stressful regardless of the actual degree of stress present in their jobs.

In their study of 91 employed women, Kelly and Houston (1985) used two self-report measures of Type A behaviour, the Jenkins Activity Scale and the Framingham Type A Scale. These were correlated with a number of perceived environmental variables and the authors also partialled out for the effect of job level. The partialling out procedure made very little difference to the correlations and the correlations were virtually identical for both measures of Type A. Type A was correlated with perceived quantitative workload 0.38, but it was also correlated 0.37 with overtime worked per week, and overtime hours desired (0.34). There was no correlation with perceived role conflict however. Thus, whilst the more Type A women appear to occupy the more demanding jobs, they also tend to see more workload. Unfortunately, it is not possible to control for hours of overtime worked as the full matrix of correlations is not presented, but there is some support here that Type As do see their work environments differently from Type Bs.

INDIVIDUAL DIFFERENCES AS A MODERATOR OF THE STRESS – STRAIN RELATIONSHIP

It has already been shown that several individual difference variables correlate with symptoms of psychological strain, and with perceptions of the stressfulness of the occupational environment. Despite the existence of these relationships several authors have treated these individual difference variables as moderators of the relationship between stress and strain. The assumptions that lie behind this analytical procedure are that the relationship between stress and strain will vary according to the level of the moderator variable. For example, it might be hypothesized that the relationship between stress and strain is very strong amongst people high on Type A. For people who are in the middle range of Type A/B it might be argued that the relationship between stress and strain is close to zero, and for extreme Type Bs it might be argued that the relationship is negative, though small in size. Many studies do not split their population/sample into three or more, but are content to compare extreme high and low groups on a given variable, or use moderated regression to demonstrate a variable is acting as a moderator without showing exactly how the moderator is affecting the relationship.

Van Dijkhuizen and Reiche (1980) divided their sample of 574 into three groups on the Type A variable, but report results only for the 47 with the highest Type A score and the 48 with the lowest Type A scores (i.e. extreme Type Bs). Apart from showing the Type As reported more quantitative workload, more responsibility for people, and more use of skills they also showed the Type As had more psychic complaints, higher diastolic blood pressure, and higher self-esteem. They also found that Type A did moderate the relationship between stress and strain. Three stressors were measured: work load, poor relationships with others and job future ambiguity. Examples of the correlations between the three measures of stress and strains for the Type A and Type B subgroups appear below:

	Type A	Type B
Poor relations with others and		
(1) psychosomatic complaints	0.45	0.02
(2) psychic complaints	0.51	0.16
Job future ambiguity and		
(1) blood pressure	0.37	−0.17
(2) cholesterol level	0.38	0.03

Workload did not act as a moderator and the authors claim that, 'It thus appears that A/B typology has a conditioning influence on the relationship between psychosocial stress and strains' (p. 129). A note of caution might be sounded, however, for both these job stressors, future ambiguity and poor relationships with others, would appear to be much more open to subjective interpretations than other stressor variables such as heavy workload or long hours. The previous section on individual differences and perceptions of the environment emphasized this problem of course.

The sample sizes of this study are relatively small too, and this is even more true of a study by Orpen (1982) who studied 91 middle-managers and compared the 30 highest with the 30 lowest on the Type A/B typology. Correlations were calculated for 15 stress–strain relationships. Five reached the 5% confidence level. All five were correlations between subjective stressors and subjective strains, e.g. role overload and physical strain, role conflict and psychological strain. None of the relationships between role stress and physical measures of strain (e.g. heart rate or blood pressure) were significant. Orpen again found the Type As experienced greater stress and strain and cautions the reader about the self-report nature of the data.

The use of the top and bottom thirds of the sample was also followed by Ivancevich, Matteson and Preston. (1982). They report two studies. The first consisted of 339 business/industrial managers who had recently completed a medical examination, and who returned a self-completion questionnaire. Six environmental stressors were measured, five about the job situation, and one about the family situation. Seven strain measures were taken, five being physiological or physical indices (e.g. serum cholesterol and per cent body fat) and two being affective (intrinsic and extrinsic satisfaction). The paper reports eight cases where there is a significant difference between the correlations of the stressor variables with the strain variables. The authors summarize their findings thus:

Type A behavior was a fairly significant moderator in study 1. As expected, managers with high Type A characteristics were more adversely affected by quantitative workload. There also was a stronger association between lack of career progression and intrinsic satisfaction, role conflict and intrinsic satisfaction, and role conflict and systolic blood pressure for managers with Type A tendencies than for their Type B counterparts. (p. 382)

Whether intrinsic and extrinsic satisfaction can be considered as valid measures of job strain seems a moot point in this study, but it does provide evidence that Type A can act as a moderator, and the usual assumptions about stress–strain relationships seem to work for Type As, but not Type Bs, for in all three studies there are virtually no relationships between stress and strain for the Type B subjects.

The second study reported by Ivancevich *et al.* involved nurses, but it suffers small sample sizes, there being 21 Type A nurses and 29 Type Bs. None of the statistical tests reached the 1% confidence interval used in the first study but seven reached the 10% level or better. Since 47 relationships were compared, however, five of these may be chance relationships. Once again, where there were significant relationships between stressors and strains it was for the Type A nurses only. Four out of the seven relationships that differed between Type A and B were for physiological strain measures and three were for satisfaction. Whilst less compelling than study 1 the weight of the evidence is in favour of a moderating effect.

Dearborn and Hastings (1987) adopted the more conservative, but perhaps more rigorous criterion for dividing their sample of employed women, by splitting it into two at the mean score on Type A/B. Using job stress and a mixture of psychological and physical symptoms as strains they found 12 out of 20 significant correlations for the Type As, and only six for the Type Bs. They did not test for the significance of the difference between the correlations that were significant in each sample, but only one looks to be significant; for Type Bs there is a correlation of 0.29 between job stress and getting colds. Where there is a correlation for the Type As, but not the Type Bs, then the majority of the seven correlations are probably significantly different from each other. The authors note that for Type Bs job stress tends to be related to work related symptoms only, but for Type As it spreads to family and other social settings.

One study which differs in some important respects from the ones considered so far is that by Caplan and Jones (1975). It dealt with a real-life stressor, the temporary shutdown of the main computer in a university, the shutdown lasting 23 days. Measure were taken from 75 computer users three days before the shutdown and six months later. The job stressors were quantitative workload (subjective) and role ambiguity, and the strains were anxiety, depression, resentment and heart-rate. The symptom measures in particular changed over time, being significantly higher just prior to the shutdown. The authors were able to investigate the moderating role of Type

A on relationships between *changes* in the variables over time. Their sample was split at the median on the Type A measure. Their findings were that:

> The correlation between changes in subjective workload and changes in anxiety was .54 for the Type A persons, but only .27 for the Type B persons ($p < .10$). The slope of the regression of changes in work load on changes in anxiety was higher ($p < .05$) for the Type A persons than for the Type B persons. There was a similar tendency for the relationship between changes in anxiety and heart rate to be higher for the Type A ($r = .45$, $p < .005$) than for the Type B persons ($r = .22$, $p < .10$) although no difference in the regression slopes of the two groups. (p. 717)

Keenan and McBain (1979) also used Type A as a moderator of the relationship between perceived stressors and strains. The three stressors were role ambiguity, role conflict and role overload, and these were related to tension at work and job satisfaction. Their sample was divided at the median on Type A/B giving 45 middle-managers in each subgroup. Out of the six comparisons only one reached the 5% confidence level. For Type As the correlation between role ambiguity was significantly greater than for Type Bs (-0.70 vs -0.26).

Without carrying out a complete survey of all published and unpublished studies, it is impossible to know for sure how good the evidence is that Type A moderates the relationship between stress and strain. Some of the studies reported here are based on quite small numbers but the weight of the evidence is that for Type A persons the relationship between reported stress and strain is stronger, and is so for both psychological strains and some physical strains. For Type Bs the relationships are either much weaker in size, or come close to zero.

The other variable which has been quite frequently used as a moderator is locus of control. Keenan and McBain also used this in their study and once again only one out of six tests showed the correlations to be significantly different. There was a correlation of 0.55 between role ambiguity and tension at work for the external group but a correlation of only 0.07 for the internal group. Amongst externals those who experience more role ambiguity also experience more tension at work.

One of the largest and most impressive studies was conducted by Krause and Stryker (1984). Their data were taken from the National Longitudinal Study of Middle-Aged Men who were aged 45–54 in 1966. Data from the 1969 and 1971 panel interviews were used. They used a shortened version of the locus of control scale which deleted items known to load on factors other than genalized locus of control (e.g. about schooling and politics). Their sample contained over 2000 men and when these are divided into internals (1339) and externals (751) they found that, 'men with external locus of control orientations experience higher levels of psychophysical distress because of stressful events (job and economic events) than men with internal locus of control' (p. 786). The effects of age, marital status, race, education, occupation, income and health status in 1969 were controlled. More detailed analyses showed some intriguing results. The sample was divided into four groups of extreme internal, moderate internal, moderate external and extreme external. The relationship between stress and distress is significantly different for the moderate internal group from all other groups. Having moderate internal locus of control beliefs reduces the impact of job and economic stress. For extreme internals and extreme externals the effects of stress on psychophysiological distress did not differ, though the two variables are related for both groups. The group most vulnerable to stress was the moderate external.

Krause and Stryker suggest that extreme externals are vulnerable to stress because they are less likely to bother taking positive actions, whilst the high internals are paralyzed by their own guilt since they believe their failure to cope is their own fault.

Krause followed the advice offered in the above paper and studied a group of a different age to see if the results were replicated (Krause, 1986). Krause found that in his sample of 351 older adults that extreme internals and extreme externals had more depressive symptoms. He also showed that internals actually reported fewer negative life events and suggested this was because they initiated actions to avoid or ameliorate them. Thus being high internal is a mixed blessing: such beliefs promote stress avoidance, but they also lead to self-blame.

In the previous study Krause used moderated regression to examine the interactive effects of locus of control and stress and strain. This has also been used by Batlis (1980) and Abdel–Halim (1980). Batlis studied 111 supermarket managers measuring job satisfaction, job related anxiety and propensity to leave as strains, and role ambiguity and role conflict as stressors. Batlis found no support for locus of control as a moderator. In his study of 89 middle-managers Abdel–Halim found that the relationship between role ambiguity and job satisfaction was moderated by locus of control. In more ambiguous jobs the internals were more satisfied than the externals. Since job satisfaction and indices of strain typically correlate over 0.30 (Kasl, 1978) this may be indirect support for a moderation of a genuine stress–strain relationship.

Another large study employed the same technique in studying 854 employed males (Syrotnick and D'Arcy, 1982). The independent variables were job autonomy, job pressure and job opportunities. Since Karasek (1979) has shown that the most stressful jobs are those with low autonomy and high demands autonomy is perhaps appropriately conceptualized as a stressor. The dependent variables were job satisfaction, the 30 item version of the General Health Questionnaire as a measure of psychological distress, a personal health rating and alcohol abuse. Few interactions were found, though they did report that externals reported using more social support when under pressure. The authors concluded that locus of control does not have extensive moderator effects on stress–strain relationships.

Parkes (1984) carried out a study of locus of control, cognitive appraisal and coping in stressful episodes. The study is not strictly speaking a test of the moderator effect in stress–strain relationships, but it is an interesting study in an occupational setting: the subjects were 171 student nurses. Parkes' findings were similar to those of Krause mentioned above. The internals reported more adaptive coping responses; this was particularly true when the situations were appraised as potentially controllable and important to the subject.

Another study which does not fall into the conventional test of the stress–strain relationship is that of Anderson (1977) who studied the effects of a natural disaster: namely a hurricane. Anderson examined the coping efforts and performance of 90 businessmen whose businesses had been disrupted by the disaster. Externals perceived their circumstances as more stressful, and relied more on emotional means of coping (denial etc.) than on problem-solving methods of coping than did the internals. Not only that, the businesses of the internals were more successful during the following three years.

There are, of course, studies that lie outside occupational contexts where locus of control has been shown to be a moderator of the stress–strain relationship. Many of them lie within the study of life-events and their possible effect on future health and well-being. Lefcourt (1983) reviews the area and confirms the overall picture described above. Externals experience greater strain than internals. Indeed, Lefcourt proposes that they do so even in the absence of stressful life events. This is consistent with the point made earlier that locus of control correlates with trait anxiety. This relationship might then be largely caused by the externals being more neurotic/anxious. Lefcourt makes an important qualification about much of this research. He says that much of it shows that in the short-term stress has an immediate impact on nearly everyone irrespective of their locus of control (or neuroticism presumably) but that given the passage of time internals succeed in leaving their disappointments behind whilst the externals use them to confirm their belief that the world is outside their control, so their effects live on for longer. It is this sort of complexity that leads Lefcourt to conclude:

the point to be taken is that although locus of control does offer some power in predicting the response to stress, the effects are not without complexity. Where research with moderator effects has recently begun to overshadow the more simple investigations linking stress with illness, more recent findings have begun to reveal higher-order interactions in which moderators of moderators are explored. (p. 265)

Another point already made concerns the small number of studies of occupational stress that have included a measure of negative affectivity/neuroticism/anxiety. None of those cited here have used it as a moderator of the stress–strain relationship. Given that such measures have such strong correlations with other measures of strain it might not act as a moderator anyway, particularly where the measures of stress are also self-report. It might be recalled that Payne (1987) showed that trait neuroticism cloaks the effects of locus of control and perceived demands, support, etc., when it is entered first in a regression predicting current affective states such as anxiety and depression. Apart from this qualification, however, the preceding paragraphs contain sufficient evidence to conclude that Type A and locus of control moderate the relationships between stressors and strains, at least when the stressors and the strains are measured by self-report. Whether this result would hold up if stressors were measured objectively and the strains were assessed physiologically is open to empirical test, but these are rare or non-existent in the occupational stress literature. The results do indicate, however, that internals cope better with higher levels of stress, and Type As cope worse. As we shall see in the next section on individual differences and coping, this raises an interesting conceptual issue.

INDIVIDUAL DIFFERENCES AND COPING

The literature on coping with occupational stress is comprehensively reviewed by Edwards (1988) in chapter 8 of this book. For the sake of completeness, however, it needs to be recognized that individual differences in personality, age, experience, gender, intellectual ability, cognitive style, etc., affect the way a person responds to stressful work environments. The attempt to develop measures of coping styles which might be related to such individual differences has accelerated during the last decade but at present there is little agreement on what constitutes dimensions of coping behaviour. Several conceptual schemes have been proposed, but the development of reliable and valid empirical measures is still in its infancy, though progress has been made by Folkman and Lazarus (1980), Pearlin and Schooler (1978), Moos and Billings (1982) and Osipow and Spokane (1984).

    One problem in this literature is whether there are styles of coping which are stable over both time and situations. If there are stable styles of coping an interesting conceptual issue is raised. What is the difference between a stable style of coping and a personality trait? Is the Type A behaviour pattern a way of coping with life's problems? Are the attributional processes inherent in being internal or external in one's beliefs different ways of coping with life? Warr's (1987) concern with distinguishing baseline mental health from current mental health is concerned with a similar issue. Coping style, conceptually, is of course different from individual difference variables such as physical strength or intelligence. The possession of great strength or great intelligence obviously enables a person to cope with life in particular ways, but they are not coping styles in the same sense as emotion focused and problem focused coping styles are (Folkman and Lazarus, 1980). People high on neuroticism also respond to problems in a particular way: they worry, become agitated, perhaps act rashly as a result of their anxiety so their characteristic behaviour is in one sense a way of coping, but their high levels of emotionality are at the same time 'built in' and thus not a coping style in that sense.

Coping is a core concept in the stress literature and it might be argued that coping should only refer to actions and reactions that present the individual with problems. The difficulty with such a definition is to define a state or situation which is not a problem; people have to 'cope' with such everyday 'problems' as preparing meals, dressing, keeping clean, getting from A to B. Whilst there is this difficulty it would be reasonable to assume that coping refers to dealing with problematic situations. Fleishman (1984) argues that, 'The distinction between personality characteristics and coping behaviours is one of generality or level of abstraction. General personality orientations may be manifest in the choice of specific coping behaviours in a particular situation' (p. 231). Like Fleishman, I will choose to leave things fuzzy and turn to him again for one of the few studies that relate coping styles to personality variables.

Drawing on the data from the large community study of stress conducted by Pearlin and Schooler (1978) in Chicago, Fleishman related four personality measures to four measures of coping. The latter comprised one problem-focused measure, and three emotion-focused measures. These were employed across four role stress areas such as work, marriage, economic circumstances and the coping items varied somewhat for each role area. The four personality variables were mastery (cf. locus of control), self-esteem, self-denial and non-disclosure of problems to others. The results are complex but in a series of 22 regressions using the four personality variables plus age, sex, education, income and role stress the percentage of variance accounted for in the coping styles varied from 8 to 28%. There was considerable variation is what predicted what according to the role situation studied. Thus self-esteem predicts selective ignoring for parental coping, but not marital coping, financial coping or occupational coping. Mastery, on the other hand predicted self-ignoring in all four role situations. Fleishman's conclusions to this study are, 'the findings highlight the importance of considering in detail how personality characteristics combine with features of the situation to shape behaviour' (p. 242).

Having raised the conceptual issues surrounding coping vs individual differences and demonstrated, not surprisingly, that they are related and both affect responses to stress we shall leave the topic. One observation is worth making, however, and that is that when coping is studied it is usually treated as if it were an individual difference variable, except in studies where coping is treated as the outcome variable itself.

CONCLUSION

Whilst a good number of studies have been referred to here they are drawn from a relatively narrow band of concepts and this is a limitation on any conclusions that might be drawn. On the other hand, these three concepts (negative affectivity, Type A and locus of control) all relate to each other, so any conclusions drawn for any of them are still open to the attack that a third variable might be the real cause. If a case were to be made for any of these three as the fundamental underlying variable then negative affectivity would appear to be the strongest candidate. It is more likely to be partly genetically determined than the other two which are more likely to be acquired dispositions or belief patterns. In an existential sense, such conceptual splitting seems artificial, but the studies reported are based on samples of individuals where the aim is to look for trends and directions rather than precise prediction of individual behaviour or experience. This all too brief review does show, however, that these variables have pervasive effects on the stress process and that they should be taken into account in future studies to check that they, rather than the environment, are not the true causes of changes in psychological well-being.

REFERENCES

Abdel-Halim, A. A. (1980). Effects of person–job compatability on managerial relations to role ambiguity, *Organizational Behaviour and Human Performance*, **26**, 193–211.

Anderson, C. R. (1977). Locus of control, coping behaviors and performance in a stress setting: a longitudinal study, *Journal of Applied Psychology*, **62**, 446–51.

Antonovsky, A. (1987). *Unravelling the Mystery of Health*, Jossey-Bass, San Francisco.

Archer, R. P. (1979). Relationships between locus of control, trait anxiety and state anxiety: an interactionist perspective, *Journal of Personality*, **47**, 305–16.

Bachman, J. G. (1970). *Youth in Transition*, Vol. 2, Institute for Social Research, Ann Arbor, M.

Batlis, N C. (1980). Job Involvement and locus of control as moderators of role–perception/individual outcome relationships, *Psychological Reports*, **46**, 111–19.

Buck, V. E. (1972). *Working Under Pressure*, Staples Press, London.

Burke, R. J. (1984). The Type A experience: occupational and life demands, satisfaction and well-being. In R. J. Burke (ed.), *Current Issues in Occupational Stress*: York University, Toronto.

Caplan, R. D. and Jones, K. W. (1975). Effects of workload, role ambiguity and Type A personality on anxiety, depression and heart-rate. *Journal of Applied Psychology*, **60**, 713–19.

Cherry, N. (1978). Stress, anxiety and work: a longitudinal study, *Journal of Occupational Psychology*, **51**, 259–70.

Conley, J. J. (1985). Longitudinal stability of personality traits: a multitrait–multimethod–multioccasion analysis, *Journal of Personality and Social Psychology*, **49**, 1266–82.

Costa, P. T., Jr and McCrae, R. R. (1985). Hypochondriasis, neuroticism and ageing, *American Psychologist*, **40**, 19–29.

Dearborn, M. J. and Hastings, J. E. (1987). Type A personality as a mediator of stress and strain in employed women, *Journal of Human Stress*, Summer 1987, 53–60.

Depue, R. A. and Monroe, S. M. (1986). Conceptualization and measurement of human disorders in life stress research: the problem of chronic disturbance, *Psychological Bulletin*, **99**, 36–51.

Edwards, J. R. (1988). The determinants and consequences of coping with stress. This volume, Chapter 8.

Eysenck, H. J. and Eysenck, S. B. G. (1964), *Manual of the Eysenck Personality Inventory*, London University Press, London.

Finlay-Jones, R. A. and Burvill, P. W. (1977). The prevalence of minor psychiatric morbidity in the community, *Psychological Medicine*, **7**, 475–89.

Fleishman, J. A. (1984). Personality characteristics and coping patterns, *Journal of Health and Social Behavior*, **25**, 229–44.

Fletcher, B. (C) (1988). The epidemiology of occupational stress. This volume, Chapter 1.

Fletcher, B. (C) and Payne, R. L. (1980). Stress and work: a review and theoretical framework, Part 1, *Personnel Review*, **9**(1), 19–29.

Folkman, S. and Lazarus, R. S. (1980). An analysis of coping in a middle-aged community sample, *Journal of Health and Social Behavior*, **21**, 219–39.

Frese, M. and Okonek, K. (1984). Reasons to leave shift-work and psychological and psychosomatic complaints of former shift-workers, *Journal of Applied Psychology*, **69**, 509–14.

Furnham, A. (1983). The A Type Behaviour Pattern, mental health and health locus of control beliefs, *Social Science and Medicine*, **20**, 1569–72.

Glick, W. H. (1985). Conceptualizing and measuring organizational and psychological climate: pitfalls in multilevel research, *Academy of Management Review*, **10**, 601–16.

Gemmill, G. R. and Heisler, W. J. (1972). Fatalism as a factor in managerial job satisfaction, job strain, and mobility, *Personnel Psychology*, **25**, 241–50.

Goldberg, D. P. (1972). *The Detection of Psychiatric Illness by Questionnaire*, Oxford University Press, Oxford.

Hackman, J. R. and Oldham, G. R. (1975). Development of the Job Diagnostic Survey, *Journal of Applied Psychology*, **60**, 159–70.

Health Promotion Research Trust (1987). *The Health and Lifestyle Survey*, Health Promotion Research Trust, London.

Hinkle, L. E., Jr (1974). The effect of exposure to culture change, social change and changes in interpersonal relationships on health. In B. S. Dohrenwend and B. P. Dohenwend (eds) *Stressful Life Events: Their Nature and Effects*, John Wiley and Sons, New York.

Henderson, S., Byrne, D. G. and Duncan-Jones, P. (1981). *Neurosis and the Social Environment*, Academic Press, London.

Hoehn-Saric, R. and McLeod, D. R. (1985). Locus of control in chronic anxiety disorders, *Acta Psychiatra Scandinavia*, **72**, 529–35.

Holland, J. L. (1976). Vocational preferences. In M. D. Dunnette (ed.) *Handbook of Industrial and Organizational Psychology*, Rand McNally, Chicago.

Ivancevich, J. M., Matteson, M. T. and Preston, C. (1982). Occupational stress, Type A behaviour and physical well-being, *Academy of Management Journal*, **25**, 2, 373–391.

Janman, K., Jones, J. C., Payne, R. L. and Rick, J. T. (1988). Clustering individuals as a way of dealing with multiple predictors in occupational stress research, *Journal of Human Stress*, in press.

Joe, V. C. (1971). Review of the internal–external control construct as a personality variable, *Psychological Reports*, **28**, 619–40.

Kahn, R. L. (1974). Conflict, ambiguity and overwork: three elements in job stress, in A. McLean (ed.) *Occupational Stress*, Charles C. Thomas, Springfield, IL.

Kahn, R. L., Wolfe, D. M., Quinn, R. P., Snoek, J. D. and Rosenthal, R. A. (1964). *Organizational Stress: Studies in Role, Conflict and Ambiguity*, John Wiley and Sons, New York.

Kasl, S. V. (1978. Epidemiological contributions to the study of work stress. In C. L. Cooper and R. Payne (eds) *Stress at Work*, John Wiley and Sons, Chichester.

Karasek, R. A. (1979). Job demands, job decision latitude and mental strain: implications for job redesign, *Administrative Science Quarterly*, 285–308.

Keenan, A. and McBain, G. D. M. (1979). Effects of Type A behaviour, intolerance of ambiguity, and locus of control on the relationship between role stress and work-related outcomes, *Journal of Occupational Psychology*, **52**, 277–85.

Kelly, K. E. and Houston, B. K. (1985). Type A behaviour in employed women: relation to work, marital and leisure variables, social support, stress, tension and health, *Journal of Personality and Social Psychology*, **46**, 1067–79.

Kesler, R. C. and Cleary, P. D. (1980). Social class and psychological distress, *American Sociological Review*, **45**, 463–78.

Kohn, M. (1969). *Class and Conformity*, Dorsey Press, Homewood, Ill.

Krause, N. (1986). Stress and coping: reconceptualizing the role of locus of control beliefs, *Journal of Gerontology*, **41**, 617–22.

Krause, N. and Stryker, S. (1984). Stress and well-being: the buffering role of locus of control beliefs, *Social Science and Medicine*, **18**, 783–90.

Lau, R. (1982). Origins of health locus of control beliefs, *Journal of Personality and Social Psychology*, **42**, 322–34.

Langner, T. S. (1962). A twenty-two item screening score of psychiatric symptoms indicating impairment, *Journal of Health and Social Behavior*, **3**, 269–76.

Lefcourt, H. M. (1983). The locus of control as a moderator variable: stress. In H. M. Lefcourt (ed.) *Research with the Locus of Control Construct*, Vol. 2, Academic Press, New York.

Maddi, S. R. and Kobasa, S. C. (1984). *The Hardy Executive: Health under Stress*, Dow Jones-Irwin, Homewood, Ill.

Matteson, M. T., Ivancevich, J. M. and Smith, S. V. (1984). Relation of Type A behaviour to performance and satisfaction among sales personnel, *Journal of Vocational Behavior*, **25**, 203–214.

Matthews, K. A. and Haynes, S. G. (1986). Type A behavior pattern and coronary disease risk: update and critical evaluation, *American Journal of Epidemiology*, **123**, 923–60.

Moos, R. H. and Billings, A. G. (1982). Conceptualizing and measuring coping resources and processes. In *Handbook of Stress: Theoretical and Clinical Aspects*, Free Press, New York.

Organ, D. W. and Greene, E. N. (1974). Role ambiguity, locus of control and work satisfaction, *Journal of Applied Psychology*, **59**, 101–2.

Orpen, C. (1982). Type A personality as a moderator of the effects of role conflict, role ambiguity and role overload on individual strain, *Journal of Human Stress*, **8** (2), 8–14.

Osipow, S. H. and Spokane, A. R. (1984). Measuring occupational stress, strain and coping. In S. Okamap (ed.), *Applied Social Psychology Annual*, Vol. 5, Sage, Beverley Hills.

Parkes, K. P. (1984). Locus of control, cognitive appraisal, and coping in stressful episodes, *Journal of Personality and Social Psychology*, **3**, 655–68.

Payne, R. L. (1979). Demands, supports, constraints and psychological health. In C. J. Mackay and T. Cox (eds). *Response to Stress: Occupational Aspects*, International Publishing Corporation, London.

Payne, R. L. (1988). A longitudinal study of the psychological well-being of unemployed men and the mediating effect of neuroticism, *Human Relations*, in press.

Payne, R. L. and Hartley, J. (1987). A test of a model for explaining the affective experience of unemployed men. *Journal of Occupational Psychology*, **60**, 31–47.

Pearlin, L. I. and Schooler, C. (1978). The structure of coping, *Journal of Health and Social Behaviour*, **19**, 2–21.

Phares, E. J. (1976). *Locus of Control in Personality*, General Learning Press, New Jersey.

Powell, L. N. (1987). Issues in the measurement of Type A behaviour pattern. In S. V. Kasl and C. L. Cooper (eds), *Stress and Health: Issues in Research Methodology* John Wiley and Sons, London.

Reker, G. T. and Wong, P. T. P. (1983). *The Salutary Effects of Personal Optimism and Meaningfulness on the Physical and Psychological Well-Being of the Elderly*, 29th Annual Meeting of the Western Gerontological Society.

Ray, W. J. and Katahn, M. (1968). Relation of anxiety to locus of control, *Psychological Reports*, **23**, 1196.

Scheier, M. F. and Carver, C. S. (1985). Optimism, coping and health: assessment and implications of generalised outcome expectancies, *Health Psychology*, **4**, 219–247.

Scheier, M. F. and Carver, C. S. (1987). Dispositional optimism and physical well-being: the influence of generalized outcome expectancies on health, *Journal of Personality*, **55**, 2, 169–210.

Schmidt, T., Dembroski, T. M. and Blümchen, G. (1986). *Biological and Psychological Factors in Cardiovascular Disease*, Springer, Berlin.

Sorensen, G., Pirie, P., Folsom, A., Luepker, R., Jacobs, D. and Gillum, R. (1985). Sex differences in the relationship between work and health: the Minnesota Heart Survey, *Journal of Health and Social Behavior*, **26**, 379–94.

Spector, P. E. (1982). Behaviour in organizations as a function of employees' Locus of Control, *Psychological Bulletin*, **91**, 482–97.

Syrotnick, J. M. and D'Arcy, C. (1982). Occupational stress, locus of control and health among men in a prairie province. *Canadian Journal of Behavioral Science*, **14**, (2), 122–133.

Van Dijkhuizen, N. and Reiche, H. (1980). Psychosocial stress in industry: a heart-ache for middle management? *Psychotherapy and Psychosomatics*, **34**, 124–34.

Waldron, I., Zyzanski, S., Shekelle, R. B., Jenkins, C. D. and Tannenbaum, S. (1977). The coronary-prone behavior pattern in employed men and women, *Journal of Human Stress*, December 1977, 2–18.

Warr, P. B. (1987). *Work, Unemployment and Mental Health*, Oxford University Press, Oxford.

Warr, P. B. and Jackson, P. R. (1985). Factor influencing the psychological impact of prolonged unemployment and of re-employment, *Psychological Medicine*, **15**, 795–807.

Warr, P. and Payne, R. (1982). Experiences of strain and pleasure among British adults, *Social Science and Medicine*, **16**, 1691–7.

Watson, D. and Clark, L. A. (1984). Negative affectivity: the disposition to experience aversive emotional states, *Psychological Bulletin*, **96**, 465–90.

Werts, C. E. and Watley, D. J. (1970). *Paternal influence on talent development*, National Merit Scholarship Corporation, Report No. 4, Evanston, II.

Causes, Coping and Consequences of Stress at Work
Edited by C. L. Cooper and R. Payne
© 1988 John Wiley & Sons Ltd

Chapter 8

The Determinants and Consequences of Coping with Stress

Jeffrey R. Edwards

In recent years, it has been acknowledged that individual well-being is influenced not only by the amount of stress experienced by the individual, but also by how the individual *copes* with stress (Antonovsky, 1979; Holroyd and Lazarus, 1982; Lazarus and Launier, 1978). While there is widespread agreement concerning the importance of coping, there is little agreement concerning the meaning of coping and the mechanisms by which it influences stress and well-being. For this reason, it is difficult to organize the existing coping literature into a cohesive whole. Measures of coping have been presented (Aldwin et al., 1980; Latack, 1986; Sidle *et al.*, 1969; Stone and Neale, 1984) and the role of coping in the stress process has been examined (Folkman and Lazarus, 1980; Newton and Keenan, 1985; Pearlin and Schooler, 1978), but we still know relatively little about the specific coping strategies individuals use in dealing with stress, the process by which individuals select and implement these strategies, or the mechanisms by which coping affects stress and individual well-being.

The purpose of this chapter is to review existing theoretical approaches to coping and, based on this review, present an alternative approach.* First, major theoretical approaches to coping will be summarized, and the advantages and drawbacks of these approaches will be noted. Following this, a theoretical approach to coping will be presented which attempts to incorporate the advantages of existing theoretical approaches and to overcome their drawbacks. We will conclude with a discussion of the implications of the theoretical approach presented in this chapter for future research into coping with stress at work.

---

* While this chapter was originally intended to focus specifically on coping with stress at work, coping with work and nonwork sources of stress are often discussed jointly in the coping literature. Therefore, this chapter discusses coping in general terms, allowing for applications in both work and nonwork settings.

THEORETICAL APPROACHES TO COPING

This section will review major theoretical approaches to the study of coping and identify advantages and drawbacks associated with these approaches. This review is intended to provide an overview of general theoretical approaches to coping rather than a critique of any specific theory. In addition, this section focuses on theoretical rather than empirical work on coping. For reviews of empirical research on coping, see Coelho, Hamburg and Adams (1974), Lazarus and Folkman (1984b), Menaghan (1983), Silver and Wortman (1980) and Suls and Fletcher (1985).

Psychoanalytic Approaches to Coping

Investigators in the area of psychoanalytic and personality psychology have long been concerned with various forms of adjustment, including coping. In this literature, coping is typically defined in terms of realistic thoughts and actions which solve problems confronting the individual. This method of adjustment is contrasted with more primitive means, such as repression, displacement, denial of reality, and so on. Several investigators have derived classification schemes to describe these various means of adjustment. For example, the writings of Freud, Adler and Jung contain classifications of adjustment and defense mechanisms by which individuals deal with intrapsychic conflict (Rychlak, 1981). More recently, investigators such as Menninger (1963), Haan (1969, 1977) and Valliant (1977) have presented hierarchical descriptions of adjustment processes. In each of these classification schemes, coping represents the highest level of adjustment, with processes further down the hierarchy representing less reality-oriented (and thus inherently inferior) methods of adjustment.

Psychoanalytic approaches to coping are noteworthy in their rich, vivid descriptions of coping processes. Nonetheless, these approaches also contain several drawbacks. First, contact with reality is considered a necessary condition for successful coping (e.g. Haan, 1977). However, there are cases where the *denial* of reality is an effective means of coping. For example, denial may help reduce stress when the individual is initially overwhelmed by a stressful situation or appraises the situation as uncontrollable (Hamburg and Adams, 1967; Lazarus, 1983; Miller and Grant, 1979). Similarly, research on the relative efficacy of avoidant and non-avoidant coping strategies indicates that, while non-avoidant coping strategies are superior in the long run, avoidant coping strategies are generally more effective in the short run (Suls and Fletcher, 1985). Second, the psychoanalytic literature typically defines coping in terms of *successful* adjustment. That is, coping refers to successfully meeting the demands of a stressful situation, while failure to meet these demands indicates a lack of coping. However, defining coping in terms of its outcome confounds these two variables and prevents meaningful tests of relationships between coping and well-being (Lazarus and Folkman, 1984b). As a result, we overlook cases where individual and situational variables cause similar coping strategies to yield different effects on well-being. In sum, by defining coping in terms of realistic thoughts and actions which resolve stress, psychoanalytic approaches to coping ignore cases where denial is an effective means of coping and obscure the relationship between coping and outcomes.

Coping as a Personal Trait or Style

A considerable amount of research has characterized coping in terms of relatively stable personal traits or styles. Studies adopting this approach examine the impact of a particular personality trait or coping style, such as hardiness (Kobasa, Maddi and Courington, 1981), locus of control (Lefcourt, 1985; Rotter, 1966), or Type A behavior pattern (Friedman and Rosenman, 1959; Glass, 1977), on the relationship between stress and well-being, under the assumption that individuals with certain predispositions (e.g. high hardiness, internal locus of control, Type B behavior pattern) are better able to cope with stress and therefore suffer fewer of its negative consequences. In spite of the intuitive appeal of this approach, there is little unequivocal evidence that particular personal traits or coping styles consistently lead to the attenuation of the relationship between stress and well-being (Cohen and Edwards, 1988).

The lack of support for the stress buffering effects of personal traits or styles may be partially explained by noting several conceptual and methodological problems associated with this approach. First, personal traits and styles are often poor predictors of actual situational appraisals and coping behaviors (Lazarus and Folkman, 1984b). For instance, studies examining the impact of locus of control on the relationship between stressful life events and symptomatology have found little correspondence between control orientation (internal vs external) and actual appraisals of control over stressful life events (Nelson and Cohen, 1983; Sandler and Lakey, 1982). Similarly, Cohen and Lazarus (1973) found no relationship between surgical patients' scores on the Byrne (1964) repression–sensitization scale and their desire for information concerning their illness and its treatment. Second, actual coping processes are rarely measured in this literature. Instead, coping processes are usually inferred from the personality measure under question (Lazarus and Folkman, 1984b). For instance, Kobasa (1979) assumes that 'hardy' persons react to stress with a sense of control, commitment and challenge. However, in a review of this literature, Cohen and Edwards (1988) did not find a single study where coping behaviors of hardy and non-hardy individuals were actually *measured*. Third, the personal trait and style approach to coping implicitly assumes that coping is, for the most part, unidimensional and stable across time and situations (Lazarus and Folkman, 1984a). However, empirical evidence indicates that coping processes are multidimensional and vary over time and across situations, suggesting that characterizing coping as a single stable dimension is overly simplistic (Folkman and Lazarus, 1985; McCrae, 1984). In sum, by characterizing coping in terms of a personal trait or style, we fail to predict actual coping behaviors, rarely measure these behaviors and ignore the multidimensional and dynamic nature of actual coping responses.

Coping as a Sequence of Stages

Several researchers have described reactions to stress in terms of a series of stages through which the individual passes. This approach is particularly common in research on reactions to life-threatening illness and injury. For example, Kubler-Ross (1969) indicates that terminally ill patients pass through stages of denial, anger, bargaining, depression and acceptance. Other variants of the stage approach focus on more general sources of stress. For example, Klinger (1975) indicates that when a goal is blocked, the individual responds with increased effort toward goal attainment. If these efforts fail, aggression, depression and eventual recovery follow. Similarly, Wortman and Brehm (1975) indicate that, when an individual loses control over an important outcome, he or she exhibits increased anger, aggression and motivation to obtain the outcome. If efforts to obtain the outcome fail, passivity, depression and decreased motivation ensue. Likewise, Janis and Mann (1977) indicate that, under conditions of threat, the coping response selected by the individual is determined by his or her answers to a sequence of four questions, including: (1) whether there are serious risks if no action is taken; (2) whether there are serious risks if the most salient course of action is taken; (3) whether there is hope to find a better course of action; and (4) whether there is sufficient time to search for and deliberate alternate courses of action. As these examples indicate, the common feature of stage approaches to coping is a series of discrete responses which occur in a specific sequence.

Stage approaches to coping present several distinct advantages. First, data used to derive these approaches were usually obtained from individuals responding to stressful situations which were authentic and, in some cases, extreme (e.g. Shontz, 1975). Second, these approaches involve multiple assessments of coping efforts over time, thereby tapping the multidimensional and dynamic aspects of coping. Third, a number of these approaches address the often neglected processes underlying the selection and implementation of coping strategies (Cummings and Cooper, 1979; Janis and Mann, 1977). However, despite these advantages, empirical evidence indicates that coping behaviors often do *not* occur in a specific sequence (Silver and Wortman, 1980). Instead, individuals seem to select from a wide array of coping strategies and implement these strategies in a variety of sequences.

The lack of empirical support for stage approaches to coping may be partially attributable to several conceptual and methodological problems associated with this approach. First, as noted by Silver and Wortman (1980), many stage approaches to coping do not specify either the exact duration of each stage or the impetus for moving from one stage to the next. Presumably, the transition from one stage to another is prompted by an internal or external cue, such as the fulfilment of some requirement or the exhaustion of some resource. However, the dimensions which influence transition from one stage to another and the thresholds which must be reached on these dimensions are rarely specified. For example, Wortman and Brehm (1975) indicate that repeated failures to obtain a desired outcome reduce the individual's expectations of control over that outcome. When a certain number of failures have been experienced, efforts to control the outcome cease, and depression, passivity and lowered motivation ensue. However, it is unclear how many failures are required or how low expectations must fall before the individual stops trying to attain the desired outcome. Similarly, the incentive–disengagement model presented by Klinger (1975) states that the duration of the stages following the obstruction of a goal may vary considerably, depending on factors such as individual differences and the nature and timing of the blocked goal. However, it is unclear what level must be attained on these factors to prompt transition to a subsequent stage. If stage models do not specify the factors influencing stage duration and transition, it is difficult to determine whether empirical data support or disconfirm these models (Silver and Wortman, 1980).

A related problem concerns whether it is reasonable to assume that individuals coping with stress pass through a predictable set of stages. Aside from the lack of empirical support for this assumption (Silver and Wortman, 1980), the complexity and variability of the person and situation factors contributing to stress suggest a corresponding complexity and variability of coping responses. Some researchers have attempted to model these person and situation factors to predict deviations from the expected sequence of stages. For example, Wortman and Brehm (1975) indicate that, if the individual does not expect control over an important outcome, he or she will not experience increased anger, aggression and motivation to obtain the outcome. Janis and Mann (1977) also indicate that individuals responding to stress may consider the predicted series of questions out of sequence. However, they do not specify the conditions under which different sequences are expected to occur. Given the extreme variability in coping responses noted above, identifying the conditions under which each permutation of coping stages occurs would be difficult, if not impossible. Again, unless the model specifies the conditions under which the individual is expected to deviate from the standard sequence of stages, empirical data cannot disconfirm the model (Silver and Wortman, 1980).

A third problem concerns classifying individual coping efforts in terms of particular stages. Placing coping efforts into discrete categories denoted by stages is both difficult and results in the loss of information. For example, consider the coping patterns of vigilance and hypervigilance discussed by Janis and Mann (1977). Vigilance is characterized in terms of a thorough consideration of alternative courses of action and their attendant consequences, followed by a selection of the best alternative. Hypervigilance, on the other hand, occurs when the time available to consider alternatives is inadequate. When this occurs, the individual frantically considers a limited number of alternatives and hastily selects one which promises immediate payoff. These descriptions imply that we should classify a coping pattern as vigilant or hypervigilant depending upon the number of alternatives considered, the quality of the selected alternative and the speed with which the decision is made. In addition, we must select thresholds for each criteria such that coping patterns may be appropriately classified. However, the selection of these thresholds raises a number of methodological questions. How many alternatives are required to classify coping as vigilant? How do we determine whether the selected alternative is optimal? How rapidly are hypervigilant coping decisions made? Furthermore, are these criteria compensatory, such that a large number of alternatives considered rapidly is equivalent to a small number of alternatives considered slowly? Finally, once coping behaviors are classified, are we to assume that the actual coping behaviors within each category are homogeneous? As this example illustrates, determining the category to which coping behaviors belong presents a major methodological challenge. Even if this challenge is successfully met, we lose information concerning the unique characteristics of coping behaviors placed in the same category.

Coping as Specific Methods or Foci

Several investigators have conceptualized coping either in terms of specific methods of coping or in terms of specific foci of coping efforts. This approach typically involves the development of a taxonomy which classifies coping efforts either according to the method used or according to the focus, or target, of coping efforts. For example, Billings and Moos (1981) distinguish between the following methods of coping: (1) *active–cognitive*, where the individual attempts to manage his or her appraisal of the stressful situation or event, (2) *active–behavioral*, which refers to overt behavioral attempts to deal directly with the situation or event and (3) *avoidance*, where the individual attempts to avoid confronting the problem altogether. Similarly, a number of investigators present categorization schemes which distinguish between the foci, or targets, of coping efforts (e.g. Kahn *et al.*, 1964; Lazarus and Launier, 1978; Moos and Billings, 1982; Pearlin and Schooler, 1978). The most common distinction made in these schemes involves the following two foci: (1) *problem-focused coping*, which involves attempts to manage or reduce stress by directly altering the situation or the individual's appraisal of the situation* and (2) *emotion-focused coping*, where attempts are made to regulate the emotional responses to a stressful situation. Several recent studies of stress and coping classify coping efforts by method (Menaghan, 1982; Menaghan and Merves, 1984; Newton and Keenan, 1985), focus (Billings and Moos, 1984; Folkman and Lazarus, 1980; Lazarus and Folkman, 1985; Pearlin and Schooler, 1978) or both (Billings and Moos, 1981), and examine the relationships between these coping methods or foci and type of stress experienced and/or outcomes of stress.

Conceptualizing coping in terms of specific methods or foci presents several advantages. First, this approach provides a useful taxonomy for describing coping behaviors. Second, investigations based on this approach typically include a fairly comprehensive assessment of actual coping behaviors (e.g. Folkman and Lazarus, 1980; Folkman *et al.*, 1986). On the other hand, there are several problems associated with conceptualizing coping in terms of specific methods or foci. One problem concerns the inherent difficulty in distinguishing between coping methods and foci. For instance, Moos and Billings (1982) classify coping efforts into appraisal-, problem- and emotion-focused efforts. However, each of these categories is described according to various *methods* used to cope with stress. For example, logical analysis (a form of appraisal-focused coping) is described as 'trying to identify the cause of the problem, paying attention to one aspect of the situation at a time, drawing on relevant past experiences, and mentally rehearsing possible actions and their consequences' (Moos and Billings, 1982, p. 218). While logical analysis may result in a reappraisal of the situation (i.e. appraisal-focused coping), it is defined in terms of specific *methods* by which the individual can accomplish this. Similarly, the 'Ways of Coping Checklist' used in various studies by the Lazarus group (Folkman and Lazarus, 1980, 1985), is intended to distinguish between problem- and emotion-focused coping. However, this instrument describes specific coping *methods* rather than the foci of coping efforts.

In addition to problems of distinguishing between coping methods and coping foci, the boundaries *within* each of these categories are often unclear. This is primarily because a particular coping attempt may involve a *variety* of methods or may be directed toward *multiple* foci. For example, a worker

---

* Moos and Billings (1982) further divide this category into (1) *problem-focused coping*, or attempts to modify or remove the source of stress and (2) *appraisal-focused coping*, or attempts to redefine the situation.

confronted with conflicting job demands may consult his or her superior in an attempt to resolve this conflict. Do we classify this method as gathering information, directly addressing the problem or seeking social support? Similarly, a given coping attempt may simultaneously address multiple foci. For instance, a student who takes a tranquilizer before a major exam may simultaneously dampen his or her emotional response and control anxiety which may interfere with exam performance. Obviously, this single act may be classified as both emotion-focused and problem-focused coping. While the difficulties associated with classifying coping methods and foci have been noted elsewhere (Lazarus and Folkman, 1984b; Moos and Billings, 1982), an adequate solution has yet to be presented.

Another problem associated with this approach is the limited attention given to the process by which individuals select specific coping methods and/ or direct coping efforts toward specific foci. This process is presumably influenced by various person and situation factors, such as the degree and type of stress, the demands of coping options relative to the abilities of the individual, the perceived potential impact of coping options on the situation and the self, the degree of ambiguity in the situation, the amount of importance associated with resolving the situation, experience with similar stressors, and so on. While the importance of these factors has been discussed (Lazarus and Folkman, 1984b; Menaghan, 1983), empirical investigations of their impact on coping methods and foci are limited. Some studies have approximated these factors by examining coping in different life roles (e.g. work, family, marriage, etc.), under the assumption that differences between these roles influence coping method and focus (e.g. Folkman and Lazarus, 1980; Menaghan and Merves, 1984; Pearlin and Schooler, 1978). Several studies by Lazarus and his colleagues have incorporated these factors more directly, examining differences in coping depending upon whether respondents indicated the situation could be changed, had to be accepted, required gathering more information, or required restraint (Coyne, Aldwin and Lazarus, 1981; Folkman and Lazarus, 1980, 1985; Folkman *et al.*, 1986). While these investigations represent an important first step, a complete understanding of the determinants of stress requires an explicit and comprehensive consideration of the decision-making process influencing the selection of coping methods and foci (e.g. Janis and Mann, 1977).

A final problem concerns the lack of attention given to the mechanisms by which coping influences stress and well-being. An example of this drawback can be found in the stress and coping paradigm developed by Lazarus and his colleagues (Lazarus and Folkman, 1984b; Lazarus and Launier, 1978). According to Lazarus, stress results when an individual appraises a situation as harmful, threatening or challenging. Lazarus further states that the degree of stress associated with this appraisal is contingent upon the strength of the commitment involved in the situation, with higher stress associated with more strongly-held commitments. With this in mind, one might argue that, in order to reduce stress, coping must influence either the situational factors contributing to the appraised harm, threat or challenge, the nature and strength of the commitment involved in the appraisal, or both. In a word, coping should influence stress by affecting the factors which *cause* stress (Edwards and Cooper, in press; Menaghan, 1983). However, investigations based on this approach which assess the relationship between coping and well-being do not examine whether this relationship is mediated by the cognitive appraisal processes described by Lazarus (e.g. Folkman and Lazarus, 1985; Folkman *et al.*, 1986). To understand the process by which coping affects well-being, we must assess the degree to which coping influences the person and situation factors presumed to cause stress.

Summary

In sum, while the approaches outlined above have provided a substantial contribution to our understanding of coping, they also present a number of conceptual and methodological problems. Psychoanalytic approaches to coping consider contact with reality to be necessary for coping to occur, even though some forms of adjustment rely upon the *denial* of reality. In addition, these approaches typically define coping in terms of successful adjustment thereby obscuring the relationship between coping and outcomes. Personal trait or style approaches to coping assume a correspondence between traits or styles and subsequent coping behaviors, though relevant studies indicate that this correspondence is often weak at best. Furthermore, the trait or style approach often describes coping as stable and unidimensional, while this is usually not the case. Stage approaches to coping often fail to specify the factors which influence stage duration and transition, underrepresent the variability found in actual coping behaviors and require the difficult task of placing these behaviors into discrete categories. Describing coping in terms of specific methods or foci also contains drawbacks, such as difficulty in distinguishing various methods and foci, incomplete consideration of the determinants of coping method and focus, and inattention to the mechanisms by which coping influences stress and well-being.

In the following section, a theoretical approach to coping will be presented which draws from the advantages of the approaches described above and attempts to overcome their drawbacks. Following this, the determinants of coping will be discussed, focusing on the process by which individuals select and implement coping strategies. Next, the consequences of coping will be discussed, focusing on how coping affects the determinants of stress and how coping itself may act as a source of stress. The chapter will conclude with a discussion of the implications of the model for research on coping with stress at work.

A THEORETICAL APPROACH TO COPING

This section presents a theoretical approach to coping which builds upon existing approaches to stress and coping and draws from the control theory, decision-making and motivation literatures. As will be seen, this approach presents the basic elements of a *process* theory of coping. That is, rather than adopting a content theoretic approach, describing specific individual and situational characteristics which may influence coping or categorizing various methods by which individuals cope, this approach emphasizes the process by which person and situation factors combine to influence coping and the mechanisms by which coping, in turn, influences stress and well-being (cf. Campbell *et al.*, 1970). A central assumption in this approach is that stress experienced by the individual produces negative impacts on well-being and motivation to minimize these impacts (Duval and Wicklund, 1972; Raynor, 1982). This motivation is reflected in coping, which is directed toward the person and situation factors which cause stress. If attempts to alter these factors are successful, stress is reduced and well-being is improved. Thus, coping is viewed as a critical component of a negative feedback loop, representing the means by which the individual affects the determinants of stress and thereby attenuates the deleterious impacts of stress on well-being (cf. Carver and Scheier, 1981, 1982; Cummings and Cooper, 1979; Katz and Kahn, 1978; Leventhal, Nerenz and Strauss, 1980; McGrath, 1976; Powers, 1973; Schwartz, 1983).

Overview of the Model

The theoretical approach to coping described in this chapter is derived from a general process theory of stress and coping currently under development. As will be seen, this model draws from the stress and coping literature and incorporates elements of the motivation, decision-making and control theory literatures.

Before presenting the model, let us first define the concepts of stress and coping. *Stress* is defined here as *a negative discrepancy between an individual's perceived state and desired state, provided that the presence of this discrepancy is considered important by the individual.* The term *negative discrepancy* indicates that stress exists when the individual's perceived state *falls short* of his or her desired state. This definition of stress is consistent with other definitions which involve the relationship between the individual's preferences and environmental characteristics (e.g. Cummings and Cooper, 1979; French, Rogers and Cobb, 1974; Schuler, 1980). These definitions may be contrasted with those which involve the relationship between environmental demands and individual abilities (e.g. Lazarus and Folkman, 1984b; McGrath, 1976; Sells, 1970).* While these two classes of definitions appear inconsistent on the surface, Harrison (1978) notes that a discrepancy between demands and abilities produces stress only when (1) the individual consciously desires to meet the demand or (2) the satisfaction of individual motives or desires is contingent upon meeting the demand. In other words, a situation where demands exceed abilities is defined as stressful only when demands actually represent a desire which the individual is unable to fulfill, or when the demands associated with the resolution of a discrepancy between perceptions and desires exceed the individual's abilities. Thus, definitions comparing demands and abilities implicitly include a discrepancy between perceptions and desires. Because of this, we will define stress explicitly in terms of a discrepancy between perceptions and desires. The comparison between situational demands and individual abilities will be incorporated into the concept of coping, as discussed below.

According to the model, stress will lead to two classes of outcomes. One class includes various dimensions of psychological and physiological well-being which represent the mental and physical health of the individual. The other class of outcomes consists of attempts to reduce the negative impacts of stress on individual well-being. We will refer to these *efforts to reduce the negative impacts of stress on individual well-being* as *coping*. These efforts are directed toward the determinants of stress, i.e. the perceptions and desires involved in the discrepancy and/or the amount of importance associated with the discrepancy. The success or failure of coping will depend upon a variety of factors, such as the magnitude and nature of the demands associated with the resolution of the discrepancy, individual resources, such as ability, energy, time, etc., and various situational factors. When the individual is able to meet the demands associated with resolving the discrepancy, stress will be reduced, and individual well-being will be improved. On the other hand, when the individual is unable to meet the demands associated with resolving the discrepancy, stress will, in most cases, persist, and individual well-being will deteriorate.

Figure 1 depicts a theoretical model which incorporates the definitions of stress and coping presented above. While this model may appear somewhat forbidding at first, its essential elements are rather straightforward. The process starts with the individual's *perception* of a particular life facet. This life facet may be a dimension of the individual's physical or social environ-

---

* This defination may also be contrasted with those which define stress in terms of environmental stimuli (e.g. Caplan et al., 1975; Dohrenwend and Dohrenwend 1974; Holmes and Rahe 1967) or individual responses (e.g. Ivancevich and Matteson, 1980; Parker and DeCotiis, 1983; Selye, 1956). The shortcomings of stimulus and response definitions of stress are aptly described elsewhere and will not be reiterated here (e.g. Lazarus and Folkham, 1984b; Schuler, 1980).

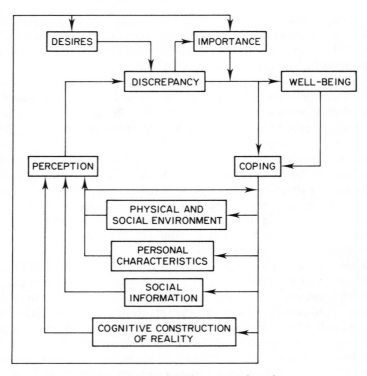

Figure 1   A model of stress and coping

ment or one of the individual's own personal characteristics or qualities. As indicated in the model, this perception is influenced not only by attributes of the individual and his or her physical and social environment, but also by social information available to the individual (Salancik and Pfeffer, 1978) and the individual's own cognitive construction of reality (Weick, 1979). Perceptions associated with the life facet are then compared against *desires* associated with this facet, resulting in the presence or absence of a *discrepancy* between perceptions and desires. This discrepancy affects *importance* such that greater importance is associated with larger discrepancies between perceptions and desires. The discrepancy also affects the two classes of outcomes noted above, including (1) the individual's psychological and physiological *well-being* and (2) *coping*, i.e. individual efforts to alleviate these negative impacts on well-being. As indicated in the model, the amount of importance associated with the presence of the discrepancy moderates the relationship between the discrepancy and both individual well-being and coping, with higher importance associated with greater impacts of the discrepancy on well-being as well as increased coping efforts (cf. Mobley and Locke, 1970; Naylor, Pritchard and Ilgen., 1980; Rice *et al.*, 1985). Coping may also be directly influenced by well-being, as when coping occurs after damage to well-being has been sustained. Coping, in turn, influences the determinants of stress through six basic pathways: (1) by directly changing relevant aspects of the individual's physical and social environment; (2) by changing an aspect of the self (i.e. a personal characteristic); (3) by challenging the social information upon which perceptions are based; (4) by affecting the individual's cognitive construction of reality, such that perceptions are either removed from awareness (i.e. denial) or are changed without actually changing the environment or the self; (5) by adjusting desires in order to reduce the discrepancy; (6) by decreasing the amount of importance associated with the presence of the discrepancy. Overall, the process depicted in the model consists of a negative feedback loop, where discrepancies between perceptions and desires affect individual well-being and lead to efforts to resolve the discrepancy, a re-evaluation of the discrepancy, and so on. The model of stress and coping presented here is consistent with other applications of cybernetic or control theory in the psychological literature (Buckley, 1968; Carver and Scheier, 1981, 1982; Miller, 1965; Powers, 1973), particularly those which focus on stress and coping (Cummings and Cooper, 1979; Katz and Kahn, 1978; McGrath, 1976; Scheier and Carver, 1985; Schwartz, 1983).

THE DETERMINANTS OF COPING

The model described above outlines the pathways by which coping may affect the determinants of stress. For each pathway, there are numerous specific coping alternatives the individual may implement to influence stress. The existence of these multiple coping alternatives indicates that an individual under stress may select from a wide variety of coping strategies. Several investigators have developed measures which attempt to reflect the variety of coping strategies available to the individual (e.g. Aldwin *et al.*, 1980; Billings and Moos, 1981; Latack, 1986; Sidle *et al.*, 1969). The present discussion is intended to complement these efforts by focusing on the decision-making process underlying the selection of coping strategies.

When considering the process by which individuals select coping strategies, it is tempting to conclude that individuals under stress consciously generate a comprehensive set of coping alternatives, evaluate the potential consequences of each alternative, and select the strategy which minimizes stress and maximizes well-being. However, research in the decision-making area suggests that individuals seldom adopt such a thorough, rational approach. Instead, people systematically violate the principles of rational decision making when generating, evaluating and selecting alternative courses of action (March and Simon, 1958; Simon, 1976; Slovic, Fischhoff and Lichtenstein, 1976, 1977). This suggests that individuals under stress will demonstrate a corresponding lack of rationality when selecting coping strategies, relying on routine programs and heuristics, simplifying assumptions, and satisficing techniques. These decision-making processes will tend to result in the selection of coping strategies which are suboptimal and, in some cases, ineffective.

While individuals will rarely, if ever, adopt a rational approach to the selection of coping strategies (Simon, 1976), such an approach provides a useful point of departure to describe and evaluate how individuals actually select coping strategies (Barclay, Beach and Braithwaite, 1971). Furthermore, by outlining the dimensions of the effective selection of coping strategies, we can derive recommendations for the facilitation of coping efforts (D'Zurilla and Goldfried, 1971; Spivack, Platt and Shure, 1976). To fulfill these objectives, the following discussion will describe a normative model of the selection of coping strategies, under the assumption of rational decision making. Following this, we will draw from the decision-making literature to determine the conditions under which individuals will depart from this rational approach to coping, resulting in a descriptive model of the selection of coping strategies.

A Normative Model of the Selection of Coping Strategies

By definition, a normative approach to the selection of coping strategies assumes an underlying rational decision-making process. Following Simon (1976), the rational selection of coping strategies requires: (1) viewing all coping strategies prior to selection, (2) considering all potential consequences of each strategy and (3) selecting one strategy which minimizes stress and maximizes well-being. To meet the first requirement, the individual must generate an exhaustive array of alternative coping strategies for consideration. As indicated earlier, these alternatives would involve altering the determinants of stress, including changing perceptions by modifying relevant aspects of the environment, the individual, social information available to the individual and the individual's own cognitive construction of reality, adjusting desires in order to reduce the discrepancy between perceptions and desires, and decreasing the amount of importance associated with the discrepancy. The generation of these alternatives may be facilitated by attempting to determine the cause of experienced stress, with specific coping behaviors focusing on the hypothesized causal factors. After deriving an exhaustive array of potential coping strategies, the individual would proceed with their evaluation, as discussed below.

The second requirement of rational coping strategy selection involves the consideration of all potential consequences of each coping strategy. This includes two primary considerations: (1) *perceived efficacy*, which refers to the individual's belief that he or she can successfully execute the coping strategy under consideration and (2) *perceived potential impact on well-being*, which refers to the individual's assessment of the potential improvement or deterioration in well-being associated with the coping strategy under consideration. As defined here, perceived efficacy is analogous to Bandura's concept of efficacy expectancy (Bandura, 1977) and the concept of expectancy found in expectancy theory and its variants (Georgopoulos, Mahoney and Jones, 1957; Porter and Lawler, 1968; Tolman, 1932; Vroom, 1964). Perceived efficacy is determined by a comparison of the demands associated with the coping strategy under consideration against individual resources (e.g. abilities, social supports, material assets) available to meet these demands, a process analogous to Lazarus' concept of secondary appraisal (Lazarus and Folkman, 1984b). The efficacy estimate produced by this comparison process often involves some degree of uncertainty (cf. Luce and Suppes, 1965), and this level of uncertainty will influence the individual's evaluation of each coping strategy, depending on his or her preference for uncertainty (cf. Archer, 1979; Berlyne, 1960; Lazarus and Folkman, 1984b; McGrath, 1976). In some cases, a given coping strategy may succeed if any of a number of independent conditions are met. In other cases, a given coping strategy may involve multiple contingencies, each of which must be met in order for the coping strategy to succeed. When multiple contingencies are involved, the individual would multiply the probabilities of satisfying each contingency to derive an overall efficacy estimate. Holding other factors constant, the individual will select a coping strategy which has the maximum likelihood of success. If this is not feasible, the individual would abstain from coping, which would typically result in the persistence of stress and the deterioration of well-being (Coyne *et al.*, 1981; Seligman, 1975).

The second consideration is the perceived potential impact of coping strategies on well-being. This refers to the individual's assessment of the potential improvement or deterioration in well-being associated with each coping strategy under consideration, similar to the concept of valence in expectancy theory (e.g. Naylor, Pritchard and Ilgen, 1980; Vroom, 1964). The perceived potential impact of coping strategies on well-being is influenced by three factors. One factor is the anticipated impact of each coping strategy on the stressful situation toward which coping efforts are directed. This refers to the assessment of whether the coping strategy under consideration, if successfully implemented, will have a beneficial or deleterious impact on experienced stress. A second factor involves the anticipated impact of each coping strategy on stress associated with other life facets. That is, a given coping strategy may benefit the stressful situation in question but threaten desires, values and goals associated with other life facets (Lazarus and Launier, 1978). A third factor concerns the anticipated impact of the implementation of each coping strategy *itself* on well-being (Cohen *et al.*, 1986; Edwards and Cooper, in press). For example, the individual may view the implementation of a coping strategy as potentially enjoyable, as when coping consists of taking an extended vacation. On the other hand, certain coping strategies may be viewed as inherently aversive, as when an individual copes with excessive job demands by working evenings and weekends. Following the normative model, the individual would rank-order the alternative coping strategies in terms of well-being by jointly considering their expected impact on experienced stress, their potential impact on stress associated with other life facets and their inherent attractiveness and aversiveness.

The third requirement of rational coping is the selection of the coping strategy which maximizes well-being. To meet this requirement, the individual must simply select and implement the coping strategy which, according to the rank-ordering process described above, is considered optimal in terms of well-being. In cases where the perceived potential damage to well-being of any coping strategy exceeds the deleterious impacts of experienced stress, the individual would abstain from coping, resulting in continued stress and further deterioration of well-being.

A Descriptive Model of the Selection of Coping Strategies

As indicated earlier, individuals will rarely adopt the rational approach to the selection of coping strategies described above. However, this approach provides a useful point of departure for deriving a descriptive model of the selection of coping strategies. To derive this descriptive model, we will consider each requirement for the rational selection of coping strategies and attempt to specify the conditions under which the individual will deviate from these requirements.

First, let us consider the generation of coping alternatives. According to the normative model, individuals under stress would generate an exhaustive array of coping alternatives and consider these alternatives simultaneously. However, in most instances, coping alternatives are not obvious, and generating feasible alternatives is difficult (MacCrimmon and Taylor, 1976). Because of this, the individual is likely to consider a very limited number of alternatives (Simon, 1976). The number and type of coping alternatives generated, and the effort the individual is willing to apply to their generation, will depend upon several factors. One factor is the level of stress experienced by the individual. Several investigators suggest that individuals experiencing low levels of stress will consider coping strategies used in similar coping instances, while individuals experiencing intense or prolonged stress will attempt to formulate new strategies (Hamburg and Adams, 1967; Janis and Mann, 1977; Weiss, Ilgen and Sharbaugh, 1982). However, while increased stress may motivate the individual to generate a broader array of coping alternatives, it may also produce emotional upset and mental confusion, thereby encouraging desperate and primitive modes of coping such as rage, panic, or defense mechanisms (Lazarus and Launier, 1978). Hence, as stress increases, motivation to generate coping alternatives would increase, while ability to generate these alternatives would decrease. A second factor is the amount of importance associated with the desire involved in the stressful situation. As importance increases, the individual will expend more energy toward the generation of coping alternatives (Simon, 1976). A third factor is the time available to generate coping alternatives. Following Janis and Mann (1977), as the time available to generate coping alternatives decreases, the individual will tend to use simple-minded decision rules (e.g. do whatever the others around you are doing, do what worked last time), thereby overlooking superior alternatives. A fourth factor is experience with the same or similar sources of stress. If the individual has had relevant experience, he or she will tend to consider coping alternatives which have worked well in the past and avoid those which have worked poorly (MacCrimmon and Taylor, 1976). A fifth factor is the availability of social information from others who have coped with similar stressful circumstances. As the amount of relevant and credible social information increases, the individual will rely more on this information rather than generating his or her own unique set of coping alternatives (Simon, 1976). A sixth factor is based on the notion that individuals consider coping alternatives *sequentially* rather than simultaneously. This is due, in part, to the fact that the number of potential coping alternatives usually far exceeds the individual's short-term memory capacity of seven, plus or minus two (Miller, 1956). Because of this, the individual will tend to consider coping alternatives sequentially and terminate the search when an acceptable alternative has been identified (Janis and Mann, 1977; Simon, 1976). The longer it takes to identify such an acceptable alternative, the more alternatives will be considered. Thus, stress, importance, time, experience, social information and the sequential process by which coping alternatives are considered may each influence the number and type of coping alternatives generated.

Let us now examine the manner in which coping alternatives are evaluated. First, consider the determination of perceived efficacy. Because perceived efficacy concerns future events, it is necessarily based on probablistic information. Following the normative model, we would assume that the individual would cognitively process this information. However, several investigators indicate that, rather than processing this information, individuals typically derive a general, often intuitive assessment of perceived efficacy (Goodman, Rose and Furcon, 1970; Kahneman and Tversky, 1973; Naylor *et al.*, 1980). The degree to which individuals attempt to process this probabilistic information, as opposed to relying on intuitive assessments, may depend upon several factors. A number of these factors were also relevant in the generation of coping alternatives, as described earlier. For example, as the level of stress experienced by the individual increases, the individual's desire to relieve this stress would increase, thereby heightening his or her efforts to identify a coping strategy with a high likelihood of success. Similarly, as the importance associated with the threatened desire increases, the individual may expend more energy determining the likelihood that each coping alternative may be successfully executed (Simon, 1976). The amount of time available should also influence the individual's desire to evaluate each coping strategy, such that increased time will prompt more reflection and thought (Lazarus and Launier, 1978; Janis and Mann, 1977). Furthermore, as prior experience with the coping strategies under consideration increases, the individual will rely more on this experience rather than attempting to re-evaluate the likelihood of success of coping strategy (Seligman, 1975; Wortman and Brehm, 1975). Finally, the individual may consider social information, drawing from the experience of similar others to determine the likelihood of success of each coping strategy under consideration (Simon, 1976).

A number of additional factors may influence the amount of effort the individual will expend in the determination of perceived efficacy. For instance, as the perceived costs associated with the implementation of each coping strategy increases, the individual will expend more energy to determine whether each coping strategy, if implemented, will indeed succeed. In addition, the level of ambiguity associated with the situation will influence perceived efficacy such that, as ambiguity increases, individuals will expend less energy to determine whether each coping strategy will succeed and will rely more on general belief systems (i.e. locus of control, self-efficacy) (Lazarus and Folkman, 1984a; Menaghan, 1983). Thus, level of stress, importance, time, experience, social information, the costs of coping and ambiguity may each influence the effort expended by the individual toward the determination of perceived efficacy.

While the factors mentioned above may influence individual effort toward the determination of perceived efficacy, actually determining all potential consequences of each coping strategy would require the individual to process so much information that his or her mental capabilities would be exceeded (Janis and Mann, 1977). Furthermore, as Tversky and Kahneman (1974) point out, individuals make systematic errors when processing such information. For example, individuals will tend to overestimate the overall likelihood of success of the coping strategy when it requires the satisfaction of multiple conditions. Conversely, individuals will tend to underestimate the overall likelihood of success of a coping strategy when it requires the satisfaction of only one of several conditions. Furthermore, the individual will often overgeneralize from very limited prior experience with the coping strategies under consideration, such that coping strategies which have worked in the past will be viewed as sure winners, while coping strategies which have not worked will be viewed as doomed to failure (Tversky and Kahneman, 1971). Aside from these constraints, the individual must determine the potential success of each coping alternative while under stress, which may further interfere with information processing (Folkman, Schaefer and Lazarus, 1979). Thus, in spite of individual efforts to assess the likelihood of success of coping alternatives, these assessments will generally be biased and inaccurate.

Let us now consider the evaluation of the perceived potential impact of each coping strategy on well-being. Following the normative model, the individual would evaluate each coping alternative in terms of its impact on experienced stress, its effect on stress associated with other life facets, and its inherent attractiveness or aversiveness, resulting in a rank ordering of each coping alternative in terms of well-being. However, the decision-making literature suggests that individuals will often employ much simpler methods in the evaluation of coping alternatives. Following Simon (1976), the individual may evaluate coping alternatives against some minimum criteria of well-being and terminate the evaluation process when an acceptable alternative has been identified. An even simpler strategy would involve sequentially considering coping alternatives until one which will minimally improve current well-being is identified (Lindblom, 1959; Miller and Starr, 1967). Alternately, the individual may sequentially consider the most important attributes of a set of coping alternatives and successively reject those alternatives which are unsatisfactory on the attribute under consideration (Tversky, 1972). Once the set of alternatives has been reduced, individuals may employ compensatory strategies, comparing the advantages and disadvantages of the remaining alternatives (Payne, 1976, 1982). Perhaps the simplest strategy would be to minimize the evaluation of coping alternatives altogether by simply selecting an alternative which has produced acceptable outcomes in the past (Merton, 1936).

As noted by Slovic *et al.* (1977), satisficing approaches, such as those described above, require less cognitive effort than the rational approach described earlier. While the individual will often prefer approaches which require less effort (Beach and Mitchell, 1978), several factors may influence the amount of effort the individual will expend in evaluating the impacts of alternative coping strategies on well-being. A number of these factors were also relevant in the generation of coping alternatives and the determination of perceived efficacy. For example, if experienced stress is severe, the individual will probably attempt to identify a coping alternative which will significantly improve well-being. Similarly, as the importance associated with desire involved in the stressful situation increases, the individual may direct more effort toward the selection of the best available coping strategy (Simon, 1976). In addition, as the time available to evaluate coping alternatives decreases, individuals are more likely to give coping alternatives only superficial consideration, thereby failing to notice obvious defects and advantages of each alternative (Hamburg and Adams, 1967; Janis and Mann, 1977). Also, as experience with the coping strategies under consideration increases, the individual will draw more from this information to determine the potential impact of each coping strategy on well-being. Furthermore, the individual may draw from social information, considering the well-being of others who have implemented similar coping strategies (Salancik and Pfeffer, 1978).

The factors described above will influence individual efforts to rank order each coping strategy in terms of well-being. However, in spite of these efforts, the fact remains that the selection of coping strategies is based on *anticipated* well-being. Following Simon (1976), the anticipation of the consequences of each coping strategy can hardly have the same emotional impact as their actual occurrence. Therefore, the evaluation of coping alternatives in terms of well-being is limited by the individual's ability to anticipate the consequences of each alternative and to give these consequences the same value in anticipation as they will receive in actual experience.

Finally, let us consider the selection of coping strategies. Following the normative model, the individual would select the coping strategy which, based on his or her evaluation of the alternatives, will maximize well-being. Again, the decision-making literature suggests that individuals under stress rarely attempt to maximize well-being through the selection of coping strategies. Instead, individuals will often select a coping strategy which will achieve a minimum acceptable level of well-being (Simon, 1976). Alternately, the individual may select a coping strategy such that well-being is marginally improved (Lindblom, 1959). Furthermore, recent research suggests that some individuals may not seek to improve well-being at all. For example, consider negative affectivity, which Watson and Clark (1984) describe as a disposition to experience negative affect across time and regardless of the situation. This construct is intuitively appealing, as it is not difficult to recall individuals who, despite both positive and negative experiences, appear chronically discontent. One mechanism behind negative affectivity may be the active selection of coping strategies which preserve a customary level of affect. That is, rather than selecting coping strategies which maximize well-being, the individual selects coping strategies which maintain a homeostatic level of affect. In cases where this homeostatic level refers to anxiety, depression, or upset, the individual will manifest a state consistent with negative affectivity. Thus, rather than selecting coping strategies which maximize well-being, individuals are likely to select coping strategies which meet some minimal criteria, which marginally improve current well-being, or, in some cases, which preserve a customary level of affect.

In sum, the descriptive model of the selection of coping strategies differs from the normative model in a number of fundamental ways. Rather than generating a comprehensive array of coping alternatives, evaluating the likelihood of success and potential consequences of each alternative and selecting the alternative which maximizes well-being, individuals will tend to consider a limited number of coping alternatives, evaluate these alternatives in a superficial and erroneous manner, and select an alternative which is suboptimal in terms of well-being. The amount of effort the individual applies to the generation, evaluation and selection of coping strategies depends on a variety of factors, including level of stress, importance, time, experience, social information and ambiguity. While these factors were discussed separately, they are certainly interrelated and are therefore likely to have direct, indirect and interactive effects on the amount of effort applied to the coping strategy selection process. However, in spite of these efforts, cognitive limits to rationality will generally preclude the selection of coping strategies as prescribed by the normative model. It is hoped that the preceding discussion will help to inform future research into the manner in which individuals actually generate, evaluate and select coping strategies, and the factors which influence this process.

THE CONSEQUENCES OF COPING

The preceding section involved the determinants of coping, focusing on the manner in which coping strategies are selected. To complement this, the present section focuses on the consequences of coping, highlighting the process by which coping affects stress and well-being. As indicated in Figure 1, coping influences well-being by affecting the determinants of stress. In other words, regardless of the particular characteristics of the coping strategy in use, its impact is mediated by the alteration of the perceptions, desires and importance which characterize experienced stress. For example, coping may reduce stress by changing perceptions. As indicated in Figure 1, this occurs through the alteration of the *determinants* of perceptions outlined earlier. For instance, the individual may alter his or her physical and social environment or change a personal characteristic, an approach typically labeled problem-focused coping (Lazarus and Folkman, 1984b; Lazarus and Launier, 1978; Moos and Billings, 1982). Alternately, the individual may alter perceptions by changing information contained in his or her social environment, either by challenging existing sources of information or by seeking new sources. Finally, the individual may alter his or her perceptions by cognitively reconstructing reality. In other words, the individual may deny a stressful situation or simply focus on a different, less stressful situation (Lazarus, 1983; Miller and Grant, 1979), a process often referred to as appraisal-focused coping (Moos and Billings, 1982). Regardless of their particular characteristics, coping strategies which focus on the alteration of perceptions reduce stress by making perceptions more consistent with desires or by removing perceptions from awareness altogether.

As indicated in Figure 1, coping may also consist of the alteration of *desires*. That is, an individual may reduce a discrepancy between perceptions and desires by adjusting desires, leaving perceptions intact (Strauss, 1974). For example, an individual may reduce a discrepancy between perceived and desired job performance by adjusting performance aspirations, deciding that his or her performance is, in fact, adequate. Coping may also consist of changing the amount of *importance* associated with a discrepancy between perceptions and desires. In other words, an individual may reduce stress by deciding that a discrepancy between perceptions and desires is not as important as once believed (Pearlin, 1980; Sherwood, 1965). In sum, the implementation of a method of coping affects stress through the alteration of the perceptions, desires and importance which constitute the stressful discrepancy under consideration. This basic assumption is crucial to the understanding of stress and coping in terms of a negative feedback loop, as described earlier (cf. Carver and Scheier, 1981; Cummings and Cooper, 1979; McGrath, 1976).

As indicated in Figure 1, personal characteristics influence the impact of the implementation of a coping strategy on the determinants of stress. Personal characteristics include skills, abilities and personality traits which may be relevant for the successful implementation of the selected method of coping (cf. Porter and Lawler, 1968). For example, a skilled mechanic is likely to cope with stress associated with an automobile malfunction more successfully than an individual with no experience in automobile repair. Personality traits may also influence the effects of coping, particularly when the situation is ambiguous (Lazarus and Folkman, 1984a). For example, individuals with an internal locus of control tend to be relatively more resistant to the deleterious impacts of stressful life events than individuals with an external locus of control (Johnson and Sarason, 1978; Lefcourt *et al.*, 1981; Sandler and Lakey, 1982). One explanation for this effect is that internals do indeed possess skills which allow them to personally control their environment. If these skills are relevant to a given stressful situation, then the likelihood of successfully coping with the stressful situation increases. In addition, individuals who display Type A behavior pattern are relatively more likely to suffer from the deleterious effects of stress, particularly when stress occurs in the context of challenging, competitive or uncontrollable situations (Glass, 1977). One possible explanation for this effect is that Type As implement coping strategies in an aggressive and impatient manner, while Type Bs adopt a slower, more methodical approach. As a result, Type As exhibit higher levels of sustained arousal while coping with stress, resulting in increased risk of disease (Jenkins, 1978). While skills, abilities and personality traits such as those described above are, by definition, relatively stable and enduring, it must be emphasized that their impacts on stress are highly variable, depending upon the specific demands elicited by the coping strategy in use.

Factors in the individual's physical and social environment also influence the effects of coping strategies (see Figure 1). Physical environmental factors include a variety of conditions, such as distance, weather and physical barriers. For example, a married couple may be physically separated for an extended period, preventing the successful resolution of marital problems. Social relationships or arrangements may also influence the impact of coping efforts on the determinants of stresss (Cohen and McKay, 1984; House, 1981). For example, a co-worker may provide material or emotional support while an individual attempts to cope with a stressful situation. On the other hand, certain social relationships may impede coping efforts, as when an individual is berated by his or her co-workers for giving up trendy but unhealthy behaviors. As with personal characteristics, physical and social environmental factors may facilitate or impede coping efforts, depending on the requirements of the selected method of coping.

In the preceding section, it was noted that coping may influence stress associated with other life facets (Lazarus and Launier, 1978). This process may be clarified through the application of the model of stress and coping presented earlier. The notion that coping may influence stress associated with other life facets is based on the assumption that coping directed toward perceptions, desires, and importance associated with a particular life facet may intentionally or unintentionally influence perceptions, desires, and importance associated with other life facets. For example, if a supervisor copes with poor subordinate performance by providing additional resources and assistance to the subordinate, the performance of other subordinates may suffer. Conversely, if a manager copes with an unfair performance appraisal system by devaluing the overall importance of his or her job, then stress associated with other job factors may be reduced. In general, the amount of stress associated with other life facets will be contingent upon the impact of coping on the magnitudes of the discrepancies between perceptions and desires associated with each life facet, weighted by the amount of importance associated with these discrepancies.

The preceding section also indicated that the implementation of a coping strategy itself may influence well-being (Cohen *et al.*, 1986). Again, this process may be clarified by applying the model of stress and coping presented earlier. In particular, the amount of stress associated with a coping strategy is determined by the magnitude of the discrepancy between perceptions and desires associated with the coping strategy, weighted by the amount of importance associated with this discrepancy. For example, a coping strategy may involve activities which the individual finds inherently undesirable, such as facing a punitive supervisor. On the other hand, coping may involve activities which are inherently enjoyable to the individual, such as watching humorous movies or engaging in relaxation techniques (Benson, 1976; Cousins, 1976). Further, the duration of the discrepancy between perceptions and desires associated with a coping strategy will affect its impact on well-being, with longer duration associated with greater cumulative effects. When the implementation of a coping strategy is rather quick, as when coping with an illness simply involves receiving an injection, the cumulative impact of the implementation of the coping strategy will be relatively limited. On the other hand, when the implementation of a coping strategy requires prolonged effort, as when coping with job demands involves working overtime for an extended period, the cumulative impact of the implementation of the coping strategy may be quite severe. Prolonged coping efforts may also lead to fatigue and exhaustion in the individual (Selye, 1956), thereby damaging well-being and preventing effective coping with other stressful situations. Thus, the implementations of a coping strategy itself may cause stress, and this process must be considered in order to understanding of the overall effect of coping on individual well-being.

In sum, the consequences of coping consist of the alteration of the basic determinants of experienced stress. That is, regardless of the particular characteristics of the coping strategy in use, its ultimate impact on stress and well-being occurs through the alteration of the perceptions, desires and importance which constitute experienced stress. In addition, coping may affect stress associated with other life facets by influencing perceptions, desires and importance associated with these facets. Furthermore, the implementation of the coping strategy itself may serve as a source of stress, producing an effect on well-being which is distinct from the effects of the stressful experience toward which coping efforts are directed. The examination of the impacts of coping on the determinants of stress, on stress associated with other life facets, and stress associated with coping itself represents a fruitful area for future research.

IMPLICATIONS FOR FUTURE RESEARCH

The discussion of the determinants and consequences of coping presented in this chapter suggests several important implications for future coping research. The determinants of coping emphasized in this chapter consist of the decision-making process underlying the selection of coping strategies and the factors which influence this process. This decision-making process has been largely overlooked in the coping literature. Studies which have examined the determinants of coping have primarily focused on coping associated with different problem areas (Folkman and Lazarus, 1980; Menaghan and Merves, 1984; Pearlin and Schooler, 1978), different types of problems (McCrae, 1984), or different phases of a problem (Folkman and Lazarus, 1985). Implicit in these studies is the assumption that factors associated with problem area, type, or phase influence the selection of one coping strategy over another. A number of studies have begun to address these factors (Coyne, Aldwin and Lazarus, 1981; Folkman and Lazarus, 1980, 1985; Folkman *et al.*, 1986), and these studies represent an important initial step. By including a broader array of factors which may influence the selection of coping strategies, such as those discussed earlier, future coping research may clarify differences in coping across individuals and within individuals across situations. The decision-making process underlying the selection of coping strategies may be further illuminated through process-tracing studies, where subjects verbalize the coping strategy selection process (cf. Payne, 1976). By explicitly considering the decision-making process underlying the selection of coping strategies and the factors which influence this process, future coping research will help uncover not only *how* individuals under stress cope, but *why* they cope as they do.

The consequences of coping discussed in this chapter also present several implications for future research. The consequences of coping emphasized in this chapter consisted of the impacts of coping in the *determinants* of stress, i.e. the discrepancy between perceptions and desires and the importance associated with this discrepancy. Previous coping research has focused primarily on the direct effects of coping on well-being (Pearlin and Schooler, 1978; Billings and Moos, 1982; Folkman and Lazarus, 1985). A limited number of studies have also examined the impact of coping on reported problem resolution, which may approximate the resolution of the discrepancy between perceptions and desires or the reduction of the importance associated with this discrepancy (Folkman *et al.*, 1986; McCrae and Costa, 1986; Menaghan and Merves, 1984). While these studies are informative, they fail to examine whether the impact of coping is *mediated* by the determinants of stress. If our models correctly specify the constructs which constitute stress, then the impact of coping on well-being should be mediated by these constructs. The model of stress and coping presented in Figure 1 makes this explicit, indicating that stress damages well-being and stimulates coping which, in turn, is directed toward the perceptions, desires and importance associated with the stressful situation. By examining the impact of coping on the determinants of stress, future coping research will help identify the *process* by which coping affects stress and influence well-being.

SUMMARY

The aim of this chapter was to review major theoretical approaches to the study of coping, identify advantages and drawbacks associated with these approaches, and present an alternative approach, focusing on the determinants and consequences of coping with stress. The intention of this discussion was not to critique the approach adopted by a particular researcher, but to evaluate general themes and approaches found in the coping literature. The alternative approach to coping presented in this chapter viewed stress and coping in terms of a negative feedback loop, where a discrepancy between perceptions and desires and the importance associated with this discrepancy combine to produce stress. Stress, in turn, influences well-being and motivates the individual to cope with coping efforts directed toward the causes of stress, i.e. the discrepancy between perceptions and desires and/or the importance associated with this discrepancy. This approach gave explicit consideration to the decision-making process underlying the selection of coping strategies and the mechanisms by which coping influences stress and well-being. Future research will determine the validity of the theoretical approach presented in this chapter and, hopefully, shed additional light on the determinants and consequences of coping with stress.

REFERENCES

Aldwin, C., Folkman, S., Schaefer, C., Coyne, J. C. and Lazarus, R. S. (1980). Ways of coping: a process measure, paper presented at the meetings of the American Psychological Association, Montreal.

Antonovsky, A. (1979). *Health, Stress, and Coping*, Josey-Bass, Washington.

Archer, R. P. (1979). Relationship between locus of control and anxiety. *Journal of Personality Assessment*, **43**, 617–626.

Bandura, A. (1977). Self-efficacy: toward a unifying theory of behavioral change, *Psychological Review*, **84**, 191–215.

Barclay, S., Beach, L. R. and Braithwaite, W. P. (1971). Normative models in the study of cognition, *Organizational Behavior and Human Performance*, **6**, 389–413.

Beach, L. R., and Mitchell, T. R. (1978). A contingency model for the selection of decision strategies, *Academy of Management Review*, **3**, 439–449.

Benson, H. (1976). *The Relaxation Response*, Avon, New York.

Berlyne, D. E. (1960). *Conflict, Arousal and Curiosity*, New York: McGraw Hill.

Billings, A. G. and Moos, R. H. (1981). The role of coping responses and social resources in attenuating the stress of life events, *Journal of Behavioral Medicine*, **4**, 139–57.

Billings, A. G. and Moos, R. H. (1984). Coping, stress, and social resources among adults with unipolar depression, *Journal of Personality and Social Psychology*, **46**, 877–91.

Buckley, W. (1968). *Modern Systems Research for the Behavioral Scientist*. Chicago: Aldine

Byrne, D. (1964). Repression-sensitization as a dimension of personality. In B. A. Maher (ed.) *Progress in Experimental Personality Research* Vol. 1, Academic Press, New York.

Campbell, J. P., Dunnette, M. D., Lawler, E. E., and Weick, K. E. (1970). *Managerial Behavior, Performance, and Effectiveness*, McGraw-Hill, New York.

Caplan, R. D., Cobb, S., French, J. R. P., Jr, Harrison, R. V. and Pinneau, S. R. (1975). *Job Demands and Worker Health: Main Effects and Occupational Differences*, Institute for Social Research, Ann Arbor, MI.

Carver, C. S. and Scheier, M. F. (1981). *Attention and Self-Regulation: A Control-Theory Approach to Human Behavior*. Springer, New York.

Carver, C. S. and Scheier, M. F. (1982). Control theory: A useful conceptual framework for personality-social, clinical, and health psychology. *Psychological Bulletin*, **92**, 111–35.

Coelho, G., Hamburg, D. and Adams, J. (eds) (1974). *Coping and Adaptation*, Basic Books, New York.

Cohen, F. and Lazarus, R. S. (1973). Active coping processes, coping dispositions, and recovery from surgery, *Psychosomatic Medicine*, **35**, 375–89.

Cohen, S. and Edwards, J. R. (1988). Personality characteristics as moderators of the relationship between stress and disorder. In W. J. Neufeld (ed.) *Advances in the Investigation of Psychological Stress*, John Wiley and Sons, New York.

Cohen, S. and McKay, G. (1984). Social support, stress, and the buffering hypothesis: A theoretical analysis. In A. Baum, J. E. Singer and S. E. Taylor (eds) *Handbook of Psychology and Health*, vol. 4, pp. 253–67, NJ. Lawrence Erlbaum, Hillsdale.

Cohen S., Evans, G. W. , Stokols, D. and Krantz, D. S. (1986). *Behaviour, health, and environmental stress*, Plenum Press, New York.

Cousins, N. (1976). Anatomy of an illness (as perceived by the patient), *New England Journal of Medicine*, **295**, 1458–63.

Coyne, J. C., Aldwin, C. and Lazarus, R. S. (1981). Depression and coping in stressful episodes, *Journal of Abnormal Psychology*, **90**, 439–47.

Cummings, T. G. and Cooper, C. L. (1979). A cybernetic framework for studying occupational stress, *Human Relations*, **32**, 395–418.

Dohrenwend, B. S. and Dohrenwend, B. P. (1974). *Stressful Life Events: Their Nature and Effects*, John Wiley and Sons, New York.

Duval, S. and Wicklund, R. A. (1972). *A Theory of Objective Self-Awareness*, Academic Press, New York.

D'Zurilla, T. and Goldfried, M. R. (1971). Problem-solving and behavior modification, *Journal of Abnormal Psychology*. **78**, 107–26.

Edwards, J. R. and Cooper, C. L. (in press). Research in stress, coping, and health: theoretical and methodological issues, *Psychological Medicine*.

Folkman, S. and Lazarus, R. S. (1980). An analysis of coping in a middle-aged community sample, *Journal of Health and Social Behavior*, **21**, 219–39.

Folkman, S. and Lazarus, R. S. (1985). If it changes, it must be a process: a study of emotion and coping during three stages of a college examination, *Journal of Personality and Social Psychology*, **48**, 150–70.

Folkman, S., Schaefer, C. and Lazarus, R. S. (1979). Cognitive processes as mediators of stress and coping. In V. Hamilton and D. M. Warburton (eds), *Human Stress and Cognition: An Information Processing Approach*, pp. 265–98, John Wiley and Sons, Chichester.

Folkman, S., Lazarus, R. S., Dunkel-Schetter, C., DeLongis, A. and Gruen, R. J. (1986). Dynamics of a stressful encounter: cognitive appraisal, coping, and encounter outcomes, *Journal of Personality and Social Psychology*, **50**, 992–1003.

French, J. R. P., Jr, Rodgers, W. L. and Cobb, S. (1974). Adjustment as person–environment fit. In G. Goelho, D. Hamburg and J. Adams (eds) *Coping and Adaptation*, Basic Books, New York.

Friedman, M. and Rosenman, R. H. (1959). Association of specific overt behavior pattern with increases in blood cholesterol, blood clotting time, incidence of arcus senilis and clinical coronary artery disease, *Journal of the American Medical Association*, **169**, 1286–96.

Georgopoulos, B. S., Mahoney, G. M. and Jones, N. W. (1957). A path-goal approach to productivity. *Journal of Applied Psychology*, **41**, 345–53.

Glass, D. C. (1977). *Behavior Patterns, Stress, and Coronary Disease*, Lawrence Erlbaum, Hillsdale, NJ.

Goodman, P. S., Rose, J. H. and Furcon, J. E. (1970) Comparison of motivational antecedents of the work performance of scientists and engineers. *Journal of Applied Psychology*, **54**, 491–495.

Haan, N. A. (1969). A tripartite model of ego functioning values and clinical research applications, *Journal of Nervous and Mental Disease*, **148**, 14–30.

Haan, N. A. (1977). *Coping and Defending: Processes of Self-Environment Organization*, Academic Press, New York.

Hamburg, D. A. and Adams, J. E. (1967). A perspective on coping behavior: seeking and utilizing information in major transactions, *Archives of General Psychiatry*, **17**, 277–87.

Harrison, R. V. (1978). Person–environment fit and job stress. In C. L. Cooper and R. Payne (eds) *Stress at Work*, John Wiley and Sons, New York.

Holmes, T. H. and Rahe, R. H. (1967). The social readjustment rating scale. *Journal of Psychomatic Research*, **11**, 213–18.

Holroyd, K. A. and Lazarus, R. S. (1982). Stress, coping and somatic adaptation. In L. Goldberger and S. Breznitz (eds) *Handbook of Stress: Theoretical and Clinical Aspects*, pp. 21–34, Free Press, New York.

House, J. S. (1981). *Work, Stress, and Social Support*, Addison-Wesley, Reading, MA.

Ivancevich, J. M. and Matteson, M. T. (1980). *Stress and Work*, Scott, Foresman, Glenview, Il.

Janis, I. L. and Mann, L. (1977). *Decision Making*, The Free Press, New York.

Jenkins, C. D. (1978). Behavioral risk factors in coronary artery disease, *Annual Review of Medicine*, **29**, 543–62.

Johnson, J., and Sarason, I. (1978). Life Stress, depression, and anxiety: Internal-external control as a moderator variable. *Journal of Psychosomatic Research*, **22**, 205–208.

Kahn, R. L., Wolfe, D. M., Quinn, R. P., Snoeck, J. D. and Rosenthal, R. A. (1964). *Organizational Stress: Studies in Role Conflict and Ambiguity*, John Wiley and Sons, New York.

Kahneman, D. and Tversky, A. (1973). On the psychology of prediction, *Psychological Review*, **80**, 237–51.

Katz, D. and Kahn, R. L. (1978). *The Social Psychology of Organizations*, 2nd Edn., John Wiley and Sons, New York.

Klinger, E. (1975). Consequences of commitment to and disengagement from incentives, *Psychological Review*, **82**, 1–25.

Kobasa, S. C. (1979). Stressful life events, personality, and health: an inquiry into hardiness, *Journal of Personality and Social Psychology*, **37**, 1–11.

Kobasa, C. S., Maddi, S. R. and Courington, S. (1981). Personality and constitution as mediators in the stress–illness relationship, *Journal of Health and Social Behavior*, **22**, 368–78.

Kubler-Ross, E. (1969). *On Death and Dying*, Macmillan, New York.

Latack, J. C. (1986). Coping with job stress: measures and future directions for scale development, *Journal of Applied Psychology*, **71**, 377–85.

Lazarus, R. S. (1983). The costs and benefits of denial. In S. Breznitz (ed.) *Denial of Stress*, pp. 1–30, International Universities Press, New York.

Lazarus, R. S. and Folkman, S. (1984a). Coping and adaptation. In W. D. Gentry (ed.) *The Handbook of Behavioral Medicine*, pp. 282–325, Guilford, New York.

Lazarus, R. S. and Folkman, S. (1984b). *Stress, Coping, and Adaptation*, Springer, New York.

Lazarus, R. S., and Launier, R. (1978). Stress-related transactions between person and environment. In L. A. Pervin and M. Lewis (eds) *Perspective in Interactional Psychology*, Plenum Press, New York.

Lefcourt, H. M. (1985). Intimacy, social support and locus of control as moderators of stress. In I. G. Sarason and B. R. Sarason (eds) *Social Support: Theory, Research, and Applications*, Martinus Nijhoff, Dordrecht.

Lefcourt, H. M., Miller, R. S., Ware, E. G., and Sherk, D. (1981). Locus of control as a modifier of the relationship between stressors and moods. *Journal of Personality and Social Psychology*, **41**, 357–369.

Leventhal, H., Nerenz, D. C and Strauss, A. (1980). Self-regulation and the mechanisms for symptom appraisal. In D. Mechanic (ed.) *Psychological Epidemiology*, Neal Watson Academic Publications, New York.

Lindblom, C. E. (1959). The science of muddling through, *Public Administration Review*, **19**, 79–99.

Luce, R. D. and Suppes, P. (1965). Preference, utility, and subjective probability. In R. D. Luce, R. R. Bush and E. Galanter (Eds.), *Handbook of Mathematical Psychology*, John Wiley and Sons, New York.

McCrae, R. R. (1984). Situational determinants of coping responses: loss, threat, and challenge, *Journal of Personality and Social Psychology*, **46**, 919–28.

McCrae, R. R. and Costa, P. T., Jr (1986). Personality, coping, and coping effectiveness in an adult sample, *Journal of Personality*, **54**, 385–405.

MacCrimmon, K. R. and Taylor, R. N. (1976). Decision making and problem solving. In M. D. Dunnette (ed.) *Handbook of Industrial and Organizational Psychology*, pp. 1397–1453, Rand McNally, Chicago.

McGrath, J. E. (1976). Stress and behavior in organizations. In M. Dunnette (ed.) *Handbook of Industrial and Organizational Psychology*, pp. 1351–95, Rand McNally, Chicago.

March, J. G. and Simon, H. A. (1958) *Organizations*. New York, John Wiley and Sons.

Menaghan, E. (1982). Measuring coping effectiveness: a panel analysis of marital problems and coping efforts. *Journal of Health and Social Behavior*, **23**, 220–34.

Menaghan, E. G. (1983). Individual coping efforts: moderators of the relationship between life stress and mental health outcomes. In H. B. Kaplan (ed.) *Psychological Stress: Trends in Theory and Research*, pp. 157–91, Academic Press, New York.

Menaghan, E. G. and Merves, E. S. (1984). Coping with occupational problems: the limits of individual efforts, *Journal of Health and Social Behavior*, **25**, 406–23.

Menninger, K. (1963). *The Vital Balance: The Life Processes in Mental Health and Illness*, Viking, New York.

Merton, R. K. (1936). The unanticipated consequences of purposive social action, *American Sociological Review*, **1**, 894–904.

Miller, D. W. and Starr, M. K. (1967). *The Structure of Human Decisions*, Prentice Hall, Englewood Cliffs, NJ.

Miller, G. A. (1956). The magical number seven, plus or minus two. *Psychological Review*, **63**, 81–97.

Miller, J. G. (1965). Living systems: basic concepts, *Behavioral Science*, **10**, 193–237.

Miller, S. M. and Grant, R. (1979). The blunting hypothesis: a view of predictability and human stress. In P. O. Sjoden, S. Bates and W. S. Dockens (eds) *Trends in Behavior Therapy*, Academic Press, New York.

Mobley, W. H. and Locke, E. A. (1970). The relationship of value importance to satisfaction, *Organizational Behavior and Human Performance*, **5**, 463–83.

Moos, R. H. and Billings, A. G. (1982). Conceptualizing and measuring coping resources and processes. In L. Goldberger and S. Breznitz (eds) *Handbook of Stress: Theoretical and Clinical Aspects*, 212–30, Free Press, New York.

Naylor, J. C., Pritchard, R. D. and Ilgen, D. R. (1980). *A Theory of Behavior in Organizations*, Academic Press, New York.

Nelson, D. W. and Cohen, L. H. (1983). Locus of control and control perceptions and the relationship between life stress and psychological disorder, *American Journal of Community Psychology*, **11**, 705–22.

Newton, T. J. and Keenan, A. (1985). Coping with work-related stress, *Human Relations*, **38**, 107–26.

Parker, D. F. and DeCotiis, T. A. (1983). Organizational determinants of job stress, *Organizational Behavior and Human Performance*, **32**, 160–77.

Payne, J. W. (1976). Task complexity and contingent processing in decision making: an information search and protocol analysis, *Organizational Behavior and Human Performance*, **16**, 366–87.

Payne, J. W. (1982). Contingent decision behavior. *Psychological Bulletin*, **92**, 382–402.

Pearlin, L. I. (1980). Life strains and psychological distress among adults. In N. J. Smelser and E. H. Erikson (eds), *Themes of Work and Love in Adulthood*, Harvard University Press, Cambridge, MA.

Pearlin, L. I. and Schooler, C. (1978). The structure of coping, *Journal of Health and Social Behavior*, **19**, 2–21.

Porter, L. W. and Lawler, E. E. (1968). *Managerial attitudes and performance*, Dorsey Press, Homewood, IL.

Powers, W. T. (1973). *Behavior: The Control of Perception*, Aldine, Chicago.

Raynor, J. O. (1982). A theory of personality functioning and change. In J. O. Raynor and E. E. Entin (eds) *Motivation, Career, Striving, and Aging*, pp. 249–302, Hemisphere, Washington, DC.

Rice, R. W., McFarlin, D. B., Hunt, R. G. and Near, J. P. (1985). Organizational work and the perceived quality of life: toward a conceptual model, *Academy of Management Review*, **10**, 296–310.

Rotter, J. B. (1966). Generalized expectancies for internal versus external control of reinforcement, *Psychological Monographs*, **80**, (1, Whole No. 609).

Rychlak, J. F. (1981). *Introduction to Personality and Psychotherapy: A Theory-Construction Approach*, Houghton Mifflin, Boston.

Salancik, G. R. and Pfeffer, J. (1978). A social information processing approach to job attitudes and task design, *Administrative Science Quarterly*, **23**, 224–53.

Sandler, I. N. and Lakey, B. (1982). Locus of control as a stress moderator: The role of control perceptions and social support, *American Journal of Community Psychology*, **10**, 65–80.

Scheier, M. F. and Carver, C. S. (1985). Optimism, coping, and health: Assessment and implications of generalized outcome expectancies, *Health Psychology*, **4**, 219–47.

Schuler, R. S. (1980). Definition and conceptualization of stress in organizations, *Organizational Behavior and Human Performance*, **25**, 184–215.

Schwartz, G. E. (1983). Disregulation theory and disease: applications to the repression/cerebral disconnection/cardiovascular disorder hypothesis. In J. Matarazzo, N. Miller and S. Weiss (eds) Special issue on behavioral medicine of *International Review of Applied Psychology*, **32**, 95–118.

Seligman, M. E. P. (1975). *Helplessness: On Depression, Development, and Death*, Freeman, San Franciso.

Sells, S. B. (1979). On the nature of stress. In J. E. McGrath (ed.) *Social and Psychological Factors in Stress*, Holt, New York.

Selye, H. (1956). *The Stress of Life*, McGraw-Hill, New York.

Sherwood, J. J. (1965). Self-identity and referent others, *Sociometry*, **28**, 66–81.

Shontz, F. C. (1975). *The Psychological Aspects of Physical Illness and Disability*, Macmillan, New York.

Sidle, A., Moos, R. H., Adams, J. and Cady, P. (1969). Development of a coping scale, *Archives of General Psychiatry*, **20**, 225–32.

Silver, R. L. and Wortman, C. B. (1980). Coping with undesirable life events. In J. Garber and M. E. P. Seligman (eds) *Human Helplessness: Theory and Applications*, pp. 279–340, Academic Press, New York.

Simon, H. A. (1976). *Administrative Behavior*, 3rd edn, Free Press, New York.

Slovic, P., Fischhoff, B. and Lichtenstein, S. C. (1976). Cognitive processes and societal risk taking. In J. S. Carroll and J. W. Payne (eds) *Cognition and Social Behavior*, Lawrence Erlbaum, Hillsdale, NJ.

Slovic, P., Fischhoff, B. and Lichtenstein, S.C. (1977). Behavioral decision theory. *Annual Review of Psychology*, **28**, 1–39.

Spivack, G., Platt, J. J. and Shure, M. B. (1976). *The Problem-Solving Approach to Adjustment*, Jossey-Bass, San Francisco.

Stone, A. A. and Neale, J. M. (1984). New measure of daily coping: development and preliminary results, *Journal of Personality and Social Psychology*, **46**, 892–906.

Strauss, G. (1974). Workers: attitudes and adjustments. In the American Assembly, Columbia University, *The Worker and the Job: Coping with Change*, pp. 73–98, Prentice-Hall, Englewood Cliffs, NJ.

Suls, J. and Fletcher, B. (1985). The relative efficacy of avoidant and non-avoidant coping strategies: a meta-analysis, *Health Psychology*, **4**, 249–88.

Tolman, E. C. (1932). *Purposive Behavior in Animals and Men*, Century, New York.

Tversky, A. (1072). Elimination by aspects: a theory of choice, *Psychological Review*, **79**, 281–99.

Tversky, A. and Kahneman, D. (1971). Belief in the law of small numbers, *Psychological Bulletin*, **76**, 105–10.

Tversky, A. and Kahneman, D. (1974). Judgement under uncertainty: heuristics and biases, *Science*, **185**, 1124–31.

Valliant, G. E. (1977). *Adaptation to Life*, Little, Brown, Boston.

Vroom, V. H. (1964). *Work and Motivation*. John Wiley and Sons, New York.

Watson, D. and Clark, L. A. (1984). Negative affectivity: the disposition to experience aversive emotional states, *Psychological Bulletin*, **96**, 465–90.

Weick, K. E. (1979). *The Social Psychology of Organizing*, Addison-Wesley, Reading, MA

Weiss, H. M., Ilgen, D. R. and Sharbaugh, M. E. (1982). Effects of life and job stress on information search behaviors of organizational members, *Journal of Applied Psychology*, **67**, 60–6.

Wortman, C. B. and Brehm, J. W. (1975). Responses to uncontrollable outcomes: an integration of reactance theory and learned helplessness model. In L. Berkowitz (ed.) *Advances in experimental Social Psychology*, pp. 277–336, Academic Press, New York.

PART IV

The Person in the Work Environment

Causes, Coping and Consequences of Stress at Work
Edited by C. L. Cooper and R. Payne
© 1988 John Wiley & Sons Ltd

Chapter 9

Promoting the Individual's Health and Well-Being

John M. Ivancevich and Michael T. Matteson

Numerous and well-respected organizations such as the American Heart Association, the American Cancer Society and the President's Council on Fitness and Sports Medicine conduct public information campaigns to increase awareness about health and well-being. These and other groups have pointed out the following:

(1) If people didn't smoke, at least 80% of the 130,000 annual deaths from lung cancer, cancer of the larynx, mouth and esophagus would be prevented. Lung cancer is not the only disease linked to smoking. According to a recent study, the mortality rate from heart disease is 3.6 times higher in smokers as compared with nonsmokers.

(2) If people cut down on the consumption of animal fat, exercised more and did not smoke, the annual death rate from heart attacks—560,000— would be considerably decreased.

(3) Regular exercise primes the immune system (the cells and antibodies that protect us against disease) and helps our brain and body resist aging. If human brain and body are kept in good condition, they deteriorate less rapidly.

Statements like these have encouraged more people to seek more information. As they learn more, individuals start to ask themselves questions like 'What can I do to help myself?', 'How can I get some control over my life?' and 'How can I discipline myself to eat better, exercise more and stop smoking?'

These and other similar questions are the result of society's growing interest in health and well-being. This interest is partially the result of the discovery that the human body is one of the most responsive organisms on earth. It responds in direct proportion to how well it is treated. The body which is abused, neglected and improperly utilized wears out faster and is not efficient. On the other hand, the body which is nurtured, cared for and pampered has fewer problems.

The activities that reflect how individuals care for or neglect their bodies are called lifestyles. In this paper individuals' roles in taking care of their bodies will be examined. The emphasis of this chapter is on understanding what people can do to improve their health and well-being. The primary focus will be on changing specific lifestyle patterns so that a person's health and well-being are enhanced. There are numerous change techniques or approaches that are being touted as successful in changing lifestyle patterns. However, as this review will indicate, some of these claims are based on anecdotes, non-empirical statements and rather weak research investigation.

DEFINITIONS

Lifestyle is perhaps even harder to define clearly than stress or stressor. In a straightforward way, it concerns how individuals live and in particular is the accumulation of choices. Lalonde (1975, p. 2) offers the following as a concise and informative definition of lifestyle:

> The sum of decisions by individuals that affect their health and that can, to some extent, be controlled by them; decisions that affect health negatively then create self-imposed risks; and in that sense individuals contribute to their own illness or health.

Preventive medicine is the branch of medicine that is concerned primarily with preventing physical, mental and emotional disease and injury, in contrast to treating the sick and injured. Prevention is said to have three components: primary, secondary and tertiary. Primary prevention means preventing the occurrence of disease or injury, for example, by use of safety equipment to protect workers in hazardous occupations. Secondary prevention means early detection and intervention, preferably before the condition is clinically apparent, and has the aim of reversing, halting, or at least retarding the progress of a condition (Last, 1986). Tertiary prevention means minimizing the effects of disease and disability by surveillance and maintenance aimed at preventing complications and premature deterioration.

Kolbe (1983) offered a typology of health related behaviors that is helpful in communicating about promotion of health and well-being. He offered these clear definitions:

> *Preventive Health Behavior*—Any activity undertaken by an individual who believes herself to be healthy for the purpose of preventing illness or detecting it in an asymptomatic state.
> *At-Risk Behavior*—Any activity undertaken by an individual who believes himself to be healthy but at greater risk than normal of developing a specific health condition for the purpose of preventing that condition or detecting it in an asymptomatic state.

The term wellness is often used synonymously with the more familiar terms health and excellent health. The term wellness was coined by Dunn (1961) in a deliberate attempt to fashion a new way of paying attention to a person's health status. Dunn intended to differentiate the realm of disease or illness dominated by the medical model and system from that of health promotion and prevention dominated by social scientists, educators and others generally outside the world of medicine.

Dunn (1961) considered wellness as the style of living that permits or facilitates an improved quality of life, human excellence and high energy life. In Dunn's view wellness and health is dynamic, not static. Health is a way of living that helps us continuously to uncover human potential.

A wellness system intends to maximize good health (Ardell, 1977). In contrast, an illness system seeks to minimize the impact of disease. The difference in a wellness approach and an illness approach are made clear in Figure 1. In the illness system approach the medical or other interventions (represented by the arrows) used are directed toward treating the disease. By focusing exclusively on illness, medical practitioners have accomplished major breakthroughs in curing disease. Many practitioners have not, however, been primarily concerned with achieving health or optimal health.

On the other hand, a wellness system approach moves beyond striving for the absence of disease. The emphasis is on self-responsibility. That is, the person is given primary responsibility for his or her achievement of health. Medical and health professionals are available as resources for the individual.

AN ILLUSTRATION OF WELLNESS

Recently, a 41-year-old junior executive was promoted to take over the international division of a Fortune 500 firm. For six years the manager worked long days, accepted difficult assignments and attended extensive

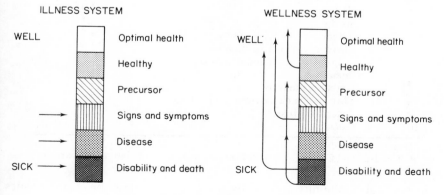

Figure 1 Emphasis in Wellness and Illness Systems

and intense training programs. The promotion committee noticed that the manager was always enthusiastic, positive and willing to do what was necessary to help co-workers and the firm. He was a true team player and a person that others enjoyed working with.

Besides being upbeat and positive the manager exuded self-confidence and adhered to a daily ritual of exercise and self-improvement. He was concerned about his health and read about, attended training sessions and participated in the firm's health promotion programs.

This person, despite a busy schedule, pressing demands and responsibilities fits Dunn's description of optimal wellness. That is, the manager maximized his potential within the environment in which he was functioning. The manager adopted an active role in engineering his lifestyle so that optimal mental and physical health could be attained.

PREVENTABLE HEALTH PROBLEMS

Table 1 depicts the major causes of death in the United States for 1981. Today most of the serious health problems individuals face are ones that develop slowly over time. As Table 1 shows, the major causes of death are no longer infectious diseases. Rather, today's major killers of Americans are heart disease (37.0% of all deaths), cancer (20.4%) and stroke (9.6%). Deaths from heart disease and stroke increased during the first half of the 20th century, but as detailed by Thorn and Kannel (1981) and Levy and Moskovitz (1982), this pattern has begun to reverse.

Table 1 Ten leading causes of death—United States, 1981

Rank	Cause of death	Rate per 100,000 population*
1	Heart disease	336.0
2	Cancer	183.9
3	Stroke	75.1
4	Accidents	45.7
5	Chronic obstructive pulmonary diseases and allied conditions	24.7
6	Pneumonia and influenza	24.1
7	Diabetes mellitus	15.4
8	Chronic liver disease and cirrhosis	13.5
9	Arteriosclerosis	13.0
10	Suicide	11.9

*Non-age-adjusted
Source: National Center for Health Statistics, 1981 (provisional) mortality rates.

The medical community uses the term risk factor to describe characteristics which increase a person's risk for each health problem (Drechsler, Bruner and Kreitter, 1987; Kannel, Capples and D'Agostino, 1987; Leon, 1987). Risk factors may be divided into three types: the controllable, uncontrollable and semicontrollable. An example of an uncontrollable risk factor would be heredity. The semicontrollable risk factor can be illustrated by environmental conditions. In some workplaces there is air pollution. This is a semicontrollable risk factor because it is one that can be eliminated even though it may not be practical to do so. For example, risk factors for heart disease include smoking, high blood pressure, elevated serum cholesterol, obesity, a family history of heart disease, Type A behavior and a lack of exercise. Most of these risk factors are under the control of the individual. That is, the individual can exercise some type of control over these traditional risk factors.

Belloc and Breslow (1972) presented the results of a survey of a representative probability sample of 6,928 American adults. The survey revealed that seven specific personal health practices were highly correlated with the physical health of the adults:

(1)   Sleeping seven to eight hours daily;
(2)   Eating breakfast almost every day;
(3)   Never or rarely eating between meals;
(4)   Currently being at or near prescribed height-adjusted weight;
(5)   Never smoking cigarettes;
(6)   Moderate or no use of alcohol;
(7)   Regular physical activity.

Those adults who followed all or most of these seven good practices were found to be in better general health than those who followed none or few. Belloc (1973) continued to probe the relationship between health practices from the time of the initial survey—1965 to 1971. The presence or absence of each of the seven health practices showed only modest levels of intercorrelation across individuals when analyzed as pairs of behavior. However, summing the practices for each individual showed a clear relationship to mortality at follow-up (Matarazzo, 1984).

Breslow and Enstrom (1980) in a 9½-year follow-up further confirmed the effect on mortality of these seven health practices. They found that men who followed all seven health practices had a mortality rate only 28% of that of men who followed zero to three practices; the comparable rate for women who followed all seven practices was 43% of that of women who followed only zero to three health practices.

Breslow (1978) and his associates (Breslow and Somers, 1977) offer a number of demonstrably valid and cost-effective steps that can be taken throughout a person's life that specifically promote health and well-being. These steps include receiving seven immunizations (e.g. chicken pox, polio), screening tests during infancy, control of smoking and obesity, and screening tests for hypertension and cancer (cervical, gastrointestinal and mammary). This prescription for actively pursuing a healthy life encourages health-related behaviors as opposed to a more passive disease response behavior (Warner, 1987).

THE GOAL OF PROMOTING HEALTH AND WELL BEING

The main goal of promoting health and well-being is behavior change, leading to changes in mediating mechanisms of health problems, and finally to changes in morbidity, mortality and longevity. Most systematic programs for achieving behavior change are based on analysis of behavior approaches and social learning theory (Jenkins, 1986). These approaches were first applied in changing health-related behavior by Ferster, Nurnberger and Levitt (1962). In more recent times Bandura's (1977) work on self-efficacy has had a significant influence.

Bandura (1977, 1982) proposed that self-efficacy expectations mediate change and maintenance of change. Self-efficacy is the belief that an individual has mastered the skills necessary to engage in the new behavior. Self-efficacy is increased by means of participant modeling and successfully engaging in behaviors without attributing the skills to external aids. Thus, both verbal messages attempting to persuade and improved knowledge are less likely to result in increases in self-efficacy compared with direct, self-guided practice of the new behavior. In the face of minor setbacks, the higher the self-efficacy the less likely a return to old habits. A critical factor in self-efficacy is attribution of responsibility for the behavior change to his or her own doing vs outside sources (Goldfried and Robins, 1982). A person who attributes a change in health or well-being to luck, a friend or a drug is likely to have low self-efficacy and is vulnerable to relapse when the external agents are withdrawn.

Experimental studies testing the premises of self-efficacy theory are beginning to emerge. Craighead, Stankard and O'Brien (1981) showed that a group of people who were given a weight-loss drug plus behavior therapy lost more weight than a behavior therapy alone group, but they relapsed more rapidly. Presumably the weight-loss participants in the combined treatment intervention group attributed their weight change to the externally administered drug even though they practiced the same behavioral skills as the other group. Since self-efficacy did not change in the combined group, they were apparently more vulnerable to relapse.

DiClemente (1981) investigated the relationship between self-efficacy and maintenance of nonsmoking. Individuals who had recently quit smoking judged their efficacy to avoid smoking in 12 situations along a range of stress levels. The participants were surveyed a few months later to determine maintenance. The findings indicated that maintainers had judged efficacy significantly higher than recidivists and that self-efficacy was a better predictor of future smoking behavior than was smoking history or demographic variables.

An important means of developing self-efficacy is through goal setting. A perceived negative discrepancy between present performance level and some desired standard can prompt individuals into action. The anticipated self-satisfaction of goal attainment sustains a person's involvement and helps develop skills.

Behavioral change in terms of promoting one's health and well-being requires a specific program on the part of the individual. Mahoney (1975) has provided such a program that relies on the individual becoming personally motivated to do something about his/her health and well-being. Some of the steps in Mahoney's program suggest the following activities:

(1) *Self-monitoring.* The person needs to keep some type of written record indicating each time a behavior occurs (e.g. snacking between meals, losing one's temper). Research has determined that keeping a record improves the probability of compliance.

(2) *Analysis of the entire behavioral sequence.* For losing one's temper, this sequence may require recording thoughts that preceded a meeting that resulted in an argument. This analysis may point to areas where intervention is most likely to have a positive impact.

(3) *Goal Setting and Contracting.* Goals that point to changing behavior are set. Moderately challenging goals must be set so that early successes can lead to later successes. The goals should be concise, include a target date for review and require the person to be actively involved.

(4) *Feedback should be included.* Feedback should be presented as an opportunity for determining how well one is progressing. Greater positive changes can be achieved if the behavior (e.g. biofeedback training, increased exercise, modification of Type A) is monitored and reinforced.

(5) *Development of a self-reward system.* Some type of tangible, intangible or self-talk reward system should be established.

(6) *Modeling of the correct behaviors.* If a person can observe others performing the desired health behaviors and being rewarded for them, it will both teach and correct technique.

(7) *Cognitive engineering.* Individuals should be encouraged to visualize the positive consequences of adhering to the health regimen and the negative consequences of failure to adhere. Visualization can clearly identify the reasons why optimal health and well-being are preferable to sickness and a poor quality of life. As Bandura (1977) argues, the determinants of behavior are largely under an individual's own control. Thus, a person can alter his or her level of arousal through self-generated

imagery and can apply foresight to situational cues in order to predict and then to modify sequences leading to future behaviors.

There is probably no behavior change in lifestyle or health behavior which can be brought about by a single activity. Instead, as Mahoney (1975) and others have vividly pointed out, a number of activities must be performed. As such activities as self-monitoring, goal setting, interpreting feedback and cognitive engineering are performed, there are likely to be successes and failures, enthusiasm and discouragement, and stability and instability. After all, learning new lifestyle and healthy behaviors, habits and skills after years of unhealthy behaviors, poor habits and a lack of skills is no easy task.

METHODS OF LIFESTYLE IMPROVEMENT

Permeating various approaches to promoting health and well-being is an important premise—namely, that people have the means of bringing about meaningful changes in their lifestyle that will persist over time. Typically, it is assumed that behaving in personally responsible ways—that is, exercising what is called self-management—requires a number of skills. However, these skills are not usually a part of everyone's preferred repertoire (Mahoney and Thoresen, 1974). People need to be taught how to be more concerned, caring and responsible for their own health and well-being, especially when co-workers, television advertisements, family members and other environmental stimuli are showing and promoting unhealthy habits and behaviors.

The respected physician imploring the patient to 'stop smoking, exercise more, control your temper and eat better balanced meals' apparently is not enough to change or improve unhealthy lifestyles (Thoresen and KermilGray, 1983). What then is the best way to change behavior and to promote well-being? Of course, a simplistic answer is that it depends on the people involved, the environment and the goals of the change strategy. One model that encourages developing change programs that considers the multiple reciprocal influences of cognitive, environmental, behavior, and physiological processes is the expanded cognitive social learning model. This model is useful for weighing the potential benefits of a particular program, designing the features of a program, and evaluating the results of a program. Figure 2 presents the model. The model suggests that when attempting to improve well-being, multiple factors need to be considered—cognitive, physiological, environmental and behavioral. Personal health and well-being is influenced by 'good habits'—exercise, relaxation, positive thoughts and an overall life-style that is supportive of health enhancement.

There are a vast array of lifestyle change intervention programs that have been studied and are of current interest to the public, organizations and researchers. Four of the most cited, discussed and critiqued programs are

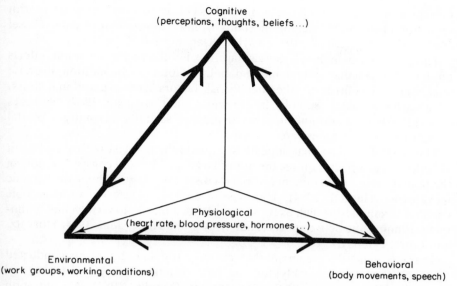

Cognitive
(perceptions, thoughts, beliefs...)

Physiological
(heart rate, blood pressure, hormones...)

Environmental
(work groups, working conditions)

Behavioral
(body movements, speech)

Figure 2   Bandura's expanded Cognitive Social Learning Model

exercise, biofeedback training, cognitive-behavioral and modification of Type A behavior pattern. Each of these programs has stimulated debate, research investigations, and some controversy.

Exercise

Common-sense supports the view that exercise and keeping fit can promote health and well-being. However, the study of the physical activity, health and illness complex encounters great difficulties. An epidemiologic prospective study, comparing a large sample of physically active subjects with a randomized, large sample of 'inactive' subjects over a long period of time has never been conducted. There is little likelihood for a 'double blind study' where physical activity can be measured. However, three types of biomedical studies have been conducted that lend some empirical support to the position that exercise can enhance health and well-being.

Training studies show that training consistently improves physical work capacity and cardiovascular and metabolic function in normal individuals and in many patients with established cardiovascular disease (Hanson, 1982). *Hypodynamic studies* of individuals after prolonged bed-rest or weightlessness in space provide significant evidence that exercise can enhance health (Pace, 1977; Saltin *et al.*, 1968). In both cases there is a rapid reduction in physical work capacity and loss of normal cardiovascular response to exercise stress. *Epidemiologic studies* of occupational physical activity have shown that jobs requiring a relatively high physical activity are associated with reduction in the incidence and mortality from cardiovascular disease (Cassel *et al.*, 1971; Morris *et al.*, 1953; Taylor, Klepetar and Keys, 1962).

The potential benefits of exercise are not limited to the favorable effects on the cardiovascular system and metabolic adaptation. In addition, exercise aids voluntary control of other health risk factors such as emotional stress, adverse dietary habits and obesity (Fremont and Craighead, 1987). At times it is difficult to determine to what degree of scientific certainty a partial benefit has been demonstrated to exist.

The type of exercise that appears to provide the greatest individual health benefits is that which requires the use of large muscles and consists of moving the body weight against gravity or over a distance using rhythmic or dynamic movements (Haskell, 1984). This type of exercise is referred to as aerobic exercise. Examples of such exercise include jogging, stationary cycling, swimming, running and active sports (Hall, Meyer and Hellerstein, 1984; Horwitz, and Groves, 1985).

There is general agreement that exercise training should be conducted three or four times weekly for the best results (Bruce, DeRowen and Hossack, 1980; Cooper, 1982; Masironi and Denolin, 1985). The duration of each session depends on the intensity and type of exercise. Most studies report that 30–40 minutes of aerobic exercise at moderate intensity is required. Balke (1974) has suggested that the energy expenditure should equal 10% of daily caloric consumption.

Since exercise sessions are optimally 30–40 minutes long they should begin with a five to ten minute warm-up period that emphasizes progressive stretching. The warm-up period helps to prevent musculoskeltal strain and prepares the cardiopulmonary system for more strenuous work. The maximum effect of exercise adaptation is attained in three to five months of consistent training.

Research indicates that approximately 15% of the United States adult population are very active and involved in exercise programs. Also, about 70% of the population are either low-active or nonactive (Belisle, Roskies and Levesque, 1987). These data suggest that most adults are not motivated to initiate or sustain an exercise program. Compliance rates in prescribed exercise programs for patients with coronary heart disease suggest that approximately 40–50% of those who enter programs drop out within six to twelve months (Oldrige, 1982). Other data suggest compliance of approximately 50–60% for six months, dropping to about 35% after two or more years (Dishman and Ickes, 1981).

Goal setting has been shown to have some success in improving exercise adherence rates. Martin and Dubbert (1982) suggest that self-set goals are more effective than external party set goals. Realistic and challenging goals need to be set by the individual. Despite some success with goal-setting programs adherence is a major problem with exercise programs. Although exercise has some benefits associated with it there are still many people who possess beliefs and attitudes that block their compliance with an exercise regimen. In fact, beliefs and attitudes are extremely important when discussing any method of lifestyle intervention.

A *belief* is a hypothetical construct that involves the assertion between some attitude object (not exercising) and some attribute of that object (e.g. causes a person to be sluggish or to have trouble sleeping). An *attitude* is a hypothetical construct used to explain consistencies within people in their affective reactions to (feeling toward) an attitude objet. Attitudes, according to Ajzen and Fishbein (1977, 1980) are evaluations made on the affective (feeling) dimension. Most theories agree that attitudes are learned and serve to motivate behavior.

The Theory of Reasoned Action formulated by Fishbein and Ajzen (1975) asserts that human behavior, such as following an exercise program, is controlled by thoughtful analysis. A person decides to engage or not to engage in an exercise program by carefully considering its implications. Behavior is under volitional control and is a function of the person's intention to perform or not to perform a particular behavior. Thus, beliefs influence attitudes and subjective norms; these two components influence intentions, and intentions influence behavior. Behavioral change is ultimately the result of changes in belief. Consequently, belief changes are needed to bring about change in attitudes. An adapted version of Ajzen and Fishbein's theory is portrayed in Figure 3.

Many studies have searched for a nonadherent personality or have attempted to correlate demographic factors into a predictive equation. In general, these efforts of attempting to identify the type of person who adheres and the type who drops out of an exercise program have been fruitless.

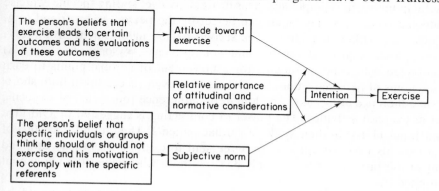

Note: Arrows indicate the direction of influence

Figure 3 Factors determining a person's behavior

Attempts to improve exercise adherence have typically focused on (a) educating the person; (b) tailoring the program to fit the person; or (c) using behavioral techniques.

Haynes (1976), after reviewing a large literature base on compliance to regimens, concluded that in terms of therapeutic outcome, educating the person achieved a success rate of about 50%. He reviewed such educational techniques as brief health messages, individual instruction, counseling plus written instructions, lecture demonstration activities and emotional role playing. A person is simply not able to adhere to any regimen (e.g. taking medication, exercising) if he or she does not understand the technique.

An effective way to improve understanding and involvement is to tailor the regimen to fit the person's schedule, preferences and tolerance levels. If a program is adapted to better fit a person's schedule and preference it is more likely to keep the individual interested and motivated. After all, exercise requires not only physical output, but also psychological discipline and commitment.

A number of behavioral techniques have been employed to improve compliance. The provision of cues or stimuli which can keep the person thinking about compliance are useful. Charts, diagrams, cartoons and other types of cues can provide a higher profile of exercise in the person's environment.

The use of self-monitoring has proved to be useful in some dietary control studies (Dunbar and Stunkard, 1979). This technique could be easily adapted for exercise programs. The person's recording of exercise times, locations, intensity and effects on such outcomes as heart rate (pulse), endurance and strength may be useful and worth evaluating.

Utilizing a goal contract is another behavioral technique that could be useful in improving compliance. This process involves stating specific exercise outcome type goals. The goals can be set by the person and a friend (e.g. spouse, co-worker, neighbor). The second person involvement promotes a more public stance, statement and commitment. Wysocki et al. (1978) contracted with college students for achievement of aerobic points to earn back items of personal value; the technique proved successful in both short-term adherence (10 weeks) and long-term adherence (one year) of a specific set of exercise activities. The power of contracting is suggested by Oldridge and Jones (1983) in their study of cardiac patients. They found that 80% of the patients who did not sign an agreement to exercise eventually dropped out of the program, whereas only 35% of those who signed the agreement dropped out.

The issue of how long a contractual arrangement will last should be considered. Reid and Morgan (1979) found that an exercise program was followed for about three months but was not adhered to at six months. This inding which differs from the Wysocki *et al.* (1978) results suggests that the length of adherence time is still a controversial and perplexing issue.

The long-term commitment to the maintenance of exercise habits is rather disappointing when research is reviewed. The recidivism rate of 70% of more after a few years seems to apply to most exercise activities. Despite the potential physiological and behavioral benefits of regular exercise most people have trouble adhering to a disciplined regimen. Since each person is responsible for their exercise behaviors, each individual will have to privately weigh the potential cost and benefits of exercise adherence.

BIOFEEDBACK

The use and effectiveness of biofeedback for treating a wide variety of disorders and for promoting well-being has been enthusiastically accepted by advocates of this approach. However, due to some flaws in the research designs of often cited studies, there is reason for using caution in concluding that biofeedback can be effective (Norris, 1986). Biofeedback does exactly that its name suggests. It feeds back biological information to an individual. Each person possesses their own intrinsic biofeedback systems. For example, food regulation is accomplished by food ingestion distending the stomach and raising blood sugar levels, as well as causing hormones to be released. All of these internal functions 'feed back' to the brain, telling the individual 'you are full'. Thus, biofeedback can be defined as receiving immediate information in the dynamic state of a physiological factor. Biofeedback training has the potential for teaching the mind to regulate the activities of the so-called automonic organs.

One of the first empirical examinations into the ability of animals to gain control over visceral processes was conducted by Miller and DiCara (1969). Initially, they were interested in exploring whether classical conditioning and instrumental conditioning were two separate phenomena or merely two manifestations of the same phenomenon. During the course of their investigations, they reported success in setting up conditions under which rats could learn to regulate their heart rate, blood pressure, rate of urine formation, vasomotor activity and intestinal contractions.

Encouraged by the success of Miller and DiCara with the visceral learning phenomenon in animals, other researchers began to examine the possibility that humans could override and control. Kamiya (1969) was interested in the ability of people to detect when they were and were not producing specific brainwave patterns. He arranged a monitor stimulus so that a light would go on when the person produced alpha waves from the occipital region of the brain. He found that by giving individuals feedback related to the presence or absence of their own alpha wave activity at a given moment, individuals could alter the amount of time they spent producing this pattern

of brainwave activity. By receiving timely, high quality feedback Kamiya'
subjects could eventually regulate their own patterns of brainwave activity.

Green (1969, 1970), in a series of experiments, demonstrated that whe
given appropriate physiological feedback, individuals could learn to regulat
skeletal muscle tension and peripheral blood flow. His experiments led t
revolutionary new treatments for muscle tension and vascular migrain
headaches.

The work of Kamiya, Green and other researchers has resulted in th
development of biofeedback training. The objective of biofeedback trainin
is to provide an individual with timely physiological information feedbac
that can then be used in acquiring control over visceral parameters. Thi
control can then be applied in three areas. First, it can be used in th
treatment of disease. An afflicted person can voluntarily alter the activity c
the troubled system and the body in fighting the problem. Second, contrc
can be used by healthy individuals to reduce disease probability or revers
a physiological problem at its earliest stages. Finally, gaining consciou
control over physical functions can help individuals achieve well-being an
health.

To gain control over internal processes, a person must first be able t
monitor them. Most internal physiological processes are not directly access
ible to our senses. Instrumentation is needed to sense internal activity an
then create a presentation that reflects the activity of the internal organ in
manner that a person can monitor. Typically, biofeedback instrument
convert physiological signals into changes such as variation in the pitch of a
auditory tone or variations in the display of flashing lights.

Biofeedback training can play three roles in stress management (Allei
1983). First, biofeedback can be used in treating psychosomatic problem:
Biofeedback training can give individuals some control over migraine heac
aches, hypertension, Raynard's syndrome and tachycardia.

Second, biofeedback training can be used in identifying so-called 'wea
organs'. Current thinking is that if weak organs can be identified in advanc
of the actual manifestation of disease, the person can learn to control th
activity of the system while it is still healthy and responsive to learning an
conditioning and thus avoid the occurrence of the disease. This 'weak orga
diagnostic approach to preventive medicine is still in its early developme
phase and in need of much more experimental research.

Finally, biofeedback training can be valuable in augmenting the effe
tiveness of systematic relaxation techniques. Biofeedback can be used
determine which forms and duration of systematic relaxation are the mo
physiologically effective. Biofeedback can provide information about wheth
a relaxation strategy is lowering visceral arousal effectively.

Biofeedback training involves the use of sensors which are attached to tl
body to monitor internal physiological activity. The electrical sensor is tl

most frequently used to monitor myocardial activity, muscular tension and brainwave activity. Other types of sensors include transducers, which convert a phsyiological activity that is not electrical into electricity so the biofeedback instrument can process the signal. Examples of transducers include thermistors and thermocouples (to measure blood flow) and photoplelhysmographs (to measure pulse pressure).

The biofeedback instruments and sensors do nothing to a person. They merely serve to monitor the activity that is going on inside a person's body. If changes within the person occur, they are accomplished by the individual. The skill to change or exercise control over the internal processes must be developed. Typically muscular tension is a process that can most readily be brought under voluntary control. Usually, four to six 20- to 30-minute training sessions are enough for a person to achieve the level of control required to produce deep relaxation at will. Altering blood flow requires significantly more training time.

There are available for individual use a varity of biofeedback training devices. The most commonly used include electroencephalography (EEG), electromyography (EMG), cardiovascular parameters and electrodermal activity. EEG refers to monitoring brainwave activity. EMG refers to the electrical activity of the muscles. Cardiovascular feedback can provide information on the activities of the heart, the vascular system, or arterial blood pressure. Electrodermal biofeedback, previously labeled GSR for galvanic skin response, involves measuring the ability of the skin surface to conduct electricity.

Many therapists and researchers consider EMG to be the most useful of the various forms of biofeedback (Burish, 1981; Fuller, 1978). Thus, because of space limitations only the EMG form will be discussed in this chapter. EMG is offered as the most effective and efficient method for helping people cope with stress and stress-related disorders; primarily because of its alleged ability to enable people to achieve a deep state of relaxation (Gaarder and Montgomery, 1977; Stoyva, 1977). In most cases, EMG biofeedback training consists of single site feedback reflecting muscle activity from the frontal region. It is assumed that such single site feedback enables the person not only to control the muscle tension at the feedback site but also to accomplish a number of other goals important for general stress reduction.

A number of studies have assessed whether EMG biofeedback reduces muscle tension in the frontal region (Beiman, Israel and Johnson, 1978; Solomon and Brehony, 1979). The conclusions of the researchers were that biofeedback training is clearly effective in reducing muscle tension levels in the target area below those of subjects not given any other type of relaxation training.

Alexander (1975) assigned subjects either to a frontal EMG biofeedback group or to a control group which recieved instructions to reduce their muscle tension. EMG levels were recorded from the frontal area, forearm and lower leg during training and nontraining sessions. Results indicated that the biofeedback training was effective in reducing frontal EMG levels, but that these reductions were not accompanied by reductions in either forearm or lower leg EMG levels.

The general tone of EMG frontal area research is that there is little empirical support that reducing EMG levels in the frontal region will reduce EMG levels in other muscle sites. Perhaps the claims of EMG supporters were physiolgoically naive in the first place when it was stated that EMG reductions in the frontal region would generalize to other muscle groups. If general muscle relaxation is the goal, it seems more reasonable that individuals will have to be given feedback from multiple muscle regions.

Several individuals have suggested that biofeedback training may help individuals to cognitively cope with stress (Lazarus, 1977; Meichenbaum, 1976). Unfortunately, little research has been conducted to examine these suggestions. Burish and Schwartz (1980) had subjects who were either given frontal EMB biofreedback training or were asked to sit quietly and relax. Half of the subjects (early threat condition) were told before the biofeedback training/relaxation period began that they would receive an electric shock later in the experiment, while the remaining subjects (late threat condition) were not told about the shock until immediately before it was delivered. After receiving the shock, subjects were asked to rate how much they worried about the shock. It was proposed that the late threat condition subjects would have less time to worry and dwell on the shock. It was also proposed that subjects in the biofeedback–early threat condition would report worrying less about the shock than subjects in the no biofeedback–early threat condition. As predicted, subjects in the biofeedback–early threat, biofeedback–late threat, and no biofeedback–late threat conditions reported worrying less about the shock than subjects in the no biofeedback–early threat condition. This finding suggests that EMG biofeedback training given during a stressful situation may help people avoid worrying about the situation, probably because it tends to channel their attention away from the aversive event and onto the biofeedback training task itself.

It is sometimes assumed that EMG biofeedback training compares favorably to other techniques used for stress reduction (Budzyaski, 1978). The research results do not equivocally support such an assumption. Haynes, Moseley and McGowan (1975), compared frontal EMG biofeedback training to passive relaxation training, active relaxation training, false feedback and no treatment control procedures. Results indicated that the biofeedback training and passive relaxation training groups both had significantly lower levels of frontal EMG than did any of the other groups. Sime and DeGood (1977) compared frontal biofeedback training, progressive relaxation training focusing on the forehead muscles and a control group listening to music as an alleged guide for relaxation. The biofeedback and relaxation groups were equally effective and produced significantly lower EMG levels than the control condition.

Fee and Gudano (1978) compared five groups including frontal EMG biofeedback, meditation, progressive relaxation, placebo and no treatment. After ten sessions of training only the biofeedback and meditation groups showed a significant decrease in frontal EMG. No group showed a consistent reduction in the autonomic indices which were collected.

The most important and consistent conclusion that can be reached at this time is that EMG biofeedback training is effective in reducing EMG levels in target muscles. However, EMG biofeedback training has little effect on EMG levels in nonfeedback areas, autonomic arousal or performance under stress. Also, EMG biofeedback training is generally no more effective than less expensive forms of relaxation training in reducing EMG levels. Thus, until new data demonstrate the usefulness of EMG biofeedback training, investigators should be cautious in what they claim it can do for promoting health and well-being. There is simply no consistent scientific support for the effectiveness of biofeedback in treating stress-related problems, disease or overall well-being (Stoney *et al.*, 1987).

Cognitive-Behavioral Approaches to Health Promotion and Well-Being

The cognitive-behavioral perspective on promoting health and well-being encompasses a number of strategies (Kendall and Turk, 1984). Instead of grand theoretical foundations for this perspective, there are a number of guiding principles (Kendall and Bemis, 1983; Mahoney, 1977). Included in the set of principles are the following:

(1) Individuals do not respond directly to their environment; they respond to their own cognitive interpretation of the environment.
(2) Cognitions (thoughts), emotions (feelings) and behaviors (actions) are causally interrelated.
(3) The prediction and understanding of negative cognitions and behaviors are enhanced by paying attention to a person's expectancies, beliefs and attributions.
(4) It is possible and desirable to combine and integrate cognitive approaches to correcting problems with performance-based and behavioral contingency management.

The exact nature of how these guiding principles are employed is not universally accepted. In fact, there are differences in what is being changed. In such approaches as rational restructuring (Goldfried, 1969), stress inoculation training (Meichenbaum, 1977) and cognitive therapy of depression

(Beck *et al.*, 1979) the intent is to change cognitions and behaviors directly. However, in using rational-emotive therapy (RET) (Ellis, 1962), the intention is to bring about a philosophical change in the person.

Cognitive-behavioral approaches to lifestyle modification tend to be fairly structured and dynamic. These approaches are designed to assist a person in identifying, reality testing and correcting improper conceptualizations, dysfunctional beliefs and incorrect patterns of thinking. A special emphasis in cognitive-behavioral approaches is on improving skill deficiencies (e.g. deficient approaches to improving health and well-being).

The role attributed to psychological factors in health and disease has waxed and waned throughout the 20th century. Recently, there is increased acceptance that the etiology of disease is multidetermined. Earlier, Mechanic (1968) noted that, in contrast to disease, illness involves three components: (a) a person's attentiveness to symptoms, (b) the process affecting how symptoms are defined and (c) the person's help-seeking behavior, alterations of lifestyle and so forth. Thus, in Mechanic's interpretation 'illness' refers to a person's subjective experience of the objective disease.

Individuals develop elaborate conceptualizations of health and disease—causes, cures, self-responsibility and control. These personal conceptualizations are largely shaped by prior experiences, friends, relatives and co-workers, mass media reports and other sources of information. The manner in which this information is conceptualized effects a person's health-protective behavior, their symptom perception, and how they generally behave (Ferguson, Discenza and Miller, 1987).

There is a growing body of literature that supports the important role that cognitive factors play in promoting health and well-being (Kirschenbaum, 1987; Turk, Meichenbaum and Genest, 1983). Since cognitive factors play an important role, cognitive-behavioral interrelations are becoming more popular. Such interventions have been used in the treatment of alcohol abuse (Chaney, O'Leary and Marlatt, 1978), modification of Type A coronary prone behavior (Jenni and Wollersheim, 1979), prevention of maladaptive responses to job-related stress (Sarason *et al.*, 1979), and enhancing coping skills for chronic illness (Weisman, Worden and Sobel, 1980).

Stress inoculation training is a cognitive-behavioral approach that focuses on altering a person's conceptualization and processing of information about a stressful situation and focuses on cognitive and behavioral coping skills to modify maladaptive ways of reacting. Stress inoculation training contains three stages: (1) preparation, (2) skills training and (3) application training (Meichenbaum, 1985; Meichenbaum and Cameron, 1983). In the preparation stage the person identifies the relationship among maladaptive cognitions (e.g. thoughts, beliefs) and maladaptive patterns of emotional response and behavior. This stage is primarily educational, with the counselor or therapist presenting the person with an explanation of the powerful role that cognitions can play. A goal of this stage is to convince the person that he or she is not helpless in coping with a health problem or a stress situation. The person is asked to explain his or her perceptions, behavioral actions and self-talk statements.

The second stage of stress inoculation training focuses on skills development. The person is taught to confront the stress with coping techniques he or she already possesses or to learn new coping techniques. A variety of techniques have been employed, including relaxation exercises, cognitive restructuring procedures and self-instructional training.

The final stage of stress inoculation training involves the person's application and practice of the newly acquired skills. Depending on the nature of the problem being treated, application targets may differ. Meichenbaum (1977) discussed using gradually increasing intensities of shock for treating fear-anxiety responses. Novaco (1977) used anger hierarchies in treating anger and depression.

Novaco (1977) proposes that anger is a stress reaction consisting of autonomic, cognitive and motor components. Anger is an emotional state that is determined partially by a person's cognitive structuring of a situation. Anger serves to energize and increase the vigor of a response. Novaco has developed a cognitive-behavioral program of anger control that uses concepts similar to stress inoculation training.

In Stage 1, anger provocation is broken down into four parts. During the educational phase, the individual is taught to self-monitor anger arousal and cognitive concomitants of anger. The person also performs a situational analysis to assess the multidimensional factors involved in anger provocation. Included are a review of the person's day prior to the provocation, job pressures and family pressures.

Stage 2 involves the acquisition of skills for coping with each aspect of the provocation sequence. Phases in the sequence include preparing for a provocation, impact and confrontation with the anger stimulus, coping with arousal and subsequent reflection on the conflict experience. The person learns to perform a cost–benefit analysis of emitting an anger response. The individual also learns self-statements designed and generated to help him or her remain task-oriented and to maintain a sense of personal control.

The third phase is the application of anger management skills learned in the second stage. The person develops an anger provocation hierarchy. Then the individual directly role plays the way anger will be handled. He or she acts out the type of coping that will be necessary to stay in control.

The cognitive-behavioral approach has appeal as a procedure for promoting health and well-being. The approach has been used with some success for fear/anxiety, uncertainty, pain and anger situations. There still remains some unanswered questions, and to date no empirically validated attempt has been made to apply an education, skills training and application type model to promoting health and well-being. The efficacy of applying a cognitive-behavioral package to promoting health and well-being needs to be tested with diverse samples. There is much to be learned from the study of the cognitions and behavior of persons who engage in a healthy lifestyle (Grigsby, 1987).

Modifying the Type A Behavior Pattern

The original description of the Type A behavior pattern (TABP) was distinctly behavioral. Friedman and Rosenman (1959) observed that men who eventually developed coronary heart disease could be identified by various clinical signs and symptoms, such as fast and emphatic speech patterns, interrupting others and easily aroused irritabilities (Williams *et al.*, 1980). Using the work of Cannon (1915), they hypothesized that these discrete behaviors were the signs of a chronic struggle against time and other people, resulting from an interplay between personality traits and specific environmental demands (Friedman and Ulmer, 1984; Friedman and Rosenman, 1974). Thus, since the struggle manifested itself in relation to time and other people, the TABP was said to have two key elements—time urgency and hostility.

Friedman and Rosenman drew on their vast clinical practice to develop their interpretation of TABP. In an attempt to determine empirically the specific individual behaviors which contribute to the development of coronary heart disease (CHD), Matthews and her colleagues (1977) studied items that discriminated between subjects who were and were not destined to develop CHD in the Western Collaborative Group Study. Items related to time urgency ('irritation in waiting lines'), hostility ('potential for hostility'), anger ('anger directed outward', 'angry more than once a week') and vigorous speech style ('explosive voice modulation') were found to have pathogenic significance in a white male population.

Another conceptual approach was taken by Glass (1977) when he attempted to isolate a central trait that serves to produce and sustain overt Type A behavior. In a series of laboratory experiments, Glass found that Type As work hard, work fast and attempt to suppress fatigue. Thus, Glass concluded that TABP is motivated by a person's exaggerated need for control over the environment.

An assumption underlying the conceptual and empirical work surrounding TABP is that perhaps Type A behavior can be reduced to a single unifying trait. If this were the case then there would be a direction pointed out for interventions aimed at reducing the negative health, disease and lifestyle aspects of TABP. However, the assumption of a unidimensional concept does not appear to fit the data. Instead the evidence available appears to suggest that TABP is a multidimensional phenomenon, including an array of overt behaviors, cognitive styles, behaviors in response to environmental demands and physiological concommitants. Under this conceptualization, the Type A perception of others may be 'hostility' and the Type A perception of self may be 'low self-esteem' (Powell, 1984). What produces the Type A reactivity may be a high 'need for control'.

Designing an intervention program to reduce TABP requires that a number of issues be considered. Who should the target population be? What should be the target behavior? What should the format for intervention be? How should change in TABP be evaluated? Each of these issues deserve special attention before undertaking any particular type of intervention.

There is a growing number of studies on Type A intervention (Powell, 1984; Roskies, 1987). Some of the studies have been directed at primary intervention (changing the TABP of healthy individuals), secondary prevention (changing the TABP of high risk individuals) and tertiary prevention (changing the TABP of post-infarct individuals).

In most intervention programs the duration of the formal modification attempt has been short, from one session to 14 sessions over a 14-week period (Roskies *et al.*, 1977). Also, most intervention programs have focused on managing stress and tension without paying attention to other components of TABP—time urgency and hostility. Thompson (1976) used a deep muscle relaxation exercise or listening to music. Suinn (1974), Suinn and Bloom (1978) and Baskin (1979) provided Anxiety Management Training (AMT) in combination with new ways of responding to stressful situations.

Suinn (1982), in summarizing seven studies that attempted to change TABP in healthy persons, stated that extremely small sample sizes and the failure of any study to include an expectancy control group made it difficult to determine if anything meaningful occurred.

A major obstacle to the increased understanding of the relationship between treatment intervention and degree of change in TABP is the absence of validated posttreatment measures of Type A in most of the intervention studies. An exception to this evaluation flaw is the Recurrent Coronary Prevention Project (RCPP) (Friedman *et al.*, 1982, 1984). The major aims of the RCPP are to determine to what degree Type A behavior can be modified in postinfarction patients and to what extent the recurrence rate of coronary catastrophes can be altered in postinfarction patients whose TABP has been modified. Over 1000 postinfarction patients are participating in this five-year study. At intake all subjects had at least one infarction, some subjects had as many as five or six.

Approximately 300 subjects in Section I receive extensive medical information about CHD and learn about diet control, exercise, adherence to medication regimens, and other steps to help them in preventing another catastrophe. These subjects meet bimonthly with a cardiologist in groups of 10 to 15 persons each with a cardiologist.

Another group of approximately 600 subjects, in addition to receiving the same advice and counseling as Section I, also learn how to alter TABP. Small groups of 10 to 15 persons each meet weekly for 90 minutes during the first two months, biweekly for months 3 to 6, and monthly for the remainder of the five-year program. A major part of the Type A counseling focused on participants' awareness of specific behaviors that they exhibit, the conditions under which these behaviors occur, the effect of Type A behaviors on the participants and those around them, and the development of alternative strategies for handling recurring situations that trigger off TABP. The participants were instructed on daily drills to reduce time urgency, hostility, impatience and excessive self-centredness.

The Section II participants were also instructed and counseled on how to change aspects of the environment that prompt Type A type reactivity. The participants received instruction in progressive muscle relaxation, behavioral learning, cognitive affective learning and restructuring of some environmental situations. Also, the program attempted to help the participants find ways to give and receive love in their home environments. The support provided by children and a spouse are invaluable in modifying TABP.

Another part of the Type A treatment section involved the identification of cognitive factors that initiate and sustain TABP. Participants learned to examine the thoughts, beliefs and expectations that promote time urgency and impatience. Attention is paid to detecting early signals or cues that suggest extreme arousal.

The two major dependent variables of the RCPP are (a) recurrent infarctions and (b) coronary death. Lower rates of recurrences and deaths at the end of five years in Section II (Type A modification group) than in Section I and the control section (i.e. approximately 150 subjects) would demonstrate in a dramatic way the efficacy of altering Type A behavior in reducing coronary risk. In the RCPP evaluation data are collected on observable behavior, physiological indices, environmental changes and modifications in cognitions.

Observable behaviors are collected via the Structured Interview. In addition, each participant names a monitor (another person) who completes a questionnaire on specific behavioral changes displayed by the subject. If the subject is married, the spouse (in addition to the monitor) fills out a questionnaire on behavioral changes.

The principal physiological measure is level of serum cholesterol which is taken every six months. Each subject is also given an annual physical examination. Self-report measures such as the Novaco Anger Scale (Novaco, 1975) and the Work Environment and Health Questionnaire are collected.

After three years, subjects randomly placed in Section II, the Type A counseling group, had a myocardial infarction recurrence rate of 7.2% compared with 13.2% in Section I and 14.0% in the control group. These results are encouraging in terms of modification of TABP. The results suggest that something in this intervention was responsible for clinically valid changes. Of course, additional intervention studies using the RCCP and other powerful designs are needed to determine if there are long-term benefits associated with Type A modification.

The RCPP preliminary results have suggested that not all the component elements of TABP operate with equal frequency, intensity and duration in all individuals. Thus, there may be a need to assess target behaviors that are defined in terms of each component and to then tailor the intervention to fit the individual's pattern. For example, a Type A person may report little Type A reaction in terms of cognitive, behavioral or emotional responses to stressors. However, this same person may show significant sympathetic nervous system response to the stressors. That is, there is only a marked physiological response indicated. Perhaps biofeedback or meditation is most likely to impact this person's response to stressors without having an impact on cognitions, behaviors and emotions. Further research examining the feasibility of designing individual focused approaches is needed.

QUESTIONS, ISSUES, AND RESEARCH DIRECTIONS FOR PROMOTING INDIVIDUAL HEALTH AND WELL-BEING

An examination of the contents of this chapter indicates that lifestyle changes are extremely difficult to achieve and maintain in any population. Even after the occurrence of a major life threatening heart attack many individuals resist information, counseling help and professional suggestions to adopt and adhere to a new lifestyle regimen. The range of programs available for modifying lifestyles involves the active participation of individuals. In this chapter four intervention programs were reviewed and discussed in terms of their effectiveness for promoting health and well-being. The review of these intervention strategies points to many unanswered questions, problems with placebo control, measurement issues and suggestions for future research.

Unanswered Questions

The majority of research on modifying lifestyles has not answered the question of 'how can healthy lifestyle behaviors be maintained?' Relapse problems in exercise regimens, biofeedback utilization and practice, cognitive–behavioral techniques and modification of TABP are significantly high (Brownell *et al.*, 1986; Cohen and Syme, 1985; Epstein and Class, 1982; Janis, 1983; Marlett, 1985; Steinberg, 1985). Specifically, how positive behavior changes in each of these four areas is an elusive and under-researched issue.

There remains the question of whether changes in lifestyle via the use of programs such as those presented in this chapter can make a difference in morbidity and mortality. Certainly, this question cannot be reliably or validly answered until changes in behavior are rigorously monitored over a long time frame using longitudinal research designs.

There is also the question of cost vs benefits (Ginzberg, 1987). Are the costs of exercise or biofeedback or any particular lifestyle modification worth the benefits achieved? If a particular lifestyle change strategy has been found to have an impact on promoting individual health and well-being, cost–benefit analysis can be conducted. It is important to specify clearly the tangible and intangible costs and benefits of a particular program. This is an area that will require careful and thorough specification of costs and benefits, but this type of analysis is invaluable in providing supportive or nonsupportive evidence.

There are also questions about what an individual can tolerate or needs in terms of exercise, biofeedback, cognitive–behavioral reengineering or modification of TABP. Requirements for change or improvement vary across individuals and with the desired outcome. For example, what is the optimal level of exercise for a 45–year-old sedentary male who wants to improve his cardiovascular conditioning? Perhaps there is an exercise level beyond which the effect on health and well-being of this man is negative. The same type of questions can be asked about other lifestyle change programs—what is the optimal level of biofeedback for a 37-year-old woman, etc.

There are also questions about the interaction effects of two or more lifestyle change techniques. For example, will exercise have an effect on anger, time impatience and/or hostility? These types of questions need to be answered in terms of cost and benefits. Perhaps it is more efficient economically and in terms of time allocation to use a robust or powerful change technique that can effect multiple physiological, behavioral and psychological factors. Is exercise such a technique? Is biofeedback training such a technique?

There is also the question of how can the benefits provided by the promotion of individual health and well-being be applied to the majority instead of an elite few? A significant number of the early organization health promotion programs were developed for top executive levels only. Lower level managers and operating employees were typically not encouraged or permitted to participate in the programs. These practices and the social determinants of good health and well-being—socioeconomic status and education level—if permitted to evolve, will create an elite in society (Carr-Hill, Hardman and Russell, 1987; Walter and Hofman, 1987). Research indicates that smoking, alcohol abuse and obesity are all more prevalent in lower socioeconomic groups. Unless some medical, governmental, labor and management emphasis is placed on reaching all classes and especially high-risk groups, the optimal impact of lifestyle changes will not be achieved (Charlton and Velez, 1986). Thus, finding strategies to involve individuals from all strata of society is an important issue to be addressed by advocates of making and sustaining positive lifestyle changes.

The Placebo Problem in Lifestyle Change Research

Since individuals may be randomly assigned to intervention groups or may be differentiated from one another on some behavioral dimension, researchers must establish studies that will permit attribution of a lifestyle change to the intervention rather than to extraneous factors such as placebo effects (Critelli and Nerrmann, 1984; Parloff, 1986). A placebo is any therapy or component of therapy that is used for its nonspecific, psychological or psychophysiological effect, but is without specific activity for the condition being treated (Shapiro and Morris, 1978, p. 371). A placebo effect, therefore, may be considered as the 'psychological or psychophysiological effect produced by placebos'. Implicit within this definition are the assumptions that (a) placebo effects may be positive or negative and (b) placebo effects are not equivalent to behavioral changes due to the passage of time, repeated testing, or other spontaneous influences occurring.

If the true impact of a lifestyle change program such as exercise or biofeedback training is to be determined, procedures for controlling placebo effects must be implemented. If placebo controls are not present or are inadequate the construct validity of the applied technique cannot be adequately determined (Cook and Campbell, 1976).

Failure to control for placebo effects may also be associated with negative consequences for subjects. For example, Hendler *et al.*, (1977) used EMG frontalis biofeedback for 13 patients with chronic pain. They assumed that if general tension and anxiety could be reduced by use of biofeedback, there would be a significant reduction in the pain. Six patients, after one month of application, reported the reduction of some pain. The lack of proper placebo controls used in this study, however, prevents one from reaching the conclusion that the positive self-reports about pain reduction were due to the application of biofeedback. Perhaps the individuals reported improvement because they made a significant financial investment in the biofeedback equipment (Prokop and Bradley, 1981).

The majority of single-subject studies assess the efficacy of a particular lifestyle change intervention by examining behavior at various times during which the intervention either is or is not being applied by the person. If positive behavioral change occurs only during intervention use periods and diminishes during baseline (nonuse) periods the change may be confidently attributed to the intervention technique rather than to extraneous factors (Prokop and Bradley, 1981).

There are two strategies that can be used to control for placebo effects in single-subject evaluation studies. The researcher can design a complex study in which the efficacies of specific and placebo control interventions may be assessed (Kazdin, 1978). Another alternative is to assess the efficacy of an intervention found to be useful with a single person in a group investigation that includes at a minimum a placebo control treatment. The strongest design described by Mahoney is the placebo and control investigation in which individuals are assigned to two experimental and no-intervention treatment control conditions are in a Solomon four-group design and two additional conditions in which an intervention is provided that does not have a specific component but is equally credible to individuals as the treatment intervention (e.g. stress inoculation training or biofeedback).

A placebo control intervention should have the same credibility and generate the same positive expectancies for outcome improvement as an experimental intervention (Burish, 1981). Unless similar realism and expectancies exist across interventions it is impossible to attribute any positive effects to the experimental intervention.

Measurement Issues

Once an adequate research design is developed and adequate placebo controls are established, the issue of measurement becomes relevant. Three crucial measurement issues must be resolved: (a) what dependent variables should be assessed, (b) how should lifestyle change be assessed and (c) what is an appropriate time period to track changes? The majority of dependent variables in the research associated with the four lifestyle change programs reported in this chapter consist of (a) self-reports, (b) individual diary or self-monitoring and (c) direct measures such as blood pressure, brainwaves.

Relying on self-reports as *the* primary measure of changes is inadequate because of psychometric problems with most paper-and-pencil instruments such as poor reliability and validity. In addition, self-reports are subject to error because of socially desirable response sets. However, it should be mentioned that even direct measures of physiological changes such as blood pressure and hormone secretion found in urine samples are subject to faulty measurement.

The use of diaries is also subject to various inaccuracies and biases. Thus, as others have already suggested, there are significant reasons to use multiple dependent measures that assess various physiological, psychological and behavioral changes. We strongly advocate that researchers use multiple dependent measures that are important not only to the investigator but also to the individual. Also, the multiple measures should continue for some time (more than a year) in order to determine whether changes are sustained or lasting. The lack of long-term evaluations of the lifestyle change programs discussed raises other questions of whether any changes have a significant lasting influence on health and well-being. Until more longitudinal research is conducted, a positive answer or guess must be treated with skepticism.

Future Research Directions

If future research is to improve the credibility and applications of the lifestyle change programs presented in this chapter, it is important for researchers to attend to the questions asked, to the placebo control problem and to various measurement issues. Perhaps the most pressing need is for researchers to incorporate control groups and some form of placebo intervention in their research design. The time has arrived for the public to be concerned about whether lifestyle change techniques have any lasting effect. If interventions are only short-lived or are very expensive or have no measurable impact then the entire issue of whether well-being can really be enhanced among adults becomes a serious concern. Research may eventually determine that children should serve as the optimal foci for lifestyle change interventions (Walter *et al.*, 1985). Since children have had fewer years to develop poor lifestyle habits and behaviors they may be the best target population for exercise programs, biofeedback, cognitive behavior exercises and application, and modification of TABP.

Although significant research and experimental challenges lie ahead, it is refreshing to trace the progress made in the past decade in public awareness about health, well-being and individual responsibility (Lamm, 1987). The public is demanding more information about what lifestyle improvement methods are scientifically sound and medically safe. It is this type of awareness and interest that will stimulate more high quality and rigorous empirical investigations of the type of techniques presented in this chapter. The opportunities for researchers to provide needed data and information to the public on exercise, biofeedback, cognitive–behavior exercises, modification of TABP and other lifestyle change programs have never been more available.

REFERENCES

Ajzen, I. and Fishbein, M. (1977). Attitude–behavior relations: a theoretical analysis and review of empirical research, *Psychological Bulletin*, **84**, 888–914.
Ajzen, I. and Fishbein, M. (1980). *Understanding Attitudes and Predicting Social Behavior*, Prentice–Hall, Englewood Cliffs, NJ.
Allen, R. J. (1983). *Human Stress: Its Nature and Control*, Burgess, Minneapolis.
Ardell, D. (1977). High level wellness strategies, *Health Education*, **8**(4), 1–10.
Balke, B. (1974). Prescribing physical activity. In A. J. Ryan and F. Allman (eds) *Sports Medicine*, Academic Press, New York.
Bandura, A. (1977). Self-efficacy: toward a unifying theory of behavioral change, *Psychological Review*, **84**, 191–215.
Bandura, A. (1982). Self-efficacy mechanism in human agency, *American Psychologist*, **37**, 122–47.

Beck, A. T., Rush, A. J., Shaw, B. F. and Emery, G. (1979). *Cognitive Therapy of Depression*, Guilford Press, New York.

Belisle, M., Roskies, E. and Levesque, J. M. (1987). Improving adherence to physical activity, *Health Psychology*, **6**, 159–72.

Belloc, N. B. (1973). Relationship of health practices and mortality, *Preventive Medicine*, **3**, 67–81.

Belloc, N. B. and Breslow, L. (1972). Relationship of physical health status and health practices, *Preventive Medicine*, **1**, 409–21.

Breslow, L. (1978). Risk factor intervention for health maintenance, *Science*, **200**, 908–12.

Breslow, L. and Enstrom, J. E. (1980). Persistence of health habits and their relationship to mortality, *Preventive Medicine*, **9**, 469–83.

Breslow, L. and Somers, A. R. (1977). The lifetime health-monitoring program: a practical approach to preventive medicine, *New England Journal of Medicine*, **296**, 601–10.

Brownell, K. D., Marlatt, G. A., Lichtenstein, E. and Wilson, C. (1986). Understanding and preventing relapse, *American Psychologist*, **41**, 765–82.

Bruce, R. A., DeRowen, T. A. and Hossack, K. F. (1980). Pilot study examining the motivational effects of maximal exercise testing to modify risk factors and health habits, *Cardiology*, **66**, 111–19.

Budzynski, T. H. (1978). Biofeedback applications to stress-related disorders, *International Review of Applied Psychology*, **27**, 73–9.

Burish, T. G. (1981). EMG biofeedback in the treatment of stress-related disorders, *International Review of Applied Psychology*, **27**, 73–9.

Burish, T. G. (1981). EMG biofeedback in the treatment of stress-related disorders. In C. K. Prokop and L. A. Bradley (eds) *Medical Psychology*, pp. 395–421, Academic Press, Orlando.

Burish, T. G. and Schwartz, D. P. (1980). EMG biofeedback training, transfer of training, and coping with stress, *Journal of Psychosomatic Research*, **24**, 85–96.

Cannon, W. B. (1915). *Bodily Changes in Pain, Hunger, Fear and Rage: An Account of Recent Research into the Function of Emotional Excitement*, Appleton, New York.

Carr-Hall, R. A., Hardman, G. F. and Russell, I. T. (1987). Variations in avoidable mortality and variations in health care, *Lancet*, **536**, 789–92.

Cassel, J., Heyden, S., Bartel, A. G., Kaplan, B., Troyler, A., Cornoni, J. and Haines, C. (1971). Occupation and physical activity and coronary heart disease, *Archives of Internal Medicine*, **128**, 420–928.

Chaney, E., O'Leary, M. and Marlatt, G. (1978). Skill training with alcoholics, *Journal of Consulting and Clinical Psychology*, **46**, 1092–1104.

Charlton, J. R. H. and Velez, R. (1986). Some international comparisons of mortality amenable to medical intervention, *British Medical Journal*, **292**, 295–301.

Cohen, S. and Syme, L. (1985). *Social Support and Health*, Academic Press, New York.

Cook, T. D. and Campbell, D. T. (1976). The design and conduct of quasi-experiments and true experiments in field settings. In M. Dunnette (ed.) *Handbook of Industrial and Organizational Psychology*, Rand McNally, Chicago.

Cooper, K. H. (1982). *The Aerobics Program for Total Well-Being*, M. Evans, New York.

Craighead, L. W., Stunkard, A. J. and O'Brien, R. (1981). Behavior therapy and pharmacotherapy for obesity, *Archives of General Psychiatry*, **38**, 763–6.

Critelli, J. and Neumann, K. (1984). The placebo: conceptual analysis of a construct in transition, *American Psychologist*, **39**, 32–9.

Drechsler, I., Bruner, D. and Kreitter, S. (1987). Cognitive antecedents of coronary heart disease, *Social Science and Medicine*, 581–8.

DiClemente, C. C. (1981). Self-efficacy and smoking cessation maintenance: a preliminary report, *Cognitive Therapy and Research*, **5**, 175–87.

Dishman, R. K. and Ickes, W. (1981). Self-motivation and adherence to therapeutic exercise, *Journal of Behavioral Medicine*, **4**, 421–38.

Dunn, H. (1961). *High Level Wellness*, R. W. Beatty, Arlington, VA.

Ellis, A. (1962). *Reason and Emotion in Psychotherapy*, Stuart, New York.

Epstein, L. H. and Cluss, P. A. (1982). A behavioral medicine perspective on adherence to long-term medical regimens, *Journal of Consulting and Clinical Psychology*, **50**, 950–71.

Fee, R. A. and Girdano, D. A. (1978). The relative effectiveness of three techniques to induce the trophotropic response, *Biofeedback and Self-Regulation*, **3**, 145–57.

Ferguson, J. M., Discenza, R. and Miller, J. A. (1987). Increasing the odds of patient compliance through prescription warning labels, *Journal of Health Care Marketing*, **7**, 37–46.

Ferster, C. B., Nurnberger, J. I. and Levitt, E. B. (1962). The control of eating, *Journal of Mathematical Psychology*, **1**, 87–109.

Fishbein, M., & Ajzen, I. (1975). *Belief, Attitude, Intention, and Behavior: An Introduction to Theory and Research*, Addison–Wesley, Reading, MA.

Fremont, J. and Craighead, L. W. (1987). Aerobic exercise and cognitive therapy in the treatment of dysphoric moods, *Cognitive Therapy and Research*, **11**, 241–51.

Friedman, M. and Rosenman, R. H. (1959). Association of specific overt behavior pattern with blood and cardiovascular findings, *Journal of the American Medical Association*, **169**, 1286–96.

Friedman, M. and Rosenman, R. H. (1974). *Type A Behavior and Your Heart*, Alfred A. Knopf, New York.

Friedman, M. and Ulmer, D. (1984). *Treating Type A Behavior and Your Heart*, Alfred A. Knopf, New York.

Friedman, M., Thoresen, C. F., Gill, J. J. Ulmer, D., Thompson, L., Powell, L., Price, V. A., Elek, S. K., Rabin, D. D., Breall, W. S., Piaget, G., Dixon, T., Bourg, E., Levy, R. A. and Tasto, D. L. (1982). Feasibility of altering Type A behaviour pattern after myocardial infarction, *Circulation*, 66, 83–92.

Friedman, M., Thoresen, C. E., Gill, J. J. *et al.* (1984). Alteration of Type A behavior and reduction in cardiac recurrences in postmyocardial infarction patients, *American Heart Journal*, 108, 237–248.

Fuller, G. D. (1978). Current status of biofeedback in clinical practice, *American Psychologist*, **33**, 39–48.

Gaarder, K. R. and Montgomery, P. S. (1977). *Clinical Biofeedback: A Procedural Manual*, Williams and Wilkins, Baltimore.

Ginzberg, E. (1987). A hard look at cost containment, *New England Journal of Medicine*, **316**, 1151–4.

Glass, D. C. (1977). *Behavior Patterns, Stress, and Coronary Disease*. Lawrence Erlbaum, Hillsdale, NJ.

Goldfried, M. R. (1979). Anxiety reduction through cognitive–behavioral intervention. In P. C. Kendall and S. D. Hollon (eds) *Cognitive–Behavioral Interactions: Theory, Research, and Procedures*, Academic Press, New York.

Goldfried, M. R. and Robins, C. (1982). On the facilitation of self-efficacy. *Cognitive Theory and Research*, **6**, 361–79.

Green, E. (1969). Feedback techniques for deep relaxation, *Psychophysiology*, **6**, 371.

Green, E. (1970). Voluntary control of internal states: psychological and physiological, *Journal of Transpersonal Psychology*, **11**, 1–26.

Grigsby, J. P. (1987). The use of imagery in the treatment of posttraumatic stress disorder, *Journal of Nervous and Mental Disease*, **175**, 55–9.

Hall, L. K., Meyer, G. C. and Helderstein, H. K. (1984). *Cardiac Rehabilitation: Exercise Testing and Prescription*, SP Medical and Scientific Books, New York.

Hanson, P. G. (1982). Exercise, In R. B. Taylor, J. R. Ureda and J. W. Denham (eds) *Health Promotion: Principles and Practical Applications*, pp. 215–32, Appleton–Century–Crofts, Norwalk, CT.

Haskell, W. L. (1984). Overview: health benefits of exercise. In J. D. Matarazzo *et al.* (eds) *Behavioral Health*, pp. 297–307, John Wiley and Sons, New York.

Haynes, R. B. (1976). Strategies for improving compliance: a methodologic analysis and review. In D. L. Sackett and R. B. Haynes (eds) *Compliance with Therapeutic Regimens*, Johns Hopkins University Press, Baltimore.

Haynes, S. N., Moseley, D. and McGowan, W. T. (1975). Relaxation training and biofeedback in the reduction of frontalis muscle tension. *Psychophysiology*, **12**, 547–52.

Hendler, N., Derogatis, L., Avella, J. and Long, D. (1977). EMG biofeedback in patients with chronic pain, *Diseases of the Nervous System*, **38**, 505–14.

Horwitz, L. D. and Groves, B. M. (1985). *Signs and Symptoms in Cardiology*, J. B. Lippincott, New York.

Janis, T. L. (1983). The role of social support in adherence to stressful decisions, *American Psychologist*, **38**, 143–60.

Jenkins, C. D. (1986). Diagnosis and treatment of behavioral barriers to good health. In J. M. Last (ed.) *Public Health and Preventive Medicine*, pp. 1109–22, Appleton–Century–Crofts, Norwalk, CT.

Jenni, M. A. and Wollershein, J. D. (1979). Cognitive therapy, stress management training, and the Type A behavior pattern, *Cognitive Therapy and Research*, **3**, 61–74.

Kannel, W. B., Capples, L. A. and D'Agostino, R. B. (1987). Sudden death in coronary heart disease: the Framingham study. *American Heart Journal*, **13**, 799–804.

Kamiya, J. (1969). Operant control of the EEG alpha rhythm and some of its reported effects on consciousness. In C. Tart (ed.) *Altered States of Consciousness*, John Wiley and Sons, New York.

Kazdin, A. E. (1978]. Methodological and interpretive problems of single-case experimental designs, *Journal of Consulting and Clinical Psychology*, **46**, 629–42.

Kendall, P. C. and Bemis, K. M. (1983). Thought and action in psychotherapy: the cognitive–behavioral approaches. In M. Hensen, A. E. Kazdin and A. S. Bellack (eds) *The Clinical Psychology Handbook*, Pergamon Press, New York.

Kendall, P. C. and Turk, D. C. (1984). Cognitive–behavioral strategies and health enhancement. In J. D. Matarazzo *et al.* (eds), *Behavioral Health*, pp. 393–405, John Wiley and Sons, New York.

Kirschenbaum, D. S. (1987). Self-regulating failure: a review with clinical implications, *Clinical Psychology Review*, **7**, 77–104.

Kolbe, L. (1983). Improving the health status of children: an epidemiologica approach to establishing priorities for behavioral research. In *Proceedings of the National Conference on Research and Development in Health Education with Special Reference to Youth*, Southampton University Press, Southampton.

Lalonde, M. (1975). *A New Perspective on the Health of Canadians*, Information Canada, Ottawa.

Lamm, R. D. (1987). The ten commandments of health care, *The Humanist*, **47**, 16–20, 34.

Last, J. M. (1986). Scope and methods of prevention. In J. M. Last (ed.) *Public Health and Preventive Medicine*, pp. 3–7, Appleton–Century–Crofts, Norwalk, CT.

Lazarus, R. S. (1977). A cognitive analysis of biofeedback control. In G. Schwartz and J. Beatty (eds), *Biofeedback theory and research*. Academic Press, New York.

Leon, A. S. (1987). Age and other predictors of coronary heart disease. *Medicine and Science in Sports and Exercise*, **19**, 159–67.

Levy, R. I. and Moskowitz, J. (1982). Cardiovascular research: decades of progress, a decade of promise, *Science*, **217**, 121–29.

Mahoney, M. J. (1975). The behavioral treatment of obesity, In A. J. Enelow and J. P. Henderson (eds) *Applying Behavioral Science to Cardiovascular Risk*, pp. 121–32, American Heart Association, Dallas.

Mahoney, M. J. (1977). Reflections on the cognitive–learning trend in psychotherapy, *American Psychologist*, **32**, 5–13.

Mahoney, M. J. and Thoresen, C. E. (1974).

Marlatt, G. A. and Gordon, J. R. (1985). *Relapse Prevention*, Guilford, New York.

Martin, J. E. and Dubbert, P. M. (1982). Exercise applications and promotion in behavioral medicine: current status and future directions, *Journal of Consulting and Clinical Psychology*, **50**, 1004–17.

Masironi, R. and Denolin, H. (eds) (1985). *Physical Activity in Disease Prevention and Treatment*, Piccin/Butterworth, Padova.

Matarazzo, J. D. (1984). Behavioral health: a 1990 challenge for the health services professions. In J. D. Matarazzo, S. M. Weiss, J. A. Herd and N. E. Miller (eds). *Behavioral Health: A Handbook of Health Enhancement and Disease Prevention*, pp. 3–40. John Wiley and Sons. New York.

Matthews, K. A., Glass, D. C., Rosenman, R. H. *et al.* (1977). Competitive drive, pattern A, and coronary heart disease: a further analysis of some data from the Western Collaborative Group Study, *Journal of Chronic Diseases*, **30**, 489–98.

Mechanic, P. (1968). *Medical Sociology*, Free Press, New York.

Meichenbaum, D. (1976). Cognitive factors in biofeedback therapy, *Biofeedback and Self-Regulation*, **1**, 201–16.

Meichenbaum, D. (1977). *Cognitive-Behavior Modification: An Integrative Approach*, Plenum Press, New York.

Meichanbaum, D. (1985). *Stress Inoculation Training*, Pergamon Press, New York.

Meichenbaum, D. and Cameron, R. (1983). Stress inoculation training: Toward a general paradigm for training coping skills. In D. Meichenbaum and M. E. Jaremko (eds) *Stress Reduction and Prevention*, Plenum Press, New York.

Miller, N. E. and DiCara, L. (1967). Instrumental learning of heart rate changes in rats: shaping and specificity to discriminative stimulus, *Journal of Comparative and Physiological Psychology*, **62**, 12–19.

Morris, J. N., Heady, J. A., Raffle, P. A. B., Roberts, C. G. and Parks, J. W. (1953). Coronary heart disease and physical activity of work. *Lancet*, **ii**, 1053–7.

Norris, P. (1986). Biofeedback, voluntary control, and human potential, *Biofeedback and Self-Regulation*, **11**, 1–20.

Novaco, R. W. (1975). *Anger Control: The Development and Evaluation of an Experimental Treatment*, Heath and Co, Lexington, MA.

Novaco, R. W. (1977). A stress inoculation approach of anger management in the training of law enforcement officers, *American Journal of Community Psychology*, **5**, 327–46.

Oldridge, N. B. (1982). Compliance and exercise in primary and secondary prevention of coronary heart disease: a review. *Preventive Medicine*, **11**, 56–70.

Oldridge, N. B. and Jones, N. L. (1983). Improving patient compliance in cardiac exercise rehabilitation: effects of written agreement and self-monitoring, *Journal of Cardiac Rehabilitation*, **3**, 257–62.

Pace, N. (1977). Weightlessness: a matter of gravity, *New England Journal of Medicine*, **297**, 32–37.

Parloff, M. B. (1986). Placebo controls in psychotherapy research: a sine qua non or a placebo for research problems, *Journal of Consulting and Clinical Psychology*, **54**, 79–89.

Powell, L. H. (1984). Area review: stress, Type A behavior, and cardiovascular disease, *Behavioral Medicine Update*, **6**, 7–10.

Prokop, C. K., and Bradley, L. A. (1981). Methodological issues in medical psychology and behavioral medicine research. In C. K. Prokop and L. A. Bradley (eds), *Medical Psychology: Contributions to Behavioral Medicine*, pp. 485–96, Academic Press, New York.

Reid, E. L. and Morgan, R. W. (1979). Exercise prescription: a clinical trial, *American Journal of Public Health*, **69**, 591–5.

Roskies, E. (1987). *Stress Management for the Healthy Type A: Theory and Practice*, Guilford, New York.

Roskies, E., Spevack, M., Surkis, A., Cohen, C. and Gilman, S. (1977). Changing the coronary prone (Type A) behavior pattern in a non-clinical population, *Journal of Behavioral Medicine*, **1**, 201–16.

Saltin, B., Blomquist, B., Mitchell, J. H., Johnson, R. L., Jr, Wildenthal, K. and Chapman, C. B. (1968). Response to exercise after bed rest and after training, *Circulation*, **38**, 1–18.

Sarason, I. G., Johnson, J. H., Berberich, J. P. and Siegel, J. M. (1979). Helping police officers to cope with stress: a cognitive-behavioral approach, *American Journal of Community Psychology*, **7**, 593–603.

Shapiro and Morris. (1978).

Sime, W. E. and DeGood, D. E. (1977). Effect of EMG biofeedback and progressive muscle relaxation training on awareness of frontalis muscle tension, *Psychophysiology*, **14**, 522–530.

Solomon, L. J. and Brehony, K. A. (1979). The effects of EMG feedback training during problem solving. *Biofeedback and Self-Regulation*, **4**, 81–6.

Steinberg, B. S. (1985). Relapse in weight control: definitions, processes, and prevention strategies. In G. A. Marlatt and J. R. Gordon (eds) *Relapse Prevention*, pp. 521–45, Guilford, New York.

Stoney, C. M., Langer, A. W., Sutterer, J. R. and Gelling, P. D. (1987). A comparison of biofeedback-assisted cardiodeceleration in Type A and B men: modification of stress-associated cardiopulmonary and hemodynamic adjustments, *Psychosomatic Medicine*, **109**, 79–87.

Stoyva, J. (1977). Why should muscular relaxation be clinically useful? Some data and 2 & ½ models. In J. Beatty and H. Legeiore (eds) *Biofeedback and Behavior*, Plenum Press, New York.

Suinn, R. M. (1974). Behavior therapy for cardiac patients: letter to the editor. *Behavior Therapy*, **5**, 569–571.

Suinn, R. M. (1982). Intervention with Type A behaviors. *Journal of Consulting and Clinical Psychology*, **50**, 933–949.

Suinn, R. M., and Bloom, L. J. (1978). Anxiety management for Type A persons, *Journal of Behavior Medicine*, **1**, 25–35.

Taylor, H. L., Klepetar, E. and Keys, A. (1962). Death rate among physically active and sedentary employees of the railroad industry, *American Journal of Public Health*, **52**, 1697–9.

Thompson, P. B. (1976). Effectiveness of relaxation techniques in reducing anxiety and stress factors in Type A, post-myocardial infarction patients, unpublished doctoral dissertation, University of Massachusetts.

Thoresen, C. E. (1984). Overview. In J. D. Matarazzo *et al.* (eds) *Behavioral Health*, pp. 297–307, John Wiley and Sons, New York.

Thoresen, C. E. and Kimil–Gray, K. (1983). Self-management psychology in the treatment of childhood asthma, *Journal of Allergy and Clinical Immunology*, **72**, 596–606.

Thorn, T. J. and Kannel, W. E. (1981). Downward trend in cardiovascular mortality, *Annual Review of Medicine*, **32**, 427–34.

Turk, D. C., Meichenbaum, D. H. and Genest, M. (1983). *Pain and Behavioral Medicine: Theory, Research, and a Clinical Guide*, Guilford Press, New York.

Walter, H. J. and Hofman, A. (1987). Socioeconomic status, ethnic origin, and risk factors for coronary heart disease in children, *American Heart Journal*, **13**, 812–18.

Walter, H. J., Hofman, A., Connelly, P. A., Barrett, L. T. and Kost, K. L. (1985). Primary prevention of chronic diseases in childhood: Changes in risk factors after one year of intervention, *American Journal of Epidemiology*, **122**, 772.

Warner, K. E. (1987). Selling health promotion to corporate America: uses and abuses of the economic argument, *Health Education Quarterly*, **14**, 39–55.

Weisman, A. D., Worden, J. W. and Sobel, J. H. (1980). *Psychosocial Screening and Intervention with Cancer Patients: Research Report*, Shea Press, Cambridge, MA.

Williams, R. B., Haney, T. L., Lee, K. L., *et al.* (1980). Type A behavior, hostility, and coronary alheroscherosis, *Psychosomatic Medicine*, **42**, 539–49.

Wysocki, T., Hall, G., Iwata, B. and Riordan, M. (1978). Behavioral management of exercise: contracting for aerobic points, *Journal of Applied Behavioral Analysis*, **12**, 55–64.

Causes, Coping and Consequences of Stress at Work
Edited by C. L. Cooper and R. Payne
© 1988 John Wiley & Sons Ltd

Chapter 10

Workplace Interventions for Stress Reduction and Prevention

Lawrence R. Murphy

This chapter reviews workplace interventions designed to reduce or prevent employee distress. Three classes of interventions are discussed: employee assistance programs (EAPs), stress management training and stressor reduction strategies. For each intervention, an historical context is offered first, followed by a description of the intervention and review of empirical research. Employee assistance programs and stress management are the most common types of interventions in work settings. Both of these approaches target the employee, not the work environment, for modification or change. Virtually no randomized controlled experiments were found examining the efficacy of EAPs. Less rigorously designed studies, however, generally have indicated beneficial effects of EAPs. Stress management has been subjected to more rigorous empirical tests, but such studies often lack long-term follow-up and usually employ few types of dependent measures. Well-designed evaluations of interventions aimed at altering work stressors, primary prevention of organizational stress, were relatively scarce in the scientific literature. Studies of this type produced consistent, positive results, but additional research is needed to make definitive statements. It is concluded that strategies which address employee *and* organizational factors as intervention points should produce the most significant and enduring reductions in employee distress.

The first edition of *Stress at Work* contained a single chapter on stress reduction entitled 'What people can do for themselves to cope with stress' (Ellis, 1978). The chapter was idiosyncratic and dealt exclusively with one individual-oriented approach to the problem, namely, rational-emotive therapy. The basic premise was that people choose to be under stress as a result of the belief system which they apply to 'stressful situations'. The recommended solution involved teaching individuals to become aware of their belief systems and to modify (irrational) beliefs as a means of reducing distress.

The present chapter reviews a wider range of stress interventions in work settings. Three types of interventions are reviewed: (1) employee assistance programs (EAPs), (2) stress management training and (3) stressor reduction strategies. EAPs have a history of application in work settings and represent a commonly used mechanism by organizations for dealing with 'troubled workers'. Stress management is a more recent intervention that is enjoying widespread application in work settings and a growing base of evaluative data. Stressor reduction represents the most direct way to reduce stress via modification of the source and flows conceptually from a good deal of research.

The three interventions selected for review represent levels of prevention: primary (stressor reduction), secondary (stress management) and tertiary (EAPs). As will be seen, the prevalence of these approaches in work settings and evaluative research on their efficacy is quite uneven. The decision to implement an intervention and the choice of a specific strategy is rarely based upon a scientific assessment of the problem(s); more often than not, it is heavily influenced by impressions of the scope (and economics) of the problem and conceptualizations of the nature of stress.

SCOPE OF THE PROBLEM

It is not unusual to encounter rather striking estimates of the total costs of stress that reach into billions of dollars annually. While such estimates seem impressive, one experiences great difficulty trying to track down the precise components of the estimation formulas. On the other hand, certain types of data provide a more concrete base upon which to gauge the scope of the problem. For example, the National Council on Compensation Insurance (1985) recently reported that mental stress accounted for 11% of occupational disease claims from 1980–1982 and represented the fastest growing type of worker compensation claim in the 1980s.

Results of a US household survey conducted in 1985 provide another type of data bearing upon the scope of the problem. This survey, the 1985 National Health Interview Survey, contained questionnaire items dealing with stress in general, and worker perceptions of stress at work, that are relevant to the discussion here. The results showed that 75% of the general population reported experiencing at least 'some' stress in the two weeks preceding the survey. About half of the respondents reported 'a lot' or 'moderate' amounts of stress during this period (Silverman, Eichler and Williams, 1987).

Currently employed workers in the survey sample were asked (1) if they were exposed to any work conditions that could endanger their health such as loud noise, extreme heat or cold, physical or mental stress, or radiation, (2) to list the condition(s) and (3) to specify how work conditions could lead to health outcomes. Using population weights derived from the sample, 35.2% of the estimated currently employed US population answered 'Yes' to the first question. Loud noise was the work condition mentioned most frequently (34.9%) followed closely by mental stress (29.7%). Physical stress was reported by 5.9% of the working population (Shilling and Brackbill, 1987). (The presentation of data on specific health conditions did not allow the reader to directly link the work conditions generated by question 2 with the attributions in question 3.) Admittedly, the data represent attributions on the part of workers and are not prevalence estimates for stress at work. Also, it is not clear to what extent the phrasing of questions (requiring a health attribution on the part of respondents) under- or over-estimates the prevalence of stress. It does seem significant that half of the estimated US population reported at least moderate stress in the two weeks prior to the interview and that an estimated 11 million currently employed workers felt that exposure to mental stress at work endangered their health.

CONCEPTUALIZATIONS OF STRESS

A telephone and mail survey sponsored by the National Institute for Occupational Safety and Health (NIOSH) in 1982 (Neale *et al.*, 1982) provided information on the perspectives of management and labor groups regarding work stress and appropriate stress reduction strategies. Information regarding stress management techniques, counselling and educational programs, work redesign and worker participation were addressed in the survey.

The results indicated that corporate and labor groups conceptualized stress in very different ways. Labor groups mentioned physical and environmental stressors (including poor ergonomic design of work) more frequently than corporate respondents. Psychosocial stressors identified by labor groups included lack of control over the work content and process, unrealistic task demands, lack of understanding by supervisors and management, and lack of predictability and security about their job future as important psychological stressors. Corporate respondents, on the other hand, rarely characterized work environment factors as stressors. Rather, emphasis was placed upon personality traits (e.g. Type A behavior), lifestyle behaviors, interpersonal relationships and familial problems as prominent sources of worker stress.

These divergent conceptualizations of stress led the two groups to advocate distinct types of stress reduction actions (see Tables 1 and 2). Labor groups advocated contractually-empowered health and safety committees as the strongest stress reduction approach. Through this mechanism, worker participation is increased by membership on such committees and control over some aspects of the work process is returned to the employee. Corporate respondents, on the other hand, advocated lifestyle modification focusing on exercise, nutrition and coronary-prone behaviors. Personal strategies to increase resistance to stress and/or improve stress coping skills such as muscle

Table 1 Union-identified stressors and recommended stress reduction actions

Stressor	Informal response	Formal response
Heat, ventilation, noise, dust, etc.	Slow down; self-regulation; prophylactic devices; frequent breaks; postural adjustments; denial; apathy and accommodation	OS&H monitoring and inspections; NIOSH health hazard research; OS&H committees with worker representation; contractual agreements re: OS&H
Office work hazards	Social support; petitions; meetings with supervisors; sick days; sabotage; quit	Request government hearings and OS&H research; lobby for legislation; unionize to obtain collective bargaining strength
Workpace, workload, job content, shiftwork, etc.	Slow down/speed up; sleep on job; sabotage; redefine task; quit	Contract language assuring grievances; OS&H committees; quality circles; supervisor training
Automation	Sabotage; develop new skills; hide redundancy; go into management	Advance notice and retraining clauses in contracts; participation in corporate planning via board membership or stock ownership
Psychological job pressures	Social support; self-help; recreation; substance abuse; vacation	Referral to health agencies; leaves of absence; negotiated alcohol and counselling programmes
Job security	Become 'indispensable'; find 'recession-proof' work; don't make waves; accept lower wages or benefits	Job security clause in contract; gain voice in corporate decisions via board membership or stock ownership

relaxation and employee counseling as well as formal EAPs were mentioned by corporate respondents.

It is evident from the above that corporate and labor groups displayed 'selective attention' in their conceptualization of stress and failed to acknowledge and appreciate opposing viewpoints. These divergent perspectives had direct effects on the type and frequency of stress programs advocated by these groups.

Table 2 Management-identified stressors and recommended stress reduction actions

Stressor	Formal response
Maladaptive health behaviors	Health education (brochures, workshops); health promotion programmes (smoking cessation, weight reduction, exercise gyms, screening)
Substance abuse	Drug and alcohol rehabilitation programmes; employee assistance programmes (EAPs) for short-term counseling and referral
Personality traits (Type A behavior, anxiety, apathy)	Stress education (time management, lifestyle changes, anger/conflict management); stress management— (relaxation, meditation, biofeedback, group discussion, yoga)
Life development	EAP counseling; retirement counseling
Interpersonal relations	EAP counseling; family therapy; support groups
Societal changes	Stress management; EAP counseling
Work setting issues	(a) Pre-screening (b) Transfer (c) EAP referral (d) Work redesign (e) Quality circles, employee involvement (f) Flexible work hours (g) Management training (h) Bring in outside consultants; do research

EMPLOYEE ASSISTANCE PROGRAMS

Levinson (1956) traced the development of nonpsychiatric industrial counseling (and assistance) programs to the now classic Hawthorne Studies conducted at Western Electric in the mid-1920s and early 1930s. (For a history of psychiatric programs in industry, see McLean, 1973.) Though the most memorable results of those studies dealt with the effects of subject factors on employee responses (e.g. productivity), the following data were additionally gleaned from interviews with approximately 20,000 employees:

The investigators reported two discoveries, both significant although elementary knowledge to anyone with clinical training: (1) The complaint, as stated, was frequently not the real source of the individual's difficulty. Consequently, action based on the manifest content of the complaint did not assure that the underlying difficulty would be eliminated. (2) With the opportunity to express themselves freely, the employees were able to more clearly formulate their complaints, and in many cases the complaints disappeared entirely. In addition, many employees developed a new enthusiasm for their work as they talked out their problems and lost some of their tensions. These considerations led to the development of the Western Electric counseling program, formally organized in 1936 as part of the Industrial Relations Branch, which became the precursor of all other nonpsychiatric industrial counseling programs. (Levinson, 1956, pp. 76–7)

The original group of counselors in the Western Electric program were supervisors and other plant employees who had participated in the earlier research and, as such, had no clinical training. The purpose of the program was to use the interview process itself to bring about adjustments in employee and supervisory attitudes. Diagnosis, prescriptions or advice-giving were specifically avoided in favor of a nondirective, confidential listener's role (Dickson, 1945).

In a survey of major industrial mental health programs conducted by the Menninger Foundation in 1954, Menninger and Levinson (1954) noted that many companies and managers were uncomfortable with businesses becoming involved in employee mental health. The attitude was that emotional problems were personal in origin and the responsibility for treatment was also personal, as indicated by the following quote:

> Finally, we found that whatever limited discussion of industrial mental health there was in the literature focused primarily on the individual employee and his presumed shortcomings. Such phrases as 'the pathological emotional attitude of employees' and 'industrial psychopathology' indicated that the writers saw many of the mental health problems in industry as the 'fault' of the individual workers. In professional circles, too, there was some question about the desirability of industry's interest in mental health problems. One writer went so far as to describe human relations in industry as 'cow sociology', designed to lull employees into placid acceptance without solving the problems that led to discontent. (Levinson, 1961, p. 3)

A shift in focus from counseling of 'normal' employees and toward treatment of 'troubled' employees, especially alcoholic employees, was reflected by the emergence of occupational alcoholism programs. The National Council on Alcoholism (formed in 1944) and the Yale Center of Alcohol Studies invested significant energy to educate companies about the merits of employee alcoholism programs (Presnall, 1967). Despite these efforts over a 16-year period, only about 50 US companies had formal programs in operation in 1959. Due to persistent efforts by the National Council on Alcoholism, its affiliates and the Yale group, the number of industrial programs increased 357% by 1965 (Presnall, 1967). Since then, the prevalence of what are now called employee assistance programs (EAPs) increased substantially totalling 500 in 1973, 2400 in 1977, 4400 in 1979–1980 (Department of Health and Human Services, 1980a), and an estimated 8000 in 1984 (MacLeod, 1985).

Parallel activities are found in the United Kingdom where, over the past 20 years, the National Council on Alcoholism established 27 local and regional councils that provide advice and counseling services in key cities (Vetter, 1981). The more recently established EAPs have been promoted as 'broad brush' programs, which purport to offer assistance to all 'troubled employees'. By and large, though, EAPs continue to focus primarily on the alcoholic employee.

The substantial increase in the number of EAPs in the US over the last 20 years was due in no small part to the involvement, since the 1970s, by the National Institute on Alcohol Abuse and Alcoholism in the form of funding for occupational program consultants (OPCs), demonstration and research grants and dissemination activities. Studies documenting the high cost of alcoholic employees to industry also had an accelerating effect on the growth of EAPs. With respect to the latter, alcoholism has long been referred to as 'industry's billion dollar hangover' (Menninger and Levinson, 1954). Studies agree that the alcoholic employe is far more costly than the non-alcoholic employee as measured by sickness absenteeism, work accidents and overall health care costs (Maxell, 1959; Thorpe and Perret, 1959; Trice, 1965; Winslow *et al.*, 1966; Pell and D'Alonzo, 1970). In addition, Pell and D'Alonzo (1968) and D'Alonzo and Pell (1968) reported that alcoholic employees had higher prevalence rates for nearly all chronic diseases, especially cardiovascular diseases. In a five-year mortality study, Pell and D'Alonzo (1973) found that alcoholic employees had mortality rates 2–3 times higher than those of a comparison group of employees after controlling for age, sex, socioeconomic status and geographical location. Excess mortality among alcoholics has been confirmed in a recent US population study (Department of Health and Human Services, 1985). Effects of alcohol on cardiovascular diseases have been reported in US longitudinal studies such as Framingham (Kannel and Sorlie, 1974) and Tecumesh (Harburg *et al.*, 1980) as well as in other countries (Savide, Grosslight and Adena, 1984).

Stress Reduction Functions of EAPs

How do EAPs function to reduce employee stress? The connection is not as direct as it could be, if these programs were truly 'broad brush'. As they currently operate, EAPs can be considered stress reduction strategies to the extent that (1) emotional stress is an etiological factor in alcohol use, (2) problem drinking itself creates employee distress and/or (3) EAPs reduce distress among supervisors who must deal with troubled employees.

The notion that anxiety or stress promoted alcohol use and that the reinforcing properties of alcohol sustain its use has been suggested by a number of empirical studies and conceptual articles. Admitting the importance of social and cultural factors in alcohol use and abuse, psychological models of alcohol use were developed to explain individual variations within given sociocultural situations. Psychological models variously specify (1) direct tension reduction (Bandura, 1969; Conger, 1956), (2) reduced cognitive self-awareness, leading to decreases in negative self-evaluation after failure and decreases in appropriate behaviors (Hull, 1981) or (3) selective impairment of emotional memory, which facilitates escape or relief from unpleasant feelings (Cowan, 1983). Each of these hypotheses views alcohol consumption as a learned behavior used to cope with stress in the environment (Pearlin and Radabaugh, 1976; Williams, Calhoun and Ackoff, 1982). Drinking is perpetuated by its reinforcing qualities and eventually leads to alcoholism.

The organizatonal stress literature contains sporadic studies linking job stressors to alcohol use. For example, data collected in the 1972–1973 Quality of Employment Survey from a nationally representative sample of 1496 employed persons indicated that escapist drinking was associated with overall levels of job stress and with worker reports of resource inadequacy, under-utilization, quantitative work overload, insecurity and nonparticipation (Margolis, Kroes and Quinn, 1974). In a survey of 1049 nurses from 10 hospitals, and 885 food processors from eight food processing plants across the United States, Tasto *et al.* (1978) reported that nurses on rotating and afternoon shifts drank significantly more beer than day shift nurses. Additionally, rotators drank more liquor of any kind than day shift nurses. These associations were not found among food processors. In a survey of 1150 police officers from 21 police organizations, Violanti, Marshall and Howe (1983) recently reported that psychological distress was an intervening variable influencing job demands and alcohol use. Of course, the validity and reliability of self-reported alcohol use are certainly questionable, especially when the questions are asked in a workplace context. Problem drinking creates distress for the alcoholic worker as a function of verbal and written disciplinary actions taken by supervisors as employee work performance deteriorates (Trice and Roman, 1972). Efforts by the alcoholic worker to 'cover up' and deny problem drinking are additional sources of distress that can be reduced by EAPs. Finally, the distress experienced by supervisors who manage alcoholic employees in an oft neglected problem. A formal EAP, with explicit policies and procedures for dealing with troubled employees, should reduce supervisory distress, permitting the supervisor to return to more productive work.

Structure of EAPs

The structure of EAPs vary widely among specific programs but any definition would include a set of company policies and procedures for identifying and responding to employee personal or emotional problems that interfere with work performance (Walsh, 1982). In a 1976 survey of Fortune 500 companies, Roman and Thomas (1978) reported wide variability among EAP program components. Most programs had a written company policy, formalized procedures for identification and referral, assurance of confidentiality and health insurance coverage for outpatient treatment. Less uniformity among programs was found for employee education and supervisory orientation and training sessions, and provision of services for employees' dependents. Walsh and Hingson (1985) enumerate the following areas of program variability: (1) content and formality of company policies and procedures, (2) mechanisms for problem identification and referral, (3) involvement of company functional units such as medical, personnel and industrial relations, as well as union activity, (4) in-house vs external resources, (5) distribution of problems (diagnoses) treated and (6) staffing (psychologists, social workers, recovered alcoholics, nurses, physicians, psychiatrists, etc.).

Despite the variation in components, the following are believed to be essential ingredients of an effective EAP (MacLeod, 1985; Walsh, 1982; Wrich, 1984):

Commitment and support from top management;

A clear, written set of policies and procedures that outlines the purpose of the EAP and how it functions in the organization;

Close cooperation with local union(s);

Training of supervisors on their role in problem identification;

Education of employees and promotion of EAP services to foster widespread utilization throughout the company;

A continuum of care, including referral to community agencies and follow-up of each case;

An explicit policy on confidentiality of employee information;

Maintenance of records for program evaluation purposes;

Coverage of EAP services by company health insurance benefits.

Function of EAPs

Functional aspects of EAPs would be expected to flow from their structure, producing a great deal of variability. However, there seems to be more consistency with respect to EAP function than structure. In this regard, 'constructive confrontation' has been the predominant strategy for dealing with alcoholics in the work setting (Trice and Roman, 1972). The confrontation is between the supervisor and the employee, and the focus is on poor work performance, not problem drinking. Indeed, the supervisor need not mention problem drinking as a causative factor. The constructive element of the strategy is the provision of EAP services to the worker while still employed. Repeated confrontations become necessary if work performance does not improve and, ultimately, the supervisor may need to precipitate a crisis specifying progressively more serious consequences (i.e. enter a treatment program or face job layoffs, reductions in pay or job termination).

The constructive confrontation strategy utilizes social controls within the work organization rather than creating a 'deviant' role for the worker. It has been suggested that confrontation and crisis precipitation are needed to maximize treatment (Trice, Hunt and Beyer, 1977). Indeed, there is evidence that while the combination of constructive and confrontive elements of the strategy predicts whether an alcoholic employee enters treatment, only the confrontive element predicts improved work performance (Trice and Beyer, 1984). For example, a Canadian study found that alcoholic employees perceive significant company pressure to enter treatment following confrontation but that perceived pressure is reduced drastically once the employee receives treatment. At the same time, fear of job loss consequent to resumption of drinking remains high after treatment (Freedberg and Johnston, 1981).

Constructive confrontation has been successful in work settings for a number of reasons. First, the focus is on work performance, not the employees' personal (non-occupational) behavior, and the former is a legitimate concern for employers. Second, the workplace has significant preventive potential since impaired job performance occurs early in the alcohol addiction process. Third, it is more difficult for the alcoholic to use denial mechanisms in view of documented evidence of impaired work performance. Finally, the threat of disciplinary actions, even job loss, is a powerful motivating factor for most workers (Beyer and Trice, 1982).

Evaluation of EAPs

Do EAPs work? Despite their prevalence in work settings, EAPs are rarely evaluated using well-controlled, scientific methodologies. At the same time, EAPs are routinely promoted as 'tried and true', successful approaches for dealing with troubled employees. To understand this apparent disparity, one needs to appreciate various levels of program evaluation and the wide range of outcome measures used to evaluate program 'success'. Indicators of EAP program success have included (1) the percentage of employees who enter treatment, (2) percentage that return to work after treatment, (3) changes in drinking activity after treatment, (4) improved work performance and (5) cost-savings to the company. Using these types of measures, EAPs achieve uniformly positive results. For example, return to work rates fluctuate around

50% (Franco, 1960; Eggum, Keller and Burton, 1980) but it is not uncommon to find rates of 70–80% (Asma, Eggert and Hilker, 1971; Asma *et al.*, 1980; Guest, 1981; Trice and Beyer, 1984). The largest alcoholism treatment center in the United Kingdom, ACCEPT (Alcoholism Community Centers for Education, Prevention and Treatment) reported that 80% of its referrals in the greater London area in 1980 were still employed (Vetter, 1981). Abstinence rates tend to be somewhat lower, about 40–50% (Asma *et al.*, 1971, 1980). In a recent national interview and questionnaire survey of 480 private sector companies with EAPs, Blum and Roman (1986) found EAP success rates of 60–68%. Cost-savings studies, focusing on changes in absenteeism, health care costs and/or disability, similarly yielded positive results (Foote *et al.*, 1978; Schramm, 1977; Wrich, 1984). It is noteworthy that evaluation studies rarely consider the benefits of the EAP to supervisors of alcoholic employees. As noted earlier, an EAP also provides supervisors with a formal mechanism for dealing with troubled employees, thus reducing supervisor distress.

Though these studies would seem to support the efficacy of EAPs, they are subject to criticism on methodological grounds. In their review of EAP evaluation research, Kurtz, Googins and Howard (1984) found relatively few studies that employed any type of comparison group and no studies that randomly assigned employees to study groups. The concern here is that without valid comparison groups or random assignment of employee to groups, there is no good reason to suspect that the treatments under study, as opposed to a host of other factors, produced the observed results. Indeed, nonspecific effects are common in the clinical literature (Kazdin and Wilcoxin, 1976) and in worksite stress management studies (Murphy, 1984a).

One obvious confounding variable is selection bias. It is possible that employees most likely to succeed are screened into the EAP while the more incorrigible or less likely to succeed are screened out. Trice and Beyer (1984) elaborated other possible selection biases and designed a study to estimate such bias. Two types of selection bias were estimated: (1) employees identified by managers as having a drinking problem but who were discharged, laid off, retired, voluntarily quit, died or were otherwise separated from the company instead of being referred to the EAP and (2) employees who were referred to the EAP but did not complete the treatment program or were 'lost to follow-up', for reasons including those listed in (1) above.

Data were collected from a stratified random sample of 19 locations of a large corporation. Interviews were conducted with 154 managers who had a subordinate with a drinking problem and 351 managers who dealt with difficult (troubled), but not alcoholic, employees. The authors estimated the referral process selection bias at 3% and the after referral bias at 5%, for a total estimated bias of 8%. The results suggest that selection biases in EAPs account for a relatively small percentage of the high success rates commonly reported for EAPs (Trice and Beyer, 1984).

Beyond the methodological criticisms, very little research has addressed other key topics, such as comparative effectiveness of alternative treatment strategies (e.g. Alcoholics Anonymous, psychotherapy, aversive conditioning, relaxation training, etc.), in-patient vs outpatient treatment plans, company in-house vs external EAPs, constructive confrontation of employees vs formal discipline, and identification and assessment of EAP selection biases (Walsh and Hingson, 1985). Notable exceptions are studies by Trice and Beyer (1984) that address the relative significance of components of EAPs (constructive confrontation vs formal discipline).

Barriers to EAP evaluation research are noteworthy. Foremost among these are limited access by evaluation researchers and issues of employee confidentiality. Indeed, Walsh and Hingson (1985) supplied convincing evidence of the former. Over a three-year period, these researchers approached 68 American companies for which they had some previous contact and proposed a randomized controlled experiment of alternative treatment for problem drinkers. All but one company declined the offer, most on the basis of logistical and ethical concerns inherent in randomized experiments. Violations of employee confidentiality, or even the impression of violation, is another significant barrier to evaluation research, especially in external EAPs. The assurance of confidentiality is crucial to the success of the EAP so EAP providers are reluctant to provide sensitive employee data to researchers. On the other hand, some providers may not want their program evaluated, and others may not feel the need to evaluate, especially if company management does not require or desire detailed evaluations.

Summary

As they currently operate, EAPs offer tertiary prevention for problem drinkers. Increasingly, EAPs are expanding their services to address other problem areas such as drug abuse and employee distress. Because of their access to organizations, EAPs have potential for reducing worker distress. For this potential to be realized, EAPs will need to add a primary prevention component and begin providing feedback to organizations with respect to stressful work environment factors. In light of the sensitivity of worker confidentiality, such feedback will have to be provided in a manner that prevents individual worker identification. Provision of summary statistics would permit organizations to pinpoint high stress departments that can serve as a starting point for more in-depth stress assessment studies.

Other types of feedback could take the form of organizational characteristics that generate worker distress. Of course, EAP counselors would need to become familiar with principles of organizational behavior and th dynamics of work environment/health relationships. This may mean adding occupational mental health specialists to the EAP staff or providing training to existing staff in these areas. At present, EAPs represent an underutilized resource for organizational stress reduction and prevention.

STRESS MANAGEMENT TRAINING

Over the past 10 years, stress management has become a popular health program offered in work settings. Stress management refers collectively to a group of worker-oriented techniques that seek (1) to foster awareness and recognition of stressors and attendant health effects and (2) to each arousal (stress) reduction skills. The latter is accomplished via training in progressive muscle relaxation, biofeedback, meditation, breathing exercises and assorted cognition-focused techniques. Each of these techniques has demonstrated effectiveness in clinical or laboratory settings for reducing arousal level Meichenbaum, 1977; Patel, 1977; Orme-Johnson and Farrow, 1977; Tarler-Benlo, 1978; Pomerleau and Brady, 1979).

As applied in work settings, stress management more often than not has been offered in a preventive, as opposed to curative, context. That is, participants were not recruited because of evident stress problems or health risks. Accordingly, these programs have a more compelling association with health promotion than with stress reduction. Stress management has ridden the coat-tails of the health promotion movement in the US that became evident in the early 1970s. Health promotion programs represent educational and motivational efforts designed to effect behavioral and lifestyle changes so as to improve health and well-being. In work settings, these programs stand in contrast to traditional workplace health activities that seek to ensure worker protection from hazardous environmental conditions. In the latter, attention is directed toward health risks stemming from occupational exposures to toxic chemicals, harmful physical agents (excess noise, heat, vibration, radiation) and strenuous job demands and work routines. Engineering control options are considered preferred approaches for dealing with such hazards.

The growing interest in health promotion programs has been attributed to soaring medical care costs and the realization that behavioral factors play a significant role in seven of the ten leading causes of death in the United States (Department of Health and Human Services, 1979). The Surgeon General's report *Healthy People* documented the preventable nature of many illnesses and established the groundwork for emphasizing disease prevention through self-help, self-care actions to make progress in enhancing the nation's health status. In particular, the report identified 15 priority areas wherein improvements could be made in the health of Americans. A follow-up publication (Department of Health and Human Services, 1980b) set forth specific and quantifiable objectives within each priority area for attainment at various points through the year 1990.

References to the workplace were made in two ways in these publications. First, the workplace was identified as priority area considering that occupational illnesses and injury were of human origin and preventable. In this regard, a host of actions were listed for ensuring improved worker health and safety. Most were cast as environmental control solutions but two made mention of lifestyle factors or health promotion issues. Second, in addressing personal lifestyle/behavioral risk factors as problem priority areas, the 1990 Objectives referenced the workplace, but only in the context of it serving as a vehicle for facilitating remedial actions. Indeed, the workplace was viewed as the ideal vehicle for health promotion programs because it offered (1) convenient access to large, relatively stable populations, (2) available staff already committed to improving worker health and safety, (3) organizational structures to support programs and (4) opportunities to utilize existing peer support systems to improve participation in and compliance with health promotion activities. A mid-course review of these objectives indicated significant progress with respect to worksite stress management (Department of Health and Human Services, 1986).

A survey of Californian companies in 1983 discovered that more companies had a functional stress management program than physical fitness, hypertension screening or smoking cessation programs. Moreover, more companies reported plans to establish stress management programs in the near future than any other health promotion activity (Fielding and Breslow, 1983). In a 1985 survey of US worksites, an estimated 26% reported some type of stress management activity (Office of Disease Prevention and Health Promotion, in press).

Research on the efficacy of worksite stress management has increased steadily since the later 1970s. A review of the literature up to 1983 found 13 studies, five of which were unpublished (Murphy, 1984a). A later review (McLeroy *et al.*, 1984) identified 19 studies. Conclusions from these reviews are summarized below:

Stress management in work settings has been narrowly defined to focus on the individual worker as the target for change. Interventions aimed at modifying stressful aspects of the work environment are rare.

Programs are preventive and seek to improve worker awareness and recognition of stress. In this sense, the label 'stress management' is misleading since neither workers nor organizations with apparent stress problems are solicited.

Programs are usually offered to workers in white collar occupations.

Training typically includes education, some type of relaxation exercise, and may additionally include meditation, biofeedback and/or a cognition-- focused technique.

Programs have been generic in nature not targeting specific work stressors or stress symptoms.

Few studies compared the relative effectiveness of different training techniques. Thus, although doing something appears to be better than doing nothing, the specific technique used may not matter much.

Evaluation has been based upon individual-oriented measures (e.g. anxiety) that have been assessed over a short post-training period.

In various studies, stress management has been associated with significant reductions in anxiety, depression, somatic complaints, sleep disturbances, muscle tension levels, blood pressure and urinary catecholamines.

The changes observed immediately after training have not always been maintained in follow-up evaluations; regression toward baseline levels has occurred in many studies that contained a follow-up.

Though the number of studies evaluating worksite stress management increased significantly since these reviews, the conclusions of the earlier reviews remain largely unchanged. The newer studies have confirmed the effectiveness of stress management for reducing subjective distress such as anxiety (e.g. Sommerville, *et al.*, 1984; West, Horan and Games, 1984) and psychophysiological indicators such as blood pressure (Charlesworth, Williams and Baer, 1984; West *et al.*, 1984) and urinary catecholamines (McNulty, Jeffrys and Singer, 1984).

Like the previous studies, the newer ones have not provided much information about the relative effectiveness of different training methods. An exception is the study by Bruning and Frew (1985) that compared the effects of management skills training (goal setting, time management and conflict resolution), clinically standardized meditation, physical exercise and combinations of these strategies on pulse rate, systolic and diastolic blood pressure and galvanic skin response. The results indicated that while each technique was effective in reducing pulse rate and systolic blood pressure, the largest reductions occurred for the group that received management skills training. Of the various combinations of techniques, exercise followed by meditation led to the greatest reductions in pulse rate but no changes on remaining physiological measures.

Information gaps and research needs noted in the previous reviews also remain unaddressed. These include the influence of nonspecific training effects, characteristics of workers who volunteer for stress management training, comparison of successful vs unsuccessful trainees, assessment of long-term benefits of training, factors affecting the post-training maintenance of benefits and the cost-effectiveness of stress management in work settings.

DeFrank and Cooper (1987) suggested that the content of work stress interventions needs to be expanded to address (1) the interface of the individual with the organizational (e.g. relationships at work, role issues, participation, and autonomy) and (2) the organization itself (organization structure, selection and placement, training, physical features of the job). Similar expansion was recommended for outcome measures to reflect the interaction of the individual with the organization or that have significant implications for organizational functioning. Examples would be job satisfaction, productivity, absenteeism, turnover, organizational health care costs, and accidents/ injuries. Examination of the effects of stress management on these types of outcomes is presented in the following sections.

Job Satisfaction and Work Performance

Of the 30 studies that evaluated stress management in work settings, nearly half (14) assessed some type of organizational outcome (see Table 3). Five of the nine studies found a significant increase in job satisfaction following stress management; three found no effects due to training, and one study (Riley, Fredericksen and Winett, 1984) found a significant *decrease* in job satisfaction among trained workers compared to controls. Four studies measured self-reported work performance; two reported improvements and two found no training-specific changes. Two additional studies found no changes in either productivity or supervisor ratings of employee performance.

As a group, these studies found inconsistent effects of stress management on job satisfaction and work performance. The study by Frew (1974) provides insight into potential response biases on these types of measures. When asked about job satisfaction, work performance and job turnover propensity, workers proficient in meditation rated the first two as high and the latter as low. Supervisor and co-worker ratings of meditators on these same scales indicated agreement with meditator ratings of job satisfaction, but not for work performance nor turnover propensity. These results could be interpreted as a generalized reporting bias among meditators; the positive effects of meditation on arousal level and psychological state (commonly reported in meditation studies) might generalize and influence attributions about the job itself. Other studies that utilized supervisory ratings of employee performance support the conclusion that training in biofeedback, muscle relaxation, or cognitive skills does not lead to significant improvements in work performance (Murphy and Sorenson, in press; Riley *et al.*, 1984).

Any effects of stress management on job satisfaction are likely to be a function of (1) the content of stress education information offered to partici-

Table 3 Organizational outcomes following stress management

Investigator(s)	Job satisfaction	Productivity/ performance	Absenteeism/ turnover	Clinic visits/ health claims	Comments
Frew (1974)	Increased	Increased performance ratings	Lower turnover propensity	—	Self-report data; workers selected based upon prior experience with TM
Peters et al. (1977 a.b.); Peters (1981)	Increased	Increased performance ratings	—	—	Satisfaction measure was not specific to work; changes also found at 6 month follow-up
Gray-Toft (1980)	Increased	—	Reduced turnover	—	Effects on satisfaction were largest for nurses on evening/night shifts
Manuso (in Schwartz, 1980)	Increased	—	No change in absenteeism	Fewer health clinic visits	Subjects were workers with stress symptoms; no control group used
Forman (1981)	Increased	—	—	—	Satisfaction measured using JDI subscales
Seamonds (1982, 1983)	—	—	Lower absenteeism	—	Intervention was a single counseling session
Alderman and Techlenburg (1983)	No change	—	—	—	Outcome measure was organizational commitment
Manuso (1983)	—	—	—	Fewer health clinic visits	Subjects were Type A and Type B workers; no control group used
Murphy (1983)	No change	No change in performance ratings	—	—	Control group reported more dissatisfaction

Table 3 (Continued)

Investigator(s)	Job satisfaction	Productivity/ performance	Absenteeism/ turnover	Clinic visits/ health claims	Comments
Charlesworth, et al. (1984)	—	—	Decreased health care claims	Subjects were hypertensive workers; no control group for claims data.	
Riley et al. (1984)	Decreased	No change in productivity	No change in absenteeism	No change in health care claims	Trained groups showed lower job satisfaction; no training effects found for other measures
Murphy (1984)	No change	No change in performance ratings	—	—	Dissatisfaction decreased in all groups.
Murphy and Sorenson (in press)	—	No change in performance ratings	Lower absenteeism for one of two trained groups	—	Records study with non-equivalent control group; changes seen for muscle relax but not biofeedback group

Note: TM=Transcendental Meditation
JDI=Job Descriptive Index.

pants and (2) the source and level of stress in the participants' organization. Regarding the former, all stress management studies reportedly contained a stress education component, but detailed descriptions of its content are rarely described in individual reports. It is reasonable to suppose that educational materials focusing on general life stressors will produce a smaller impact on job satisfaction than materials that additionally describe the nature and sources of work stress. With respect to the second point, *decreases* in job satisfaction might be expected if, as a result of improved awareness, participants felt that some of the significant stressors that they face were work-related and yet not being addressed by the intervention strategy. (See Steinmetz, Kaplan and Miller, 1982, for description of other unanticipated outcomes). In view of these speculations, consistent effects of stress management on job satisfaction across studies would be the exception, not the rule.

Turnover and Absenteeism

Too little data exist to support general statements about the effects of stress management on job turnover. The Frew (1974) study described above produced inconclusive data on turnover propensity. Gray-Toft (1980) reported lower turnover in the hospice unit that participated in a stress counseling program than in other hospital units. The author also noted that there was a striking correlation between stress levels and turnover percentage among five hospital units and that the hospice unit had the lowest stress levels. It is noteworthy that the hospice unit was less than two years old and may not have been the most appropriate unit for comparison with older hospital departments with respect to turnover. Nevertheless, these results are provocative and encourage replication in other organizations.

No studies evaluating the effects of stress management on employee absenteeism were found in the published literature. The absenteeism studies listed in Table 3 represent (1) a secondary account of a study (Schwartz, 1980), (2) as yet unpublished studies (Murphy and Sorenson, in press; Riley et al., 1984) or (3) an intervention that did not involve stress management training as defined earlier (Seamonds, 1982, 1983). Schwartz (1980) described a study conducted at the Equitable Life Assurance Company where 15 employees with recurring headaches and 15 employees with chronic anxiety received stress management training (a combination of EMG biofeedback, muscle relaxation, breathing exercises and imagery techniques). A control group was not included in the study design. Three months after training, participants reported significant decreases in stress symptoms and symptom interference with work, along with increases in work satisfaction and effectiveness. Absenteeism rates for the trained workers were not significantly different from the corporate average.

The two unpublished studies produced somewhat different results. The intervention in Riley *et al.* (1984) was a cognitive-behavioral program that emphasized the development of problem-solving skills to manage stress. The six-session program focused on acknowledging and changing cognitions (negative self-statements, irrational beliefs), assertiveness, and fostering social support. Twenty-eight workers received the training, and an additional 20 workers served as waiting-list controls. Outcome measures included productivity, absenteeism and health care claims. The results indicated that both trained and control groups showed significant increases in productivity and decreases in absenteeism over the course of the study; there was no differential change as a function of training. Health care claims were too infrequent to permit statistical analysis but the number of claims was similar for both groups through the evaluation period.

The other unpublished study (Murphy and Sorenson, in press) gathered data from organizational records on absenteeism, performance ratings, equipment accidents and job injuries for workers trained in EMG biofeedback (N=17) or muscle relaxation (N=21), and for a group of workers who had not volunteered for the training program (N=80). Employee records encompassed the 30 months before training and 18 months after training. Multiple regression analyses indicated that muscle relaxation (but not biofeedback) training explained additional variance in each of the four absenteeism indicators during the first post-training year. The amount of variance explained was small, accounting for between 3 and 9% of the variance. Analysis of the following half-year period yielded insignificant results for both trained groups. Neither group entered regression models for performance ratings, equipment accidents or work injuries for the first year after training, or the following half year.

The intervention in the two studies by Seamonds (1982, 1983) did not involve stress management training as defined earlier. Rather, the intervention involved a single health education interview that focused on sources of stress and ways to maintain or improve individual health and well-being. Following the interview, referrals were made to community agencies or to resources for educational materials. Forty-one percent of the interviewees were provided with information and resources for exercise programs; 32% received information on relaxation techniques (10.5% did not require referrals).

Absenteeism rates (number of days absent) for employees that received health interviews were significantly lower six months after the interview compared with pre-interview levels. The pre- vs post-interview change was nearly 50%. A control group of workers matched on sex, job level and job stress scores showed a slight increase in absenteeism during this same interval. In a questionnaire mailed to 'high absentee' interviewees six weeks after the interview, 80% felt that their ability to cope with stress had improved since the interview and 90% reported being able to determine, as a result of the interview, areas of their health care that they had neglected.

Health Clinic Visits/Health Insurance Claims

Three published studies and one unpublished report evaluated health clinic visits or health insurance claims following stress management. Schwartz (1980) reported that workers with chronic anxiety or recurring headaches made 50% fewer health clinic visits during the three months after stress management training than the three months before training. Similar results were reported by Manuso (1983) in a second study. The lack of a control group in both of these studies warrants a cautious interpretation. Charlesworth *et al.* (1984) selected hypertensive workers and compared health insurance claims (in dollars) before and after training in muscle relaxation, imagery, cognitive restructuring and assertiveness. Mean claim values were calculated for the year before training (Time 1), the year during which training took place (Time 2) and the half year following training (Time 3). Mean claim dollars were reduced by more than 50% ($225.00 vs $97.00) at Time 2 ($p<0.05$). Levels at Time 3 were not significantly different from those at Time 2 (85 vs 97), suggesting maintenance of post-training gains. However, as in previous studies, no control or comparison group was used.

Finally, Riley *et al.* (1984) found no significant changes in health insurance claims between workers who received stress management training compared with controls. However, the authors noted that too few claims were filed to permit statistical analyses but that levels remained constant throughout the study period and similar between groups.

Summary

A number of authors have argued that stress management represents a limited approach to the problem of work stress and that organizational stressors should be the primary targets of worksite stress programs (e.g. Beehr and O'Hara, 1987; DeFrank and Cooper, 1987; Ganster *et al.*, 1982; Murphy, 1984a; Rosch and Pelletier, 1987). The characterization of stress management as a 'band-aid' solution to the problem assumes, of course, that the 'problem' is organizational stress and not stress from other sources nor the interaction of work and nonwork stress. The success of worksite stress management, with respect to psychological and physiological outcomes, may be due in part to its applicability to work and nonwork problems. In contrast, organizational change interventions deal only with work stressors (usually restricted to one or two presumed stressors) and may actually increase stress for some workers, depending upon the nature of the intervention.

Ganster *et al.* (1982) suggested that stress management might be a useful supplement to organizational change interventions, especially in work situations where some stressors cannot be eliminated. Given the preventive orientation adopted in most studies (neither organizations nor employees with evident stress problems were actively recruited), Murphy (1984a) suggested that stress management has a more compelling association with health promotion than with stress reduction. Accordingly, treating stress management like other organizational training programs or integrating stress management into EAPs would more accurately mirror their application in research studies. In this regard, Murphy and Hurrell (1987) described an approach to organizational stress reduction that capitalized on the the strong points of stress management and stressor-focused tactics. The study was conducted in an organization with apparent problems of employee dissatisfaction, low morale, and stress. An intervention was recommended that contained four phases: (1) a stress management workshop, (2) a survey of employee strain, (3) organizational change actions and (4) evaluation. In this conceptualization, stress management was not the 'treatment', but rather served to legitimize stress in the work setting, foster awareness about the nature, sources and consequences of stress, and provide workers with cognitive and relaxation skills useful in reducing arousal. (It is noteworthy that only the latter aspect of stress management is presumed to be the 'active ingredient' in most evaluation studies.) Workshop leaders provided feedback to the department management on job features perceived as stressful and this data was used to develop a stressor evaluation survey.

An employee committee was then formed with representatives from each of four departmental work groups plus the management office. The committee commissioned the stressor survey and was responsible for making organizational change recommendations. The survey indicated (1) that, compared with national norms, job dissatisfaction was significantly lower in the sample and (2) that supervisory support, job involvement, autonomy, task orientation and clarity were interrelated stressors that predicted job dissatisfaction. Based upon these data and results of worker interviews, the committee submitted a list of recommendations to management for consideration. The committee plans to re-administer the stressor survey when (if?) any changes are implemented.

STRESSOR REDUCTION INTERVENTIONS

Reducing stress through actions aimed at work environment stressors is the most straightforward organizational stress reduction intervention. They also can be costly and difficult to implement in organizations. Stressor reduction requires an identification of the stressors followed by planned changes in organizational structure or function. Organizations, more so than individuals, resist change. This inertia is reinforced by the belief prevalent in many organizations that the work environment contributes little to employee distress and that stress is a personal problem requiring worker-oriented and worker-initiated solutions (Neale *et al.*, 1982). For these and other reasons, studies that evaluate organizational interventions designed to reduce employee distress are uncommon in the published literature.

This section will review stressor reduction interventions and evidence of their effectiveness. The review will focus on interventions that aim for, or result in, increases in worker control. (Though much of the job enrichment literature dealt with the concept of increased worker participation and control, the aim of these interventions was to improve job satisfaction, employee morale and productivity, not health, and thus are not reviewed here.) Interventions involving increased worker discretion over job tasks or work processes, formation of autonomous work groups, worker participation in decision making, or flexibility in work schedules all offer potential for improved worker control and form the basis for this review. The relationship of control to stress is dealt with first, followed by a review of the relationship between worker control and psychological, behavioral and physiological outcomes. Finally, organizational interventions that increased worker control or perceptions of control are reviewed.

Control and Stress

Various typologies of control have been postulated (e.g. Averill, 1973; Miller, 1979) but the definition suggested by Thompson (1981) is used here. Control is defined as the belief that one has at one's disposal a response that can influence the aversiveness of an event. This definition emphasizes the importance of perceived control (belief) and instrumentality (one can do something to influence the aversiveness of the event). Controllable events 'hurt less' than uncontrollable events (Miller, 1979).

The concept of control has been closely tied to stress. Cognitive appraisal is thought to be a function of the amount of control the person believes he/she has in the situation (Lazarus, 1966). Perceived control is an essential ingredient of coping (Folkman and Lazarus, 1980) and a psychological resource that people draw upon during stressful events (Pearlin and Schooler, 1978).

A great deal of animal and human research indicates that the presence or absence of control has profound effects on health and well-being (Abramson, Seligman and Teasdale, 1978; Averill, 1973; Glass and Singer, 1972; Miller, 1979; Seligman, 1975). When faced with uncontrollable events or situations (or ones perceived as uncontrollable), a host of physiological changes can occur including increased heart rate, excess production of adrenocortical and adrenomedullary hormones and decreased immunological activity, Glass, Reim and Singer, 1971; Weiss, 1971). The pattern of changes resembles the 'fight or flight' response (Cannon, 1929) characteristic of stress (Selye, 1936, 1956). Lack of control also has been shown to foster helplessness, a syndrome of cognitive, motivational and emotional deficits produced by learning that events are not under one's personal control (Seligman, 1975). Losing control (relative to never having had control) has been associated with frustration and prolonged depression (Stroebel, 1969) and elevated cortisol levels (Hanson, Larson and Snowdon, 1976). Evidently, it is less stressful never to have had control than to have had it and lost it. (This has implications for organizations that may 'experiment' with increased worker control or participation without a long-term commitment to the process.)

Degree of control, directly or as engendered by participation in decision making, has occupied a central position in theories of job design and organizational behavior. For example, the Job Characteristics Model of task design considers autonomy a core job dimension that leads to positive affect via experienced responsibility for work outcomes (Hackman and Lawler, 1971; Hackman and Oldham, 1976). Worker participation in decision making, which presumably increases control (or perhaps perceived control), is a fundamental element of sociotechnical systems theory (Emery and Trist, 1969) and quality circles (Barra, 1983). Finally, two major theories relating organizational stress to health feature control as a central concept, either explicitly (Karasek, 1979) or implicitly (Caplan *et al.*, 1975; Harrison, 1978).

In light of the above, it should not be surprising that workers desire increased control and participation in decision making. Interviews conducted by the Work in America Task Force in the 1970s illustrate this point:

> Task force member James Wright, a former steelworker himself, took a small team of interviewers into the field and came back with a large and surprising body of taped discussions with truck drivers, auto workers, steel workers, clerks, and secretaries. . . . What was particularly memorable about the interviews was that time and time again the workers told of suggesting to their employers that there were better ways to organize their tasks—and of these suggestions invariably being met with indifference, disdain, or contempt. Finally, the workers gave up trying. They began to make the minimum possible commitment to their jobs that would still ensure a paycheck at the end of the week. (O'Toole, 1974, p. 711)

Worker Control and Health

The empirical relationship between control and worker health has only recently been investigated and then usually via cross-sectional surveys. For example, in a US survey of employed adults, perceived nonparticipation exhibited stronger associations with lack of motivation to work, job dissatisfaction, reduced self-esteem, absenteeism and turnover intention than other potential work stressors (Margolis *et al.*, 1974).

A good deal of evidence indicates that machine-paced work is a potent work stressor (Cox, 1985; Frankenhauser and Gardell, 1976; Salvendy and Smith, 1981). Early field studies reported a variety of adverse psychological states linked to machine-pacing, including lack of self-respect and personal growth due to underutilization of abilities (Kornhauser, 1965), feelings of anonymity (Walker and Guest, 1952) and job dissatisfaction (Wyatt and Marriott, 1951). In a study of job stress and health relationships in 23 occupations (Caplan *et al.*, 1975), machine-paced assembly line workers reported heavier workload, less utilization of abilities and skills, less participation in decision making, more boredom and more health complaints compared with remaining occupations. Interestingly, assembly line workers that worked in teams reported better utilization of skills and abilities, higher job complexity and more participation in decision making.

It is no coincidence that it is in precisely these types of short cycle, repetitive, work situations that outbreaks of mass psychogenic illness (MPI) tend to occur. Affected workers tended to be employed in boring, repetitive jobs, under high production pressure, in physical surroundings judged as uncomfortable and in an atmosphere of poor labor–management relations. Common characteristics among affected workers included symptoms of headache, lightheadedness, dizziness and weakness that seemed to spread through the workplace in an epidemic-like fashion (Colligan and Murphy, 1979).

The Construct of Control in Work Settings

The most explicit statement of the relationship of job control to worker health was offered by Karasek and associates (Karasek, 1979; Karasek *et al.*, 1981). Karaek hypothesized that psychological strain results from the joint effects of psychological job demands (workload) and the degree of worker control (decision latitude). The model predicts that (1) worker strain increases as job demands increase relative to decreasing job decision latitude and (2) worker competency increases when job demands and decision latitude are simultaneously high. The model was first tested using mental health indicators obtained from nationally representative surveys in the US and Sweden (Karasek, 1979), and later with coronary disease (and its risk factors) in both cross-sectional and longitudinal studies (Karasek *et al.*, 1981; Karasek, Schwartz and Theorell, 1982).

Control is also a central feature of person–environment (P–E) fit theory, though it is less explicit than in Karsek's model. P–E fit theory (Caplan *et al.*, 1975; Harrison, 1978) predicts worker distress as a function of the congruence between objective job demands and subjective worker needs. For example, the degree of fit between, say, perceived workload and desired workload should be a better predictor of distress than perceived workload alone. It follows that workers with more job control can (re)structure jobs to optimize fit with their needs and abilities.

It has been argued that control is not a unidimensional construct but, rather, that facets or domains of worker control coexist (Breaugh, 1985; Fisher, 1984; Ganster, 1985). The question 'Control over what?' seems particularly important in work settings and suggests consideration of discrete aspects of work over which workers may exert control. Examples here would include (1) how the job is done, (2) how work is scheduled, (3) selection of methods used in performing tasks, (4) timing of work-rest breaks, (5) arrival and departure times, (6) modification of unpleasant physical conditions and (7) job mobility.

In summary, it seems clear that people seek to control their environment, particularly when faced with adverse situations. It seems equally clear that there are facets or domains of control at work and that individual differences can be expected in facets over which control is sought (or relinquished). For example, a worker who does not seek to participate in decision making (i.e. exert influence) with respect to production schedules may desire control over arrival and departure times or determination of work-rest breaks. The intervention studies reviewed in the next section manipulated different facets of control and evaluated effects on worker distress.

Intervention Studies

The most striking feature of studies evaluating the effects of worker control manipulations on employee strain is the sheer lack of them. Increased worker control generated via participation in decision making, autonomous work groups, or gainsharing plans have been examined with respect to job satisfaction, employee attitudes and productivity outcomes (Bullock and Lawler, 1984; Locke and Schweiger, 1979; Spector, 1986). However, changes in worker health were rarely evaluated, so that general statements of efficacy are not possible. (Though not included in this review, a good case could be made for considering job satisfaction as a mental health outcome thereby substantially increasing the number of studies that report beneficial effects of increased participation and autonomy.) Having said that, the few studies that did assess health changes following manipulations of worker control are reviewed.

Participation in decision making (Jackson, 1983)

Decision making has been traditionally vested in the upper echelons of organizations. Scientific management theory espoused the hierarchical concentration of control (power) as efficient since workers would not be distracted by the need to make decisions and could concentrate on their job duties. The wisdom of this approach has been challenged by a good deal of research (primarily cross-sectional) indicating that (1) workers desire to participate in decisions that affect their jobs, (2) lack of participation is associated with negative affective states and physical health outcomes and (3) increased worker participation leads to higher job satisfaction, motivation and productivity.

Among other things, participation in decision making (PDM) serves to increase information available to employees and enhances workers' feelings of influence and control. Provision of information functions to reduce employee ambiguity and, therefore, distress. Improved control allows workers the opportunity to influence job demands (to improve 'fit') and in this way may mitigate role conflicts/ambiguities to reduce distress.

Jackson (1983) designed a careful evaluation of the effects of PDM and potential intervening variables on role stressors and employee distress. It was hypothesized that PDM would improve perceived ability to influence the environment (reducing role conflict) and increase job-related communications (reducing role ambiguity) leading to lower employee distress, absenteeism and turnover intention. The study was conducted in an outpatient hospital facility that consisted of 25 semi-autonomous specialty clinics. Workers (nurses, nursing assistants, technicians and clerical personnel) were randomly assigned to intervention/no intervention and pretest/post-test groups in a Solomon four group experimental design. The intervention involved increased frequency of staff meetings, from once a month or less to at least two per month. Questionnaire data were gathered two months prior to the intervention and again three and six months after the intervention. Three months post-intervention, workers in the PDM group reported higher perceived influence, lower emotional distress, and lower turnover intention than workers in the the nonparticipation groups. No significant changes were found for role conflict or ambiguity, job satisfaction, absence frequency, job related or personal communications, or social support. Six months post-intervention, perceived influence remained significant, turnover intention and emotional distress became nonsignificant, and role ambiguity and role conflict were significantly reduced. Jackson (1983) concluded that PDM reduced role stressors and that perceived influence was a mediating variable.

Increased job autonomy (Wall and Clegg, 1981)

Wall and Clegg (1981) reported a work redesign study that evaluated emotional distress and job characteristics following an intervention designed to increase worker autonomy. Participants in the study were members of one department that the organization felt had problems of low morale, poor work attitudes and low work motivation. The investigators' approach to the problem involved a blending of action research, sociotechnical systems theory and the Job Characteristics Model. Due to the nature of the jobs in the department, an approach based upon group redesign was sought.

The study involved three phases (1) problem assessment, (2) implementation of redesign intervention and (3) short- (six months) and long-term (18 months) post-intervention follow-up. An assessment revealed low scores on three job chracteristics, namely, autonomy, task identity and feedback. The investigators also found low levels of internal work motivation and job satisfaction along with high levels of emotional distress. The intervention involved increasing group autonomy, group task identity and group feedback. The changes aimed at group autonomy were the most elaborate and involved shifting of responsibility and control from the supervisor to the work teams. Each team had control over the pace of the work, organization of rest breaks and allocation of work assignments and overtime. (Supervisors assumed support function roles with respect to daily operations.)

Significant increases were found on measures of group autonomy and work-group identity but not on group feedback at the first post-intervention period (six months). No changes were found in skill variety or task significance, which were not targets for change. The results indicated that the interventions were successful in increasing autonomy and identity but not feedback. Long term (18 months) follow-up indicated maintenance of the changes in autonomy and task identity but no additional increases beyond the six-month levels.

Emotional distress (along with all other outcome measures) was significantly reduced at both follow-up periods, the largest decrease occurring 18 months post-intervention. Though a more rigorous experimental design would have been preferred (as Wall and Clegg admit), the pattern of obtained results (intervention-specific vs generalized outcomes) and inclusion of short- and long-term follow-ups, lend credence to the authors' conclusions of the benefits of improved autonomy and task identity on employee mental health.

Work schedule autonomy (Pierce and Newstrom, 1983).

Alternative work schedules such as flextime have become common in organizations over the past 15 years. Flextime allows employees to vary (control), within prescribed limits, work arrival and departure times. In the context of the present chapter, flextime can be considered an intervention that increases employee control over one aspect of their work: scheduling. The relationship of flextime to a variety of work, nonwork, individual and organizational variables has been examined but much of this literature is anecdotal and descriptive so that the validity of obtained results and stated conclusions is questionable (see Golembiewski and Proehl, 1978; Hurrell and Colligan, 1985).

Several studies did examine mental health changes following the introduction of flexible work schedules (Barling and Barenbrug, 1984; Krausz and Freidbach, 1983; Pierce and Newstrom, 1983). Of these, only the Pierce and Newstrom study provided sufficient methodological detail and produced interpretable results (in spite of certain design flaws discussed later).

Pierce and Newstrom (1983) examined six features of flexible work schedules, namely, core minutes, band width, band length, schedule flexibility, schedule variability and supervisory approval, using data taken from organizational records. Due to the high intercorrelation among these variables (except bandwidth), composite scales were created that reflected (1) schedule flexibility and (2) discretionary time. Organizational commitment, psychological stress symptoms, absenteeism, work performance and perceived time autonomy were measured.

Zero-order correlations indicated that psychological stress symptoms correlated significantly with all schedule features except bandwidth, most highly with time autonomy, supervisory change approval, schedule variability, discretionary time. Multiple regression analyses indicated that absenteeism, performance and organizational commitment were the only variables related to the six flexible work schedule features. When perceived autonomy was added to the model, psychological stress symptoms and job satisfaction became significant ($R^2 = 0.08$ and 0.10, respectively). In this model, the percentage of variance explained by performance and absenteeism variables was similar to the model without time autonomy but the R^2 for organizational commitment increased in the latter model. Pierce and Newstrom (1983) concluded that perceived time autonomy mediated the relationship among flexible work schedules and worker attitudes and responses.

The most important deficiency of the study was its design: a single group, post-test only. As Cook and Campbell (1979) point out, this type of study design generally does not permit adequate tests of causal hypotheses. Lack of pre-intervention data and the absence of comparison groups allow for a wide range of potential threats to internal validity. Pierce and Newstrom were careful in enumerating methodological limitations of the study, consequent threats to internal and external validity, and the need for constructive replication. However, their use of multiple dependent variables (that may show differential sensitivity to the intervention) and use of an intervening variable (time autonomy) strengthened the study design and produced interpretable results.

Summary

Obviously, definitive conclusions regarding the effects of interventions that increase worker control on employee well-being cannot be made based upon the few studies reviewed here. It is axiomatic that additional research is necessary, especially studies that manipulate control directly and provide some indication that the intervention actually influenced worker control. Among the three studies reviewed here, only one (Wall and Clegg) manipulated worker control over significant aspects of the work process. The manipulation in the Jackson study produced, at best, modest increases in worker control. The autonomy engendered in the Pierce and Newstrom study was restricted to what some might consider a minor aspect of work. Nevertheless, the results suggest that freedom to determine arrival/departure times and other aspects of scheduling may be a significant intervention for improving worker control. This type of discretion has traditionally been reserved for professional and managerial positions. The acquisition of such discretion may be a more significant intervention than more traditional approaches (e.g. PDM). Certainly there should be less variability in employee preferences for flexible work hours than for PDM, the latter being preferred by some but certainly not all workers.

Though the results of the three studies reviewed here were consistent with theoretical formulations and with empirical studies reviewed earlier, there are indications that the *process* can be as important as the nature of the intervention. Lawler and Hackman's (1969) study of worker participation in the development and introduction of incentive pay plans illustrates this point. In this study, identical incentive pay plans resulted in different effects on worker attendance as a function of *how* the plans were introduced to workers. The three work groups that participated in the development of pay plans showed increased attendance in the 16 weeks after the plans were introduced relative to the 12 weeks before the plans went into effect. A year later, two of the three pay plans were discontinued. Interviews with the managers who discontinued the plans revealed that they felt little commitment to the plans and had not themselves participated in their development (Scheflen, Lawler and Hackman, 1971). The authors concluded that lasting, effective change in organizations requires involvement of individuals at all levels in the organization.

The experience in Germany with co-determination illustrates the same point. German employers are required by law to consult with workers regarding aspects of the employment relationship, such as hours of work and payment plans. Dworkin *et al.*, (1983) reported results of a survey of German workers that assessed (1) satisfaction with work and with the joint decision making process and (2) elements of the co-determination system that are deemed most important by workers. The results indicated that workers were generally satisfied with their jobs but expressed least satisfaction with their ability to influence decisions affecting their work. Apparently, though participation was mandated by law, workers felt little involvement in the representative form of participation and no commitment to the policy.

Given the varieties of stressors that have been identified in work settings (see Holt, 1982), it is apparent that interventions other than those reviewed here hold promise for reducing work stress. Examples here include changes in role relationships, (re)design of physical environment features based upon ergonomic principles, provision of child-care facilities at the workplace, pre-retirement seminars, lateral promotion schemes to supplement vertical ones, and so on.

CONCLUDING REMARKS

As an area of scientific inquiry, organizational stress reduction and prevention is in its infancy. This state of affairs contrasts with the burgeoning and increasing literature associating organizational stressors with mental and physical outcomes. Admittedly, the organizational stress/health literature has produced more 'associations' than 'effects' and studies are not without methodological flaws (e.g. Kasl, 1978). Nevertheless, the data point to work stress as a prevalent and costly organizational problem requiring research attention to strategies for its alleviation or prevention.

In this regard, actions aimed at changing the worker, as opposed to changing the work environment, are by far the most prevalent strategies. EAPs have an indirect link to worker distress via problem drinking (despite 'broad brush' claims), and their approach to the problem is tertiary. Though EAPs are increasingly prevalent in work settings, well-controlled studies are needed to determine their 'active ingredient(s)' and long-term benefits. Stress management has a more direct link with employee distress and the approach is secondary prevention (assuming, of course, that the 'problem' is work stress and not general life stress). Evaluations of stress management have become more common in recent years and have used more rigorous experimental designs than EAPs. However, these studies suffer from short-term evaluation periods and a restricted range of outcome measures. Studies evaluating actions aimed at reducing or preventing work stressors, primary prevention approaches, are quite rare in the literature but have produced consistent and provocative results.

Additional research is needed for each of the approaches reviewed in this chapter. In this regard, the use of experimental designs with random assignment of workers to intervention and (one or more) comparison groups would certainly facilitate interpretation of results. When this is not feasible, a properly designed quasi-experiment can produce interpretable results (Cook and Campbell, 1979).

It is probable that worker-oriented approaches will continue to be more prevalent in work settings relative to organizational change interventions. These approaches involve less disruption of organization structure/function, can be tailored to individual needs, and 'fit' a management view of stress as a personal, not work, problem. Worker-oriented approaches offer a limited solution to the problem of work stress and are considered by some to be 'blaming the victim'. There is a need for organizational change interventions designed to reduce or prevent stress. Researchers interested in manipulating work environment stressors to reduce employee distress often have a problem with entree into organizations, for some of the reasons listed above. One way to facilitate entree would be to design experiments around 'natural' organizational change(s) as exemplified by the Jackson (1983) study.

The costs of stress, reflected in part by worker compensation claims, and the prevalence of stress in the workplace has led more and more organizations to seek out stress reduction and prevention strategies. This interest may increase opportunities for stress intervention studies in work settings. In light of the studies reviewed in this chapter, interventions that are comprehensive and address individual worker and organizational factors hold the greatest promise for effective reduction and prevention of stress at work.

REFERENCES

Abramson, L. Y., Seligman, M. E. P. and Teasdale, J. D. (1978). Learned helplessness in humans: critique and reform, *Journal of Abnormal Psychology*, **87**, 49–74.

Alderman, M. and Techlenburg, K. (1983). Effect of relaxation training on personal adjustment and perceptions of organizational climate, *Journal of Psychology*, **115**, 185–91.

Asma, R. E., Eggert, R. L. and Hilker, R. R. J. (1971). Long-term experience with rehabilitation of alcoholic employees, *Journal of Occupational Medicine*, **13**, 581–5.

Asma, R. E., Hilker, R. R. J., Shevlin, J. J. and Golden, R. G. (1980). 'Twenty-five years of rehabilitation of employees with drinking problems, *Journal of Occupational Medicine*, **22**, 214–44.

Averill, J. R. (1973). Personal control over aversive stimuli and its relationship to stress, *Psychological Bulletin*, **80**, 286–303.

Bandura, A. (1969). *Principles of Behavior Modification*, Holt, Rinehart and Winston, New York.

Barling, J. and Barenburg, A. (1984). Some personal consequences of 'flextime' work schedules, *Journal of Social Psychology*, **123**, 137–8.

Barra, R. J. (1983). *Putting Quality Circles to Work*, McGraw-Hill, New York.

Beehr, T. A. and O'Hara, K. (1987). Methodological designs for the evaluation of occupational stress interventions. C. L. Cooper and S. V. Kasl. In *Stress and Health: Issues in Research Methodology*, John Wiley and Sons, Chichester.

Beyer, J. M. and Trice, H. M. (1982). Design and implementation of job based alcoholism programs: constructive confrontation strategies and how they work. In *Occupational Alcoholism: A Review of Research Issues*, DHHS (ADM) Publication No. 82–1184, US Government Printing Office, Washington, DC.

Blum, T. C. and Roman, P. M. (1986) Alcohol, drugs and EAPs: new data from a national study, *The Almacan*, May 1986, 20–3.

Breaugh, J. A. (1985). The measurement of work autonomy, *Human Relations*, **38**, 551–70.

Bruning, N. S. and Frew, D. R. (1985). The impact of various stress management training strategies: a longitudinal experiment, In R. B. Robinson and J. A. Pearce. (eds) *Academy of Management Proceedings*, Academy of Management, San Diego, California.

Bullock, R. J. and Lawler, E. E. (1984). Gainsharing: a few research questions and fewer answers, *Human Resource Management*, **23**, 23–40.

Cannon, W. B. (1929). *Bodily Changes in Pain, Hunger, Fear, and Rage*, C. T. Branford, Boston, MA.

Caplan, R. D., Cobb, S., French, J. R. P., Jr, Harrison, R. V. and Pinneau, S. R. (1975). *Job Demands and Worker Health*, DHHS (NIOSH) Publication No. 75–160, US Government Printing Office, Washington, DC.

Charlesworth, E. A., Williams, B. J., and Baer, P. E. (1984). Stress management at the worksite for hypertension: compliance, cost-benefit, health care, and hypertension-related variables, *Psychosomatic Medicine*, **46**, 387–97.

Colligan, M. J. and Murphy, L. R. (1979). 'Mass psychogenic illness in organizations: an overview, *Journal of Occupational Psychology*, **52**, 77–90.

Conger, J. J. (1956). Alcoholism: theory problem, and challenge—II. Reinforcement theory and the dynamics of alcoholism, *Quarterly Journal of Studies on Alcoholism*, **17**, 296–305.

Cook, T. D. and Campbell, D. T. (1979). *Quasi-experimentation: Design and Analysis Issues for Field Settings*, Rand-McNally, Chicago.

Cowan, J. D. (1983). Testing the escape hypotheses: alcohol helps users to forget their feelings, *Journal of Nervous and Mental Disease*, **171**, 40–8.

Cox, T. (1985). Repetitive work: occupational stress and health, In C. Cooper and M. J. Smith, (eds) *Blue Collar Stress*, John Wiley and Sons, Chichester.

D'Alonzo, C. A. and Pell, S. (1968). Cardiovascular disease among problem drinkers, *Journal of Occupational Medicine*, **10**, 344–50.

DeFrank, R. S. and Cooper, C. L. (1987). Worksite stress management interventions: their effectiveness and conceptualization, *Journal of Managerial Psychology*, **2**, 4–10.

Department of Health and Human Services. (1979). *Healthy People: The Surgeon General's Report on Health Promotion and Disease Prevention*, DHHS (PHS) Publication No. 79–55071, US Government Printing Office, Washington, DC.

Department of Health and Human Services (1980a). *Fourth Special Report to Congress on Alcohol and Health*, Washington, DC, Public Health Service, National Institute on Alcohol Abuse and Alcoholism.

Department of Health and Human Services. (1980b) *Promoting Health/Preventing Disease: Objectives for the Nation*, US Government Printing Office, Washington, DC.

Department of Health and Human Services (1985). Surveillance and assessment of alcohol-related mortality—United States, 1980, *Morbidity and Mortality Weekly Report*, **34**, 161–163.

Department of Health and Human Services. (1986). *The 1990 Objectives for the Nation: A Midcourse Review*, US Government Printing Office, Washington, DC.

Dickson, W. J. (1945). The Hawthorne plan of personnel counseling, *American Journal of Orthopsychiatry*, **15**, 343–7.

Dworkin, J. B., Hobson, C. J., Frieling, E. F. and Oakes, D. M. (1983). How

German workers view their jobs, *Columbia Journal of World Business*, Summer 1983, 48–54.

Eggum, P. E., Keller, P. J. and Burton, W. N. (1980). Nurse/health counseling model for a successful alcoholism assistance program, *Journal of Occupational Medicine*, **22**, 545–48.

Ellis, A. (1978). What people can do for themselves to cope with stress. In C. L. Cooper and R. Payne (eds), *Stress at Work*, John Wiley and Sons, Chichester.

Emery, F. E. and Trist, E. L. (1969). Sociotechnical systems, in F. E. Emery (ed.) *Systems Thinking*, Penguin, Harmondsworth.

Fielding, J. E. and Breslow, L. (1983). Health promotion programs sponsored by California employers, *American Journal of Public Health*, **73**, 538–42.

Fisher (1984). *Stress and the Perception of Control*. Lawrence Erlbaum, Hillsdale, NJ.

Folkman, S. and Lazarus, R. S. (1980). An analysis of coping in a middle-aged community sample, *Journal of Health and Social Behavior*, **21**, 219–39.

Foote, A., Erfurt, J., Strauch, P. and Guzzardo, T. (1978). *Cost Effectiveness of Occupations EAPs — Test of an Evaluation Method*, Worker Health Program, Institute of Labor and Industrial Relations, University of Michigan-Wayne State University, Ann Arbor, MI.

Forman, S. G. (1981). Stress-management training: evaluation of effects on school psychological services, *Journal of School Psychology*, **19**, 233–41.

Franco, S. C. (1960). A company program for problem drinking, *Journal of Occupational Medicine*, **2**, 157–62.

Frankenhauser, M. and Gardell, B. (1976). 'Underload and overload in working life: outline of a multidisciplinary approach, *Journal of Human Stress*, **2**, 35–46.

Freedberg, E. J. and Johnston, W. E. (1981). The effectiveness of confrontation procedures before and after treatment of employed alcoholics, *Journal of Occupational Medicine*, **23**, 193–7.

Frew, D. R. (1974). Transcendental meditation and productivity, *Academy of Management Journal*, **17**, 362–8.

Ganster, D. J. (1985). Exploring the role of control in occupational stress, *Paper presented at NIOSH Workshop on Occupational Stress Management*, New Orleans, L. A.

Ganster, D. C., Mayes, B. T., Sime, W. E. and Tharp, G. D. (1982). Managing occupational stress: a field experiment, *Journal of Applied Psychology*, **67**, 533–42.

Glass, D. C. and Singer, J. E. (1972). *Urban Stress: Experiments on Noise and Social Stressors*, Academic Press, New York.

Glass, D. C., Reim, B., and Singer, J. R. (1971). Behavioral consequences of adaptation to controllable and uncontrollable noise, *Journal of Experimental Social Psychology*, **7**, 244–257

Golembiewski, R. T. and Proehl, C. W. (1978). A survey of the empirical literature on flexible work hours: character and consequences of a major innovation, *Academy of Management Review*, **3**, 837–53.

Gray-Toft, P. (1980). Effectiveness of a counseling support program for hospice nurses, *Journal of Counseling Psychology*, **27**, 346–54.

Guest, J. (1981). An active employee assistance program, in R. M. Schwartz (ed.). *New Developments in Occupational Stress*. DHHS (NIOSH) Publication No. 81–102, US Government Printing Office, Washington, DC.

Hackman, J. R. and Lawler, E. E. (1971). Employee reactions to job characteristics, *Journal of Applied Psychology Monograph*, **55**, 259–86.

Hackman, J. R. and Oldham, G. R. (1976). Motivation through the design of work: test of a theory, *Organizational Behavior and Human Performance*, **16**, 250–79.

Hanson, J. D., Larson, M. E., and Snowdon, C. T. (1976). The effects of control over high intensity noise on plasma cortisol levels in rhesus monkeys, *Behavioral Biology*, **16**, 333.

Harburg, E., Ozgoren, F., Hawthorne, V. M., and Schork, M. A. (1980). Community norms of alcohol usage and blood pressure: Tecumseh, *American Journal of Public Health*, **70**, 813–20.

Harrison, R. V. (1978). Person–environment fit and job stress. In C. Cooper and M. J. Smith (eds) *Blue Collar Stress*, John Wiley and Sons, Chichester.

Holt, R. R. (1982). Occupational Stress. In L. Goldberger and S. Breznitz (eds), *Handbook of Stress*, Free Press, New York.

Hull, J. G. (1981). A self-awareness model of the causes and effects of alcohol consumption, *Journal of Abnormal Psychology*, **90**, 586–590.

Hurrell, J. J., Jr and Colligan, M. J. (1978). Alternative work schedules: flextime and the compressed work week, In C. Cooper and M. J. Smith (eds) *Blue Collar Stress*. John Wiley and Sons, Chichester.

Jackson, S. E. (1983). Participation in decision making as a strategy for reducing job-related strain, *Journal of Applied Psychology*, **68**, 3–19.

Kannel, W. B. and Sorlie, P. (1974). Hypertension in Framingham, In *Epidemiology and Control of Hypertension*, Stratton International Medical Book Corporation, New York.

Karasek, R. A. (1979). Job demands, job decision latitude, and mental strain: implications for job redesign, *Administrative Science Quarterly*, **24**, 285–308.

Karasek, R. A., Schwartz, A. J. and Theorell, T. (1982). Job characteristics, occupation, and coronary heart disease, Final Report on Grant No. RO1-OH-00906, National Institute for Occupational Safety and Health, Cincinnati, OH.

Karasek, R. A., Baker, D., Marxer, F., Ahlbom, A. and Theorell, T. (1981). Job decision latitude, job demands, and cardiovascular disease: a prospective study of Swedish men, *American Journal of Public Health*, **71**, 694–705.

Kasl, S. V. (1978). Epidemiology contributions to the study of work stress. In C. L. Cooper and R. Payne (eds), *Stress at Work*, John Wiley and Sons, Chichester.

Kazdin, A. E. and Wilcoxin, L. A. (1976). Systematic desensitization and non-specific treatment effects: a methodological evaluation, *Psychological Bulletin*, **83**, 729–56.

Kornhauser, A. W. (1965). *Mental Health of the Industrial Worker*, John Wiley and Sons, New York.

Krausz, M. and Frieback, M. A. (1983). Effects of flexible working time for employed women upon satisfaction, strains, and absenteeism, *Journal of Occupational Psychology*, **56**, 155–9.

Kurtz, N. R., Googins, B. and Howard, W. C. (1984). Measuring the success of occupational alcoholism programs, *Journal of Studies on Alcohol*, **45**, 33–45.

Lawler, E. E. and Hackman, J. R. (1969). Impact of employee participation in the development of pay incentive plans: a field experiment, *Journal of Applied Psychology*, **53**, 467–71.

Lazarus, R. S. (1966). *Psychological Stress and the Coping Process*, McGraw-Hill, New York.

Levinson, H. (1956). Employee counseling in industry: observations on three programs, *Bulletin of the Menninger Clinic*, **20**, 76–84.

Levinson, H. (1961). Industrial mental health: progress and prospects, *Menninger Quarterly*, Winter 1961.

Locke, E. A. and Schweiger, D. M. (1979). Participation in decision making: one more look. In B. Staw (ed.) *Research in Organizational Behavior*, Vol. 1, JAI Press, Greenwich, CT.

McLean, A. A. (1973). Occupational mental health: review of an emerging art, In R. L. Noland (ed.) *Industrial Mental Health and Employee Counseling*, Behavioral Publications, New York.

MacLeod, A. G. S. (1985). EAPs and blue collar stress, In C. Cooper and M. J. Smith (eds) *Blue Collar Stress*, John Wiley and Sons, Chichester.

McLeroy, K. R., Green, L. W., Mullen, K. D., and Foshee, V. (1984). Assessing the effects of health promotion in worksites: a review of the stress program evaluations, *Health Education Quarterly*, **11**, 379–401.

McNulty, S., Jeffrys, D., Singer, G., and Singer, L. (1984). Use of hormone analysis in the assessment of the efficacy of stress management training in police recruits, *Journal of Police Science and Administration*, **12**, 130–2.

Manuso, J. S. J. (1983). The Equitable Life Assurance Society programme, *Preventive Medicine*, **12**, 658–662.

Margolis, B. L., Kroes, W. H. and Quinn, R. P. (1974). Job stress: an unlisted occupational hazard, *Journal of Occupational Medicine*, **16**, 659–61.

Maxell, M. A. (1959). A study of absenteeism, accidents, and sickness payments in problem drinkers in one industry, *Quarterly Journal of Studies on Alcohol*, **19**, 24–32.

Meichenbaum, D. (1977). *Cognitive-Behavior Modification*, Plenum Press, New York.

Menninger, W. C. and Levinson, H. (1954). The Menninger foundation survey of industrial mental health, *Menninger Quarterly*, **8**, 1–13.

Miller, S. M. (1979). Controllability and human stress: method, evidence, and theory, *Behavior Research and Therapy*, **17**, 287–304.

Murphy L. R. (1983). A comparison of relaxation methods for reducing stress in nursing personnel, *Human Factors*, **25**, 431–40.

Murphy, L. R. (1984a). Occupational stress management: a review and appraisal, *Journal of Occupational Psychology*, **57**, 1–15.

Murphy, L. R. (1984b). Stress management in highway maintenance workers, *Journal of Occupational Medicine*, **26**, 436–42.

Murphy, L. R. and Hurrell, J. J. (1987). Stress management in the process of organizational stress reduction, *Journal of Managerial Psychology*, **2**, 18–23.

Murphy, L. R. and Sorenson, S. (in press). Employee behaviors before and after stress management training, *Journal of Occupational Behavior*.

National Council on Compensation Insurance (1985). *Emotional Stress in the Workplace: New Legal Rights in the Eighties*, National Council on Compensation Insurance, New York.

Neale, M. S., Singer, J., Schwartz, G. E. and Schwartz, J. (1982). Conflicting perspectives on stress reduction in occupational settings: a systems approach to their resolution, Report to NIOSH on P.O. No. 82–1058, Cincinnati, OH.

Office of Disease Prevention and Health Promotion (in press). *National Survey of Worksite Health Promotion Activities*, US Government Printing Office, Washington, DC.

Orme-Johnson, D. W., and Farrow, J. T. (1977). *Scientific Research on the Transcendental Meditation Program*, Collected Papers, Vol. 1, MIU Press, Livingston Manor, New York.

O'Toole, J. (1974). Work in America and the great job satisfaction controversy, *Journal of Occupational Medicine*, **16**, 710–15.

Patel, C. H. (1977). Biofeedback-aided relaxation and meditation in the management of hypertension, *Biofeedback and Self-Regulation*, **2**, 1–41.

Pearlin, L. and Radabaugh, C. (1976). Economic strain and the coping function of alcohol, *American Journal of Sociology*, **82**, 652–63.

Pell, S. and D'Alonzo, C. A. (1968). The prevalence of chronic disease among problem drinkers, *Archives of Environmental Health*, **16**, 679–84.

Pell, S. and D'Alonzo, C. A. (1970). 'Sickness absenteeism of alcoholics', *Journal of Occupational Medicine*, **12**, 198–210.

Pell, S. and D'Alonzo, C. A. (1973). A five-year mortality study of alcoholics, *Journal of Occupational Medicine*, **15**, 120–5.

Peters, R. K. (1981). Daily relaxation response breaks: follow-up of a work-based stress management program, National Technical Information Service, No. PB 83–175364, Springfield, VA.

Peters, R. K., Benson, H. and Porter, D. (1977a). Daily relaxation response breaks in a working population—I. Effects on self-reported measures of health, performance, and well-being, *American Journal of Public Health*, **67**, 946–53.

Peters, R. K., Benson, H. and Peters, J. M. (1977b). Daily relaxation response breaks in a working population—II. Effects on blood pressure, *American Journal of Public Health*, **67**, 954–9.

Pierce, J. L. and Newstrom, J. W. (1983). The design of flexible work schedules and employee responses: relationships and processes, *Journal of Occupational Behavior*, **4**, 247–62.

Pomerleau, D. F. and Brady, J. P. (1979). *Behavioral Medicine. Theory and Practice*, Williams and Wilkins, Baltimore., MD

Presnall, L. F. (1967). Folklore and facts about employees with alcoholism, *Journal of Occupational Medicine*, **9**, 187–92.

Riley, A. W., Frederickson, L. W., and Winett, R. A. (1984). Stress management in work settings: a time for caution in organizational health promotion. Report to NIOSH on P.O. No. 84–1320, Cincinnati, OH.

Roman, P. M. and Thomas, L. A. (1978). Structure and outcome in occupational programs; exploratory and comparative observations, *Labor Movement Journal on Alcoholism*, **8**, 42–52.

Rosch, P. and Pelletier, K. (1987). Designing workplace stress management programs, In L. R. Murphy and T. F. Schoenborn (eds) *Stress Management in Work Settings*, DHSS (NIOSH) Publication No. 87–111, US Government Printing Office, Washington, DC.

Salvendy, G. and Smith, M. J. (1981). *Machine Pacing and Occupational Stress*, Taylor and Francis, London.

Savide, E., Grosslight, G. M. and Adena, M. A. (1984). Relation of alcohol and cigarette consumption to blood pressure and serum creatinine levels, *Journal of Chronic Disease*, **37**, 617–23.

Scheflin, K. C., Lawler, E. E. and Hackman, J. R. (1971). Long-term impact of employee participation in the development of pay incentive plans: a field experiment revisited, *Journal of Applied Psychology*, **55**, 182–6.

Schramm, C. J. (1977). Measuring return on program costs: evaluation of a multi-employer alcoholism treatment program, *American Journal of Public Health*, **67**, 50–1.

Schwartz, G. (1980). Stress management in occupational settings, *Public Health Reports*, **95**, 99–108.

Seamonds, B. C. (1982). Stress factors and their effects on absenteeism in a corporate employee group, *Journal of Occupational Medicine*, **24**, 393–7.

Seamonds, B. C. (1983). Extension of research into stress factors and their effect on illness absenteeism, *Journal of Occupational Medicine*, **25**, 821–2.

Seligman, M. E. P. (1975). *Helplessness: On Depression, Development, and Death*, Freeman, San Francisco.

Selye, H. (1936). A syndrome produced by diverse noxious agents, *Nature*, **138**, 32.

Selye, H. (1956). *The Stress of Life*, McGraw-Hill, New York.

Shilling, S. and Brackbill, R. M. (1987). Occupational health and safety risks and potential health consequences perceived by U.S. workers, *Public Health Reports*, **102**, 36–46.

Silverman, M. M., Eichler, A. and Williams, G. D. (1987). Self-reported stress: findings from the 1985 National Health Interview Survey, *Public Health Reports*, **102**, 47–53.

Sommerville, A. W., Allen, A. R., Noble, B. A. and Sedgwick, D. L. (1984). Effects of a stress management class: one year later, *Teaching of Psychology*, **11**, 82–5.

Spector, P. E. (1986). Perceived control by employees: a meta-analysis of studies concerning autonomy and participation at work, *Human Relations*, **39**, 1005–16.

Steinmetz, J. I., Kaplan, R. M. and Miller, G. L. (1982). Stress management: an assessment questionnaire for evaluating interventions and comparing groups. *Journal of Occupational Medicine*, **24**, 923–31.

Stroebel, C. (1969). Biologic rhythm correlates of disturbed behavior in the monkey, *Bibliography Primatology*, **9**, 91–105.

Tarler-Benlo, L. (1978). The role of relaxation in biofeedback training: a critical review of the literature, *Psychological Bulletin*, **85**, 727–55.

Tasto, D., Coligan, M. J., Skjei, E. W., and Polly, S. J. (1978). *Health Consequences of Shiftwork*, DHHS (NIOSH) Publication No. 78–154, US Government Printing Office, Washington, DC.

Thompson, S. C. (1981). Will it hurt less if I can control it? A complex answer to a simple question, *Psychological Bulletin*, **90**, 89–101.

Thorpe, J. J. and Perret, J. T. (1959). Problem-drinking: a follow-up study, *American Medical Association Archives of Industrial Health*, **19**, 24–32.

Trice, H. M. (1965). Alcoholic employees—A comparison of psychotic, neurotic, and 'normal' personnel, *Journal of Occupational Medicine*, **7**, 94–9.

Trice, H. M. and Beyer, J. M. (1984). Work related outcomes of the constructive-confrontation strategy in a job based alcoholism program, *Journal of Studies on Alcoholism*, **45**, 393–404.

Trice, H. M. and Roman, P. (1972). *Spirits and Demons at Work: Alcohol and Other Drugs on the Job*, Cornell University, Ithaca, NY.

Trice, H. M., Hunt, R. E., and Beyer, J. M. (1977). Alcoholism programs in unionized settings: problems and prospects in union–management cooperation, *Journal of Drug Issues*, **7**, 103–15.

Vetter, C. (1981). Alcohol and drug misuse, In J. Marshall and C. Cooper (eds) *Coping With Stress at Work*, Gower, Aldershot.

Violanti, J., Marshall, J. and Howe, B. (1983). Police occupational demands, psychological distress, and the coping function of alcohol, *Journal of Occupational Medicine*, **25**, 455–8.

Walker, C. R. and Guest, R. H. (1952). *The Man on the Assembly Line*, Harvard University Press, Cambridge, Mass.

Wall, T. D. and Clegg, C. W. (1981). A longitudinal study of group work redesign, *Journal of Occupational Behavior*, **2**, 31–49.

Walsh, D. C. (1982). Employee assistance programs, *Millbank Memorial Quarterly*, **60**, 492–517.

Walsh, D. C. and Hingson, R. W. (1985). Where to refer employees for treatment of drinking problems, *Journal of Occupational Medicine*, **27**, 745–52.

Weiss, J. M. (1971). Effects of coping behavior in different warning signal conditions on stress pathology in rats, *Journal of Comparative and Physiological Psychology*, **77**, 1–13.

West, D. J., Horan, J. J., and Games, P. A. (1984). Component analysis of occupational stress inoculation applied to registered nurses in an acute care hospital setting, *Journal of Counseling Psychology*, **31**, 209–18.

Williams, T. A., Calhoun, G. and Ackoff, R. L. (1982). Stress, alcoholism, and personality, *Human Relations*, **6**, 491–510.

Winslow, W. W., Hayes, K., Prentice, L., Powles, W. E., Seeman, W. and Ross, D. (1966). Some economic estimates of job disruption, *Archives of Environmental Health*, **13**, 213–19.

Wrich, J. (1984). *The Employee Assistance Program*, Hazelden Educational Foundation, Minnesota.

Wyatt, S. and Marriott, R. (1951). A study of some attitudes to factory work, *Occupational Psychology*, **March**, 181–191.

PART V

Issues in Research on Stress at work

Causes, Coping and Consequences of Stress at Work
Edited by C. L. Cooper and R. Payne
© 1988 John Wiley & Sons Ltd

Chapter 11

The Future of Physiological Assessments in Work Situations

*Yitzhak Fried**

In recent years there has been a noticeable growth in studies examining the effect of stress in work situations on a variety of physiological criteria. It appears, however, that while more and more scholars recognize the potential advantages of using physiological indicators as criteria for work stress, not much recognition has been given in the literature to serious problems regarding the measurement of physiological variables and their effect on studies' results. The present chapter discusses these problems and provides recommendations where research may develop in the future.

Few subjects in organizational behavior research have attracted as much attention as the study of stress at work (see e.g. Beehr and Schuler, 1982; Fried, Rowland and Ferris, 1984). Research in the area of work stress has typically focused on common causes of stress in the work environment and their effect on personal and organizational outcomes (e.g. Beehr and Newman, 1978; Cooper and Marshall, 1976). More specifically, studies have traditionally examined the impact of work stressors on three major response categories: psychological, behavioral and physiological (Beehr and Newman, 1978; Schuler, 1980). In particular, researchers have focused on the first two categories of response; considering variables such as job dissatisfaction, absenteeism and turnover as symptoms of stress (Fried *et al.*, 1984).

In recent years, however, more and more scholars have employed physiological measures in studies of work stress (Fried *et al.*, 1984). The growing interest concerning physiological reactions to work stress seems to be based on several factors. First, there is empirical evidence to suggest a potential relationship between stressful events and physiological variables (see e.g. Levine, 1986). Second, many researchers have appeared to adopt the concept that physiological reactions are less likely to be affected by uncontrolled personal or contextual factors compared to self-report or behavioral criteria (Fried *et al.*, 1984). Third, some evidence suggests that physiological indi-

* The author would like to thank Robert Tiegs and Blake Ashforth for their helpful comments on earlier drafts of this manuscript and Dawn Havard for her diligent clerical work.

cators might detect a situation of stress among individuals who are not consciously aware of it because of the operation of defensive mechanisms (e.g. Eden, 1982; Gale and Edwards, 1986).

It appears, however, that the continual growth of research on the relationship between work stress and physiological reactions has not been fully recognized by scholars in the field of organizational behavior, possibly because much of this research has been published in journals not typically read by organizational scientists (for more on this issue, see Beehr and Newman, 1978; Cox, 1987). Moreover, while the potential advantages of physiological measures in the area of stress have been discussed, not much recognition has been given to serious difficulties regarding the measurement of physiological variables and their effects on studies' results (Fried *et al.*, 1984). It follows, then, that in the area of work stress research there is a great need for critical analysis concerning the assessment of physiological variables.

The purpose of this chapter is, therefore, to discuss the difficulties of studies exploring the relationship between work stress and physiological reactions and to indicate where research may develop in the future. Specifically, the paper consists of two major parts. The first part analyzes the potential problems concerning the measurement of physiological variables commonly used in work stress research. This analysis is followed by a review of the extent to which work stress studies have actually considered these measurement problems. The second part discusses several approaches that could be adopted by researchers in the future to reduce difficulties and problems associated with physiological assessment in work stress studies.

Note that although much of what is to be discussed appears to be relevant to data obtained both in clinics and work situations, the primary emphasis here is on the latter. This emphasis is consistent with a continual growth in work stress studies employing physiological measures in work situations (see e.g. Astrand *et al.*, 1973; Barnard and Duncan, 1975; Caplan *et al.*, 1975; Caplan, Cobb and French, 1979; Dutton *et al.*, 1978; Ganster *et al.*, 1982; Jenner, Reynolds and Harrison, 1980; Johnasson and Aronsson, 1984; Kaufman and Beehr, 1986; Korhonen and Kuorinka, 1981). Collecting data in work situations enhances the researcher's capacity to detect physiological changes under specific stressors occurring during work time. Moreover, employing physiological measures at work enables researchers to collect data from many subjects in a relatively short period of time. However, the process of data collection at work is associated with great difficulties, many of which are unanalyzed in the literature. Such difficulties are, for example, work interruptions (which often result in organizational resistance to measurement) time pressure and inadequate facilities to collect the data (e.g. small and non-private toilet facilities for collecting urine samples; see, e.g. Christie and Woodman, 1980). It follows then that in the future researchers should place greater emphasis on developing methods to minimize the difficulties associated with physiological measurement in work situations.

PHYSIOLOGICAL INDICATORS OF WORK STRESS AND MEASUREMENT PROBLEMS

Typology of Measurement Problems

The literature has focused on several methodological problems concerning the measurement of stress as well as the measurement of psychological and behavioral criteria of stress (see, e.g. Beehr and Newman, 1978; Fried *et al.*, 1984; McGrath, 1982). However, much less attention has been given in the literature to the potential methodological problems concerning physiological measurement (Fried *et al.*, 1984). Specifically, it appears that stress research has tended to neglect the potentially threatening or confounding factors that might affect the level of a given physiological variable. This tendency might be a central cause of the weak, inconsistent results reported by studies on the relationship between work stressors and physiological symptoms (Fried *et al.*, 1984; Kasl, 1978).

Work stress studies have focused on a variety of physiological indicators.* The most commonly used indicators include:

(1) Cardiovascular indicators (most popular), particularly of heart rate and blood pressure;
(2) Biochemical indicators, such as levels of uric acid, blood sugar, steroid hormones (especially cortisol), and, most of all, cholesterol and catecholamines (especially adrenalin and noradrenaline);
(3) Gastrointestinal indicators, primarily peptic ulcer.

The literature appears to suggest three major categories of factors, independent of work stress, that if not considered or controlled might adversely

---

* Studies in the area of work stress have previously explored the relative changes in physiological indicators under different levels of stress. The issue of whether work stressors actually lead to abnormal physiological symptoms has been largely neglected. Although research on the association between stress and abnormal levels of physiological variables, can certainly provide useful information, it is difficult to conduct because of the problem of identifying the exact line that differentiates between normal and abnormal levels of a given physiological symptom. Any attempt to do so in a simplistic way might be misleading. For example, what is considered high blood pressure is dependent, in part, on such individual differences as age and health. Moreover, focusing on *absolute* levels of physiological symptoms in work stress research might bias studies' results and conclusions because stress might have a *relative* effect on these symptoms. For example, subjects of a particular study might all be classified as having normal blood pressure, but still show differences in blood pressure contingent upon the level of stress they experience at work. However, it is hoped that future studies will elaborate upon our current knowledge regarding the association between stress at work and abnormal physiological symptoms.

affect the validity of physiological stress measurement (Fried *et al.*, 1984). These three categories are as follows:

Stable or permanent factors: refers to factors which represent differences among individuals and groups in their *susceptibility* to certain physiological symptoms. Examples of such factors are familial (i.e. genetic) tendency, race, sex and diet or habitual nutrition.

Transitory factors: refers to factors which are time and situation-specific such as time of the day, room temperature, postural position, or consumption of caffeine or nicotine before or during the time of measurement.

Procedural factors: unlike the above two sets of factors which focus on the external or contextual factors (to measurement) that might affect the recorded level of physiological variables, the emphasis here is on problems associated with measurement procedures such as the number of times measurements are taken or the duration of time between measurements.

In the following sections these factors are discussed with regard to the measurement of commonly-used physiological variables: (1) blood pressure and cardiac activity (heart rate and EKG),* (2) cholesterol in the blood, (3) urinary catecholamines and (4) peptic ulcer. (For a more detailed discussion see Fried *et al.*, 1984). It should be noted that although cholesterol and catecholamines can be collected from other systems in the body, studies on work stress and physiological indicators have generally collected cholesterol from the blood and catecholamines from the urine (Fried *et al.*, 1984). Thus, the analysis and critique in this paper will be restricted to blood cholesterol and urinary catecholamines.

Stable or Permanent Factors

Familial tendency

Studies have shown that familial (genetic) tendencies tend to affect blood pressure and cardiac activity as well as cholesterol and peptic ulcer (see, e.g. Chapman, 1978; Christian and Kang, 1977; Hennekens *et al.*, 1980; Light, 1981; Wolf *et al.*, 1979; Zinner, Levy and Kass, 1971). For example, research has indicated that cholesterol levels in children are positively correlated with those of their parents and siblings (e.g. Christian and Kang, 1977; Hennekens *et al.*, 1980). Some of these studies have shown that familial tendencies explain about half of the variance in plasma cholesterol (see Fried *et al.*, 1984). Research has further indicated that peptic ulcer tends to occur more than twice as frequently among the siblings of patients with an ulcer compared with the general population, and that those subjects with blood group O are approximately 40% more likely to develop a duodenal ulcer

---

* Since the literature suggests that blood pressure and cardiac activity are generally highly correlated (e.g. Steptoe, 1980), they are discussed together.

(which is a specific type of peptic ulcer) than are people of other blood groups (see, e.g. Chapman, 1978; Wolf *et al.*, 1979).

Demographics

After reviewing the literature, Siddle and Turpin (1980) concluded that sex, race and age appear to affect blood pressure and cardiac activity. The effect of age on blood pressure, however, is more pronounced in industrial societies. There is also some evidence indicating that sex might be related to cholesterol and catecholamines (see e.g. Frankenhaeuser, 1975a; Sabine, 1977). For example, males tend to have higher concentrations of cholesterol than females, although after 50 years of age this trend may be reversed (see Sabine, 1977).

Health disorders

It appears that heart disease in particular may significantly alter blood pressure and cardiac activity (Jennings *et al.*, 1981). There are also large numbers of inheritable disorders of lipid metabolism in humans that can influence the level of cholesterol (e.g. cholesterol ester shortage disease and tangier disease). In addition, there are non-inheritable diseases, such as liver disorders, that affect the level of blood cholesterol (Sabine, 1977).

Diet

There appears to be clear evidence that the quantity and the quality of fatty acids in the diet can highly influence men's level of circulation cholesterol (Sabine, 1977). Regarding peptic ulcer, there is some evidence that the consumption of caffeine and nicotine over long periods of time increases the incidence of duodenal ulcer (see Chapman, 1978; Wolf *et al.*, 1979).

Transitory Factors

There is suggestive evidence that such factors as temperature, humidity, postural change, time, exercise before or during measurement and consumption of caffeine, nicotine and alcohol before or during measurement influence the level of cardiovascular measures, serum cholesterol and catecholamines (see Christie and Woodman, 1980; Dimsdale and Moss, 1980a,b; Frankenhauser, 1975b, Jennings *et al.*, 1981; Sabine, 1977; Siddle and Turpin, 1980; Statland, Bokelund and Winkel, 1974). To illustrate, studies have shown that change in room temperature from one period of time to another (e.g. from one day to the next) can affect the measurement results of the cardiovascular system (e.g. Siddle and Turpin, 1980). Similarly, the time of day when a urine sample is taken has been demonstrated to affect the level of catecholamines obtained (Christie and Woodman, 1980). For example, it was shown that night urine values of noradrenaline were reduced by 50% while adrenalin concentrations were reduced by 10%. Furthermore, the level of cardio-vascular activity, blood cholesterol and urinary catecholamines tends to be higher if subjects smoke before or during measurement as well as if subjects are standing rather than sitting (e.g. Sabine, 1977; Statland *et al.*, 1974). Similarly, physical exertion and consumption of caffeine prior to or during measurement also appears to affect the recorded level of cardiovascular variables and urinary catecholamines. Further, venous occlusion, even for a short time period, can significantly increase the measured level of blood cholesterol. Blood cholesterol appears also to be higher in the second sample than the first sample, if both samples are taken through the same venipuncture. Finally, research has indicated that the lowest levels of cholesterol occur in the autumn or winter, while the highest levels occur in the spring or summer (Sabine, 1977).

The above review clearly indicates that unless the factors of the two categories (i.e. stable or permanent factors and transitory factors) are controlled or taken into account they are likely to add error variance to the physiological variables explored. This, in turn, might obscure the results and conclusions concerning the effect of work stress on physiological reactions.

Procedural Factors

Research has indicated that there is a natural variation in the cardiovascular system (e.g. Rosner and Polk, 1979, 1981; Stern, Ray and Davis, 1980). Specifically, a normal person's blood pressure can vary as much as 30 mm Hg during a one-minute recording (Tursky, 1974). This inherent variability suggests that a single assessment of blood pressure is not sufficiently reliable for conclusions on the level of an individual's blood pressure. Evidence has further indicated that numerous hormones in the blood such as catechol-amines and cortisol fluctuate so rapidly that the results supplied by a single sample or samples taken at intervals of several hours can be highly variable, depending upon the point(s) in the secretion–action–cataclysm sequence the people were in when examined (see Christie and Woodman, 1980). Because of this inherent variability, a single sample of blood or numerous samples taken at large intervals might lead to invalid conclusions regarding the level of catecholamines or cortisol drawn from blood.

Finally, the literature has identified two major problems concerning the study of peptic ulcer. First, there appears to be a lack of commonly accepted definitions of peptic ulcer. Specifically, peptic ulcer is not a single disease but rather a heterogeneous group of diseases of diverse etiology and pathogenesis (Wolf *et al.*, 1979). For example, a gastric ulcer is not identical to a duodenal ulcer, which implies that these two types of ulcers should be treated separately in research. Moreover, there appears to be some vagueness as to which criteria to consider in identifying an ulcer disorder: patient symptoms, doctor diagnosis, radiologic evidence or surgical evidence (Wolf *et al.*, 1979). Each of these definitions might lead to a different conclusion concerning the existence of peptic ulcer. For example, relying only on patient symptoms as a diagnostic criterion would tend to overstate the existence of the illness. On the other hand, relying only on surgery would seriously underestimate its existence (Wolf *et al.*, 1979).

Table 1 summarizes to what extent studies of work stress and physiological indicators have considered the potential effect of the various confounding factors.*

Table 1 clearly indicates that studies have generally failed to systematically control for or take into account confounding factors. It can be seen, for example, that out of the 37 studies reviewed on cardiovascular variables none has considered the effect of humidity, two studies have considered the effect of alcohol consumption (i.e. Howard, Cunningham and Rechnitzer, 1986; Ivancevich, Matteson and Preston, 1982) and four studies have attempted to control for the consumption of caffeine and nicotine (i.e. Caplan *et al.*, 1975; Howard *et al.*, 1986; Ivancevich *et al.*, 1982; Johannson and Aronsson, 1984). In addition, relatively few studies have considered the effect of familial tendency (four studies), health conditions (eight) or postural position (eight) on cardiovascular measures. Regarding postural position, two studies (i.e. Orth-Gomer and Ahlbom, 1980; Rose, Jenkins and Hurst, 1978) have averaged the readings of blood pressure which were taken while subjects were in different postural positions (lying down, sitting up, standing up). The six other studies which attempted to control for postural position have reported observing the level of heart rate or blood pessure while all subjects were in one position.

It also appears that most studies focusing on blood pressure have failed to adequately measure this variable. Specifically, some studies assessed blood pressure only once (e.g. Brousseau and Mallinger, 1981; Crump, Cooper and Maxwell, 1981; Ivancevich *et al.*, 1982; Shirom *et al.*, 1973). Other studies assessed blood pressure several times; however, these multiple measures were taken on only one occasion or during only one visit (e.g. Caplan, 1971; Caplan *et al.*, 1975; Howard *et al.*, 1986; Kaufman and Beehr, 1986; Rose *et al.*, 1978). In addition, in many of these studies the several measurements

---

* The reviewed studies have concentrated on the effect of a variety of stressors in work situations on physiological criteria. Specifically, some studies have focused on role stressors; primarily role conflict, role ambiguity, and role overload. Others have focused on occupational stressors which supposedly are inherent in the work of such groups as managers, pilots, or air traffic controllers. Finally, studies have also been concerned with situational or environmental stressors such as computer shutdowns, plant closings, or space vehicle launchings (see also Fried *et al.*, 1984).

Table 1 Potential confounding factors of physiological measurements considered by work stress studies*
(This table updates the information that appeared in Fried et al., 1984)

(a) Cardiovascular measures

Studies	Race	Sex	Age	Familial tendency	Health conditions	Postural position	Consumption of caffeine and nicotine*	Humidity	Alcohol consumption	BP variability
Astrand et al. (1973)		+	+							
Aunola et al. (1978, 1979)	+	+	+							
Barnard and Duncan (1975)	+	+			+					
Brousseau and Mallinger (1981)	+	+	+							
Caplan (1971)		+	+	+						
Caplan and Jones (1975)		+			+	+				
Caplan et al. (1975)	+	+	+			+				
Chapman et al. (1966)		+					+			
Cobb and Kasl (1972)		+			+					
Cobb and Rose (1973)	+	+	+							
Crump et al. (1981)		+	+	+						
Dougherty (1967)		+								
Eden (1982)	+									
Ferris (1983)										
French and Caplan (1970)	+	+								
Harburg et al. (1979)	+	+	+							

(a) Cardiovascular measures (continued)

Studies	Race	Sex	Age	Familial tendency	Health conditions	Postural position	Consumption of caffeine and nicotine*	Humidity	Alcohol consumption	BP variability
Hennigan and Wortham (1975)					+					
House et al. (1979)	+					+				
Howard et al. (1976)		+	+							
Howard et al. (1986)	+	+				+	+		+	
Ivancevich et al. (1982)										
Study 1										
Study 2		+					+		+	
Johannson and Aronsson (1984)	+	+				+	+			+
Kasl and Cobb (1970)	+	+	+				+			+
Kaufman and Beehr (1986)	+	+				+				
Kuorinka and Korhonen (1981)	+	+	+	+	+					
Orth–Gomer and Ahlbom (1980)	+	+	+		+	+				
Payne and Rick (1986a)		+	+							
Payne and Rick (1986b)		+	+		+					
Reeder et al. (1973)	+	+	+							
Reynolds (1974)	+	+	+			+				
Rose et al. (1978)		+								
Sales (1970)		+								
Schar et al. (1973)	+	+	+	+						
Shirom et al. (1973)	+	+	+							
Waldron (1978)	+	+			+					
Warheit (1974)		+								

(b) Serum cholesterol

Studies	Sex	Age	Familial tendency	Health condition	Diet	Postural position	Consumption of caffeine*	Season	Venous occlusion
Caplan (1971)	+			+				+	
Caplan et al. (1975)	+	+				+	+		
Chapman et al. (1966)	+		+	+	+				
Cobb and Kasl (1972)	+								
Crump et al. (1981)	+	+	+					+	
Eden (1982)	+								
French and Caplan (1970)	+							+	
Friedman et al. (1958)	+				+				
Gore (1978)	+								
Hendrix et al. (1985)	+	+		+	+		+	+	
Howard et al. (1976)	+							+	
Howard et al. (1986)	+						+		
Ivancevich et al. (1982)									
Study 1	+						+	+	
Study 2	+						+	+	
Orth-Gomer and Ahlbom (1980)	+							+	
Reeder et al. (1973)	+			+				+	
Rubin and Rahe (1974)	+	+	+						
Schar et al. (1973)	+	+	+					+	
Shirom et al. (1973)	+	+						+	

(c) Catecholamines

Studies	Sex	Health conditions	Time of day	Postural position	Consumption of caffeine and nicotine*	Physical exertion
Astrand et al. (1973)	+					
Dutton et al. (1978)	+		+	+	+	+
Frankenhaeuer and Gadell (1976)	+		+	+	+	+
Ganster et al. (1982)	+		+		+	
Grandjean et al. (1971)	+					
Hale et al. (1971a)	+					
Hale et al. (1971b)	+					
Jenner et al. (1980)	+		+	+	+	+
Johansson et al. (1978)	+		+	+	+	+
Johansson and Aronsson (1984)	+		+		+	
Payne and Rick (1986b)			+			
Rubin (1974)	+	+				

(d) Peptic ulcer

Studies	Familial tendency	Longitudinal consumption of caffeine and nicotine	Peptic ulcer definition	Peptic ulcer illness criteria
Caplan et al. (1975)				
Cobb and Kasl (1972)				
Cobb and Rose (1973)				
Dunn and Cobb (1962)				
Gosling (1958)				
House et al. (1979)			+	
Johansson et al. (1978)				
Sandberg and Bliding (1976)			+	

* Before or during measurement
The + sign indicates the confounding factor(s) considered in each study.

of blood pressure were taken repeatedly or during a short period of time. This might have caused erroneous results because repeated measurements of blood pressure within too short a time period are likely to produce, through the inflation and deflation of the pressure cuff, temporary tissue changes which in turn cause different blood pressure readings (see Stern, Ray and Davis, 1980). Only Johansson and Aronsson (1984) and Kasl and Cobb (1970) appeared to adequately measure blood pressure by assessing it on several different days with multiple measurements per day with sufficient time intervals between measurements.

None of the 19 studies on serum cholesterol reviewed has reported controlling for the possible effect of venous occlusion, and only one study (Caplan *et al.*, 1975) ruled out the effect of postural position. Furthermore, only three studies have considered the effect of diet while four studies have taken into account the possible effect of caffeine consumption, familial tendency and health condition. Seven studies out of the 19 reviewed (Caplan *et al.*, 1975; Chapman *et al.*, 1966; Cobb and Kasl, 1972; Eden, 1982; Friedman, Rosenman and Carroll, 1958; Gore, 1978; Rubin and Rahe, 1974) have collected blood cholesterol across different seasons without taking into account the possible effect of the seasonal factors on the cholesterol analysis. Consequently, the internal validity of these studies and the ability to generalize or compare their results with other studies must be seriously challenged. In the remaining studies the effect of season was controlled to some extent because all of them appeared to collect their data within one season. However, attempting to generalize these studies' results beyond the specific season or meaningfully compare them with the results of studies conducted during another season might result in invalid conclusions.

Concerning the measurement of urinary catecholamines, only one study (Rubin, 1974) out of the 12 reviewed considered the effect of health conditions while four studies appeared to control for the effects of postural position and physical exertion. Six studies have controlled for the consumption of caffeine and nicotine during the time of measurement and seven have considered the effect of time of day. To illustrate: Dutton *et al.*, (1978) collected 24 hourly urine samples from firemen and paramedics during both a work day and a rest day. The majority of studies, however, failed to do so. Astrand *et al.*, (1973), for example, reported that fishermen's levels of catecholamines were significantly higher during daytime work hours than during rest hours at night. However, the authors themselves recognized that it was impossible to conclude whether the difference was caused primarily by the physical and mental stress fisherman were exposed to at work, by the time difference of urine collection, or by the difference in subject's body posture.

There is evidence which suggests that researchers have also failed to recognize the problem of hormone fluctuations in the blood. Specifically, six work stress studies have been found to deal with cortisol from the blood (see Fried *et al.*, 1984). Out of these six studies only one (Rose *et al.*, 1978) coped with the problem of fluctuations in measurement by collecting blood samples from their subjects continuously over several periods.

Concerning peptic ulcer, most studies have failed to deal with the problem of its definition. Specifically, only two out of the eight studies examined (i.e. Cobb and Rose, 1973; Sandberg and Bliding, 1976) dealt explicitly with duodenal ulcer. The other studies either seemed to be dealing with different types of ulcers, or were not specific as to what type of disease they were discussing. None of the focal studies have considered the issues of familial tendency, longitudinal (i.e. habitual) consumption of caffeine and nicotine or peptic ulcer illness criteria. Studies have tended to ignore the illness criteria problems by arbitrarily choosing different criteria (such as subject's self-report, medical record, chemical test or radiographic examination) for determining the existence of peptic ulcer.

Finally, the overwhelming majority of the studies reviewed have dealt exclusively with *males* and significant numbers of these studies with *white* males (see also, Kasl, 1978). This implies that the confounding effect of sex has been controlled for by the majority of the studies and that a significant portion of these studies have also controlled for the contaminating effect of race.

The above portrait appears to raise serious questions concerning the validity of physiological assessments in work stress studies, and consequently the validity of the obtained results on the relationship between work stress and physiological symptoms. It further suggests that changes in future research are essential for confronting the measurement problems of physiological variables.

FUTURE ASSESSMENT OF PHYSIOLOGICAL VARIABLES

It is argued here that future studies concerning the assessment of physiological indicators under work related stressors should progress in three areas in order to significantly improve the validity of their results. Specifically, changes are recommended in the following three areas:

(1) *Research design*: refers to the design characteristics of a study on work stress and physiological indicators that would minimize the effect of confounding factors.
(2) *Measurement standards of physiological indicators*: refers to the selection and application of measurement standards concerning physiological indicators that would improve research control over the effect of confounding factors.
(3) *Range of physiological substances and measures*: refers to a range of physiological substances and measures (some of which have not been

commonly used) that might be considered by work stress research in an attempt to broaden the base of knowledge regarding an individual's physiological activity.

Research Design

It appears that the majority of studies on work stress and physiological symptomology are cross-sectional in nature. More specifically, out of the 54 studies reviewed in Table 1 26 are cross-sectional. In these studies data on both the independent and dependent variables are collected at one point in time. Only 13 studies are truly longitudinal in the sense that they examine the changes in physiological criteria under different levels of stress at work over a period of several months or years. The remaining 15 studies focus on the existence of physiological symptoms in stressful vs non-stressful situations over a relatively short-term interval. Only some of the above studies appear to include control group(s) in addition to the experimental group(s).

One might argue that the discussion concerning the potential threats of the three sets of confounding factors (i.e. stable or permanent factors, transitory factors and procedural factors) is more relevant to cross-sectional studies with no control group(s) than other more sophisticated designs. However, as the discussion below indicates, this claim can be supported only to a certain degree (see also, Fried *et al.*, 1984).

Shortcomings of cross-sectional studies

Because of their design characteristics, cross-sectional studies with no control group(s) appear to be more vulnerable to the effect of inadequate measurement procedures. For example, measuring blood pressure once instead of several times might confound the results of these studies. Cross-sectional studies are also more vulnerable to the effect of transitory factors. To illustrate, if subjects in a given study are permitted to consume caffeine prior to measurement of cardiovascular symptoms, it could be generally expected that some subjects will consume caffeine while others will not. Consequently, different levels of cardiovascular activity, if found, might be largely the result of differences in caffeine consumption rather than work stress.

Finally, stable or permanent factors might also confound the measurement of physiological criteria in cross-sectional studies For example, people with a lower physiological tolerance to stress (due to such factors as familial tendency, age or nutritional habits) are expected to find it more difficult to cope with certain work demands than those with a higher physiological tolerance to stress. Consequently, although the objective level of work stress might be similar for both groups, the group with the lower physiological tolerance is likely to experience a higher level of work stress.

Advantages and weaknesses of more advanced research designs

In contrast to the above, one might argue that the threat of potentially confounding factors would be substantially lower if studies attempt to validate the results through the use of control group(s) and/or if they are conducted over extended time periods. In other words, results are expected to be more valid if studies compare physiological indicators under different levels of work stress over different periods of time and/or between experimental group(s) and control group(s).

This argument is based on the assumption that in sophisticated research designs with multiple conditions of measurement, potentially confounding factors are likely to be similarly distributed, and thus have similar effects on physiological assessments across the different conditions of measurement. This, in turn, enables the researcher to validly analyze the main effects of work stress on physiological symptoms, beyond the possible effect of the confounding factors. More specifically, one may argue that if individuals are randomly assigned to experimental and control groups, potentially confounding personal factors such as genetic tendency for high blood pressure or individual habits of smoking and coffee drinking are expected to be similar in both the experimental and control groups (i.e. no systematic differences are expected to be found in the different groups in regard to the number of people with high blood pressure tendency or number of people who are smokers or coffee drinkers). Consequently, one need not find systematic differences in the effect of these factors on physiological data obtained in the various groups. Similarly, in studies with multiple measurements taken over days, weeks, or several months, personal characteristics such as the above can be expected to remain largely stable, and consequently to have similar effect on measurement results across the different periods of measurement.

One may further argue that the prevalence and thus the effect of potentially measurement-related confounding factors on physiological data need not be systematically different across the various conditions of measurement. For example, the number of times blood samples are drawn with venous occlusions as well as the time length of such venous obstructions would not be significantly different in the experimental vs control groups or across measurements over time. On this basis the apparently confounding effect of venous occlusions on blood analysis (Sabine, 1977) need not be different across the various measurement conditions.

The above appears to suggest that the use of experimental designs which incorporate control groups and repeated measurements over time can enable scholars to study the independent effects of focal work related stressors on physiological criteria beyond the possible biasing effects of contaminating factors. However, it is argued here that although sophisticated research designs should be encouraged as a mechanism to reduce biasing effects of some confounding factors, such designs *cannot* control for all possible effects of all threatening factors (see also, Fried *et al.*, 1984). To begin with, random distribution of subjects across the different conditions of measurement does not necessarily mean a similar effect of potentially confounding personal factors on physiological measurement results. To illustrate, a random selection of subjects across experimental and control groups is expected to lead to a similar number of people in both groups that are potential coffee drinkers and smokers. However the potential coffee drinkers and smokers in the experimental group (i.e. the group under stress) are expected to *implement* their coffee drinking and smoking habits significantly more than their counterparts in the control (i.e. 'nonstressful' group). This is because of a common tendency among people with habits of smoking and drinking to practice those habits more under stressful situations as stress-coping mechanisms. Similarly, subjects under different levels of work stress over different points in time are expected to smoke or consume coffee to a higher degree under stressful conditions (e.g. during a working day) than in more calm situations (e.g. during leisure time). Obviously, because smoking and coffee drinking prior to or during measurement tend to affect the level of a variety of physiological indicators, differences in the amount of coffee drinking and smoking among the different conditions of measurement can obscure the results and conclusions regarding the effect of stress on physiological criteria.

Another example would be that people with a familial tendency toward high blood pressure might show significantly higher blood pressure under stressful situations than under nonstressful situations because of the possible interaction between stress and tendency toward high blood pressure. It follows then that results of a study in which a relatively large portion of the participants have a genetic tendency toward high blood pressure, might lead to erroneous conclusions regarding the independent effect of work stress on blood pressure. Once again, advanced research designs cannot be expected to eliminate the biasing effect of high blood pressure tendency. Specifically, in a study which consists of experimental and control groups, results might support the predicted effect of stress on blood pressure by indicating, on the average, higher blood pressure in the experimental ('stressful') group than in the control ('nonstressful') group. However, this finding could be largely related to the *interaction* between stress and tendency for high blood pressure rather than to the main effect of stress. Similarly, in a longitudinal study with a number of measurements over time under different levels of stress, subjects with high blood pressure tendency might show higher blood pressure when exposed to the stressful situations than when exposed to the nonstressful situations. Similar to the previous example, the finding might be largely a function of the interaction between stress and the focal genetic tendency, rather than of the main effect of stress, as one might erroneously conclude.

Moreover, advanced research designs do not seem to control for possible confounding effects of all contextual factors. It can be argued that since scholars, in general, tend to be unaware of the need to equalize such factors as room temperature, postural position, or time of the day, these factors are likely to be dissimilar across the different conditions of measurement, at least in some studies. For example, a situation where the control group is located in a different place (e.g. different building) from the experimental group and the research team is small and restricted for time increases the probability that the measurement of the two groups will be taken at different times.

Finally, advanced research designs cannot remove the *procedural* problems often present in the measurement of stress-related physiological symptoms. To illustrate: taking only a single measure of blood pressure or collecting blood samples for the purpose of hormone analysis only once is likely to bias results even under experimentally-designed studies with multiple measurements.

The above discussion supports a recommendation for future research to rely more on longitudinal designs which include both experimental and control groups. However, as discussed, an appropriate research design can help only to a certain degree, and it clearly cannot replace the direct responsibility of the researcher to actively take into account, or rule out, the effect of relevant confounding factors.

Measurement Standards of Physiological Indicators

An obvious goal of future work stress research is to increase its standards concerning the measurement of phsyiological reactions. These higher standards can be achieved by scholars recognizing the importance of considering potential confounding factors while assessing physiological symptoms, as well as by professional journals imposing strict criteria regarding physiological measurement. It appears that professional journals in both organizational sciences and health and social sciences have generally paid too little attention to the critical elements of physiological measurements in the work stress area. While the professional journals in these fields have generally imposed rigid requirements on issues of research design and measurement in many areas of investigation, they have failed to do so with regard to physiological measurement in work stress research. Thus, one would expect scholarly journals to use the review process as a mechanism to improve approaches to the assessment of physiological criteria.

Researchers might control some of the potentially confounding factors of physiological measurement using statistical methods to analyze the collected data. For example, researchers might explore for statistical differences between males and females or blacks and whites concerning physiological reactions to work stress. Similarly, researchers might search for a possible difference in physiological responses to work stress based on familial tendencies, time of day or season of the year.

However, the research is also obligated to take steps to assure appropriate measurement procedures and minimize confounding effects of factors that are irrelevant to the research. Clearly, it seems that in most cases the researcher is expected to design his/her study so that he/she would be able to draw more than one sample of blood or urine, as well as to conduct multiple assessments of the cardiovascular system. Concerning the measurement of peptic ulcer, the researcher is expected to define and specifically describe the type of peptic ulcer he/she is interested in studying (e.g. duodenal ulcer vs gastric ulcer), as well as the criteria used to determine ulcer disorders (e.g. patient symptoms vs doctor diagnosis vs surgical evidence). Doing so will enable more valid comparisons among studies' results. Moreover, because of the difficulty in deciding which type of peptic ulcer to explore and what criteria to use for assessing an ulcer disorder, the researcher might choose to focus on several ulcer diseases using multiple diagnostic criteria and then statistically analyze the relationship between the focal work stressors and each of the explored ulcer diseases as assessed by different diagnostic criteria.

It is further argued that one could rule out in the process of measurement the confounding effect of transitory factors such as smoking or consumption of caffeine and alcohol (by forbidding subjects to smoke or drink coffee and alcohol before and during measurement), postural position (by enforcing one postural position for all subjects during measurement, or by averaging the results across different postural positions) or time of day (by attempting to collect physiological information of all subjects at a similar time of day).

Finally, the accuracy of physiological measurement in work situations can be improved by researchers adopting, whenever possible, advanced technological devices for the purpose of assessing physiological reactions. To illustrate, recording cardiac activity is commonly done indirectly by a surface-placed bipolar electrode configuration (Siddle and Turpin, 1980). Using this technique in the 'field' (e.g. work setting) might lead to inaccurate recording because of movement artifacts from freely moving subjects (Siddle and Turpin, 1980). A possible solution for this problem is the use of radiotelemetry to transmit the EKG signal to a receiver and preamplifier or on the use of a portable tape recorder such as Medilog (Oxford Instruments Company) which is attached to the subject in order to record the EKG signals on tape for the purpose of analysis (see Rolfe, 1973; Siddle and Turpin, 1980; Payne and Rick, 1986a,b).

Concerning blood pressure, the common device used to detect blood pressure is the sphygmomanometer, which consists of a pressure cuff connected to a tube containing mercury (Fried *et al.*, 1984; Stern *et al.*,

1980). The reliability and validity of this method might be adversely affected by factors such as the recorder's subjective judgment regarding the presence or absence of Korotkoff sounds. To some degree the measurement problems associated with the assessment of blood pressure can be reduced by the use of the more recently developed automated devices for assessing blood pressure (Steptoe, 1980). Furthermore, there is a direct measure of blood pressure, which involves inserting a catheter into a blood vessel. This technique appears to provide much more accurate information regarding blood pressure (Lywood, 1967). However, it should be recognized that using such a technique is likely to create undesirable psychological stress as well as growing resistance to subsequent measurement.

Range of Physiological Substances and Measures in Work Stress Studies

Subjects' typical resistance to a direct measure of blood pressure as mentioned above can be generalized to include all physiological measurements that are uncomfortable or intrusive in nature. Such resistance seems to be particularly prevalent when samples of blood or urine are collected as a basis for biochemical analysis (see, e.g. Christie and Woodman, 1980). Moreover, organizations might also object to research involved with physiological measurement because the process of measurement might often disrupt work schedules and work objectives. It is conceivable that the difficulty of gaining access to organizations and employees for research purposes has led researchers to adopt lower measurement standards (e.g. collecting blood or urine samples once instead of several times as needed) and to focus on few physiological criteria (primarily on cardiovascular symptoms which are relatively easy to obtain). The literature, however, appears to caution against relying on one physical system or one physiological measure as a basis for detecting stress, because different individuals might develop different physiological responses to a given stressor (see e.g. Gale and Edwards, 1986; Lacey and Lacey, 1958; Levine, 1986).

It follows that researchers should attempt to achieve two important objectives: (1) to improve the validity of physiological measurement by adopting higher measurement standards and by broadening the base of information on individual's physiological response to work stress; and (2) to improve the cooperation of organizations and employees regarding their participation in research on stress and phsyiological aspects. One might argue that these two objectives are largely contradictory. That is, using multiple physiological measures and adopting high measurement standards are likely to make the measurement process more disturbing and uncomfortable for both organizations and employees, and thus reduce their willingness to participate in research. However, it is argued here that some workable balance between the two objectives is feasible.

The following discussion portrays three possible approaches that might help to achieve such a balance. Specifically, it is argued that a researcher might rely on the characteristics of the focal work stressors to improve selection of the physiological criteria used in the study. Moreover, future research might choose to rely more on such substances as saliva and sweat for the purpose of biochemical analysis, because the general procedures for collecting these substances are relatively simple and nonintrusive compared with the procedures used to collect blood or urine. Finally, there is some evidence to suggest that researchers might extend their knowledge of an individual's physiological state by relying on some self-report measures of physiological and psychological activity (see Mackay, 1980, for a review). These self-report measures are expected to be especially beneficial when the researcher (possibly due to a strong resistance by the organizations or employees) finds it difficult to record any, or a sufficient number of, physiological variables in the research setting. These three approaches are now discussed.

Work stress characteristics and the selection of physiological variables

Using multiple physiological measures in work stress research is associated with a substantial increase of measurement problems compared with the use of a single physiological criterion. This fact appears to emphasize the importance of a careful examination by scholars regarding which physiological criteria are to be selected for a specific work stress study.

It is argued here that a major factor in determining which physiological criteria to select should be the characteristics of the examined work stressors. Namely, whether the study focuses on *acute* work stressors such as a computer shutdown with only a short warning, or *chronic* work stressors, such as continual exposure to role ambiguity or role overload over months or years (see also, Fried *et al.*, 1984).

Specifically, cardiovascular variables are highly responsive to transient events (e.g., Drescher, Gantt and Whitehead, 1980; Lynch, Long, Thomas, Malinow and Katcher, 1981). Moreover, while there is strong empirical evidence supporting the effects of acute stressful events on cardiovascular reactions, effects of chronic stressors on these reactions appear to be vague or inconclusive (for further discussion see Shapiro *et al.*, 1979). It follows that cardiovascular symptoms should be used primarily as criteria for identifying acute, rather than chronic, work stressors.

Similar to the cardiosvascular system, plasma catecholamines change very rapidly in response to sympathetic stimulation, and thus appear to be an appropriate index for acute stressors.

On the other hand, urinary catecholamines tend to be substantially more stable (i.e. less sensitive) to transient events compared with plasma catecholamines. This, in turn, suggests that urinary catecholamines can serve as better criteria for chronic stressors than for acute stressors. (On the differences between urinary and plasma catcholamines see, e.g. Dimsdale and Moss, 1980a,b; Jenner et al., 1979; Yamaguchi and Kopin, 1979.)

Lastly, gastrointestinal symptoms, such as peptic ulcer, tend to be developed over months or years. This implies that gastrointestinal symptoms potentially can be used as criteria for identifying chronic work stressors, but not for acute stressors.

Body fluid and biochemical analysis

Biochemical analysis in work stress research has been based primarily on samples of blood or urine (Fried et al., 1984). However, it appears that the collection of these substances in work situations tend to cause work disturbances, psychological strain, and in the case of drawing blood phsyiological discomfort. Consequently, organizations and their employees often resist the whole process of sampling blood or urine.

It seems, however, that scholars might reduce some of the problems associated with biochemical analysis if they rely more on saliva and to some degree sweat, both of which can be collected with much less disruption and discomfort than urine and especially blood.

Blood and urine. Drawing blood samples seems to be particularly complex, disruptive and intrusive when it is collected through the vein. The usual point of collection is from a superficial arm or antecubital vein. The collection of a venous sample is cumbersome because it requires medical facilities and the availability of sterilized syringes and needles (Christie and Woodman, 1980). Moreover, the process of blood collection, the appearance of the syringe and needle, as well as the anticipation of adverse effects might cause participants to experience psychological stress. Such a threatening experience might affect the blood constituent to be analyzed and thus add error variance to the data (Christie and Woodman, 1980).

An alternative to the venous blood sample is capillary blood samples. Here blood is drawn from either the ball or nail bed of a finger or thumb. Relative to venous samples, capillary samples are easier to collect and are less threatening and intrusive for the involved individuals.

On the surface, collecting urine samples seems to be simple and easy because unlike drawing blood samples there is no need for outside intervention, which is stressful in nature. Also, relatively large volumes are made available with little effort, and medical help is not needed in the process of collection. However, a more careful examination appears to indicate that requests to produce urine samples within work situations for analysis purposes might be stressful to the individual. This is particularly so because the toilet facilities at work tend to be inadequate to enable numerous participants to void a sample is a given period of time in a quiet and private way. Individuals might also experience stress because of the knowledge that they are expected to produce urine at specific times. These stressors might cause some subjects to be unable to void a sample as requested (Christie and Woodman, 1980).

Saliva and sweat. There is evidence to suggest that saliva might be a useful body fluid for exploring physiological reactions to stress. Specifically, saliva can serve as a basis for electrolyte analysis, especially with regard to changes of sodium/potassium ratio (Na/K) in stress situations (Christie, 1975; Christie and Woodman, 1980; Rick and Payne, 1987). It also appears that the hormonal context of saliva makes it a suitable basis for the study of cortisol which is a stress related hormone (e.g. Landman, Sanford and Howland, 1976). Finally, saliva analysis might provide information regarding duodenal ulcer. Specifically, those nonsecretors of blood group substances in their saliva are 50% more likely to develop duodenal ulcer (e.g. Chapman, 1978; Vesley, 1968).

Although it seems that blood or urine analysis can provide more interpretable information compared with saliva analysis (e.g. Christie and Woodman, 1980; Shannon, Katz and Beering, 1967) the latter has been proven to be useful in the field, (e.g. De Marchi, 1976; Fowles and Venables, 1970). A major advantage of saliva as a basis for analyses is that this fluid can be conveniently collected, and it generally does not cause adverse interferences or noticeable psychological stress among participants. Moreover, analyzing the saliva appears to be relatively uncomplicated (e.g. Bovard, 1959; Christie and Woodman, 1980). However, researchers should be aware of some measurememt problems concerning saliva collection and analysis. Specifically, the 'spitting procedure' of saliva collection appears to be potentially stressful for some individuals, which might affect the analysis results (Wenger, 1966). This procedure can be replaced with the use of the Lashley disk which seems to be a stress-free method (Terry and Shannon, 1964; Fowles and Venables, 1970). Moreover, variables such as position of subjects, room temperature, smoking or diet might affect the salivary analysis and thus should be controlled in the process of measurement (Christie and Woodman, 1980; Jenkins, 1978).

Another fluid that can potentially provide information on physiological reaction to stress is sweat (Christie and Woodman, 1980). Although to date little use has been made of sweat analysis, such an analysis offers possibilities for exploration of electrolyte shifts under stress conditions as well as drug use, which is a possible indicator of an individual's experience of stress (Bell, Christie and Venables, 1975; Christie and Venables, 1971; Christie and Woodman, 1980). Bell *et al.* (1975) devised a method in which the electrolyte content of palmar surface film is collected when sweat glands are inactive. This procedure of collection appears to be, similar to the collection of saliva, simple and nonintrusive. In this method sweat is collected from the palmar surface using gauze or filter papers which are placed on a cleansed palm and pressed by concave disk and a pressure pad. (For more detailed discussion on this measurement technique, see Bell *et al.* 1975.) One should recall, however, that variables such as age, season, site of collection and diet can all affect the explored electrolyte content of the palmar sweat. Thus, these variables should be controlled in the process of measurement to reduce error variance (Christie and Woodman, 1980).

Physiological activity and self-report measures

The problems and difficulties associated with the measurement of physiological variables in work stress studies have led researchers to use self-report measures that supposedly provide information regarding an individual's physiological activity during stressful, work-related situations (see, e.g. studies by Brenner and Bartell, 1984; Cherry, 1984; Kemery, Mossholder and Bedeian, 1987; Frese, 1985; Ganster, Fusilier and Mayes, 1986; Johansson and Aronsson, 1984; Sykes and Eden, 1985). A major advantage of self-report measures is that it is easy to administer them without causing much interference to, or resistance from, the involved organizations and employees. However, the extent to which self-report measures actually reflect the physiological state of an individual is clearly a serious concern. There appear to be three major types of self-report measures which supposedly relate to a person's physiological activity. One type attempts to detect an individual's level of activation (i.e. arousal); the second type concentrates on an individual's mood; and the third type focuses on an individual's somatic state (see MacKay, 1980, for a more detailed discussion). Specifically, several scholars headed by Thayer (1967; 1978a,b) have attempted to develop a measure that would detect the individual level of intensity (i.e. arousal) on a scale ranging from 'extreme excitement' to 'deep sleep'. Traditionally, the different questionnaires on arousal have been based on a number of adjectives of activational content such as 'active', 'energetic', 'vigorous' or 'alert' (see e.g. Thayer, 1967 MacKay, Cox, Burrows and Lazzarini, 1978). Research has generally indicated a consistent relationship between self-reported arousal and various physiological variables. Specifically, studies have shown that self-report measures of arousal are positively correlated with such physiological reactions as skin resistance, body temperature, heart rate, pulse rate, respiration rate, muscle action potentials and finger blood volume (see Thayer, 1967; Bohlin and Kjellberg, 1973; Clements, Hafer and Vermillion, 1976). Moreover, it appears that self-reported arousal correlates more strongly with a variety of physiological measures than individual physiological measures correlate among themselves (see Thayer, 1967; MacKay, 1980). This might suggest that self-report measures of arousal are better indicators of general physiological activation than any of the physiological measures (MacKay, 1980).

Two other relevant self-report measures are mood and somatic state. Mood refers to the general well-being of an individual (e.g. Meddis, 1969). Mood states have been assessed by adjective checklists, rating scales and question-naires (e.g. 'I am doing as well as I really can today'— response can range from 'very true' to 'very false') (see Catell, 1973).

The self-report measures of somatic states attempt to assess subjects' awareness of *visceral changes* in their body activity. The focus might be on perceived visceral changes which are later correlated with various sources of stress (e.g. 'I am sometimes troubled by "cold sweats"'—on a scale ranging from 'very inaccurate' to 'very accurate'), or on perceived visceral changes directly under states of stress and strain (e.g. 'when you feel anxious, do you get a sinking or heavy feeling in your stomach?'—on a scale ranging from 'never' to 'always') (see e.g. Caplan *et al.*, 1975; MacKay, 1980). Evidence seems to indicate, however, an inconsistent relationship between the percep-tual measures of mood and somatic state with physiological variables (see MacKay, 1980 for further discussion). It follows then that the overall useful-ness of these measures as a basis for detecting physiological activity is highly questionable at present.

SUMMARY

In the past decade there has been a growing interest in research concerning the relationship between work stress and physiological reactions. However, it appears that much of this research has failed to consider systematically the effect of potentially confounding factors on the measurement of physiological indicators.

It seems that three major factors have contributed to the general failure of work stress researchers to consider these potentially confounding factors:

(1) Lack of sufficient knowledge and understanding regarding the scope and nature of the confounding factors;
(2) Lack of sufficient pressure from scholarly journals to enforce more rigid standards in the area of physiological measurement;
(3) Resistance from organizations and/or subjects to be involved in the measurement of physiological indicators. This, in turn, might have led researchers at times to compromise on measurement standards in order to gain better cooperation with organizations and subjects for research purposes.

It is hoped that this paper, together with other relevant materials in the literature (see, e.g. Fried *et al.*, 1984), will help researchers to develop more informed understanding of the measurement of physiologicial activities. Such an increase in knowledge and understanding is expected to improve operational standards regarding the process of physiological measurement, particularly if it is combined with more rigid requirements imposed by scholarly journals through the review system. On the surface the two goals of keeping high standards of physiological measurement and gaining the cooperation of organizations and employees seem to be largely contradictory. However, it is argued that scholars might be able to find a workable balance between these two goals by searching and implementing alternative strategies of measurement. Thus, for example, scholars can expect to reduce the range of measurement problems they face by excluding from research those physiological criteria that do not match the chronic or acute characteristics of the focal work stressors. Moreover, scholars might consider using sweat and particularly saliva as either supplementary or alternative sources of data to that provided by blood and urine for the purpose of biochemical analysis. The reasons are that both saliva and sweat are easy to collect and seem to cause only minimal interference or disturbance. Finally, scholars might also consider using some self-report measures which are easy to administer as another basis for assessing an individual's physiological state.

REFERENCES

Astrand, I., Fugelli, P., Karlsson, C. G., Rodahl K., and Vodak, Z. (1973). Energy output and work stress in coastal fishing, *Scanadinavian Journal of Clinical and Laboratory Investigation*, **31**, 105–13.

Aunola, S., Nykyri, R. and Rusko, H. (1978). Strain of employees in the machine industry in Finland, *Ergonomics*, **21**, 509–19.

Aunola, S., Nykyri, R. and Rusko, H., (1979). Strain of employees in the manufacturing industry in Finland, *Ergonomics*, **22**, 29–36.

Barnard, R. J. and Duncan, H. W. (1975). Heart rate and ECG responses of fire fighters, *Journal of Occupational Medicine*, **17**, 247–62.

Beehr, T. A. and Newman, J. D. (1978). Job stress, employee health, and organizational effectiveness: a facet analysis, model, and literature review, *Personnel Psychology*, **31**, 665–99.

Beehr, T. A. and Schuler, A. S., (1982). Stress in organizations. In K. M. Rowland and G. R. Ferris (eds) *Personnel Management*, Allyn and Bacon, Boston.

Bell, B., Christie, M. J. and Venables, P. H. (1975). Menstrual cycle variation in body fluid potassium, *Journal of Interdisciplinary Cycle Research*, **6**, 113–20.

Bohlin, G. and Kjellberg, A. (1975). Self-reported arousal: factorial complexity as a function of the subject's arousal level, *Scandinavian Journal of Psychology*, **14**, 78–86.

Bovard, E. W. (1959). The effects of social stimuli on the response to stress, *Psychological Review*, **66**, 267–77.

Brenner, S. D. and Bartell, R. (1984). The teacher stress process: a cross-cultural analysis, *Journal of Occupational Behavior*, **5**, 183–95.

Brousseau, K. R. and Mallinger, M. A. (1981). Internal–external locus of control, perceived occupational stress and cardiovascular health, *Journal of Occupational Behavior*, **2**, 65–73.

Caplan, R. D. (1971). *Organizational stress and individual stress*: a socio-psychological study of risk factors in coronary heart disease among administrators, engineers, and scientists, unpublished doctoral dissertation, University of Michigan, Ann Arbor.

Caplan, R. D. and Jones. K. W. (1975). Effects of work load, role ambiguity, and type A personality on anxiety, depression, and heart rate, *Journal of Applied Psychology*, **60**, 713–19.

Caplan, R. D., Cobb, S. and French, J. R. P., Jr (1979). White collar work load and cortisol: disruption of a circadian rhythm by job stress? *Journal of Psychosomatic Research*, **23**, 181–92.

Caplan, R. D., Cobb, S., French, J. R. P., Jr, Harrison, R. U. and Pinneau, S. R., Jr (1975). *Job Demands and Worker Health*, NIOSH Research Report, Washington, D. C.

Cattell, R. B. (1973). *Personality and Mood by Questionnaire*, Jossey-Bass, San Francisco.

Chapman, M. L. (1978). Peptic ulcer: a medical perspective. In H. D. Janowitz (ed.) *The Medical Clinics of North America*, Saunders, New York.

Chapman, J. M., Reeder, L. G., Massey, F. J., Jr, Borun, E. R., Picken, B., Browning, G. D., Coulson, A. A. and Zimmerman, D. H., (1966). Relationships of stress tranquilizers and serum cholesterol levels in a sample population under study for coronary heart disease, *American Journal of Epidemiology*, **83**, 537–47.

Cherry, N. (1984). Nervous strain, anxiety and symptoms amongst 32-year-old men at work in Britain, *Journal of Occupational Psychology*, **57**, 95–105.

Christian, J. C. and Kang, K. W. (1977). Maternal influence on plasma cholesterol variation, *American Journal of Human Genetics*, **20**, 462–7.

Christie, M. J., (1975). The psychosocial environment and precurors of disease. In P. H. Venables and M. J. Christie (eds) *Research in Psychophysiology*, John Wiley and Sons, London.

Christie, M. A. and Venables, P. H. (1971). Effects on 'basal' skin potential level of varying the concentration of an external electrolyte, *Journal of Psychosomatic Research*, **15**, 343–8.

Christie, C. W. and Woodman, D. D. (1980). Biochemical methods. In I. Martin and P. H. Venables (eds) *Techniques in Psychophysiology*, John Wiley and Sons, New York.

Clements, P. R., Hafer, M. D. and Vermillion, M. E. (1976). Psychometric, diurnal and electrophysiological correlates of activation, *Journal of Personality and Social Psychology*, **33**, 387–94.

Cobb, S. and Kasl, S. V. (1972). Some medical aspects of unemployment. *Industrial Gerontology*, **12**, 8–16.

Cobb, S. and Rose, R. (1973). Hypertension, peptic ulcer and diabetes in air traffic controllers, *Journal of the American Medical Association*, **224**, 489–92.

Cooper, C. L. and Marshall, J. (1976). Occupational sources of stress: a review of the literature relating to coronary heart disease and mental ill health, *Journal of Occupational Psychology*, **49**, 11–28.

Cox, T. (1987). Editorial, *Work and Stress*, **1**, 1–4.

Crump, J. H., Cooper, C. L. and Maxwell, V. B. (1981). Stress among air traffic controllers: occupational sources of coronary heart disease risk, *Journal of Occupational Behavior*, **2**, 293–303.

De Marchi, G. W. (1976). Psychophysiological aspects of the menstrual cycle, *Journal of Psychosomatic Research*, **20**, 279–87.

Dimsdale, J. E. and Moss, J. (1980a). Plasma catecholamines in stress and exercise, *Journal of the American Medical Association*, **243**, 340–2.

Dimsdale, J. E. and Moss, J., (1980b). Short-term catecholamine response to psychological stress, *Psychosomatic Medicine*, 42, 493–512.

Dougherty, J. D. (1967). Cardiovascular findings in air traffic controllers, *Aerospace Medicine*, 38, 26–30.

Drescher, M., Gantt, W. H. and Whitehead, W. E. (1980). Heart rate response to touch, *Psychosomatic Medicine*, 42, 559–74.

Dunn, J. P. and Cobb, S. (1962). Frequency of peptic ulcer among executives, craftsmen and foremen, *Journal of Occupational Medicine*, 4, 343–8.

Dutton, L. M., Smolensky, M. H., Leach, C. S., Lorimer, R. and Hsi, B. P. (1978). Stress levels of ambulance paramedics and firefighters, *Journal of Occupational Medicine*, 20, 111–20.

Eden, D. (1982). Critical job events, acute stress, and strain: a multiple interrupted time series, *Organizational Behavior and Human Performance*, 301, 312–29.

Ferris, G. R. (1983). Activation–increasing properties of task performance, *Psychological Reports*, 52, 731–4.

Fowles, D. C. and Venables, P. H. (1970). The effects of epidermal hydration and sodium reabsorption on salmar skin potential level, *Psychological Bulletin*, 73, 363–78.

Frankenhaeuser, M. (1975a). Sympathetic-adrenomedullary activity, behavior, and the psychosocial environment. In P. H. Venables and M. J. Christie (eds) *Research in Psychophysiology*, John Wiley and Sons, New York.

Frankenhaeuser, M. (1975b). Experimental approach to the study of catecholamines and emotion. In L. Levy (ed.) *Emotions, their Parameters and Measurement*, Raicen Press, New York.

Frankenhaeuser, M. and Gardell, B. (1976). Underload and overload in working life: outline of a multidisciplinary approach, *Journal of Human Stress*, 2, 35–46.

French, J. R. P., Jr and Caplan, R. D. (1970). Psychological factors in coronary heart disease, *Industrial Medicine and Surgery*, 39, 31–45.

Frese, M. (1985). Stress at work and psychosomatic complaints: a causal interpretation, *Journal of Applied Psychology*, 70, 314–28.

Fried, Y., Rowland, K. M. and Ferris, G. R. (1984). The physiological measurement of work stress: a critique, *Personnel Psychology*, 37, 583–615.

Friedman, M. D., Rosenman, R. D. and Carroll, V. (1958). Changes in serum cholesterol and blood clotting time in men subject to cyclic variation of occupational stress, *Circulation*, 17, 852–61.

Gale, A. and Edwards, J. A. (1986). Individual differences. In M. G. H. Coles E. Donchine and S. W. Porges) (eds) *Psychophysiology: Symptoms, Processes and Applications*, pp. 431–507, Guilford Press, New York.

Ganster, D. C., Fusilier, M. R. and Mayes, B. T. (1986). Role of social support in the experience of stress and work, *Journal of Applied Psychology*, 71, 102–110.

Ganster, D. C., Mayes, B. T., Sime, W. E. and Tharp, G. D. (1982). Managing organizational stress: a field experiment, *Journal of Applied Psychology*, 67, 533–42.

Gore, S. (1978). The effect of social support in moderating the health consequences of unemployment, *Journal of Health and Social Behavior*, 19, 157–65.

Gosling, R. H. (1958). Peptic ulcer and mental disorder, *Journal of Psychosomatic Research*, 2, 285–301.

Grandjean, E. P., Wotzka, G., Schaad, R., and Gilgen, A. (1971). Fatigue and stress in air traffic controllers. *Ergonomics*. 14, 159–165

Hale, H. B., Williams, E. W., Smith, B. N. and Melton, C. E., Jr (1971a). Excretion patterns of air traffic controllers, *Aerospace Medicine*, 42, 127–38.

Hale, H. B., Williams, E. W., Smith, B. N. and Melton, C. E., Jr (1971b). Neuroendocrine and metabolic responses to intermittent night shift work, *Aerospace Medicine*, **42**, 156–62.

Harburg, E., Blakelock, E. H. and Roeper, P. J. (1979). Resentful and reflective coping with arbitrary authority and blood pressure, *Psychosomatic Medicine*, **41**, 189–202.

Hendrix, W. H., Ovalle, N. K. and Troxler, R. G. (1985). Behavioral and physiological consequences of stress and its antecedent factors. *Journal of Applied Psychology*, **70**, 188–201.

Hennekens, C. H., Levine, R. S., Rosner, B., Klein, B. E., Gourley, J. E., Gelband, H. and Jessie, M. J. (1980). Aggregation of cholesterol among young families of men with premature myocardial infarction, *Journal of Chronic Diseases*, **33**, 359–64.

Hennigan, J. K. and Wortham, A. W. (1975). Analysis of workday stresses on industrial managers using heart rate as a criterion, *Ergonomics*, **18**, 675–81.

House, J. S., McMichael, A. J., Wells, J. A., Kaplan, B. H. and Landerman, L. R. (1979). Occupational stress and health among factory workers, *Journal of Health and Social Behavior*, **20**, 139–60.

Howard, J. H., Cunningham, D. A. and Rechnitzer, P. A. (1976). Health patterns associated with type A behavior: a managerial population, *Journal of Human Stress*, **2**, 24–31.

Howard, J. H., Cunningham, D. A. and Rechnitzer, P. A. (1986). Role ambiguity, type A behavior, and job satisfaction: moderating effects on cardiovascular and biochemical responses associated with coronary risk, *Journal of Applied Psychology*, **71**, 95–101.

Ivancevich, J. M., Matteson, M. T. and Preston, C. (1982). Occupational stress, type A behavior, and physical well-being, *Academy of Management Journal*, **25**, 373–91.

Jenkins, G. N. (1978). *The Physiology of the Mouth*, Blackwell, Oxford.

Jenner, D. A., Reynolds, V. and Harrison, G. A. (1979). Population field studies of catecholamines. In C. MacKay and T. Cox (eds) *Response to Stress: Occupational Aspects*, IPC Science and Technology Press, London.

Jenner, D. A., Reynolds, V. and Harrison, G. A. (1980). Catecholamine excretion rates and occupation, *Ergonomics*, **23**, 237–46.

Jennings, J. R., Berg, W. K., Hutchenson, J. S., Orbist, P., Portes, S. and Tupin, G. (1981). Publication guidelines for heart rate studies in man. *Psychophysiology*, **18**, 226–31.

Johansson, G. and Aronsson, G. (1984). Stress reactions in computerized administrative work, *Journal of Occupational Behavior*, **5**, 159–81.

Johansson, G., Aronsson, G. and Lindstrom, B. O. (1978). Social psychological and neuroendocrine stress reactions in highly mechanized work, *Ergonomics*, **21**, 583–99.

Kasl, S. V. (1978). Epidemiological contributions to the study of work stress. In D. L. Cooper and R. Payne (eds) *Stress at Work*, John Wiley and Sons, Chichester.

Kasl, S. V. and Cobb, S. (1970). Blood pressure changes in men undergoing job loss: a preliminary report, *Psychosomatic Medicine*, **32**, 19–38.

Kaufman, G. M. and Beehr, T. A. (1986). Interactions between job stressors and social support: some counterintuitive results, *Journal of Applied Psychology*, **71**, 522–6.

Kemery, E. R., Mossholder, K. W. and Bedeian, A. R. (1987). Role stress, physical symptomology, and turnover intention: a causal analysis of three alternative specifications, *Journal of Occupational Behavior*, **8**, 11–23.

Kuorinka, I. and Korhonen, O. (1981). Firefighters' reaction to alarm, an ECG and heart rate study, *Journal of Occupational Medicine*, **23**, 762–6.

Lacey, J. I. and Lacey, B. C. (1958). Verification and extension of the principle of autonomic response-stereotyping, *American Journal of Psychology*, **71**, 50–73.

Landman, A. D., Sanford, L. M. and Howland, B. E. (1976). Testosterone in human saliva, *Experientia*, **32**, 940–1.

Levine, P. (1986). Stress, In M. G. H. Coles, E. Donchine and S. W. Porges (eds) *Psychophysiology: Systems, Processes and Applications*, pp. 331–353, Guilford Press, New York.

Light, K. C. (1981). Cardiovascular responses to effortful active coping: implications for the role of stress in hypertension development, *Psychophysiology*, **18**, 216–25.

Lynch, J. J., Long, J. M., Thomas, S. A., Malinow, K. L. and Katcher, A. H. (1981). The effects of talking on the blood pressure of hypertensive and normotensive individuals, *Psychosomatic Medicine*, **43**, 25–33.

Lywood, D. W. (1967). Blood pressure. In P. H. Venables and I. Martin (eds) *A Manual of Psychophysiological Methods*, John Wiley and Sons, New York.

MacKay, C. J. (1980). The measurement of mood and psychophysiological activity using self-report techniques. In I. Martin and P. H. Venables (eds) *Techniques in Psychophysiology*, pp. 501–562, John Wiley and Sons, New York.

MacKay, C. J. Cox, T., Burrows, G. C. and Lazzarini, A. J. (1978). An inventory for the measurement of self-reported stress and arousal, *British Journal of Social and Clinical Psychology*, 283–284.

McGrath, J. E. (1982). Methodological problems in research on stress. In H. W. Krohn and L. Laux (eds) *Achievement, Stress, and Anxiety*, McGraw-Hill, New York.

Meddis, R. (1969). The analysis of mood ratings, doctoral dissertation, University of London.

Orth–Gomer, K. and Ahlbom, A. (1980). Impact of psychological stress and ischemic heart disease when controlling for conventional risk indicators, *Journal of Human Stress*, **6**, 7–16.

Payne, R. L. and Rick, J. T. (1986a). Heart rate as an indicator of stress in surgeons and anaesthetists. *Journal of Psychosomatic Research*, **30**, 411–20.

Payne, R. L. and Rick, J. T. (1986b). Psychological markers of stress in surgeons and anaesthetists. In T. H. Schmidt, T. M. Dembroski and G. Blumchen (eds) *Biological and Psychological Factors in Cardiovascular Disease*, Springer–Verlag, Berlin.

Reeder, L. G., Schrama, P. G. M. and Dirken, J. M. (1973). Stress and cardiovascular health: an international cooperative study—I, *Social Science and Medicine*, **7**, 573–84.

Reynolds, R. C. (1974). Community and occupational influences in stress at Cape Kennedy: relationships to heart disease. In R. S. Eliot (ed.) *Stress and the Heart*, Futura, Mount Kisco, NY.

Rick, J. T. and Payne, R. L. (1987). *Acute and chronic stress in cardio-thoracic anaesthetists*. Working paper, Department of Psychology, University of Sheffield, England.

Rolfe, J. H. (1973). Symposium on heart rate variability. *Ergonomics*, **16**, 1–112.

Rose, M., Jenkins, C. D. and Hurst, M. W. (1978). Health change in air traffic controllers: a prospective study, *Psychosomatic Medicine*, **40**, 142–65.

Rosner, B. and Polk, B. F. (1979). The implications of blood pressure variability for clinical and screening purposes, *Journal of Chronic Diseases*, **32**, 451–61.

Rosner, B. and Polk, B. F. (1981). The instability of blood pressure variability over time, *Journal of Chronic Diseases*, **34**, 135–41.

Rubin, R. T. (1974). Biochemical and neuroendocrine responses to severe psychological stress. In E. K. E. Gunderson and R. H. Rahe (eds) *Life Stress and Illness*, C. C. Thomas, Springfield, IL.

Rubin, R. T. and Rahe, R. H. (1974). U. S. Navy underwater demolition team training; biochemical studies. In E. K. E. Gunderson and R. H. Rahe (eds) *Life Stress and Illness*, C. C. Thomas, Springfield, IL.

Sabine, J. R. (1977). *Cholesterol*. Marcel Dekker, New York.

Sales, S. M. (1970). Some effects of role overload and role underload. *Organizational Behavior and Human Performance*, **5**, 592–608.

Sandberg, B. and Bliding, A. (1976). Duodenal ulcer in army trainees during basic military training, *Journal of Psychosomatic Research*, **20**, 61–74.

Schar, M., Reeder, L. G. and Dirken, J. M. (1973). Stress and cardiovascular health: an international cooperative study—II. The male population of a factory at Zurich, *Social Science and Medicine*, **7**, 585–603.

Schuler, R. S. (1980). Definition and conceptualization of stress in organizations. *Organizational Behavior and Human Performance*, **25**, 184–215.

Shannon, I. L., Katz, F. H. and Beerling, S. C. (1967). Steroids in parotid saliva, serum and urine of normal and diseased human subjects. In Schneyer, L. H. and Schneyer, C. A. (eds) *Secretory Mechanisms of Salivary Glands*, Academic Press, New York.

Shapiro, A. P., Benson, H., Chobanian, A. V., Herd, J. A., Julius, S., Kaplan, N., Lazarus, R. S., Ostfeld, A. M. and Syme, S. L. (1979). The role of stress in hypertension, *Journal of Human Stress*, **5**, 7–26.

Shirom, A., Eden, D., Silberwasser, S. and Kellermann, J. J. (1973). Job stresses and risk factors in coronary heart disease among five occupational categories in Kibbutzim, *Social Science and Medicine*, **7**, 875–92.

Siddle, D. A. T. and Turpin, G. (1980). Measurement quantification, and analysis of cardiac activity. In I. Martin and P. H. Venables (eds), *Techniques in Psychophysiology*, John Wiley and Sons, New York.

Statland, B. E., Bokelund, H. and Winkel, P. (1974). Factors contributing to intraindividual variation of serum constituents. 4. Effects of posture and tourniquet application on variation of serum constituents in healthy subjects, *Clinical Chemistry*, **20**, 1513–19.

Stern, R. M., Ray, W. J. and Davis, C. M. (1980). *Psychophysiological Recordings*, Oxford University Press, New York.

Steptoe, A. (1980). Blood pressure. In I. Martin and P. H. Venables (eds) *Techniques in Psychophysiology*, 247–73, John Wiley and Sons, New York.

Sykes, I. J. and Eden, D. (1985). Transitional stress, social support, and psychological strain, *Journal of Occupational Behavior*, **6**, 293–8.

Terry, J. M. and Shannon, I. L. (1964). Modification of self-positioning device for the collection of parotid fluid, Tech. Des. Rep. No. SAM–TDB–64–71.

Thayer, R. E. (1967). Measurement of activation through self-report, *Psychological Reports*, **20**, 663–78.

Thayer, R. E. (1978a). Towards a psychological theory of multidimensional activation (arousal), *Motivation and Emotion*, **21**, 1–34.

Thayer, R. E. (1978b). Factor analytic and reliability studies on the activation–deactivation adjective checklist. *Psychological Report*, **42**, 747–56.

Tursky, B. (1974). The indirect recording of human blood pressure. In P. Obrist, A.

H. Black, J. Brenner and L. DiCara (eds) *Cardiovascular Psychophysiology*, Aldine, Chicago.

Vesely, K. T. (1968). Clinical data and characteristics differentiating types of pepic ulcer, *GUT*, 9, 57–68.

Waldron, I. (1978). The coronary-prone behavior pattern, blood pressure, employment and socio-economic status in women, *Journal of Psychosomatic Research*, 22, 79–87.

Warheit, C. J. (1974). Occupation: a key factor in stress at the manned space center. In R. S. Eliot (ed.) *Stress and the Heart*, Mount Kisco, Futura, NY.

Wenger, M. A. (1966). Studies of the autonomic balance: a summary, *Psychophysiology*, 2, 173–86.

Wolf, S., Almy, T. P., Bachrach, W. H., Spiro, H. M., Sturdevant, R. A. L. and Weiner, H. (1979). The role of stress in peptic ulcer disease, *Journal of Human Stress*, 5, 27–37.

Yamaguchi, I. and Kopin, I. (1979). Plasma catecholamines and blood pressure responses to sympathetic stimulation in pithed rates, *American Journal of Physiology*, 237, H305–H310.

Zinner, H. S., Levy, P. S., and Kass, E. H. (1971). Familial aggregation of blood pressure in childhood, *New England Journal of Medicine*, 284, 401–12.

Causes, Coping and Consequences of Stress at Work
Edited by C. L. Cooper and R. Payne
© 1988 John Wiley & Sons Ltd

Chapter 12

Methodological Issues in the Study of Work Stress: Objective vs Subjective Measurement of Work Stress and the Question of Longitudinal Studies*

Michael Frese and Dieter Zapf

INTRODUCTION

Since the book *Stress at Work* appeared in 1978, a number of methodological advances have been made in stress research. Some of the main criticisms discussed (e.g. by Kasl, 1978) were: (1) the (self-) selection effect has not been controlled (e.g. higher smoking among blue collar workers); (2) the studies were not longitudinal and, therefore, little in terms of causal analysis could be done; (3) the independent and the dependent measures were similar in content, therefore leading to trivial results; (4) there should be more than just a stressor–dependent variable correlation— potential moderators like coping strategies or social support should be entered into the equation as well. These criticisms have led to a higher use of longitudinal studies (e.g. Frese, 1985; Karasek *et al.*, 1981; Kohn and Schooler, 1982; Parkes, 1982), more inclusion of moderators (e.g. Beehr, Walsh and Taber, 1976, Frese, 1986; House, 1981; Howard, Cunningham and Rechnitzer, 1986; Karasek *et al.*, 1981; Semmer, 1982) and to an attempt to measure work situations in an objective way (Frese, 1985; Greiner *et al.*, 1987; Jenkins *et al.*, 1975; Kannheiser, 1987; Semmer, 1982, 1984; Volpert *et al.*, 1983; Zapf, 1987). Although there are still many studies that can be criticized in the same way as in 1978, there appear to be worthwhile methodological advances in the better studies on stress at work.

Since there are still many studies that could be improved methodologically, it would be possible to write a repeat of the analysis done in 1978. However, we would end the chapter with the same demands made in 1978 and actually Kasl has been able to repeat many criticisms as late as 1986 and 1987. Therefore, we chose not to do a general review that would just repeat what

* Thanks are due to F. Glover, F. Nerdinger, R. Payne and I. Waldron for critically reading a first draft of this paper.

has been done before. Rather we want to concentrate in this chapter on the problems that appear when a more advanced methodology is used. In such a case, problems appear that are different from those associated with a less advanced conceptual and methodological approach.

We are not interested in covering methodological problems from a statistical point of view. Rather, we want to concentrate on two methodological issues that encompass the boundaries between conceptual and methodological thinking. One such problem area occurs when using objective and subjective measures of work stressors. Furthermore, we discuss the consequences of using longitudinal designs, which have ramifications for both theory and methodology.

OBJECTIVE AND SUBJECTIVE MEASURES OF STRESS AT WORK

Why is it useful in stress research to use objective measures and conceptualizations? The driving forces behind using 'objective' conceptualizations and measures in stress research are threefold: practical, theoretical and methodological.

The *practical* reasons are concerned with being able to reduce the stressors after one has done the appropriate research. There are essentially two ways to reduce stress: by focusing on the individual or by focusing on the institution. The institutional approach can only be used if the objective stressors at work are shown to produce ill-health. If stress were idiosyncratic and just related to an individual's perception or cognitive appraisals, it would not make sense to redesign working conditions; the only sensible approach would be to change the individual.

Thus, the question, whether there are objective stressors at all, has vast policy implications. For example, the approach favored by the work restructuring and job democracy movement, namely to redesign the job, would just be a waste of money from the 'subjective' point of view in the stress field.

In terms of *theory*, the cognitive 'revolution' has led to a devaluation of the importance of the objective environment. Concentrating on the objective environment 'smacked' of a purely mechanistic viewpoint that does not take into account the importance of the cognitive person variables, like appraisal processes or coping strategies. This has led to a constructivistic approach best espoused by Neisser (1967). However, there is a recent trend away from this constructivistic approach, most clearly discussed within an action theory framework (e.g. Frese and Sabini, 1985). Again Neisser (1976) has shown how perception is related to 'reality'. Moreover, acting and receiving feedback from the environment helps to produce realistic cognitions as well (von Hofsten, 1985; Neisser, 1985; Sabini, Frese and Kossmann, 1985). Thus, this approach has led to an integration of a cognitive viewpoint with a more behavioral one. The concepts of action theory are cognitive as well; the individual's perceptions and appraisals are important, however, they do not override reality but put reality into perspective. Given such an action theory approach, objective conceptualizations and measures have again received an important theoretical status in industrial psychology (Hacker, 1985, 1986; Volpert, 1987).

The *methodological* reasons for using objective measures are intimately related to the problem that trivial correlations could occur between subjective stress measures and ill-health (e.g. Kasl, 1978) either because of method variance or because there is an overlap between the items in terms of content. Only objective measures lead the way out of this triviality trap.

Thus, there are good reasons to concentrate on the objective side of work stress. However, it is not yet quite clear what is meant by 'objective' or 'subjective' in the stress field. Indeed, we think that there is some muddled thinking going on in this area. Furthermore, the question of what is objective and subjective has to be dealt with from a conceptual and a measurement point of view.

Conceptions of Objective and Subjective Stressors

There are several different ways of using the concepts subjective and objective. Three different conceptualizations of subjective and objective are used in the literature. Often they are not clearly differentiated, leading to confusions.

(1) Objective can be used to mean material objects and processes in the world, irrespective of psychological processes. Correspondingly, subjective means that psychological processes are involved. In some studies on technology, and time and motion studies, the concept of objective in this first sense is used. We find this concept of subjective and objective of little use, because it defines psychological processes to be purely subjective and does not allow the conceptualization of psychological stressors as objective.

(2) The second use of objective is in the sense of being real, being part of reality. Correspondingly, subjective means illusory or unreal. This is an overinclusive conception of objective. Stressor-perceptions that are essentially illusory seldom appear in the work sphere; therefore, this concept would not allow many differentations between objective and subjective in our area.

(3) The third concept of objective is in the sense of not being related to one specific individual's perception. Subjective in this sense is tied to one individual's cognitive and emotional processing (e.g. perceptions and appraisals). Thus, objective means that a particular individual's cognitive and emotional processing does not influence the reporting of social and physical facts. In this sense, objective stressors include physical and social character-

istics of the environment. This concept is in contrast to sense (1) stated above (objective materials and processes) as psychological processes can be called objective as long as they are independent of a person's cognitive and emotional processings. Thus, to be rebuked by a supervisor is a non-material but yet objective event, (potentially) perceivable by others. Similarly, a high degree of demand for concentration is objective in this sense. It is this definition that we find most useful.

However, one problem with this conceptualization is that the most prominent elements in the stress process are cognitive: the cognitions (appraisals) of the individual are the focus of these theories. How can one have such a concept of the stress process and still talk about objective stressors? The conceptual trick is to think of an 'average person's' cognitive and emotional processing. The 'average' has to be conceptualized to exist within a given society (or subgroup) at a given time (since, for example, aspirations change in the historical process). This 'average person' is, of course, an abstract person in the same sense as in general and experimental psychology. This conceptualization may sound like circular reasoning. A stressor is that stimulus that leads to a stress-reaction. However, such a procedure allows us to develop an objective concept of stressors (objective in the third sense) because the average person's stressor is not related to the concrete individual's cognitive and emotional processings.

Our discussion shows that it is possible (and useful) to talk about objective stressors although we know, of course, that an objective stressor does not mechanically lead to a stress reaction. As Lazarus and Folkman (1986) point out, there are perceptions, appraisals, coping strategies, personal prerequisites that all play a role in the stress process. Thus, objective stressors lead only *potentially* to a stress reaction.

In summary, we use the following terms:

Objective stressor: the objective stressors are conceptualized (and operationalized) not to be influenced by an individual's cognitive and emotional processing; an example is that the job requires the average worker to react very quickly to a danger signal and for the majority of workers this would be stressful.

Stressor perception: the objective stress situation has to be perceived in order for it to have a psychological effect on the individual (although it does not necessarily have to be conscious and reportable); for example, the perception that one has to react quickly to the danger signal.

Stressor appraisal: the perceived stressor can be seen to be stressful, if it taxes the capacities of the person or is threatening or aversive (cf. Lazarus' concept of stress); in our example, missing the danger signal would lead to negative consequences to the worker.

Short-term stress reaction: there are behavioral, emotional and physio-logical effects on the person, e.g. the worker has a 'cramped stomach' when working on this job.

Long-term stress reaction: over a period of time the stress situation may lead to psychosomatic complaints or illness or psychological dysfunctioning.

Empirically, it is not easy to differentiate these aspects of the stress process. However, it is useful to conceptually keep the different parts of the process clear, even if the empirical work is much more messy.

Measuring Objective and Subjective Stressors

A measure is, of course, an operationalization of a construct. But this oper-ationalization may be more or less well related to the concept. If one thinks in terms of structural models, one construct is operationalized with different empirical indicators. Within the concept of multiplism (Cook, 1985, Houts *et al.*, 1986 that is in some ways based on Campbell and Fiske, 1959), the demand was developed that there should be more than just one operationaliz-ation of a construct because any one measurement cannot be perfect and it always includes methodological and other sources of error.

Stress research has typically conceptualized subjective methods to be ques-tionnaire measures filled out by the subjects and objective methods to be ratings done by expert raters, as well as document analyses and physical methods (Algera, 1983; Frese, 1985; Gardell, 1971; Hackman and Lawler, 1971; Hackman and Oldham, 1974, 1975; Jenkins *et al.*, 1975; Kannheiser, 1987; Martin *et al.*, 1980; Semmer, 1982; Volpert *et al.*, 1983; Wells, 1982).

Strictly speaking, this common differentiation is not quite adequate. For example, when a person tells us (in a questionnaire) that he is 25, we take it to reflect objective reality. On the other hand, if he tells us that he does not like his job, we tend to assume that a lot more appraisal processes have taken place to arrive at his judgment. Thus, any kind of 'subjective' questionnaire report can be placed somewhere on a dimension from 'low in dependency on cognitive and emotional processing' to 'high in dependency on cognitive and emotional processing'. Similarly, the 'objective' ratings of an observer may be more or less influenced by cognitive and emotional processing as well (e.g. depending on whether the observer is contrasting the workplace with a particular 'bad' or 'good' job that she has rated before). These sorts of processes may lead to different degrees of interrater agreement in the judgment even of 'objective' stressor dimensions.

Since cognitive and emotional processing is done by both the subjects and the observers to a certain degree, 'subjective' as well as 'objective' measurements of job stressors can lead to a series of problems. The problems of the subjective measurements (based on the subjects' responses) have been emphasized repeatedly in the literature (e.g. recently again by Contrada and Krantz, 1987; Kasl 1986; Leventhal and Tomarken, 1987) and have led to the demand that observers' ratings should be used.

For example, the problems of interpreting a correlation between subjective measures of stressors and a questionnaire on psychological dysfunctioning are: (1) method variance as discussed in classical test theory (e.g. central tendency, acquiescence effect, halo effect, etc.), (2) overlap in content between independent and dependent measures, (3) problems associated with a third variable that influences both the dependent and the independent variables, e.g. a personality trait or a tendency to complain, (4) current well-being influences the judgment of stressors, (5) demand characteristics encouraging the respondent to give the researchers what they are perceived to want (Orne, 1962). Using objective indicators of work stressors will, in fact, reduce these problems and it has been shown that a substantial correlation between objective stressors and dysfunctioning remains (e.g. Frese, 1985; Greiner *et al.*, 1987).

While these problems of subjective questionnaire research have been prominently discussed, the problems associated with observers' ratings have been less clearly demarcated even in research that has used observed ratings of stressors. Here, the main problem is that the correlation between stressors and dysfunctioning is systematically underestimated. As pointed out, the observers' ratings are dependent on their cognitive and emotional processing of information. Thus, the same questionnaire effects as discussed above, apply here as well, but in the case of observers they lead to pure error variance because observers' deviations from the 'true score' are not associated with the subjects' questionnaire responses of dysfunctioning. This error variance decreases the correlation between observers' judgments of stressors and the subjects' reports of their dysfunctioning. Additionally, there are a host of other problems that appear when using observers' judgments (Zapf, 1987).

(1)*Limited time of observation.* Any observation time has to be limited. Thus, only a certain segment of work can be observed. Since peak stressors appear seldomly but are then quite powerful, they are most likely to be missed by the observer. Furthermore, practical constraints of research often forbid that observers are present when work is most stressful. It was our experience that supervisors sometimes told us not to come for observations on certain days, because work would be too hectic and we would disturb production. Furthermore, the bias of stressor observation may be systematically skewed. It is easier to observe jobs with small work cycle times (e.g. as in jobs on an assembly line) in contrast to jobs with long work cycles, because here whole work cycles cannot be observed within a period of a few hours (Baars *et al.*, 1981; Greif *et al.*, 1983; Semmer, 1984).

(2) *Unobservability of mental processes.* Sometimes, the observer has to estimate stressors that are intimately related to mental processes, e.g. high

concentration. Such mental processes cannot be observed directly and, therefore, there is much leeway for errors. This issue is more important for highly skilled blue collar work, office work and computer-aided work than for low skilled jobs.

(3) *Effects of observation on work behavior.* In our experience, people work differently when they are observed. They may work in a more leisurely way, take more rest periods to explain things, and sometimes they may even work on their preferred machine (or be asked by the supervisor to do that). Similarly, accident prevention rules are more often obeyed when one is observed. Sometimes, there may even be some anxiety to be observed as well (evaluation apprehension effect, cf. Rosenberg, 1969). Gilardi, Weber and Liepmann (1985) report their impression that in their long-term observations, people started to work normally after two, to three days.

(4) *Representativeness of workplaces.* In terms of practical constraints for research, it appears that companies with particularly bad working conditions are usually off limits for researchers and even in companies willing to participate in research, there may be a tendency for supervisors to restrict research to the more presentable workplaces.

All of these four reasons lead to a decrease of the correlation between observed stressors and dysfunctioning (compared with the true correlation) because in each case, peak or normal stressors cannot be observed and thus an important impact on dysfunctioning is not reported. In methodological terms the observed variance of the stressors is underestimated. This makes it very hard to get significant correlations empirically. Therefore, it is not surprising that there are some reports of nonsignificant findings in this area (Gardell, 1971; Seibel and Lühring, 1984, Tielsch and Hettinger, 1984; Wells, 1982). It is all the more remarkable that there are a number of studies that show clear-cut correlations (Algera, 1983; Frese, 1985; Greiner *et al.*, 1987; Hacker, Iwanowa and Richter, 1983; Iwanowa and Hacker, 1984).

In summary, there is evidence that the use of subjective judgments of stressors can lead to an overestimate of the correlation between stressors and dysfunctioning (we shall later see that there are actually also conservative constraints at work). On the other hand, the use of objective (observers') judgments of stressors leads to an underestimate of the 'true' correlation.

Consequences for the Measurement of Stressors

There are some theoretical and practical consequences that follow from our discussion of subjective and objective stressors: First, how much do cognitive and emotional processing interfere in the measurement; second, what different measurement models exist and which ones are correct; third, are there alternatives to observers' ratings that give objective measures of work stressors.

(1) As pointed out, the term subjective is dependent on whether or not cognitive and emotional processing is implicated. This means that any kind of measure can be placed on the dimension 'low on cognitive and emotional processing' to 'high on cognitive and emotional processing'. Some researchers seem to suppose that all subjects' responses lead to a subjective bias because of cognitive and emotional processes. We disagree–because it depends on the wording of the item whether there is high cognitive and emotional procesing. For example, an item like 'I feel overwhelmed by the burden of this job' is high on this dimension, an item 'How many pieces of work do you complete in a shift?' is low. Therefore, it is useful to develop items that require a minimum of cognitive and emotional processing and are therefore more objective.

The same reasoning applies to the observers. The researcher has to make sure, of course, that the observers' judgments are made with as little interference from their cognitive and emotional processing as possible. However, if the researcher does not succeed, then he or she will probably get more underestimated correlation because the observer's cognitive and emotional processing is not related to the reactions of the subjects.

An empirical indication of what we have just described can be seen in Semmer (1982, 1984); Dunckel and Semmer (1987) and Zapf, Greif and Semmer (in press). In these studies work characteristics were examined. This was done by asking several workers of one workplace and observing this workplace by two or more observers. The interrater observer's agreement was higher for the resources (control, skill level needed and variety) than for stressors. The resources can be well observed and without much interference from cognitive and emotional processing; among two observers these correlations have a mean of 0.75 in each of two studies. In contrast, the judgment of stressors is more private and therefore more strongly related to cognitive and emotional processing. Therefore, the average interrater agreements are lower for the stressors (organizational problems, environmental stressors, uncertainty, danger of accidents and intensity) with $r=0.57$ in one study and $r=0.58$ in the second. (Note, however, that the interrater agreements are in general quite substantial for complex judgments.) The same pattern appears when one correlates the agreements of two workers who work in the same job (Zapf *et al.*, in press). The correlations between observers and subjects again show a similar pattern. For resources, the average correlations are $r=0.59$ and $r=0.48$ in the two studies; the means of the correlations for the stressors are only $r=0.37$ and $r=0.33$. Other studies showed similar results, e.g. for interrater agreements and for the correlations between observers and subjects (Algera, 1983; Jenkins *et al.*, 1975).

(2) Taking the impact of cognitive and emotional processing on the meas-

ures as a starting point, it is possible that psychological dysfunctioning itself influences the (subjective) measurement of stressors. Zapf (in press) has compared different measurement models with a structural equation approach. Three different approaches to measure work stressors were used, observers' ratings, a group median of three or more people who were doing the same type of job (both are objective in our sense) and subjects' ratings. Four models were compared.

(a) The *trait model*. This model assumes that each stressor is measured by three methods: individual, group and observer measures. These measures have convergent validity. The stressors are correlated with dysfunctioning, which is measured by subjective data. The main assumption of this model is schematically shown in Figure 1.

(b) The *method model*. This model implies a complete lack of convergent validity between the measures of the stressors. The latent variables in this case are the measurement methods, i.e. questionnaires, observers' ratings and group ratings. These measurement methods stand for themselves and have little relationship to the theoretical content. This means that, for example, questionnaire data correlate essentially among themselves; the same is true of observers' ratings. Any indicator is determined by the measurement method. For questionnaire data this is in line with Kasls' (1978) critique, which argued that questionnaire data of stressors and dysfunctioning measure essentially the same thing (cf. Figure 2).

(c) The *stress perception model*. This model implies that observers' ratings and group data measure objective stressors and that subjects' responses measure perceived stressors (cf. Figure 3). In addition, this model implies that there is a path from objective stressors to perceived stressors and a path from the perceived stressors to psychological dysfunctioning (no direct path from the objective stressor to dysfunctioning). Thus, this is a model in the spirit of Lazarus's theory; (Lazarus and Lannier, 1978) the objective stressors are appraised (primary appraisal as subjective stressors) and this in turn leads to dysfunctioning.

(d) The *multitrait–multimethod model* (in the sense of Campbell and Fiske, 1959) assumes that a combination of the trait model (a) and the method model (b) is correct. It turns out that the multitrait–multimethod model fits the data best. This means that the subjective measures have some common method variance. Every time one uses questionnaire responses for relating independent and dependent variables, there is some common method variance. This claim assumes that there may also be an influence of the dependent measures of dysfunctioning on the reporting of stressors. However, the data cannot be interpreted as purely determined by method factors because there is also convergent validity of the stressor measures. This means that different measures (subjective, observed and group data) are each reflections of a construct, to a certain extent. This multitrait–multimethod model supports

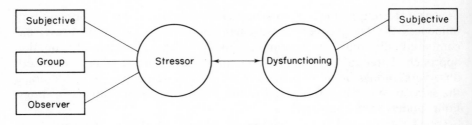

Figure 1 The trait model

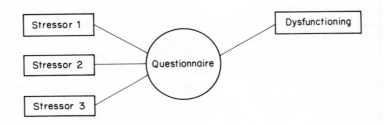

Figure 2 The method model

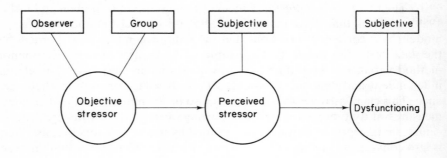

Figure 3 The stress perception model

our hypothesis that objective and subjective measures have something to do with each other but that there is noise in the data that derives from classical error variance and the cognitive and emotional processing of the subjects. Within a multitrait–multimethod model it can be shown (Figure 4) that correlations (x1,x2) between stressors and dysfunctioning (both measured by questionnaire) can be decomposed into one part that is true covariance between the stressor and dysfunctioning (path x1 – stressor – dysfunctioning – x2) and a second part that consists of method variance due to the common method (path x1 – questionnaire – x2). One implication of this is that correlations between stressors and dysfunctioning that are based on questionnaire data overestimate the true correlation to a certain extent. Another implication is that the correlation based on observers' ratings underestimate the true correlation. Thus, there is a true and substantial correlation between stressors and dysfunctioning.

A similar model applies to the measurement of resources (complexity, variety, control at work) although there are also substantial differences (Zapf, 1987). The resources measures show very little variance due to cognitive and emotional processing. The impact of the dependent variables of psychosomatic dysfunctioning on self-report measures of resources is negligible. In other words, the paths from the latent variable 'questionnaire' to the indicators for psychological dysfunctioning are zero. Thus, the error variance due to cognitive and emotional processing (as reflected in the dysfunctioning's impact) is unimportant for resources.

(3) Up to this point, we have mainly referred to observations as the more objective method of measuring work stressors. However, we actually think that group measures are very useful, adequate and possibly more practical

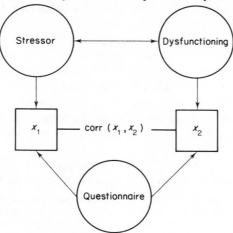

Figure 4 Decomposition of correlations (e.g. of questionnaire data) within a multitrait-multimethod model

measures of the objective side of stressors. By group data we mean that the responses of two or more workers who do the same job, are combined into one score (i.e. a median is taken). These group data are objective in our sense, because the influence of idiosyncratic responses is decreased; they take the expert role of the worker seriously, they are better at grasping infrequent but potentially strong stressors, they tap non-observable cognitions, there is no observation effect and representativeness issues are less severe. However, there are also three potential weaknesses of this procedure. First, there may be a group consensus of what is stressful and what is not, and this consensus may not be related to reality. Second, in contrast to the observers, the respondents can hardly be trained in theoretical concepts and on the use of anchors in answering the scales. Third, there may be problems because workplaces are only very seldomly really identical. There is some noise in these data because machines are of different quality, there may be more or less draft or noise in different parts of a factory hall. Many workplaces are also in some way adjusted to the specific capabilities of the individual worker (this is particularly so in office work). And even in cases where the workplaces are identical, people tend to perform work tasks in different ways. For all of these reasons, a conservative criterion for what constitutes the same workplace, has to be used.

The difficulty of finding really identical jobs makes us skeptical about studies that use a broad criterion of what constitutes the same workplace (e.g. Hackman and Lawler, 1971, Hackman and Oldham, 1975, Wells, 1982) or studies that just put together workers from the same occupation. The results of these studies may be unduly conservative and zero correlations prove little in these cases (e.g. Wells, 1982).*

It is curious to note, by the way, that Hackman and Lawler (1971) and Hackman and Oldham (1975) do not discuss the different status of individual and aggregated data with respect to objectivity. They seem to conceptualize the group data to be the subjective responses in their reports on the correlations between observers and subjects. We would conceptualize their correlations between aggregated individual data and observers' judgments to be correlations between two different objective measures. This may be one reason, why their correlations are a bit higher than those found in our study (additionally, they also averaged observers' ratings which contributed to higher correlations as well).

Our claim that the group data are more objective is substantiated by two findings. First, in terms of structural models, a stress perception model

---

* There may be practical reasons for using occupations as an independent variable in epidemiological studies. For example Karasek and Theorell (in preparation) have grouped occupations according to the mean of stressors and mean control. This gives them a tool to be used in different representative studies without having recourse to the actual working conditions. Nevertheless, such procedures are very conservative when it comes to the study of the impact of stress at work.

mentioned above (cf. Figure 3) that conceives of the group data as measures of subjective stressors is worse than one that relates them to the objective stressor (Zapf, 1987). Second, the group data show similar patterns in their correlations with dysfunctioning to the observers' data (Algera, 1983; Frese, 1985).

In summary, we have discussed the advantages and disadvantages of different objective measures of work stressors. We think that research on stress at work will profit when more objective indicators of work stressors are used but one should be aware that they may still underestimate the true effect size.

We have concentrated on the independent variables of stress research. We could have developed a similar discussion on objective indicators of dysfunctioning. It is possible to develop ratings of psychological dysfunctioning (cf. e.g. Kornhauser, 1965) or use psychophysiological measures (e.g. Frankenhaeuser and Gardell, 1976; Levi, 1967). In many ways a similar reasoning could be made for these measures as was used with reference to ratings of work stressors. Issues on physiological measures of work stress are also dealt with by Fried (1988) in Chapter 11.

THE PROBLEMS OF LONGITUDINAL STUDIES

It has been suggested that longitudinal studies can be used to reduce the problems associated with cross-sectional studies, particularly empirical validations of causal inferences. Once one used longitudinal designs, however, the problems of conceptualizing how causes can have effects, really start. In the following, we do not present methodological problems in the narrow sense of those that appear when doing longitudinal studies, for example cohort and selection effects, third variable problems, etc. (cf. Dwyer, 1983; Nesselroade and Baltes, 1979), but we want to discuss some plausible conceptual models of how a stressor can lead to ill-health, and some ramifications of this issue.

In line with Cook and Campbell (1979) we speak of a causal effect as existing if there is covariation of the stressor with ill-health, if the stressor appeared before ill-health developed, and if other plausible explanations can be ruled out (e.g. a weakening of the body's constitution that led first to more stress *and* later to an increase in the manifest ill-health).

Different Models of the Time Course of Cause and Effect

In the following, we want to present different models of how a stressor may affect ill-health in the course of time and to analyze how different theoretical reasonings might influence longitudinal panel designs. We use the simplified assumption that one stressor can lead to dysfunctioning.

Initial impact Vs exposure time models of stress effects

Within the area of job socialization (Frese, 1983, 1984), two basic kinds of causal conceptualization can be distinguished.

(a) The literature on the long term effects of the workplace assumes implicitly the *exposure time effect* (cf. Figure 5), for example, the longer a stressor impacts on the person, the higher should be the incidence of ill-health. This reasoning is similar to the one in occupational medicine, e.g. with regard to industrial deafness. The longer one is exposed to noise, the higher is the probability of deafness (Bürck, 1974).

(b) The *initial impact* concept is more dominant in the job transition literature (Nicholson, 1984). Just after a person has started a new job (or is exposed to a new stressor), there is some kind of 'reality shock' (Louis, 1980; van Maanen, 1977) because of the unexpected nature of the new stressor and because useful coping strategies for dealing with the stressor have not been developed. This effect is reduced after one gets to know the job better (cf. Figure 6).

Empirical studies of these two effects need different designs in terms of the time lags between the measurement points. The initial impact concept implies that the measurement points are relatively near to each other (e.g. at most a few months apart) in contrast to the exposure time concept with its long time periods between the onset of stressors and the appearance of the effects (e.g. one or two years).

Variants of the exposure time model

Up to this point, we have contrasted the initial impact and the exposure time effects. However, there are many plausible variants of the exposure time

Figure 5 The exposure time model of stress effects

Figure 6 The initial impact model of stress effects

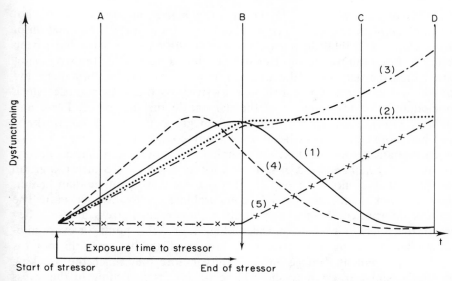

Figure 7 Variants of the exposure time model: (1) stress reaction model, (2) accumulation model, (3) dynamic accumulation model, (4) adjustment model, (5) sleeper effect model

effect displayed in Figure 7. All of these variants assume that a stressor has some impact on psychological and psychosomatic dysfunctioning:

(1) *Stress reaction model.* According to this model, the impact of a stressor increases and leads to psychological dysfunctioning after a certain time. However, once the stressor is removed there is an improvement in psychological functioning. We have found such an effect in a longitudinal study on unemployment in which older unemployed male blue collar workers were reinterviewed 1½ years after the first wave of interviews (Frese and Mohr, 1987). After this time, there was a higher degree of depression in the unemployed while the ones who had found work, or who had retired in the meantime, were less depressed than during their original period of unemployment. The same results were replicated in a longitudinal study by Baltz *et al.* (1985) with a different group of workers. Thus, the stressor has a direct impact of dysfunctioning and the effect is stronger the longer there is exposure to the stressors.

A similar effect is reported by Gardell (1978) in which a Swedish firm stopped using a piece rate system—a stressor—in favor of monthly pay. This led to a reduction of sick leave and accidents.

Similarly Wall and Clegg (1981) report in their study of the effects of introducing semi-autonomous work groups, that there are long-term increases of health in the participants in these work groups.

(2) *Accumulation model*. Psychosomatic *illnesses* (in contrast to psycho-somatic *complaints*) probably come about as a result of the accumulation of stress effects and they do not go away even after the stressors have been reduced. For example, if an ulcer has developed because of the stress situation, then the damage to the stomach membranes may be permanent and the illness may flare up in response to stressors other than those which precipitated the development of the damage in the first place. Frese and Okonek (1984) have shown that a certain group of former shiftworkers, who had stopped shiftwork because of health complaints, showed a level of psychosomatic problems that was similar to shiftworkers. This was so although they had been out of shiftwork for nine years. In contrast, a group of shiftworkers, who had stopped shiftwork for reasons other than health, showed fewer health problems (a comparable level to day-workers). The authors interpreted the findings within a vulnerability-stress model. They argue, that there is a psychological–biological breaking point for every individual. This breaking point cannot be easily predicted but when this point is reached, permanent damage ensues. Thus, before they reach the breaking point, the shiftworkers may show ill-health effects according to the stress reaction effect model [i.e. when they leave shiftwork, complaints go down (cf. also Akerstedt and Torsvall, 1978)]; after reaching the breaking point the accumulation model is a more adequate representation of the results because ill-health is not reduced even after leaving the stress situation.*

(3) *Dynamic accumulation model*. In contrast to the accumulation model, it is assumed in this model that there is an inner dynamic that leads to a further increase even after the stressor has been removed although this increase is probably decelerated. This may be so because the original stressor had a general weakening effect on the psychophysical system so that new stressors have a higher impact than normally. In such a case an individual may also be more vulnerable to stressors not related to the work situation at all (e.g. in leisure time, Bamberg, 1986). Additionally, the dynamic effect could appear in psychosomatic illnesses because the illness itself may represent an additional problem. Such a dynamic accumulation model has also been suggested for depression and irritation. Beck (1972) argued that depressives are involved in a vicious cycle. Because of negative cognitions they become sad and the negative emotions themselves lead to additional

* Depue and Monroe (1986) have argued that stressful life events have little impact on dysfunctioning because most of dysfunctioning is chronic. While we agree that much of dysfunctioning is chronic this does not presuppose that stressors do not have an influence. In contrast, the accumulation model may apply. Their article actually warrants a more intensive discussion than we can have here. However, it is interesting to note that they do not quote any studies on stress at work. This is unfortunate because many of the methodological problems they touch upon are smaller in the stress at work literature than in the literature on stressful life events since objective measures of stressors can be and have been used in the workplace.

negative cognitions, etc. Similarly, chronic irritation may increase irritation because of the dynamics with other people reacting to the irritation shown.

(4) *Adjustment model.* The adjustment model is related to the stress effect model. Similarly, there is at first a linear increase of dysfunctioning with the duration of the stressor. However, after a certain point, an adjustment process sets in and the dysfunctioning decreases although the stressor is still present. There is some overlap between this model and the initial impact model. Both assume that there is a reduction of ill-health in spite of the presence of the stressor. However, these two models are different in the time courses they suggest. The adjustment model assumes a longer increase time of dysfunctioning till an adjustment or effective coping strategies to the stressor develop. Evidence for the adjustment model may be found in a study with samples of secretaries in two different German cities (Frese, Saupe and Semmer, 1981). The younger subject showed a much higher multiple correlation of the stressors on psychosomatic complaints and depression than the older ones. Although other interpretations are possible (e.g. that older secretaries have better jobs) adjustment may have been operative in the older secretaries.

The adjustment model can be described quite well within Lazarus' theory (Lazarus, 1966): one develops coping strategies towards the stressors (e.g. denial or help seeking) which reduce ill-health. At this point, it may be useful to recall, however, that coping strategies may have only a limited impact on work stressors because stressors at work are not easily avoided (e.g. in comparison with leisure time stressors). There is some longitudinal evidence that coping strategies are not very successful in changing later work stressors and stressor perceptions (Menaghan and Merves, 1984).

(4) *Sleeper effect model.* The sleeper effect model implies that dysfunctioning appears a long time after exposure to the stressor. It is possible that the stressor is not present any more when dysfunctioning appears. It also assumes that the effect is higher with longer exposure to and stronger intensity of the stressor. There are some examples in occupational medicine for the sleeper effect, e.g. cancer caused by radioactive radiation. The manifest cancer appears long after the person has been exposed to the 'stressor'. Post-traumatic stress disorders follow this kind of pattern as well (e.g. Archibald and Tuddenham, 1965). Although, there is more evidence on war related stressors in this area, it is conceivable that occupational stressors might lead to similar problems (e.g. industrial accidents).

Frankenhaeuser (1981) showed that stressors lead to higher catecholamines *after* the stressor has been reduced. In her study, female employees of an insurance firm were studied during and after an extended period of overtime. The peak adrenaline level was after overtime was reduced. Within a much smaller time range, Frankenhaeuser and Gardell (1976) have shown that workers with more stress do not show an adjustment effect to the work in the course of a day but show an increase of catecholamines at the end of the day. Thus, the 'unwinding' after a period of stressful work takes time. A similar effect (on a yet smaller time scale) could also be shown experimentally. Glass and Singer (1972) demonstrated after-effects of stressors in their experimental studies (cf. also Cohen, 1980). While these examples clearly have a different (smaller) time range from what is implied by the sleeper effect, there is some overlap in meaning.

The five models discussed so far assume that the stressor would have a clear-cut beginning and end. This is certainly not quite realistic; people tend to anticipate and prepare for stressors (thus, it is unclear where the actual beginning lies) and it is often unclear when a stressor is removed.

Furthermore, we assumed that the increases of dysfunctioning would be essentially linearly with exposure time (except in the adjustment model). This is also not quite realistic. Most probably, there is some asymptotic, or ceiling, effect that decelerates the increases. The level of the asymptote may be higher if the intensity of the stressor is higher. The ceiling may also be more or less quickly reached depending upon which dependent variable we study (compare, for example, irritation and psychosomatic illness). Our assumption that there must be some asymptote is plausible because, for example, it is not possible to become more depressed than a certain (more or less) fixed amount of depression for every one person. Similarly, there is probably some ceiling effect for the degree of psychosomatic complaints that an individual can develop. However, note that most of the subjects in occupational stress research are, by and large, not extremely sick. Therefore, there is quite some room to move upwards on an ill-health variable and the ceiling is not reached very quickly.

A combination of the initial impact model and an exposure time model

It is possible that there are combination effects of any of these five exposure time models just discussed with the initial impact model. The effects shown in Figure 8 may occur when the initial impact effect and a simple exposure time effect appear in the same person. A person might experience a reality shock at first and then develop some coping and defense strategies to deal with the new stressor. Using these strategies, ill-health is reduced. However, these coping strategies may turn out to be inefficient in the long term (cf. Schönpflug, 1985) and may, therefore, contribute to an exposure time effect. A wave-shaped curve might appear as a result of these processes. Frese (1984) reports some results on stress at work and Warr (1984) on the effects of unemployment that appear to conform to this kind of curve quite well. In Frese, the correlations between stress at work and psychosomatic complaints are high in the first two job tenure years; these correlations reduce in the next eight years and then increase again. On a different level, Warr

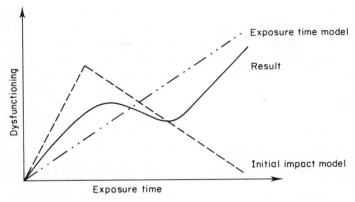

Figure 8 The combination of the initial impact and the exposure time models

reports a high incidence of ill-health in the first two months of unemployment; this percentage is reduced in the second to third month and increases again afterwards. While these data are not conclusive, they show at least that it might be worthwhile to take a close look at curve differences of this kind.

Time as a theoretical variable

We know very little about the exact timeframe that is needed for a stressor to have an impact on dysfunctioning. As a matter of fact, since stress research tended to be cross-sectional, theoretical consideration of the factor time did not matter much. Now that there is more longitudinal research, we are much more interested in the factor time. However, time is not a psychological variable *per se* as developmental psychology shows (Neugarten, 1977; Wohlwill, 1970). Rather, we have to be interested in how people spend their time, how they conceptualize time and what events occur, etc.

We have been careful not to suggest specific time spans that are needed to develop dysfunctioning. We do not know how long the exposure time to a stressor (or stressors) has to be before one develops psychosomatic complaints, or when adaptation might set in. Moreover, exposure time is not the only factor but exposure intensity is very important as well.

Fortunately, there is one line of research (on unemployment) in which time factors have been researched explicitly. Apparently, unemployment leads to psychological dysfunctioning between about three months and a year (Balz *et al.*, 1985, Brinkmann, 1985, Frese and Mohr, 1987; Warr and Jackson, 1984, 1985). This time span is related to a psychologically meaningful time period. After a few months to a year (depending upon country and job history), unemployment compensation is often reduced in Western countries, people perceive the unemployed to be 'long-term unemployed' after this time period, there is less hope, financial resources dwindle, etc.

Another area in which the timeframe was shown to be of importance is helplessness research. If the time lag between helplessness 'training' and the testing phase was less than 24 hours, helplessness behavior was seen in dogs. If the time between the two phases was longer than 24 hours, helplessness did not appear (Overmier and Seligman, 1967).

We urgently need a more detailed conceptualization of the time component in research on stress at work. It would be useful to explicate the time variable and include it into the design of studies.

This is a difficult task. Reality is actually much more complicated, because different kinds of stressors may be related to different models. Similarly, different dependent variables (e.g. psychomatic complaints vs psychosomatic illness) may follow different models. Finally, intervening variables like moderators and mediators may complicate the models even more. These issues are taken up next.

Different Kinds of Stressors and of Dysfunctioning and the Time Course of the Models

Different stressors and different types of dysfunctioning may follow different models. For example, the stressor 'danger of accident' may be easily (and sometimes all too quickly) adjusted to (adjustment model) because one can divert one's attention away from the dangers. On the other hand, this is not so for social stressors; social stressors may follow the stress reaction model because an improvement in the social climate often leads to improved well-being. Finally, shiftwork may lead to permanent damage of the psychophysical system consistent with an accumulation model (Frese and Okonek, 1984).

The time spans may be different for different stressors. We already suggested that 10 years of shiftwork may be a typical problematic time span in the development of psychosomatic problems (Frese and Semmer, 1986) and that the period of six months to a year is a cut-off point in unemployment. In contrast, we assume that mental load (e.g. concentration, vigilance tasks) has an impact on dysfunctioning within a range of some months. One explanation for these differences in time span between stressors might be that they pose different degrees of stress intensity. However, different time courses may also be associated with different kinds (contents) of stressors.

Obviously, the typical workplace is characterized by more than just one stressor. Occupational stressors tend to follow the 'law of the dung-heap'. The more dung there is, the more is added to it. The more stressors there are already, the more there are added. In a cluster-analytic study on the combinations of stressors, Dunckel (1985) found that workplaces are often either uniformly high on different stressors or low. Thus, there is a multitude of stressors that impinge on the worker in particular jobs. Since these stressors operate at the same time but may follow a different time course and different models, the complexity of this picture becomes quite high. Furthermore, the stressors can work interactively (multiplicative model), additively or may mask each other in their effects on ill-health. The masking function became clear to us during an observation of bricklayers who put up walls in a steel converter. This work was done at temperatures of about 70°C. In their subjective report, they only talked about one stressor—the heat—that was so important that all other ones were 'masked' by this one particularly severe stressor.

Different stressors lead to differences in the time course. But even more important may be the dependent variable. We can only sketch out some thoughts on this matter here. One can distinguish the following relevant aspects of dysfunctioning (cf. also Broadbent, 1985; Mohr, 1986): irritation (anger reaction), anxiety (flight and avoidance reaction), depression (passive reaction), psychomatic complaints and psychosomatic illness (bodily reaction) and reality denial (a defense mechanism). There is some indication that depression is a precursor of somatic illness (Murphy and Brown, 1980). Thus, depression should develop within a smaller time span than illness. Similarly, psychosomatic *complaints* should develop more quickly than psychosomatic *illness*. We suggest that irritation and reality denial are aspects of dysfunctioning that react even more quickly than depression and psychosomatic complaints.

It is also plausible that illness follows a different model from complaints. Illness will probably not go away immediately after the stressors have been removed (the problem of chronicity) and the presence of stressors is not a necessary precondition for the *onset* of illness; therefore, the accumulation effect and the sleeper effect probably fit better here. In contrast, irritation and psychosomatic complaints are more likely to follow an adjustment or a stress reaction model. The development of depression and anxiety may be described with any kind of model depending upon whether some kind of 'functional autonomy' or a vicious circle develops.

Person and Environmental Parameters and their Mediating and Moderating Effect on the Time Course and the Models

All of the above models are affected by intervening variables; these may be internal to the person or external in the environment (Schönpflug, 1979). Of particular importance are the intervening variables coping strategies, social support and control. Within the last three years, there has been some kind of consensus in the literature that two types of intervening variables have to be distinguished although a different nomenclature is used to describe them (James and Brett, 1984; Frese, 1986; Wheaton, 1985). We think the terms mediators and moderators are the most useful. The *mediators* relate the stressor to dysfunctioning. The causal path leads from the stressor via the mediator to dysfunctioning (cf. Figure 9). An example would be that stressors increase the degree of social support at the workplace, which in turn has an influence on depression. In the pure case of mediating relationships, the direct relationship between the stressor and depression breaks down, when the mediator (social support in our case) is statistically removed with a partial correlation procedure (Simon, 1954). The mediator is related to the independent and dependent measures. In the pure case, the mediator does not really change the relationships in the models discussed above. An example of a (nearly pure) mediator is blood alcohol level. It is determined by the intake of alcohol and it in turn determines the amount of tipsiness. If one does not measure blood alcohol level, the empirical relationship between alcohol intake and tipsiness still exists (although weight and metabolic differences may still affect this relationship).

In contrast, *moderators* change the empirical relationships of independent and dependent variables and are, therefore, of more practical importance. We shall, therefore, concentrate on moderators. The most important moderators in stress research are: social support (e.g. Frese, in preparation; House, 1981; Payne and Jones, 1987), control (job discretion or autonomy) (e.g. Karasek, 1979; Karasek *et al.*, 1981; Semmer and Frese, 1987), and coping (e.g. Cohen, 1987; Frese, 1986; Pearlin and Schooler, 1978). Figure 10 gives an illustration of a moderator effect. The high social support groups shows a weaker association between the stressor and dysfunctioning. The low social

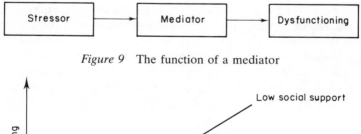

Figure 9   The function of a mediator

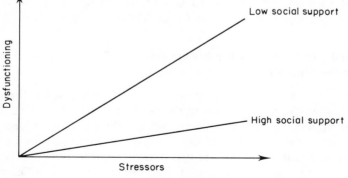

Figure 10   The function of a moderator

support group exhibits a stronger association. The moderators do not have to be correlated with the independent and dependent measures. This moderator effect can be analyzed by comparing the correlations of stressors with dysfunctioning between different subgroups (high or low on the moderator) or by using an interaction term in a regression analysis (Zedeck, 1971). Since the latter method leads to a rather conservative estimate, suggestions have been made for alternative approaches of analysis (e.g. Morris, Sherman and Mansfield, 1986).

The moderators have some impact on the models discussed above in terms of peaks of dysfunctioning, the time course of the development of dysfunctioning and switching on and off of different models.

Moderators can, for example, influence the *peak* of dysfunctioning. For example, effective coping strategies may not be able to eliminate the effects of the stressors on dysfunctioning but may lead to a smaller amount of dysfunctioning (thus to a lower peak). There is some evidence of this in our study on coping. We differentiated between under- and overreporters of stressors (Frese, 1986). Underreporters were people who reported a smaller amount of stressors in comparison with observers and other workers who were doing the same job. The underreporters showed a small impact of stressors on psychosomatic complaints than the overreporters. This effect only shows up in a longitudinal study, not in cross-sectional studies. Thus, a long-range adjustment effect may have been operative for the underreporters.

Moderators can also affect the *time course* of the development of dysfunctioning. There may be biological reasons (in the sense of an 'inferior organ') or psychological reasons like stability, hardiness (Kobosa, Maddi and Kahn, 1982) sense of coherence (Antonovsky, 1979) that impact on the time variable. For example, a person with high hardiness may suffer from stressors later than a person with low hardiness.

Moderators can have a *switch-on or -off function* between the models. Figure 11 gives an example, where both, the initial impact and the exposure time effects are operative in different people. Such a picture could emerge if there are differences between repressors or blunters and sensitizers or monitors of stressors (cf. Byrne, 1961; Miller and Mangan, 1983). Repressors do not react right away to a stressor but behave according to the exposure time effect in the long range while sensitizers react immediately to the new stressor and therefore conform to the initial impact effect.

CONSEQUENCES

In the following, we want to discuss some consequences that follow from our discussion. Our discussion of the different causal models has implications on the size of correlations in traditional stress research. Furthermore, our

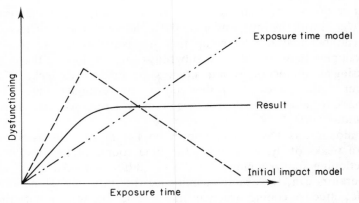

Figure 11   Exposure time model and initial impact model valid for
different subgroups of a sample

treatment leads to a new outlook on doing stress research. Finally, we present a general viewpoint.

The Problem of Small Correlations in Stress Research

Typically, there are small correlations between subjective and objective measurements of stressors and psychosomatic and psychological dysfunctioning in traditional stress research. This has led some authors to suggest that the workplace may not be important at all in the etiology of ill-health or at least it was deplored that only small correlations could be found (Kasl, 1978).

As long as correlations are computed between stressors at work and ill-health, without any further subdivisions of the sample, we suggest a completely different way of thinking about this problem: it is not the small correlation that should make us skeptical but rather the large correlations. Given the complexity of the measurement problems, the complexity of different kinds of causal models involved in a longitudinal study, the role of moderators, and the fact that the workplace is only *one* (albeit an important) area of stress in the life of people, one should only expect small correlations. In contrast, high correlations should make us suspicious that the researcher might have fallen into the triviality trap (Kasl, 1978) of using independent and dependent measures that have similar content and thereby producing high correlations. There are two classes of reasons that speak for the necessity of achieving small correlations in research: those methodological and theoretical issues that exist generally and those that can be eliminated by better design and conceptual understanding.

In terms of theory, ill-health is a multiply determined variable. The work situation is only one of the many areas of life (besides leisure activities, relations to the spouse, etc.) which have an influence on the development of ill-health. Additionally, biological factors and early life experiences also contribute to dysfunctioning. Therefore, it would be quite implausible to assume that there should be a high correlation.

In terms of methodology, there are also inherent problems in the study of stress at work. First, all of the measures have a large unsystematic error variance [according to Schmitt (1978) and Zapf (1987) about 50% even in good measures]. While this ratio can be reduced, there is some error variance left in any case. Unsystematic error variance leads to lower correlations. Second, it is nearly impossible to assess all of the stressors present at work; this leads to an underrepresentation of stressors and hence to small correlations. Again, one can try to increase the number of stressors measured (and thus get an increase in the multiple correlation). But often researchers have good theoretical reasons to concentrate on one set of stressors. This is legitimate but it should not lead reviewers of the field to the general conclusion that stressor–dysfunctioning relationships are small. Third, we strongly urge researchers to use objective methods of measuring stressors. This means that care should be taken that cognitive and emotional processing of the subjects does not intervene into stressor measurement. However, all of the objective measures lead to underestimates of the correlation as discussed above. Fourth, many studies carry out research in one factory or one branch and, therefore, produce a restriction of variance. Fifth, there is a selection effect in research on stress. Those who are ill (possibly because of work stress) may have left the workplace, are absent more often, are unemployed more frequently or will retire sooner. Therefore, they are underrepresented in the sample (healthy worker effect, Frese and Okonek, 1984; McMichael, 1976; Waldron *et al.*, 1982). Sixth, there are factors, related to our discussion of different models on how stressors can cause ill-health, that influence the size of correlations. They are discussed in more detail next.

Let us assume we make cross-sectional studies with homogeneous groups of subjects in a homogeneous work environment. In such a case, Figure 7 (on the different models) can give us a clue on what size of correlations we can expect. We have added some potential measurement points A, B, C and D in Figure 7. If one does a cross-sectional study at time A and if the exposure time models are correct, one does not find any correlations, because exposure time has not been long enough to produce ill-health. (However, if the initial impact model is correct one might find a correlation, cf. Figure 6.) At time B of Figure 7, the clearest results should appear, as long as the adjustment, the stress reaction and the accumulation models apply. However, if the sleeper effect is correct or the adjustment effect has been fully operative, the correlation will be low even at this point. Note, that a cross-sectional study will at no time point produce a correlation if the sleeper effect model applies. At times C and D, there are no correlations between the stressor and ill-health, since we assume in Figure 7 that the stressor has ceased to operate.

Our assumptions for this discussion are, of course, not quite realistic. Subjects will not be so homogeneous and the beginning and the end of stressor exposure are not so clearly demarcated. Thus, the typical study involves subjects who are situated at different points in Figure 7 and who have different stressor histories with different psychophysical prerequisites, coping dispositions, etc. Nevertheless, our rather abstract analysis shows that at any one point the different models lead to different degrees of 'loss of correlational power' in traditional cross-sectional studies. There is no conceivable design in which the full causal impact of the stressor on ill-health is present at any one point. When these different models apply to different people, to different stressors and to different moderators, some kind of correlation-reducing mechanism will always be operative.

A longitudinal study may also lead to conservative results. Figure 12 presents plausible cross-lagged panel correlations, depending upon whether one has studied stress at work with the two waves A and B or with B and D (the measurement points again refer to Figure 7). We are not concerned here with the cross-lagged panel correlation's problems in a narrow methodological sense (cf. Rogosa, 1980) or the power of cross-lagged panel correlations to decide between alternative causal models (Dwyer, 1983; Kenny, 1979). We just want to use them for a simple illustration of a point. Let us assume that the stability of the stressor fluctuates and that the stability of

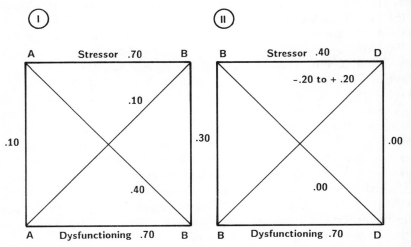

Figure 12 Potentially valid cross-lagged panel correlations (discussion in text)

dysfunctioning is relatively high (meaning that changes appear in all people in a relatively similar way). Figure 12/I leads to a causal dominance of the path from the stressor on dysfunctioning, i.e. the path from Stressor/A to Dysfunctioning/B is higher than the other cross-lagged correlation. This causal dominance holds under all models except the sleeper effect. This causal dominance may actually reverse itself, if the time lag between the times B and D is studied (as shown in Figure 12/II). Depending upon whether dysfunctioning leads to better workplaces (e.g. because of disability or protective work places) or worse ones (e.g. by a social drift downwards), the causal correlations from earlier dysfunctioning to later stressor may be either negative or positive. If the adjustment model or the stress reaction model is correct, one may even get the paradoxical result that Dysfunctioning/B leads to a smaller or a stronger Stressor/D but that the Stressor/B only as a zero path on Disfunctioning/D. This would be so under all conditions because the stressor has stopped to function at time B.

Thus, the problems of different models may lead to conservative results and even to clearly wrong ones: the result that there is an artificial impact of dysfunctioning on the stressor that is higher than the one from the stressor on dysfunctioning. This is so even though all of our models assume an impact of stressors on dysfunctining.

Thus, there is a whole gamut of methodological and theoretical reasons why the correlations between work stressors and dysfunctioning should be low. We, therefore, find the small but significant correlations between objective stressors and dysfunctioning that have been achieved in some studies (Algera, 1983, Frese, 1985; Greiner *et al.*, 1987; Zapf, in press) quite remarkable. The fact that some other studies show a very small and insignificant correlation (e.g. Wells, 1982) proves our point that correlations will only occur under certain conditions.

Moreover, even small correlations can be of substantial importance. Abelson (1985) and Frese (1985) have used extreme groups (successful baseball players and people with high psychosomatic impairment, respectively) and showed that a small correlation translated into a substantial practical impact. For example, a correlation of $r=0.19$ between observed psychological stressors at work and psychosomatic impairment translated into a ratio of 1 to 3 (Frese, 1985).

Thus, our discussion shows that one has to expect small correlations between the stressor and ill-health and that differing and even contradictory evidence is likely to develop if one uses a traditional approach to designing and analyzing cross-sectional and longitudinal studies. Since we assume that there is some evidence for all the models that we talked about and since we further argue that moderators can have a switch-on/-off function for differing models, we are not surprised by the diversity of differing results.

A New Research Perspective

Up to this point, we have essentially argued in defense of conventional stress research. However, our treatment of the different causal models may lead to a new research agenda that should be briefly described here. While traditional research has mainly asked the question, which correlation exists between the stressor and some variable of dysfunctioning, the different models and their use in longitudinal studies may lead to a whole series of new questions and new research programmes.

(1) New theoretical questions arise. The time component becomes an important variable in the formulation of a theory of stress effects. Hitherto the time variable has been very unimportant and should be more central now. Again, we refer to the study of former shiftworkers. It is theoretically and practically important to know at which point people will reach their breaking point. After having passed this point, the development of ill-health in former shiftworkers functions according to the accumulation model (i.e. dysfunctioning does not decrease after the stressor is taken away). This stands in contrast to shiftworkers who had not reached this point before they left shiftwork (here they might function according to the stress reaction model).

(2) Old and well-established concepts may be thought of differently. For example, the variable social support was usually conceived to be a variable that linearly changes the quantitative impact of the stressor on dysfunctioning. Within our conception this variable may change the ways a stressor has an impact on dysfunctioning. A high degree of social support may conform to the adjustment model (i.e. dysfunctioning is reduced even though the stressor is still present) or to the reaction model (i.e. after the stressor is removed, dysfunctioning is reduced), a low degree to the accumulation model (dysfunctioning becomes chronic). Or a high degree may just set the time component differently leading to a quicker adaptation time than a low degree of social support. These and similar questions change the function of the concept of moderators considerably.

(3) This kind of reasoning can be made more general. Our question is less whether or not, or how strongly, but rather *how* and *in which time period* stressors lead to dysfunctioning. This reasoning is more oriented to sorting out qualitative differences between the models than the traditional correlational quantitative approach. This means that we have to ask the theoretical and empirical question of how each stressor affects psychological and psychosomatic dysfunctioning, and also how different aspects of dysfunctioning follow different models.

(4) Our discussion implies that research has to take into account when a stressor has its first impact. This means that we should be more interested to do research with people who have just started work. This is quite different

from other approaches in stress research, which started with people who already had been in work for quite a while, excluding those who had a job tenure of less than half a year or a year (cf. e.g. Frese, 1985; Gardell, 1971; Greif *et al.*, 1983; Kornhauser, 1965). 'Natural experiments' often have used the right approach by getting people at the entry of a certain stressor change (e.g. Parkes, 1982). However, it is not easy to find the point where a stressor starts to operate. Since people anticipate stressors, psychological confrontation with a stressor may be earlier than material confrontation. In terms of anticipatory socialization (Frese, 1982), people attempt to construe what they will experience in their future job (or in their future job change) and will try to adapt themselves to these anticipated changes— this is the reason why the method of 'realistic job preview' works (Wanous, 1977). In any case, it is useful to start studies at a point where the stressors appear for the first time, e.g. in the case of people starting a new job, after an introduction of a new organizational scheme or new technology, etc.

(5) Results of longitudinal studies should be analyzed with these different models in mind. This leads to different questions: rather than answering the research question, whether or not a particular hypothesis is correct (e.g. that a stressor has an impact on this dysfunctioning, at all), one might test different kinds of models against each other.

(6) Methodologically, the following recommendations follow from our discussion.

(a) There should be more exploratory studies on how stressors have an impact on dysfunctioning. They can take the form of single case studies over time.

(b) It is useful to combine micro- and macro-studies. The micro-studies may for example tell us how stressors change after a new machine is introduced at a given workplace. Such micro-studies could also be done as single case studies over long time periods. Similarly time series studies can give us some information on the time lag and on the exact curve functions. Building on the results of these studies, one would have a more rational decision criterion for deciding on the time lags in longitudinal studies.

(c) More analyses should be done for subgroups. Since different groups may follow different models (depending, for example, upon longer or shorter confrontation with stressor, upon job history, upon moderator, etc.) the question should be asked whether different subgroups show different results.

(d) There should be more attempts at curve fitting. Since the models differ in their curvature, these different curves should be fitted to different subgroups or samples to determine whether or not they conform to a certain model. It is particularly useful to look at individual response curves to stress and to fit these curves to the thereotically advanced curves of Figure 7.

(e) Longitudinal studies should be designed so that one is able to explore different models. An ideal field study design would start just before the introduction of a new stressor and would have in the first period short time ranges between the waves, slowly broadening the timeframe afterwards. An example would be to have two or three waves in the first three months, then every three months till about 1½ years, then bi-yearly till the third year and then a yearly study for the next ten years. Such a study design is, of course, quite expensive. Nevertheless, even such a design poses some problems. From a methodological and statistical point of view Dwyer (1983) and Kessler and Greenberg (1981) point out that time misspecifications lead to serious problems if the time lag is too short. Moreover, the workplaces usually do not stay constant and the workers fluctuate in and out of certain jobs. Finally, we already pointed to the difficulties in determining when a person in fact is first confronted with a stressor. Thus, although an ideal design may not be feasible and not all of the problems can be coped within a single study, it pays off to test these models and develop designs that approximate an ideal design.

The General Concept: A Dynamic View

Stress research has come a long way within the last ten years and it is now time to take multiple measures (including objective measures) more seriously and to use designs that allow to study different causal relationships in detail and with a sophisticated conceptual background.

We have concentrated on two issues in this article: the question of objectivity and the question of longitudinal studies. Both are related to a general dynamic view of stress. This dynamic view is exemplified in our assumption that dysfunctioning can have an influence on the measurement of the stressor when assessed by the subjects. At the same time, the objective stress situation must in most cases influence the subjective perception.

Similarly, concerning the issue of longitudinal studies we could develop different dynamic models of the stress-dysfunctioning relationship. We are more interested in different models of how the dynamics between a stressor and dysfunctioning works than in a simple correlation between the stressor and ill-health. Although we have not discussed non-recursive models in which dysfunctioning has a true impact on the development of the stressors, the study of non-recursive relationships would be one part of such a dynamic viewpoint. While our thoughts point to the complexity of the research area, they also suggest a possible framework in which one can integrate different results, develop a new research perspective and eventually develop a cohesive theory concerning the questions: which models apply, under what circumstances, and in what period of time, for whom?

REFERENCES

Abelson, R. P. (1985). A variance explanation paradox: when a little is a lot, *Psychological Bulletin*, **97**, 129–33.

Akerstedt, T., Torsvall, L. (1978). Experimental changes in shiftwork: their effects on well-being, *Ergonomics*, **21**, 849–56.

Algera, J. A. (1983). 'Objective' and perceived task characteristics as a determinant of reactions by task performers, *Journal of Occupational Psychology*, **56**, 95–107.

Aneshensel, C. S., Fredichs, R. R. and Huba, G. J. (1984). Depression and phsyical illness: a multiwave, nonrecursive causal model, *Journal of Health and Social Behavior*, **25**, 350–71.

Antonovsky, A. (1979). *Health, Stress, and Coping*, Jossey-Bass, San Francisco.

Archibald, H. C. and Tuddenham, R. D. (1965). Persistent stress. Reaction after combat, *Archives of General Psychiatry*, **12**, 475–81.

Baars, A., Hacker, W., Hartmann, W., Iwanowa, A., Richter, P. and Wolf, S. (1981). Psychologische Arbeitsanalysen zur Erfassung der Persönlichkeitsförderlichkeit von Arbeitsinhalten. In F. Frei and E. Ulich (eds). *Beiträge zur psychologischen Arbeitsanalyse*, pp. 127–64), Huber, Bern.

Balz, H. -J., Drewski, R., Schulz-Gambard, J. and Mowka, K. H. (1985). Psychische Auswirkungen andauernder Arbeitslosigkeit—Erste Ergebnisse der Bielefelder Längsschnittstudie. In T. Kieselbach and A. Wacker (eds) *Individuelle und gesellschaftliche Kosten der Massenarbeitslosigkeit*, pp. 91–106, Beltz, Weinheim.

Bamberg, E. (1986). *Arbeit und Freizeit. Eine empirische Untersuchung zum Zusammenhang zwischen Stress am Arbeitsplatz, Freizeit und Familie*, Beltz, Weinheim.

Beck, A. T. (1972). *Depression*, University of Pennsylvania Press, Philadelphia.

Beehr, T. A., Walsh, J. T. and Taber, T. D. (1976). Relationship of stress to individually and organizationally valued states: higher order needs as a moderator, *Journal of Applied Psychology*, **61**, 41–7.

Brinkmann, C. (1985). Psychosoziale und gesundheitliche Folgen der Arbeitslosigkeit—Ergebnisse einer repräsentativen Längsschnittuntersuchung des IAB. In T. Kieselbach and A. Wacker (eds) *Individuelle und gesellschaftliche Kosten der Massenarbeitslosigkeit* (pp. 186–206, Beltz, Weinheim.

Broadbent, D. E. (1985). The clinical impact of job design, *British Journal of Clinical Psychology*, **24**, 33–44.

Bürck, W. (1974). Lärm—Der Mensch und akustische Umgebung. In H. Schmidtke (ed) *Ergonomie*, vol. 2, pp. 174–93, Hauser, München.

Byrne, D. (1961). The Repression–Sensitization Scale: rationale, reliability and validity, *Journal of Personality*, **29**, 334–49.

Campbell, D. T. and Fiske, D. W. (1959). Convergent and discriminant validation by the multitrait–multimethod matrix, *Psychological Bulletin*, **56**, 81–105.

Cohen, F. (1987). Measurement of coping. In S. V. Kasl and C. L. Cooper (eds) *Stress and Health: Issues in Research Methodology*, pp. 283–305, John Wiley and Sons, Chichester.

Cohen, S. (1980). Aftereffects of stress on human performance and social behavior: A review of research and theory, *Psychological Bulletin*, **88**, 82–108.

Contrada, R. J. and Krantz, D. S. (1987). Measurement bias in health psychology research designs. In S. V. Kasl and C. L. Cooper (eds), *Stress and Health: Issues in Research Methodology*, John Wiley and Sons, New York.

Cook, T. D. (1985). Post-positivist critical multiplism. In L. Shotland and M. M. Mark (eds) *Social Science and Social Policy*, Sage, Beverly Hills.

Cook, T. D. and Campbell, D. T. (1979). *Quasi-Experimentation. Design and Analysis for Field Settings*, Houghton Mifflin, Boston.

Depue, R. A. and Monroe, S. M. (1986). Conceptualization and measurement of human disorder in life stress research: the problem of chronic disturbance, *Psychological Bulletin*, **99**, 36–51.

Dunckel, H. (1985). *Mehrfachbelastungen an Arbeitsplatz und psychosoziale Gesundheit*, Peter Lang, Frankfurt A. M.

Dunckel, H. and Semmer, N. (1987). Streßbezogene Arbeitsanalyse: Ein Instrument zur Abschätzung von Belastungsschwerpunkten in Industriebetrieben. In Kh. Sonntag (ed.) *Arbeitsanalyse und Technikentwicklung*, pp. 163–77), Wirtschaftsverlag Bachem, Köln.

Dwyer, J. E. (1983). *Statistical Models for the Social and Behavioral Sciences*, Oxford University Press, New York.

Fahrenberg, J., Walschburger, P., Foerster, F., Myrtek, M. and Müller, W. (1979). *Psychophysiologische Aktivierungsforschung*, Minerva, München.

Frankenhaeuser, M. (1981). Coping with job stress—a psychobiological approach. In B. Gardell and G. Johansson (eds) *Working Life*. John Wiley and Sons, Chichester.

Frankenhaeuser, M. and Gardell, B. (1976). Underload and overload in working life: outline of a multidisciplinary approach, *Journal of Human Stress*, **2**, 35–46.

Frese, M. (1982). Occupational socialisation and psychological development: an underemphasized research perspective in industrial psychology, *Journal of Occupational Psychology*, **55**, 209–24.

Frese, M. (1983). Der Einfluß der Arbeit auf die Persönlichkeit. Zum Konzept des Handlungsstils in der beruflichen Sozialisation. *Zeitschrift für Sozialisationsforschung und Erziehungssoziologie*, **3**(1), 11–28.

Frese, M. (1984). Job transitions, occupational socialization, and strain. In V. Allen and E.v.D. Vliert (eds) *Role Transitions*, Plenum Press, New York.

Frese, M. (1985). Stress at work and psychosomatic complaints: a causal interpretation, *Journal of Applied Psychology*, **70**, 314–28.

Frese, M. (1986). Coping as a moderator and mediator between stress at work and psychosomatic complaints. In M. H. Appley and R. Trumbull (eds), *Dynamics of Stress*, Plenum Press, New York.

Frese, M. (in preparation). Social support as a moderator of the relationship between stress at work and psychological dysfunctioning.

Frese, M. and Mohr, G. (1987). Prolonged unemployment and depression in older workers: a longitudinal study on intervening variables, *Social Science and Medical*, **25**, 173–8.

Frese, M. and Okonek, K. (1984). Reasons to leave shiftwork and psychological and psychosomatic complaints of former shiftworkers, *Journal of Applied Psychology*, **69**, 509–14.

Frese, M. and Sabini, J. (eds) (1985). *Goal Directed Behavior: The Concept of Action in Psychology*, Lawrence Erlbaum, Hillsdale, NJ.

Frese, M., Saupe, R. and Semmer, N. (1981). Stress am Arbeitsplatz von Schreibkräften: Ein Vergleich zweier Stichproben. In M. Frese (ed.) *Stress im Büro*, Huber, Bern.

Frese, M. and Semmer, N. (1986). Shiftwork, stress, and psychosomatic complaints: a comparison between workers in different shiftwork schedules, non-shiftworkers, and former shiftworkers, *Ergonomics*, **29**, 99–114.

Fried, Y. (1988). The future of physiological assessments in work situations. This volume, Chapter 11.

Gardell, B. (1971). Alienation and mental health in the modern industrial environment. In L. Levi (ed.) *Society, stress, and disease.* Vol. 1. *The Psychosocial Environment and Psychosomatic Diseases*, Oxford University Press, London.

Gardell, B. (1978). Arbeitsgestaltung, intrinsische Arbeitszufriedenheit und Gesundheit. In M. Frese, S. Greif and N. Semmer (eds) *Industrielle Psychopathologie*, Huber, Bern.

Gilardi, R. v., Weber, G. and Liepmann, D. (1985). Untersuchung der Lernmöglichkeiten an metalltechnischen und elektrotechnischen Arbeitsplätzen während der Ausbildung. 2. Zwischenbericht an das Bundesinstitut für Berufsbildung, unpublished manuscript, Free University of Berlin.

Glass, D. C. and Singer, J. E. (1972). *Urban Stress: Experiments on Noise and Social Stressors*, Academic Press, New York.

Greif, S., Bamberg, E., Dunckel, H., Frese, M., Mohr, G., Rückert, D., Rummel, M., Semmer, N., Zapf, D. et al. (1983). *Abschlußbericht des Forschungsprojektes Psychischer Stress am Arbeitsplatz — hemmende und fördernde Bedingungen für humanere Arbeitsplätze*, Unveröffentlicher Bericht, Universität Osnabrück, Osnabrück.

Greiner, B., Leitner, K., Weber, W.–G., Hennes, K. and Volpert, W. (1987). RHIA — Ein Verfahren zur Erfassung psychischer Belastung. In Kh. Sonntag (ed.) *Arbeitsanalyse und Technikentwicklung*, pp. 145–61, Wirtschaftsverlag Bachem, Köln.

Hacker, W. (1985). Activity: a fruitful concept in industrial psychology. In M. Frese and J. Sabini (eds) *Goal Directed Behavior: The Concept of Action in Psychology*, Lawrence Erlbaum, Hillsdale, NJ.

Hacker, W. (1986). *Arbeitspsychologie*, Huber, Bern.

Hacker, W., Iwanowa, A. and Richter, P. (1983). *Tätigkeits-Bewertungssystem*, Diagnostisches Zentrum, Berlin, GDR.

Hackman, J. R. and Lawler, E. E. (1971). Employee reactions to job characteristics, *Journal of Applied Psychology*, **55**, 259–86.

Hackman, J. R. and Oldham, G. R. (1974). The job diagnostic survey: an instrument for the diagnosis of jobs and the evaluation of job redesign projects, Technical Report No. 4, Department of Administrative Sciences, Yale University.

Hackman, J. R. and Oldham, G. R. (1975). Development of the job diagnostic survey, *Journal of Applied Psychology*, **60**, 259–70.

Hofsten, C. v. (1985). Perception and action. In M. Frese and J. Sabini (eds) *Goal Directed Behavior: The Concept of Action in Psychology*, Lawrence Erlbaum, Hillsdale, NJ.

House, J. S. (1981). *Work Stress and Social Support*, Addison-Wesley, London.

Houts, A. C., Cook, T. D. and Shadish, W. R. (1986). The person–situation debate: a critical multiplist perspective. *Journal of Personality*, *54*, 52–105.

Howard, J. H., Cunningham, D. A. and Rechnitzer, P. A. (1986). Role ambiguity, Type A behavior, and job satisfaction: moderating effects on cardiovascular and biochemical responses associated with coronary risk, *Journal of Applied Psychology*, **71**, 95–101.

Iwanowa, A. and Hacker, W. (1984). Das Tätigkeitsbewertungssystem—ein Hilfsmittel beim Erfassen potentiell gesundheits- und entwicklungsfördernder objektiver Tätigkeitsmerkmale, *Psychologie und Praxis. Zeitschrift für Arbeits- und Organisationspsychologie*, **28**, 57–66.

James, L. R. and Brett, J. M. (1984). Mediators, moderators and tests for mediation, *Journal of Applied Psychology*, **69**, 307–21.

Jenkins, G. C., Nadler, D. A., Lawler, E. E., III. and Camman, C. (1975). Standardized observations: an approach to measuring the nature of jobs, *Journal of Applied Psychology*, **60**, 171–81.

Kannheiser, W. (1987). Neue Techniken und organisatorische Bedingungen: Ergebnisse und Einsatzmöglichkeiten des Tätigkeits-Analyse-Inventars (TAI). In Kh. Sonntag (ed.) *Arbeitsanalyse und Technikentwicklung*, pp. 69–85, Wirtschaftsverlag Bachem, Köln.

Karasek, R. A. (1979). Job demands, job decision latitude and mental strain: implications for job redesign, *Administrative Science Quarterly*, **24**, 385–408.

Karasek, R. A., Baker, D., Marxer, F., Ahlbom, A. and Theorell, T. (1981). Job decision latitude, job demands, and cardiovascular disease: a prospective study of Swedish men, *American Journal of Public Health*, **71**, 694–705.

Karasek, R. A., Theorell, T. (with Schwartz, J.) (in preparation). *Job Design, Productivity and Heart Disease*, Basic Books, New York.

Kasl, S. V. (1978). Epidemiological contributions to the study of work stress, in C. L. Cooper and R. Payne (eds) *Stress at Work*, pp. 3–48, John Wiley and Sons, Chichester.

Kasl, S. V. (1986). Stress and disease in the workplace: a methodological commentary on the accumulated evidence. In M. F. Cataldo and Th.J. Coates (eds) *Health and Industry. A Behavioral Medicine Perspective*, John Wiley and Sons, New York.

Kasl, S. V. (1987). Methodologies in stress and health: past difficulties, present dilemmas, future directions. In S. V. Kasl and C. L. Cooper (eds) *Stress and Health: Issues in Research Methodology*, John Wiley and Sons, New York.

Kenny, D. A. (1979). *Correlation and Causality*, John Wiley and Sons, New York.

Kessler, R. C. and Greenberg, D. F. (1981). *Linear Panel Analysis: Models of Quantitative Change*, Academic Press, New York.

Kobosa, S. C., Maddi, S. R. and Kahn, S. (1982). Hardiness and health: a prospective study, *Journal of Personality and Social Psychology*, **42**, 168–77.

Kohn, M. L. and Schooler, C. (1982). Job conditions and personality: a longitudinal assessment of their reciprocal effects, *American Journal of Sociology*, **87**, 1257–86.

Kornhauser, A. (1965). *Mental Health of the Industrial Worker*. John Wiley and Sons, New York.

Lazarus, R. S. (1966). *Psychological Stress and the Coping Process*. McGraw-Hill, New York.

Lazarus, R. S. and Folkman, S. (1986). Cognitive theories of stress and the issue of circularity. In M. L. Appley and R. Trumbull (eds) *Dynamics of Stress*, Plenum Press, New York.

Lazarus, R. S. and Launier, R. (1978). Stress-related transactions between person and environment. In L. A. Pervin and M. Lewis (eds) *Perspectives in International Psychology*, Plenum Press, New York.

Leventhal, H. and Tomarken, A. (1987). Stress and illness: perspectives from health psychology. In S. V. Kasl and C. L. Cooper (eds) *Stress and Health: Issues for Research Methodology*, John Wiley and Sons, New York.

Levi, L. (1967). *Emotional Stress*, Karger, Basel.

Louis, M. R. (1980). Surprise and sense making: what new-comers experience in entering unfamiliar organizational settings, *Administrative Science Quarterly*, **25**, 226–251.

Maanen, J.v. (1977). Experiencing organizations: notes of the meanings of careers and socialization. In J. v. Maanen (ed.) *Organizational Careers: Some New Perspectives*, John Wiley and Sons, New York.

McMichael, A. J. (1976). Standardized mortality ratios and the 'healthy worker effect': scratching beneath the surface, *Journal of Occupational Medicine*, **18**, 165–8.

Martin, E., Udris, I., Ackermann, U. and Oegerli, K. (1980). *Monotonie in der Industrie. Eine ergonomische, psychologische und medizinische Studie an Uhrenarbeitern*, Huber, Bern.

Menaghan, E. G., Merves, E. (1984). Coping with occupational problems: the limits of individual efforts, *Journal of Health and Social Behavior*, **25**, 406–23.

Miller, S. M. and Mangan, C. E. (1983). Interacting effects of information and coping style in adapting to gynecologic stress: should the doctor tell all? *Journal of Personality and Social Psychology*, **45**, 223–36.

Mohr, G. (1986). Die Erfassung psychologischer Befindensbeeinträchtigungen bei Arbeitern. *Europäische Hochschulschriften*, Peter Lang, Frankfurt a.M.

Morris, J. H., Sherman, J. D. and Mansfield, E. R. (1986). Failures to detect moderating effects with ordinary least squares-moderated multiple regression: some reasons and a remedy, *Psychological Bulletin*, **99**, 282–8.

Murphy, E. and Brown, G. W. (1980). Life events, psychiatric disturbance and physical illness, *British Journal of Psychiatry*, **136**, 326–38.

Neisser, U. (1967). *Cognitive Psychology*, Appleton-Century-Crofts, New York.

Neisser, U. (1976). *Cognition and Reality. Principles and Implications of Cognitive Psychology*, W. H. Freeman, San Francisco.

Neisser, U. (1985). The role of invariant structures in the control of movement. In M. Frese and J. Sabini (eds) *Goal Directed Behavior: The Concept of Action in Psychology*, Lawrence Erlbaum, Hillsdale, NJ.

Nesselroade, J. R. and Baltes, P. B. (eds) (1979). *Longitudinal Research in the Study of Behavior and Development*, Academic Press, New York.

Neugarten, B. L. (1977). Personality and aging. In J. E. Birren and K. W. Schaie (eds) *Handbook of the Psychology of Aging*, pp. 626–649, van Nostrand, New York.

Nicholson, N. A. (1984). A theory of work role transitions, *Administrative Science Quarterly*, **29**, 172–91.

Orne, M. T. (1962). On the social psychology of the psychological experiment: with particular reference to demand characteristics and their implications, *American Psychologist*, **17**, 776–83.

Overmier, J. B. and Seligman, M. E. P. (1967). Effects of inescapable shock upon subsequent escape and avoidance responding, *Journal Comparative Physiological Psychology*, **63**, 28–33.

Parkes, K. R. (1982). Occupational stress among student nurses; a natural experiment, *Journal of Applied Psychology*, **67**, 784–96.

Payne, R. L. and Jones, J. G. (1987). Measurement and methodological issues in social support. In S. V. Kasl and C. L. Cooper (eds) *Stress and Health: Issues in Research Methodology*, pp. 167–205, John Wiley and Sons, Chichester.

Pearlin, L. I. and Schooler, C. (1978). The structure of coping, *Journal of Health and Social Behavior*, **19**, 2–21.

Rogosa, D. (1980). A critique of cross-lagged correlation, *Psychological Bulletin*, **88**, 245–58.

Rosenberg, M. J. (1969). The conditions and consequences of evaluation apprehension. In R. Rosenthal and R. L. Rosnow (eds) *Artifact in Behavioral Research*, Academic Press, New York.

Sabini, J., Frese, M. and Kossman, D. (1985). Some contributions of action theory to social psychology: social action and social actors in the context of institutions and an objective world. In M. Frese and J. Sabini (eds), *Goal Directed Behavior: The Concept of Action in Psychology*, Lawrence Erlbaum, Hillsdale, NJ.

Schmitt, N. (1978). Path analysis of multitrait-multimethod matrices. *Applied Psychological Measurement*, **2**, 157–78.

Schönpflug, W. (1979). Regulation und Fehlregulation im Verhalten. I. Verhaltensstruktur, Effizienz und Belastung—theoretische Grundlagen eines Untersuchungsprogramms, *Psychologische Beiträge*, **21**, 174–202.

Schönpflug, W. (1985). Goal directed behavior as a source of stress: psychological origins and consequences of inefficiency. In M. Frese and J. Sabini (eds), *Goal Directed Behavior: The Concept of Action Theory in Psychology*, Lawrence Erlbaum, Hillsdale, NJ.

Seibel, H. D. and Lühring, H. (1984). *Arbeit und psychische Gesundheit*, Hogrefe, Göttingen.

Semmer, N. (1982). Stress at work, stress in private life, and psychological well-being. In W. Bachmann and I. Udris (eds) *Mental Load and Stress in Activity*, North Holland, Amsterdam.

Semmer, N. (1984). *Streßbezogene Tätigkeitsanalyse*, Beltz, Weinheim.

Semmer, N. and Frese, M. (1987). Control at work as moderator of the effect of stress at work on psychosomatic complaints: a longitudinal study with objective measurements, unpublished paper, München.

Simon, H. A. (1954). Spurious correlation: a causal interpretation, *Journal of the American Statistical Association*, **49**, 467–79.

Tielsch, R. and Hettinger, Th. (1984). Probleme und Ergebnisse subjektiver und objektiver Arbeitsplatzanalysen, *Zeitschrift für Arbeitswissenschaft*, **38**, 71–7.

Volpert, W. (1987). Psychische Regulation von Arbeitstätigkeiten In U. Kleinbeck and J. Rutenfranz (eds) *Arbeitspsychologie. Enzyklopädie der Psychologie, Themenbereich D. Serie III Band 1*. Hogrefe, Göttingen.

Volpert, W., Oesterreich, R., Gablenz-Kolakovic, S., Krogoll, T. and Resch, M. (1983). *Verfahren zur Ermittlung von Regulationserfordernissen in der Arbeitstätigkeit (VERA)*, TÜV- Rheinland, Köln.

Waldron, I., Herold, J., Dunn, D. and Staum, R. (1982). Reciprocal effects of health and labor force participation among women: Evidence from two longitudinal studies, *Journal of Occupational Medicine*, **24**, 126–32.

Wall, T. P. and Clegg, C. W. (1981). A longitudinal study of group work design, *Journal of Occupational Behavior*, **2**, 31–49.

Wanous, J. P. (1977). Organizational entry: newcomers moving from outside to inside, *Psychological Bulletin*, **84**, 601–18.

Warr, P. (1984). Job loss, unemployment and psychological well-being. In V. L. Allen and E. v. d. Vliert (eds) *Role Transitions. Explorations and Explanations*, pp. 263–88, Plenum Press, New York.

Warr, P. and Jackson, P. (1984). Men without jobs: some correlates of age and length of unemployment, *Journal of Occupational Psychology*, **57**, 77–85.

Warr, P. and Jackson, P. (1985). Factors influencing the psychological impact of prolonged unemployment and of re-employment, *Psychological Medicine*, **15**, 795–807.

Wells, J. A. (1982). Objective job conditions, social support and perceived stress among blue collar workers, *Journal of Occupational Behaviour*, **3**, 79–94.

Wheaton, B. (1985). Models for the, stress-buffering functions of coping resources. *Journal of Health and Social Behavior*, **26**, 352–64.

Wohlwill, J. F. (1970). The age variable in psychological research, *Psychological Review*, **77**, 49–64.

Zapf, D. (1987). Selbst- und Fremdbeobachtung in der psychologischen Arbeitsanalyse. Methodische Probleme bei der Erfassung von Streβ am Arbeitsplatz, Dissertation an der Freien Universität Berlin, Berlin.

Zapf, D. (in press). Analysis of self report data, group data and observer data in psychological stress research.

Zapf, D., Greif, S. and Semmer, N. (in press). Die Erfassung von Streβ am Arbeitsplatz durch Befragte und Beobachter: Meβmodelle mit vier Indikatoren.

Zedeck, S. (1971). Problems with the use of 'moderator' variables, *Psychological Bulletin*, **76**, 295–310.

Conclusions

Several themes recur in the chapters in this book and justify their emphasis in these concluding comments. They are that occupational stress is a significant problem which deserves the continuing investment of research resources. There is some concern expressed that some groups of workers deserve more attention than they have received in the past: these include less skilled/ autonomous occupations, new technology jobs and women in general.

A second theme is that the evidence on how to decrease stress and/or improve peoples' ability to cope with it is less than adequate, and much needs to be done to increase our knowledge based in this area. This said, there are encouraging signs that the high profile 'stress' has acquired in the media is playing a part in educating people about the importance of life style in determining health/illness.

Alongside these calls for more research there is a concern throughout the book with improving the quality of research that is done. Much emphasis is given to the fact that stress, occupational stress in particular, is a process that takes place over time. Understanding this process needs much more detailed, longitudinal designs with multiple measures of stresses/causes, coping and consequences whether they are assessed by self-report means or physiological measures. The call is not just for longitudinal studies with more measures, however. It is also for better measurement procedures, and there are particularly strong exhortations to avoid reliance on subjective measures of stressors. Even physiological measurement, however, has been much less rigorous than is required for acceptable scientific standards in this area. Frese and Zapf bring many of these issues together in their chapter on methodological issues but they also emphasize the need to test competing models rather than the oversimplified causes, coping and consequences sequence implicit in our title.

It is our aspiration that this volume will accelerate achievement of these aims, difficult though they are in an academic environment, which encourages efficiency (more for less) rather than effectiveness. Ten years ago in *Stress at Work*, Kasl (1978) warned about the triviality trap of relying on self-report studies to assess both sources of stress and reactions to it but that warning seems almost as relevant today as it was then. Perhaps stress researchers need to do some interventions in their own domain if their research efforts are to be commensurate with the complexity of the stress process.

We hope these changes in research practice will be possible to achieve and believe this book is one of several recently produced that indicates that that kind of commitment is emerging. It seems apposite, nay just, that researchers of occupational stress should themselves be stressed by its intellectual and practical demands.

Index